D1383682

TOWARD A JUST SOCIETY

TOWARD A JUST SOCIETY

Joseph Stiglitz and Twenty-First Century Economics

EDITED BY

Martin Guzman

COLUMBIA UNIVERSITY PRESS

NEW YORK

Columbia University Press
Publishers Since 1893
New York   Chichester, West Sussex
cup.columbia.edu

Copyright © 2018 Columbia University Press
All rights reserved

Library of Congress Cataloging-in-Publication Data
Names: Guzman, Martin, editor.
Title: Toward a just society : Joseph Stiglitz and twenty-first century
economics / edited by Martin Guzman.
Description: New York : Columbia University Press, [2018] |
Includes bibliographical references and index.
Identifiers: LCCN 2017057518 (print) | LCCN 2018012806 (ebook) |
ISBN 9780231546805 (ebook) | ISBN 9780231186728
(hardcover : alk. paper)
Subjects: LCSH: Stiglitz, Joseph E.—Political and social views. |
Poverty. | Social policy. | Finance. | Economic development.
Classification: LCC HC79.P6 (ebook) | LCC HC79.P6 T69 2018 (print) |
DDC 330—dc23
LC record available at https://lccn.loc.gov/2017057518

Columbia University Press books are printed on permanent
and durable acid-free paper.

Printed in the United States of America

Cover design: Noah Arlow

CONTENTS

Preface ix
Joseph Stiglitz

Introduction 1
Martin Guzman

PART I Inequality

1. A Firm-Level Perspective on the Role of Rents in the
Rise in Inequality   19
Jason Furman and Peter Orszag

2. Parents, Children, and Luck: Equality of Opportunity
and Equality of Outcome   48
Ravi Kanbur

3. The Middle Muddle: Conceptualizing and Measuring
the Global Middle Class   63
Arjun Jayadev, Rahul Lahoti, and Sanjay Reddy

PART II Microeconomics

4. Companies Are Seldom as Good or as Bad as They Seem
at the Time   95
Gary Smith

5. What's So Special About Two-Sided Markets?   111
Benjamin E. Hermalin and Michael L. Katz

6. Missing Money and Missing Markets in the
Electricity Industry   131
David Newbery

PART III Macroeconomics

7. Thoughts on DSGE Macroeconomics: Matching
   the Moment, But Missing the Point?   159
   Anton Korinek

8. The "Schumpeterian" and the "Keynesian" Stiglitz: Learning,
   Coordination Hurdles, and Growth Trajectories   174
   Giovanni Dosi and Maria Enrica Virgillito

9. Deleterious Effects of Sustained Deficit Spending   196
   Edmund Phelps

10. The Rediscovery of Financial Market Imperfections   201
    John C. Williams

11. Ambiguity and International Risk Sharing   207
    Brian Hill and Tomasz Michalski

PART IV Networks

12. Use and Abuse of Network Effects   227
    Hal Varian

13. Financial Contagion Revisited   240
    Franklin Allen and Douglas Gale

14. The Economics of Information and Financial Networks   277
    Stefano Battiston

PART V Development

15. Joseph Stiglitz and China's Transition Success   309
    Justin Yifu Lin

16. The Sources of Chinese Economic Growth Since 1978   323
    Lawrence J. Lau

17. Knowledge as a Global Common and the Crisis
    of the Learning Economy   353
    Ugo Pagano

PART VI Law and Economics

18. Conservatism and Switcher's Curse   377
    Aaron Edlin

19. The "Inner Logic" of Institutional Evolution:
Toward a Theory of the Relationship Between Formal
and "Informal" Law 422
Antara Haldar

PART VII Public Policies

20. Joe Stiglitz and Representative and Equitable
Global Governance 443
José Antonio Ocampo

21. The Fiscal Opacity Cycle: How America Hid
the Costs of the Wars in Iraq and Afghanistan 457
Linda J. Bilmes

22. It Works in Practice, But Would It Work in Theory?
Joseph Stiglitz's Contribution to Our Understanding
of Income Contingent Loans 479
Bruce Chapman

23. The Public Economics of Long-Term Care 493
Pierre Pestieau and Gregory Ponthiere

24. Jomo E. Stiglitz: Kenya's First Nobel Laureate
in Economics 508
Célestin Monga

List of Contributors 523
Index 531

Joseph Stiglitz

The papers collected here were presented at a 2016 conference at Columbia University to commemorate my fifty years of teaching. Normally such events, and the festschrifts that result, are organized to celebrate the research contributions of a scholar. However, I wanted a chance to celebrate a lifetime of conversations, research, and collaboration with my students. These students are long grown; they have moved on to their own careers, and they have made tremendous contributions to the world and to the field of economics but have stayed close and been part of my life for decades.

I was moved both by the decision of Columbia University's Graduate School of Business to host this event as part of their seventy-five-year celebration, and by the enthusiastic response of so many of my former students and colleagues.

In the life of a scholar, research and teaching are inextricable. Throughout my career, I have bounced my ideas off my students and tested them in class. My students had to suffer from unformulated ideas while I benefited from seeing what they did and did not understand. I saw my role as a teacher not as pouring well-established ideas into brains that were not yet saturated with knowledge but as bringing my students along our shared creative process in order to motivate them and excite them about the power of ideas and the potential of a young scholar to make a contribution—not just to the academic literature but to society. As scholars, we have to pursue ideas wherever they lead us. And yet, we have to be aware that our research findings, as tentative as they may be, can have effects on our society. For instance, research on how inequality is created and perpetuated may give us tools by which to address it. Of course I had views about what a just society might look like and how to create it—views that evolved over the fifty years of my teaching. I shared those views, and hoped to inculcate those values. My students sustained and challenged me and presented arguments that helped us develop and refine our ideas. And these enthusiastic collaborators turned into life-long friends. I have watched them develop intellectually and become active contributing members of society. I have watched them get married, have children and grandchildren. I often feel like a proud parent. There is something special about the relationship between a teacher and his students.

My teachers at Amherst College, both in economics (Arnold Collery—who went on to become Dean at Columbia College—as well as Jim Nelson and Ralph Beals) and in other subjects, emphasized the importance of asking the right questions and the questioning of authority and received wisdom. The right question is, of course, hard to define. Minimal criteria are that it is a question, the answer to which makes a difference—possibly a big difference—and that with the tools at our disposal, it is answerable. I wanted to pass along those views as well as the technical tools needed to answer the questions that they would raise. While I entered economics wanting to make a more just society, I also loved the academic enterprise itself—a beautiful proof, an elegant argument, an unexpected result. So I always pushed my students gently toward thinking about problems that would make a difference for our society and toward thinking about those where they might obtain elegant and generalizable results. I have always had a certain revulsion toward excessively parametric models. They are good as examples and homework assignments, helping develop our understanding of a problem. But they leave us uncertain about the general applicability of the results. Only by relying on quite general functional forms can we have some confidence in the generality of our analyses. I also tried to convey some feeling for the research process, breaking big problems into smaller ones, formulating overly simple models and then generalizing them, but even then keeping them simple enough—stripped bare, so that we could see what was at play—and testing them to ensure that the results were robust. Such thought experiments can often be more insightful than field experiments, even when there are random controls; they are certainly less expensive.

I was especially pleased that so many people from each of the phases of my life were able to attend, from the first tutorials I gave at Cambridge in 1966 (David Newbery and Geoff Heal); to the first class I taught at MIT in 1966–1967 (Hal Varian); through my years at Yale, Princeton,

Oxford, and Stanford; to my years in the White House and the World Bank (where while I wasn't formally teaching, I was still mentoring—with some of my mentees going on to enormous success in public policy); to the past two decades at Columbia.

My teachers had a huge influence on me and I am grateful. My eighth-grade mathematics teacher in Gary, Indiana, Miss Davidson, pulled me out of class to study on my own, setting me on a trajectory involving a love of mathematics. In my third year at Amherst, my professors sent me off to MIT, and there I was taught and advised by the greatest minds in the profession, which included Robert Solow, Paul Samuelson, Ken Arrow, Franco Modigliani, Evsey Domar, as well as a host of other great teachers. At Cambridge, Joan Robinson was initially assigned as my tutor—one of my motivations for going to Cambridge (United Kingdom) was to see "the other side;" but Frank Hahn (whose long list of distinguished students included Atkinson, Heal, Mirrlees, and Dasgupta) at Churchill College took an interest in me and got me a Junior Research Fellowship at Gonville and Caius College, improving my standard of living in every way. Although Nicky Kaldor would fall asleep in his own seminar, his trenchant questions and his nonorthodox perspectives kept us on our toes and were enormously stimulating, I first met some of his children at Sunday lunch in his home, and two of them, Francis Stewart and Mary Kaldor, are still good friends. Kaldor's lectures inspired Tony Atkinson and my first paper, "A New View of Technological Change."[1] The energetic response that David Champernowne and James Meade, leaders in the analysis of income distribution, gave to my first forays was heartening: nothing could have been more motivating to a graduate student.[2] Frank Hahn was a demanding supervisor, simultaneously encouraging me to think about big questions and to get the details of the models I formulated correct. It was motivating too when such a hard taskmaster, after explaining all that was wrong with a paper I turned in, got it accepted for publication three weeks later (in early 1966) in the *Review of Economic Studies*.[3] When I returned to modeling the increase in inequality that has occurred over the past third of a century, those models became my point of departure.

The festschrift conference "For a Just Society" came about because of the hard work of the organizers. Thanks are due to Columbia University for giving me a wonderful home for the past two decades—a place where I have had bright and engaged students, interactive colleagues, intellectual freedom to pursue ideas wherever they have led, and financial support to develop and help disseminate these ideas. In particular, the Graduate School of Business has given me the opportunity to continue my lifelong collaboration with Bruce Greenwald, one of the greatest teachers of his generation. As noted, this festschrift conference was a part of Columbia Business School's seventy-fifth anniversary celebration and I especially want to thank Dean Glenn Hubbard. Merit Janow at the School of International and Public Affairs hosted a dinner at which Eric Verhoogen made some warm remarks while Terri Thompson and Donna Rosato presented a moving video tribute. Columbia University's Provost John Coatsworth and Vice Provost Troy Eggers generously supported the conference.

Kate Baxter and Marisa Totino in the Business School, along with Sarah Thomas, Hannah Assadi, and an enthusiastic young intern, George Grun, deftly and efficiently handled the massive logistics essential to the conference. It would not have been possible without their hard work.

Columbia University Press has once again done a magnificent job in the publication of the papers, and I want to acknowledge the help and support of Bridget Flannery-McCoy, the economics editor, and her assistant, Christian Winting. I also want to thank Gabriela Plump, in my office, who played a vital role in the production of the book, serving as the liaison between the authors and the publisher.

None of this would have been possible without my students and colleagues who came to Columbia to celebrate fifty years of my teaching. I especially want to thank the authors who worked so hard to convert their exciting presentations of that day into the papers that are published here.

I have saved the last for my deepest debt: to Anya Schiffrin and Martin Guzman who conceived, shaped, and constructed the whole event. Martin wrote the wonderful introduction to this festschrift. Of course, my debt to each of them goes well beyond this event and this volume. Martin came to Columbia as a postdoctoral research fellow, but he has become one of my principal co-authors and collaborators; we have worked together, for instance, on the analytics of macroeconomics when agents differ in their beliefs and fluctuations in pseudo-wealth give rise to economic fluctuations and on the theory and practice of sovereign debt restructuring. We have also been fighting together (successfully) to get the United Nations to adopt a set of principles for sovereign debt restructuring that promote economic efficiency and social justice; and, so far with less success, to get a fair deal for Puerto Rico, America's last big colony that is currently overburdened by debt and with an unsatisfactory economic and political relationship with the United States. There, we have both contributed with technical analysis to the understanding of what is needed and actively engaged in the public debate.

And most of all: to Anya, my life's companion. Her loving kindness and lively conversation make each day together fun and interesting.

NOTES

1. *Economic Journal* 79 (315), September 1969: 573–578. We were pleasantly surprised when it was listed as one of the top ten articles in the *Economic Journal* in the first hundred years of the journal's publication.

2. After presenting a first draft of the paper to an evening seminar in Cambridge, James Meade sent a thirteen-page comment the next morning.

3. "A Two-Sector, Two Class Model of Economic Growth," *Review of Economic Studies* 34 (April 1967): 227–238.

TOWARD A JUST SOCIETY

Introduction

Martin Guzman

This is a selection of the papers presented at an unusual event: The celebration of *Joseph E. Stiglitz's 50 Years of Teaching*, on October 15–18, 2015, as part of Columbia University's Graduate School of Business 100th Anniversary Celebration, co-hosted by the School of International and Public Affairs. While it is common to have a *festschrift* celebrating a scholar's research achievements, the celebration of fifty years of teaching was notable partly because few reach that milestone, and even fewer reach it with the number and quality of students that Joe has had: from his first year of teaching at Cambridge University in 1965–1966, where he supervised Tony Atkinson, Geoff Heal, and David Newbery; to his year at MIT, where his students included Hal Varian; to the following year at Yale, where his students included Janet Yellen, Ric Levin, Steve Salop, and a host of others too numerous to name; on through Stanford, Oxford, Princeton, and Columbia. Even when he left academia to join the government, he continued his mentoring, hiring two young Harvard graduate students, Jason Furman (later Chairman of the Council of Economic Advisers) and Peter Orszag (later Director of the Office of Management and Budget), onto the staff of the Council of Economic Advisers. We were joined by many of Joe's students, postdocs, co-authors, classmates, and advisors—as well as a number of Nobel Prize recipients, including George Akerlof, Ned Phelps, and Bob Solow. Some of the participants have interacted with Joe in multiple roles—as student and co-author, advisor and co-author, classmate and co-author, and in one case even as advisee and advisor (Ravi Kanbur, who was supervised in his PhD at Oxford by Joe, and became Joe's principal advisor at the World Bank in the late 1990s).

The range of Joe's interests over those fifty years is reflected by the range of interests of his students—from micro to macro, from pure theory to policy, from the economics of advanced countries to that of development. His career has been unusual as well, combining rigorous economic theory, playing an active role in policy making, and influential engagement as a public intellectual. This diversity provided a challenge in developing a common theme for the gathering. The event was entitled simply "A Just Society." For what motivated Joe to become an economist was to help create a more just society, and in one way or another, most of the papers presented at the conference, and those selected for this volume, fall within that theme. The event was the gathering of a group of scholars from different generations who shared a sense of community, who have been spending their lives trying to understand some very important and complex problems; a group that experienced together an academic journey inspired by the desire to make the world a better place—a journey that required breathing not only *economics* but also *politics*. A journey that Joe, through his teaching has inspired and through his intellectual contributions has led.

In the fifty years of Joe's teaching we learned enormous amounts from him. We learned about economics in virtually every single field except for econometrics. But despite the huge legacy he leaves in economic science, what he taught us goes well beyond economics. He taught us how to *be* scientists, and how to *behave* as scientists in the much broader sphere that surrounds us, in the society we live. He taught us values. It was not surprising that the tone of the talks was emotional at times. It all added up. This event was not an isolated instance; Joe and Anya have together created a *New Yorker Belle Époque*, constructing a community with the same ambience that we felt at the conference.

I had the enormous privilege of spending three years as Joe's postdoc at Columbia University, from 2013–2016. A postdoc is a very special time in the life of an academic. It is at an early stage of the career, but not too early, as it follows five years of hard training in a PhD program; it also occurs at a time when one's energy is at its peak. Imagine if one happens to live those years with Joe as one's supervisor: *that* is a life changer. And as part of it, a brain changer, because one gets to absorb the way of thinking and working of one of the most influential thinkers in the history of the social sciences. This experience perhaps puts me in a privileged position to talk about Joe as a teacher.

As hard as it is to transmit how it feels and what it means for the learning process, let me try. To begin, there is the generosity of Joe's attention. Even though he is one of the most sought after and busiest people on the planet, when one discusses research with him, nothing else seems to matter. This absolute presence resonates with whomever he speaks to. For me, there is nothing comparable. My adrenaline and motivation was piqued by time spent with him discussing our research.

His style is as clear as it is effective. First, he pushes you to define the question of interest—but that question must be important, it must aim at understanding a relevant economic phenomenon. Relevance is a must. Life is short and there are too many important problems that call for a solution, so one better get to the ones that matter first. He pushes you to formalize the relevant mechanisms that underlie the problem under analysis through simple and concrete models. But he is never wedded to a particular model. He is a scientist who emphasizes how the range of validity of a model is limited by the range of validity of the assumptions on which it is built. That is why he pushes his advisees to test their models *in theory*, changing one assumption at a time, to gain insight into what drives the propositions that have been derived—and to what extent the results are robust to minor changes in the assumptions. Thought experiments are a constant part of the research process when working with Joe.

The reader will notice throughout the chapters of this volume the sense of community that reflects Joe's style. The volume compiles most of the presentations from the event. The twenty-four chapters are organized into seven sections that are connected to the tour that Joe has followed throughout his life, first as an academic; then as a scholar who contributed from the public policy arena, as he did as Chair of the U.S. Council of Economic Advisers during Bill Clinton's administration and as Chief Economist and Vice President of the World Bank; and finally as a public intellectual who reached massive global audiences through his books, journalism, and speeches.

Part I includes three chapters on the issue of *inequality*. As Joe has written, he entered economics partly because he was disturbed by the enormous inequality which he saw around him as he grew up in Gary, Indiana. His PhD thesis was on growth and inequality, and one of his widely cited papers from his thesis, "The Distribution of Income and Wealth Among Individuals," is enjoying renewed interest with the resurgence of research in the economics of inequality. (In three of his most recent books, *The Price of Inequality*, *The Great Divide*, and *Rewriting the Rules of the American Economy*, Joe has returned to these themes that absorbed him in his youth. Much of his more recent theoretical work, including his four-part National Bureau of Economics (NBER) paper, "New Theoretical Perspectives on the Distribution of Income and Wealth Among Individuals," is concerned with how to interpret the enormous increase in inequality observed over the last third of a century, its causes and consequences, and what can be done about it.)

In chapter 1, "A Firm-Level Perspective on the Role of Rents in the Rise in Inequality," Jason Furman and Peter Orszag explore two of Joe's core interests: the rise in inequality and imperfections in competition. Joe has been a leading advocate of the hypothesis that the rising prevalence of economic rents—payments to factors of production above what is required to keep them in the market—and the shift of those rents away from labor and toward capital, have played a critical role in the rise of inequality. This chapter advances a related hypothesis: using firm-level data, it shows that there has been a trend of increased dispersion of returns to capital across firms, with an increasingly large fraction of firms getting returns over 20 or 30 percent annually. It shows that increases in interfirm inequalities in wages are far more important in explaining the growth of inequality than the growth of intrafirm inequalities. It thus suggests that "a rising share of firms are earning supra-normal returns on capital and workers at those firms are both producing and sharing in those super-normal returns, driving up wage inequality."

In chapter 2, "Parents, Children, and Luck: Equality of Opportunity and Equality of Outcome," Ravi Kanbur reviews three perspectives on the concepts of equality of opportunity: the relationship between parents' outcomes, that of their children, and luck. The first perspective focuses on the intergenerational elasticity (IGE) of income transmission. There are two strands to this older literature, the first one going back at least as far as Gibrat's work in the early 1930s; it traces the consequences of higher or lower IGEs for the evolution of inequality of income; and the other from the 1970s, which sees the causality running the other way, from current inequality to IGE. Recent literature on "The Great Gatsby Curve," showing the strong connection between inequality of outcomes and inequality of opportunity, revives these older strands. The second perspective approaches intergenerational mobility through transition matrices and sets out views on "greater mobility" through this lens. A social welfare function approach is needed to make comparisons between societies (i.e., between different mobility matrices). Taking a dynastic inequality approach, Kanbur and Stiglitz had shown that full "equality of opportunity" does not necessarily lead to lower dynastic inequality than other transition matrices. Finally, the third perspective on parents, children, and luck is that of Roemer (1998; see reference list in chapter 2). There have been many applications of his framework in an attempt to quantify "inequality of opportunity." Kanbur argues that each of these approaches has serious empirical and conceptual flaws, and that each may understate the true degree of inequality of opportunity.

In chapter 3, "The Middle Muddle: Conceptualizing and Measuring the Global Middle Class," Arjun Jayadev, Rahul Lahoti, and Sanjay Reddy ask what it means to be in the global middle class and if it is growing in size (especially in the emerging markets). They compare three competing interpretations of what it means to be in the global middle class, providing estimates using data from the Global Consumption and Income Project. Looking at the global distribution of income, it is clear that citizens of the advanced countries in Europe and North America are still at the top. A second perspective is more sociological and looks at trends in mobility into the "middle." China has gained at the expense of much of the developing world. While countries like Vietnam may have gained from proximity to China and by helping produce Chinese exports, in many other countries the middle class has been eroded by competition from Chinese exports and cheap labor. Here, the key problem—beyond that of getting comparable data—is adjusting for differences in relative prices of nontraded goods. In an expansive definition, there have been substantial increases in the numbers in the middle class in some emerging countries, but even by the expansive definition, the fractions in South Asia or Africa remain low. The third concept defines the middle class as those who demand international goods and services. As they note, "Across the world, only 12 percent enjoy consumption levels of the middle class of the OECD." In this perspective, while the numbers in the middle class have been growing, the growth is at best modest.

Part II includes three chapters on *microeconomics*. It was, perhaps, in this area that Joe's reputation was most firmly established, with his work on imperfect and asymmetric information and imperfect risk markets. But Joe was interested in a whole range of market imperfections, including imperfect competition (exemplified by his work with Avinash Dixit on monopolistic competition). In some of his more recent work, Joe explores aspects of behavioral economics, including equilibrium fictions that may arise in the presence of confirmatory bias, and equilibria with endogenous preferences.

In chapter 4, "Companies Are Seldom as Good or as Bad as They Seem at the Time," Gary Smith takes on one of Joe's most explored topics, namely the implications of imperfect information. Professional forecasts of corporate earnings are not correlated perfectly with actual earnings. Those companies where forecasters are very optimistic usually do not do as well as predicted, while companies given pessimistic forecasts typically do better than predicted. Smith claims that insufficient appreciation of this statistical principle may help explain the success of contrarian investment strategies, in particular why stocks with relatively optimistic earning forecasts underperform those with pessimistic forecasts. The fact that markets do not sufficiently take into account these distortions is further evidence that markets are not efficient. While Joe emphasized asymmetries of information in his work, this chapter shows the importance of limitations in the processing of information that is publicly available.

In the past decade or so, economists have devoted considerable attention to understanding markets in which an enterprise (a "platform") facilitates exchange between two or more parties ("platform users"). Examples of this are singles bars and hook-up apps (e.g., Tinder), which facilitate romantic and/or sexual encounters among their users. This also includes payment-card networks (e.g., Visa), which facilitate exchanges between merchants and customers. Such markets have come to be called *two-sided*, in part because a platform's strategy, if well designed, must concern itself with users on both sides simultaneously. In chapter 5, Benjamin Hermalin and Michael Katz answer "What's So Special About Two-Sided Markets?" The answer is important; in recent antitrust cases (e.g., involving American Express) some courts have suggested that standard doctrines need to be rethought for two-sided markets. But in this important paper, Hermalin and Katz explain that many of the often-noted features of two-sided markets are present in ordinary firms. What is distinctive about two-sided markets, they argue, is that the marginal decision made by a user on one side of a platform affects the surplus enjoyed by users on the other side. They show that these surplus effects arise when there is inefficient rationing and/or idiosyncratic matching.

In chapter 6, "Missing Money and Missing Markets in the Electricity Industry," David Newbery addresses a key issue that arises in the absence of perfect (or even good) risk markets: how to ensure reliability, and at the same time, that there is adequate investment in energy. He argues that capacity auctions tend to overprocure capacity, exacerbating the "missing money problem" they were designed to address. He claims that the bias is further exacerbated by failing to address some of the missing market problems (those besides the absence of risk markets) also neglected in the debate, and examines the case for, criticisms of, and outcome of the first British capacity auction and the problems that arise in trading between different capacity markets.

Part III includes five chapters on *macroeconomics*. Joe was always interested in how the entire economic system worked. That was why he focused so much on the issue of the Pareto efficiency of the market economy. Obviously, an economy in which there was a high level of unemployment was not efficient. From his early work on efficiency wages and his joint work with Bob Solow, Joe sought to explain wage rigidities. He held out against the prevailing winds in the economics profession, as they moved to dynamic stochastic general equilibrium (DSGE) models, he worked with Bruce Greenwald to create alternative frameworks in which imperfections in labor, capital, and product markets were central.

In chapter 7, "Thoughts on DSGE Macroeconomics: Matching the Moment, But Missing the Point?"—Anton Korinek critically evaluates the dominant methodology in macroeconomics, the DSGE approach. He claims that although the approach has led to great progress in some areas, it has also created biases and blind spots in the profession that hold back our understanding and ability to govern the macroeconomy. He provides a cogent critique of not only the assumptions that go into the model, but also the dominant methodology for testing models—as he puts it, "matching the moment but missing the point?"—explaining how they are not well-founded methodologically and result in models that are not very useful for forecasting. But perhaps the most forceful criticism is of the complexity, which he explains, introduces a number of biases into the macroeconomic profession. Finally, he argues that there is great scope for progress in macroeconomics by judiciously pushing the boundaries of some of the methodological restrictions imposed by the DSGE approach, and abandoning the "groupthink" which has prevailed for the last two decades. He ends by recalling "that even in physics—the science which is perhaps closest to reaching a single unifying framework—mankind has not yet managed to find a theory of everything."

In chapter 8, "The 'Schumpeterian' and the 'Keynesian' Stiglitz: Learning, Coordination Hurdles, and Growth Trajectories," Giovanni Dosi and Maria Enrica Virgillito classify Joe as a "closet evolutionist" who highlighted and explored many evolutionary properties of contemporary economics in a Schumpeterian spirit. They link Joe's research on the economics of information with that on the economics of knowledge and innovation, going back to one of his earliest contributions, the Atkinson–Stiglitz concept of localized learning. They then link this work with the "Keynesian Stiglitz," with his identification of structural rigidities associated with imperfect information (Stiglitz–Weiss and Shapiro–Stiglitz). When combined with dynamic increasing returns, learning and coordination failures, the result is the possibility of multiple growth paths, fluctuations, and small and big crises.

In chapter 9, "Deleterious Effects of Sustained Deficit Spending," Edmund (Ned) Phelps contrasts his views on macroeconomic policy with Keynesians like Joe. He provides a critique of sustained deficit spending, showing that the bloating of wealth will crowd out private capital. He concludes that in a richer model, greater unemployment and reduced innovation might result.

In chapter 10, "The Rediscovery of Financial Market Imperfections," John Williams offers a set of remarks that focus on the subset of Joe's body of research that deals with financial market imperfections and the macroeconomy. Williams's perspective is from his seat at the Federal Reserve, both as an economist and policy maker. His tour over the evolution of macroeconomics in recent decades leads him to conclude that the profession has come full circle over the past fifty years, bringing institutional details and market imperfections back into macro thinking and models. He also concludes that having economists with diverse perspectives at the Federal Reserve—who learned from inspiring teachers like Joe—served the United States well during the difficult eight years that followed the 2008 U.S. financial crisis and will continue to do so in the future.

In chapter 11, "Ambiguity and International Risk Sharing," Brian Hill and Tomasz Michalski address the problem of risk sharing in international finance in a novel way. Instead of studying investors with standard risk-averse preferences that allocate capital across different countries, they assume investors exhibit ambiguity aversion—meaning that they have a preference for known risks (i.e., gambles with known probability distributions) over unknown risks (i.e., gambles with unknown or ambiguous probability distributions)—and perceive ambiguity in assets issued in foreign locations. To finance risky projects, firms issue contracts that can have an equity participation and a debt component with a fixed payment. They describe how changes in the variance of their risky production and investors' perceived ambiguity affect financial structure. Entrepreneurs from capital-scarce countries finance themselves relatively more through debt than equity. They are thus exposed to higher volatility. Increases in perceived ambiguity lead to lower across-border capital flows.

Part IV includes three chapters on *networks*. This is an area Joe began working on in the late 1990s, while he was Chief Economist of the World Bank. During the East Asia crisis of 1997, he saw default cascades firsthand—how the default in one company or bank could lead to another. Chapter 7 of Joe's book with Bruce Greenwald, *Towards a New Paradigm of Monetary Economics*, provided an early exploration. He was subsequently joined by a number of Italian colleagues in what turned out to be a fruitful research program—anticipating in many ways the problems that were uncovered in the 2008 financial crisis, and which the group has continued to explore since.

In chapter 12, "Use and Abuse of Network Effects," Hal Varian provides a clarification of the term "network effects." The term has a clear meaning in the context of economic models, but it is sometimes confused with other concepts like "increasing returns to scale" and "learning-by-doing." He uses this framework to examine competition among the major high-tech online firms, concluding that there is not a natural monopoly: " . . . we see intense competition among firms . . . these firms invest heavily in learning . . . they learn quickly, and the knowledge that they have accumulated is the fundamental source of competitive advantage."

As Franklin Allen and Douglas Gale, whose paper "Financial Contagion" published in 2000 by the *Journal of Political Economy* was among the first to examine the consequences of network structure for financial stability, observe in chapter 13, "The financial crisis of 2007–2009 has demonstrated the importance of dislocation in the financial sector as a cause of economic fluctuations. The prevalence of financial crises has led many to conclude that the financial sector is unusually susceptible to shocks. One theory is that small shocks, which initially only affect a few institutions or a particular region of the economy, spread by contagion to the rest of the financial sector and then infect the larger economy." In their chapter, "Financial Contagion Revisited," Allen and

Gale focus on contagion through interbank markets. They study the role of small shocks in bringing down the financial system through interbank market connections, and show that, generally, complete networks are more robust than incomplete networks.

In chapter 14, "The Economics of Information and Financial Networks," Stefano Battiston tries to bring together two strands of work in which Joe has made contributions: his recent work on networks with his earlier work on asymmetric information, and especially the externalities that arise whenever information is imperfect or risk markets incomplete. Battiston argues that more should be done to clarify and formalize the relationship between these two streams of literature. He relates Greenwald and Joe's early work on default cascades in a general equilibrium theory of credit, to more recent work showing how more complex systems may lead to more fragile financial systems, and greater uncertainty about default risk. These conclusions have direct policy implications. For instance, he explains why "ring fencing" may fail, and it may be desirable to foster a more diverse market structure.[1] Battiston's contribution here is part of a broader ongoing research program in complex financial networks supported by the Institute for New Economic Thinking, in which Joe and Battiston have been collaborating.

Part V focuses on *development*. Joe's interest in development goes back to his days as a graduate student. Joe's interest in inequality and poverty naturally led him to think about development—the vast majority of those in poverty live in the developing world. At the same time, from Joe's earliest experiences with developing countries—his trip to Asia in 1967 and his work in Kenya under the auspices of the Rockefeller Foundation beginning in 1969, he found thinking about developing countries enormously insightful and helpful even for understanding developed countries. One of his early famous papers was that on sharecropping, used as a model for thinking more generally about risk and incentive problems. While in Kenya in 1969 he developed the general theory of efficiency wages.

Later, in 1980, Joe was asked by China's Academy of Social Sciences to join a small group discussing China's transition to a market economy. He became further engaged with China's development in the process of co-authoring *The East Asia Miracle* for the World Bank, and then further as Chief Economist of the World Bank. Since leaving the Bank, he has continued his deep engagement with development, including in China, a country he visits a couple of times a year.

Justin Yifu Lin begins chapter 15, "Joseph Stiglitz and China's Transition Success," by saying that China is the most successful transition economy in the world and that Joe is the most influential and respected foreign economist in China. Lin's chapter discusses the achievements of China's transition since 1979, the reasons for China's success, the unaccomplished transition agenda, and the contributions Joe made to China's transition success.

In chapter 16, "The Sources of Chinese Economic Growth Since 1978," Lawrence Lau goes further, decomposing the sources that explain the impressive Chinese growth record since 1978. His analysis suggests that growth can be attributed to (1) the realization of the surplus potential output from the initial economic slack that resulted from the mandatory central planning prior to 1978 (12.65 percent); (2) the growth of inputs, tangible capital (55.71 percent) and labor (9.67 percent); (3) technical progress (growth of total factor productivity [TFP]) (7.97 percent); and (4) the effect of economies of scale (13.99 percent). He claims that in the context of China an important way in which self-fulfilling expectations can be created and changed is through the pronouncement of policy changes and actual actions by a government with credibility.

In chapter 17, "Knowledge as a Global Common and the Crisis of the Learning Economy," Ugo Pagano focuses on the effects that learning has on inequality and development—a theme that has also been extensively discussed by Joe. Pagano analyzes two main interrelated problems that characterize a learning society. On the one hand, there is a tension between the nonrival nature of knowledge and its private appropriation. On the other hand, there is an institutional mismatch between the global nature of the public good that is knowledge and the fragmentation of political power among different nations. There are policies that can help resolve these tensions—creating a global economy with faster growth and more equality. But these involve moving knowledge more into the public space—the opposite of the direction in which things have been going. He claims that the global enforcement of *intellectual property rights*, coupled with the national fragmentation of public investments, has induced each nation to free ride on the production of the global pool of knowledge, and argues that to overcome the global underinvestment in the production of public knowledge, some international institutions must change—for example, each member of the World Trade Organization (WTO) would be committed to investing in open science a minimal fraction of its gross national product (GNP)—with the fruits of that knowledge being made freely available as part of the global commons.

Part VI offers two chapters on *law and economics*. The law sets the rules of the game for the economy, and Joe has become increasingly concerned about the manner in which those rules are set—and their impact on equity and efficiency. See, for instance, his recent book *Rewriting the Rules of the American Economy*. In *Law and Economic Development with Chinese Characteristics: Institutions for the 21st Century*[2] (edited with David Kennedy of Harvard Law School), Joe expressed unease with the excessive influence of the Chicago School in this arena; that book attempted to provide an alternative framework for law and economics.

In chapter 18, "Conservatism and Switcher's Curse," Aaron Edlin formally models the virtues of Edmund Burke's conservatism, the idea that there should be a presumption in favor of the status quo—or as Burke put it (quoted by Edlin): "the longer [our old prejudges] have lasted, and the more generally they have prevailed, the more we cherish them." Edlin characterizes the optimal level of conservatism, and applies the model to management, law, and policy. He begins by introducing "switcher's curse," a trap in which a decision maker systematically switches too often. Decision makers suffer from switcher's curse if they forget the reason that they maintained incumbent policies in the past and if they naively compare rival and incumbent policies with no bias for incumbent policies. Conservatism emerges as a heuristic to avoid switcher's curse. The longer a process or policy has been in place, the more conservative one should be. On the other hand, if past decision makers were extremely conservative, little is learned from their decision to keep a policy, therefore it will pay to be relatively more progressive today.

In chapter 19, "The 'Inner Logic' of Institutional Evolution: Toward a Theory of the Relationship Between Formal and 'Informal' Law," Antara Haldar takes an initial step in the direction of systematizing a theory of the relationship between formal and "informal" law, where *law* is defined as any set of underlying rules that systematically influence patterns of behavior, and the informal aspect of law refers to the social norms, conventions and other nonformal rules that influence behavior.

Finally, part VII includes five chapters on *public policies*. While Joe wrote extensively about public policy, beginning with his early work with Partha Dasgupta and with Tony Atkinson in public economics, it was only in 1993, at the request of President Clinton, that he entered into full-time public service, as a member of Clinton's Council of Economic

Advisers, then as Chairman, moving in 1997 to become the Chief Economist of the World Bank.

In chapter 20, "Joe Stiglitz and Representative and Equitable Global Governance," José Antonio Ocampo analyzes Joe's contributions to the debates on globalization and global economic governance. The chapter refers first to his major books on the subject: *Globalization and Its Discontents* and *Making Globalization Work*. It then focuses on two issues on which Ocampo has interacted with Joe in the past: the creation of an apex mechanism of global economic governance within the United Nations system, and the need to strengthen cooperation on international corporate taxation. Ocampo argues that two common features of Joe's ideas are the need to fill major gaps in global cooperation, and to do so through representative institutions and fair and effective international judicial systems.

Between 2006 and 2013, Joe and Linda Bilmes co-authored a series of papers, articles, congressional testimonies and a best-selling book[3] investigating the full budgetary and economic costs of the U.S. wars in Iraq and Afghanistan. The full scale of those costs exceeded $3 trillion, including long-term disability benefits and medical care for veterans, war-related increases in the Pentagon base budget, social-economic burdens on veterans, and costs to the economy. Most of this amount was hidden from public view. In chapter 21, "The Fiscal Opacity Cycle: How America Hid the Cost of the Wars in Iraq and Afghanistan," Linda Bilmes examines how it was possible for the United States to commit trillions of dollars to the "post–9/11" conflicts with almost no public debate or accounting for the expenditures. The chapter shows that these conflicts were paid for with different methods than those used in previous U.S. wars such as Vietnam and Korea. The current wars have been funded through emergency and other mechanisms that circumvented the congressional budget process and kept war spending outside regular budget caps, bypassing standard systems of reporting that ensure transparency and accountability. The chapter examines several contributing factors to this lack of fiscal transparency, including: (a) a disengaged public who neither fought in the military, nor bore the cost of the conflicts in the form of higher taxes; (b) a military that relied on private contractors to an unprecedented degree; and (c) weak oversight that failed to provide accountability for spending. This led to a "fiscal opacity cycle" in which Congress and the executive branch were able to fund the wars without any budgetary trade-offs against other national priorities. The chapter shows that the lack of accountability for war spending had a significant impact on policy choices and outcomes. The impact included increased waste, profiteering and corruption, poor provision for military veterans, and the introduction of nonstrategic cuts to the military budget.

Income contingent loans (ICLs) are a particular form of government intervention that can improve how an economy works. They provide access to services (like education) to those who might not otherwise be able to afford them; and they provide risk mitigation in an important context in which risk markets typically fail. But the potential of ICLs has yet to be properly and formally recognized in the profession. In chapter 22, "It Works in Practice, But Would It Work in Theory? Joseph Stiglitz's Contribution to Our Understanding of Income Contingent Loans," Bruce Chapman offers an account of Joe's influence in the understanding of ICLs, the design of ICL programs, and their policy potential in other arenas. Joe's contribution occurred in 2013 through the auspices of a workshop organized by the International Economic Association (IEA), held at Dhurajik Pundit University in Bangkok and has been subsequently developed further in a series of formal papers. Chapman explains that although the first nationally based loan system of this type had been introduced in Australia nearly twenty-five years before the 2013 workshop, and the conceptual understanding of the economics of ICLs had been progressing, the theoretical underpinning of the instrument lacked a critical insight related to the role of the public sector in loan collection. Joe provided this final piece of the jigsaw puzzle.

With the rapid increase in long-term care (LTC) needs, the negligible role of the market and the declining role of informal family care, one would hope that the government would take a more proactive role in the support of dependent elderly, particularly those who cannot, whatever the reason, count on assistance from their families. In chapter 23, "The Public Economics of Long-Term Care," Pierre Pestieau and Gregory Ponthiere analyze the possibility of designing a sustainable public LTC scheme integrating both the market and the family.

In chapter 24, "Jomo E. Stiglitz: Kenya's First Nobel Laureate in Economics," Célestin Monga argues that Joe is a formidable example of brain circulation, and that the people of Kenya, where he spent some of his most formative intellectual years, have the right to claim him as their own. The chapter outlines Joe's philosophical itinerary. It highlights his rebellious nature and thirst for discovery, which led him to use his intellect not only to change the discipline of economics several times, but also to make the world a better place. According to Monga, Joe's inexhaustible quest for truth and justice has made him a powerful spokesperson for developing countries and the voice of the African voiceless on issues of economic development and global governance. Monga even claims that some African intellectuals and professionals, simply refer to Joe as Jomo Stiglitz—giving him a typical Kenyan first name to acknowledge the fact that he has indeed become one of them. As we celebrate Joe in this volume, Monga asks us to remember that we celebrate an African economist, as the continent claims him proudly.

Most, but not all of the authors of this volume were Joe's students. Even those who did not have the privilege of being his direct students recognize the influence that Joe has had throughout their careers—and how much they learned from him. The power of the expressions of respect and admiration reminded me of a recent incident. In 2015, Joe and I presented a co-authored paper at the Annual Meeting of the American Economic Association in Boston. The discussant was another great economist, Professor John Geanakoplos from Yale University. As usual, Geanakoplos delivered a set of outstanding remarks, but before offering his comments on the paper, he told the audience: "I learned more from Joe's papers than from any other economist outside of my direct mentors. Many of his papers have been an inspiration to me." Luckily for us, he added that he "learned a lot from this one as well." And he concluded that he hoped that "young Guzman will be another Stiglitz." But after having spent numerous hours in many different situations with Joe, I know it's impossible. Joe has brains, heart, and courage. There have been many bright minds in the world. Only a few of those minds come with a heart that calls the brain to humanity. Even fewer people can articulate what has to change to make the world a better place in addition to also having the courage and sense of fairness needed to fight to make those changes a reality.

This volume is a small celebration from some of those who accompanied Joe during his academic life. We all thank Joe for what he has given us. At the end of the conference that inspired this volume, Joe received a long, spontaneous standing ovation that epitomized how we all felt.

We are fortunate for the opportunity to honor him in life; an experience future generations will not have. But they will be able to learn from his legacy, and that will be the best celebration he receives because if future generations learn from Joe and take his teachings to heart, it will surely make the world a better place for many, fulfilling the dreams and ambitions Joe had when he first entered economics a little more than a half-century ago.

NOTES

Anya Stiglitz assisted with the editing of this introduction.

1. As suggested by the Stiglitz UN Commission in 2010 (see the *Report of the Commission of Experts of the President of the United Nations General Assembly on Reforms of the International Monetary and Financial System*).

2. Oxford: Oxford University Press (2013).

3. *The Three Trillion Dollar War: The True Cost of the Iraq Conflict*, by Joseph E. Stiglitz and Linda J. Bilmes (New York: Norton 2008) was a *New York Times* best seller and has been translated into more than twenty languages. See also Joseph E. Stiglitz and Linda J. Bilmes, "The Long-Term Costs of Conflict: The Case of the Iraq War" in *The Handbook on the Economics of Conflict*, edited by Derek L. Braddon and Keith Hartley (Cheltenham, UK: Edward Elgar, 2011) and "Estimating the Costs of War: Methodological Issues, with Applications to Iraq and Afghanistan" in *The Oxford Handbook of the Economics of Peace and Conflict*, edited by Michelle Garfinkel and Stergios Skaperdas (Oxford: Oxford University Press, 2012).

PART I

Inequality

CHAPTER 1

A Firm-Level Perspective on the Role of Rents in the Rise in Inequality

Jason Furman and Peter Orszag

Joseph Stiglitz has been an intellectual mentor to both of us for the past two decades, a period that looms large in our lives, but which today's celebration reminds us is just a fraction of the fifty years that Joe has been teaching students and inspiring policy makers. In Joe's honor, we thought it appropriate to collaborate on a paper that explores two of his core interests: the rise in inequality and how the assumption of a perfectly competitive marketplace is often misguided.

Joe has been a leading advocate of the hypothesis that the rising prevalence of economic rents—payments to factors of production above what is required to keep them in the market—and the shift of those rents away from labor and toward capital has played a critical role in the rise in inequality (Stiglitz 2012). The aggregate data are directionally consistent with this story, including the fact that the share of income going to capital has risen and the profit rate has risen. But this aggregate story does not fully explain the timing and magnitude of the increase in inequality. Inequality started rising in the 1970s, while the capital share of income and the profit rate did not begin its rise until around 2000. Moreover, the majority of the increase in inequality can be accounted for by an increasingly skewed distribution of labor income, not the division of income between workers and owners of capital.

This chapter advances another hypothesis using firm-level data to argue that there has been a trend of increased dispersion of returns to capital across firms, with an increasingly large fraction of firms getting returns over 20 or 30 percent annually—a trend that somewhat precedes the shift in the profit share. Long-standing evidence (e.g., Krueger and

Summers 1988) has documented substantial interindustry differentials in pay—a mid-level analyst may have the same marginal product wherever he or she works but is paid more at a high-return company than at a low-return company. Newer evidence (e.g., Barth et al. 2014) suggests that at least some and perhaps even most of the rise in earnings inequality represents the increased dispersion of earnings *between* firms rather than *within* firms. This is consistent with the combination of a rising dispersion of returns at the firm level and the inter-industry pay differential model, as well as with the notion that firms are wage *setters* rather than wage *takers* in a less-than-perfectly-competitive marketplace.

These various factors raise the question of whether another perspective on inequality trends—which is consistent with the data we present—is that a rising share of firms are earning supranormal returns on capital and workers at those firms are both producing and sharing in those supernormal returns, driving up wage inequality. Our hypothesis highlights the potential role of rents in the rise in inequality, extending their role to explain the increase in earnings inequality and pushing back the date of their importance to about 1990—when the distribution of returns on capital across firms began to grow increasingly skewed.

To be sure, many other factors have contributed to rising inequality and in advancing this argument, we seek to add to the existing list, not to displace or rebut any of the existing arguments. And even these data have alternative interpretations. For example, even if inequality were entirely the result of competitive markets in which the returns to skills have risen, it could still appear to be "firm driven" if there were increased sorting of workers across firms, with high-return firms hiring high-skill workers and vice versa. The only conclusion about which we have a high degree of conviction is simply that more attention needs to be paid to what is driving firm-level trends in the United States, and in particular, whether such trends reflect economic rents at the firm level.

THE DEFINITION OF RENTS AND THEIR POTENTIAL ROLE IN INCREASED INEQUALITY

Economic rents are the return to a factor of production in excess of what would be needed to keep it in the market. Rents can accrue to any of the factors of production. As just one example, rents can arise from anticompetitive behavior that produces revenues well in excess of the opportunity cost of capital. A rent can also be created by the pairing of a worker and firm in a manner that produces higher returns on capital and higher wages than either could otherwise earn and that are in excess of what would be necessary to keep the worker in the labor market and the firm in the product market. Those rents are then divided between labor and capital based on their respective bargaining power and other institutional arrangements.

A central feature of rents is that, by themselves, they are statically unproductive. By definition, they are excessive returns to market activity that would have occurred anyway in their absence. Moreover, the allocation of time and energy to the pursuit of rents ("rent seeking") hurts productivity by diverting that capital and labor away from more innovative pursuits. But in some cases, rents can be dynamically efficient: for example, our patent system effectively promises monopoly rents to innovators should they successfully bring a new technology to market. While the patent-protected rent is not necessary to encourage a producer to sell once the innovation has taken place, it is designed to encourage the initial innovation that leads to the product in the first place, with benefits for aggregate productivity.

Rents can also affect the income distribution in indirect ways. For example, if labor increases its ability to bargain for a larger share of the rent generated in the labor market, overall social welfare could potentially increase, depending on one's particular social welfare function.

Rents could play a role in increasing inequality through two principal channels. The first would occur if rents themselves are rising—if, for example, increased concentration led to greater monopoly power in product markets and thus a greater ability to extract supernormal returns. Second, for any given level of aggregate rents, they could be divided increasingly unequally—for example, reduced collective bargaining coverage could have led to a shift in the share of rents generated in the labor market away from labor and toward capital, or from nonsupervisory labor to management.

ACCOUNTING FOR THE RISE IN INEQUALITY

In order to show the ways in which rents might or might not explain rising inequality, it is helpful to begin with a decomposition of the rise in inequality. This is not a causal explanation but is instead a way to show where inequality has increased in order to focus on potential explanations for that increase.

Specifically, if income is defined as the sum of labor and capital income, then the increase in the dispersion of income can be understood as deriving from three sources:

- Increased share of income going to capital, which increases inequality because high-income households, on average, derive a larger share of their income from capital
- Increased capital income dispersion, which is the disparity of income from sources like capital gains and dividends between earners at different levels of the overall income distribution
- Increased labor income dispersion, which is the disparity of earnings between earners at the different levels of the overall income distribution

There are currently no official statistics that provide a breakdown of income into these three sources. Nevertheless, a combination of data sources can offer some insights (see Furman 2014).[1] In the United States, the top 1 percent's share of total income rose from 8 percent in 1970 to 17 percent in 2010, according to data from Thomas Piketty and Emanuel Saez available on the World Wealth and Income Database. Throughout this period, the top 1 percent's share of labor income rose steadily, while its share of capital income only began a sustained rise around 1985, as shown in figure 1.1. Overall, the 9-percentage-point increase in the share of income going to the top 1 percent in the World Wealth and Income Database from 1970 to 2010 is attributable to the three factors discussed above in the following dimensions: 68 percent due to increased inequality within labor income; 32 percent due to increased inequality within capital income; and 0 percent due to a shift in income from labor to capital.

These data exhibit no change in the share of income going to capital and labor from 1970 to 2010 in part due to source and definitional differences from the standard National Income and Product Accounts (NIPA) data. Assuming the NIPA data are correct in aggregate, we find that the income shift from labor to capital is responsible for roughly 20 percent of the increase in inequality since 1970, still a considerably smaller factor than the changing distribution within labor income or within capital income.

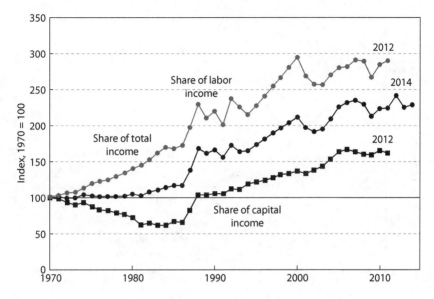

Figure 1.1   Share of Total Labor and Capital Income Accruing to Top 1 Percent

Source: World Wealth and Income Database; Saez and Zucman (forthcoming); CEA calculations.

THE RISE IN THE CAPITAL SHARE: AN AGGREGATE EXPLANATION THAT PLAYS A MINOR ROLE

This taxonomy of the rise in inequality suggests that if the cause of inequality is limited to the division of income between capital and labor, then this definition can only explain at most 20 percent of the increase in the share of income going to the top 1 percent since 1970, including none of the increase in inequality prior to 2000. Further analysis of the sources of the fall in the labor share of income casts additional doubt that this perspective plays a large role in the story.

First, the capital stock itself has not grown meaningfully relative to total output. Figure 1.2 shows that simple metrics of the size of the capital stock relative to economic output have not shown a clear directional trend in recent decades. The ratio of the nominal value of the private fixed asset stock to business sector value added is only slightly above its historical average in the wake of the financial crisis. And most of the slight increase we have seen is attributable to the housing sector: when excluding residential assets, the capital stock is even more closely in line with its historical average.

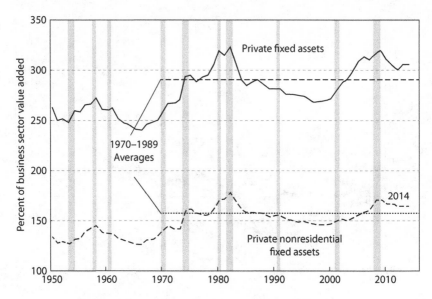

Figure 1.2   Nominal Capital Stock Relative to Economic Output

Note: Shading denotes recession.

Source: Bureau of Economic Analysis (Fixed Asset Accounts, National Income, and Product Accounts); CEA calculations.

Second, the decline in the labor share of income is not due to an increase in the share of income going to productive capital—which has largely been stable—but instead is due to the increased share of income going to housing capital, a point analyzed by Rognlie (2015) and shown in figures 1.3a and 1.3b.

As the share of total income paid to labor in the form of compensation has decreased since 2000, housing capital has captured most of the offset. Returns to private nonhousing capital have increased only slightly, as shown in figure 1.4.

The above observations are consistent with some role for aggregate rents in explaining the trends. Increased rents in housing markets due to land-use restrictions that create artificial scarcity may be part of the cause of the rise in the share of income going to housing and land (see box 1.1). It is also noteworthy that the return to productive capital has risen recently, despite the large decline in yields on government bonds,

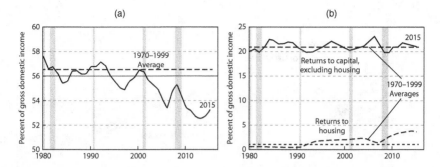

Figure 1.3 (a) Labor Share of Gross Domestic Income; (b) Capital Shares of Gross Domestic Income

Note: The labor share is defined as compensation of employees by domestic employers as a share of gross domestic income. Shading denotes recession.

"Returns to housing" are defined as the sum of rental income of persons in the housing sector, corporate profits in the housing sector, and proprietors' income in the housing sector. "Returns to capital excluding housing" are defined as the net operating surplus of all domestic enterprises excluding returns to housing.

Source: Bureau of Economic Analysis (National Income and Product Accounts); CEA calculations.

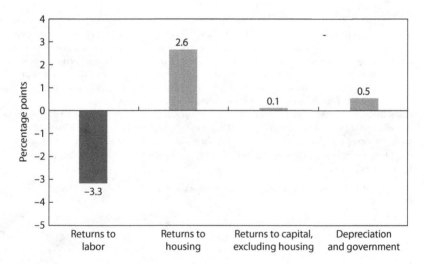

Figure 1.4 Change in Shares of Gross Domestic Income, 2015 versus 1970–1999 Average

Note: "Returns to labor" are defined as compensation of employees by domestic employers. "Returns to housing" are defined as the sum of rental income of persons in the housing sector, corporate profits in the housing sector, and proprietors' income in the housing sector. "Returns to capital excluding housing" are defined as the net operating surplus of all domestic enterprises excluding returns to housing. "Depreciation and government" is the sum of the consumption of fixed capital and government tax receipts for production and imports, less government subsidies. These four defined terms sum to the gross domestic income, and all changes are expressed as a share of gross domestic income.

Source: Bureau of Economic Analysis; CEA calculations.

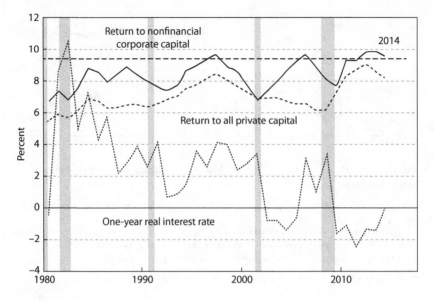

Figure 1.5 Returns to Capital

Note: The rate of return to all private capital was calculated by dividing private capital income in current dollars by the private capital stock in current dollars. Private capital income is defined as the sum of (1) corporate profits ex. federal government tax receipts on corporate income, (2) net interest and miscellaneous payments, (3) rental income of all persons, (4) business current transfer payments, (5) current surpluses of government enterprises, (6) property and severance taxes, and (7) the capital share of proprietors' income, where the capital share was assumed to match the capital share of aggregate income. The private capital stock is defined as the sum of (1) the net stock of produced private assets for all private enterprises, (2) the value of total private land inferred from the Financial Accounts of the United States, and (3) the value of U.S. capital deployed abroad less foreign capital deployed in the United States. The return to nonfinancial corporate capital is that reported by the Bureau of Economic Analysis, and the one-year real interest rate is that reported by Robert Shiller at Yale University.

Sources: Bureau of Economic Analysis; Federal Reserve Board of Governors; Robert Shiller, Yale University; CEA calculations.

as shown in figure 1.5. One potential explanation of the disparity between these two variables is the increased prevalence of rents, although changing risk characteristics of returns to private capital or government bonds could also be playing a role.

An aggregate analysis of rents leaves many questions unanswered, though, motivating an examination of rents at the firm level.

buildings that can be built in a given area. This is accomplished either through direct categorical restrictions or imposing prohibitive costs on investors.

While land-use restrictions are perhaps the most salient example of rents in the housing market, broader trends may be at work and a broad range of factors affect housing rents. The demographic trend of urbanization, for example, may confer rents on housing owners in places like New York and San Francisco, where housing values far exceed construction costs. Such trends are likely exogenous to the housing market itself, reflecting cultural shifts that boost demand for urban living. But they certainly provide returns to housing owners well above their reservation price. These housing rents would take the form of increased producer surplus in response to an exogenous positive demand shock, rather than the negative supply shock induced by land-use restrictions.

Researchers have also linked land-use restrictions directly to lost productivity and output growth, recognizing that such constraints limit worker access to the highest productivity U.S. cities. Hsieh and Moretti (2015) observe that high-productivity cities including New York and San Francisco tend to have increased constraints on housing supply, resulting in a suboptimal level of human capital being allocated to these high-productivity cities. Hsieh and Moretti find that reducing such restrictions to the level of the median city would expand an individual city's labor force and boost U.S. gross domestic product (GDP) almost 10 percent.

To the extent that cities with especially stringent land-use restrictions tend to have especially high upward mobility—and high-mobility cities do tend to have less income inequality (Chetty et al. 2014)—these rents have important implications for inequality itself and the persistence of inequality. Zoning and land-use restrictions can potentially discourage low-income families from moving to high-mobility areas—a prediction consistent with the decline in migration observed in the United States since the 1980s (Molloy et al. 2014)—effectively relegating them to lower-mobility areas, reinforcing inequality. Accordingly, housing rents have important implications for both aggregate growth and its distribution.

THE FIRM-LEVEL DISTRIBUTION OF RETURNS

The limitations of the rents hypothesis at the aggregate level suggest the importance of looking also at the firm level. Firm-level analysis of returns underscores the possibility of an increased prevalence of super-normal returns over time. We examine this issue from two perspectives: the return on equity and the return on invested capital. First, with regard to equity returns, the distribution among publicly traded corporations appears to have grown more skewed to the high end with time. Figure 1.6 compares the distribution of returns on equity across the firms that compose the S&P 500 in 1996 and 2014, two roughly comparable years in the business cycle. The modal return on equity is subtracted from each firm's return such that both distributions are centered approximately at zero and

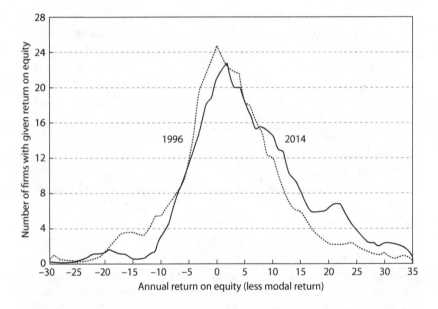

Figure 1.6   Distribution of Annual Returns on Equity Across S&P 500

Note: The annual return to common equity is displayed for the stated year (i.e., 1996 or 2014) for all members of the S&P 500 as of the last week of May the following year (i.e., 1993 or 2015). The distribution of returns covers all members of the S&P 500 in the year indicated and buckets firms by single percentage-point intervals, smoothed by averaging over five percentage-point 20 intervals. The modal return in a given year was subtracted from each firm's return such that both distributions are centered approximately at zero. The tail ends of the distribution (above or below a 60 percent or 20 percent return on equity, respectively) were trimmed for optical clarity.

Sources: Bloomberg Professional Service; CEA calculations.

skewness can be most clearly observed. The distribution has skewed to the high end over time as more supernormal returns are being earned by those firms at the high end of the distribution.[2]

The return on equity, however, can be affected by changes in the debt-equity mix and other factors. A more comprehensive measure of the return on capital is the return on invested capital, defined as net after-tax operating profits divided by capital invested in the firm. This measure reflects the total return to capital owners, independent of financing mix. Below, we present new data on the distribution of the return on invested capital at the firm level, as compiled by the McKinsey Corporate Analysis tool.

Figure 1.7 presents the distribution of the return on invested capital (ROIC) for publicly traded nonfinancial U.S. firms from 1965 through 2014, excluding goodwill (an intangible asset reflecting the excess of the price paid to acquire a company over the value of its net assets).

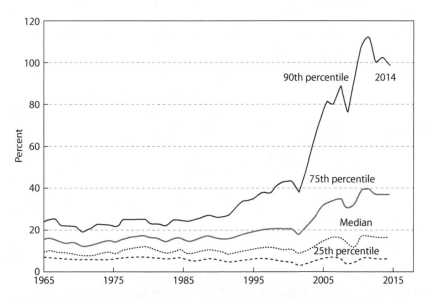

Figure 1.7   Return on Invested Capital Excluding Goodwill, U.S. Publicly Traded Nonfinancial Firms

Note: The return on invested capital definition is based on Koller et al (2015), and the data presented here are updated and augmented versions of the figures presented in chapter 6 of that volume. The McKinsey data include McKinsey analysis of Standard & Poor's data and exclude financial firms from the analysis because of the practical complexities of computing returns on invested capital for such firms. For further discussion of that point, see Koller et al. (2015).

Sources: Koller et al. (2015); McKinsey & Company.

This analysis excludes financial firms, where ROIC data is considerably more scarce. As the chart shows, the 90th percentile of the return on invested capital across firms has grown markedly since around the early 1990s. The 90/50 ratio—that is, the ratio of the 90th percentile of the distribution of capital returns to the median—has risen from under 3 to approximately 10. In addition, the dramatic returns on invested capital of roughly 100 percent apparent at the 90th percentile, and even 30 percent apparent at the 75th percentile, at the very least raise the question of whether they reflect economic rents.

The data including goodwill are somewhat less dramatic, as shown in figure 1.8. Nonetheless, even on this basis, the variance has risen over time. And more importantly for our purposes, we believe the measure excluding goodwill is more insightful to use, since supernormal operating returns on capital can be partially dissipated in value-reducing

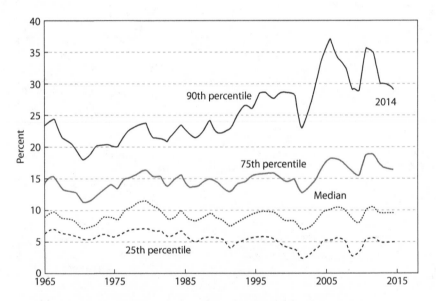

Figure 1.8 Return on Invested Capital Including Goodwill, U.S. Publicly Traded Nonfinancial Firms

Note: The return on invested capital definition is based on Koller et al (2015), and the data presented here are updated and augmented versions of the figures presented in chapter 6 of that volume. The McKinsey data include McKinsey analysis of Standard & Poor's data and exclude financial firms from the analysis because of the practical complexities of computing returns on invested capital for such firms. For further discussion of that point, see Koller et al. (2015).

Source: Koller et al. (2015); McKinsey & Company.

acquisitions. Our focus is on the emergence of the high returns in the first place, so excluding goodwill seems more appropriate.

The ROIC measure is not perfect; the treatment of R&D, for example, can cause biases. But it seems unlikely that any such biases have grown so much that they can explain the dramatic trends shown here.

Figures 1.7 and 1.8 raise the question of what factors are associated with these very high capital returns.[3] The McKinsey data show that two-thirds of the nonfinancial firms enjoying an average return on invested capital of 45 percent or higher between 2010 and 2014 were in either the health care or information technology sectors.

The dramatic increase in the dispersion of annual returns is not, in and of itself, evidence of an increase in rents. First, the returns need not be persistent—if all firms in the economy went from returns of 5 percent to random draws of 0 or 10 percent each year, we would not say that rents had risen, even if annual returns were more dispersed. Second, consistently higher average returns for some firms could reflect compensation for the greater risk they are bearing. Both of these explanations merit further exploration, but some tentative evidence on the persistence of returns suggests that there is at least more to the story than these two possibilities. An analysis of the set of firms underlying figures 1.8 and 1.9 suggests relatively low probabilities of transition out of their return bucket for high-returning firms. For example, of firms with a return on invested capital above 25 percent in 2003, only 15 percent had a return on invested capital below 25 percent in 2013, while 85 percent remained in the 25-percent-plus bucket in 2013.

Consolidation may be a contributing factor to the changing distribution of capital returns shown in figures 1.7 and 1.8 as well as the increased share of firms with apparently supernormal returns (see the Council of Economic Advisers [CEA] 2016 and *The Economist* 2016).[4] Data from the Census Bureau's Economic Census on firm concentration show a trend of pronounced consolidation across most broad industry categories in the nonfarm business sector. Table 1.1 shows that in nearly all of the industries for which data are available, the fifty largest firms gained revenue share between 1997 and 2012. We use the Census Bureau's data here because it includes private and public firms, whereas Compustat includes only public firms (Ali et al. 2009). Consistent data from the Census Bureau only start in 1997 and the most recent data go through 2012.[5] However, other industry-specific studies document similar trends over longer periods of time. A study by the Congressional Research Service shows that

Table 1.1 Change in Market Concentration by Sector, 1997–2012

Industry	Percentage Point Change in Revenue Share Earned by the Fifty Largest Firms
Transportation and warehousing	11.4
Retail trade	11.2
Finance and insurance	9.9
Wholesale trade	7.3
Real estate rental and leasing	5.4
Utilities	4.6
Educational services	3.1
Professional, scientific, and technical services	2.6
Administrative/support	1.6
Accommodation and food services	0.1
Other services, nonpublic admin	–1.9
Arts, entertainment, and recreation	–2.2
Health care and assistance	–1.6

Note: Concentration ratio data is displayed for all North American Industry Classification System (NAICS) sectors for which data are available from 1997 to 2012.

Sources: Economic Census (1997 and 2012), Census Bureau.

the revenue share held by the top four firms rose between 1972 and 2002 in eight of the nine agricultural industries it tracks (Shields 2010). In a study of a related set of industries, Fuglie et al. (2012) find an increase in market concentration among upstream agricultural supply industries worldwide. In financial services, Corbae and D'Erasmo (2013) find that loan market share (measured on a national level) of the top 10 banks increased from about 30 percent in 1980 to about 50 percent in 2010, and deposit market share of the top 10 banks increased from about 20 percent in 1980 to almost 50 percent in 2010. By 2010, these shares had grown to 38 and 37 percent, respectively.

National metrics of concentration are an imperfect tool for examining trends in geographically differentiated industries where national firms play a comparatively small role, like health care and social assistance. For these types of industries, it is often more meaningful to examine trends in the average level of local market concentration. Notably, research examining hospital markets, the largest subindustry of health care and social assistance, finds that the average local hospital market has become more concentrated, despite the fact indicated in table 1.1 that the share of revenue earned by the fifty largest firms nationwide has fallen (Gaynor, Ho, and Town 2015).

A number of market-level studies also find evidence of increasing concentration. Vogt and Town (2006) find that the average hospital Herfindahl-Hirschman Index (HHI, a common measure of market concentration) increased from 1576 to 2323 between 1990 and 2003, a result further supported by Gaynor, Ho, and Town's (2015) finding that the average hospital HHI rose by roughly 50 percent between the 1990s and 2006 to nearly 3200. For wireless markets, a study by the U.S. Federal Communications Commission (FCC 2015) finds HHIs increasing from under 2500 in 2004 to over 3000 in 2014. And in the railroad industry, Prater et al. (2012) conclude that there was an increase in market concentration between 1985 and 2007.

The overall point is that to the extent that industries look more like oligopolies than perfectly competitive markets, they will generate economic rents. In the absence of some countervailing public purpose, such rents reflect an erosion of the surplus that would otherwise accrue to consumers in a competitive market. These rents can become manifest in the form of higher prices for consumers, reduced quality and variety of products and services, and even a reduction in innovative activity, which translates into lower productivity.

It should be noted that just as rents in general are not in and of themselves harmful, not all increases in concentration are either. A firm that realizes economies of scale may achieve lower operating costs that benefit consumers through lower prices. Productive innovative activities can lead to monopolies through the patent system, and this result is by design— as noted above, the patent system is based on the premise that offering inventors a temporary monopoly for their invention encourages innovation. Network effects may mean that in some markets (particularly those dominated by new technologies), market share may tip to a single provider of the network good, at least temporarily. What makes the recent trend of decreased competition more concerning, however, is that it has occurred at the same time that labor market and firm dynamism are also in decline. Moreover, mergers and acquisitions activity is at an all-time high, and the size of such deals is on the rise as well. In and of itself, that does not necessarily imply reduced competition but it is not inconsistent with such a reduction despite efforts by the relevant enforcement agencies (the Department of Justice's Antitrust Division and the Federal

Trade Commission) in the domains of merger review and combating criminal anticompetitive behaviors, such as collusion, as highlighted by CEA (2016).

THE ROLE OF WITHIN- AND BETWEEN-FIRM EARNINGS INEQUALITY

As noted above, much of the increase in the share of income going to the top 1 percent, and especially to the top 10 percent, over the past several decades is due to increased inequality within labor income. Recent research has generally found that the increase in earnings inequality is, in turn, explained by increased divergence in the average earnings of workers in different firms rather than the increased divergence of earnings within individual firms. This evidence also suggests that we should be looking to firm-level analysis, not just an aggregate story, to understand the rise in inequality.

Barth et al. (2014) merge data from the Current Population Survey, the Longitudinal Business Data Base, and Longitudinal Employer-Household Dynamics data to examine changes in the variance of average earnings across establishments and the variance within establishments. They estimate that increasing inequality between establishments explains more than two-thirds of the increase in overall earnings inequality between 1992 and 2007. Among workers who continued at the same establishment from one year to the next, the increased spread in average pay between establishments explained 79 percent of the rise in earnings inequality over that period. As they conclude, "In short, the pattern of change in pay and potentially other economic outcomes in the establishments where people work has been a major factor in the much-heralded increase in inequality. We have shown that establishments matter but have only scratched the surface of analyzing the economics that have pulled establishments apart in earnings space" (22).

Song et al. (2016) similarly examine the trend in earnings inequality between 1981 and 2013 at the level of the firm (and not the establishment, as in Barth et al. 2014). They find that 70 percent of the rise in earnings inequality has occurred because of wider dispersion of earnings between firms rather than within firms. (The results are somewhat attenuated for the very largest firms, with about half the rise in earnings inequality for firms with more than 10,000 employees due to within-firm effects.) The underlying driver of these results, however, remains unclear. In particular, although Song et al. find that the bulk of the rise in earnings inequality has occurred between rather than within firms, they conclude that this is more a reflection of workers sorting themselves across firms (with high wage workers increasingly working with other high wage workers) rather than a reflection of the firms themselves. The authors note, however, that this sorting may still reflect a growing level and variance of rents: if rents increasingly accrue to higher earners, for example, they may have an increased incentive to isolate themselves in high-wage firms.

Additional research on this topic is crucially important, given the fact that both Barth et al. (2014) and Song et al. (2016) agree that most of the rise in wage inequality has occurred between rather than within firms. Furthermore, the perspective that this is not all, or even necessarily primarily, grounded in the sorting of workers with different skills, but instead reflects the consequences of firms with different degrees of profitability is grounded in the inter-industry wage differentials research pioneered by Krueger and Summers (1988). This literature has found that industry-specific wage premia cannot be explained by differences across industries in nonwage compensation, compensating differentials for working conditions, or differences in the propensity of unionization. This conclusion has been debated—for example, Gibbons and Katz (1992) stressed the role of unmeasured worker heterogeneity. But recent work including Abowd et al. (2012) also finds that firm-level effects explain more of the variance in inter-industry wage differentials than worker-level effects. Krueger (2013) found that the correlation between managers' and janitors' wages across industries remained high, at 0.8, consistent with the rent-sharing stories discussed here, but that the correlation had fallen relative to earlier decades, suggesting that even at high-profit firms janitors are getting a smaller share of the rents.

All of this evidence could help explain the rise in inequality of earnings. Some firms, for example in the technology sector or the financial sector, could generate consistently high supernormal returns. Workers at these firms would share in these returns in the form of higher wages than they would get for similar work at other firms that did not receive supernormal returns.

The literature on deregulation in the airline and trucking industries supports the notion that firms and workers share product market rents. Card (1996) found that following the 1978 deregulation of the airline industry, airline workers' wages fell about 10 percent relative to wages in the rest of the economy. The declines were similar across most occupation types, including for industry-specific positions (such as pilots and flight attendants) and more general positions (such as managers and secretaries). These patterns suggest that prior to deregulation, the airline industry was characterized by rent sharing with employees. Rose (1987) tested the rent-sharing hypothesis in the trucking industry, finding that following deregulation, union wages declined substantially and the wage premium (union wages relative to nonunion wages) fell from 50 percent before deregulation to under 30 percent after deregulation. This supports the notion of rent sharing, at least in the context of unionized workers.

The rent-sharing argument, however, hinges on some immobility in labor. To the degree that labor was perfectly mobile, it would compete away the portion of these rents going to workers, sorting workers into firms according to their marginal products and leaving the full benefit of these rents for capital. In general, however, there are frictions in labor markets that can generate persistent rents, and there is some evidence that these frictions may have grown over time, the topic we turn to next.

THE DECLINE IN LABOR AND BUSINESS FLUIDITY AND THE PERSISTENCE OF RENTS

JOB AND GEOGRAPHIC MOBILITY

One potential outcome of an increased variance in capital returns at the firm level along with increased rent seeking in the U.S. economy could be a reduction in the overall dynamism of U.S. labor markets. An increasing number of researchers have noted this trend, with varying levels of concern, in part because the emerging literature has not reached a consensus on its causes. Labor market dynamism (or "fluidity" or "churn") refers broadly to the frequency of changes in who is working for whom in the labor market.

We know relatively more about job flows (job creation and destruction) than worker flows (hires and separations) since series data are available back to the 1980s. Literature based on these data concludes that job flows have markedly declined over the last twenty to thirty years. For example, Decker et al. (2014) and Davis and Haltiwanger (2014) document that job creation and job destruction fell from the late 1980s to just before the 2007 recession, as shown in figure 1.9. Hyatt and Spletzer (2013) find larger declines, of roughly one-quarter to one-third, for both job creation and destruction between the late 1990s and 2010.

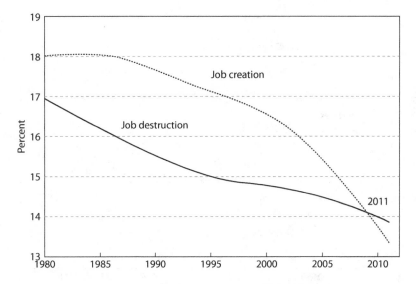

Figure 1.9   Job Creation and Destruction Rates: 1980–2011

Source: Decker et al. (2014), based on Census Bureau (Business Dynamics Statistics).

Worker flows have declined since at least the late 1990s, including the entire period for which the best direct data on these flows are
available from the Job Openings and Labor Turnover Survey (JOLTS;
Bureau of Labor Statistics). Hyatt and Spletzer (2013) document declines
of 10 percent (using Current Population Survey data) to 38 percent
(using Longitudinal Employer-Household Dynamics [LEHD] data)
in hires and separations since 2001, as shown in figure 1.10. Davis and
Haltiwanger (2014) have a longer series on hires and separations that
extends back to 1990, which shows a decline in worker flows over this
longer period.

Long-distance migration in the United States, which typically involves
a change of employer or labor force status, has also been in a decades-long
decline, falling by as much as 50 percent since the late 1970s (Molloy et
al. 2014; Kaplan and Schulhofer-Wohl 2012). Both intra- and intercounty
migration have followed similar patterns, as shown in figure 1.11.

Recent work by Molloy et al. (2016) combines these disparate
measures—worker flows, job flows, and interstate migration—into a
single measure going back to the late 1960s. Using principle component
analysis, the authors find that a single factor has driven most of the long-
run trends in each of these measures, with a decline in overall fluidity of

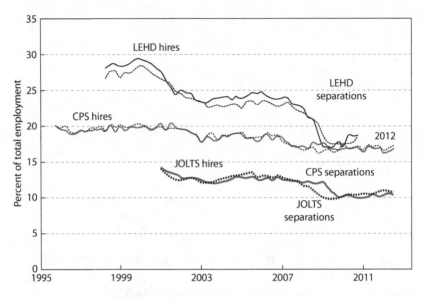

Figure 1.10   Trends in Hires and Separations, 1995–2012

Sources: Hyatt and Spletzer (2013); Bureau of Labor Statistics (Current Population Survey); Bureau of Labor Statistics (Job Openings and Labor Turnover Survey [JOLTS]); Census Bureau (Longitudinal Employer-Household Dynamics [LEHD]).

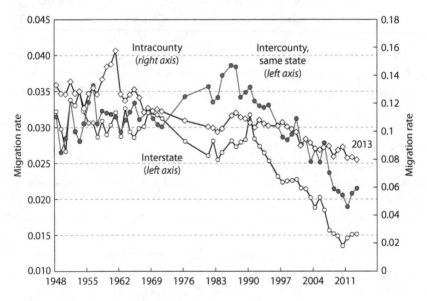

Figure 1.11   Migration Rates by Distance

Source: Raven Molloy, Christopher L. Smith, and Abigail K. Wozniak, "Declining Migration within the U.S.: The Role of the Labor Market." NBER Working Paper No. 20065.

10 to 15 percent since the early 1980s (though declining fluidity may have begun in the late 1970s).

The empirical literature has only recently begun to examine why job and worker transitions have fallen. Some explanations, like demographic changes including the rise of two-earner couples, have been ruled out because the declines in transitions are occurring for a wide range of demographic groups. Two basic hypotheses have been explored: that either firms or workers have changed over time in ways that lower fluidity.

Evidence shows that changes in firms can explain a portion of declining fluidity, while changes in worker characteristics can explain far less of the decline. The average age and number of associated establishments per firm have both risen in recent decades (Davis and Haltiwanger 2014; CEA 2015). Older, larger firms are associated with lower job flows, as these firms are less likely to contract or expand rapidly. The decline in firm entry and exit rates noted above are consistent with this change in firm composition. Because the change in the composition of firms has shifted in a way that, all else equal, would suggest fewer worker hires and separations, researchers have tested to see how much of the shift in worker flows can be explained by changes in firm composition.

Hyatt and Spletzer (2013) and Davis and Haltiwanger (2014) decompose changes in worker flows into those due to job flows and those due to worker movements between existing jobs. They find that changes in job flows account for between one-third to one-half of the decline in worker flows. Because job flows are determined in part by firm size and age, changing firm characteristics contribute to the decline in worker flows (Hyatt and Spletzer 2013). In contrast, changes in the characteristics of the average worker, like age and education, have been found to contribute little to declines in fluidity (Molloy et al. 2014; Davis and Haltiwanger 2014; Molloy et al. 2016). Molloy et al. (2016) also provide suggestive evidence that decreases in fluidity are unlikely to be the result of a number of potential explanations, including changes in industrial composition, a shrinking fraction of younger workers, formalization of hiring practices, and increased regulatory barriers to labor market transitions (see box 1.2 for a discussion of the role of occupational licensing regulations).

The implications of reductions in dynamism are less clear than the trends themselves. On the one hand, reduced dynamism may be a sign of better matching in job markets or increased efforts by firms to reduce employee turnover. (It is worth noting, however, that Molloy et al. [2016] find no evidence that decreased fluidity has been driven by better worker-firm matching, increased flexibility in compensation, or more employer-provided training.) On the other hand, reduced flows may preclude employees from realizing the wage gains of switching jobs or make it difficult for part-time workers to find full-time work, reducing overall labor productivity. As recent working papers suggest, heterogeneity in the cyclical responsiveness of worker flows among firms may play a role in slowing wage growth among workers.[6] Other research suggests that more fluid labor markets may be more resistant to cyclical shocks, or, at a minimum, experience faster recoveries after a recession (Blanchard and Wolfers 2000).

Although this literature has not reached definitive conclusions, one general theme is the importance of firm behavior in contributing to the decline in job and geographic mobility—and the ways in which this, in turn, reinforces increased wage disparities for workers. The role of the firm also appears to loom much larger in explaining wage inequality trends than the popular wisdom suggests, as we noted earlier.

Box 1.2: Occupational Licensing

Declines in worker mobility—in particular, geographic mobility—may also be in part driven by another decades-long trend in the U.S. economy: the steady increase in the number of workers whose occupations require some sort of license or certification (Davis and Haltiwanger 2014). Work by Morris Kleiner and Alan Krueger (2013) charting the historical growth in licensing from a number of different data sources shows that the share of the U.S. workforce covered by state licensing laws grew fivefold in the second half of the twentieth century, from less than 5 percent in the early 1950s to 25 percent by 2008. Although state licenses account for the bulk of licensing, the addition of local and federal licensed occupations further raises the share of the workforce that was licensed in 2008 to 29 percent. Notably, there is considerable variation across states, suggesting that licensing can help explain reduced geographic mobility.

In part, the increase in licensing is due to growth in the number of employees in occupations that typically require a license, such as health care occupations, over the last few decades. But it is also due to a large increase in the number of occupations that have been licensed.

Analysis from a recent CEA report finds that roughly two-thirds of the growth in the number of licensed workers is attributable to growth in the number of licensed occupations, with a little over one-third due to changes in the occupational composition of the workforce (CEA et al. 2015). While often based on sound concerns for health and safety protections for consumers, some occupational licensing regimes can also present a classic case of rent seeking by incumbents, who may successfully lobby government entities to erect barriers to entry to would-be competitors. Whatever its benefits or costs, the rise of licensing may be one contributing factor behind the decades-long decrease in interstate mobility, though it is unlikely that licensing is the sole driver of this change (CEA et al. 2015).

CONCLUSION

As we stated at the outset, our principal conclusion is that more work needs to be done combing questions of inequality, deviations from perfect competition, and the role of rents in both arenas. Such work needs to be done at the firm level to potentially help explain the rise in inequality—including inequality in earnings, inequality in capital returns, and the shift in income from labor to capital. Joe has shined a spotlight on these questions, advanced the theory, and pointed to a range of important evidence. The next stages of this important discussion should dig deeper into the nuances of these questions at the level of the firm and of individual workers.

NOTES

The authors thank Harris Eppsteiner, Sam Himel, Rob Seamans Gustav Sigurdsson, Peter Tillman, Eric Van Nostrand, and William Weberfor assistance; Tim Koller and Bin Jiang of McKinsey & Company for updating the data in McKinsey & Company, Koller et al. (2015) for us; and Steve Braun, Larry Katz, Alan Krueger, Claudia Sahm, and Jay Shambaugh for comments.

1. The analysis that follows considers the dispersion of labor income and of capital income across earners ordered by overall income, rather than separate orderings of labor income and capital income. Put differently, the group depicted in figure 1.1 as the "Top 1 Percent" is the same group for all three time series. Therefore, an increase in the correlation of labor income and capital income across earners would appear as a shift in labor or capital income dispersion, rather than an independent source of inequality.

2. As with the other returns on capital discussed below, it is worth noting that to the extent that some share of a supernormal return is shared with labor, the measured returns to capital (which are net of labor compensation) will be correspondingly reduced.

3. An important question is the degree to which these figures are affected by the declining prevalence of publicly listed firms in this period. Indirect evidence suggests that composition effects do not drive the results, but in the absence of a complete set of ROIC data for both public and private firms, it remains possible that changes in the type of firm publicly listed could affect the results.

4. In the spring of 2016, both the Council of Economic Advisers and *The Economist* separately explored this hypothesis and associated data and literature in greater detail, the former in an issue brief entitled "Benefits of Competition and Indicators of Market Power," which also discussed potential policy remedies.

5. This metric of concentration is an imperfect tool for examining trends in geographically differentiated industries where national firms play a comparatively small role, like health care and social assistance. For these types of industries, it is often more meaningful to examine trends in the average level of local market concentration. Notably, research examining hospital markets, the largest subindustry of health care and social assistance, finds that the average local hospital market became more concentrated from 1997 to 2007, despite the fact that the share of revenue earned by the fifty largest firms nationwide fell (Gaynor et al. 2014).

6. Very recent work suggests that changes in firm-side behavior may be deeply linked to decreases in dynamism through heterogeneity in the cyclical responsiveness of worker flows among firms. First, in a paper released in February 2015, Giuseppe Moscarini and Fabien Postel-Vinay (2015) use JOLTS data and link job flows to firm size, showing that while hires were declining even before the Great Recession, around the time of the financial crisis they collapsed among large establishments but remained stable at small establishments. Along with cyclical effects on other job and workflow measures, Moscarini and Postel-Vinay offer suggestive evidence that the "job ladder"—the process by which workers move from smaller firms to larger firms as they search for higher-quality jobs—broke down during the Great Recession and has yet to recover. The drop in hiring among larger firms and the decline in larger establishments' "poaching" workers from smaller establishments has led to reduced incentives for smaller employers to hire the unemployed, both prolonging the average duration of unemployment and causing persistent slack in the labor market.

One limitation of Moscarini and Postel-Vinay's study is that they can only examine heterogeneity by firm size, and cannot study other firm characteristics—such as firm wages. Looking over a slightly longer time frame, Haltiwanger et al. (2015) use matched employer-employee LEHD data to test Moscarini and Postel-Vinay's hypothesis. They find little support for the "job ladder" between smaller and larger firms. Instead, they find evidence of a "job ladder" along which workers reallocate from *lower-paying* firms to *higher-paying* firms. However, this firm-wage "job ladder" collapsed in the Great Recession. Likewise, Lisa Kahn and Erika McEntarfer (2014) find that separations—and particularly separations followed by employment, which are most likely to be voluntary—tend to drop more sharply in recessions among lower-paying firms. Business cycle contractions thus tend to prevent workers from progressing "up the job ladder" to higher-paying firms.

REFERENCES

Abowd, John M. et al. 2012. "Persistent Inter-Industry Wage Differences: Rent Sharing and Opportunity Costs." *IZA Journal of Labor Economics* 1 (7).

Ali, Ashiq et al. 2009. "The Limitations of Industry Concentration Measures Constructed with Compustat Data: Implications for Finance Research." *Review of Financial Studies* 22 (10):3839–3871.

Barth, Erling et al. 2014. "It's Where You Work: Increases in Earnings Dispersion Across Establishments and Individuals in the U.S." NBER Working Paper No. 20447.

Been, Vicki et al. 2014. "Preserving History or Hindering Growth? The Heterogeneous Effects of Historic Districts on Local Housing Markets in New York City." NYU Furman Center Working Paper.

Blanchard, Olivier, and Justin Wolfers. 2000. "The Role of Shocks and Institutions in the Rise of European Unemployment: The Aggregate Evidence." *Economic Journal* 110 (462):C1–C33.

Bureau of Labor Statistics. "Job Openings and Labor Turnover Survey." Dataset, https://www.bls.gov/jlt/. Accessed February 16, 2018.

Card, David. 1996. "Deregulation and Labor Earnings in the Airline Industry." NBER Working Paper No. 5687.

Chetty, Raj et al. 2014. "Where Is the Land of Opportunity? The Geography of Intergenerational Mobility in the United States." *Quarterly Journal of Economics* 129 (4):1553–1623.

Corbae, Dean, and Pablo D'Erasmo. 2013. "A Quantitative Model of Banking Industry Dynamics." Working paper. https://sites.google.com/site/pabloderasmo/home /research/a-quantitative-model-of-banking-industry-dynamics.

Council of Economic Advisers (CEA). 2015. "Chapter 3: Achievements and Challenges in the U.S. Labor Market." *Economic Report of the President.*

Council of Economic Advisers (CEA) et al. 2015. "Occupational Licensing: A Framework for Policymakers." *White House Occupational Licensing Report* (July).

Council of Economic Advisers (CEA). 2016. "Benefits of Competition and Indicators of Market Power." *Council of Economic Advisers Issue Brief* (April).

Davis, Steven J., and John Haltiwanger. "Labor Market Fluidity and Economic Performance." NBER Working Paper No. 20479.

Decker, Ryan et al. 2014. "The Role of Entrepreneurship in U.S. Job Creation and Economic Dynamism." *Journal of Economic Perspectives* 28 (3):3–24.

Economist, The. 2016. "Too Much of a Good Thing. Profits Are Too High. America Needs a Giant Dose of Competition." *The Economist* (March 26).

Fuglie, Keith et al. 2012. "Rising Concentration in Agricultural Input Industries Influences New Farm Technologies." U.S. Department of Agriculture (USDA).

Furman, Jason. 2014. "Global Lessons for Inclusive Growth." Council of Economic Advisers.

Gaynor, Martin, Kate Ho, and Robert J. Town. 2015. "The Industrial Organization of Health-Care Markets." *Journal of Economic Literature* 53 (2): 235–84.

Gibbons, Robert, and Lawrence Katz. 1992. "Does Unmeasured Ability Explain Inter-Industry Wage Differentials?" *Review of Economic Studies* 59:515–535.

Glaeser, Edward L., and Joseph Gyourko. 2003. "The Impact of Building Restrictions on Housing Affordability." *Economic Policy Review* 9 (2):21–39.

Glaeser, Edward L., Joseph Gyourko, and Raven Saks. 2005. "Why Have Housing Prices Gone Up?" *American Economic Review* 95 (2):329–333.

Gyourko, Joseph, and Raven Molloy. 2015. "Regulation and Housing Supply." In *Handbook of Regional and Urban Economics, Volume 5B,* edited by Gilles Duranton, J. Vernon Henderson, and William C. Strange. Amsterdam: Elsevier Science.

Haltiwanger, John et al. 2015. "Cyclical Reallocation of Workers Across Employers by Firm Size and Firm Wage." NBER Working Paper No. 21235.

Hsieh, Chang-Tai, and Enrico Moretti. 2015. "Why Do Cities Matter? Local Growth and Aggregate Growth." NBER Working Paper No. 21154.

Hyatt, Henry R., and James R. Spletzer. 2013. "The Recent Decline in Employment Dynamics." *IZA Journal of Labor Economics* 2 (1):1–21.

Kahn, Lisa, and Erika McEntarfer. 2014. "Employment Cyclicality and Firm Quality." NBER Working Paper No. 20698.

Kaplan, Greg, and Sam Schulhofer-Wohl. 2012. "Understanding the Long-Run Decline in Interstate Migration." NBER Working Paper No. 18507.

Kleiner, Morris M., and Alan B. Krueger. 2013. "Analyzing the Extent and Influence of Occupational Licensing on the Labor Market." *Journal of Labor Economics* 31 (2):S173–S202.

Krueger, Alan B. 2013. "Land of Hope and Dreams: Rock and Roll, Economics, and Rebuilding the Middle Class." Remarks at the Rock and Roll Hall of Fame.

Krueger, Alan B., and Lawrence H. Summers. 1988. "Efficiency Wages and the Inter-Industry Wage Structure." *Econometrica* 56 (2):259–293.

McKinsey & Company, Tim Koller et al. 2015. *Valuation: Measuring and Managing the Value of Companies,* 6th ed. Hoboken, NJ: Wiley.

Molloy, Raven et al. 2014. "Declining Migration within the U.S.: The Role of the Labor Market." NBER Working Paper No. 20065.

Molloy, Raven et al. 2016. "Understanding Declining Fluidity in the U.S. Labor Market." *Brookings Papers on Economic Activity.* BPEA Conference Draft (March 10–11).

Moscarini, Giuseppe, and Fabien Postel-Vinay. 2015. "Did the Job Ladder Fail After the Great Recession?" Working Paper. https://campuspress.yale.edu/moscarini/files/2017/01/job_ladder_GR-1lsgaa3.pdf.

Prater, Marvin E., Ken Casavant, Eric Jessup, Bruce Blanton, Pierre Bahizi, Daniel Nibarger, and Isaac Weingram. 2012. "Rail Competition Changes Since the Staggers Act." *Journal of the Transportation Research Forum* 49 (3):111–132.

Rognlie, Matthew. 2015. "Deciphering the Fall and Rise in the Net Capital Share." *Brookings Papers on Economic Activity.* BPEA Conference Draft (March 19–20).

Rose, Nancy L. 1987. "Labor Rent-Sharing and Regulation: Evidence from the Trucking Industry." *Journal of Political Economy* 95 (6):1146–1178.

Shields, Dennis A. 2010. "Consolidation and Concentration in the U.S. Dairy Industry." *Congressional Research Service.*

Song, Jae, David Price, Fatih Guvenen, Nicholas Bloom, and Till von Wachter. 2016. "Firming Up Inequality." Stanford University (mimeo).

Stiglitz, Joseph E. 2012. *The Price of Inequality: How Today's Divided Society Endangers Our Future.* New York: Norton.

U.S. Federal Communications Commission (FCC). 2015. "Eighteenth Mobile Wireless Competition Report."

Vogt, William, and Robert Town. 2006. "How Has Hospital Consolidation Affected the Price and Quality of Hospital Care?" The Synthesis Project, Report No. 9. Robert Wood Johnson Foundation.

World Wealth and Income Database. "The World Wealth and Income Database." Alvaredo, Facundo et al. Accessed April 19, 2016. http://wid.world.

CHAPTER 2

Parents, Children, and Luck

EQUALITY OF OPPORTUNITY AND EQUALITY OF OUTCOME

Ravi Kanbur

ABSTRACT

This paper considers three perspectives on parents, children, and luck (PCL), each with a venerable pedigree. The first perspective focuses on the intergenerational elasticity (IGE) of income transmission. Within this perspective, the older literature traces the consequences of higher or lower IGE for the evolution of inequality of income. The more recent literature, on the "Great Gatsby Curve," sees the causality running the other way, from current inequality to IGE. The second tradition (PCL II) approaches intergenerational mobility through transition matrices and sets out views on *greater mobility* through this lens. But these views are not necessarily consistent with each other, and a social welfare function approach is needed to pronounce on comparisons between societies. Taking a dynastic inequality approach, Kanbur and Stiglitz (2016) show that "equality of opportunity"—a transition matrix with identical rows—does not necessarily lead to lower dynastic inequality than all other transition matrices. Finally, the third perspective on parents, children, and luck (PCL III) is presented by Roemer (1998), and in particular, by applications of the framework to quantify "inequality of opportunity." It is argued here that these approaches have serious empirical and conceptual flaws, and may understate the true degree of inequality of opportunity.

1. MOTHERHOOD AND APPLE PIE

Who could possibly be against equality of opportunity, especially when compared to equality of outcomes? Not, it would seem, many egalitarian thinkers, for whom the development of egalitarian theory, since Rawls, may be characterized as an effort to replace equality of outcomes with equality of opportunities, where opportunities are interpreted in various ways. Metaphors associated with this view are "leveling the playing-field," and "starting gate equality"—Wagstaff and Kanbur (2015) call equality of opportunity the new motherhood and apple pie in policy discourse. There are many translations of this metaphor into concrete specifications. Roemer (1998), following Dworkin (1981a,b) and others, famously distinguishes between "circumstances" and "effort" as characterizing those factors that are respectively outside and within the control of the individual in determining outcomes. Equality of opportunity is then the equalization of the impact of circumstances on outcome, without touching the difference in outcome induced by effort.

There are many possible types of circumstances but two stand out in the literature. The first is the characteristics of parents, over which presumably children have no control. The second, "brute luck," to use Dworkin's phrase, in other words random events over which the individual has had no influence. There are other circumstances such as gender or ethnicity, although the latter could equally well be treated as the consequence of parental characteristics. Leaving to one side complex questions on the social construction of categories, gender is outside the control of an individual at birth, depending on parental genetic characteristics combined with the random processes of chromosomal crossover in reproduction. But then so, presumably, are all of the genetic traits that go under the label of "talent." Pushed to the limit, this chain of reasoning would leave very little outside of the realm of circumstance.

But in a narrower economic setting, let us think of the circumstances of a child as being parental income, and let us describe economic processes as leading to a stochastic outcome for the child, conditional on the parents' income. This simple formulation leads to a stochastic process through which the income distribution evolves over time, depending on the conditional distribution of the child's income given the parents' income. The tightness of the conditioning can be thought of as a measure of the *inequality of opportunity*, and naturally leads to the question of whether greater inequality of opportunity leads to greater inequality of outcome, and vice versa.

It is these interactions between parents, children, and luck in the determination of the equality of opportunity and equality of outcome which are reviewed and explored in this paper. Section 2 begins with the simplest well-known setting in which parental income determines child income but with shocks. The implications for long-run income distribution of different degrees of mobility are traced. Section 3 takes up an alternative tradition in the literature on the measurement of intergenerational mobility, based on transition matrices, and asks how common views on "greater mobility" match perspectives on dynastic inequality. Section 4 returns to the recent literature inspired by Roemer (1998) and presents a brief critique. Section 5 concludes the discussion.

2. PCL I

The first strand of literature linking parents, children, and luck goes back at least as far as Gibrat (1931). Gibrat set out a stochastic dynamic process that in his view led to a size distribution of firms that matched reality. The application of such stochastic processes to income distribution goes back at least as far as Champernowne in the 1930s (Champernowne 1973) and again Champernowne and Kalecki in the 1940s and 1950s (Kalecki 1945; Champernowne 1953). The topic was revived in the 1970s by the work of Creedy (1974) and Hart (1976). Economic models of intergenerational transmission usually have Becker and Tomes (1979) as a starting point, but have been developed considerably since then, for example, by Solon (2004, 2015).

Forty years ago, Hart (1976) set out a model of income dynamics which is now easily recognizable. The standard income transition equation between log income y of generation $t - 1$ and generation t is given by

$$y_t = \beta y_{t-1} + \varepsilon_t; \ \varepsilon_t \text{ is } N(0, \sigma_\varepsilon^2) \qquad (2.1)$$

where ε_t is a stochastic disturbance term independent of y_{t-1} and normal distributed with a mean of 0 and the variance σ_ε^2. Here, β is a conventional measure of intergenerational mobility—the extent to which generation t's outcome is influenced by the outcome for generation $t - 1$. It is also known as the intergenerational elasticity (IGE) of income. As Krueger (2012, 3) notes: "Another handy statistic for summarizing the connection between parents' and children's income is the Intergenerational Income Elasticity (IGE). Recent studies put the IGE for the United States around 0.4. This means that if someone's parents earned 50 percent more than the average, their child can be expected to earn 20 percent above the average in their generation."

Let the variance of y_t be denoted σ_t^2. Then, of course

$$\sigma_t^2 = \beta^2 \, \sigma_{t-1}^2 + \sigma_\varepsilon^2 \qquad (2.2)$$

Hart (1976) used this apparatus to derive predictions on the time path of inequality (measured by the variance of log income):

> If $\beta^2 \geq 1$ we have the result, as in Gibrat (1931), where $\beta = 1$, that the inequality of incomes must always increase over time. Gibrat's model was criticised in 1936 by Champernowne (1973) on the grounds that continuously increasing inequality of incomes does not occur very often in practice and, moreover, it is unreasonable to suppose that the chance of a given proportionate change in income was independent of the size of income, as implied by . . . $\beta = 1$. But if $\beta < 1$, the percentage increase in earnings tends on average to fall as you go up the income distribution. With this "regression" towards the median or mean, to use Galton's . . . term, it is possible for the inequality of incomes to decrease, a result rediscovered by Kalecki (1945). (Hart 1976, 556)

When $\beta < 1$, the process in (2.2) leads to a steady state level of inequality given by

$$\sigma_y^2 = \sigma^2/(1 - \beta^2) \qquad (2.3)$$

Thus, observed steady state inequality σ_y^2 is higher, the higher is the variance of the stochastic shocks to log income, σ_ε^2. But σ_y^2 also depends on β. If $\beta = 0.4$ as suggested by Krueger (2012), then inequality of income in the steady state will be around 20 percent higher than the pure variation coming from the shocks. Further, as β increases, so does inequality σ_y^2. The elasticity of inequality with respect to mobility is given by

$$d(\log \sigma_y^2)/d(\log \beta) = 2\beta^2/[1 - \beta^2] \qquad (2.4)$$

Thus for $\beta = 0.4$, the elasticity of inequality with respect to mobility is around 40 percent, and this elasticity is increasing in the level of mobility itself.

If "success breeds success," to quote Hart (1976) and shocks are serially correlated, it should be intuitively clear that the inequality effect of mobility is further intensified. To see this, let ε_t be an AR(1) process with autocorrelation parameter θ:

$$\varepsilon_t = \theta\varepsilon_{t-1} + \xi_t \; ; \; \xi_t \text{ is } N(0, \sigma\xi^2) \tag{2.5}$$

In this case

$$y_t = (\beta + \theta)y_{t-1} - \beta\theta y_{t-2} + \xi_t \tag{2.6}$$

For this second-order autoregressive process it can be shown using standard methods that the steady state variance is given by

$$\sigma_y^2 = \{(1 + \beta\theta) \, \sigma\xi^2\}/\{(1 - \beta\theta)[(1 + \beta\theta)^2 - \beta^2]\} \tag{2.7}$$

Solon (2004) derives this equation from a model of parents investing in their children's human capital, as well has public provisions of human capital. Taking the cross-section regression of y_t on y_{t-1} as being the usual estimate of IGE, it can now be shown that this IGE is increasing in the underlying parameters β and θ, which in the Solon model are themselves functions of the raw parameters of the model. Further, the variance of log income in this second-order autoregressive process is also shown to be increasing in these raw parameters: "cross-sectional income inequality is greater in the presence of stronger heritability, more productive human capital investment, higher returns to human capital, and less progressive public investment in human capital" (Solon 2004, 9).

The positive association, between a measure of inequality and a measure of intergenerational mobility, as shown in (2.3) and expanded by Solon (2004) for higher-order processes, has been dubbed "The Great Gatsby" relationship, christened as such by Krueger (2012) based on the empirical work of Miles Corak (2013):

Recent work by Miles Corak finds an intriguing link between the IGE and income inequality at a point in time. Countries that have a high degree of inequality also tend to have less economic mobility across generations. We have extended this work using OECD data on after-tax income inequality, as measured by the Gini coefficient. . . . I call this the

"Great Gatsby Curve." The points cluster around an upward sloping line, indicating that countries that had more inequality across households also had more persistence in income from one generation to the next.

Notice of course the difference in implied causal interpretation of the association shown in the steady state relationship (2.3). The Gibrat-Champernowne-Kalecki-Hart interpretation would see the causality as running from β to σ_y^2. The parameter β is the key driver of the stochastic process, leading to the outcome σ_y^2. But in Krueger's interpretation, the causality is the other way around:

> The U.S. has had a sharp rise in inequality since the 1980s. If the cross-sectional relationship displayed in this figure holds in the future, we would expect to see a rise in the persistence in income across generations in the U.S. as well. While we will not know for sure whether, and how much, income mobility across generations has been exacerbated by the rise in inequality in the U.S. until today's children have grown up and completed their careers, we can use the Great Gatsby Curve to make a rough forecast. . . . The IGE for the U.S. is predicted to rise from .47 to .56. In other words, the persistence in the advantages and disadvantages of income passed from parents to the children is predicted to rise by about a quarter for the next generation as a result of the rise in inequality that the U.S. has seen in the last 25 years. It is hard to look at these figures and not be concerned that rising inequality is jeopardizing our tradition of equality of opportunity. (Krueger 2012, 4)

Corak (2013) also has the causality running from inequality to mobility, and he uses the argument of Roemer (2004) to make the case:

> First, parents may transmit economic advantages through social connections facilitating access to jobs, admission to particular schools or colleges, or access to other sources of human capital. Second, parents may influence life chances through the genetic transmission of characteristics like innate ability, personality, and some aspects of health that are valued in the labor market. Third, parents may influence the lifetime earnings prospects of their children in subtle ways, like through a family culture and other monetary and nonmonetary investments that shape skills, aptitudes, beliefs, and behavior. (Corak 2013, 98)

It should be noted, however, that in these arguments it is not inequality per se, which is the cause of low mobility (a high β). There is not a model here that leads from a higher σ_y^2 to a higher β. One way to think of this is to go back to (2.1) and make β itself a function of y. If β is simply an increasing linear function of y, which is consistent with the arguments above, then the average value of β depends on the average value of y and does not depend on inequality in y. For inequality in y to matter for the average value of β in society, the relationship has to be nonlinear. Solon (2004) presents a model in which the relationship is in effect nonlinear, but he then linearizes it to approximate the standard mobility equation. This then raises an interesting empirical question—is the transmission of advantage disproportionately higher at higher levels of advantage? Furthermore, in his model with public investment in human capital, he shows that "less progressive public investment in human capital" leads to a lower value of the mobility estimate. Is the link then from greater inequality, through a political economy model to less progressive public investment? Such models need to be developed in order to flesh out the causality from high inequality to lower mobility.

3. PCL II

There is a complementary literature on parents, children, and luck, also with quite old roots, which is not regression based. Rather, the basic analytical device is the transition matrix. Consider the square matrix A whose typical element a_{ij} gives the probability of the child of a parent with income y_i having an income y_j. So we have parents, we have children, and we have luck. The rows of the matrix add up to unity, and we assume the matrix remains unchanged, in other words, a Markovian setting. Of special interest, as we shall see, are a class of matrices which satisfy the bistochastic property—their columns as well as their rows sum to unity. The question then becomes, comparing two transition matrices A and B (the latter with typical element b_{ij}), which displays "more mobility?"

In an important paper, Shorrocks (1978) formalized a number of views which were, and still are, prevalent in the literature. One such view is what might be termed the "diagonals" view, based on the fact that each diagonal element of a transition matrix gives the probability of staying in the same income state from generation to generation. If every diagonal element of A is smaller than the corresponding diagonal element of B one might say that A is "more mobile" than B, although of course this only induces a partial ordering on the class of transition matrices. Shorrocks calls this relation "monotonicity." The identity matrix is then the extreme of immobility, with children inheriting the income of their parents exactly, with no possibility of escape.

If the identity matrix is the most immobile, what then is the most mobile? Pushing the "diagonals" view to the other extreme, this would be a matrix with zeros in the diagonal, so that no child stays where his or her parent was in terms of income. The child's income could be higher, it could be lower, but it will not be the same. Atkinson (1981) calls this "complete reversal." This is clearest in the 2×2 case where the identity matrix and the complete reversal matrices are given respectively by

$$\begin{bmatrix} 1 & 0 \\ 0 & 1 \end{bmatrix} \text{ and } \begin{bmatrix} 0 & 1 \\ 1 & 0 \end{bmatrix} \tag{2.8}$$

Relative status therefore switches every generation.

Shorrocks (1978) contrasts the diagonals view with what he calls "perfect mobility," where the rows of the transition matrix are identical to each other. In other words, the prospects for the children are the same no matter what the parents' income. Atkinson (1981) calls this the "equality of opportunity" view, partly in reference to a large popular literature which reached then, and still reaches now, for this characterization, albeit in a nontechnical way. Shorrocks (1978) motivates his search for a measure of mobility by observing that "monotonicity" and "perfect mobility" cannot be satisfied simultaneously. This is seen straight away by considering the two matrices:

$$A = \begin{bmatrix} 0 & 1 \\ 1 & 0 \end{bmatrix} \text{ and } B = \begin{bmatrix} 1/2 & 1/2 \\ 1/2 & 1/2 \end{bmatrix} \tag{2.9}$$

Clearly, A dominates B on "monotonicity," while B dominates A on "perfect mobility."

How is a conflict like the one above to be resolved? Atkinson (1981) and Atkinson and Bourguignon (1982) propose that we have to be more explicit about the precise sense in which society prefers one matrix over another. In other words, the social welfare function needs to be specified. This set off a large literature at that time. Atkinson and Bourguignon (1982) considered a two-period social welfare function and derived dominance conditions related to the property of the social welfare function. Kanbur and Stiglitz (1986, 2016) also followed the social welfare route, but in the context of infinitely lived dynasties. The Kanbur-Stiglitz approach and results can be illustrated easily in the 2×2 bistochastic case with

$$A = \begin{bmatrix} a & 1-a \\ 1-a & a \end{bmatrix} \text{ and } B = \begin{bmatrix} b & 1-b \\ 1-b & b \end{bmatrix} \tag{2.10}$$

Clearly, with $a = 0$ and $b = 1/2$, we have the situation depicted in (2.9).

Let the vector of the two incomes be $y = (y1, y_2)$ with $y2 < y_1$. Let the discount factor be $r < 1$. Then the present discounted value vector $v = (v_1, v_2)$ for the transition matrix A is given by

$$v^A = y + rAy + r^2A^2y + r^3A^3y........ = [I - rA]^{-1}y \tag{2.11}$$

with the corresponding expression for B. Expression (2.11), with A and with B, gives us the vector of "dynastic inequalities" in the two societies characterized by mobility patterns A and B. Noting that for a bistochastic matrix the steady distribution is equal population share at each income level, in the 2×2 case we can simply look at the ratio $z = v_1/v_2$ as the measure of dynastic inequality.

For the 2×2 case in (2.10), using the expression (2.11), the dynastic inequality measures for society A can be can be written as:

$$z = \frac{(1-ra)k + r(1-a)}{(1-ra) + r(1-a)k} \tag{2.12}$$

where $k = y_1/y_2 > 1$.

If a is replaced by b in z we get the dynastic inequality in society b. Now, it can be shown that

$$v_1 + v_2 = (y_1 + y_2)/(1 - r) \tag{2.13}$$

and that

$$\frac{dz}{da} > 0 \tag{2.14}$$

In other words, an increase in a induces a mean preserving spread in the vector of dynastic inequalities.

The result in (2.14) provides a clear ranking of 2×2 matrices using the criterion of dynastic inequality. It also resolves, then, the conundrum of ranking the two matrices A and B given in (2.9). Clearly, A delivers greater dynastic equality than does B, even though B is often labeled "equality of opportunity." The intuition behind this should be clear. With discounting of the future, the present matters. Equalizing prospects from now on does not handle the fact that there is inequality in the here and now. But reversal of fortunes from generation to generation addresses this asymmetry of time, and delivers a more equitable dynastic outcome. Starting from the identity matrix (a close to unity), decreasing a will indeed decrease dynastic inequality up to the point where the rows are identical. But decreasing a further will decrease dynastic inequality further still. For dynastic inequality, therefore, we need to go beyond equality of opportunity.

For the 2×2 bistochastic case we get a complete ordering of transition matrices according to the criterion of dynastic inequality. Kanbur and Stiglitz (1986, 2016) provide a generalization for the $n \times n$ case. They show that the dynastic inequality of a society with a bistochastic transition matrix B is a mean preserving spread of the dynastic inequality of a society with bistochastic transition matrix A, if and only if there exists a bistochastic matrix Q such that

$$B = \{(1/r)I\} \{I - Q\} + AQ \tag{2.15}$$

where, as before, I denotes the identity matrix. Expression (2.15) can be interpreted as saying that B can be written as a weighted sum of the identity matrix (suitably adjusted for the discount factor r) and A, the weights being given by the matrix Q. In other words, in this generalized sense, B is "closer" to the identity matrix than is A. This is thus a generalization of the 2×2 case, where an increase in a moves the matrix closer to the identity matrix and increases dynastic inequality. Once again, however, it can be shown that in the $n \times n$ case the equal opportunity matrix is dominated by the complete reversal matrix (Kanbur and Stiglitz 2016).

For this framing of parents, children, and luck, dynastic equality requires going beyond equality of opportunity; it requires an actual correction of parental advantages, in the other direction. Thus the dynastic inequality perspective supports the "less weight in diagonals" view rather than the "rows are closer to being identical" (or "equality of opportunity") view of a "better society." To eliminate dynastic inequality, it is not enough to give the poor the same opportunity as the rich. "Clogs to clogs in three generations" is what is needed.

4. PCL III

Roemer (1998) introduced a formalization of inequality of opportunity. As stated in Roemer (2008), the key step is to "separate the influences on the outcome a person experiences into *circumstances* and *effort*: the former are attributes of a person's environment for which he should not be held responsible, and effort is the choice variable for which he should be held responsible" (Roemer 2008). The practical implementation of this conceptual frame to derive a quantitative measure of inequality of opportunity is well described by Paes de Barros et. al. for their study on Latin America:

> To measure inequality of opportunity for a certain outcome, total inequality in the outcome can be decomposed into two parts: one resulting from circumstances beyond individual control and a second part resulting from unequal individual effort and luck. . . . First, six variables related to circumstances exogenous to the individual were identified from the most comprehensive data sets available: gender, race or ethnicity, birthplace, the educational attainment of the mother, the educational attainment of the father, and the main occupation of the father. . . . Then the sample was partitioned (in each country) into groups or "cells," such that all individuals in any given cell have exactly the same combination of circumstances. The resulting subgroups are known in the literature as "types." These cells are then compared with one another. The difference in outcomes between cells can be attributed to inequality of opportunity, while the differences within cells can be considered the result of effort or luck. (2009, 125–126)

There are also, of course, parametric analogs to the nonparametric method above (see, for example, Hufe et. al. 2015).

Kanbur and Wagstaff (2016) and Wagstaff and Kanbur (2015) provide a comprehensive critique of the Paes de Barros et al. (2009) method from a technical and a conceptual standpoint. Here I focus on just two aspects of this critique, which relate to parents, children, and luck. Let us start with luck. Here again there are many related avenues one could follow, including that of the distinction made by Dworkin (1981a,b) between "brute luck" and "option luck"—as the names suggest, the latter is chosen by the individual, the former is not. Take, for example, a risk willingly and fully chosen by two individuals—let it be a sum of money on the toss of a fair coin (Kanbur 1987). After the lottery, the winner has everything, the loser nothing—sheer destitution. Would we not want to address the outcome of destitution even though it was the result of option luck rather than brute luck? Following Kanbur (1987), Kanbur and Wagstaff argue that

> in the case of destitution as an outcome of the lottery choice, our moral intuitions do indeed veer towards ex post redistribution and support for the destitute. To emphasize the point, imagine yourself serving on a soup line of the indigent. Consider then the idea that we would condition the doling out of soup on an assessment of whether it was circumstance or effort which led to the outcome of the individual in front of us to be in the soup line. Surely this is morally repugnant, and it establishes that at least for extreme outcomes the outcome-based perspective dominates any considerations of opportunity. Indeed, this point is taken on board by Bourguignon, Ferreira and Walton (2007) in their definition of equitable development policy which "makes avoidance of severe deprivation a constraint that must be satisfied in the process of pursuing the broader objective of equal opportunity. (2006, 134–135)

Thus, extreme outcomes from luck test our intuitions on opportunity and on just reward to choices. Even if a person knew that one of the outcomes of risky choice was destitution, we would not leave that person destitute if that outcome actually comes about. Against the call of "he knew what he was doing" is pitted the call of "tomorrow's hunger cannot be felt today," or "there but for the grace of God go I." Of course, redistribution after the event will have incentive effects. So be it. These will have to be taken into account in the final design of policy. The point, however, is that just because luck is option luck does not mean that its outcomes should not be addressed. Finally, of course, much of the luck that people face is in fact residual brute luck—insurance markets are not complete for well understood economic reasons (for a classic exposition, see Rothschild and Stiglitz 1976). Variations in outcome due to these circumstances should then be included in the estimate of inequality of opportunity.

Luck aside, what happens when one person's effort becomes another person's circumstance? Let us return to parents and children. If parents choose to exert little effort and indulge profligate tastes, so they do not have sufficient resources to educate their children, the "circumstances" doctrine would say that the education outcome for the children should be corrected. But this would surely violate the "effort and tastes" doctrine applied to parents, which would say that the outcomes are fine as they are. As Kanbur and Wagstaff comment: "Equality of opportunity, it would seem, is caught between two inconsistent Old Testament Biblical injunctions from Deuteronomy: 'for I, the Lord your God, am a jealous God, visiting the iniquity of the fathers on the children, and on the third and the fourth generations of those who hate Me' versus 'Fathers shall not be put to death for their sons, nor shall sons be put to death for their fathers; everyone shall be put to death for his own sin' " (2016, 135).

If our moral intuitions side with the argument that irrespective of parental effort which led to them, inequality in circumstances for children is a legitimate target for correction, what then is left of the "effort and tastes" component of the distinction between "inequality of opportunity" and "inequality of outcome?"

5. WHAT'S LEFT OF EQUALITY OF OPPORTUNITY?

This is not the place for a root-and-branch critique of the equality of opportunity doctrine. There is a large literature, with illustrious philosophers and economists weighing in. It connects also to Sen's (1985) "capabilities approach," as discussed for example in Kanbur (2016). But in the narrow confines of parents, children, and luck, the links between equality of outcome and equality of opportunity are interesting, and shed light on the broader debate.

This chapter has considered three perspectives on parents, children, and luck (PCL), each with a venerable pedigree. The first perspective (PCL I) focuses on the intergenerational elasticity of income transition. Within this perspective, the older literature traces the consequences of higher or lower IGE for the evolution of inequality of income. The more recent literature, on the "Great Gatsby Curve," sees the causality running the other way, from current inequality to IGE. The second perspective (PCL II) approaches intergenerational mobility through transition matrices and sets out views on "greater mobility" through this lens. But these views are not necessarily consistent with each other, and a social welfare function approach is needed to pronounce on comparisons between societies. Taking a dynastic inequality approach, Kanbur and Stiglitz (2016) show that "equality of opportunity"—a transition matrix with identical rows—does not necessarily lead to lower dynastic inequality than all other transition matrices. Finally, the third perspective on parents, children, and luck (PCL III) is presented by Roemer (1998) and in particular by applications of the framework to quantify "inequality of opportunity." It is argued here that these approaches have serious empirical and conceptual flaws, and may understate the true degree of inequality of opportunity.

So, inequality of outcome leads to inequality of opportunity; equality of opportunity does not lead to highest dynastic equality; and extreme outcomes trump equality of opportunity. What, then, is left of equality of opportunity?

REFERENCES

Atkinson, A. B. 1981. "The Measurement of Economic Mobility." In *Inkomensverdelingenopenbarefinancien—Essays in Honour of Jan Pen*, edited by P. J. Eigjelshoven and L. J. van Gemerden, 9–24. Utrecht: Het Spectrum. Also published in Atkinson, A. B. (ed.). 1983. *Social Justice and Public Policy*, 61–75. London: Wheatsheaf.

Atkinson, A. B., and F. Bourguignon. 1982. "The Comparison of Multi-Dimensional Distributions of Economic Status." *Review of Economic Studies* 49:183–201. Also published in Atkinson, A. B. (ed.). 1983. *Social Justice and Public Policy*, 37–59. London: Wheatsheaf.

Becker, Gary S., and Nigel Tomes. 1979. "An Equilibrium Theory of the Distribution of Income and Intergenerational Mobility." *Journal of Political Economy* 87 (6):1153–1189.

Bourguignon, Francois, Francisco Ferreira, and Michael Walton. 2007. "Equity, Efficiency and Inequality Traps: A Research Agenda." *Journal of Economic Inequality* 5:235–256.

Champernowne, David. 1953. "A Model of Income Distribution." *Economic Journal* 63:318–351.

Champernowne, David. 1973. *The Distribution of Income Between Persons*. Cambridge: Cambridge University Press.

Corak, Miles. 2013. "Income Inequality, Equality of Opportunity, and Intergenerational Mobility." *Journal of Economic Perspectives* 27 (3):79–102.

Creedy, J. 1974. "Income Changes Over the Life Cycle." *Oxford Economic Papers* 26:405–423.

Dworkin, R. 1981a. "What Is Equality? Part 1: Equality of Welfare." *Philosophy and Public Affairs* 10:185–246.

Dworkin, R. 1981b. "What Is Equality? Part 2: Equality of Resources." *Philosophy and Public Affairs* 10:283–345.

Gibrat, R. 1931. *Les Inegalités économiques*. Paris: Sirey.

Hart, Peter. 1976. "The Dynamics of Earnings, 1963–1973." *Economic Journal* 86:551–565.

Hufe, Paul, Andreas Peichl, John Roemer, and Martin Unger. 2015. "Inequality of Income Acquisition: The Role of Childhood Circumstances." ZEW Working Paper 15–084. http://ftp.zew.de/pub/zew-docs/dp/dp15084.pdf.

Kalecki, M. 1945. "On the Gibrat Distribution." *Econometrica* 13:161–170.

Kanbur, Ravi. 1987. "The Standard of Living: Uncertainty, Inequality and Opportunity." In *The Standard of Living*, edited by Geoffrey Hawthorn. Cambridge: Cambridge University Press.

Kanbur, Ravi. 2016. "Capability, Opportunity, Outcome—And Equality." Dyson Working Paper 16–05. http://publications.dyson.cornell.edu/research/researchpdf/wp/2016/Cornell-Dyson-wp1605.pdf.

Kanbur, Ravi, and J. E. Stiglitz. 1986. "Intergenerational Mobility and Dynastic Inequality." Woodrow Wilson School Discussion Paper in Economics, Number 111. Princeton University.

Kanbur, Ravi, and J. E. Stiglitz. 2016. "Dynastic Inequality, Mobility and Equality of Opportunity." *Journal of Economic Inequality* 14 (4):419–434.

Kanbur, Ravi, and Adam Wagstaff. 2016. "How Useful Is Inequality of Opportunity as a Policy Construct?" In *Inequality and Growth: Patterns and Policy, Vol. I: Concepts and Analysis*, 131–148. London: Palgrave Macmillan.

Krueger, Alan. 2012. "The Rise and Consequences of Inequality." Center for American Progress. http://www.americanprogress.org/events/2012/01/12/17181/the-rise-and-consequences-of-inequality/.

Paes de Barros, Ricardo, Francisco H. H. Ferreira, Jose R. Molinas Vega, and Jaime Saavedra Chanduvi. 2009. *Measuring Inequality of Opportunities in Latin America and the Caribbean*. Washington, DC: World Bank.

Roemer, John E. 1998. *Equality of Opportunity*. Cambridge, MA: Harvard University Press.

Roemer, John E. 2004. "Equal Opportunity and Intergenerational Mobility: Going Beyond Intergenerational Income Transition Matrices." In *Generational Income Mobility in North America and Europe*, edited by Miles Corak, chap 3. Cambridge: Cambridge University Press.

Roemer, John. 2008. "Equality of Opportunity." In *The New Palgrave Dictionary of Economics*, edited by S. Durlauf and L. Blume. New York: Macmillan.

Rothschild, Michael, and Joseph Stiglitz. 1976. "Equilibrium in Competitive Insurance Markets: An Essay on the Economics of Imperfect Information." *Quarterly Journal of Economics* 90 (4):629–649.

Sen, A. 1985. *Commodities and Capabilities*. Amsterdam: North Holland.

Shorrocks, A. F. 1978. "The Measurement of Mobility." *Econometrica* 46 (5):1013–1024.

Solon, Gary. 2004. "A Model of Intergenerational Mobility Variation Over Time and Place." In *Generational Income Mobility in North America and Europe*, edited by Miles Corak, chap. 2. Cambridge: Cambridge University Press.

Solon, Gary. 2015. "What Do We Know So Far About Multigenerational Mobility?" NBER Working Paper No. 21053.

Wagstaff, Adam, and Ravi Kanbur. 2015. "Inequality of Opportunity: The New Motherhood and Apple Pie?" *Health Economics* 24 (10):1243–1247.

CHAPTER 3

The Middle Muddle

CONCEPTUALIZING AND MEASURING THE GLOBAL MIDDLE CLASS

Arjun Jayadev, Rahul Lahoti, and Sanjay Reddy

ABSTRACT

Interest in the emergence of a global middle class has resulted in a number of attempts to identify and enumerate who belongs to it. Current research provides wildly different estimates about the size and evolution of the global middle class because of a lack of consensus on appropriate identification criteria for a person to be deemed to be middle class. We identify three competing and often conflated understandings in the literature on the subject. We further argue that for at least two of these understandings, the literature has been using inappropriate thresholds for identification. Using data from the Global Consumption and Income Project, we provide estimates of the size, composition, and evolution of the global middle class for three competing understandings and contrast these to existing estimates.

INTRODUCTION

Simply put, the American middle class is under great strain today, and the outlook for major improvements in the near future is somewhat grim unless we take action. This is a matter of great concern for our country. The middle class is the backbone of America's economy and its democracy. So the state of the middle class is in many ways a proxy for the state of the union.

Joseph E. Stiglitz,
Testimony to U.S. Congress (February 24, 2015)

For Joseph Eugene Stiglitz, whose extraordinary contributions to intellectual inquiry and the pursuit of social justice we honor in this chapter, the condition and prospects of the middle class have always been topics of great interest. From his earliest work on credit and labor markets to his most recent work on the often savage costs of inequality, the economic and social condition of the middle class has always been an urgent intellectual and political concern, underpinned by his personal origins in Gary, Indiana. In this, as with other topics, Joe's insights have contributed immensely to clarifying problems and solutions and to opening lines of inquiry.

The pivotal role of the middle class in society been a long-standing theme in social theory and political analysis, from Aristotle's description of the ideal state as comprising a large middle grouping that moderates political extremes[1] to modern considerations of the median voter theorem in political and economic decision making. Furthermore, there may be economically instrumental reasons to be concerned about the middle class as the grouping that generates new entrepreneurs, emphasizes economically "useful" values such as education and thrift, and is the main source of consumption and aggregate demand for goods and services.

Changing patterns of income and consumption distribution within and across countries have brought these concerns to contemporary popular consciousness. Thus, for example, anxieties about the disappearance of a middle class, increasing job and income polarization, and the attendant impacts on social and political stability and on aspirations for individual and collective progress have been an important theme in academic and popular discourse, especially in the United States, where the American Dream has been seen as being at stake.[2] At the same time, increased global trade and international financial integration, accompanied by reductions in the cost of communication and transportation have resulted in increases in economic interdependence. As one consequence there has been substantial interest in the emergence of a "global middle class." This grouping, it has been suggested, is a new social formation of world historical importance, its emergence portending huge implications, for consumption, growth, political dynamics within and between countries, cultural flows and norms, and the ecological health of the planet. The undoubtedly critical changes in the structure of the world economy, in particular in terms of the growing role of the developing countries and of newly affluent populations within them (with the developing countries beginning to account for the majority of global growth beginning in the first decade of the current century), have given great relevance to this question.

Nevertheless, we have a tenuous and contested understanding of the size, composition and evolution of the middle class within given societies and the world as a whole. This is despite great improvement in the availability and quality of relevant data from across the world in the last two decades.

The primary reason for this is that the middle class is a complex and contested concept and one that defies easy conceptual clarity and measurement although this is not always acknowledged. Surveys in the United States show a large fraction of people in the upper tenth and the bottom tenth of the distribution often self-identify as "middle-class" (Cashell 2008; Taylor et al. 2008). Although this may be an especially pronounced phenomenon in the United States, in light of the role within it of the Republican ideal of social equality (commented on by early observers such as Alexis de Tocqueville), it is indicative of the difficulties involved in empirical analysis of social concepts that have both "objective" and subjective elements.[3] Similarly, very small fractions of the population identify as lower or upper class. Even if one were to eschew subjective identification in favor of objective, measurable categories, it is unclear what characteristics to take into account. An individual's race, education, income, wealth, consumption patterns, family background, manners and habits, and ability to engage in social and political life can all be components of perceived or actual belonging to the middle class and it is certainly not clear how to integrate these different considerations into a single concept.

If identifying a middle class is difficult within a country, problems of identification multiply when trying to capture the middle class in a global context. Even if one were to find broad agreement on the characteristics of middle-class living in the United States, say, it would not be clear that these ought to be made the same when applied to other high-income countries and it would be even less so for other countries. The appropriate criteria to use when going beyond individual countries to determine membership in a cross-national global middle-class, spanning diverse social, cultural, and political contexts, is all the more obscure. In particular, criteria relating to command over resources may be compatible with a separate country-by-country assessment, but criteria relating to the ability to participate in a common social, cultural, and political sphere of global interactions, call for the identification of the requirements of such participation globally.[4]

Perhaps in light of the difficulties associated with conceptualizing and operationalizing broader sociological interpretations of class efforts by economists aimed at measuring the size of the middle class, which have usually relied on purely income-based definitions.[5] These measures include ranges based on absolute income or consumption, incomes relative to the median or to the mean, incomes relative to the poverty line or to a specified percentile or proportion of the income distribution (for example, the middle 40 percent).

While using an income-based measure within a country may be reasonable for certain purposes and given certain constraints (in particular the severe limitations of internationally comparable data on the intranational distribution of nonincome attainments); doing so in a global context is fraught with conceptual difficulties. A review of the academic and policy literature and the popular press suggests at least three competing definitions of an emerging global middle class that are often inappropriately conflated in the economic literature. Indeed, these may be at the source of the somewhat elusive and seemingly chimerical quality of the global middle class.

First, when speaking about the emerging global middle class, a researcher may be using a purely relative concept, referring to "middle" of the global income or consumption distribution (see, for example, Easterly 2001; Quah 1996). This perspective has the most apparent straightforwardness but is not very easy to justify in the global context. It corresponds to absolutely very low thresholds, which might not suffice for even basic attainments, let alone the conditions for meaningful participation in world society.

Second, and more commonly, the emerging global middle class is defined according to absolute income thresholds, as a grouping that enjoys a certain standard of living (e.g., those who now enjoy income levels in their home countries which enable them to be free from severe economic deprivation and to spend their income in ways that reflect broader aspirations as a result of growth) without rising above the threshold of affluence. This idea might be given a justification involving, for instance, freedom from certain forms of material lack combined with discretionary resources for various purposes, or the requirements for being perceived as a certain sort of "respectable" consumer or citizen. Absolute money thresholds can still therefore ultimately be linked to contextual considerations. Although economic, social, and cultural considerations are complexly linked in relation to this concern, for simplicity we refer to absolute thresholds based on these motivations as corresponding to a "sociological" conception of the middle class.

Third, and perhaps most obscurely, the emerging global middle class is sometimes viewed as a category of persons responsible for constituting a consumer market possessing certain quantitative or qualitative features (e.g., in terms of its contribution to global aggregate demand or the demand of specific industries). We can think of this as involving the idea of the middle class as a mover (whether or not a prime mover). Although these ideas can overlap descriptively and be connected causally, they are distinct.

In what follows we refer to these as the Global Middle-Class Concept 1, Global Middle-Class Concept 2, and Global Middle-Class Concept 3 (with apologies to Branko Milanovic) (Milanovic 2006). These are certainly not the only ways of identifying members of the middle class using economic data but they are prominent in the literature and so we focus on them in order to provide clarification. A focus on any one of these concepts must be suitably justified and moreover what follows, or doesn't, from a specific choice must be understood in order to use them as a basis for generating thresholds for operationalization and measurement.

The conceptual underpinnings are important because they form the basis for deciding the thresholds for operationalization and measurement. Perhaps in part because the underlying motivations of the exercise have been both conflated and left unclarified, researchers have employed wildly differing income or consumption thresholds in defining the global middle class. It is interesting in this regard to note that the first two empirical examinations of the global middle class employ income intervals (defined by lower and upper thresholds) that have no overlap! Thus, Banerjee and Duflo (2008) define these thresholds as occurring between $2 and $10 PPP (purchasing power parity) (in 2005 PPP terms) per day on the grounds that this corresponds to those who are not defined as poor by the World Bank's poverty line thresholds while not being wealthy,[6] while Milanovic and Yitzhaki (2002) define the threshold as between $12 and $50 PPP (in 1993 PPP terms) per day on the basis of the average incomes of Brazil and Portugal, respectively. In the recent past, there have been more entrants and contestants in the definition of this group: Kharas (2010), Kharas and Gertz (2010), and Lopez-Calva and Ortiz-Juarez (2014) use $10 as the lower cutoff for the middle class; with the latter defending this on the basis that at that level, the nonpoor in Latin America have only a one in ten chance of returning to poverty (Ferreira et al. 2012). At the upper end, the two differ—with Kharas and Gertz setting it at $100 PPP per day (the upper bound is chosen as twice the median income of Luxembourg, the richest advanced country), while Lopez-Calva and Ortiz-Juarez set it at $50 PPP (which excludes only the top 5 percent of Latin American households). Ravallion (2010) defines the middle-class group as possessing incomes between $2 and $13 PPP across the developing world. Nancy Birdsall (2010) uses a hybrid definition, again choosing $10 PPP as the absolute lower threshold and using a relative cutoff at the upper end by excluding the richest 5 percent of individuals within any country. Researchers from the International Labor Organization (ILO) specify cutoffs of $4 to $13 PPP per day (Kapsos and Bourmpoula 2013). Finally, there are other approaches which eschew dollar values altogether and use indicators such as car consumption (Dadush and Ali 2012) to identify the global middle class.

Unsurprisingly, these different approaches and intuitions give rise to wildly differing estimates and understandings of the global middle class. Figure 3.1 shows that the global middle class in 2013 could be as large as

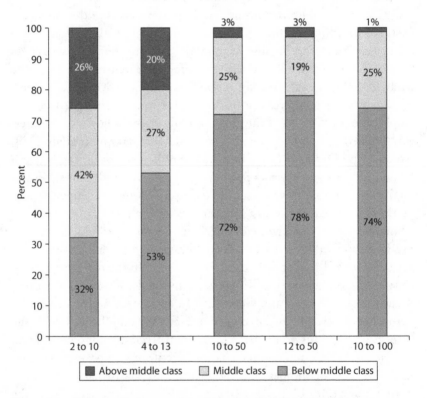

Figure 3.1 Different Estimates of the Size of the World Middle Class

Note: 2–10 (2005 PPP): Banerjee and Duflo (2008) cutoffs based on the "Developing World Middle Class"; 10–50 (2005 PPP): Lopez-Calva and Ortiz-Juarez (2014) cutoffs based on the "Latin American Middle Class"; 12–50 (1993 PPP): Milanovic and Yitzhaki (2002) cutoffs based on "Brazil and Italy Comparison"; 10–100 (2005 PPP): Kharas (2010) definition based on "Developing World Middle Class."

42 percent of the global population or as small as 19 percent depending on which of the extant definitions we use. One might be forgiven for seeing these results as reflecting something of a free for all. There is almost no overlap between the Banerjee and Duflo, Ravallion, and ILO definitions on the one hand, and the Milanovic and Yitzhaki, Kharas, Birdsall, and Lopez-Calva and Ortiz-Juarez definitions on the other. Thus, using the Kharas (2010) definition suggests that the global middle class includes 1.5 billion people while the Banerjee and Duflo (2008) definition would peg it as 2.9 billion. In addition, middle-class definitions based on relative incomes add another layer of confusion. As Birdsall (2012) notes: "Depending on your point of view, the middle class in Brazil includes everyone in the three middle quintiles (Easterly 2001) about 114 million people in 2009 or everyone with per capita daily income between $10 and $50 about 61 million people, with an overlap in the case of Brazil in 2009 of only 36 million people." It is of no surprise then that popular articles describe the global middle class as "elusive" and researchers often dismiss attempts to define it are "arbitrary." Needless to say, not only the level but also the regional and national composition and trend over time of the number of persons in the middle class can be greatly affected by the choice of identification criteria, so this is no mere distinction without a difference.[7] If it matters to assess the membership of the global middle class at all, then these sizable variations ought to give reason for concern.

Our purpose in this paper is to suggest that these somewhat pessimistic conclusions are primarily due to an unhelpful conflation of understandings of the global middle class. We wish, therefore, to accomplish two interrelated objectives. First, we seek to clarify possible definitions and understanding of the middle class based on the three categories we have outlined above. All three have a potentially valid underlying motivation, but they are distinct conceptions which direct us to pay attention to different data in different ways.

We will argue that the literature has thus far been using conceptually inappropriate thresholds, especially with regard to Global Middle-Class Concept 2 and Global Middle-Class Concept 3. For Global Middle-Class Concept 1, based on population-based relative criteria, we will discuss possible choices of threshold and their motivation, and argue that some are better founded than others. For Global Middle-Class Concept 2, based on absolute criteria, we do similarly, and argue that we ought to more carefully identify substantively meaningful "middle-class-specific consumption baskets" to obtain a better understanding of its size and evolution across the world over time. Finally, for Global Middle-Class Concept 3, after surveying the considerations involved, we suggest that it may not be appropriate to use PPP rates at all and that the appropriate comparison would be to use market exchange rates. Using preferred definitions for each of the concepts, we use material from the newly developed Global Consumption and Income Project (GCIP) to identify the size and composition of the global middle class and its evolution over time based on thresholds that we consider more plausible, although they should still be viewed as highly tentative.

The Global Consumption and Income Project consists of two linked databases—the Global Income Dataset and the Global Consumption Dataset, which together allow for a more detailed portrait of consumption and income of persons over time, within and across countries around the world, than has previously been available. The benchmark version estimates the monthly real consumption and income (in $2005 PPP) for quantiles of the population (a consumption/income profile) of the vast majority of countries in the world (around 145) for every year for more than half a century (1960–2013). For a detailed discussion of the relative strengths and limitations of the dataset, see Lahoti, Jayadev, and Reddy (2014). Because of the coverage and flexibility of the dataset, we are able to generate portraits using standard PPP comparisons, but also market exchange rates and other concepts, as discussed in section 3.

1. THE GLOBAL MIDDLE CLASS AS THE MIDDLE OF THE GLOBAL CONSUMPTION DISTRIBUTION

One plausible definition of the global middle class is that it literally involves those who comprise the middle of the global consumption or income distribution. (We focus on consumption here, although our argument also applies to income.) The thought experiment here is to treat the world as a country and to identify bounds around a median. This is in essence the approach espoused by Easterly (2001), who takes the middle to refer to those in the middle three expenditure quintiles. The Palma ratio, which can be used to identify the relatively poor as those below the 40th percentile and the relatively rich as those above the 90th percentile, can be used similarly to identify a middle class specified in relative terms as those with expenditures between the 40th and 90th percentiles. A third approach associated with Lester Thurow (1987), and subsequently Birdsall, Graham, and Pettinato (2000), is to define the middle as 75 to 125 percent of the median.

Table 3.1 identifies the evolution of the global middle class, and the regional contributions to this grouping at three points in time: 1990, 2000, and 2010, as defined by the Thurow criterion. A few points bear mentioning at the outset.

First, when one uses this definition of the "global middle class," the bounds are narrow and more importantly low, from between $1.23 to $2.05 in 2005 PPP terms in 1990 to between $1.47 to $2.45 in 2000 to $2.22 to $3.69 in 2010. Put another way, even in 2015, the vast majority of the world's population live on less than $4 in 2005 PPP terms. This has enormous implications for the global poverty debate. Because this is such a low level of consumption, it seems strange to call someone who has attained it, a member of the middle class.[8] The difficulties of a purely relative interpretation of the middle class in the global context, where this entails very low absolute levels, are made stark.

Second, in an exercise of this kind involving relative ranking, East Asia and the Pacific play the starring role in terms of movement into the middle class, reflecting (primarily) the very rapid growth of China. While in 1990, 56 percent of the East Asian/Pacific region was below the middle class defined according to these thresholds (stringent in absolute terms), by 2010, only 33 percent was below, with the majority (48 percent) actually being above the global middle class. South Asia's relative ranking had fallen, with 75 percent being below the threshold of the global middle class in 2010 as compared to 64 percent in 1990. Seen another way, the East Asia Pacific region has managed to reduce the absolute numbers of people considered below the world middle class (from 980 million in 1990 to 700 million in 2010), while in South Asia, the reverse has occurred, with 1.2 billion people in 2010 being considered below the world middle class compared to 720 million in 1990. The relative rise of East Asia and the Pacific has come at the expense of all non-OECD (Organization for Economic Cooperation and Development) regions: only 10 percent of the Sub-Saharan population was above the middle-class threshold in 2010 compared with nearly a quarter in 1990; in the Middle East and North Africa over 20 percent of its population in 2010 were considered below the threshold for the middle class compared to only 4 percent in 1990; and in Latin America, while 83 percent were over the global middle-class threshold in 1990, that number was only 70 percent in 2010. Interestingly, the share of East Asia and the Pacific region in the global middle class has remained the same (around 40 percent in the global middle are from the region), but the proportion above and below the global middle class has

Table 3.1 World Middle Class as Defined by 75 to 125 Percent of the Global Median

	Below Middle	Middle	Above Middle	Share Below	Share Middle	Share Above	Pop. Below	Pop. Middle	Pop. Above
1990 [1.23-2.05]									
East Asia & Pacific	0.56	0.18	0.26	0.48	0.41	0.2	980334464	315107520	455155264
Europe & Central Asia	0.03	0.04	0.93	0.01	0.04	0.33	24843076	33124102	770135424
Latin America & Caribbean	0.06	0.11	0.83	0.01	0.06	0.15	25751196	47210528	356224896
Middle East & North Africa	0.04	0.19	0.77	0	0.06	0.07	8957002	42545760	172422288
North America	0	0	1	0	0	0.12	0	0	277441016
South Asia	0.64	0.24	0.12	0.35	0.35	0.06	726384896	272394336	136197168
Sub-Saharan Africa	0.55	0.21	0.24	0.13	0.13	0.05	270326624	103215616	117960720
World	0.4	0.15	0.45	1	1	1	2054281984	770355776	2311067136
2000 [1.47-2.45]									
East Asia & Pacific	0.44	0.2	0.36	0.36	0.41	0.27	865491200	393405056	708129152
Europe & Central Asia	0.07	0.07	0.86	0.03	0.06	0.28	60196996	60196996	739563136
Latin America & Caribbean	0.07	0.13	0.8	0.01	0.07	0.16	35643844	66195712	407358240
Middle East & North Africa	0.07	0.22	0.71	0.01	0.06	0.07	19211896	60380244	194863520
North America	0	0	1	0	0	0.12	0	0	312932096
South Asia	0.71	0.18	0.11	0.41	0.26	0.06	981358912	248795232	152041536
Sub-Saharan Africa	0.67	0.17	0.16	0.18	0.12	0.04	432653504	1097777728	103320256
World	0.4	0.16	0.44	1	1	1	2380606208	952242432	2618666752

East Asia & Pacific	0.33	0.19	0.48	0.25	0.4	0.35	700288960	403196608	1018602176
Europe & Central Asia	0.04	0.05	0.91	0.01	0.04	0.27	35475544	44344436	807068608
Latin America & Caribbean	0.12	0.18	0.7	0.03	0.1	0.14	69446688	104170040	405105696
Middle East & North Africa	0.21	0.26	0.53	0.02	0.08	0.06	68326240	84594392	172442416
North America	0	0	1	0	0	0.12	0	0	34331584
South Asia	0.75	0.16	0.09	0.44	0.26	0.05	1205129216	257094272	144615456
Sub-Saharan Africa	0.77	0.13	0.1	0.23	0.11	0.03	645700288	109014328	83857200
World	0.41	0.15	0.44	1	1	1	2747739648	1005270656	2948793856

reversed (with 40 percent above the middle and 20 percent below in 2010 compared with 20 percent above and 40 percent below in 1990). The use of purely relative thresholds implies that movement into the middle class (in this case, China in particular) necessarily implies that others (such as those living in South Asia and in the Middle East and North Africa or Latin America) must move out of it, either by falling beneath the relative thresholds or rising above them. This could be true even if their incomes had not changed at all, which may seem a somewhat implausible implication of the choice of purely relative thresholds.

Third, despite anxieties as to the Chinese ascent, the relative position of Europe and North America in the global order has barely budged. The whole population of North America has enjoyed and continues to enjoy consumption and income levels above the global middle, while about 90 percent of Europe and Central Asia does. These numbers have not changed over the entire period under consideration.

Second, since this involves relative rankings, East Asia and the Pacific region has been the major mover at the expense of all the other non-industrialized regions, reflecting (primarily) the very rapid growth of China. While in 1990, 56 percent of the East Asian/Pacific region was below the middle class, by 2010, only 33 percent was below, with the majority (48 percent) actually being above the global middle class. South Asia's relative ranking has fallen with 75 percent below the threshold of the global middle class in 2010 compared to 64 percent in 1990. Seen another way, the East Asia/Pacific region has managed to reduce the absolute numbers of people considered below the world middle class (from 980 million in 1990 to 700 million in 2010), while in South Asia, the reverse has occurred, with 1.2 billion people in 2010 being considered below the world middle class compared to 720 million in 1990. The relative rise of East Asia and the Pacific region has come at the expense of all non-OECD regions: only 10 percent of the Sub-Saharan population was above the middle-class threshold in 2010 compared with nearly a quarter in 1990, in the Middle East and North Africa over 20 percent of their population in 2010 were considered below the threshold for the middle class compared to only 4 percent in 1990; and in Latin America, while 83 percent were over the global middle-class threshold in 1990, that number was only 70 percent in 2010. Interestingly, the share of East Asia and the Pacific region in the global middle class has remained the same (around 40 percent in the global middle are from the region), but the proportion above and below the global middle class has reversed (with 40 percent above the middle and 20 percent below in 2010 compared with 20 percent above and 40 percent below in 1990).

Third, despite the anxieties in the West as to the Chinese ascent, the relative rankings of Europe and North America have barely budged. The whole population of North America enjoys consumption and income levels above the global middle, while about 90 percent of Europe and Central Asia does. These numbers have not changed over the entire period under consideration.

Taken as a whole then, the story of the global middle class (understood as the middle of the global distribution) in the last three decades has been the rapid rise of the (from this point of view, truly) middle kingdom. This can also be seen in the relative positions of distributions as seen in figure 3.2. The major mover between 1980 and 2010 was China. In 1980, the entire distribution was below every other country depicted. By 2010, nearly the entire Chinese population was ranked higher than the populations of India, Indonesia, and Nigeria, and around half its population enjoyed a ranking higher than the lower third of Brazil's population. This noted, the entire Chinese population, based on percentile data, was still ranked below the entire population of the United States.

2. GLOBAL MIDDLE-CLASS MEMBERSHIP AS A SOCIOLOGICAL CATEGORY

Assigning membership to the middle class is a difficult task, but one can certainly imagine some common attributes, sociologically understood, that might broadly inform such a definition: e.g., income of a sufficient level, some income security, ownership of durable goods deemed useful for freeing one from drudgery or for providing social status, some disposable income that can be applied to discretionary consumption and leisure activities, access to technology, some level of school education, the perception of being respectable, the ability to participate with a degree of confidence in the life of one's society, and so on.

Conceiving of the middle class as a sociological category with an attendant set of economic attributes, without reducing one to the other, is a plausible approach. Indeed, it is at the core of some of the attempts to describe the global middle class. However, trying to do so using a money-metric at the outset, without first attempting to assess what the relevant achievements are (as most studies do) is bound to lead to some difficulties.

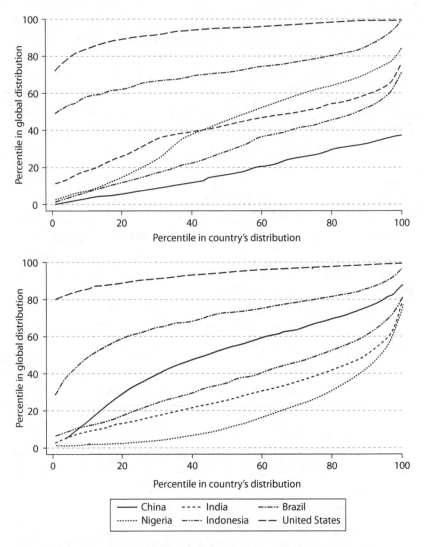

Figure 3.2   Relative Rankings of Countries and Percentiles in the World Distribution: 1980 and 2010

Note: The Chinese catchup. *Upper panel*: Distribution in 1980. *Lower panel*: Distribution in 2010. All figures in $2005 PPP according to the authors' calculations.

This can be made clear by a very simple example. Consider first the lower threshold for membership in the global middle class used by several researchers ($10 PPP per day). This threshold, as noted earlier was chosen because it represented the lowest required level of income to ensure some level of economic security in Latin America according to the researchers concerned. However, think now of that threshold as applied to the numeraire country, the United States (since the international dollar used to define standard PPPs is deemed by definition to be equal in purchasing power to the U.S. dollar). Those living on $10 a day in the United States cannot conceivably be called middle class. If one presumes a forty-hour workweek at minimum wage, an individual with $10 PPP income a day would be making eight times less than the prevailing federal minimum wage, and would be making about a third of the $12,071 poverty line specified by the Census Bureau (not to mention much less than unofficial estimates of the living wage)! It is not a defense, as might be thought of at first, to argue that such a comparison is wrongly using Latin American standards to apply to the U.S. case. While it is certainly true that if a U.S. individual earning $10 a day were somehow able to teleport to Nicaragua and use the PPP equivalent in local currency, he or she could conceivably have a (low) middle-class life (as defined by income security), this is not the counterfactual being considered—we are interested in the number of people enjoying income security *wherever they happen to be in the world*. In addition, it can be shown that the minimum cost of nutritional adequacy alone in the United States approaches $4 to $5 per person per day (in $2005 PPP).[9] The remainder in the $10 assumed adequate for middle-class membership could hardly suffice for all the other purposes required.

That this kind of identification problem is not simply the result of inappropriately applying developing country patterns to developed counties, which can be seen by the application of some of these thresholds to other developing countries. Birdsall's (2010) hybrid definition suggests that India has no middle class at all (since the entire population whose consumption is above $10 PPP per day is in the top 5 percent of the population and hence excluded by her definition). And yet it is evident that there are several dozens of millions of people who enjoy some level of income security, leisure, possess consumer durables, and whose children go to school and have aspirations to a better life and career.[10] This tells us, among other things, that there is something wrong not only with the thresholds used but the PPPs.

Why do these thresholds lead to such troubling anomalies? The answer is simply that the cost structures for obtaining a "middle-class life" differs from country to country. In India, $8 PPP may be sufficient to generate income security, allow an individual to obtain some consumer durables, and attain other capabilities associated with being middle class; but in order to do this, $10 PPP may not be sufficient in Latin America, and certainly insufficient in the United States or elsewhere. The key point is one that has been made with respect to the poverty line debate.

This presumes, in the first place, however, a careful assessment and definitions of the capabilities associated with the status of middle class, and while this can certainly be contested, it is necessary to do so prior to identifying thresholds. Such exercises have in fact been undertaken in different contexts (Atkinson and Brandolini 2011) and Blank (2010) seeking to identify how individuals could achieve middle-class status given different demographic and cultural factors. Another approach that may not require as much deliberation would be to follow the lead of Deaton and Dupriez (2011), who use an Engel curve methodology to identify poverty-specific PPPs.

Given the computational and deliberative difficulty of these two approaches, we propose here a rough and ready alternative, primarily as a proof of concept providing an initial demonstration of what might be done more carefully in the future. Specifically, we define a basic set of goods and services required for entering the "middle-class" life and use an online dataset (Numbeo: www.numbeo.com) to identify the cost of these goods and services across the world in 2015. Numbeo is a "crowd-sourced" online database that collects self-reported data on a bundle of goods and services from different cities in the world. The database is generated from approximately 2 million self-reported observations across cities in about 130 countries. Data are reported only if there is a sufficient number of observations and outliers (defined as prices that are above the 80th percentile and below the 20th percentile of all observations for a city) are dropped. Despite these safeguards, given that the data are entirely self-reported their reliability is therefore potentially questionable. In addition, they are likely to be biased upward given that individuals likely to input data are typically higher income. While Numbeo is not the only dataset that compares a market basket across cities and countries, others available are either proprietary or have much more limited coverage.

Having noted this, we conducted a Spearman rank correlation test of the most expensive cities in the world as defined by the Numbeo cost of living index on the one hand, and two proprietary datasets: the Mercer cost of living database and the UBS cost of living database, respectively. (We will extend this in subsequent work to the UN International Civil Service Commission Post Adjustment database.) The Spearman rank correlation coefficient was 0.63 between Numbeo and the first and an impressive 0.92 between Numbeo and the second, and the test of independence was decisively rejected in both cases. Despite reasonable misgivings therefore, in our judgment there is no *a priori* reason to reject the data on the basis of quality.

Since our task is to define a middle-class level of material attainment, we begin by defining the floor for the middle class as the threshold at which a person can cover food and living expenses at a certain level. Specifically, we use the Numbeo data for the cost of an "Asian" food basket required to obtain a day's consumption (2300 calories), translate this to monthly costs and add the cost of renting a one bedroom apartment and utilities shared between two people. We take the average cost for the living and food basket as specified across all the cities in the Numbeo database to get a country-wide estimate of the lower-end threshold.

At the other end, to be considered as having achieved middle-class status but not to belong to the upper class (i.e., to have not surpassed the middle-class ceiling), in our definition a person needs to not be able to afford more than the following market basket of goods: First, a "Western" market basket of goods that yields 2300 calories (Numbeo provides this data) for a person for a thirty-day period. Second, rent and basic utilities for a three bedroom apartment in the city center/two (on the assumption that two people share this three bedroom apartment). Third, the person should be able to afford entertainment defined as a meal at a mid-range restaurant/two (since the meal in Numbeo is for two people) per week and one movie ticket per week to an international release for four weeks each. Fourth, the person should be able to afford a monthly transportation pass. We use the average across all the cities in each country to generate the average cost of this basket of goods. Anyone whose income is higher than this threshold is considered above the middle class. No provision is made for savings or any other expenditures, and so this is a very conservative range.

The result is that for each country we get a different range in current U.S. dollar (USD) exchange rates associated with the thresholds. (See table 3.2) This is as we should expect if we are interested in the actual achievements (as we are). The estimates we obtain for the U.S. lead, for example to an interval between $27 per person per day and $63 per person per day. For India, by contrast, the estimates suggest that to be in this category requires one to have income in an interval between Rs. 345 (at current exchange rates) and Rs. 830. In Germany, the thresholds

Table 3.2 Middle-Class Threshold as Defined by Numbeo Basket Cost: Selected Countries

Country	Floor ($)	Ceiling ($)	Percent Below	Percent in Middle	Percent Above
India	5.3	12.7	98.6%	1.2%	0.2%
Pakistan	6.0	15.1	99.2%	0.7%	0.1%
Egypt	6.6	20.8	95.6%	3.9%	0.5%
Bangladesh	6.6	16.4	99.2%	0.8%	0.0%
Uganda	7.7	19.9	99.3%	0.6%	0.1%
Turkey	8.2	20.7	62.4%	31.8%	5.7%
Brazil	8.6	23.4	74.4%	22.0%	3.6%
Mexico	8.9	24.1	78.2%	18.5%	3.3%
Romania	9.0	20.4	90.1%	9.9%	0.0%
Malaysia	9.5	21.8	82.6%	15.4%	2.0%
Kenya	10.4	34.0	98.8%	1.1%	0.1%
South Africa	10.7	25.9	94.8%	3.6%	1.6%
Thailand	11.0	31.0	92.2%	7.3%	0.6%
Portugal	11.9	31.0	35.8%	49.8%	14.4%
Greece	11.9	27.1	21.7%	55.5%	22.8%
Russian Federation	12.4	34.5	91.1%	8.9%	0.0%
Peru	12.7	30.7	91.0%	8.0%	1.1%
Ecuador	13.0	27.3	93.3%	5.5%	1.2%
China	14.1	43.2	92.7%	7.3%	0.0%
Nigeria	15.6	58.8	99.8%	0.2%	0.0%
Spain	15.8	37.2	33.5%	53.7%	12.8%
Germany	19.5	53.4	12.4%	66.4%	21.2%
Sweden	19.7	56.7	12.3%	71.2%	16.5%
Italy	20.0	50.8	40.8%	51.5%	7.6%
France	21.4	52.9	18.5%	64.3%	17.2%
Canada	22.0	48.7	14.3%	51.4%	34.3%
New Zealand	22.1	55.2	0.0%	23.3%	76.7%
Netherlands	22.7	59.6	24.0%	64.1%	11.9%
Denmark	23.0	65.7	7.5%	68.4%	24.1%
Belgium	23.3	57.0	22.2%	62.0%	15.8%
Korea, Rep.	23.4	61.9	57.4%	39.1%	3.5%
Japan	24.4	67.0	31.1%	61.1%	7.8%
Australia	26.3	66.4	12.6%	57.8%	29.6%
United Kingdom	27.5	66.7	18.9%	58.5%	22.7%
United States	27.7	62.3	17.7%	50.0%	32.3%
Norway	31.4	82.7	25.3%	64.4%	10.2%

correspond from 17.4 to 47.6 euros per person per day at current (2015) market exchange rates.

A few points should be noted. First, the range of thresholds to achieve middle-class status as defined by the market basket of goods is very wide between countries and within them, when compared at market exchange rates. Second, industrialized countries have a substantial proportion of their population in this middle class (from around 50 percent in the United States to 71 percent in Sweden). Interestingly, the Anglo-Saxon countries have smaller middle classes than continental Europe, but a larger proportion that is above. Another important consideration is that by this measure poorer countries do not have a meaningful middle class to speak of—with only 1 to 2 percent of the population enjoying consumption levels that would put them in this range. This is not surprising however, given that the countries are, indeed poorer—but it is also likely partly the artifact of the data collection procedure, since the data are generated from cities which will likely underestimate the number of people who have a middle-class lifestyle in countries with larger rural populations. There are also reasons to think that survey data in developing countries may generally underestimate middle- and upper-class consumption and income, perhaps severely in many cases.

Partly in response to this, we undertake a rudimentary adjustment and define the lower threshold to be 0.5 times the floor market basket of goods to account for the middle class who are not in cities or who are otherwise under represented by survey data. This multiplicative factor is admittedly arbitrary and further refinements can certainly be made. Note in particular that for richer countries in which the population does live in cities, this has the effect of including people who are below the threshold required for a middle-class basket of goods in urban areas. This measure may underestimate the urban poor in developing countries, potentially counting some of them as belonging to the urban middle class (if we take the view that falling beneath the lower threshold for middle class membership makes one poor, which is a separate taxonomic decision and is not a necessary one; one might, for instance think of some people who are just above the poverty line still not having attained the requirements for "respectable" middle-class membership).

At the other threshold, given that people have disposable income for vehicles or clothing or other goods as well as some savings and still be broadly middle class but not affluent according to prevailing perceptions (consider, for instance, a middle-tier civil servant living on her official salary alone), we suggest an expanded threshold of 1.5 times the ceiling required. This multiplicative factor is arbitrary too, but the range of the (0.5 floor basket of goods to 1.5 ceiling basket of goods) provides an expanded middle-class definition which we think is roughly plausible and informative.

Using this expanded understanding of the middle class, we arrive at another set of estimates by country for 2015 as shown in table 3.3.

Predictably, the adjustment leads to a sharp fall in the number of people considered to be below middle class in advanced industrialized countries (often to zero) while expanding the proportion of the middle class in lower income countries. This may be too expansive a definition for advanced countries, but on the other hand, may be more effective in capturing the middle class in less urbanized and poorer countries.

Finally, we can repeat the exercise we did with PPP rates that shows the size and contribution of various regions to the global middle class in 2015 by using this achievement-based definition of the middle class. The results are given in figure 3.3.

The urban middle-class thresholds provided by Numbeo suggest a widely variant membership across the world. Overall, only about 13 percent of the world's population enjoy this status. Unsurprisingly, North America (with 50 percent of its population) and Europe with 33 percent have the largest numbers, while South Asia and Sub-Saharan Africa have very small numbers (on the order of 1 percent) who attain this consumption level. Even if one were to use more generous bounds (as in the second panel of figure 3.3), this does not greatly improve the portrait for those two regions. By contrast, with the more expansive bounds, majorities in Europe and North America achieve such a status, while sizable groups in East Asia, Latin America, and the Middle East and North Africa do as well.

3. THE GLOBAL MIDDLE CLASS AS CONSUMERS OF AN INTERNATIONAL BASKET OF GOODS

We move finally to the third consumer market-specific definition of the global middle class. This is a notion that is the staple of the business press: the global middle class defined as those who demand international goods and services.[11] Attempts to measure the size of this group in different countries have been varied and use different approaches and regional foci, but all aimed to examine the size of the global consuming middle class (Corrales, Barberena, and Schmeichel 2006; Court and Narsimhan 2010; Dadush and Ali 2012; Kamakura and Mazzon 2013).

Table 3.3 Expanded Middle-Class Threshold as Defined by Numbeo Basket Cost: Selected Countries

Country	Floor ($)	Ceiling ($)	Percent Below	Percent in Middle	Percent Above
India	2.7	19.0	93.6%	6.3%	0.1%
Pakistan	3.0	22.6	95.3%	4.7%	0.0%
Egypt	3.3	31.2	83.3%	16.5%	0.2%
Bangladesh	3.3	24.7	95.3%	4.7%	0.0%
Uganda	3.9	29.9	97.2%	2.8%	0.0%
Turkey	4.1	31.0	25.2%	72.6%	2.2%
Brazil	4.3	35.1	39.3%	59.2%	1.5%
Mexico	4.4	36.2	44.6%	53.9%	1.5%
Romania	4.5	30.6	45.0%	55.0%	0.0%
Malaysia	4.8	32.7	41.8%	57.9%	0.3%
Kenya	5.2	51.1	95.0%	4.9%	0.1%
South Africa	5.3	38.9	87.0%	12.1%	0.9%
Thailand	5.5	46.5	70.2%	29.7%	0.0%
Portugal	6.0	46.4	7.1%	87.1%	5.8%
Greece	6.0	40.7	1.2%	91.1%	7.7%
Russian Federation	6.2	51.7	57.3%	42.7%	0.0%
Peru	6.4	46.0	63.0%	36.7%	0.3%
Ecuador	6.5	41.0	74.1%	25.5%	0.4%
China	7.1	64.8	68.9%	31.1%	0.0%
Nigeria	7.8	88.2	98.5%	1.5%	0.0%
Spain	7.9	55.8	6.3%	89.8%	3.9%
Germany	9.7	80.1	0.0%	93.0%	7.0%
Sweden	9.9	85.1	0.0%	95.0%	5.0%
Italy	10.0	76.3	8.0%	89.7%	2.3%
France	10.7	79.4	0.9%	94.8%	4.2%
Canada	11.0	73.0	0.0%	87.2%	12.8%
New Zealand	11.0	82.8	0.0%	48.9%	51.1%
Netherlands	11.3	89.3	0.3%	96.2%	3.6%
Denmark	11.5	98.5	0.0%	92.3%	7.7%
Belgium	11.7	85.6	0.0%	94.8%	5.2%
Korea, Rep.	11.7	92.9	10.4%	88.5%	1.1%
Japan	12.2	100.6	0.0%	97.5%	2.5%
Australia	13.2	99.7	0.0%	89.8%	10.2%
United Kingdom	13.7	100.1	0.0%	92.1%	7.9%
United States	13.9	93.4	0.0%	87.2%	12.8%
Norway	15.7	124.1	0.5%	96.5%	3.0%

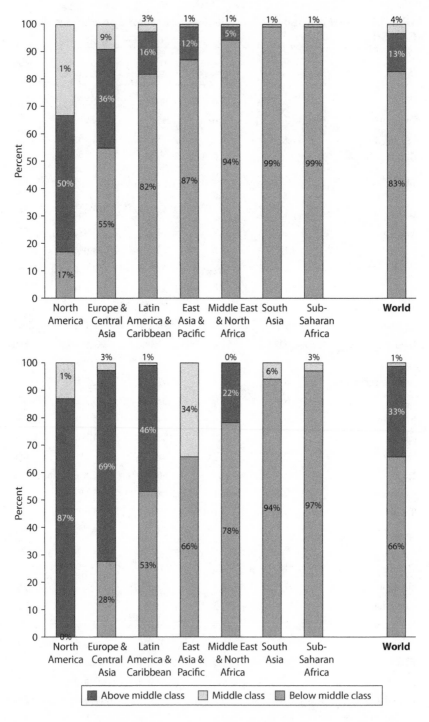

Figure 3.3   Global Middle Class with Numbeo Basket—Basic and Expanded

Note: *Upper panel*: Distribution for Numbeo basket. *Lower panel*: Distribution for 0.5 lower basket to 1.5 upper basket. Based on authors' calculations.

This is certainly a valid grouping to be concerned with, but it is not entirely clear how to measure their size. If the global elite and possibly the global middle class increasingly consume very similar things, even more similar perhaps than the various "subsistence" levels around the world, then the correct strategy is not to use PPP-adjusted measures but simply use exchange rates and identify those who achieve a certain level of consumption of an international basket of goods. If the goods are tradeable, one should not expect vast differences in the international cost of these goods across countries. Given that the major interest is in the ability to purchase goods and services that could be afforded by the OECD, we estimate the global middle class defined as the middle of the OECD distribution (the middle 40 percent) of OECD consumption, this time using market exchange rates rather than PPP values. This is shown in table 3.4.

Table 3.4 Global Middle Class as Defined by Exchange Rates

Year 1990 (bounds $13.31 to $25.58 1990 US$)	Below Middle	Middle	Above	Share Below	Share Middle	Share Above Middle
East Asia & Pacific	93%	5%	2%	37%	21%	11%
Europe & Central Asia	46%	30%	24%	9%	60%	64%
Latin America & Caribbean	97%	2%	1%	9%	2%	1%
Middle East & North Africa	87%	8%	5%	4%	4%	4%
North America	22%	41%	37%	1%	28%	33%
South Asia	100%	0%	0%	26%	0%	0%
Sub-Saharan Africa	98%	0%	2%	11%	0%	3%
World	86%	8%	6%	100%	100%	100%
Year 2010 (bounds $25.31 to $48.60 2010 US$)						
East Asia & Pacific	93%	4%	3%	33%	18%	19%
Europe & Central Asia	65%	23%	12%	10%	43%	32%
Latin America & Caribbean	97%	2%	1%	10%	2%	2%
Middle East & North Africa	98%	1%	1%	5%	1%	1%
North America	19%	40%	41%	1%	29%	42%
South Asia	100%	0%	0%	27%	0%	0%
Sub-Saharan Africa	98%	0%	2%	14%	0%	5%
World	88%	7%	5%	100%	100%	100%

The startling point to note here is the fact that the (only) movement is within the wealthy countries. Latin America has only about 3 percent of its population in the OECD middle class, East Asia and the Pacific region has only about 7 percent of its population, while Sub-Saharan Africa and India have none, whether one is using 1990 exchange rates or 2010 exchange rates to compare the relative distributions. Across the world, only 12 percent enjoy consumption levels of the middle class of the OECD.

The breathless anticipation of the new consumer global order centered in China and other emerging economies, endlessly repeated in the business press then, may be a case of willful self-delusion. But the implications go beyond the fact that multinationals will not find as large markets as the business press has suggested exists in emerging markets. The critical issue from the macroeconomic perspective is that at least in the medium term, one cannot expect any replacement from the rest of the world for consumer demand from the OECD. Given this, if one needs to conceive of sources of global aggregate demand, the consumer in the OECD remains the key element in any sort of rebalancing of demand.

CONCLUSION

We see our attempt in this article as doing precisely that, and trying to disentangle a muddle that has been created by an inappropriate conflation of the many relevant and competing definitions of the global middle class. In doing so we identified three major definitions: the global middle class as the middle of the global income distribution, the global middle class as a sociological category of people who enjoy some level of common achievement of goods and services, and the global middle class as consumers of an international basket of goods. For the second, we undertook an analysis which fixed a set of achievements but that allowed for a relevant implicit substantive interpretation. This elides some of the problems associated with the use of PPPs. For the third, we showed that the rest of the world still does not have a substantial proportion of people who can replace the OECD middle class as consumers of a global basket of goods when looked at (as is appropriate) with market exchange rates.

That these distinctions have very strong material impacts on the measurement of the middle class within and between countries can be seen in table 3.5. Depending on the definition, for example, the United States has anything between 60 and a 100 percent of its population enjoying an income or above that of the global middle class.

Table 3.5 Middle Class Using Various Thresholds

Country	GMC1			GMC2			GMC3		
	Below	Middle	Above	Below	Middle	Above	Below	Middle	Above
Brazil	7.8%	16.3%	75.9%	74.4%	22.0%	3.6%	93.9%	4.5%	1.6%
China	35.7%	19.4%	44.9%	92.7%	7.3%	0.0%	100.0%	0.0%	0.0%
France	0.0%	0.0%	100.0%	18.5%	64.3%	17.2%	22.3%	49.5%	28.2%
Germany	0.0%	0.0%	100.0%	12.4%	66.4%	21.2%	25.1%	47.7%	27.2%
India	79.2%	14.3%	6.5%	98.6%	1.2%	0.2%	100.0%	0.0%	0.0%
South Africa	49.0%	18.0%	33.0%	94.8%	3.6%	1.6%	97.6%	1.4%	1.0%
Sweden	0.0%	0.0%	100.0%	12.3%	71.2%	16.5%	21.9%	49.4%	28.8%
United Kingdom	0.0%	0.0%	100.0%	18.9%	58.5%	22.7%	21.6%	44.6%	33.8%
United States	0.0%	0.0%	100.0%	17.7%	50.0%	32.3%	19.4%	40.4%	40.2%

Note: GMC 1: PPP middle class ($2005 PPP) for 2010;

GMC 2: Numbeo middle class (2015); and

GMC 3: OECD-based global middle class ($2010 ER, 2010).

Moving forward, it is important that we obtain more disaggregated and spatially differentiated PPPs and that we fully examine the relevant basket of goods to achieve a middle-class status across contexts. Joseph Stiglitz's concern with a just society has always been a global one. Correctly identifying and understanding the global middle class may be a necessary step therefore to achieving this.

NOTES

1. As he put it in his *Politics* ". . . a city ought to be composed, as far as possible, of equals and similars; and these are generally the middle classes. Wherefore the city which is composed of middle-class citizens is necessarily best constituted in respect of the elements of which we say the fabric of the state naturally consists . . ." (see Benjamin Jowett's translation, Book Four, Part XI, http://classics.mit.edu/Aristotle/politics.4.four.html).

2. Some representative academic explorations of the disappearing middle class, very far from exhaustive, include Frank 2007; Esteban and Ray 1994; Duclos, Esteban, and Ray 2004; Pressman 2007; Autor, Katz, and Kearney, 2008; Wolfson 1994. For a characteristic meditation on the impact of the thinning of the middle class on politics and society, see Ed Luce, "It's Still the Middle Class, Dumbo," *Financial Times*, October 4, 2015.

3. Here, of course, the distinction between a class-for-itself and a class-in-itself from Lukács (1971) is relevant.

4. This is not a simple matter of absolute and relative classification. A given absolutely defined capability (e.g., to be able to participate meaningfully in the sphere of cultural production of consequence to one's society) may depend on commodity requirements that are relative in the space of commodities and dependent upon specified contextual boundaries. For instance, whereas previously it may have required knowledge of and ability to relate and modify an oral tradition in one's own language, in today's global context it might require access to a computer and knowledge of the English language or another prevalent tongue.

5. (Bardhan 1999, 1984) uses broader Marxian categories to analyze Indian class formations. The work of social theorists and others, although enormously influential in sociology, appears not to have much impact in economics (Bourdieu 2011; Aron 1950; Parsons 1940; Runciman 1974). Some thoughtful recent exceptions include Atkinson and Brandolini (2011) and Blank (2010).

6. This definition is also used by Sumner (2012) in his analysis of the global middle class.

7. This dependence of patterns upon thresholds is well-known in the case of poverty assessment, where for instance the choice of a higher global poverty line leads to a much less favorable trend of poverty reduction for recent years (within the prevailing money-metric approach) precisely because it affects the regional composition of poverty and different regions have had very different trends of poverty reduction. See, for instance, Jayadev, Lahoti, and Reddy (2015).

8. See Reddy and Lahoti (2015), http://ineteconomics.org/ideas-papers/blog/1-90 -per-day-what-does-it-say for a detailed explanation of exactly how low this is.

9. See the Thrifty Food Plan: http://www.cnpp.usda.gov/sites/default/files/usda _food_plans_cost_of_food/TFP2006Report.pdf.

10. Birdsall (2010) calls the grouping of Indians who possess incomes of between $4 and $10 PPP per day a "catalytic class" which is neither poor nor middle class.

11. An academic, when interviewed notes for example that "There is a demand argument, and if I were at VW, Nestle, Dunkin' Donuts or Ikea, that's what I would be interested in" (Christian Meyer quoted in (Rosenbaum 2013).

REFERENCES

Aron, R. 1950. "Social Structure and the Ruling Class: Part 1." *British Journal of Sociology* 1 (1):1–16.

Atkinson, A., and A. Brandolini. 2011. "On the Identification of the Middle Class." Working Paper 217, ECINEQ, Society for the Study of Economic Inequality.

Autor, D. H., L. F. Katz, and M. S. Kearney. 2008. "Trends in U.S. Wage Inequality: Revising the Revisionists." *Review of Economics and Statistics* 90 (2):300–323.

Banerjee, A. V., and E. Duflo. 2008. "What Is Middle Class about the Middle Classes around the World?" *Journal of Economic Perspectives* 22 (2):3.

Bardhan, P. K. 1984. *Land, Labor, and Rural Poverty: Essays in Development Economics.* New York: Columbia University Press.

Bardhan, P. 1999. *The Political Economy of Development in India: Expanded Edition with an Epilogue on the Political Economy of Reform in India.* New Delhi: Oxford University Press.

Birdsall, N. 2010. "The (Indispensable) Middle Class in Developing Countries; or, the Rich and the Rest, Not the Poor and the Rest." In *Equity in a Globalizing World,* edited by Ravi Kanbur and Michael Spence. Washington, DC: World Bank.

Birdsall, N. 2012. "Oops: Economists in Confused Search for the Middle Class in the Developing World." Views from the Center Blog, Center for Global Development. https://www.cgdev.org/blog/oops-economists-confused-search-middle-class-developing -world.

Birdsall, N., C. Graham, and S. Pettinato. 2000. "Stuck in the Tunnel: Is Globaliza- tion Muddling the Middle?" Working Paper 14, Center on Social and Economic Dynamics. Washington, DC: Brookings Institution.

Blank, R. 2010. "Middle Class in America." Working Papers, U.S. Department of Commerce Economics and Statistics Division.

Bourdieu, P. 2011. "The Forms of Capital (1986)." In *Cultural Theory: An Anthology,* edited by I. Szeman and T. Kaposy, 81–93. Hoboken, NJ: Wiley.

Cashell, B. W. 2007. "Who Are the 'Middle Class'?" Congressional Research Service (March).

Corrales, B., M. Barberena, and N. Schmeichel. 2006. "Latin American Profile, Demographics and Socio Economic Strata." Research Paper, European Society for Opinion and Marketing Research (ESOMAR).

Court, D., and L. Narsimhan. 2010. "Capturing the World's Emerging Middle Class." *McKinsey Quarterly*. https://www.mckinsey.com/industries/retail/our-insights /capturing-the-worlds-emerging-middle-class.

Dadush, U. B., and S. Ali. 2012. "In Search of the Global Middle Class: A New Index." Carnegie Endowment for International Peace.

Deaton, A., and O. Dupriez. 2011. "Purchasing Power Parity Exchange Rates for the Global Poor." *American Economic Journal: Applied Economics* 3 (2):137–166.

Duclos, J.-Y., J. Esteban, and D. Ray. 2004. "Polarization: Concepts, Measurement, Estimation." *Econometrica* 72 (6):1737–1772.

Easterly, W. 2001. "The Middle Class Consensus and Economic Development." *Journal of Economic Growth* 6 (4):317–335.

Esteban, J.-M., and D. Ray. 1994. "On the Measurement of Polarization." *Econometrica* 62 (4):819–851.

Ferreira, F. H., J. Messina, J. Rigolini, L.-F. López-Calva, M. A. Lugo, R. Vakis, L. F. Ló et al. 2012. *Economic Mobility and the Rise of the Latin American Middle Class*. Washington, DC: World Bank Publications.

Frank, R. H. 2007. *Falling Behind: How Income Inequality Harms the Middle Class*. Berkeley: University of California Press.

Jayadev, A., R. Lahoti, and S. G. Reddy. 2015. "Who Got What, Then and Now? A Fifty Year Overview from the Global Consumption and Income Project." Technical Report. Courant Research Centre: Poverty, Equity and Growth Discussion Papers.

Kamakura, W. A., and J. A. Mazzon. 2013. "Socioeconomic Status and Consumption in an Emerging Economy." *International Journal of Research in Marketing* 30 (1):4–18.

Kapsos, S., and E. Bourmpoula. 2013. "Employment and Economic Class in the Developing World." ILO Research Paper No. 6. Geneva: International Labor Office.

Kharas, H. 2010. "The Emerging Middle Class in Developing Countries." Washington, DC: Brookings Institution.

Kharas, H., and G. Gertz. 2010. "The New Global Middle Class: A Crossover from West to East." Wolfensohn Center for Development at Brookings (1–14).

Lahoti, R., A. Jayadev, and S. G. Reddy. 2014. "The Global Consumption and Income Project (GCIP): An Introduction and Preliminary Findings." Working paper. https://papers.ssrn.com/sol3/papers.cfm?abstract_id=2480636..

Lopez-Calva, L. F., and E. Ortiz-Juarez. 2014. "A Vulnerability Approach to the Definition of the Middle Class." *Journal of Economic Inequality* 12 (1):23–47.

Lukács, G. 1971. *History and Class Consciousness: Studies in Marxist Dialectics, Vol. 215*. Cambridge, MA: MIT Press.

Milanovic, B. 2006. "Global Income Inequality: What It Is and Why It Matters." World Bank Policy Research Working Paper 3865.

Milanovic, B., and S. Yitzhaki. 2002. "Decomposing World Income Distribution: Does the World Have a Middle Class?" *Review of Income and Wealth* 48 (2):155–178.

Parsons, T. 1940. "An Analytical Approach to the Theory of Social Stratification." *American Journal of Sociology* 45 (6):841–862.

Pressman, S. 2007. "The Decline of the Middle Class: An International Perspective." *Journal of Economic Issues* 41 (1):181–200.

Quah, D. T. 1996. "Twin Peaks: Growth and Convergence in Models of Distribution Dynamics." *Economic Journal* 106 (437):1045–1055.

Ravallion, M. 2010. "The Developing World's Bulging (But Vulnerable) Middle Class." *World Development* 38 (4):445–454.

Rosenbaum, E. 2013. "A New Species? The Elusive Nature of the Global Middle Class." CNBC Online. https://www.cnbc.com/id/100949800

Runciman, W. G. 1974. "Occupational Class and the Assessment of Economic Inequality in Britain." In *Poverty, Inequality, and Class Structure*, edited by D. Wedderbrun, 93–106. New York: Cambridge University Press.

Stiglitz, J. 2012. *The Price of Inequality*. London: Penguin.

Sumner, A. 2012. "The Buoyant Billions: How 'Middle Class' Are the New Middle Classes in Developing Countries? (and Why Does It Matter?)." Center for Global Development Working Paper 309.

Taylor, P., R. Morin, R. F. D'Vera Cohn, R. Kochhar, and A. Clark. 2008. "Inside the Middle Class: Bad Times Hit the Good Life." Pew Research Center.

Thurow, Lester C. 1987. "A Surge in Inequality." *Scientific American* 256 (5):30.

Wolfson, M. C. 1994. "When Inequalities Diverge." *American Economic Review* 84 (2):353–358.

PART II

Microeconomics

Companies Are Seldom as Good or as Bad as They Seem at the Time

Gary Smith

ABSTRACT

Professional forecasts of corporate earnings are not correlated perfectly with actual earnings. Those companies that forecasters are optimistic about usually do not do as well as predicted, while companies given pessimistic predictions typically do better than predicted. Insufficient appreciation of this statistical principle may help explain the success of contrarian investment strategies, in particular, why stocks with relatively optimistic earnings forecasts underperform those with pessimistic forecasts.

⎯⎯∞⎯⎯

Joseph Stiglitz has explored widely and deeply the implications of imperfect information. Sometimes, the information is asymmetric; sometimes, it is just imperfect. The most obvious implications are that even completely rational people may make decisions they later regret and that those who are more informed may take advantage of the less informed. More subtly, and perhaps more importantly, actions often reveal information—which, at times, provides an incentive for information-revealing action and, at other times, inaction. Companies pay dividends to demonstrate that their profits are not illusory, guarantee products to demonstrate confidence in their durability, and are reluctant to reward valuable employees publicly lest they be targeted by other firms.

To focus on the profound implications of relaxing the ingrained, yet wildly implausible, classical assumption that everyone is informed perfectly, Stiglitz typically maintains the similarly implausible classical assumption that everyone makes completely rational decisions based on the information they do possess. The current paper looks at one implication of the fact that stock market investors are not only imperfectly informed, but also imperfectly rational. The result documents yet another reason to question the efficient market claim that "given the available information, actual [stock] prices at every point in time represent very good estimates of intrinsic values" (Fama 1965, 34).

There is a useful distinction between investors *possessing* information and investors *processing* information. Stiglitz's work often explores situations in which two sides to a transaction possess different information; for example, when bidding for oil leases, pricing medical insurance, and governing corporations.

Possessing valuable information in the stock market means knowing something about a company that others do not know. Processing information valuably is thinking more clearly about things that are well known; for example, not letting large losses affect one's investment decisions (Smith, Levere, and Kurtzman 2009).

This paper examines a more subtle possible source of error in processing information. Professional corporate earnings forecasts are widely publicized, yet it is apparently not widely recognized that because of the imperfect correlation between predicted and actual earnings, the most extreme predictions are likely to be too extreme. The subsequent adjustment of stock prices when earnings turn out to be less extreme than predicted may partly explain the success of contrarian investment strategies.

1. CONTRARIAN STRATEGIES

"Value" investment strategies identify stocks that are out of favor, as gauged by their low market prices relative to dividends, earnings, book value, or cash flow (early research includes O'Higgins and Downes 1992; Basu 1977; Rosenberg, Reid, and Lanstein 1985; Chan, Hamao, and Lakonishok 1991). Fama and French (1992) argue that because the stock market is efficient, the high returns from value strategies must be risk premia—even if we cannot pinpoint why value stocks are risky. An obvious alternative to this circular argument is that investor foibles in processing information (such as the incautious extrapolation of earnings growth rates or a failure to distinguish between a good company and a good stock) create opportunities for contrarian investors (Lakonishok, Shliefer, and Vishny 1994).

The success of contrarian strategies is also documented by the mean-reversion literature. For example, DeBondt and Thaler (1985, 1987) found that portfolios of poorly performing "loser" stocks outperformed portfolios of previous winners by substantial margins, even though the winner portfolios were riskier.

One way to tie together the empirical success of value strategies and the mean reversion of stock prices is the possibility that investors have an insufficient appreciation of the statistical principle of regression to the mean, both with respect to fluctuations in actual earnings and, also, in the imperfect relationship between predicted and actual earnings.

2. REGRESSION TO THE MEAN

Regression to the mean commonly occurs when observed data are an imperfect measure of an underlying trait. For example, because observed heights are an imperfect estimate of the genetic influences that parents pass on to their children, parents whose heights are far from the mean tend to have children whose heights are closer to the mean (Galton 1889). Similarly, because test scores are an imperfect measure of mastery, students whose scores are far from the mean on one test tend to score closer to the mean on a second test of the same material (Lord and Novick 1968).

In business, Secrist (1993) found that the most and least successful companies (as measured, for example, by the ratio of profits to assets) tended to become more nearly average as time passed. Secrist (1993, 24) speculated that firms with "superior judgment, merchandizing sense, and honesty" were undermined by competition from "unfit" firms, causing businesses to converge to mediocrity. The initial reviews (for example, Riegel 1933; Elder 1934; King 1934) of Secrist's book, *The Triumph of Mediocrity in Business*, were glowing; then Hotelling (1933) pointed out that Secrist had been fooled by regression toward the mean.

In any given year, the most successful companies are more likely to have had good luck than bad, and to have done well not only relative to other companies, but also relative to their own "ability." The opposite is true of the least successful companies. This is why the subsequent performance of the top and bottom companies is usually closer to the average company. At the same time, their places at the extremes are taken by other companies experiencing fortune or misfortune. These up-and-down fluctuations are part of the natural ebb and flow of life and do not mean that all companies will soon be mediocre. As Hotelling put it, Secrist's calculations "really prove nothing more than that the ratios in question have a tendency to wander about" (1933, 164).

3. ARE WE AWARE OF REGRESSION TO THE MEAN?

Secrist is not alone. An anonymous reviewer for a paper (Schall and Smith 2000) on regression to the mean in baseball wrote that "There are few statistical facts more interesting than regression to the mean for two reasons. First, people encounter it almost every day of their lives. Second, almost nobody understands it. The coupling of these two reasons makes regression to the mean one of the most fundamental sources of error in human judgment."

People often do not anticipate statistical regression and, when it occurs, they search for causal explanations. If pilots who excel in a training session do not do as well in the next session, it is because the flight instructors praised them for doing well (Kahneman and Tversky 1973). If students who do poorly on one test do better subsequently, it was because they were given special attention (Thorndike 1942).

Mean reversion in stock returns may be due to this insufficient appreciation of regression to the mean in earnings, cash flow, and other fundamental determinants of stock prices. Keynes observed that "day-to-day fluctuations in the profits of existing investments, which are obviously of an ephemeral and nonsignificant character, tend to have an altogether excessive, and even absurd, influence on the market" (1936, 138).

For simplicity, suppose that a company's return on assets (ROA) fluctuates randomly about a constant expected value. The firm's ROA will consequently exhibit regression to the mean (extreme values tend to be followed by values that are closer to the mean) and the *change* in ROA will exhibit mean reversion (ROA increases tend to be followed by ROE decreases, and vice versa).

Now suppose that investors do not fully appreciate regression to the mean. They see an increase in earnings and bid up the price of the stock. When earnings regress to the mean, the stock price takes a hit. Thus, a price increase (and high return) tends to be followed by a price decrease (and low return). This argument that regression to the mean in earnings causes a mean reversion in prices explains the conclusion of Lakonishok, Shliefer, and Vishny (1994):

> First, a variety of investment strategies that involve buying out-of-favor (value) stocks have outperformed glamour strategies over the April 1968 to April 1990 period. Second, a likely reason that these value strategies have worked so well relative to the glamour strategies is the fact that the actual future growth rates of earnings, cash flow, [and sales] etc. of glamour stocks relative to value stocks turned out to be much lower than they were in the past, or as the multiples on those stocks indicate the market expected them to be. (1574)

We can apply the same logic to earnings forecasts if we think of the forecasts as predictors of actual earnings in the same way that parents' heights are predictors of their children's heights, test scores are predictors of future test scores, and current earnings are predictors of future earnings. The most optimistic predictions are more likely to be overly optimistic than to be excessively pessimistic; so, the companies with the most optimistic forecasts probably won't do as well as predicted—nor are the companies with the most pessimistic forecasts likely to do as poorly as predicted.

4. A MODEL OF REGRESSION TOWARD THE MEAN

Let μ_i be the statistical expected value of company i's earnings growth rate and Y_i be the median of the expert forecasts of this growth rate. Even if the forecasts are unbiased with Y_i equal to μ_i plus a random error term,

$$Y_i = X_i + \varepsilon_i \qquad (4.1)$$

the variance of the forecasts across firms is larger than the variance of the actual expected values. Extreme forecasts tend to be too extreme.

If μ_i were known, we could use it to make unbiased predictions of actual earnings growth. Because μ_i is not observable, we use the analysts' forecasts. If we had the forecast for only one company, we might use that forecast as is. However, looking at the forecast for one company in relation to the forecasts for other companies, we should take into account the statistical argument that those forecasts that are optimistic relative to other companies are probably also optimistic relative to this company's own prospects. It would be unusual if analysts were unduly pessimistic about a company and it still had one of the highest predicted growth rates.

This line of reasoning suggests that the accuracy of earnings predictions for any one company may be enhanced by shrinking the prediction toward the average prediction for all companies. But by how much?

In educational testing literature, μ_i is the expected value of a person's test score (fittingly labeled this person's "ability") and Y_i is this person's observed score on a single test that is intended to measure this ability.

Truman Kelley (1947) showed that the optimal estimate of a person's ability is a weighted average of this person's score and the average score of the group the person came from:

$$\hat{\mu}_i = RY_i + (1 - R)\bar{Y} \tag{4.2}$$

The term r is the test's reliability, which measures the extent to which performances are consistent. If a group of students take two comparable tests, reliability is the correlation between their scores on these two tests.

If test scores were completely random, like guessing the answers to questions written in a language the test-takers don't understand, the reliability would be zero, and the best estimate of a person's ability is the average score of the group. At the other extreme, a perfectly reliable test would be one where some people do better than others, but any single person gets the same score, test after test. Now, the best estimate of a person's ability is the test score, regardless of the group score.

In between these extremes, Kelley's equation is a weighted average of the individual score and the group score, with the weight given to the individual score increasing as the test's reliability increases. Kelley's equation not only recognizes that performances tend to regress to the mean, but it tells us how much regression to expect.

Although Kelley derived the equation named after him by using the thoroughly conventional approach to statistics that prevailed in the 1940s (and for many decades afterward), Kelley's equation can also be derived using Bayesian reasoning. If the error term in equation (4.1) is normally distributed and our prior distribution for a person's ability is normally distributed with a mean equal to the average score, the mean of the posterior distribution for ability is given by equation 4.2.

Applying Kelley's equation to corporate earnings forecasts, the optimal estimate of the expected value of a company's earnings growth is a weighted average of the analysts' forecast for this company and the average forecast for all companies, with the weights depending on the correlation between actual and predicted earnings growth across companies.

If forecast and actual growth rates were perfectly correlated, we would not shrink the forecasts at all. If the forecast and actual growth rates were uncorrelated, the forecasts would be useless in predicting earnings and we would shrink each forecast to the mean completely, making no effort to predict which companies will have above-average or below-average growth rates.

Analysts' forecasts need not be unbiased. Several studies have documented that analysts tend to be too optimistic (for example, Dreman and Berry 1995; Easterwood and Nutt 1999). I will consequently work with standardized actual and predicted growth rates, each normalized to have a mean of zero and standard deviation of one.

Kelley's equation now simplifies to

$$\hat{\mu}_i = rY_i + (1-r)\bar{Y} \tag{4.3}$$

where Z_i is the standardized expert forecast and $\hat{Z}_i$ is the adjusted forecast, taking regression to the mean into account.

5. DATA

Some companies have higher earnings per share than other companies simply because they have fewer shares outstanding. I consequently analyze the predicted and actual growth rates of earnings per share, both normalized across firms each year to have a mean of zero and a standard deviation of one. Regression to the mean applies to growth rates across firms, and implies that firms whose growth rates are predicted to be far from the mean will probably have growth rates closer to the mean, regardless of whether the average growth rate is high or low.

All forecasts were taken from the Institutional Brokers' Estimate System (IBES) database, which records the forecast, the forecaster, and the time and date when the forecast is announced. Since all forecasts are entered contemporaneously, there are no backfilling issues. The IBES database maintains a record of every forecast made by each forecaster so that it is possible to identify a forecaster's most recent forecast as of any specified date.

I used the median of the analysts' forecasts for all companies with December fiscal years so that all earnings results are buffeted by the same macroeconomic factors. Companies with December fiscal years are required to file 10-K reports by March 31; I used the most recent forecasts as of April 30 to ensure that earnings for the preceding fiscal year were available to analysts. I looked at both the current-year and year-ahead forecasts. For April 30, 2005, for example, the current-year forecasts are for fiscal year 2005 and the year-ahead forecasts are for fiscal year 2006.

I restricted my analysis to companies with forecasts from at least twenty-five analysts to ensure that these companies are prominent, highly visible, and closely scrutinized. Any systematic inaccuracies in analyst forecasts cannot be explained away as careless guesses about unimportant companies. I used the median prediction to reduce the influence of outliers. I also excluded companies that did not have stock return data in the Center for Research in Security Prices (CRSP) database because I wanted to track the stock performance of the companies I analyzed.

I excluded situations in which percentage changes were meaningless because base-year earnings were negative. I also excluded situations in which earnings are predicted to increase or decrease by more than 100 percent, as these are presumably special situations or rebounds from special situations and the large values might unduly influence the results.

These various restrictions limited the years studied to 1992 through 2014, with an average of fifty-four companies per year for the current-year forecasts and thirty-eight companies per year for the year-ahead forecasts.

6. RESULTS

Kelley's equation was used to adjust the forecasts for regression to the mean. The correlation between forecasts and actual earnings was estimated using the most recent data available at the time of the forecast. For example, for the current-year forecasts on April 30, 2005, I estimated the correlation between current-year forecasts on April 30, 2004, and actual 2004 earnings—both of which were available on April 30, 2005. For the year-ahead forecasts on April 30, 2005, I estimated the correlation between year-ahead forecasts on April 30, 2003, and actual 2004 earnings.

Forecasting accuracy was measured in two ways: by the number of adjusted or unadjusted forecasts that were closer to the actual values, and by the mean absolute error (MAE) for the adjusted and unadjusted forecasts. Tables 4.1 and 4.2 show the results.

Table 4.1 Current-Year Forecasts of Standardized Percentage Changes in Earnings, 1992–2014

Mean No. of Companies	Mean No. of Analysts	Mean Forecast, Percent	Mean Actual, Percent	Correlation	More Accurate		MAE	
					Z	rZ	Z	rZ
53.9	29.9	10.57	9.86	0.57	516	724	0.48	0.43

Table 4.2 Year-Ahead Forecasts of Standardized Percentage Changes in Earnings

Mean No. of Companies	Mean No. of Analysts	Mean Forecast, Percent	Mean Actual, Percent	Correlation	More Accurate		MAE	
					Z	rZ	Z	rZ
38.1	29.9	17.09	12.99	0.05	276	601	0.90	0.58

Overall, the average median forecast earnings growth is 10.57 percent and 17.09 percent for the current year and year ahead, respectively, compared with average actual values of 9.86 percent and 12.99 percent. The question addressed here, however, is not whether the forecasts should be uniformly adjusted downward, but rather whether the forecasts should be compacted by making the relatively optimistic predictions less optimistic and the relatively pessimistic predictions less pessimistic.

It is striking that, over the entire period, the correlation between predicted and actual growth rates across firms was 0.57 for the current-year forecasts and 0.05 for the year-ahead forecasts. Remember, the current-year predictions are as of April 30, four months into the fiscal year being forecast. The year-ahead forecasts are evidently little better than dart throws.

Whether gauged by the number of more accurate predictions or by the mean absolute errors, the adjusted forecasts are more accurate than the unadjusted forecasts. Overall, the adjusted forecasts are more accurate for 58 percent of the current-year predictions and 69 percent of the year-ahead forecasts. The shrunken forecasts reduce the mean absolute errors by about 10 percent and 35 percent, respectively. We can use the binomial distribution to test the null hypothesis that each method is equally likely to give a more accurate prediction. The two-sided p-value is 2.0×10^{-9} for the current-year predictions and 4.7×10^{-29} for the year-ahead predictions.

7. PORTFOLIO RETURNS

The previous section showed that analysts are, on average, excessively optimistic about the companies that they predict will have relatively large earnings increases and overly pessimistic about the companies predicted to have relatively small increases. If investors pay attention to analysts (or make similar predictions themselves), stock prices may be too high for companies with relatively optimistic forecasts and too low for the companies with relatively pessimistic forecasts—mistakes that will be corrected when earnings regress to the mean relative to these forecasts. If so, stocks with relatively pessimistic earnings predictions may outperform stocks with relatively optimistic predictions.

To test this conjecture, four portfolios were formed on April 30 of each year based on the analysts' predicted earnings growth for the current fiscal year. Portfolio 1 consisted of the quartile of stocks with the highest predicted growth, Portfolio 4 contained the quartile with the lowest growth. Equal dollar amounts were invested in each stock. If the stock was taken private or involved in a merger during the next twelve months, the proceeds were reinvested in the remaining stocks in the portfolio. At the end of twelve months, the portfolio returns were calculated and new portfolios were formed.

For the year-ahead predictions, four portfolios were formed on April 30 of each year based on the forecast quartiles, but now the stock returns were tracked over the next twenty-four months. I also looked at two annual strategies. In the first strategy, the portfolios were formed on April 30 of each year and held for one year. They were consequently liquidated a year ahead of the actual earnings announcement. In the second strategy, the portfolios were formed one year after the prediction and held for the one year.

For example, the year-ahead forecasts on April 30, 2005, are for fiscal year 2006. In the first annual strategy, the portfolio is formed on April 30, 2005, based on the year-ahead forecasts at that time, and held until April 30, 2006, at which time the proceeds are invested based on the year-ahead forecasts on April 30, 2006, which are for fiscal year 2007. In the second annual strategy, the portfolio is formed on April 30, 2006, based on the year-ahead forecasts made on April 30, 2005, and held until April 30, 2007, at which time the proceeds are invested based on the year-ahead forecasts on April 30, 2006. These two strategies are easily implemented in practice and can help determine whether performance

Table 4.3   Four Portfolios Based on Current-Year Earnings Forecasts

	Portfolio			
	1	2	3	4
Average Number of Stocks	13.39	13.26	13.78	13.48
Average Forecast, Z	1.20	0.23	−0.24	−1.17
Average Actual, Z	0.82	0.13	−0.17	−0.77
Annual Return				
Mean, Percent	11.84	11.39	14.27	14.00
Standard Deviation, Percent	27.30	24.53	19.93	19.89
Beta Coefficient	0.94	1.25	0.91	0.88
Geometric Mean, Percent	8.56	8.58	12.46	12.05

differences based on year-ahead forecasts occur during the first or second twelve months after the forecasts are made.

Just as I looked at relative earnings, I looked at relative stock returns. I am not trying to predict the direction of the stock market, but rather how a portfolio of stocks with optimistic earnings forecasts does relative to a portfolio of stocks with pessimistic forecasts.

Table 4.3 shows the results for the current-year forecasts. As expected, the actual growth rates are closer to zero than are the predicted growth rates. In addition, the portfolio with the lowest forecast earnings growth rates outperformed the portfolio with the highest forecast growth rates, on average, by about 2 percentage points a year, though the matched-pair two-sided p-value is 0.60. The difference in geometric returns (12.05 versus 8.56 percent), means that over the complete period 1992 through 2014, the most-pessimistic portfolio would have grown to more than twice the value of the most-optimistic portfolio. A $10,000 investment in the most-optimistic stocks would have grown to $66,000, while a $10,000 investment in the most-pessimistic stocks would have grown to $137,000.

Table 4.4 shows the results for the year-ahead forecasts. The actual growth rates are much closer to zero than are the predicted growth rates, reflecting the near-zero correlation between the predicted and actual growth rates. In addition, the average two-year returns are substantially higher for the most-pessimistic portfolio than for the most-optimistic portfolio, and the matched-pair two-sided p-value is 0.0264.

Table 4.4 Four Portfolios Based on Year-Ahead Earnings Forecasts

	Portfolio			
	1	2	3	4
Average Number of Stocks	9.35	9.48	9.65	9.65
Average Forecast, Z	1.33	0.07	−0.34	−1.02
Average Actual, Z	0.10	0.03	−0.05	−0.08
Two-Year Return				
Mean, Percent	23.57	30.48	32.27	35.99
Standard Deviation, Percent	41.85	40.85	35.23	39.21
Beta Coefficient	1.18	1.13	1.06	1.01

Table 4.5 breaks the year-ahead performance into the first and second years following the predictions, as explained above. The most-pessimistic portfolios do better than the most optimistic portfolios in both years, though the differences are more pronounced during the second year. The matched-pair two-sided p-values are 0.23 for the first-year portfolios and 0.03 for the second-year portfolios. For the first-year strategy, a $10,000 investment in the most-optimistic stocks would have grown to $46,000, while a $10,000 investment in the most-pessimistic stocks would have grown to $179,000. For the second-year strategy, a $10,000 investment

Table 4.5 Year-Ahead Portfolios: First-Year and Second-Year Annual Returns

	Portfolio			
	1	2	3	4
First Year				
Mean, Percent	11.09	14.16	14.48	15.25
Standard Deviation, Percent	28.33	24.34	18.54	20.44
Beta Coefficient	1.36	0.99	0.81	0.89
Geometric Mean, Percent	6.90	11.56	13.01	13.37
Second Year				
Mean, Percent	9.63	14.83	15.28	17.02
Standard Deviation, Percent	25.82	22.58	23.30	20.97
Beta Coefficient	1.01	1.06	1.01	0.91
Geometric Mean, Percent	7.87	12.26	12.05	14.80

in the most-optimistic stocks would have grown to $40,000, while a $10,000 investment in the most-pessimistic stocks would have grown to $221,000.

8. A RISK PREMIUM?

It is unlikely that the superior performance of the pessimistic portfolios reflects some kind of risk premium. Growth stocks are not only likely to have relatively uncertain cash flows but, because of their long durations, they are also more sensitive to changes in required rates of return. Tables 4.3, 4.4, and 4.5 show that the annual returns for the most optimistic portfolios have higher standard deviations and more systematic risk (as measured by beta in relation to the S&P 500).

The timing patterns documented in table 4.5 further indicate that the cumulative return differences between Portfolios 1 and 4 are not a risk premium. If it were a risk premium why would the return differential be larger in the second year of the holding period? A more plausible explanation is that stock prices adjust as investors learn that earnings will be closer to the mean than was predicted.

Nonetheless, I gauged the riskiness of the portfolios by estimating the Fama-French (1993) three-factor model using daily percentage-return data from Ken French's website (2015):

$$R = \alpha + \beta_1 MKT + \beta_2 SMB + \beta_3 HML + \beta_4 UMD + \varepsilon$$

where

$R =$ return on portfolio minus the return on Treasury bills
$MKT =$ the value-weighted return on all NYSE, AMEX, and NASDAQ stocks (from CRSP) minus the return on Treasury bills
$SMB =$ average return on three small-stock portfolios minus the average return on three large-stock portfolios (size factor)
$HML =$ the average return on two value portfolios minus the average return on two growth portfolios (value factor)

This model reflects the historical evidence that stock returns are affected by common macro factors; small stocks tend to outperform large stocks (Banz 1981; Reinganum 1981); and value stocks tend to outperform growth stocks (Rosenberg, Reid, and Lanstein 1985).

Chan (1988) and Fama and French (1992) argue that any systematic differences in returns attributable to these factors must represent risks that matter to investors who must be rewarded for bearing these risks. Others, including Lakonishok, Shliefer, and Vishny (1994), interpret the above-average returns as evidence of investor errors—for example, value stocks generally outperform growth stocks because investors overreact to news, causing stocks to be mispriced temporarily. Either way, the question here is whether the relatively strong performance of the pessimistic portfolios can be explained by these three factors.

The estimates are shown in table 4.6. The alphas are negative for the most optimistic portfolios and positive for the most pessimistic portfolios, although the only value that is statistically significant at the 5-percent level is for the year-ahead pessimistic portfolio. A daily excess return of 0.02 percent is roughly 5 percent on an annual basis.

There is no consistent pattern for the size (small-minus-big [SMB]) factor. The coefficients of the value factor tend to be negative for the

Table 4.6   Fama-French Factor Model

		Intercept	$R_M - R_f$	SMB	HML	R^2
Current Year	Portfolio 1	−0.01	1.21	0.09	−0.10	0.65
		[0.07]	[99.82]	[3.70]	[4.26]	
	Portfolio 2	0.00	1.11	−0.04	−0.28	0.73
		[0.18]	[119.72]	[2.18]	[15.37]	
	Portfolio 3	0.01	0.99	−0.10	0.22	0.68
		[1.08]	[109.03]	[5.41]	[11.99]	
	Portfolio 4	0.01	1.02	0.11	0.28	0.59
		[0.68]	[90.87]	[4.89]	[12.82]	
Year Ahead	Portfolio 1	−0.01	1.18	0.05	0.04	0.63
		[0.61]	[135.83]	[2.70]	[2.37]	
	Portfolio 2	0.01	1.07	−0.03	−0.07	0.65
		[1.35]	[139.79]	[2.25]	[4.62]	
	Portfolio 3	0.01	0.96	0.22	0.61	0.61
		[1.71]	[129.41]	[11.25]	[15.16]	
	Portfolio 4	0.02	1.01	−0.09	0.07	0.61
		[2.24]	[128.26]	[5.83]	[4.77]	

Note: [ ] = *t*-values.

optimistic portfolios and positive for the pessimistic portfolios, indicating (not surprisingly) that analysts tend to be more optimistic about growth stocks than value stocks.

9. SUMMARY

Warren Buffett's (2008) succinct summary of a contrarian investment strategy is, "Be fearful when others are greedy and be greedy when others are fearful." His aphorism is generally thought to apply to market bubbles and panics. The evidence presented here suggests a similar mind-set for individual stocks, even during normal times: "Companies are seldom as good or as bad as they seem at the time."

The evidence is persuasive that earnings forecasts are systematically too extreme—too optimistic for companies predicted to do well and too pessimistic for those predicted to do poorly. The accuracy of these forecasts can be improved consistently and substantially by shrinking them toward the mean. These are not fly-by-night companies. They are prominent, widely followed, and closely scrutinized firms.

In addition, portfolios of stocks with relatively optimistic earnings predictions underperform portfolios of stocks with relatively pessimistic predictions. Most tellingly, the return differentials for the year-ahead portfolios are concentrated in the second year of the holding period, when investors are learning that earnings will be closer to the mean than was predicted.

It is not just corporate earnings and it is not just stock prices. Whenever there is imperfect information—whenever there is uncertainty—people may make flawed decisions based on an insufficient appreciation of regression to the mean.

REFERENCES

Banz, R. 1981. "The Relationship Between Return and Market Value of Common Stocks." *Journal of Financial Economics* 9 (1):3–18.

Basu, S. 1977. "Investment Performance of Common Stocks in Relation to Their Price-Earnings Ratios: A Test of the Efficient Market Hypothesis." *Journal of Finance* 32 (3):663–682.

Buffett, W. 2008. "Buy American. I Am." *New York Times*, October 16, 2008.

Chan, K. 1988. "On the Contrarian Investment Strategy." *Journal of Business* 61 (2):147–163.

Chan, L., Y. Hamao, and J. Lakonishok. 1991. "Fundamentals and Stock Returns in Japan." *Journal of Finance* 46 (5):1739–1764.

DeBondt, W. F. M., and R. Thaler. 1985. "Does the Stock Market Overreact?" *Journal of Finance* 40 (3):793–805.

DeBondt, W. F. M., and R. Thaler. 1987. "Further Evidence on Investor Overreaction and Stock Market Seasonality." *Journal of Finance* 42 (3):557–580.

Dreman, D. N., and M. A. Berry. 1995. "Analysts Forecasting Errors and Their Implications for Security Analysis." *Financial Analysts Journal* 51 (3):30–40.

Easterwood, J. C. and S. R. Nutt. 1999. "Inefficiency in Analysts' Earnings Forecasts: Systematic Misreaction or Systematic Optimism?" *Journal of Finance* 54: 1777–1797.

Elder, R. F. 1934. "Review of the Triumph of Mediocrity in Business by Horace Secrist." *American Economic Review* 24 (1):121–122.

Fama, E. F. 1965. "The Behavior of Stock Market Prices." *Journal of Business* 38 (1):34–105.

Fama, E. F., and K. R. French. 1992. "The Cross-Section of Expected Stock Returns." *Journal of Finance* 47 (2):427–465.

Fama, E. F., and K. R. French. 1993. "Common Risk Factors in the Returns on Bonds and Stocks." *Journal of Financial Economics* 33 (1):3–56.

French, K. R. Data Library. Retrieved July 14, 2015, from http://mba.tuck.dartmouth.edu/pages/faculty/ken.french/data_library.html.

Galton, F. 1889. *Natural Inheritance.* New York: Macmillan.

Hotelling, H. 1933. "Review of the Triumph of Mediocrity in Business." *Journal of the American Statistical Association* 28 (184):463–465.

Kahneman, D., and A. Tversky. 1973. "On the Psychology of Prediction." *Psychological Review* 80 (4):237–251.

Kelley, T. L. 1947. *Fundamentals of Statistics.* Cambridge, MA: Harvard University.

Keynes, J. M. 1936. *The General Theory of Employment, Interest and Money.* New York: Macmillan.

King, W. I. 1934. "Review of the Triumph of Mediocrity in Business by Secrist H." *Journal of Political Economy* 42 (3):398–400.

Lakonishok, J., A. Shliefer, and R. W. Vishny. 1994. "Contrarian Investment, Extrapolation, and Risk." *Journal of Finance* 49 (5):1541–1578.

Lord, F. M., and M. R. Novick. 1968. *Statistical Theory of Mental Test Scores.* Reading, MA: Addison-Wesley.

O'Higgins, M. B., and J. Downes. 1992. *Beating the Dow.* New York: HarperCollins.

Reinganum, M. 1981. "Misspecification of Capital Asset Pricing: Empirical Anomalies Based on Earnings' Yields and Market Values." *Journal of Financial Economics* 9 (1):19–46.

Riegel, R. 1933. "Review of the Triumph of Mediocrity in Business by Horace Secrist." *Annals of the American Academy of Political and Social Science* 170 (November):178–179.

Rosenberg, B., K. Reid, and R. Lanstein. 1985. "Persuasive Evidence of Market Inefficiency." *Journal of Portfolio Management* 11 (3):9–16.

Schall, T., and G. Smith. 2000. "Baseball Players Regress Toward the Mean." *American Statistician* 54 (4):231–235.

Secrist, H. 1933. *The Triumph of Mediocrity in Business.* Evanston, IL: Northwestern University.

Smith, G., M. Levere, and R. Kurtzman. 2009. "Poker Player Behavior After Big Wins and Big Losses." *Management Science* 55 (9):1547–1555.

Thorndike, R. L. 1942. "Regression Fallacies in the Matched Group Experiment." *Psychometrika* 7 (2):85–102.

CHAPTER 5

What's So Special About Two-Sided Markets?

Benjamin E. Hermalin and Michael L. Katz

INTRODUCTION

A man walks into a bar . . . What happens next is the subject of many bad jokes and good economics papers. In the past decade or so, economists have devoted considerable attention to understanding markets in which an enterprise (a "platform") facilitates exchange between two or more parties ("platform users"). Singles bars and hookup apps (e.g., Tinder), which facilitate romantic and/or sexual encounters among their users, are examples. So are payment-card networks (e.g., Visa), which facilitate exchange between merchants and customers. Such markets have come to be called *two sided*, in part because a platform's strategy, if well designed, must concern itself with users on both sides simultaneously.

An unusual feature of two-sided markets is that there is no consensus regarding what they are. There have been many attempts to offer precise definitions of two-sided markets, but none is fully accepted. The name itself is unhelpful: aren't all markets two sided, bringing buyers and sellers together? Such an expansive conception would provide no guidance for either scholarship or public policy (parties in antitrust litigation and regulatory proceedings frequently invoke two-sidedness as a reason to deviate from traditional antitrust principles).

One might argue that no formal definition is needed and that two-sidedness is like pornography: you know it when you see it. However, like pornography, two people may look at the same thing differently. There is consensus that advertising supported media (e.g., newspapers and internet search engines), payment-card networks, and online commerce and social networking platforms (e.g., eBay and Facebook, respectively) constitute two-sided markets. But there is less agreement that communications networks (e.g., telephone networks and internet service providers) and health insurance plans (which bring together care providers and patients) are two sided, even though their structures are equivalent to many that are regarded as two sided. And the literature has excluded manufacturers (even though a manufacturer facilitates exchange between input suppliers and final product consumers) and tended to exclude retailers.[1] There is little value in having a signifier if there is no agreement what it signifies. Moreover, deriving a meaningful definition may generate insight into the underlying economic phenomenon and clarify its relationship with other distinct phenomena, such as network effects.

Our approach to deriving a definition is to identify examples that have been found to represent an interesting phenomenon in common and then reverse engineer the outcomes to determine the drivers of what are perceived to be the distinguishing or interesting features of equilibrium. In our view, the central focus of the two-sided markets literature has been on identifying and analyzing settings in which the actions of one set of participants affect the surplus of another set, so that the possibility of externalities arises. The goal of our definition thus is to isolate what factors give rise to externalities that are not internalized by end users when the platform engages in "conventional" pricing. Below, we identify two critical features: *idiosyncratic matching* and *inefficient rationing*.

1. PAST DEFINITIONS OF TWO-SIDED MARKETS

Before offering our own (implicit) definition, we first review existing definitions. There is agreement that the central role of a platform is to facilitate transactions among its users, and that it may undertake a variety of actions to do so. However, this is true of any intermediary. So what—if anything—distinguishes a platform?

Rochet and Tirole (2003) identify the importance of the externalities that can arise when a user on one side of a platform cares about the number of users on the other side and how they behave (e.g., how intensively they utilize the platform):

> The interaction between the two sides gives rise to strong complementarities, but the corresponding externalities are not internalized by end users, unlike in the multiproduct literature (the same consumer buys the razor and the razor blade). In this sense, our theory is a cross between network

economics, which emphasizes such externalities, and the literature on (monopoly or competitive) multiproduct pricing, which stresses cross-elasticities. (991)

Two types of external effects potentially arise: *access externalities* and *usage externalities*. An access externality (referred to as a "membership externality" by Rochet and Tirole 2006) is the benefit a user on one side generates for users on the other by joining the platform, thereby making himself accessible or available for transactions. A usage externality is the benefit a user on one side generates for a user on the other by actually engaging in transactions on the platform. As an example, your acquisition of a mobile phone generates an access externality for others because they find you easier to reach. Your calling someone on that phone generates an externality (positive or negative) for that person depending on her value from hearing from you.

A common view is that two-sided markets are those in which network effects or access externalities are present. A network effect is said to arise when the value of a good or service to a given user rises as the number of other users of that good or service rises. For example, a given subscriber's value of belonging to a communications network depends on the number of other subscribers on the network. This is a direct effect in that users directly interact with one another. Network effects can also be indirect: the value a user places on an operating system for a computer or smartphone, for example, tends to rise with the number of users because the greater that operating system's total number of users, the greater the incentive for application providers to produce for that operating system. With both direct and indirect network effects, the literature on network effects has focused on how a network effect drives members of one side (e.g., communicators or device users) to cluster together.[2]

The two-sided market literature offers a somewhat different perspective on network effects. Instead of focusing on how the presence of members of one group makes the network more desirable to other members of that same group, the focus has been on intergroup network effects. That is, the two-sided markets literature focuses on how the presence of members of group *A* attracts members of group *B*, and vice versa. For example, how does having more merchants willing to accept Visa cards affect consumers' acquisition and use of Visa cards? Because members of the two groups are on opposite sides of the platform this phenomenon has come to be known as a *cross-platform* network effect.

Some researchers have suggested that intergroup or cross-platform network effects are the defining feature of two-sided markets. Indeed, Parker and Van Alstyne's (2005) seminal paper was titled "Two-Sided Network Effects: A Theory of Information Product Design." However, as Rochet and Tirole (2006) illustrate, there is more to the literature than the study of cross-platform network effects: for instance, a cross-group network effects definition fails to capture usage externalities.[3] Rochet and Tirole make a platform's pricing to the two sides a central part of their definition: they identify two-sided markets by the presence of cross-platform welfare effects that the users would not internalize absent pricing by the platform, and these welfare effects can arise from membership or usage decisions or both. Rochet and Tirole (2006, 648) offer the following definition for the case of pure usage externalities:[4]

> Consider a platform charging per-interaction charges p_1 and p_2 to the two sides. The market is *not* two sided if the volume of transactions realized on the platform depends only on the aggregate price level, $P \equiv p_1 + p_2$; that is, if it is insensitive to reallocations of the total price P between the two sides. If, in contrast, volume varies with p_i holding P constant, the market is said to be two-sided.

They extend their definition to encompass membership decisions and the corresponding access, subscription, or membership fees. To paraphrase this definition, a two-sided market is one in which the *structure* of prices, as well as their levels, matter.

Although this definition has much to recommend it, it is not perfect. First, it should—and readily can—be extended to consider nonprice strategies targeted at the two sides of the market; the structure of these nonprice strategies can matter even in situations where the structure of a platform's pricing does not. Second, it may be too broad: any firm can be viewed as facilitating "transactions" between its input suppliers and output buyers. Specifically, consider a firm that sets both input and output prices. The difference between those prices is the sum of the fees the firm charges its input suppliers and output buyers for facilitating transactions between them. Holding that difference constant, the volume of transactions is affected by raising or lowering the two prices by equal amounts. In other words, the pricing structure matters, holding the net level constant. Hence, this example falls within Rochet and Tirole's definition. Yet we suspect that few authors would consider the theory of two-sided markets to be equivalent to the theory of the firm.[5]

Rysman (2009) suggests that the focus of a definition of a two-sided market should be on the strategies employed rather than prices. Specifically, if the platform's optimal strategy vis-à-vis users on one side of the platform is independent of the strategy it adopts vis-à-vis users on the other side, then this is *not* a two-sided market. Otherwise, it is. This definition encompasses a key aspect of a two-sided market, namely that the platform must consider both sides simultaneously. At the same time, we believe Rysman's definition—like Rochet and Tirole's—is too broad, capturing any firm that has market power in both the input and output markets in which it participates. For example, a manufacturer with market power cannot decide its willingness to pay for inputs without estimating the demand for its output, and it cannot set the price of its output without estimating input prices.

Rather than offer a definition that creates bright-line boundaries, Weyl (2010, 1644) identifies a set of market characteristics that lead to interesting phenomena. One characteristic is that a platform has market power with respect to users on both sides of the market. However, Weyl narrows the set of firms considered to be platforms by also requiring that: (a) the platform provides distinct services—and can charge distinct prices—to the two sides of the market, and (b) there are cross-platform network effects. We believe this is a very useful perspective but that it is also useful to derive a sharper delineation of what distinguishes a platform from other intermediaries.

Hagiu (2007) seeks to develop a definition that would expressly rule out retailers and would, by extension, rule out many other types of firms as well. In his view, the key differences between a retailer and a platform are that: (a) the former takes possession (assumes ownership) of the manufacturer's product and has control over its sale to consumers, whereas the latter does not, and (b) the latter, unlike the former, shares control rights over the implementation of the final sale to the consumer with the manufacturer. For example, Walmart has very considerable discretion over the prices and other aspects of the transactions with consumers vis-à-vis products it previously purchased from manufacturers. In contrast, on eBay, sellers retain considerable control over prices and other aspects of the transaction, such as mode of shipment (although eBay does set policies with which sellers must abide). Furthermore, in many instances, a dissatisfied consumer who buys from Walmart tends to deal with Walmart, whereas a dissatisfied consumer who buys on eBay often deals directly with the seller.

In our view, lack of possession is not the defining feature of a two-sided market. For example, U.S. bookstores traditionally had contractual rights to return, for a refund, unsold books to their publishers. Yet bookstores would presumably not be seen by many as examples of two-sided markets. Moreover, if possession were the defining feature, then it could be difficult to distinguish a two-sided market from agency. For example, a realtor does not take possession of the seller's house, yet many aspects of what a realtor does to facilitate a transaction between a buyer and seller (e.g., staging a house, holding an open house) seem better modeled using the tools of agency theory than those from the two-sided markets literature.

In addition, there are certain types of retailing that would seem to encompass, in part, aspects of a two-sided market. Consider, for instance, Apple's iTunes (an example also given by Hagiu 2007). At one point, iTunes set the price at 99 cents per song, which in Hagiu's view makes iTunes a retailer, not a platform. Possession, though, is not a clear concept with respect to digital goods—it is not obvious that iTunes has taken possession of any music in the same way a record store of yore took possession of LPS. Furthermore, there are many aspects of iTunes that appear to encompass two-sidedness, in particular important network effects. For instance, attracting music companies to iTunes was critical to Apple's ability to sell iPods and the number of iPods sold influenced music companies' willingness to license their music to iTunes.

Hagiu and Wright (2011) offer a definition that builds on the notion that platform users retain considerable autonomy with respect to their transactions with one another while also accounting for network effects: "[a multisided platform is] an organization that creates value primarily by enabling direct interactions between two (or more) distinct types of affiliated customers." By "affiliated," Hagiu and Wright mean the customers—end users—must deliberately choose to join the platform. The notion of user autonomy is captured by the reference to "direct" interactions (as opposed to the case of a retailer, whose suppliers may never directly interact with its customers). Although network effects are not explicit in this definition, the principal way—at least in modeling—the platform creates value is by internalizing, in part, the relevant externalities when it sets (negotiates) terms with the end users.

Below, we will offer a definition that also focuses on internalizing potential cross-platform externalities but that more fully isolates the relevant factors that make platforms an interesting, distinct phenomenon. We do so by examining the pricing decision of a monopoly platform and identifying market characteristics that give rise to unique market outcomes.

2. ANONYMOUS PAIRING AND EFFICIENT RATIONING

We begin by examining an important special case in which platform pricing corresponds to that of conventional firms. Suppose that a user cares about completing a transaction, but not about with whom. Specifically, the user derives utility v from completing a transaction independent of the identity of the user on the other side of the transaction. We call this property *anonymous pairing*. Because exchange is voluntary, a transaction takes place if and only if a pair of users, one from each side, desires it. Let t_i denote the number of transactions that users on side i of the platform, $i = 1$ or 2, would collectively like to undertake. The fact that it takes two to tango is captured by assuming the total number of transactions actually completed equals min $\{t_1, t_2\}$. Observe that, when $t_i > t_j$, it will be necessary to ration side-i users. We say that there is *efficient rationing* if the i-side users who transact are the t_j of them with the highest values of transacting. As we will demonstrate in the remainder of this section, in situations satisfying efficient rationing and anonymous pairing, a platform's pricing is like that of any other firm.

A platform may set both per-exchange, or transaction, prices and membership, or access, prices. For expositional ease, we follow much of the literature in examining the two types of pricing separately even though they can interact.

2.1. TRANSACTION PRICING

Consider a platform that employs a linear tariff with prices p_1 and p_2 to sides 1 and 2, respectively. The realized utility of an individual on side i with value v is $v - p_i$ if he transacts and 0 otherwise. Hence, an individual agrees to transact only if $v \geq p_i$. Note that v and p_i can be positive or negative. Let $p_i(t)$ denote the tth-highest value of v for users on side i of the market (i.e., the inverse demand curve of type-i users).

The total surplus is

$$W(t_1,t_2) \le \int_0^{\min\{t_1,t_2\}} \{P_1(z) + P_2(z)\}\, dz - c\min\{t_1,t_2\},$$

where c denotes the incremental cost of a transaction. The inequality is an equality under efficient rationing, and rationing is necessarily efficient at prices $p_1(t)$ and $p_2(t)$ because trade is desired by the same number on each side and the value of any completed transaction exceeds the value of any transaction forgone. Because $W(t_1,t_2) \le W(\min\{t_1,t_2\}, \min\{t_1,t_2\})$, there is no loss in welfare from restricting attention to prices that induce $t_1 = t_2$. Therefore, the welfare maximizer's program is equivalent to choosing $t \in$ arg max $W(t, t)$, which has the first-order condition[6]

$$P_1(t) + P_2(t) = c. \tag{5.1}$$

Equation (5.1) states that the sum of the prices equals marginal cost. With efficient rationing and anonymous pairing, the problem is equivalent to an excludable public good problem: the optimal quantity is the one at which the sum of marginal benefits equals the marginal cost of completing another pairing. Observe that the efficient prices are not personalized—all users on a given side of the platform face the same price.

Next, consider a profit-maximizing platform. The platform's profits are

$$\pi(t_1,t_2) \equiv \big(P_1(t_1) + P_2(t_2) - c\big)\min\{t_1,t_2\}.$$

A profit-maximizing platform will also induce $t_1 = t_2$: if, counterfactually, $t_i > t_j$, then reducing t_i would raise the price paid by side-i users without affecting the set of completed transactions. The first-order condition for the common value, t, is

$$t\big(P_1'(t) + P_2'(t)\big) + P_1(t) + P_2(t) = c. \tag{5.2}$$

Comparing (5.1) and (5.2), one sees that the platform chooses higher overall prices, which induce a lower level of transactions. *Given the level of transactions*, a profit-maximizing platform chooses the same *structure* of prices as would a welfare maximizer: each chooses prices that equalize the two sides' desired levels of transactions.[7] This property is similar to Joe's observation in Stiglitz (1977, 410) that a profit-maximizing multi product monopolist sets Ramsey prices conditional on the resulting profit level.

An examination of equations (5.1) and (5.2) reveals the following:

- Efficient prices do not rely on assigning some or all of the marginal costs to one side of the market or the other based on notions of which side caused or triggered the costs. Instead, the costs are common costs of facilitating a transaction.
- Profit and welfare maximization depend on demand conditions on both sides of the market simultaneously.
- Because of the usage externality, either a welfare- or profit-maximizing platform may find it optimal to charge one side of the market a zero or even negative price. Negative prices can arise when completing a transaction is beneficial to one side of the market but costly to the other, so that the latter must be subsidized in order to transact voluntarily.
- The socially optimal prices for the platform's services sum to marginal cost.

In our experience, the first three findings above are often key results highlighted by researchers studying two-sided markets. We note, however, that these results apply to any firm! To see this fact, interpret $p_1(t)$ as the firm's customers' willingness to pay for t units of the firm's output, and $-p_2(t)$ as the firm's input suppliers' price for supplying the inputs needed to produce the tth unit of output. Then the firm chooses its output level, t, to maximize

$$t\left(P_1(t) - \left(c - P_2(t)\right)\right),$$

where $c - p_2(t)$ is the firm's marginal cost of supplying output. Although the literature often highlights the "unusual" possibility of levying negative prices on one side of the market, there is nothing unusual about such prices when that side comprises input suppliers (i.e., that a supplier is paid—not charged—for what it supplies).[8] In our view, it is the violation of the fourth finding that distinguishes platforms from other firms, at least as objects of economic analysis: in the key cases of interest in the two-sided markets literature, the socially optimal platform prices do *not* sum to marginal cost.

2.2. ACCESS PRICING

Now suppose access to the platform is priced, but transactions are free to platform members. Users decide whether to join the platform and then how much to transact. As we will see, the mapping from membership decisions to transaction levels is critical for the results obtained. To help fix intuition, suppose the platform is a singles bar or a hookup app, and the two sides are heterosexual men and women. A type-v individual receives utility v from being paired off regardless of the partner. The utility of an individual on side i with value v who pays admission fee f_i to join the platform is $v - f_i$ if paired off and $-f_i$ if not. Suppose that the transaction-determination technology is the following: each user can transact with at most one user of the other side of the platform, and transactions are determined by random pairing. If there are n_1 side-1 users and n_2 side-2 users, with $n_i \geq n_j$, then n_j transactions occur; each side-j user transacts with probability 1, but each side-i user transacts with probability $n_j/n_i < 1$. Faced with admission fee f_i, an i-side user who obtains v from transacting will join the platform if and only if $v \min \{n_j/n_i, 1\} \geq f_i$.

Consider the welfare-maximizing prices. First, note that $n_1 = n_2$ is necessary for welfare optimization: if one started with unequal numbers and reduced the number of people on the more populous side by raising the access fee to that side, then the total number of transactions would not change, but costs would fall and the average value of a transaction would rise, where we have used the fact that those users with the highest values of v are the ones that will choose to pay the admission fee and join the platform (i.e., rationing is efficient). With equal numbers of members on the two sides, total welfare (surplus) is equal to

$$W(n,n) \equiv \int_0^n \left(P_1(z) + P_2(z) \right) dz - \left(k_1 + k_2 \right) n,$$

where k_i is the marginal cost of a side-i user's joining the platform and $p_i(n)$ is the nth-highest value of v among side-i individuals. The first-order condition for welfare maximization is

$$P_1(n) + P_2(n) = k_1 + k_2. \tag{5.3}$$

Equation (5.3) closely parallels the finding for transaction pricing, equation (5.1). In particular, note the efficient prices sum to the marginal cost of facilitating a transaction through membership.

Next, consider a profit-maximizing platform. Without loss of generality assume $n_1 \leq n_2$. The marginal side-1 user is willing to pay $p_1(n_1)$, and the marginal side-2 user (who is not certain to transact) is willing to pay $p_2(n_2)n_1/n_2$, so the platform's profit is

$$\pi(n_1, n_2) \equiv \left(n_1 P_1(n_1) + n_2 \tfrac{n_1}{n_2} P_2(n_2) \right) - k_1 n_1 - k_2 n_2 .$$

If $n_1 < n_2$, then—given demand curves slope down and costs are increasing—the "solution" to maximizing profit would entail $n_2 = 0$, which is nonsense. The platform must choose $n_1 = n_2 = n$. The associated first-order condition is

$$n\left(P_1'(n) + P_2'(n) \right) + P_1(n) + P_2(n) = k_1 + k_2, \qquad (5.4)$$

which closely parallels the finding for transaction pricing in equation (5.2).

3. INEFFICIENT RATIONING

As we will see, the assumptions of efficient rationing and anonymous pairing made above are critical to the result that the welfare-maximizing prices for the platform's services sum to marginal cost. In the present section, we first examine the usage and then access externalities that arise when efficient rationing is violated, which is the case examined by most of the two-sided markets literature. In the section following this one, we present an example in which there is idiosyncratic matching rather than anonymous pairing.

3.1. TRANSACTION GAMES AND USAGE EXTERNALITIES

Above, we considered a particular technology that generated potential transactions among platform users. We now consider alternative technologies and demonstrate that they can give rise to externalities that affect socially and privately optimal platform pricing.

As above, assume users do not care about the identity of the user with whom they transact. Now, however, assume a user on one side can transact with *every* member of the other side willing to transact with him or her. For example, if we divide phone users into call initiators and call recipients, with each of the former potentially calling each of the latter, then the number of completed calls is the product of the number of those willing to initiate times the number willing to answer.[9] As we will now show, this multiplicative transaction technology has a profound effect on the nature of privately and socially optimal platform pricing.

Suppose that a *given* user on one side of the market gets a constant benefit per transaction, v, but this value varies across the population on each side. Without loss of generality, normalize the number of users on each side to one. Let $1 - D_i(v)$ denote the distribution function of benefits across side-i users. The use of the letter "D" is not accidental—the survival function, $D_i(v)$, is like a demand curve: $D_i(p_i)$ is the number of side-i users who want to transact when side-i users are charged p_i per transaction. Each user on the *other* side, side j, who wants to transact will thus complete $D_i(p_i)$ transactions, and the total number of transactions is $D_i(p_i)D_j(p_j)$.[10]

The aggregate surplus that members of side i gain from their transactions with any given member of side j is, as usual, the area beneath their demand curve for transactions with that individual and above price; that is, it is

$$S_i(p_i) = \int_{p_i}^{\infty} D_i(p)\,dp.$$

Because $S_i(p_i)$ is the aggregate surplus side-i users obtain from each side-j user with whom they transact, the total side-i surplus over *all* transactions is $D_j(p_j)S_i(p_i)$. The platform's cost per exchange is c, so its profit (surplus) is $(p_1 + p_2 - c)D_1(p_1)D_2(p_2)$. Summing the platform's and the two sides' surpluses, the total surplus is

$$W(p_1, p_2) \equiv D_2(p_2)S_1(p_1) + D_1(p_1)S_2(p_2) + (p_1 + p_2 - c)D_1(p_1)D_2(p_2).$$

We have expressed this model in terms of prices because that is how it has been developed in the literature.[11] However, it is useful to express it in the same terms we used above. Let $p_i(n)$ denote the nth-highest per-transaction value for users on side i of the market. Faced with a per-transaction price of $p_i(n)$, n side-i users will make themselves available for transactions (e.g., n merchants will accept a credit card or n consumers will wish to pay using that card). Hence, we can write

$$W(n_1, n_2) \equiv n_2 S_1\big(P_1(n_1)\big) + n_1 S_2\big(P_2(n_2)\big) + \big(P_1(n_1) + P_2(n_2) - c\big)n_1 n_2.$$

Because $S_i'(p_i) = -n_i$, the first-order conditions for maximizing welfare can be given as

$$P_1(n_1) + P_2(n_2) = c - \frac{S_1(P_1(n_1))}{n_1} = c - \frac{S_2(P_2(n_2))}{n_2}.$$

Observe that the welfare-maximizing prices sum to less than marginal cost. Specifically, the sum of the prices is less than marginal cost by an amount equal to the average surplus that transactions generate for side-i users.[12]

An obvious question is: Why do efficient prices sum to less than marginal cost here, but summed to marginal cost above? The answer is the lack of efficient rationing. In the present model, the transactions forgone due to a reduction in n_i include transactions that are, from side-j's perspective, inframarginal: they generate positive average surplus for side j. This fact is relevant for pricing to side i because, when users on side i reduce their willingness to transact by δ, users on the other side of the market lose surplus $\delta S_j(p_j) > 0$. By contrast, with efficient rationing, the transactions forgone due to a reduction in n_i are solely the ones that were marginal from side-j's perspective; that is, they yielded side j no consumer surplus.

Now consider a platform that seeks to maximize its profit,

$$\pi(n_1, n_2) \equiv \left(P_1(n_1) + P_2(n_2) - c\right) n_1 n_2.$$

The corresponding first-order conditions can be expressed as

$$P_1(n_1) + P_2(n_2) = c - n_1 P_1'(n_1) = c - n_2 P_2'(n_2). \tag{5.5}$$

Because demand curves slope downward, (5.5) implies that profit-maximizing prices sum to more than marginal cost. Equation (5.5) also implies

$$\frac{-D_1'(p_1)}{D_1(p_1)} = \frac{-D_2'(p_2)}{D_2(p_2)}. \tag{5.6}$$

The left-hand (respectively, right-hand) side of (5.6) is the hazard rate associated with the distribution of benefits for side-1 (respectively, side-2) users. Expression (5.6) thus states that, at the profit-maximizing prices, the probabilities a random user is indifferent between transacting and not conditional on his being a user willing to transact must be the same for the two sides.

An additional issue is whether, *conditional* on the sum of its prices, the platform chooses an efficient price structure. Rochet and Tirole (2003) and Hermalin and Katz (2004) show that the answer may be "yes" or "no." When "no," a second distortion arises: for a given margin, a profit-maximizing platform chooses prices to maximize transaction volume, while the social planner takes into account the surplus those transactions generate for users. In essence, a profit-maximizer is concerned with generating value on the margin, whereas the social planner is also concerned with inframarginal value, a familiar source of distortion (see, e.g., Spence 1975).

3.2. MEMBERSHIP GAMES AND ACCESS EXTERNALITIES

We now return to a setting in which transaction prices are taken as given (for convenience, equal to zero) and focus on membership pricing. We consider a platform having a matching technology that results in the number of transactions being $n_1 n_2$ rather than $\min\{n_1, n_2\}$ as above. Interpreted in terms of a singles bar, every transaction is a conversation, and every man in the bar converses with every woman there, and vice versa. Under this interpretation, $P_i(n)$ is the valuation placed on a transaction (e.g., a conversation) by the member of side i with the nth-highest valuation. Note the user obtains this value from each transaction in which s/he engages. Hence, the nth user on side i derives total benefits $n_j P_i(n)$.

With this pairing technology, total surplus is equal to

$$W(n_1, n_2) \equiv n_2 \int_0^{n_1} P_1(z)\, dz + n_1 \int_0^{n_2} P_2(z)\, dz - k_1 n_1 - k_2 n_2.$$

Hence, the first-order condition for welfare maximization with respect to n_i is

$$n_j P_i(n_i) + \int_0^{n_j} P_j(z)\, dz = k_i.$$

Notice that, faced with admission fee f_i, a user on side i who values a transaction at v will choose to join the platform if and only if $n_j v \geq f_i$. This fact implies that the welfare-maximizing admission fee satisfies

$$f_i = k_i - \int_0^{n_j} P_j(z)\, dz < k_i.$$

Here, too, the sum of the socially optimal prices is less than (total) marginal cost.

As Armstrong (2006) observes, this analysis yields the expected result that, in an efficient equilibrium, each member of side i should pay his or her social cost of entering, where the social cost is physical cost, k_i, less the social benefit his or her entering provides to members of the other side, $\int_0^{n_j} P_j(z)\, dz$. Unlike the special case considered above, the marginal benefit to the other side is not zero: a change in the decision by the marginal person on one side of the market has effects on the welfare of inframarginal users on the other side.

Recalling that the entry fee on side i is $n_j P_i(n_i)$, a profit-maximizing platform acts to maximize:

$$\pi(n_1, n_2) \equiv n_1 n_2 \big(P_1(n_1) + P_2(n_2) \big) - k_1 n_1 - k_2 n_2.$$

The corresponding first-order conditions can be expressed as

$$f_i = n_j P_i(n_i) = k_i - n_j P_j(n_j) - n_1 n_2 P_i'(n_i).$$

The profit-maximizing price is equal to marginal cost adjusted downward by the effect on the other side's willingness to pay, $-n_j P_j(n_j)$, and upward by the market-power effect, $-n_1 n_2 P_i'(n_i) > 0$.

4. IDIOSYNCRATIC MATCHING

So far, we have assumed a user cares about the number of transactions with users on the other side of the market, but not the identities or types of those users. For instance, in the singles bar examples above, one partner (for the evening or just a conversation) was assumed to be as good as any other. In this section, we will suppose that the partner does matter. We will consider an access-pricing example, but similar considerations arise with transaction pricing as well.

Specifically, return to a model of a singles bar in which a transaction is pairing (i.e., an individual who enters the bar engages in at most one transaction) and suppose that the bar charges only for admission. Further, as before, suppose that all women are equally good matches, but now suppose there are two types of men: cads and princes. As the names suggest, a woman derives greater value from being matched with a prince than a cad. Consider the n men with the highest willingnesses to pay and let $A(n)$ denote the fraction among them who are princes. Let $P_1(n, A)$ denote the value that the nth woman places on being matched with a prince with probability A and a cad with probability $1 - A$. Suppose that value is additively separable and the premium placed on princes (normalized to 1) is the same for all women; that is,

$$P_1(n, A) = u(n) + A, \tag{5.7}$$

where $u(\cdot)$ is decreasing. As above, the nth-man's value of being matched with certainty is $P_2(n)$. Observe the women's side is indexed by 1 and the men's by 2.

Weakly more men than women must patronize the bar at the social optimum. To see why, suppose instead that there were more women than men and, thus, some unmatched women. By raising the admission fee charged to women, the platform could reduce the number of women slightly without affecting the behavior or well-being of men. The women who would stop patronizing the bar would be the ones with the lowest values of matching. Hence, costs would fall, the number of matches would remain constant, and the average value of a match would rise. In other words, benefits would rise and costs would fall.

Restricted to values for which $n_1 < n_2$ (i.e., there are more men than women), the expected welfare is

$$W(n_1, n_2) \equiv \int_0^{n_1} P_1(z, A(n_2))\, dz + \frac{n_1}{n_2} \int_0^{n_2} P_2(z)\, dz - k_1 n_1 - k_2 n_2. \tag{5.8}$$

Using (5.7) and differentiating (5.8) with respect to n_2 yields

$$\frac{\partial W(n_1, n_2)}{\partial n_2} = n_1 A' + \frac{n_1}{n_2}\left[P_2(n_2) - \frac{1}{n_2} \int_0^{n_2} P_2(z)\, dz \right] - k_2. \tag{5.9}$$

The term in square brackets is the difference between the marginal and average valuations men have for being paired with a woman, which is negative. Initially assume that the platform is characterized by beneficial selection in that inducing more men to participate lowers the average quality (i.e., $A' < 0$). In this case, it readily follows that (5.9) is negative for all $n_1 < n_2$. In other words, the social optimum entails equal numbers of men and women patronizing the bar.

Differentiating $W(n, n)$ with respect to n yields the first-order condition

$$P_1(n, A(n)) + P_2(n) = k_1 + k_2 - nA'(n). \tag{5.10}$$

Given the assumption that $A' < 0$, equation (5.10) implies that the socially optimal platform prices sum to *more* than marginal cost. Intuitively, charging men a high admission fee leads to a better quality pool of men, and the benefits of the higher average quality of matches outweighs the loss in benefits from forgone matches. Given the reduced number of men, it is efficient to raise the admission fee to women in order to equalize the numbers of users on the two sides.

Now, suppose that the platform is characterized by adverse selection, so that inducing more men to participate raises the average quality (i.e., $A' > 0$). Assume, however, that effect is sufficiently weak that

$$A'(n_2) + \frac{1}{n_2}\left[P_2(n_2) - \frac{1}{n_2}\int_0^{n_2} P_2(z)\, dz \right] < 0 \tag{5.11}$$

for all positive n_2. Then (5.9) remains negative for all $n_1 < n_2$, so the social optimum again entails $n_1 = n_2$. Correspondingly, (5.10) remains the first-order condition for the optimal n. In this case, (5.10) implies that the socially optimal platform prices sum to strictly less than marginal cost, a result more typically found in models of two-sided pricing.

For some parameter values, it is socially optimal to have more men than women patronize the singles bar. This is readily seen by considering a slightly modified version of the model: there are n women and $n + m$ men, where the n men with the highest values for matching are all cads. Assume, unlike the previous analysis, that women derive no utility if matched with a cad (i.e., $u\,(\cdot) \equiv 0$), but considerable utility if matched with a prince. Then unless prices induce more than n men to patronize the bar, there is no value to women from entering the bar. If women gain enough from matches with princes, and the marginal costs of admission are low enough, it will be efficient to induce more than n men to patronize the bar. In other words, it will be efficient to set prices that lead women to be rationed. This result is an example of a general phenomenon identified by Joe and Andrew Weiss in Stiglitz and Weiss (1981): prices play two roles—screening the market participants to induce high-quality users to participate and clearing the market. In the presence of adverse selection, these roles can be in conflict.

In our view, the case of idiosyncratic matching is underexplored in the two-sided markets literature, and there are several directions in which the analysis could be extended.[13] In the analysis considered here, all women agreed on which type of man was the more desirable match: men varied along a vertical quality dimension. One could also imagine horizontal differentiation: users on side i of the market have heterogeneous preferences with respect to the types of users on side j of the market. In such a market, the quality of one's match may increase with the number of potential partners. In other words, a network effect arises because of the prospect of a superior idiosyncratic match.

CONCLUSION

The literature on two-sided markets has led to many important insights. In our view, these insights arise from two primary factors. One is the recognition that users on one side of a platform can usefully be viewed as inputs to the production of benefits for users on the other side of the platform. Although this recognition does not give rise to entirely new phenomena, it has proven to be a very useful framework for examining a wide variety of business and public policy issues. In this chapter, we have focused on the second factor: the literature has concentrated on situations that give rise to unique features of equilibrium. Specifically, the literature has examined settings in which the marginal decision made by a user on one side of a platform affects the surplus enjoyed by users on the other side. As we have demonstrated, these surplus effects arise when there is inefficient rationing and/or idiosyncratic matching.

NOTES

1. There are exceptions. For example, Armstrong (2006, 684) considers a supermarket to be a platform operating in a two-sided market.

2. See, for example, Rohlfs (1974) and Katz and Shapiro (1985). For a review of the network effects literature, see Farrell and Klemperer (2007).

3. Rochet and Tirole (2006, 657) also observe that, because the effects are mediated through prices, the statement that members of group A benefit from an increase in the number of members of group B is a statement about the relative utility levels in two different equilibria. Whether or not members of group A benefit from additional members of group B will depend, in part, on what price changes accompanied the increase. We observe that this critique applies to any model of indirect network effects, and calls for care in interpretation as opposed to undermining the utility of the concept.

4. We have slightly edited the stated definition in Rochet and Tirole (2006) so it better accords with the conventions and notation of this paper.

5. A third shortcoming is somewhat more technical in nature. Proposition 2 of Hermalin and Katz (2004) shows that, whether only the level P matters for the volume of message exchange in a telecommunications setting depends on the specific distribution of the benefits the sender and receiver derive from such exchange. Many authors, including Rochet and Tirole, would consider platform-mediated communication a two-sided market and there is, thus, something unsatisfactory about a definition that holds except for certain distributions of benefits.

6. The second-order conditions hold because demand curves slope down.

7. Rochet and Tirole (2003) demonstrate that, holding the sum of the prices to the two sides constant, a profit-maximizing platform may not choose the same price structure as a welfare-maximizing one.

8. This is not to say that these insights are unimportant. That the users on one side of a market can be seen as suppliers of services to users on the other side can be a useful change in perspective. For example, in telecommunications, it has proved useful to recognize that the calling party is not the sole cost causer and, hence, that it can be efficient to charge the calling party less than the cost of a call and have the receiving party pay a positive price.

9. See Hermalin and Katz (2004) for a discussion of the complications that arise for the analysis if there is a correlation in who calls whom.

10. Alternatively, one could interpret the analysis as being conducted pairwise across the population. In this interpretation, $D_i(p_i)$ is the probability that a given individual on side i obtains a benefit greater than p_i from a transaction with a given individual on side j, $j \neq i$.

11. See, for example, Rochet and Tirole (2003, 2006), Hermalin and Katz (2004), and Bolt and Tieman (2006).

12. Notice, too, that the welfare-maximizing prices equilibrate the average surplus members of one side derive from transacting with the average surplus members of the other side derive from transacting.

13. Within the two-sided market literature, Damiano and Li (2007, 2008) examine platforms' use of pricing strategies to induce sorting through self-selection. Following the seminal paper of Gale and Shapley (1962), there is a large literature that examines institutions to facilitate matching when users have idiosyncratic benefits. However, this literature tends to focus on mechanism design rather than taking the matching technology as given and examining how admissions fees and/or transaction prices affect welfare and profits, which has been the focus of most of the two-sided market literature. For surveys of the matching literature, see Roth and Sotomayor (1990) and Sönmez and Ünver (2010).

REFERENCES

Armstrong, M. 2006. "Competition in Two-Sided Markets." *RAND Journal of Economics* 37 (3):668–691.

Bolt, W., and A. F. Tieman. 2006. "Social Welfare and Cost Recovery in Two-Sided Markets." *Review of Network Economics* 1 (article 7), http://www.bepress.com/rne /vol5/iss1/7.

Damiano, E., and H. Li. 2007. "Price Discrimination and Efficient Matching." *Economic Theory* 30 (2):243–263.

Damiano, E., and H. Li. 2008. "Competing Matchmaking." *Journal of the European Economic Association* 6 (4):789–818.

Farrell, J., and P. Klemperer. 2007. "Coordination and Lock-In: Competition with Switching Costs and Network Effects." In *Handbook of Industrial Organization, Vol. 3*, edited by M. Armstrong and R. Porter, 1967–2072. Amsterdam: Elsevier.

Gale, D., and L. Shapley. 1962. "College Admissions and the Stability of Marriage." *American Mathematical Monthly* 69:9–15.

Hagiu, A. 2007. "Merchant or Two-Sided Platform." *Review of Network Economics* 6 (2):115–113.

Hagiu, A., and J. Wright. 2015. "Multi-Sided Platforms." *International Journal of Industrial Organization* 43:162–174.

Hermalin, B. E., and M. L. Katz. 2004. "Sender or Receiver: Who Should Pay to Exchange an Electronic Message?" *RAND Journal of Economics* 35 (3):423–448.

Katz, M. L., and C. Shapiro. 1985. "Network Externalities, Competition, and Compatibility." *American Economic Review* 75 (June):424–440.

Parker, G., and M. Van Alstyne. 2005. "Two-Sided Network Effects: A Theory of Information Product Design." *Management Science* 51 (10):1494–1504.

Rochet, J.-C., and J. Tirole. 2003. "Platform Competition in Two-Sided Markets." *Journal of the European Economic Association* 1 (4):990–1029.

Rochet, J.-C., and J. Tirole. 2006. "Two-Sided Markets: A Progress Report." *RAND Journal of Economics* 37 (3):645–667.

Rohlfs, J. 1974. "A Theory of Interdependent Demand for a Communications Service." *Bell Journal of Economics* 5 (1):16–37.

Roth, A. E., and M. A. Oliveira Sotomayor. 1990. *Two-Sided Matching: A Study in Game-Theoretic Modeling and Analysis.* Cambridge: Cambridge University Press.

Rysman, M. 2009. "The Economics of Two-Sided Markets." *Journal of Economic Perspectives* 23 (3):125–143.

Sönmez, T., and M. U. Ünver. 2010. "Matching, Allocation, and Exchange of Discrete Resources." In *Handbook of Social Economics*, edited by J. Benhabib, A. Bisin, and M. Jackson, 781–852. Oxford: Elsevier.

Spence, A. M. 1975. "Monopoly, Quality, and Regulation." *Bell Journal of Economics* 6(2):417-429.

Stiglitz, J. E. 1977. "Monopoly, Non-Linear Pricing, and Imperfect Information: The Insurance Market." *Review of Economic Studies* 44:407–430.

Stiglitz, J. E., and A. Weiss. 1981. "Credit Rationing in Markets with Imperfect Information." *American Economic Review* 71 (3):393–410.

Weyl, E. G. 2010. "A Price Theory of Multi-Sided Platforms." *American Economic Review* 100 (4):1642–1672.

CHAPTER 6

Missing Money and Missing Markets in the Electricity Industry

David Newbery

ABSTRACT

In the energy trilemma of reliability, sustainability, and affordability, politicians treat reliability as overriding. The European Union (EU) assumes the energy-only Target Electricity Model will deliver reliability but the United Kingdom argues that a capacity remuneration mechanism is needed. This chapter argues that capacity auctions tend to overprocure capacity, exacerbating the missing money problem they were designed to address. The bias is further exacerbated by failing to address some of the missing market problems also neglected in the debate. It examines the case for, criticisms, and outcome of the first Great Britain (GB) capacity auction and problems of trading between different capacity markets.

INTRODUCTION

In 1976, while visiting Stanford University at the invitation of Joe Stiglitz, and during a period of commodity price instability precipitated by the first oil price shock, the U.S. Agency for International Development (USAID) invited us to write a report on the impact of commodity price stabilization (Newbery and Stiglitz 1977). That invitation caused us to think carefully about the market failures that justified intervening in risky commodity markets. Over the next few years, in an exciting collaboration that moved from Stanford to Oxford, Cambridge, and Princeton, we wrote a series of articles setting out the theory (Newbery and Stiglitz 1979, 1982a,b,c) and combined them into a lengthy book (Newbery and Stiglitz 1981). Two key insights were the concept of constrained Pareto efficiency, constrained by the existing set of institutions such as the set of futures and risk markets; and the consequence of the absence of a complete set of risk markets. Rational expectations and risk neutrality implied that competitive equilibria were constrained Pareto efficient (Newbery and Stiglitz 1982a, *Proposition*). If agents are not risk neutral, "in the absence of a complete set of risk markets, prices provide incorrect signals for guiding production decisions" (Newbery and Stiglitz 1982b).

That basic insight still appears to be missing from much of the debate on the efficiency of the market economy, which was much fostered by disillusionment with state ownership and the move to roll back the frontiers of the state (Newbery 2003). While risk neutrality may be a good approximation for large diversified publicly quoted energy companies, and while one might legitimately be skeptical at the superior forecasting abilities of states over private investors, the particular forms of risk inhabiting markets impacted by politically motivated subsidies and interventions create other obstacles that are the subject of the present contribution.

1. ELECTRICITY MARKET DESIGN

Britain restructured and privatized its electricity industry starting in 1989, with a wholesale market design that sensibly recognized the difference between energy and capacity, which were separately priced in the electricity pool, with capacity declared available, paid a scarcity price reflecting the probability of a loss of load (normally very low). After both massive entries of new gas-fired generation and an obstinate failure of competition to break out (at least until late 1999), the electricity pool was replaced with an energy-only market, and instead of procuring and rewarding capacity day ahead, generators were required to submit balanced bids and offers to the System Operator, or pay an imbalance price determined by a balancing mechanism (a pay-as-bid procurement auction with distinct high buy and low sell prices, designed to incentivize self-balancing).

Fortunately, entry and divestiture in the last part of the 1990s had delivered a potentially competitive wholesale market with six vertically integrated generating and supply companies, so the inefficiencies of the New Electricity Trading Arrangements, as they were called, were modest. Over time, as the gross inefficiencies in the Balancing Mechanism were rectified (through over 200 modifications painfully consulted on and implemented) the wholesale market evolved to deliver workably competitive outcomes (CMA [Competition and Markets Authority] 2016).

However, this market design came under stress with the growing emphasis on decarbonizing the electricity sector and the passage of the *Climate Change Act 2008* (HoC 2008).

Newbery (2012a, 2013) documents the analysis that led to the UK's Electricity Market Reform (EMR) and its embodiment in the *Energy Act 2013*. Briefly, in response to the consultation on the *Renewables Directive* (2009/28/EC), the UK government accepted one of the most challenging renewables targets (relative to its initial position) of 15 percent and promised to source 40 percent of electricity from low-carbon sources and around 30 percent of electricity from renewables by 2020 (DECC 2009). These ambitious targets undermined confidence that there would be any support for conventional generation, much of which was due to retire as a result of the EU *Large Combustion Plant Directive* (LCPD) and the EU *Industrial Emissions Directive*.

Between 2008 and 2014, 6 gigawatts (GW) of coal plants closed, and 1.9 GW were converted to biomass, reducing the total coal capacity by 8 GW (out of a total nonrenewable capacity in 2008 of 69 GW). In addition, 1.6 GW of nuclear power and 2.8 GW of large oil-fired capacity plants closed, or in total 10.4 GW, with more expected to exit before 2016.[1] By 2014, nuclear power's share of output had fallen to 18 percent, gas to 29 percent, but coal held at 39 percent as coal and carbon prices fell, and renewables rose to 13 percent (DECC 2015).

Faced with the exit of a large fraction of coal and life-expiring nuclear capacity, the hope of market advocates was that rising forward prices would encourage suitable replacement generation to be built. However, forward electricity markets are illiquid more than a year out, and wholesale prices were increasingly seen as the plaything of policy makers, intervening to support renewables, impose carbon price floors (HM Treasury 2011) or threatening to impose price caps (CMA 2016), so the utilities and their financiers considered the investment climate uninvestable.

Ofgem (2010), concerned about the lack of government action, investigated this failure to invest and concluded that "[T]he unprecedented combination of the global financial crisis, tough environmental targets, increasing gas import dependency and the closure of ageing power stations has combined to cast reasonable doubt over whether the current energy arrangements will deliver secure and sustainable energy supplies" (1).

In response, the *Energy Act 2013* that set out the Electricity Market Reform rejected relying on an energy-only market and legislated for auctions to deliver capacity adequacy. As a result, Britain was the first country to introduce a capacity auction after the EU Third Package2 (to deliver the Target Electricity Model [TEM]) was announced. The TEM is designed as an energy-only market that leaves the delivery of capacity adequacy to profit-motivated investment decisions by liberalized and unbundled generation companies.

This paper examines the case for a capacity auction in a liberalized electricity market, and argues that the conventional argument that these markets suffer from missing money obscures the deeper problem of missing markets. The more these problems can be addressed, the smaller will be the problem of missing money, and capacity auctions will then evolve toward surrogates for the missing futures markets, providing insurance against opportunistic regulatory and government intervention. Conversely, by ignoring the missing market problem they perversely exacerbate the missing money problem. As such, they should not be viewed with skepticism as heavy-handed government interventions guiding the market and overriding market signals, but as attempts to remedy the absence of increasingly required futures and insurance markets.

The paper also criticizes aspects of the design chosen by the UK government, specifically the understudied issue of how the amount of capacity to procure was determined. It argues that typical capacity auction designs have a bias toward excess procurement, in contrast to fears that the energy-only market would lead to underprocurement. Capacity auction design also raises important questions for cross-border trading and the role of interconnectors, which this paper addresses. It argues that it is less important to harmonize capacity remuneration mechanisms across borders than to ensure that trade between countries is governed by clear market signals or clear out-of-market agreements between System Operators (when markets reach price caps or otherwise fail), without the fear of political or regulatory overrides in stress situations. A better alternative design that addresses these issues is to auction reliability options, as proposed for the island of Ireland, to provide insurance while continuing to give efficient market signals from cross-border transactions (Newbery 2017).

As a number of countries are now considering whether, and if so how, to introduce or reform their Capacity Revenue Mechanisms it is timely to examine the British experience. Eurelectric is the latest organization to recognize that not all EU countries will be happy with the reference energy-only markets of the TEM, and "recognizes that properly designed capacity markets, developed in line with the objective of the Integrated Electricity Market, are an integral part of a future market design" (Eurelectric 2015, 4).

2. MISSING MONEY AND MISSING MARKETS

While ensuring short-term security of supply is normally the duty of the System Operator (SO), capacity adequacy is often the subject of regulatory and political concern. EU electricity markets are now liberalized and generation is, for the most part, not regulated but subject to normal competition policy. If markets were not subject to policy interventions or price caps, it is plausible that capacity adequacy could be delivered by profit-motivated generation investment without explicit policy guidance. For this to be the case, investors need confidence that the revenue they earn from the energy markets (including those supplying the ancillary services that the SO needs to ensure short-term stability) will be adequate to cover investment and operating costs.

If this revenue is systemically inadequate, there is a "missing money" problem (Joskow 2013), but if it is potentially adequate but not perceived to be so by generation companies or their financiers, then there is a "missing market" problem (Newbery and Stiglitz 1982b; Newbery 1989). *Missing money* problems arise if price caps are set too low (below the Value of Lost Load [VoLL]); or ancillary services, such as flexibility, ramp rates, frequency response, black start capability, etc., and/or balancing services are inadequately remunerated; and/or energy prices are inefficiently low. Inefficiently low wholesale prices seem less likely as the normal problem is one of market power raising prices above their competitive level, and prices are not necessarily *inefficiently* low just because there is excess capacity.

Missing markets create problems if risks cannot be efficiently borne or allocated with minimal transaction costs through futures and contract markets, or if important externalities such as CO_2 and other pollutants are not properly priced. The concept of missing markets can be usefully extended to cases in which politicians and/or regulators are not willing to offer hedges against future market interventions that could adversely affect generator profits. The various arguments for capacity markets have been extensively covered in the literature, recently in the *Symposium on "Capacity Markets,"* (Joskow 2013; Cramton, Ockenfels, and Stoft 2013). Almost all the discussion about capacity mechanisms concentrates on the missing money problem and whether the various market and regulatory/

political failures are sufficient to justify a capacity mechanism, and if so, what form it should best take.[3]

Both the missing money and missing market failures have risen in salience as renewable electricity targets have become more ambitious at the same time as the EU Emissions Trading System has failed to deliver an adequate, durable, and credible carbon price, and as such is under constant threat of reform. Absent a futures market with a credible counterparty it is hard to be confident that future electricity prices will be remunerative for unsubsidized generation, and harder to convince bankers or shareholders of the credibility of investment plans based on forecast revenues. If renewables continue their planned increase in market share mandated by the EU *Renewables Directive* (2009/28/EC) they will depress average energy prices. This does not in and of itself give rise to an adequacy problem, although utilities may justifiably complain that their past investment decisions have been partially expropriated by unanticipated political actions. However, it increases the demand for existing balancing services such as primary reserves, fast-frequency response, and inertia, and may also increase the need for additional ancillary services. If these services are not yet adequately defined and/or their future prices are hard to predict there is a missing market problem. If these services are underpriced by SOs whose powers of balancing supply and demand may be met by administrative or regulatory means (e.g., by requiring those connecting to the grid to make some of these services available as part of the grid code), there is a missing money problem. In either case these may precipitate a capacity adequacy problem.

2.1. MARKET FAILURES IN DELIVERING RELIABILITY

The *reliability* of an electricity system also requires *security*: "The ability to withstand sudden disturbances, such as electric short circuits or unanticipated losses of system components . . ." (ENTSO-E 2015).[4] Security is a public good supplied by the SO through his acquisition of a range of ancillary and balancing services, while adequacy could, in principle, be delivered by competitive energy-only markets, as the TEM envisages (Oren 2000).

Eurelectric (2015) provides a useful summary of the various ways used to measure reliability. Most EU electricity systems specify the "Loss of Load Expectation" (LoLE), which for most and for GB is three hours per year. Averaging over a large number of possible events (cold weather, plant failures, high demand, etc.) for some future period, the electricity system should perform better than averaging "Losses of Load events" of three hours per year. The former Central Electricity Generating Board (CEGB) had a standard of disconnections in three winters in 100 years (Webb 1977). Before the electricity industry was liberalized and unbundled, the SO had ownership control of generation and transmission and was responsible for both system security and adequacy. Planned investment ensured that both capabilities would be assessed, which was also much easier when essentially all plants had (at least in aggregate) a predictable and controllable output.

The main security problem to address was very short-run increases in demand (notably during intermissions in major sporting events when consumers all simultaneously switch on their electric kettles) or those caused by the loss of a large station or transmission link. This was addressed by specifying a reserve margin and ensuring adequate short-run flexibility by the choice of plant type. Thus, the CEGB, that predated the British restructuring of 1989, computed the required gross reserve margin at 19 percent based on a Loss of Load Probability (LoLP) calculation and its reliability measures. It built pumped storage systems to provide fast-response peaking capacity and to use surplus nighttime nuclear power (Williams 1991), as well as jet-derivative gas turbines for fast ramping.

With liberalization and unbundling, all these security services had to be separately procured by the SO. Some, such as inertia and the additional security offered by interconnectors, came at no cost to the SO. Others had to be procured through balancing and contract markets, just when the challenges of handling increasing volumes of intermittent and less predictable wind were increasing (Newbery 2010, 2012b). As problems of intermittency increase, so does the challenge of ensuring that these services are efficiently priced and procured (Pöyry 2014).

The Single Electricity Market (SEM) of the island of Ireland is probably at the forefront of addressing these problems, as it is a small moderately isolated system in which individual power stations are large and lumpy relative to peak demand (up to 10 percent) and the system is being adapted to handle up to 70 percent nonsynchronous wind penetration.[5] One (implausible) solution would be to have price signals vary over very short periods of time. A sudden fall in frequency caused by a sudden fall in supply relative to demand means that the value of power in the next cycle (1/50th of a second) has increased, and the speed of response is key to minimizing the disruption. Fast responders would enjoy the sudden increase in price which slower responders would miss.

If prices were to move in response to instantaneous system conditions, then it would be potentially profitable to have the capability to respond on the appropriate timescale. In practice, market designs vary in their granularity, with the most flexible having five-minute settlement periods (Australia). Some continental balancing markets have a fifteen-minute settlement period,[6] while GB and the SEM have a half-hourly settlement period in the day-ahead market (DAM), and most continental power exchanges and the EUPHEMIA auction platform have an hourly resolution in the DAM. Increasing granularity improves the accuracy of the temporal pattern of price signals to guide the choice of flexibility, but runs up against the practical constraint that the system state requires a finite amount of time to reestimate, probably on the order of minutes, while the transaction costs of dealing at a high frequency make very short-term markets illiquid.

Given the inability and absence of energy markets at this level of time granularity, new products are needed to supplement existing products, as set out in SEM (2014). For these new products, markets are missing as their procurement is still undecided, making it hard to estimate their future value to potential investors who might supply them bundled in different mixes with new capacity.

The other more market-oriented approach to reliability is to specify the Value of Lost Load, the amount that consumers should be willing to pay to avoid disconnection. In a future with sufficiently smart meters, consumers would be able to sign a contract with the electricity supplier stating the maximum amount they would be willing to pay for each tranche of firm power, with the smart meter disconnecting appliances at each specified price point, leaving some lights, television, and electronic equipment until last. That would create the currently largely absent demand side and provide a private good market solution to the problem. It could avoid the missing money if not the missing (future) market problem, provided the short-run prices were set at their efficient scarcity value. This is the sum of the System Marginal Cost (SMC) plus a Capacity Payment, CP, where

$$CP = LoLP^*(VoLL - SMC) \qquad (6.1)$$

The relationship between the security standard and the VoLL is symmetric, in that if capacity investment decisions are based on revenues determined by (6.1) and the VoLL is pre-determined, then the resulting capacity will give rise to an LoLE. If the standard is a predetermined LoLE, the cost of new capacity implies a cost of delivering the LoLP and hence an implied VoLL.

Britain has followed both models. The English pool from 1989 to 2001 set the VoLL at £(2012)5000/MWh [(€6250)/MWh], letting the market determine capacity. After the pool was replaced with an energy-only market in 2001, the Department of Energy & Climate Change (DECC) specified the LoLE. National Grid (2014a) deduced the 2018 VoLL as £(2012)17,000/MWh [€(2012)21,250/MWh], which was higher than the direct estimates of the willingness to pay to avoid disconnections (London Economics 2013).

2.2. CAN ENERGY-ONLY MARKETS DELIVER ADEQUATE RELIABILITY?

One completely legitimate case for a capacity payment is that if generators are required to bid their Short-Run Marginal Cost (SRMC, mostly fuel costs), as under the Bidding Code of Practice of the SEM (SEM 2007), they will fail to recover their fixed costs without such an addition. The electricity pool of England and Wales also added the CP of (6.1), but allowed generators to offer an unrestricted supply function (which, given their market power, was often above SRMC) (Green and Newbery 1992; Newbery 1995; Sweeting 2007). In this period of benign liberalization, high electricity prices and low gas prices led to considerable entry and an excessive reserve margin.

In the energy-only market envisaged by the TEM, generators will offer supply functions that should reflect the scarcity value of electricity (and their degree of market power). Figure 6.1 shows the day-ahead price duration curves for several European power exchanges in 2012. What is striking is that most exchange prices do not exceed €200/MWh, and even the most peaky, France, only does so 0.25 of 1 percent of the time (about twenty-two hours per year). Given that the VoLL in the English pool until 2001 was €(2012)6250/MWh and the current implied VoLL in GB is €(2012)21,250/MWh, these prices indicate a low LoLP or high reliability. Given existing capacity levels, high reliability is a reasonable inference, but the problem again is one of missing (futures) markets. Investment lags in delivering capacity adequacy are two to four years for peaking plants (longer for most base-load plants), beyond the time horizon of adequately liquid futures markets (and they only offer one-year hedge).

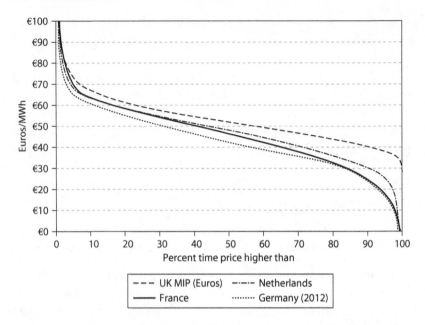

Figure 6.1   Price Duration Curves of Day-Ahead Hourly Prices, 2012

Sources: MIP (Market Index Price) and NL prices from APX, Germany and France from EEX.

On the other hand, figure 6.2 shows that the 2008 balancing buy prices[7] in the energy-only market that replaced the pool were considerably peakier than the old pool prices (which included an explicit CP and also probably reflected more market power). Thus, energy-only markets can reflect scarcity, and properly calculated capacity payments may be very low if the reserve margin is adequate, as the LoLP is roughly exponential in demand less de-rated capacity (Newbery 2005). However, by 2013–2014, the GB Balancing Mechanism had a price duration curve quite similar to those shown in figure 6.1, with prices above €200/MWh for less than 0.25 of 1 percent of the time, and well below the French day-ahead price duration curve.

Thus, one might conclude that energy-only markets (which include balancing markets) can deliver sufficiently sharp scarcity prices that should signal the profitability of adequate new investment, provided all the other security services are adequately remunerated (i.e., resolving any of those missing market problems). This might be plausible if all investment decisions were taken on commercial grounds as in the 1990s, that prices were not capped, that the policy environment were predictable and

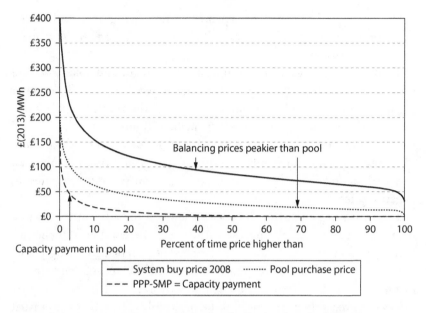

Figure 6.2   Scarcity Pricing in GB Under the Pool and in the Balancing Mechanism

Sources: National Grid, Elexon.

stable, and that either a liquid forward market existed for a reasonable fraction of the proposed plant life (i.e., twenty-plus years ahead of the final investment decision) or credible long-term power purchase agreements could be signed with creditworthy counterparties. Unfortunately, hardly any of these conditions hold in the TEM.

2.3. MARKET, INSTITUTIONAL, AND POLITICAL/REGULATORY FAILURES

While price caps are set at rather low levels in the United States, exacerbating the "missing money" problem, there are also, if much higher, price caps in the EUPHEMIA auction platform (for day-ahead at €3000/MWh, a price that France has hit on numerous occasions). The lack of forward markets and long-term contracts might not be so critical if the future was reasonably predictable and stable, but this is far from the case at present. EU climate change policy is failing, in conflict with the *Renewables Directive* (2009/28/EC), and surely ripe for as yet uncertain reform. Large volumes of variable renewables increase the need for flexible reserves, which in the past came from obsolescing plants, mostly oil or coal. These plants are now being decommissioned because of the *Large Combustion Plant Directive* and the *Integrated Emissions Directive*.

Increasing volumes of renewables (mainly wind and solar PV) add little to reliable capacity, as it is unavailable on windless cold, dark winter nights, but reduces average wholesale prices. If the average capacity factor of onshore wind is 25 percent, then the GB target of 30 percent of electricity from wind requires a capacity of 30/25 times or 120 percent of average demand. In windy conditions that would often displace all conventional plants and could lead, under present subsidy structures, to negative prices.

Intermittent generation increases the need for additional flexible plants that can be called up at short notice if the wind falls or the sun fades. In addition, new plants will be needed to replace retiring plants (not just coal, but in the UK, France, and Germany, substantial volumes of nuclear plants as well). These plants will need considerably higher prices than recently experienced to be profitable. The EU is committed to an 80 percent reduction in greenhouse gas emissions by 2050. Coal has twice the carbon intensity of gas, so utilities are unlikely to build durable (forty to sixty years) coal-fired plants that would face tight future emissions limits, leaving gas-fired plants as the only alternative. Unfortunately, crashed electricity prices and high gas prices precipitated by the closure of Japan's nuclear fleet have made their economics very unattractive.

The UK introduced a carbon price floor in the 2011 Budget (HMT 2011) that would support the price of CO_2 at £16/tonne in 2013, rising to £30/tonne (€35/tonne) in 2020, and projected to rise to £70/tonne by 2030 (all at 2009 prices). As an example of policy instability, the 2014 budget froze the carbon price floor—clearly an instrument subject to the whim of chancellors, creating additional investment uncertainty. It would be a brave politician who trusted these markets to deliver reliability.

3. THE DESIGN OF THE GB CAPACITY AUCTION

Capacity Auctions were introduced by the *Energy Act 2013* to addresses the issue of capacity adequacy. The government (specifically the Secretary of State for Energy & Climate Change) advised by DECC,

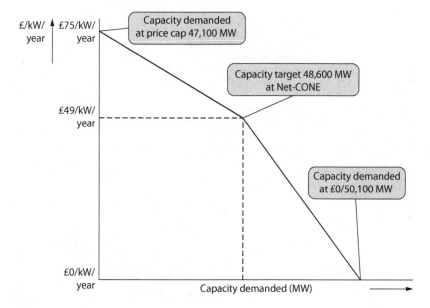

Figure 6.3   The T-4 2014 Auction Demand Curve

Source: Ofgem (2015).

decides how much capacity is required. The capacity auction is a single-price descending clock auction with a demand schedule as shown in figure 6.3. National Grid as an SO was charged to recommend the target volume of capacity to secure four years after the auction (which was termed the T-4 auction).

National Grid (2014a) chose the amount to procure, balancing the cost of additional capacity against the cost of the Expected Energy Unserved, as shown in figure 6.4. National Grid (2014a) projected that the auction clearing price would likely be set at the Net Cost of New Entry (CONE), estimated at £49/kW-yr as shown in figure 6.3. This was the missing money a combined cycle gas turbine (CCGT) might need given its revenues from all other markets and after paying the Transmission Network Use of System (TNUoS) charges. These range from £30/kW-yr (in NW Scotland), to negative (–£5/kW-yr in Cornwall) (National Grid 2013), and are designed to guide new generation to where most needed. Entrants are given fifteen-year indexed contracts, while existing plants receive one-year contracts to defer exit decisions until the next auction.

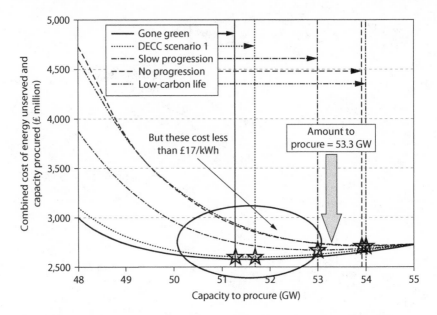

Figure 6.4 Capacity Needed to Minimize Total Cost in the Slow Progression Scenario

Note: Stars mark the lowest point on each curve and the corresponding capacity to procure.

Source: After National Grid (2014a, 50, fig 12) with additions by the author.

The missing money can be roughly estimated from the VoLL (£17/kWh) *less* the maximum the SO pays for balancing actions (£6/kWh) to give £11/kWh, *times* three hours LoLE, or £33/kW-yr. The effective cap in the Balancing Mechanism of £9999/MWh would reduce the missing money to £21/kW-yr. Both numbers suggest a Net CONE of £49/kW-yr is high or that other energy services are under-rewarded.

The auction was sensibly designed (Newbery and Grubb 2015) but flawed in requiring the SO to advise the minister on the procurement amount. The SO stands accountable if "the lights go out" but does not pay for the capacity. The minister wishes to avoid newspaper headlines predicting blackouts resulting from his decision. Both argue for excess procurement. DECC appointed an independent panel of technical experts (PTE) to comment on the analysis, and they made a number of strong (but, for the 2014 auction, ineffective) criticisms.

3.1. CRITICISMS OF THE CAPACITY TO PROCURE

The PTE first criticized the terminology of "Loss of Load" as emotive and misleading. The GB regulator, Ofgem, defines a "Loss of Load event" as one in which market demand exceeds market supply and as such the SO has to intervene to balance the system. For that purpose, the SO can call on a range of increasingly expensive options: asking generators to temporarily exceed rated capacity; invoking "new balancing services;"[8] cutting interconnector exports to zero; requesting imports; reducing voltage ("brown outs");[9] before finally resorting to selective disconnections. The crucial point is that these actions cost less, often much less, than VoLL and hence bias the unserved load cost upward, moving the minimum value to the right and thus increasing the target capacity as seen in figure 6.4.

Successful Capacity Market Units in the auction receive a capacity agreement that requires them to be available in "stress events," which are signaled four hours ahead. The DECC (2014b, §391) defines these events as "any settlement periods in which either voltage control or controlled load shedding are experienced at any point on the system for 15 minutes or longer. . . . Periods of voltage control or load shedding resulting from failures or deficiencies in the transmission or distribution systems are not considered as stress events." However, these "notices of inadequate system margin" are issued "based on the available capacity (declared 'maximum export limit' [MEL] minus transmission system demand and reserve for response capacity)" (2014b, box 107).

National Grid (2014a) chose the amount to procure using a Least Worst Regrets approach as it was unwilling to attach explicit probabilities to the various scenarios considered. The result of overvaluing the cost of "Loss of Load" is to increase the capacity at which the Least Worst Regret cost schedule is minimized (figure 6.4). The PTE (DECC 2013) strongly criticized National Grid for assuming no net imports in stress periods, despite 3.75 GW interconnection capacity and a potential new interconnector capacity of 2.25 GW that might be available by 2018–2019. This seemed perverse, as all parties (Ofgem, DECC, and National Grid) agreed that interconnectors increased security. Three reports commissioned by these parties (Pöyry 2012, 2013; Redpoint 2013) argued that interconnector capacity could displace domestic capacity by 50 to 80 percent of its value. Even DECC's *Final Impact Assessment*, published just before the procurement decision (DECC 2014a), estimated the amount of interconnector capacity to include in the total procurement amount at 2.9 GW. Ignoring interconnectors could move the auction clearing price from the net cost of new entry of £49/kW-yr to that set by existing plants (maximum of £25/kW-yr), *increasing* the expected cost of procurement by £1.3 billion per year for the following fifteen years.

Ignoring interconnectors seemed particularly perverse as the TEM aims to integrate markets across borders. Market coupling already dispatches GB continental interconnectors in the EUPHEMIA day-ahead market (DAM). Interconnector flows already reflect a willingness to pay in the DAM, and will do so in the intra-day and real-time markets when network codes are agreed upon (perhaps by 2018). In response to the criticism of the Panel of Technical Experts (DECC 2013; Newbery and Grubb 2013), the European Commission urged the UK government to include interconnectors in future capacity auctions. As a result, the two existing interconnectors with a de-rated capacity of 1.9 GW secured capacity agreements in the 2015 T-4 auction at the clearing price of £18.00/kW-yr (Ofgem 2016). De-rating measures the equivalent amount of firm GB capacity that the interconnector could displace, and will depend on both its technical reliability and the likelihood that it is available to import into GB.

3.2. POSSIBLE CONSEQUENCES OF EXCESSIVE CAPACITY PROCUREMENT

Excess procured capacity will lower future wholesale prices with a number of effects, not all immediately obvious. First, lower prices reduce the revenue that new entrants can expect from the energy markets, increase the Net CONE and raise the auction price. Second, it undermines the old market design in which investment in conventional generation was at the discretion of private companies making commercial decisions. No company would invest in conventional generation without a capacity agreement given its large disadvantage compared to those with agreements. The amount of new plants will therefore be entirely determined by the minister, ending a key element of the liberalized market. All non-fossil generation will also be granted long-term Contracts for Differences (CfDs)[10] under the EMR, moving Britain to the single-buyer model ruled out in earlier EU electricity directives.

Third, lower prices increase payments to low-carbon CfDs, which receive the difference between the contracted strike and wholesale price.

As the government limits total renewables payments through the Levy Control Framework, the perverse effect is to support less renewable electricity, although the EMR was designed to remove obstacles to meeting the renewables target.

Fourth, the commercial case for interconnectors depends on price differences, with GB typically importing from cheaper continental markets. Lower GB prices reduce arbitrage profits, undermining the investment case for the additional interconnectors when they are increasingly needed to balance growing intermittent generation across wider market areas. Ignoring interconnectors risks a self-fulfilling but expensive policy of autarky.

Fifth, although the future wholesale prices will be lower, offsetting possibly a large part of the consumer cost, it will be hard to convince consumers of this. They will see the gross cost, which is estimated at 53.3 GW × £49m/GW-yr = £2.6 billion per year.

3.3. THE OUTCOME OF THE 2014 CAPACITY AUCTION

The auction cleared at £(2012)19.40/kW-yr (National Grid 2014b). The auction produced several surprises. First, the auction cleared at less than 40 percent of the predicted Net CONE value of £49/kW-yr (although close to the missing money estimated above, assuming a balancing cap of £9999/ MWh). The estimated Net CONE was based on new entry of CCGT, and two CCGTs that entered, supplying about 60 percent of the total 2795 MW, new entry. They later withdrew and paid a penalty when their bankers were unimpressed with their profitability at this capacity price. Second, the next largest (28 percent) entry category was open cycle gas turbines (OCGTs)/ reciprocating engines, average size 11 MW. These small units connect to the distribution networks, where they receive an additional "embedded benefit" of about £50/kW-yr, the average cost of the avoided transmission charges for delivering power to the distribution network. As the efficient price (the marginal cost) of avoided transmission costs is closer to £5/kW-yr this resulted in a massive distortion of the type and location of new capacity. After several years of pressure by the Panel of Technical Experts this was finally changed in 2017, after several further auctions.

The final point is that the auction demonstrates the value of market-based methods of revealing entry costs, and the danger of leaving such decisions to SOs or regulators (as in the SEM,[11] where the regulators calculate the cost of Best New Entry and set it at a high price).

4. BIASES IN CAPACITY AUCTIONS AND
ENERGY-ONLY MARKETS

The arguments above strongly suggest that if procurement decisions are left to politicians advised by the SO, they will err on the high side, and tend to ignore supplies from outside their control area (over interconnectors). Their caution is exacerbated by the emotive and misleading terminology of "Loss of Load." Some of these shortcomings can be addressed by requiring the SO to cost and quantify the actions that are taken in stress events that fall short of controlled disconnections. Delegating the decision to independent agencies, perhaps to an Independent Planning and System Operator, could de-politicize the decision (but might not remove the fear of disconnections through inadequacy, nor the bias of not paying for capacity).

There is a more fundamental problem in that if future energy prices are competitively delivered and if all security services (ancillary and balancing) are properly priced, the missing market and missing money problems can both be addressed by offering suitable hedging contracts, of which the auctioned capacity agreement is an excellent example. Price caps could be replaced by reliability options or one-way CfDs that have a high-strike price, and which allow consumers or their suppliers to hedge against high prices while allowing the spot and balancing market prices to reach the scarcity levels needed for efficient actions (in demand reduction and interconnector trade) (see, e.g., Vásquez, Rivier, and Pérez-Arriaga 2002; Bidwell 2005; Newbery 2017).

Now consider the costs of under- or overspecifying the amount to procure. Overprocurement, as noted above, risks depressing future prices and hence reducing future energy and ancillary service revenues, requiring a higher auction price in compensation. While addressing the missing markets problem, it risks amplifying the missing money problem. In contrast, underprocurement leads to expectations of higher future prices, requiring a lower capacity auction bid as the capacity agreement does not preclude earning revenues in all the energy markets. If the price is very low, investors may conclude that investing without a capacity agreement has a relatively low risk, particularly as the design of the GB auction offers a T-4 contract of fifteen years for new plants, but successive T-1 contracts of one year for existing plants at the same clearing price, for which speculative plants would be eligible. A signal to err on the side of underprocurement would be underwritten by the ability to true up closer to delivery, reducing risks, as any overprocurement would merely delay the moment at which more capacity was needed in the auction, and should limit the period of inadequate revenue to a year or so.

5. IS THERE A NEED FOR REGIONAL COORDINATION?

Eurelectric (2015) argues strongly for a design of regional capacity markets that places the obligation on generation (or demand) regardless of national location. This would require a common regional capacity adequacy assessment and no double payment (i.e., if capacity has an agreement from country A it would be denied one from B and would be excluded from B's capacity assessment, subject to adequate interconnector capacity from B to A). As such it may well be suited to the meshed continental network where power flows according to Kirchhoff's laws, but not necessarily to DC-linked systems.

For markets interconnected over DC links it is not the simplest way of addressing the problem. The underlying problem is that investors lack confidence that they will secure an adequate return. This has two dimensions—future prices may not properly reflect scarcity and other attributes of security, and future prices cannot be hedged and therefore are risky. Long-term contracts address the latter, efficient short-run pricing the former. Provided the auction platform can accommodate efficient scarcity prices (i.e., provided at least the intra-day and balancing markets are not capped at too low a level), then trading over any interconnector will only benefit a country that ensures that the relevant prices are efficient, as in equation (6.1). Suppose A and B trade, but A has a higher VoLL than B, and hence a larger reliability margin. If A and B both have stress events, A can outbid B to secure imports, with B accepting a higher LoLP reflecting its lower willingness to pay to avoid disconnections. Country A can ensure that domestic consumers are insulated from these high-trading prices via *reliability options*.

The logic of making adequacy as close as possible to a private market good (through allowing efficient pricing) is that there can be gains from trade for the efficiently priced market even when market designs are different. If prices are inefficient in B, then it is they who lose, not A. That provides incentives to reform and avoids the need for politically fraught agreements on harmonization. The important design question to address is how best to ensure that prices for trading over interconnectors properly reflect scarcity. It may be that a scarcity adder (e.g., the CP in equation [6.1] or an amount to bring the supply schedule up to the full price in [6.1]) must be administratively added, or there may be other ways in which the SO can ensure that the trading country acquires all it needs up to the VoLL before controlled disconnections, but such design issues can be devolved to member states.

CONCLUSIONS

Missing money and missing markets provide compelling reasons for a capacity payment in competitive electricity markets dominated by politically determined and subsidized unreliable generation, where investors lack confidence in future revenue adequacy. Some countries may have surplus capacity and may be under no immediate pressure to encourage new investment, and can defer addressing these questions, but many countries need to encourage efficient, more flexible investment if only to address increasing intermittent renewables penetration. It may be that well-designed markets can secure the required flexible capacity but it is more likely that tender auctions/contracts will also be needed, and these have much in common with capacity auctions.

Capacity auctions (GB provides a good example) address the missing money problem and part of the missing market problem (the missing futures markets). Other signals for location, flexibility, etc., needed to deliver security, still need efficient solutions, which may be best supplied by markets, auctions, or procurement contracts but will also need efficiently set regulated transmission and distribution tariffs. The part of the adequacy debate that has been neglected is how to, and who should, determine the amount and type of capacity to procure (generation, DSR, interconnection), a problem that is exacerbated by misunderstandings over what a "Loss of Load event" means and what it might cost.

This paper argues that this neglect biases toward overprocurement, which leads to a self-fulfilling prophecy that merchant generation investment can no longer be relied upon. Perversely, this exacerbates the missing money problem that capacity auctions were designed to address. The bias is further exacerbated by failing to address some of the missing market problems that have also been neglected in the debate.

NOTES

This is a revised version of the paper presented to *A Just Society* honoring Joseph Stiglitz at Columbia University, October 16–17, 2015, and published as Newbery (2016). I am indebted to Elsevier for permission to reprint large parts of that paper.

The author was a member of the Panel of Technical Experts advising the DECC on the delivery of Electricity Market Reform but this article is written entirely in his personal capacity, drawing solely on published material. I am indebted to two excellent referees for helpful comments.

1. National Grid provides annual updates of the capacity and fuel of every grid-connected generator at http://www2.nationalgrid.com/UK/Industry-information /Future-of-Energy/Electricity-Ten-Year-Statement/.

2. See, for example, http://www2.nationalgrid.com/UK/Industry-information /Europe/Third-energy-package/.

3. See, for example, Adib, Schubert, and Oren (2008), Batlle et al. (2007), Batlle and Rodilla (2010), Bowring (2008, 2013), Chao and Wilson (1987, 2002), Cramton and Ockenfels (2011), Cramton and Stoft (2008), Joskow (2008), Joskow and Tirole (2007), O'Neill at al. (2006), Platchkov, Pollitt, and Shaorshadze (2011), and de Vries (2007).

4. Bompard et al. (2013) provide a useful taxonomy of terms used to describe security.

5. Conventional rotating generation turbines are synchronized to the grid frequency and have substantial inertia, so that if there is a momentary loss of supply, that inertia prevents the frequency from falling too fast. Wind power has effectively no inertia, which has to be provided in some form to maintain frequency within acceptable limits.

6. Also suggested by Mott MacDonald Group (2013). California is interested in five-minute granularity.

7. For a description of the British Balancing Mechanism, see Newbery (2005).

8. "The new balancing services are Demand Side Balancing Reserve (DSBR) and Supplemental Balancing Reserve (SBR)." National Grid announced its tender for these new services on June 10, 2014 (http://www.nationalgrid.com/uk/electricity /additionalmeasures).

9. The CEGB estimated that voltage reductions reduce loads by 7.5 percent in the 1970s (Bates and Fraser 1974) but National Grid now estimates only 1.5 percent in the absence of firm evidence.

10. The CfD specifies a strike price and pays the shortfall of the market price less the strike price, but obliges the holder to pay any excess of the market price over the strike price.

11. See http://www.allislandproject.org/en/cp_current-consultations.aspx?article =75c548a7-34ee-497c-afd2-62f8aa0062df.

REFERENCES

Adib, P., E. Schubert, and S. Oren, S. 2008. "Resource Adequacy: Alternate Perspectives and Divergent Paths." In *Competitive Electricity Markets: Design, Implementation, Performance*, edited by F. P. Sioshansi, 327–362. Oxford: Elsevier. http://dx.doi .org/10.1016/B978-008047172-3.50013–1.

Bates, R., and N. Fraser. 1974. *Investment Decisions in the Nationalised Fuel Industries.* Cambridge: Cambridge University Press.

Batlle, C. and P. Rodilla. 2010. "A Critical Assessment of the Different Approaches Aimed to Secure Electricity Generation Supply." *Energy Policy* 38:7169–7179. https://doi.org//10.1016/j.enpol.2010.07.039.

Batlle, C., C. Vazquez, M. Rivier, and I. J. Perez-Arriaga. 2007. "Enhancing Power Supply Adequacy in Spain: Migrating from Capacity Payments to Reliability Options." *Energy Policy* 35 (9):4545–4554. http://dx.doi.org/10.1016/j.enpol.2007.04.002.

Bidwell, M. 2005. "Reliability Options: A Market-Oriented Approach to Long-Term Adequacy." *Electricity Journal* 185:11–25.

Bompard, E., T. Huang, Y. Wu, and M. Cremenescu. 2013. "Classification and Trend Analysis of Threats Origins to the Security of Power Systems." *International Journal of Electrical Power and Energy Systems* 50:50–64. ISSN 0142–0615, http://dx.doi.org/10.1016/j.ijepes.2013.02.008 .

Bowring, J. 2008. "The Evolution on PJM's Capacity Market." In *Competitive Electricity Markets: Design, Implementation, Performance,* edited by F. P. Sioshansi, chap. 10, 363–386. Oxford: Elsevier.

Bowring, J. 2013. "Capacity Markets in PJM." *Economics of Energy and Environmental Policy* 22:47–64.

Chao, H. P., and R. Wilson. 1987. "Priority Service: Pricing, Investment and Market Organization." *American Economic Review* 77 (5):89–116.

Chao, H. P., and R. Wilson. 2002. "Multi-Dimensional Procurement Auctions for Power Reserves: Robust Incentive-Compatible Scoring and Settlement Rules." *Journal of Regulatory Economics* 22 (2):161–183. http://dx.doi.org/10.1023/A:1020535511537.

CMA (Competition and Markets Authority). 2016. *Energy Market Investigation.* Competition and Markets Authority Final Report (June 24). https://assets.publishing.service.gov.uk/media/5773de34e5274a0da3000113/final-report-energy-market-investigation.pdf.

Cramton, P., and A. Ockenfels. 2011. "Economics and Design of Capacity Markets for the Power Sector." http://www.cramton.umd.edu/papers2010-2014/cramton-ockenfels-economics-and-design-of-capacity-markets.pdf [published in 2012 in *Zeitschrift für Energiewirtschaft* 36 (2):113–134].

Cramton, P., and S. Stoft. 2008. "Forward Reliability Markets: Less Risk, Less Market Power, More Efficiency." *Utilities Policy* 16 (3):194–201. http://dx.doi.org/10.1016/j.jup.2008.01.007.

Cramton, P., A. Ockenfels, and S. Stoft. 2013. "Capacity Market Fundamentals." *Economics of Energy and Environmental Policy* 22:27–46.

DECC (UK Department of Energy & Climate Change). 2009. "The UK Low Carbon Transition Plan." https://www.gov.uk/government/uploads/system/uploads/attachment_data/file/228752/9780108508394.pdf.

DECC. 2013. *Annex F: EMR Panel of Technical Experts Final Report for DECC.* HMG (July). https://www.gov.uk/government/uploads/system/uploads/attachment_data/file/223656/emr_consultation_annex_f.pdf.

DECC. 2014a. "Impact Assessment" (June). https://www.gov.uk/government/uploads /system/uploads/attachment_data/file/324430/Final_Capacity_Market_Impact _Assessment.pdf.

DECC. 2014b. "Implementing Electricity Market Reform (EMR): Finalised Policy Positions for Implementation of EMR" (June). https://www.gov.uk/government /uploads/system/uploads/attachment_data/file/324176/Implementing_Electricity _Market_Reform.pdf accessed 25.8.15.

DECC. 2015. "Historical Electricity Data: 1920 to 2014." https://www.gov.uk/government /statistical-data-sets/historical-electricity-data-1920-to-2011 (updated 2015, accessed August 8, 2015).

EC. 2009. *Directive on the Promotion of the Use of Energy from Renewable Sources* (2009 /28/EC). http://eur-lex.europa.eu/legal-content/EN/ALL/?uri=CELEX:32009L0028 (accessed July 17, 2015).

ENTSO-E. 2015. "Metadata Repository. Glossary of Terms, Statistical Glossary." https://emr.entsoe.eu/glossary/bin/view/GlossaryCode/GlossaryIndex (accessed March 31, 2015).

Eurelectric. 2015. "A Reference Model for European Capacity Markets" (March). http://www.eurelectric.org/media/169068/a_reference_model_for_european _capacity_markets-2015-030-0145-01-e.pdf.

Green, R. J., and D. M. Newbery. 1992. "Competition in the British Electricity Spot Market." *Journal of Regulatory Economics* 1005:929–953.

HM Treasury. Budget 2011. HC 836 (March).

HoC. 2008. *Climate Change Act 2008.* http://www.legislation.gov.uk/ukpga/2008/27 /contents (last accessed July 17, 2015).

HoC. 2013. *Energy Act 2013.* 2013. http://www.legislation.gov.uk/ukpga/2013/32 /contents/enacted/data.htm.

Joskow, P. L. 2008. "Capacity Payments in Imperfect Electricity Markets: Need and Design." *Utilities Policy* 163:159–170. http://dx.doi.org/10.1016 /j.jup.2007.10.003.

Joskow, P. 2013. "Symposium on Capacity Markets." *Economics of Energy and Environmental Policy* 22:v–vi.

Joskow, P. L., and J. Tirole. 2007. "Reliability and Competitive Electricity Markets." *RAND Journal of Economics* 381:68–84. http://dx.doi.org/10.1111/j.1756-2171.2007 .tb00044.x.

London Economics. 2013. *The Value of Lost Load VoLL for Electricity in Great Britain.* Final Report for OFGEM and DECC (July). https://www.gov.uk/government /uploads/system/uploads/attachment_data/file/224028/value_lost_load_electricty _gb.pdf.

Mott MacDonald Group. 2013. "Impact Assessment on European Electricity Balancing Market." http://ec.europa.eu/energy/gas_electricity/studies/doc/electricity/20130610 _eu_balancing_master.pdf.

National Grid. 2013. "TNUoS Tariffs for 2013/14" (January). http://www2.nationalgrid .com/UK/Industry-information/System-charges/Electricity-transmission /Approval-conditions/Condition-5/.

National Grid. 2014a. *Electricity Capacity Report.* http://www2.nationalgrid.com /UK/Our%20company/Electricity/Market%20Reform/Announcements /June%202014%20Auction%20Guidelines%20publication/.

National Grid. 2014b. *Provisional Auction Results: T-4 Capacity Market Auction 2014.* https://www.gov.uk/government/uploads/system/uploads/attachment_data/file /389832/Provisional_Results_Report-Ammendment.pdf.

Newbery, D. M. 1989. "Missing Markets: Consequences and Remedies." In *Economics of Missing Markets, Information, and Games,* edited by F. H. Hahn, chap. 10, 211–242. Oxford: Clarendon Press.

Newbery, D. M. 1995. "Power Markets and Market Power." *Energy Journal* 163:41–66.

Newbery, D. M. 2003. "Risk, Reform and Privatisation." In *Economics for an Imperfect World: Essays in Honor of Joseph Stiglitz,* edited by R. Arnott, B. Greenwald, R. Kanbur, and B. Nalebuff, chap. 29, 535–548. Cambridge, MA: MIT Press.

Newbery, D. M. 2005. "Electricity Liberalisation in Britain: The Quest for a Satisfactory Wholesale Market Design." *Energy Journal* (Special Issue on European Electricity Liberalisation): 43–70. http://www.iaee.org/en/publications/speciali.aspx.

Newbery, D. M. 2010. "Market Design for a Large Share of Wind Power." *Energy Policy* 387:3131–3134. http://dx.doi.org/10.1016/j.enpol.2009.07.037.

Newbery, D. M. 2012a. "Reforming Competitive Electricity Markets to Meet Environmental Targets." *Economics of Energy and Environmental Policy* 11:69–82.

Newbery, D. M. 2012b. "Contracting for Wind Generation." *Economics of Energy and Environmental Policy* 12:19–36.

Newbery, D. M. 2013. "Evolution of British Electricity Market and the Role of Policy for the Regulation Toward Low Carbon Future." In *Evolution of Global Electricity Markets: New Paradigms, New Challenges, New Approaches,* edited by F. P. Sioshansi, 3–33. Oxford: Elsevier.

Newbery, D. M. 2016. "Missing Money and Missing Markets: Reliability, Capacity Auctions and Interconnectors." *Energy Policy* 94:401–410.

Newbery, D. M. 2017. "Tales of Two Islands—Lessons for EU Energy Policy from Electricity Market Reforms in Britain and Ireland." *Energy Policy* 105:597–607. http://doi.org/10.1016/j.enpol.2016.10.015.

Newbery, D. M., and M. Grubb. 2015. "Security of Supply, the Role of Interconnectors and Option Values: Insights from the GB Capacity Auction." *Economics of Energy and Environmental Policy* 4 (2):65–81. doi http://dx.doi.org /10.5547/2160-5890.4.2.dnew.

Newbery, D. M. G., and J. E. Stiglitz. 1977. *The Economic Impact of Price Stabilization.* Report presented to the U.S. Agency for International Development (USAID), Washington, DC.

Newbery, D. M., and J. E. Stiglitz. 1979. "The Theory of Commodity Price Stabilisation Rules: Welfare Impacts and Supply Responses." *Economic Journal* 89 (December):799-817.

Newbery, D. M., and J. E. Stiglitz. 1981. *The Theory of Commodity Price Stabilization: A Study in the Economics of Risk.* Oxford: Clarendon Press.

Newbery, D. M., and J. E. Stiglitz. 1982a. "Optimal Commodity Stock-Piling Rules." *Oxford Economic Papers* 34 (3):403–427.

Newbery, D. M., and J. E. Stiglitz. 1982b. "The Choice of Techniques and the Optimality of Market Equilibrium with Rational Expectations." *Journal of Political Economy* 90 (2):223–246.

Newbery, D. M., and J. E. Stiglitz. 1982c. "Risk Aversion, Supply Response, and the Optimality of Random Prices." *Quarterly Journal of Economics* 97 (1):1–26.

Ofgem. 2010. "Project Discovery: Options for Delivering Secure and Sustainable Energy Supplies." https://www.ofgem.gov.uk/ofgem-publications/40354/projectdiscovery febcondocfinal.pdf.

Ofgem. 2015. *Annual Report on the Operation of the Capacity Market.* https://www .ofgem.gov.uk/sites/default/files/docs/2015/06/annual_report_on_the_operation _of_the_cm_final_0.pdf.

Ofgem. 2016. *Annual Report on the Operation of the Capacity Market in 2015.* https:// www.ofgem.gov.uk/publications-and-updates/annual-report-operation-capacity -market-2015.

O'Neill, R., U. Helman, B. F. Hobbs, and R. Baldick. 2006. "Independent System Operators in the USA: History, Lessons Learned and Prospects." In *Electricity Market Reform: An International Perspective*, edited by F. P. Sioshansi and W. Pfaffenberger, 479–528. Amsterdam: Elsevier.

Oren, S. 2000. "Capacity Payments and Supply Adequacy in a Competitive Electricity Market." Paper presented at VII SEPOPE, Curitiba-Parana, Brazil (May 21–26). www.ieor.berkeley.edu/~oren/workingp/sepope.pdf.

Platchkov, L., M. Pollitt, and I. Shaorshadze. 2011. *The Implications of Recent UK Energy Policy for the Consumer: A Report for the Consumers' Association.* http://www .eprg.group.cam.ac.uk/tag/l-platchkov/.

Pöyry. 2012. *Impact of EMR on Interconnection: A Report to Department of Energy & Climate Change* (December 3). https://www.gov.uk/government/uploads/system /uploads/attachment_data/file/252744/Poyry_Report_on_Impact_of_CM_on _Interconnection.pdf

Pöyry. 2014. "Revealing the Value of Flexibility: How Can Flexible Capability Be Rewarded in the Electricity Markets of the Future?" http://www.poyry.com/sites /default/files/imce/files/revealing_the_value_of_flexibility_public_report_v1_0.pdf.

Redpoint. 2013. *Impacts of Further Electricity Interconnection on Great Britain.* https:// www.gov.uk/government/uploads/system/uploads/attachment_data/file/266307 /DECC_Impacts_of_further_electricity_interconnection_for_GB_Redpoint _Report_Final.pdf.

SEM. 2007. "The Bidding Code of Practice—A Response and Decision Paper." AIP-SEM-07-430 (July 30). www.allislandproject.org.

SEM. 2014. "DS3 System Services—Procurement Consultation—Final." http://www .allislandproject.org/en/transmission_current_consultations.aspx?article=11d55fa2 -e9cd-454c-aaa5-d689d434db20&mode=author.

Sweeting, A. 2007. "Market Power in the England and Wales Wholesale Electricity Market 1995–2000." *Economic Journal* 117:654–685. doi: 10.1111/j.1468-0297.2007 .02045.

Vázquez, C., M. Rivier, and I. J. Pérez-Arriaga. 2002. "A Market Approach to Long-Term Security of Supply." *IEEE Transactions on Power Systems* 17 (2):349–357.

de Vries, L. J. 2007. "Generation Adequacy: Helping the Market to Do Its Job." *Utilities Policy* 15:20–35. doi:10.1016/j.jup/2006.08.001.

Webb, M. G. 1977. "The Determination of Reserve Generating Capacity Criteria in Electricity Supply Systems." *Applied Economics* 9:19–21.

Williams, E. 1991. *Dinorwig: The Electric Mountain*. London: National Grid.

PART III

Macroeconomics

Thoughts on DSGE Macroeconomics

MATCHING THE MOMENT, BUT MISSING THE POINT?

Anton Korinek

PROLOGUE

The most important lessons that an advisor can teach his students are neither about the techniques nor about the substantive insights of his field, but about how to ask the questions that matter. There are few people in the world who know how to ask the right questions as well as Joe Stiglitz. Even more importantly, Joe also knows the importance of asking the questions that no one else is asking because they conflict with conventional wisdom.

During my PhD studies in the early 2000s, Joe was both tireless in his critique of mainstream macroeconomics[1] and unmoved by the fact that his words largely fell on deaf ears. Although I found his critique intellectually convincing, I did not understand its full significance until September 2008 when the *Great Financial Crisis* demonstrated that there were, to put it mildly, gaping holes in the prevailing paradigm of macroeconomics, the dynamic stochastic general equilibrium (DSGE) approach.

In line with what Joe taught me, this article critically evaluates the benefits and costs of the dominant methodology in macroeconomics, the DSGE approach. Although the approach has led to great progress in some areas, I argue that its conceptual restrictions, numerical methods, and the resulting complexity have created biases that risk holding back progress in macroeconomics. There is great scope for making further progress by judiciously pushing the boundaries of some of the methodological restrictions imposed by the DSGE approach. A richer set of methodologies would also make macroeconomics more robust and better prepared for new challenges in understanding and governing our economies.

⸺∞⸺

Modern macroeconomics relies heavily on dynamic stochastic general equilibrium models of the economy. In the aftermath of the Great Financial Crisis of 2008/2009, DSGE macroeconomists have faced scathing criticism both within their profession and from outsiders of the field, and the DSGE approach has come under heavy fire. In this article, I will evaluate this criticism and discuss what I view as the main benefits and shortcomings (also illustrated in figure 7.1) of the DSGE approach for macroeconomic analysis.

Curiously, a majority of the critics of dynamic stochastic general equilibrium macroeconomics agree that it is, in principle, desirable for macroeconomic models to (i) incorporate dynamics, i.e., a time dimension, (ii) deal with stochastic uncertainty, and (iii) study general equilibrium effects. It seems the critique of DSGE macroeconomics therefore does

Figure 7.1   Progress and Incentives in Macroeconomics

Comic © 2015 Anton Korinek

not refer to models being dynamic, stochastic, and featuring general equilibrium analysis, but rather to broader methodological concerns about modern macroeconomics.

At its most basic level, the DSGE approach can be described as a research methodology for the field of macroeconomics. A research methodology defines the general strategy that is to be applied to research questions in a field, defines how research is to be conducted, and identifies a set of methods and restrictions on what is permissible in the field.

A methodology consists not only of a set of formal methods, such as the powerful set of DSGE methods taught in graduate school, but also of a less explicit set of requirements and restrictions that are imposed on the researcher and that sometimes act more like unspoken social conventions. When teachers tell their students to make their macroeconomic models "more rigorous" or to "impose more discipline" on their model, they frequently refer to such unspoken restrictions. For example, it is not acceptable to call a dynamic stochastic general equilibrium model with two time periods a DSGE model. This article will consider both the explicit and implicit, unspoken requirements and restrictions imposed by the DSGE approach.

The methodological restrictions imposed by the DSGE approach can be distinguished into two categories, which I discuss in turn in the remainder of this article. First, in section 1, I consider the conceptual restrictions, such as the requirement for models to be dynamic, stochastic, and general equilibrium (as captured by the name of the approach), the use of microfoundations, the analysis of stationary equilibria, etc. Then, in section 2, I turn to the quantitative methods and restrictions that are part of the DSGE approach.

To evaluate benefits and costs, we need to have an objective in mind against which these benefits and costs are measured. I will take this objective to be a sound understanding of the functioning of the macroeconomy, with an eye toward guiding economic policy and predicting the future course of the economy.

Although some of the methodological restrictions imposed by the DSGE approach are useful, I will argue that others are counterproductive for the profession. Dogmatically applying these methodological restrictions to all macroeconomic problems, risks biasing the scientific progress in macroeconomics in a single direction. This comes at the expense of other approaches that would have led to a deeper and more robust understanding of the real world.

I expect that most of the progress in macroeconomics will come from evaluating the merits of individual methodological restrictions imposed by the DSGE approach—and judiciously removing them if warranted. This holds much promise for the macro profession in future years and will ultimately allow us to develop new theories that improve our understanding and the robustness of our understanding of the macroeconomy.

Going beyond the benefits and costs of specific methodological restrictions, this article also analyzes two broader implications of the widespread use of the DSGE approach. In section 3, I investigate the way in which the complexity of DSGE models limits the scope of our analysis in macroeconomics. In section 4, I discuss the lack of robustness of our understanding ("groupthink") that is generated by having a single dominant methodological approach.

Before proceeding, let me emphasize two caveats that I want to point out as a member of the macro profession who himself at times employs DSGE models to analyze interesting macroeconomic questions.

First, the field of DSGE macroeconomics is incredibly diverse. Many modern macroeconomists who employ the DSGE approach have a deep appreciation of the methodological concerns that I discuss below. They have been—and are—working hard on addressing them to expand the frontiers of our knowledge. I do not intend to criticize those individual research programs. I rather want to argue that the DSGE approach has led to shortcomings in the macro profession as a whole that deserve, in my view, more attention in future research.

Second, I do not think it is desirable to offer a single unified alternative approach to DSGE macroeconomics. In this article, I deliberately abstain from advocating any specific alternative approaches (including the ones I am employing in my own research) to push the boundaries of DSGE. I believe instead that the most desirable future direction for macroeconomics would be less dogma, more diversity and more acceptance of diversity of thought within the macro profession.

1. CONCEPTUAL RESTRICTIONS . . . D, S, GE, AND MORE

Three of the conceptual methodological restrictions imposed by the DSGE approach are apparent from its name: the DSGE approach requires macro models to be dynamic, stochastic, and analyze general equilibrium. Few critics question that these three elements are useful in principle, as mentioned in the introduction. However, the three elements carry an interpretation that is far more specific than a naïve understanding of the words abbreviated by "DSGE" suggests.

Dynamic means that a model following the DSGE approach is expected to be an infinite horizon model—it is socially unacceptable to call a stochastic general equilibrium model in which the dynamics consist of two time periods, a DSGE model, even though it technically contains the elements D, S, and GE. Using infinite horizon models carries both large benefits and costs. On the positive side, they allow for elegant and parsimonious descriptions of economic models since each period can be described as following the same laws of motion. In some respects, this makes infinite horizon models even simpler than two period models—in which, by their very nature, the two periods are asymmetric.

On the downside, an infinite time horizon introduces far greater complexity in solving models and creates a bias toward models that have a well-behaved ergodic steady state that is not present in models with a finite time horizon. On the first issue, it is rarely possible to explicitly solve stochastic infinite horizon models, which makes it necessary to use approximations and computer simulations even to solve simple DSGE models. Further consequences of this complexity are discussed below in a separate section.

On the second issue, an infinite horizon model is only well behaved and can be subjected to the standard methods of economic analysis if it has an ergodic steady state. This is problematic because there are many real-world processes for which it is not obvious that they follow a defined ergodic distribution. In fact, some of the most important phenomena facing humanity are not usefully described as ergodic, ranging from the Industrial Revolution to problems such as global warming or nuclear proliferation. If an economic system is assumed to always revert back toward its steady state, there is much less concern about destabilizing dynamics than there is in the real world, where individuals as well as, potentially, humanity as a whole, have a finite life span.

Stochastic means not only that models should take account of uncertainty, but in the conventional DSGE approach (inherited from real business cycle analysis), that a fundamental driving force of uncertainty is productivity shocks. Although DSGE researchers have long ventured beyond productivity shocks and introduced all other kinds of shocks, productivity shocks are still the most common source of uncertainty in DSGE models, and the first type of shocks we typically tell our students to incorporate in their macroeconomic models. This prevalence stands in marked contrast to the much less robust empirical evidence on the relevance of productivity shocks.

Shocks to productivity also introduce a bias regarding the efficiency of equilibria: when macroeconomic fluctuations are driven by changes in productivity and no other frictions are present, the first welfare theorem applies and there is no role for policy makers to intervene. It is not clear that this is the best benchmark for economic shocks.

General equilibrium means that the economy is described as a closed system in which all variables of interest are determined endogenously. Crucially, the behavior of all agents is modeled from the bottom up based on solid microfoundations. This is one of the main characteristics that distinguish DSGE models from the preceding methodology in macroeconomics that was dominant up to the 1970s. At the time, macroeconomists used structural equations that were based on empirical relationships between macroeconomic variables to describe the path of the economy. It was the exclusive sphere of microeconomists to develop theories based on the notion that individual economic behavior was the result of an optimization problem that described how economic actors maximized their objective (profits, or utility) given the constraints that they faced.

(Curiously, DSGE models need to be micro-founded, but they don't really need to be full general equilibrium models in the strict sense of the word to be called "DSGE"—it is, for example, perfectly acceptable to speak of small, open economy DSGE models even though they take world prices as a given and are thus partial equilibrium models.)

One of the driving forces to employ microfoundations in macroeconomics was to use more consistent methodologies in economics and to allow 1970s macroeconomics to benefit from the great methodological innovations in microeconomics in the preceding decades. As a first approximation, the thought was that we can describe the aggregate behavior of the macroeconomy simply by adding up the actions of all the individual agents in the economy as described by microeconomics. It turns out that doing so carries both large benefits and disadvantages. But before evaluating these in detail, let us consider the question on the desirability of more consistent methodologies for micro- and macroeconomics from a more general perspective.

There are many sciences that employ different methodological approaches at the micro level and the macro level. For example, the following pairs of scientific fields describe micro- and macro-level aspects of the same processes: nuclear physics and chemistry, chemistry and microbiology, microbiology and medicine. In all these fields, macro-level researchers use different methodologies than micro-level research-ers. They commonly use approximate laws that hold at the macro level, even though they are not (yet) able to derive them in detail from the underlying microfoundations. In general, many macro phenomena in the described fields are what systems theorists call "emergent phenomena" that emerge from the interactions of entities at the micro level but are too complex to be satisfactorily described from a micro perspective given our current state of knowledge.

To put it more starkly, we know that physicists understand the micro-level processes that occur in our bodies in much greater detail and preci-sion than medical doctors—but would you rather see your physician or your physicist if you are sick, on the basis that the latter better under-stands the microfoundations of what is going on in your body?

In macroeconomics, there are a number of emergent phenomena that are still difficult to trace back to their precise micro origins. One of the most important such concepts is aggregate demand, which does not have a clear counterpart in microeconomics.

In any given field, micro and macro approaches inform each other, but in most fields, macro-level researchers (say engineers or medical doctors) would not be willing to throw out the set of macro laws and heuristics that their field has accumulated over centuries and use exclusively the microfoundations of their field. This is, however, what happened in mac-roeconomics when the DSGE approach became the dominant approach.

While highlighting the desirability of different methodological approaches for micro- and macro-level researchers in principle, I also want to stress the desirability for the two subfields to learn from each other. For example, much of the progress in medicine over the past decades has been driven by insights from biochemistry.

Rational expectations were considered one of the most important areas of progress of the DSGE approach in the 1970s, after Robert Lucas, Jr., pointed out (in what became known as the Lucas critique) that ratio-nal agents would update their expectations and change their behavior in response to policy changes. If macroeconomic models employ statistical relationships between macroeconomic variables that were derived from past observed behavior that ignore such changes in expectations, then they are bound to be wrong. This was an important insight, especially in the 1970s when policy makers and macroeconomists around the world battled with high inflation that was, in part, driven by unmodeled inflationary expectations.

The Lucas critique led to an innovation in macroeconomics that was clearly driven by a microeconomic insight, i.e., the effects of rational expectations in optimizing models. DSGE models are based on microeconomic fundamentals such as preferences and technologies that are assumed not to be affected by policy action. Along this dimension, policy analysis in a DSGE model has the potential to be more robust. For example, in New Keynesian DSGE models, monetary policy cannot permanently increase output since economic agents have rational expectations and foresee that permanently expansive monetary policy only leads to inflation.

From a somewhat broader perspective, the Lucas critique is an application of the principle that if you leave something out of your model and that thing changes, you will get things wrong. DSGE models are neither necessary nor sufficient to deal with this broader problem—for example, many of the macroeconometric models used by central banks have explicitly incorporated inflation expectations in response to the Lucas critique, without relying on full microfoundations. Furthermore, there are many dimensions along which the DSGE literature falls short of capturing the true microeconomic foundations of economic behavior. For example, it is common to employ assumptions and parameter values that are clearly at odds with actual measured microeconomic behavior in order to fit aggregate economic behavior. This includes, among others, assumptions on the homogeneity of economic agents (or heterogeneity along only a small number of groups or dimensions), on the elasticity of labor supply, which is typically assumed to be an order of magnitude higher than what is observed in micro data so as to fit the observed response of employment in recessions, or on utility functions that exhibit a strong habit persistence in the New Keynesian literature so as to fit the behavior of the inflation rate.

If models abstract from certain features of reality or, even more, if they employ fundamental parameter values that are at odds with empirical estimates at the micro level in order to replicate certain aggregate summary statistics of the economy, then they are not actually capturing the true microeconomic incentives faced by economic agents, but are *bent* to fit the data, as was the case with 1970s-style macroeconomic models. Since they are not capturing the true underlying preferences and technologies of the agents in the economy, the described behavior is not robust to changes in policy regimes or other external factors.

The broader point of the "Lucas critique," that models can only make useful predictions if they do not leave out some of the most important effects of the policies under consideration, applies to any model, including DSGE models. Researchers who employ DSGE models have to keep in mind that any macro model is bound to make some simplifications that destroy its robustness to some types of policy intervention. When investigating a specific research question, the art of being a good researcher is to distinguish which simplifications matter and which ones don't.

Welfare experiments are a second aspect of DSGE models that are made possible by building on microfoundations and that has proven very useful. In the context of the traditional macroeconomic models of the 1970s, it was not possible to make direct statements about welfare, although the models could be used to speak about real variables that matter for welfare such as growth or unemployment. Since DSGE models explicitly assume utility functions for all economic agents, evaluating the impact of different economic policies on the utility of agents is a useful way to study welfare effects.

What we discussed in the context of the Lucas critique equally applies here: any welfare calculation is only as reliable as the macroeconomic model it is derived from. If a model makes the wrong simplifications, the welfare implications derived from it will not capture reality. A typical example is the low cost of business cycle fluctuations that is obtained in standard real business cycle models—if periods of unemployment correspond to voluntary and symmetric reductions in hours worked by all agents, then it is unsurprising that the costs of unemployment are low, but it is questionable if the model is a useful guide to reality. Again, the art of being a good researcher is to make sure that those aspects of the model that matter for welfare in a given policy experiment are included in one's model.

More generally, microfoundations are a useful tool for many types of questions in macroeconomics, but they are not a goal in itself. For some questions, microfoundations are indispensable, for others they may be misplaced.

2. QUANTITATIVE MACROECONOMICS . . . MATCHING THE MOMENT, BUT MISSING THE POINT?

The second important aspect of DSGE methodology that I want to discuss is its quantitative ambitions. DSGE models aim to quantitatively describe the macroeconomy in an engineering-like fashion.

A typical approach to writing a paper in DSGE macroeconomics is as follows:

- To establish "stylized facts" about the quantitative interrelationships of certain macroeconomic variables (e.g., moments of the data such as variances, autocorrelations, covariances, . . .) that have hitherto not been jointly explained;
- To write down a DSGE model of an economy subject to a defined set of shocks that aims to capture the described interrelationships; and
- To show that the model can "replicate" or "match" the chosen moments when it is fed with stochastic shocks generated by the assumed shock process.

The last described step is used to test the fitness of DSGE models by comparing the simulated moments from the model to the observed moments in the data. Models that roughly match the observed moments are accepted; models that are not consistent with the data are rejected.

However, the test imposed by matching DSGE models to the data is problematic in at least four respects.

First, the time series employed are typically de-trended, using methods such as the Hodrick-Prescott (HP) filter to focus the analysis on stationary fluctuations at business cycle frequencies. Although this is useful in some applications, it risks throwing the baby out with the bathwater as many important macroeconomic phenomena are nonstationary or occur at lower frequencies. An example of particular relevance in recent years includes the growth effects of financial crises.

Second, for given de-trended time series, the set of moments chosen to evaluate the model and compare it to the data is largely arbitrary— there is no strong scientific basis for one particular set of moments over another. The macro profession has developed certain conventions, focusing largely on second moments, i.e., variances and covariances. However, this is problematic for some of the most important macroeconomic events, such as financial crises, which are not well captured by second moments. Financial crises are rare tail events that introduce a lot of skewness and fat tails into time series. As a result, a good model of financial crises may well distinguish itself by not matching the traditional second moments used to evaluate regular business cycle models, which are driven by a different set of shocks. In such instances, the criterion of matching traditional moments may even be a dangerous guide for how useful a model is for the real world. For example, matching the variance of output during the 2000s does not generally imply that a model is a good description of output dynamics over the decade.

Third, for a given set of moments, there is no well-defined statistic to measure the goodness of fit of a DSGE model or to establish what constitutes an improvement in such a framework. Whether the moments generated by the model satisfactorily match the moments observed in the real world is often determined by an eyeball comparison and is largely at the discretion of the reader. The scientific rigor of this method is questionable.

Fourth, the evaluation is complicated by the fact that, at some level, all economic models are rejected by the data. All macroeconomic models, whether DSGE or not, simplify complex social interactions into a small set of variables and interrelationships. In addition, DSGE models, as I emphasized in the previous section, frequently impose a number of restrictions that are in direct conflict with micro evidence. If a model has been rejected along some dimensions, then a statistic that measures the goodness of fit along other dimensions is meaningless.

Should we have greater confidence in DSGE models that match more moments and that achieve a closer match to certain moments of the data than other models? Are these likely to provide a more useful guide to reality? There is no scientific basis to answer this question affirmatively.

The *Theory of the Second Best* asserts that in an economy with multiple market failures, correcting one market failure may actually reduce overall economic efficiency. A meta-theory of the second best applies to economic models: since our models of the real world are never "first best" and always contain simplifications, improving the fit of a model along one dimension may make it a worse guide to reality.

Focusing on the quantitative fit of models also creates powerful incentives for researchers to (i) introduce elements that bear little resemblance to reality for the sake of achieving a better fit, (ii) introduce opaque elements that provide the researcher with free (or almost free) parameters, and (iii) introduce elements that improve the fit for the reported moments but deteriorate the fit along other unreported dimensions.

Albert Einstein observed that "not everything that counts can be counted, and not everything that can be counted counts." DSGE models make it easy to offer a wealth of numerical results by following a well-defined set of methods that requires a few years of investment in graduate school, but is relatively straightforward to apply thereafter. There is a risk for researchers to focus too much on numerical predictions of questionable reliability and relevance that absorb a lot of time and effort rather than focusing on deeper conceptual questions that are of higher relevance for society.

3. THE COMPLEXITY OF DSGE MODELS . . . LIMITING THE SCOPE OF OUR INVESTIGATION?

DSGE models are not easy to solve: economic agents confront an infinitely forward-looking optimization problem; value and policy functions typically do not have an explicit representation; rational expectations imply that the expectations and actions of all agents have to be mutually consistent; etc. The simplest benchmark real business cycle (RBC) model is nontrivial to solve for beginners; each friction that is introduced on top of that benchmark makes the model exponentially more difficult to solve, especially if global solution methods need to be employed.

Many times, the conceptual requirements and the quantitative ambitions of DSGE models are in direct conflict with each other—the conceptual restrictions make quantitative analysis more difficult and vice versa. As a result, some conceptual insights in macroeconomics that are difficult to simulate numerically are not spelled out; some numerical simulations that are difficult to square with the conceptual restrictions of DSGE model are not performed.

Biases: The complexity of DSGE models thus risks introducing a number of biases into the macroeconomic profession.

First, there is a bias in the positive mechanisms that the profession is able to describe in DSGE models. Mathematical and computational complexity impose serious restrictions on the set of models that DSGE macroeconomists can analyze. In other words, the set of ideas that we can describe in rigorously quantified DSGE models is smaller than the set of ideas that we can express in simpler models. These methodological restrictions limit our modeling and, ultimately, limit our thinking.

There is a danger that ideas that are at present too complex to capture in DSGE models (for example, because numerical simulations are beyond our computational capabilities) get discounted as "unscientific" just because they do not fit into the dominant prevailing methodological apparatus.

Second, complexity also introduces a normative bias. When adding frictions into economic models, it is easiest to assume them in well-behaved analytical forms, e.g., as reduced-form shocks to technology or other parameters, as fixed wedges, or as convex constraints. Oftentimes, these assumptions automatically imply that the welfare theorems in the described system hold. In other words, the assumptions that keep a model numerically more tractable and the assumptions that assure that a model economy is constrained efficient, frequently overlap. But it is dangerous to derive normative implications from a model that was designed to be constrained efficient just so it can be solved more easily. The desire to channel economic frictions into well-behaved analytical forms therefore introduces a normative bias into macroeconomics that makes the welfare theorems hold more frequently than an accurate description of the economy would suggest.

Third, the complexity introduced by the DSGE approach conflicts with Occam's razor, i.e., with the scientific principle that models should be as simple as possible. This implies that ideas are presented in a fashion that is less clear than possible and that some economic insights are clouded or obscured by complexity. This is especially problematic in graduate education—some graduate students who have successfully passed qualifying exams in macroeconomics are unable to reproduce basic macroeconomic relationships that have been known for generations.

A fourth and related bias introduced by the complexity of solving DSGE models occurs in the amount of time spent on methods versus substance. This starts during graduate education but carries over into the profession at large. Since the methods of DSGE macroeconomics require a significant investment, graduate education in macroeconomics often focuses so heavily on methods that it gives insufficient attention to content. More broadly, the average DSGE macroeconomist spends a considerable amount of time, energy, and effort dealing with the complexity generated by satisfying simultaneously the conceptual and numerical requirements of the DSGE approach. At the margin, society may benefit more if some of these resources were spent on tackling macroeconomic problems without being subject to the methodological restrictions imposed by the DSGE approach.

Methodological innovations frequently create methodological traps. After every methodological innovation, some works are more concerned with incorporating the latest techniques than with the underlying questions themselves. However, applying the latest methodology does not guarantee economic insight—not every mathematical truism is a useful economic theory. In fact, the two all too often get confused. Ultimately, the main criterion to judge the usefulness of macroeconomic models must be their potential to contribute to our understanding of the real world and to improve our ability to govern the macroeconomy.

Finally, the complexity of DSGE models also introduces a selection bias into who becomes a macroeconomist. If we believe that the distribution of technical skills and conceptual economic skills across the population is not perfectly correlated, then the increasing technical demands of DSGE models cause the pool of macroeconomists to be on average less well-endowed with conceptual economic skills.

4. UNIFORMITY IN MACROECONOMICS . . . DANGERS OF GROUPTHINK?

An interesting property of scientific methodologies, including of the DSGE approach, is that they generate network externalities. The more people use a given methodology, the greater the payoffs to using it. A methodology provides a common framework of thought that facilitates the exchange of ideas and the incremental nature of scientific progress. These forces, by themselves, lead to natural monopolies in scientific methodologies. By some accounts, they have catapulted the DSGE approach into the position of a natural monopoly. Indeed, some macroeconomists tend to dismiss any conceptual macroeconomic model that's not DSGE as unscientific.

The uniformity created by a single dominant methodology in a scientific field is desirable if that methodology is able to efficiently encompass all the important phenomena to be described in a given field. However, the macroeconomics profession is far from this goal. Each of the restrictions imposed by the DSGE approach that we discussed in the previous sections has some clear benefits, but there are also situations when they are unnecessary for the insights to be gained, inconvenient because of the additional mathematical burden imposed, or outright misplaced in the sense that they do not represent the most fitting restrictions to capture empirical evidence.

Robustness: If a methodology becomes dominant but is not sufficiently broad to capture all the phenomena of interest in a given field, then it exposes the field to a dangerous lack of robustness. Macroeconomics has arguably suffered from such a lack of robustness: Prior to 2008, mainstream macroeconomics was unprepared to understand the roots, mechanisms, and policy solutions to the financial crisis of 2008/2009.

The reasons arguably included the focus on models with a well-behaved ergodic steady state and on second moments of macroeconomic variables rather than on extreme tail events.

The importance of robustness creates a powerful countervailing force to the network externalities that we discussed earlier, which makes methodological diversity desirable from a social point of view. However, it is not clear if private and social incentives for diversity are aligned.

In the end, methodological uniformity may not be very desirable for macroeconomics. If we want to build a useful quantitative model of the economy, it is not clear that imposing the conceptual restrictions of the DSGE approach is always a good idea—for example, no major central bank in the world uses a DSGE model as their main model of the economy. Similarly, if we want to understand a conceptual economic mechanism, it is not clear how useful it is to subject it to the requirement to perform detailed numerical simulations if these are costly to implement.

In short, as in many other scientific disciplines that study macro phenomena, it may be better for macroeconomists to embrace more diversity of methodological approaches, some of them focusing on quantitative insights, others on conceptual insights, and yet others working on combining the two. Recall that even in physics—the science that is perhaps closest to reaching a single unifying framework—mankind has not yet managed to find a theory of everything.

NOTE

This paper was prepared for the 2015 Conference "A Just Society" honoring Joseph Stiglitz's fifty years of teaching. It has benefited greatly from detailed comments by Joseph Stiglitz and Martin Guzman, as well as interesting conversations with Boragan Aruoba, Wouter den Haan, and Erick Sager.

1. An excellent example is Greenwald and Stiglitz (2003), *Towards a New Paradigm in Monetary Economics*, Cambridge: Cambridge University Press.

CHAPTER 8

The "Schumpeterian" and the "Keynesian" Stiglitz

LEARNING, COORDINATION HURDLES, AND GROWTH TRAJECTORIES

Giovanni Dosi and Maria Enrica Virgillito

INTRODUCTION

The analysis of economies characterized by persistent learning and coordination hurdles has been and is a major unifying theme in Joe Stiglitz's monumental work. Such a world is plausibly the mecca of evolutionary theorizing, bounded rationality, and out-of-equilibrium dynamics. Joe, however, until recently has chosen to use rather conventional instruments and indeed went a long way with them in exploring crucial properties of economic realities as one observes them. In the fiftieth anniversary party that led to this fest, one of us (G.D.) offered the analogy with Paganini, the famous composer and violinist, who was able to play a whole concert on a single violin chord. But Paganini used at least one chord of the appropriate instrument, the violin, while Joe's task has been even harder: he has been mostly using equilibrium assumptions on the state of the system and maximization assumptions on the side of behaviors, still reaching profoundly insightful conclusions. In that, Joe has been extremely subversive in "the use of the unflinching application of the combined postulates of maximizing behaviour, stable preference, and market equilibrium" (Becker 1978, 6), which are indeed the core pillars of the mainstream paradigm. And he has done that basically by studying the properties of highly stylized systems which, however, are *information rich*, wherein information itself is asymmetrically and incompletely distributed, but can be and is persistently augmented over time.

In all that, Joe is in many respects a "closet evolutionist" who in fact highlighted and explored many evolutionary properties of contemporary economics in a Schumpeterian spirit. And he went further introducing genuinely Keynesian properties, e.g., coordination failures and the possibility of path-dependent multiplicity of growth trajectories which are far and beyond Schumpeterian concerns.

In this short essay, we shall illustrate this point with reference to some of Stiglitz's works, out of many, linking them with significantly overlapping contributions from the evolutionary camp, grouping them by two major themes, namely, the consequences of learning and dynamic increasing returns, and "Keynesian" coordination failures with the ensuing possibility of multiple growth paths, fluctuations, and small and big crises.

1. THE "SCHUMPETERIAN" STIGLITZ

Learning and in particular technological learning is at the core of the interpretation of why for the first time in human history per capita income started to grow exponentially since the Industrial Revolution, first in England, and later in other parts of the globe. And learning is indeed at the core of the analyses of classic thinkers, including Adam Smith and Malthus.

However, as Chris Freeman (1982) noted, since the classics, little progress has been made for almost two centuries in our understanding—both empirically and theoretically—of the ways new technological knowledge has been generated and of its economic impact. Karl Marx and Joseph Schumpeter stand out as major exceptions, but they were sort of mavericks in the economic discipline. The importance of technological change only reappeared almost by default, in Bob Solow's analysis of growth dynamics in the 1950s.

Since then, major advances have been made toward the understanding of what happens "inside the blackbox" of technology—using the felicitous expression of Nate Rosenberg. The huge advances in the interpretation of the evidence are reviewed in Dosi and Nelson (2010). Here we restrict ourselves to the theory side, pioneered by the explorations of the properties of technological knowledge, and its augmentation by Nelson (1959), Arrow (1962a,b), and indeed, Atkinson and Stiglitz (1969).

Let us focus on two fundamental properties of technological learning, namely (i) its *cumulativeness*, and (ii) its *locality* in some knowledge space, at least. Both are quite straightforward.

Individuals and organizations augment their knowledge by building, refining, and modifying what they already know. Trivially, one learns the Calculus II course more easily if she has already mastered the Calculus

I program. And most likely, there are *dynamic increasing returns* in the process. Advances in knowledge tend to be multiplicative. Indeed, such property of technological learning is overwhelming documented in the literature on the empirics of technological innovation. This applies to whole technologies and indeed to individual firms.

Together, learning is *local*. Trivially, if you learn about mathematics you do not learn about playing football: on the contrary, learning about the former might make you neglect the latter. Even nearer to our technological concerns, learning about the production and/or use of an electromechanical lathe might well be uncorrelated (or even anticorrelated if attention is selective) with learning on say, CAD/CAM machinery.

Both points are strongly made by Atkinson and Stiglitz (1969), which could be taken indeed as a "general theorem on the impossibility of convex production costs," and as a consequence, as a demonstration on the generic existence of multiple equilibria, or, more broadly, of no equilibrium at all (see below).

Consider figure 8.1 from Atkinson and Stiglitz (1969). Suppose that in some Paradise Lost, humans were originally endowed with the proper techniques as assumed in any micro manual, as depicted by the activities B-A-C. Suppose also that, given the incumbent relative prices, say, the tangent to point A, Adam and Eve chose technique A. It happened, however, that for known reasons, they got kicked out of Paradise, and, as a consequence, they were also made less than omniscient in their technical

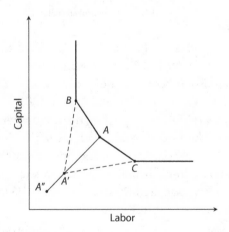

Figure 8.1 From Ancestral Convex Cost Functions to Nonconvexities and Technological Trajectories

Source: Modified from Atkinson and Stiglitz (1969, fig. 3).

knowledge. They had to learn locally thereafter, so for example, given the initial equilibrium technique A at the time of their deportation, they had to learn just in its neighborhood, and got, say to A'.

As emphasized by Atkinson and Stiglitz (1969), note that learning does not move the whole isoquant but just introduces a new technique superior to the old one *irrespectively of relative prices*. Suppose that the process went on and Adam and Eve searched in the neighborhood of A', finding A". The moral of the story is indeed that learning turned out to occur along *technological trajectories* both in the space of input coefficients and of output characteristics (Dosi 1982).

A *first* major consequence is *path-dependence*, and thus the importance of history in selecting particular technologies or variations thereof. The adoption of the keyboard QWERTY is possibly the most famous example (David 1985) but the property is shared by all cases where dynamic increasing returns are present (see Arthur, Ermoliev, and Kaniovski 1983 and Dosi, Ermoliev, and Kaniovski 1994 for formalizations based on generalized Pólya urn models).

In a nutshell, consider the case of two competing technologies A and B. Let x and $(1-x)$ be their "initial" shares among adopters and the adoption process be sequential. Let $f(x)$ be the probability of adoption of the $n-th$ adopter. If the choice function is positively dependent on the share of past adopters, as in figure 8.2, due say, to network externalities or

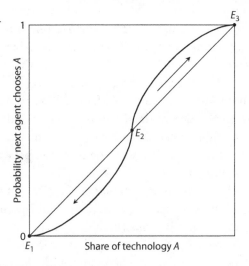

Figure 8.2   Competing Technologies

Source: Arthur, Ermoliev, and Kaniovski (1983).

technological-specific learning by doing, then, under dynamic increasing returns, one may well attain a lock-in into technologies which are Pareto-dominated (see David 1985; Arthur 1989; Dosi, Ermoliev, and Kaniovski 1994; Dosi and Kaniovski 1994; and this is also an implication of Stiglitz and Greenwald 2014).

Second, and relatedly, learning by doing is a general property of individual firms, whole industries, and economies (see Stiglitz and Greenwald 2014, for an impressive analysis across all three levels, and also Cimoli, Dosi, and Stiglitz 2009).

Third, micro heterogeneity is a ubiquitous consequence of firm-specific idiosyncratic learning on every dimension one is aware of—ranging from productivities to propensity to innovate, profitability, growth rates, and so on (for some review of the literature, see Dosi and Nelson 2010 and Syverson 2011).

Joe is well aware of that, as repeatedly remarked also in the cited tour de force on learning economies (Stiglitz and Greenwald 2014). Yet, it is still one of the less formalized intuitions in Joe's work, and in our view, this entirely goes to Joe's merit, fully aware as he is, that any reasonable formalization of heterogeneity implies an explicit acknowledgment of some sort of disequilibrium dynamics. Short of that, Joe has always masterly used max-cum-equilibrium assumption as a sort of *a fortiori tool*: "I show you properties which hold *even* under such far-fetched assumptions, which would apply, *much more so*, under more realistic set-ups." Or, putting it the other way round, we are not aware of any Stiglitz contribution attempting to rationalize micro heterogeneity as an equilibrium phenomenon: in that he has stayed far away from the "Counter-Reformation tide," which has recently tried to marry innovation and micro heterogeneity with some industry level (or General) Equilibria (examples among many, are Melitz 2003 and Acemoglu 2015). More generally, a good deal of the recent literature in industrial economics, finally aware of micro heterogeneity has restlessly attempted to build Ptolemaic epicycles to reconcile it with the Becker imperative cited above. Joe never had anything to do with it.

Fourth, Joe Stiglitz, together with one of the giants of the contemporary economic discipline, Ken Arrow, have forcefully pointed out one of the most devastating implications (for the standard theory, of course!) of information/knowledge and learning taken seriously: as already mentioned, nonconvexities are everywhere, and with that, multiplicity of equilibria/growth paths or even no equilibrium at all.

As discussed in Stiglitz (2000), while Economics of Invention and Innovation is meant to analyze the process of creation and appropriation on *new knowledge*, the Economics of Information is meant to study the influence of *asymmetries in information* when new products, processes, and behaviors emerge. Both theories recognize a limited scope for prices as a means to convey information and for price competition to shape economic dynamics.

The known properties of information (its nonrival use, nonperishability, scale-freeness in its application, etc.), when taken seriously, imply that the usual general equilibrium (GE) results are not guaranteed any longer. In fact as discussed in Radner and Stiglitz (1984), whenever there are nonconvexities in the production function, discontinuities arise and information is naturally associated with nonconvexities because of the fixed cost of acquiring it. Then, the benefits of information increase with the scale of its production. But given nonconvexities, the existence of equilibrium is not guaranteed (see Rothschild and Stiglitz 1976, and its manual-level acknowledgment in Mas-Colell, Whinston, and Green 1995). In fact, under nonconvex technologies, the supply curve is not equivalent to the marginal cost function and the intersection with the demand curve is not ensured. Arrow (1996) clearly states how the introduction of information in the production possibility set induces increasing returns:

> [c]ompetitive equilibrium is viable only if production possibilities are convex sets, that is do not display increasing return . . . with information constant returns are impossible. . . . The same information [can be] used regardless of the scale of production. Hence there is an extreme form of increasing returns.
>
> Arrow (1996, 647–648)

In fact, the existence of conventional general equilibria is undermined in the presence of innovation even neglecting increasing returns properties of innovation itself (see Winter 1971).

Indeed, in the presence of information, the very *existence of equilibrium* is undermined. Together, what is undermined is the miraculous equilibrating property of markets; as shown by the seminal contribution of Grossman and Stiglitz (1980) as knowledge diffuses among traders, traders themselves lose the incentive of bearing the cost of acquiring new information yielding the paradoxical result of *no trade under informationally efficient markets*. But, that implies that even when a notional equilibrium exists, nothing ensures that both the *first and the second welfare theorems* are satisfied. Competitive markets are not constrained Pareto efficient; some individuals could, in principle, be made better off without making anyone worse off. The economy cannot be efficient decentralized (II Welfare Theorem) whenever welfare effects are present and the standard separation of equity and efficiency does not hold—the Coase conjecture on the irrelevance of the distribution of property rights (see also Shapiro and Stiglitz 1984, for a labor market application of the latter results).

Unfortunately, the Arrow/Stiglitz message is still largely neglected in most of the current theoretical practice, and worse, especially among young scholars, whose urge to publish well and quickly blinds them from exploring more daring routes which nonetheless are more respectful of both incumbent theorems and incumbent evidence.

The argument so far has been made on the full equivalence between technological knowledge and sheer information. However, an exploration of the differences between the two is also crucial and bears far-reaching implications (much more in Dosi and Nelson 2010). In the perspective of "knowledge equals information," one is inclined to focus on the links between patterns of *distribution of information* and the ensuing *incentive* problems. Conversely, in the perspective of Economics of Knowledge and Innovation the focus tends to be on the role of individuals and especially organizational *capabilities*. Organizations are not seen primarily as a collection of contracts for which one should design the right scheme of incentives, in order to align, e.g., manager and worker interests, but they are the result of practices, norms, behavior, and unwritten conducts meant to "doing something," and learning has to do with improvements thereof.

The two perspectives are far from being mutually exclusive, but to date, little dialogue has been going on. Indeed, putting it emphatically, one badly needs Stiglitz and Greenwald (2014) meeting Nelson and Winter (1982), and vice versa.

2. THE "KEYNESIAN" STIGLITZ

Joe Stiglitz is deeply and genuinely Keynesian. However, *formally*, Stiglitz is largely a *supply side* theorist. How come?

Well, in our view, it is the virtuosity of Joe's "*a fortiori* epistemology" mentioned earlier. With information taken seriously, even if with only two functionally or informationally different agents, "quasi-equilibria" or, as Joe puts it, setups with an "equilibrium amount of disequilibrium" (Stiglitz 2000) generally arise, characterized by, e.g., efficiency wages and involuntary unemployment; the impossibility of efficient markets; credit rationing; systematic underinvestment in learning, etc. All properties whose identification led to a more than deserved Nobel Prize.

Take two of the best known results. On the labor market side, unemployment can be the result of the design of contracts whereby high efficiency wages are paid in order to make shirking not optimal for workers. However, if one accepts a standard production function as Shapiro and Stiglitz (1984) do—for rhetorical purposes we believe—when high wages are paid, labor demand turns out to be weak, and vice versa. Under relatively low employment rates, whenever shirking workers are caught, they expect to be unemployed for long spells. As a result, they will not shirk, reaching a behavior compatible with the objectives of the firm. But, nonshirking wages are not consistent with full employment, hence a (*persistent*) equilibrium amount of involuntary *unemployment* will arise. Indeed, it is Marx put into asymmetric information shoes.

Similarly, in Stiglitz and Weiss (1992), whenever both asymmetric information and adverse selection are present, credit rationing equilibria are likely to arise. The chosen/offered contracts are the *equilibrium one* because they satisfy a Nash condition: nobody increases her utility or profit by deviating from the chosen equilibrium contract. But, of course, under the equilibrium contracts, market clearing does not occur; in this case, a persistent amount of credit rationing will be observed, so that excess demand for credit will be the norm, not the exception.

Notice that these and many other Stiglitzian results are *not* obtained as "frictions" vis-à-vis the standard GE model. It is not, for example, that involuntary unemployment stems from some lack of "flexibility" on some markets. That is, nominal (or less often) real rigidities, typically in the labor market, but sometimes also in the product market are by no means the cause of the "bad" equilibria. In this, Joe is anything but a good-hearted, *ante litteram*, "New Keynesian" dynamic stochastic general equilibrium model (DSGE) guy.

On the contrary, the foregoing properties come from *structural* features of contemporary economic systems, while more "flexibilization," that is, attempts to render the world more akin to GE may well make things in the aggregate *worse*.

Together, capitalist systems are characterized by massive and huge *coordination failures* also in the demand side. Coordination failures are a clear-cut example of the absence of any isomorphism between the micro adjustments and the macro outcomes. A simple and vivid illustration, which in the literature has been almost ostracized, is Cooper and John (1988):

> Strategic complementaries are associated with the presence of "Keynesian features" such as multiple equilibria and a multiplier process. . . . When this occurs a *coordination failure* is present: mutual gain from an all-around change in strategies may not be realised because no individual player has an incentive to deviate from an initial equilibrium.
>
> Cooper and John (1988, 442–443)

Consider an economy with many agents, wherein $e_{i,j}$ are the j strategies of the i agent (say, in terms of demand levels). Call $\bar{e}$ the action of the other agents, and $V_{i,j}(e_i, \bar{e})$ the payoff function of agent i when strategy j is chosen. If $V_{i,j}(e_i, \bar{e}) > 0$ there are strategic complementaries and with that, also Pareto-rankable equilibria. Under this setup, demand shocks tend to be amplified; that is, they have *multiplier effects*. Such complementaries are a fundamental ingredient of a genuine Keynesian world which allow, indeed *imply*, demand-driven or at least demand-propagated small and big crises (Stiglitz 2016).

And in fact, such coordination hurdles are even stronger in the presence of a financial sector which is not just a "veil" upon real dynamics. Here, Minskyian intuitions (the so-called *financial fragility hypothesis*) significantly overlap with Stiglitzian ones; while for the former high interest rates signal euphoria in financial markets, as a prelude of the emergence of Ponzi scheme traders; and for the latter, high interest rates in capital markets induce both a *sorting effect*, reducing the proportion of low risk borrowers, and an *incentive effect*, inducing borrowers in using riskier techniques (see Stiglitz and Weiss 1992), then triggering the emergence of crashes.

The static concept of strategic complementarity (or more humbly, complementaries among many agents of whatever kind) can be rephrased in a dynamic perspective, as suggested by Cooper and Haltiwanger (1993). Dynamically, even the very simple Keynesian worlds of the foregoing kind are characterized by positive co-movements across agents; temporal agglomeration (agents have an incentive to synchronize discrete decisions); and magnification and propagation of aggregate demand shocks.

Indeed, in our view, evolutionary Agent-Based Models (ABMs) are the mecca where the conjecture of the "demand-side Keynesian Stiglitz" can be fully vindicated. In fact, the ABM route has been increasingly explored by Joe himself (see Caiani et al. 2015; Landini, Gallegati, and Stiglitz 2015; Dosi et al. 2016a).

In this perspective, let us flag some of the results from Dosi, Fagiolo, and Roventini (2010) to Dosi et al. (2016b), which can be robustly shown as emergent properties out of the interaction of heterogeneous agents. Quite remarkably, *all* the properties inherently linked with macroeconomic externalities listed in Cooper and Haltiwanger (1993) emerge in a "Schumpeter meeting Keynes" (K+S) family of models, and many more as shown in table 8.1.

Table 8.1 Stylized Facts Matched by the K+S Family of Models

Firm Level SF	Aggregate Level SF
Skewed firm size distribution	Endogenous self-sustained growth with persistent fluctuations
Fat-tailed firm growth rate distribution	Fat-tailed GDP growth rate distribution
Productivity heterogeneity across firms	Relative volatility of GDP, consumption and investment
Persistent productivity differentials among firms	Cross-correlation of macro variables
Lumpy investment rates at firm level	Procyclical aggregate R&D investment
Firm bankruptcies are countercyclical	Cross-correlations of credit-related variables
Firm bad-debt distribution fits a power law	Cross-correlation between firm debt and loan losses
	Banking crises duration is right skewed
	Fiscal costs of banking crises to GDP
	Distribution is fat tailed
	Persistent unemployment
	Wage curve
	Beveridge curve
	Okun curve
	Separation and hiring rate volatility
	Matching function
	Productivity, unemployment, and vacancy rate volatility
	Unemployment and inequality correlation

Another profoundly Keynesian proposition, offered by Joe, concerns the perverse effect of "making the word more alike the theory:"

> The problem that Keynes recognized was that wages can be *too flexible*. Indeed, when wages fall, people's income falls and their ability to demand goods falls as well. Lack of aggregate demand was the problem with the Great Depression, just as lack of aggregate demand is the problem today. Imposing more wage flexibility can result in exacerbating the underlying problem of lack of aggregate demand.
>
> Stiglitz (2013, 10)

Again, such a proposition can be naturally vindicated on the grounds of our K+S modeling platform with an explicit interaction between microfounded labor market dynamics and aggregate demand. So, in Dosi et al. (2016c) we show that more flexibility in terms of variations of monetary wages and labor mobility is prone to induce systematic coordination failures, higher macro volatility, higher unemployment, and a higher frequency of crises. In fact, it is precisely the downward flexibility of wages and employment and the related higher degrees of inequality—as profitable as it might be for individual firms—that lead recurrently, *as system-level emergent properties*, to small and big aggregate demand failures. Conversely, the model shows that seemingly more rigid labor markets and labor relations are conducive to *coordination successes* with higher and smoother growth.

Finally, a major genuine Keynesian—and, even more so Kaldorian—theme in Joe's work has been the importance of income distribution in terms of growth patterns. While on somewhat more arcane debates like the famous one on "capital theory" he has been relatively agnostic or mildly for the American side of the controversy, on the short and long-term relevance of distributive dynamics he is certainly on the side of Cambridge, England, and beyond, with a sensitivity to the added deep social damages of inequality almost unique among economists (see Stiglitz 2012, 2015; Gallegati, Landini, and Stiglitz 2016).

3. STIGLITZ AND THE STANDARD PARADIGM

As known, for more than three decades after World War II (WWII) there were more or less three tenets of an uneasy intellectual compromise that dominated the economic discipline, based on the division of labor between (i) microfounded general equilibrium models, (ii) short-run macroeconomics, and (iii) growth theories.

3.1. THE MICRO

The coordination research program, as known—with its early roots more in Leon Walras than in Adam Smith—culminated into the Arrow-Debreu-Meckenzie general equilibrium model, indeed an elegant and institutionally very parsimonious demonstration of the possibility of equilibrium coordination among decentralized agents.

In fact, subsequent, basically negative, results have shown, *even in the absence of innovation*, the general impossibility of moving from existence theorems to the implicit dynamics captured by proofs of global or local stability—loosely speaking, the ability of the system, when scrambled, to get back to its equilibrium state. Quite the contrary, even empirically far-fetched processes such as *tatonnements* (with the omniscient Walrasian auctioneer proclaiming equilibrium transaction when he sees them) in general do not converge.

Even more powerfully, some of the founding fathers of GE themselves have shown that existence does not bear any implication in terms of the shape of excess demand functions (this is what the Sonnenschein-Mantel-Debreu theorem implies). Putting it shortly, in general forget even local stability.

Conversely, any careful look at the toll requirements, which sheer existence entails—in terms of information and rationality—highlights the extent to which GE is a beautiful but extremely fragile creature, certainly unable to withhold the weight of any account of the dynamics of the economy as a whole and even less so to offer any serious microfoundation to transforming economies undergoing various forms of innovation.

In fact, even forgetting search and innovation, it is quite ill-founded to claim that standard GE models can be an account, no matter how utterly stylized, paraphrasing Adam Smith, of why the butcher offers meat day after day more or less at the same price, mainly motivated by self-interest. If the conditions—in terms of rationality, characteristics of the exchanges, etc.—required in reality were even vaguely as stringent as those required in GE models, probably no one would ever offer meat or whatever else.

In any case, that was the *micro* for the standard paradigm.

3.2. THE MACRO

Then there were basically two *macros*. One was (equilibrium) growth theory that largely lived until the end of the 1970s a life of its own. While it is the case that models à la Solow invoked maximizing behaviors in order to establish equilibrium input intensities, no claim was made that such allocations were the work of any representative agent, in turn taken to be the synthetic version of some underlying general equilibrium. By the same token, the distinction between positive (i.e., descriptive) models, on the one hand, and normative ones before Lucas and companions, was clear to the practitioners. Finally, in the good and in the bad, technological change was kept separate from the mechanisms of resource allocation; the famous Solow residual was, as well known, the statistical counterpart of the drift in growth models with an exogenous technological change.

Together, in some land between purported GE microfoundations and equilibrium growth theories, lived for at least three decades a macroeconomics sufficiently Keynesian in spirit and quite neoclassical in terms of tools. It was the early neo-Keynesianism—pioneered by Hicks, and shortly thereafter by Modigliani, Patinkin, and a few other American Keynesians, who Joan Robinson contemptuously defined as "bastard Keynesians." It is the combination of short-term macro (fixed prices) "IS-LM" curves—meant to capture the aggregate relations between money supply and money demand, interest rates, savings and investments—with the Phillips curve on the labor market, which yields the "AS-AD" aggregate equilibrium.

The quick Keynesian synthesis presented by Hicks had been offered as a seemingly sensible and parsimonious account of Keynes's General Theory—cutting out all the detours and qualifications. In fact, it was its most rudimentary general equilibrium translation with an implicit representative agent and various sorts of frictions added up. However, it took almost half a century for the American macro mainstream to further sterilize, reformulate, refine the neo-Keynesian apparatus, and baptize it as the dynamic stochastic general equilibrium (DSGE) model.

3.3. *TAKE NO PRISONERS*: THE LUCAS REVOLUTION

What happened next?

First, New Classic Economics (even if the reference to the Classics cannot be more far away from the truth) fully abolished the distinction between the normative and positive (i.e., descriptive) domains—between models à la Ramsey versus models à la Harrod, Domar, Solow, and so on (notwithstanding the differences among the latter ones).

In fact, the striking paradox for theorists who are in good part market fanatics is that one starts with a model which is essentially of a benign, forward-looking, central planner, and only at the end, one claims that the solution of whatever intertemporal optimization problem is in fact supported by a decentralized market equilibrium.

The reasoning could be much easier for this approach if one could legitimately summarize a genuine general equilibrium (that is, with many agents, heterogeneous at least in their endowments and preferences) into some representative agent. But the fact is that one cannot (Kirman 1992). By doing that nonetheless, one simply assumes away as solved by construction the coordination problem. Notwithstanding the name, there is very little of general equilibrium in the DSGE models, and earlier antecedents. All that irrespectively of the trust in the ability of GE to capture the essentials of the coordination hurdles, mentioned above, in market economies, which is very low indeed.

The representative agent holds all the micro and macro on its shoulder, folding together the expectation-augmented Phillips curve (for the labor market), the Euler equation (for the intertemporal allocation between consumption and saving, and leisure and working time), and finally the Taylor rule (for monetary policy), in order to build DSGE models.

Second, but relatedly, the last three decades have seen the disappearance of the distinction between long term and short term—with the latter as the locus where all frictions, liquidity traps, Phillips curves, some (temporary) real effects of fiscal and particularly monetary policies, could all hazardously survive. Why would a representative agent be able to solve sophisticated intertemporal optimization problems from here to infinity display frictions and distortions in the short run? We all know the outrageously silly propositions, sold as major discoveries, associated with the rational expectation revolution, concerning the ineffectiveness of fiscal and monetary policies and the general properties of markets to yield Pareto first-best allocations. In this respect, of course, it is easier for that to happen if the market is squeezed into a representative agent; in that case, coordination and allocation failures would involve serious episodes of "schizophrenia" by that agent itself.

It is easy to appreciate the "light-years" distance between Stiglitz's perspective and the standard paradigm, especially in its more extreme version. Even if Joe generally assumes maximizing agents, the system-level properties he identifies are more the outcome of structural features of the *distribution of information among types of agents/techniques of production*, rather than the outcome of rational agents optimizing over an intertemporal horizon.

4. ALTERNATIVE PARADIGMS: KEYNES MEETING SCHUMPETER

What about the alternatives? Well, Joe's work has been a bastion throughout, suggesting an *alternative economic theory* which never interpreted any difference between observed dynamics of any economy and the prediction of the "economic model" as frictions, rigidities, etc., but rather as properties of the inner workings of information-rich, innovating, capitalist systems.

On a parallel track, evolutionary, Schumpeterian-inspired models went a long way in interpreting processes of endogenous innovation-driven growth. The literature spurring from the seminal Nelson and Winter (1982) has been impressively blossoming.

All this notwithstanding, these two alternative streams rarely interacted with each other. Worse than that, as a significant contributor of one of the latter stream, one of us (G.D.) easily admits that evolutionary theorists have tended to be far too "Schumpeterian," in their neglect of any Keynesian coordination hurdle in both the short and the long run.

Certainly, here there is no betrayal of Schumpeter, his book review of Keynes's *General Theory* (Schumpeter 1936) sounds, more often than not, as a note by a grudging, solid but not-too-insightful, Chicago-style PhD student. So, after suggesting that Keynes's *General Theory* "expresses forcefully the attitude of a decaying civilization" and "invites sociological interpretation in the Marxian sense" (1936, 792), he shows no understanding at all of involuntary unemployment, whose notion is considered by Schumpeter equivalent to "artificial definitions which . . . produce paradoxical-looking tautologies" and, relatedly, of the relation between demand for labor and aggregate demand:

> The definition of involuntary unemployment, page 15, may serve as an example. Taken literally (which of course would be unfair to do) it would mean that there is no practically conceivable case in which workmen are not partially unemployed by definition. For if prices of wage good rise a little, other things being equal, it is clear that both the demand for, and

the supply of, labor will increase under competitive conditions, the latter at least as long as the flexibility of the marginal utility of income to the workmen is what present statistics lead us to believe. [*sic*]

Schumpeter (1936, 792, footnote 1)

Indeed, well in tune with the later "neo-Schumpeterian" perspective, he handwaves us "the most powerful propeller of investment, the financing of changes in that production functions" ridiculing demand-based multiplier and investment accelerators, as "having no greater practical importance than a proof that motor cars cannot run in the absence of fuel" (1936, 793).

Two outstanding exceptions, focusing on the crucial interactions between coordination-demand generation, on the one hand, and innovative dynamics, on the other, are Christopher Freeman on the one side of the Atlantic, and Joe Stiglitz on the other, despite different but quite complementary interpretative lenses.

Here, let us flag the pioneering emphasis of the contribution by Joe to the World Conference of the International Schumpeter Society in Japan (Stiglitz 1994). His point counters any rough Schumpeterianism as it can: *there are positive feedbacks between levels of aggregate activities and innovative search.* To reinforce the point, Chris Freeman would have added that there are also powerful interactions between aggregate demand and *diffusion* of innovations. Indeed, both Stiglitz and C. Freeman agree that alone neither Schumpeter nor Keynes are enough (see Freeman and Soete 1994).[1]

Whenever one abandons the unfortunate idea that the macro economic system is held up to some mysteriously stable, unique equilibrium path, it could well be that *negative demand shocks exert persistent effects,* because less aggregate demand entails less innovative search, which in turn entails less innovation stemming from technological shocks:

> [During recessionary phases], typically firms also reduce their expenditures in R&D and productivity-enhancing expenditures. The reduction in output reduces opportunities to "learn by doing." Thus, the attempt to pare all unnecessary expenditures may have a concomitant effect on long-run productivity growth. In this view, the loss from a recession may be more than just the large, but temporary, costs of idle and wasted resources: the growth path of the economy may be permanently lowered.

Stiglitz (1994, 122)

Despite the 2008 crisis, many economists continue to believe in some version of the model underlying example *A* in figure 8.3; the economy is bound to spring back, with no permanent loss to its long-run equilibrium rate of growth. The econometric side of this belief is the Frisch-like idea of the economy as a "pendulum," responding to exogenous shocks.[2] In this perspective, it seems almost miraculous that in the empirical literature one recently finds impulse response function implying multipliers significantly greater than one; as such, we suggest, a witness of the depth of the current crisis (see, Blanchard and Leigh 2013).

However, a small but significant minority of the profession has been forced by the evidence to buy case *B* in figure 8.3, recession-induced output losses are permanent, and even if the system goes back to the precrisis *rates* of growth, that implies an exponentially growing *absolute level gap*. Moreover, as discussed in Stiglitz (1994), imperfect capital markets and credit rationing may exacerbate the effect of recessions, hampering the recovery.

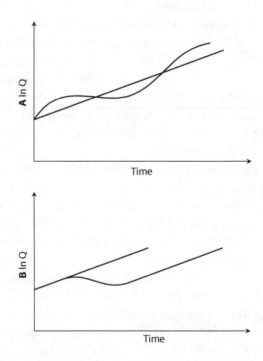

Figure 8.3   Positive Feedbacks Between Levels of Aggregate Activities and Innovative Search: Short-Run (A) and Long-Run (B) Effects of Recessions

Source: Stiglitz (1994, 123).

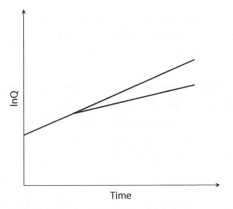

Figure 8.4 Divergent Growth Trajectories: Permanent Losses in Output Growth Rates

Source: A stylized version from Dosi et al. (2016b; 2016c).

But, more than that, recurrent negative demand shocks implied by austerity policies or labor market flexibilization, might well yield *lower long-term rates of growth* (see figure 8.4); this is what we show in Dosi et al. (2016b) and in Dosi et al. (2016c). In the latter scenario, presented in figure 8.4, the growth trajectories diverge, implying a decaying long-run rate of output growth.

CONCLUSIONS: BUILDING BRIDGES

This short essay has been mainly focused on the links between the research program of the Economics of Information, to which Stiglitz has offered seminal contributions and the one of Economics of Knowledge and Innovation (more broadly, Evolutionary Economics). We tried to highlight the bridges and overlappings between the two, including the very emphasis on knowledge-information and the implications for "learning economies." In environments populated by multiple learning and interacting agents, coordination hurdles are likely to emerge together with feedback mechanisms linking crises driven by shortages in aggregate demand, and changing intensity of innovative search; hence, the possibility of persistent losses in the levels and/or rates of growth of output, giving rise to multiplicity of growth trajectories. The analysis of these properties of the economy represents a powerful file rouge between the Economics of Information and Evolutionary Economics.

Stiglitz (2000) proposes two priority areas of investigation common both to the Economics of Information and the Economics of Knowledge, namely:

> But perhaps the most important advances will be in two areas . . . on *dynamics* and on . . . *organizations*, on how and how well organizations and societies absorb new information, learn, adapt their behaviour, and even their structures; and how different economic and organizational designs affect the ability to create, transmit, absorb, and use knowledge and information.
>
> Stiglitz (2000, 1471)

In our view, between the two domains of Economics of Information and Knowledge there are also largely unexplored complementaries in the modeling approach. Bridges between "reduced forms," low-dimensional models, often amenable to analytical solutions, on the one hand, and fully fledged agent-based evolutionary models with explicit links between micro *interactions* and macro *emergent properties*, on the other, are markedly necessary. They hold the promise to allow a deeper understanding of worlds where "Keynes meets Schumpeter" and well beyond.

NOTES

The contribution is based on the presentation by G. Dosi to the Conference "A Just Society. Honoring Joseph Stiglitz" held at Columbia Business School, New York City, on October 16, 2015. We gratefully acknowledge the support by the European Union's Horizon 2020 Research and Innovation Programme under Grant Agreement No. 649186—ISIGrowth.

1. See the latter contribution for a more general argument on the relationship between technological innovation, aggregate demand, and employment.

2. For an enticing reconstruction of the discussion between Frisch and Schumpeter on the "pendulum" metaphor, see Louca (2001).

REFERENCES

Acemoglu, D. 2015. "Localised and Biased Technologies: Atkinson and Stiglitz's New View, Induced Innovations, and Directed Technological Change." *Economic Journal* 125 (583):443–463.

Arrow, K. 1962a. "The Economic Implications of Learning by Doing." *Review of Economic Studies* 29 (3):155–173.

Arrow, K. 1962b. "Economic Welfare and the Allocation of Resources for Invention." In *The Rate and Direction of Inventive Activity: Economic and Social Factors*, edited by R. Nelson, 609–626. Princeton, NJ: Princeton University Press.

Arrow, K. 1996. "Technical Information and Industrial Structure." *Industrial and Corporate Change* 5 (2):645–652.

Arthur, B. 1989. "Competing Technologies, Increasing Returns, and Lock-In by Historical Events." *Economic Journal* 99 (394):116–131.

Arthur, B., Y. Ermoliev, and Y. Kaniovski. 1983. "On Generalized Urn Schemes of the Pólya Kind." *Cybernetics* 19:61–71.

Atkinson, A., and J. Stiglitz. 1969. "A New View of Technological Change." *Economic Journal* 79 (315):573–578.

Becker, G. 1978. *The Economic Approach to Human Behavior*. Chicago: University of Chicago Press.

Blanchard, O., and D. Leigh. 2013. "Growth Forecast Errors and Fiscal Multipliers." NBER Working Paper No. 18779. Cambridge, MA: National Bureau of Economic Research.

Caiani, A., A. Godin, E. Caverzasi, M. Gallegati, S. Kinsella, and J. E. Stiglitz (2016). "Agent Based- Stock Flow Consistent Macroeconomics: Towards a Benchmark Model." *Journal of Economic Dynamics and Control* 69:375–408.

Cimoli, M., G. Dosi, and J. Stiglitz (eds.). 2009. *Industrial Policy and Development: The Political Economy of Capabilities Accumulation*. Oxford: Oxford University Press.

Cooper, R., and J. Haltiwanger. 1993. "Evidence on Macroeconomic Externalities." NBER Working Paper No. 4577. Cambridge, MA: National Bureau of Economic Research.

Cooper, R., and A. John. 1988. "Coordinating Coordination Failures in Keynesian Models." *Quarterly Journal of Economics* 103 (3):441–463.

David, P. 1985. "Clio and the Economics of QWERTY." *American Economic Review* 75 (2):332–337.

Dosi, G. 1982. "Technological Paradigms and Technological Trajectories." *Research Policy* 11 (3):147–162.

Dosi, G., Y. Ermoliev, and Y. Kaniovski. 1994. "Generalized Urn Schemes and Technological Dynamics." *Journal of Mathematical Economics* 23 (1):1–19.

Dosi, G., and Y. Kaniovski. 1994. "On 'Badly Behaved' Dynamics." *Journal of Evolutionary Economics* 4 (2):93–123.

Dosi, G., G. Fagiolo, and A. Roventini. 2010. "Schumpeter Meeting Keynes: A Policy-Friendly Model of Endogenous Growth and Business Cycles." *Journal of Economic Dynamics and Control* 34 (9):1748–1767.

Dosi, G., and R. Nelson. 2010. "Technical Change and Industrial Dynamics as Evolutionary Processes." In *Handbook of Economics of Innovation, Vol. 1*, edited by B. Hall and N. Rosenberg, 51–127. Amsterdam: North Holland.

Dosi, G., M. Napoletano, A. Roventini, J. Stiglitz, and T. Treibich. 2017a . "Expectation Formation, Fiscal Policies and Macroeconomic Performance When Agents Are Heterogeneous and the World Is Changing." LEM Working Papers Series n. 2017/31. Laboratory of Economics and Management (LEM). Pisa, Italy: Sant'Anna School of Advanced Studies.

Dosi, G., M. Napoletano, A. Roventini, and T. Treibich. 2016. "The Short- and Long-Run Damages of Austerity: Keynes Beyond Schumpeter." In *Contemporary Issues in Macroeconomics*, edited by J. Stiglitz, 79–100. London: Palgrave.

Dosi, G., M. C. Pereira, A. Roventini, and M. E. Virgillito. 2017 b. "When More Flexibility Yields More Fragility: The Microfoundations of Keynesian Aggregate Unemployment." *Journal of Economic Dynamics and Control* 81: 162–186.

Freeman, C. 1982. *The Economics of Industrial Innovation,* 2nd ed. London: Frances Pinter.

Freeman, C., and L. Soete. 1994. *Work for All or Mass Unemployment? Computerised Technical Change Into the 21st Century.* London: Pinter Publisher.

Gallegati, M., S. Landini, and J. Stiglitz. 2016. "The Inequality Multiplier." Columbia Business School Research Paper No. 16-29.

Grossman, S., and J. Stiglitz. 1980. "On the Impossibility of Informationally Efficient Markets." *American Economic Review* 70 (3):393–408.

Kirman, A. 1992. "Whom or What Does the Representative Individual Represent? *Journal of Economic Perspectives* 6 (2):117–136.

Landini, S., M. Gallegati, and J. Stiglitz. 2015. "Economies with Heterogeneous Interacting Learning Agents." *Journal of Economic Interaction and Coordination* 10 (1):91–118.

Louca, F. 2001. "Intriguing Pendula: Founding Metaphors in the Analysis of Economic Fluctuations." *Cambridge Journal of Economics* 25:25–55.

Mas-Colell, A., M. Whinston, and J. Green. 1995. *Microeconomic Theory, Vol. 1.* Oxford: Oxford University Press.

Melitz, M. 2003. "The Impact of Trade on Aggregate Industry Productivity and Intra-Industry Reallocations." *Econometrica* 71 (6):1695–1725.

Nelson, R. 1959. "The Simple Economics of Basic Scientific Research." *Journal of Political Economy* 67:297–306.

Nelson, R., and S. Winter. 1982. *An Evolutionary Theory of Economic Change.* Cambridge, MA: Harvard University Press.

Radner, R., and J. Stiglitz. 1984. "A Nonconcavity in the Value of Information." In *Bayesian Models in Economic Theory: Studies in Bayesian Econometrics, Vol. 5,* edited by M. Boyer and R. Kihlstrom, 421–452. Oxford: Elsevier Science.

Rosenberg, Nathan. *Inside the black box: technology and economics.* Cambridge, Cambridge University Press, 1982.

Rothschild, M., and J. Stiglitz. 1976. "Equilibrium in Competitive Insurance Markets: An Essay on the Economics of Imperfect Information." *Quarterly Journal of Economics* 90 (4):629–649.

Schumpeter, J. 1936. "Review on the General Theory of Employment, Interest and Money by John Maynard Keynes." *American Statistical Association* 31 (196):791–795.

Shapiro, C., and J. Stiglitz. 1984. "Equilibrium Unemployment as a Worker Discipline Device." *American Economic Review* 74 (3):433–444.

Stiglitz, J. 1994. "Endogenous Growth and Cycles." In *Innovation in Technology, Industry and Institutions,* edited by Y. Shionoya and M. Perlman, 121–156. Ann Arbor: University of Michigan Press.

Stiglitz, J. 2000. "The Contributions of the Economics of Information to Twentieth Century Economics." *Quarterly Journal of Economics* 115 (4):1441–1478.

Stiglitz, J. 2012. *The Price of Inequality.* New York: Norton.

Stiglitz, J. 2013. "The Global Crisis, Social Protection and Jobs." *International Labour Review* 152 (Supplement S1):93–106.

Stiglitz, J. 2015. *The Great Divide.* New York: Norton.

Stiglitz, J. 2016. "The Capitalist Economy as a Credit Economy." Chapter 3 of Stiglitz, *Towards a General Theory of Deep Downturns: Presidential Address from the 17th World Congress of the International Economic Association in 2014*, 47–60. London: Palgrave Macmillan.

Stiglitz, J., and B. Greenwald. 2014. *Creating a Learning Society: A New Approach to Growth, Development, and Social Progress.* New York: Columbia University Press.

Stiglitz, J., and A. Weiss. 1992. "Asymmetric Information in Credit Markets and Its Implications for Macro-Economics." *Oxford Economic Papers* 44 (4):694–724.

Syverson, C. 2011. "What Determines Productivity? *Journal of Economic Literature* 49 (2):326–65.

Winter, S. 1971. "Satisficing, Selection, and the Innovating Remnant." *Quarterly Journal of Economics* 85 (2):237–261.

CHAPTER 9

Deleterious Effects of Sustained Deficit Spending

Edmund Phelps

Let me first say that I am in awe of Joe's vast contribution to economics. His ability to build a model with which to analyze some behavior, its causes and effects, is phenomenal. I am going to talk about a disagreement I have with him in *macroeconomic policy*—his choice models—but that takes *nothing* away from my admiration for his gigantic contribution to the stock of economic knowledge.

It's good to have a session on macroeconomics in view of the long slide in almost all the economies of the West. Labor force participation rates of men have suffered a particularly serious decline: In the United States, the rate slid from nearly 94 percent in the mid-1960s to around 86 percent around 2005 to around 84 percent now; in Italy, from nearly 89 percent in the mid-1970s to nearly 85 percent in the mid-1980s, and 81 percent around 2005; in France, from 86 percent in the early 1980s to around 83 percent in 2005.[1] Wage rates have slowed in one country after another since the 1960s—first in the United States and later in most of Europe. What is at issue is the *cause* and *cure.*

Joe Stiglitz says that the U.S. wage slowdown results from a weakness of "demand"—brought on by increases in inequality. Larry Summers speaks of "secular stagnation," which he says results from a deficiency of "demand." They and many other economists see increases in *deficit spending* to be a solution to the losses of prosperity.

Apparently, they are both relying on *Keynesian* theory—the family of Keynesian models. But, as I heard Bob Solow tell MIT students (in a course I had the honor of teaching with him in 1963), macroeconomics is a *collection* of theories. The Keynesian theory is just one of *several* theories. (In a little book of lectures, I identified seven schools of macroeconomic thought.) Joe knows this, but Keynesian theory evidently dominates his thinking on macroeconomic matters.

In the 1960s—a decade of extraordinary creativity, as Duncan Foley once commented—a number of macroeconomists started to venture away from the Keynesian doctrine that had grown dominant in the 1940s and 1950s. As you know, some upstart theorists built "microeconomic foundations" for a link from demand to employment dynamics. In arguing that the level of aggregate demand had no sustained effect on aggregate activity, they were subversive of Keynesian activism in monetary policy making. Another line of new models implied that sustained deficit spending was not just ineffective at sustaining high employment; it was actually damaging for employment—and not only employment.

I don't know who was first. I recall that sometime in the 1960s, Franco Modigliani presented a diagram in which the public debt creates a wedge between wealth and capital. A helicopter drop of public debt adds to wealth and depresses capital. He argued that the "loss of capital" reduced labor productivity, thus wages and maybe employment.

I also recall my 1965 book, *Fiscal Neutrality toward Economic Growth.*[2] In the model discussed there, public debt makes people feel richer than they are really are—they own debt on top of their ownership of capital—thus inducing households to consume more than they would have had they understood their lifetime consumption possibilities had not been increased by the public debt they held. My emphasis was on the corollary that, feeling richer, they cut back their supply of labor—entering the labor force later or retiring sooner. Of course, people might have been oversaving and overworking out of anxiety before the public debt was created. But, absent such anxiety, I concluded that public debt creation is damaging for our economic health.

In the second half of the 1960s, Ken Arrow and my former student Mordecai Kurz published several papers on fiscal policy, culminating in their 1970 book, *Public Investment, the Rate of Return, and Optimal Fiscal Policy.*[3] They note that the "viewpoint" in my book is "similar" to theirs while noting that my book "emphasizes the labor-leisure margin" and their book the "saving-consumption margin" (1970, 180).

There was another difference. I had worked within the framework of a finite-lifetime saving model while they worked with Frank Ramsey's infinite horizon. So, in my work the question didn't arise of whether *infinitely lived* worker-savers would be led to save less and work less by the increase of public debt. There was another unanswered question: I argued from my model that government *capital* expenditures ought to be *tax-financed*, just as the government's current expenditures ought to be tax-financed. I said that if the government creates an uncrowded bridge, then it's right to deficit finance the construction and service the debt with tolls for use of the bridge. But if in a rainy country the government creates sunshine with no possibility of user fees, there is no such case for deficit financing. The sunshine project ought to be tax-financed. Jim Tobin thought I was wrong about that—at least in Frank Ramsey's infinite-horizon framework.[4]

So, what is the answer? Would even the super-intelligent *Ramsey savers* be led to under-save and under-work when the government *deficit finances* its expenditures—even investment expenditure? I take an extreme case in which the state is engaging in sustained investment in some sort of public capital good—one that does not get into households' utility and production functions.

In the following appendix, I show that even in the steady-growth state, a *wedge* has been driven between *wealth* and *capital* in two ways: First, the steady-growth deficit *shifts up* the steady-growth path of private wealth. Second, the steady-growth public capital investment, in crowding out private investment, *shifts down* the steady-growth path of private capital. See the steady-state equations. In the phase diagram, the stationary locus of normalized wealth is shifted *rightward* and that of normalized capital per worker is shifted *leftward*. The saddle path in terms of normalized wealth is shifted up (and the corresponding path of normalized capital is shifted down). If the economy would have been in the *Golden Rule* state or short of that, the bloating of wealth would be harmful, and so would the crowding out of private capital. In a richer model, greater unemployment and reduced innovation might result.

APPENDIX:
INCIDENCE OF GOVERNMENT SPENDING AND PUBLIC DEBT

$$F(K, \Lambda L) = \Lambda f(k, L) \text{ where } k = K/\Lambda$$

$$\mathcal{L}_i = max \ \{U(C_i) * Z(1 - L_i) + Q_i \ [V L_i + r B_i - X_i - C_i]\}$$

where $U(C_i) = \dfrac{C_i^{1+E}}{1+E}$ and $Z'(1 - L_i) > 0, Z''(1 - L_i) < 0.$

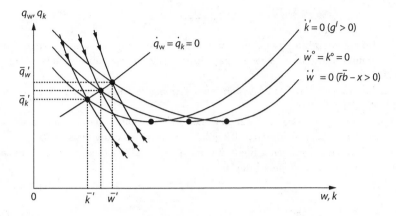

Figure 9.1   Time Path of Capital and Wealth, Given the Public Debt

$$\dot{w} = f(k,L) + rb - x - c - \lambda w, w = \frac{W}{\Lambda}$$

$$\dot{k} = f(k,L) - g^I - c - \lambda k, g^I = \frac{G^I}{\Lambda}$$

$$Z(1 - L_i) \, U'(C_i) = Q_i, \, U(C_i)Z'(1 - L_i) = Q_i V$$

$$Z(1 - L_i) \, U'(c) = q_w, \, U(c) \, Z'(1 - L)$$

$$= q_w v, \frac{\dot{q}w}{qw} = -(r - \rho) - E\lambda$$

where $c = \dfrac{C}{\Lambda}, v = \dfrac{V}{\Lambda}, q_w = Q\Lambda^{-E}, \dfrac{\dot{\Lambda}}{\wedge}, E < 0.$

Suppose $\Lambda = e^{\lambda t}$. In steady-growth sate,

$$\lambda \overline{w} = f\left(\overline{k}, \overline{L}\right) + \overline{rb} - \overline{c} - \overline{x}$$

$$\lambda \overline{k} = f\left(\overline{k}, \overline{L}\right) - g^I - \overline{c}$$

$$\overline{w} - \overline{k} = \frac{1}{\lambda}\left[\overline{r}_\lambda \overline{b} - \overline{x} + g^I\right](> 0)$$

$$\overline{r} = \rho - E\lambda$$

NOTES

1. Immigration into France and more strongly Germany has turned participation rates around. But one suspects the participation rates of the native population have declined.

2. Edmund Phelps, *Fiscal Neutrality toward Economic Growth*, New York: McGraw-Hill, 1965.

3. Kenneth J. Arrow and Mordecai Kurz, *Public Investment, the Rate of Return, and Optimal Fiscal Policy*, Baltimore, MD: Johns Hopkins University Press, 1970.

4. We discussed this on a flight, but our plane landed without our reaching an agreement. We never discussed the issue again.

CHAPTER 10

The Rediscovery of Financial Market Imperfections

John C. Williams

This conference is a fitting way to recognize Joe Stiglitz's numerous accomplishments and profound contributions across the field of economics as a researcher, a teacher, and a renowned figure not just within the academic community, but in the public arena as well. My remarks will focus on one small subset of Joe's vast body of research, that which deals with financial market imperfections and the macroeconomy. My perspective is from my seat at the Federal Reserve, both as an economist and policy maker. Before I go any further, I have to state that the views I express are mine alone and do not necessarily reflect those of anyone else in the Federal Reserve System.

In thinking about this topic, I am transported back twenty-five years to one spring day at Stanford, my first class of Joe's first-year graduate macroeconomics course. The required text was Olivier Blanchard and Stanley Fischer's *Lectures on Macroeconomics*, which, I should add, cost a credit-constrained graduate student a bundle. Joe began the lecture with the offhand remark that he assigned this book only so we could see what mainstream macro looked like, but in this course we were going to learn how the economy really worked. For the next ten weeks we were immersed in theories of imperfect information, moral hazard, adverse selection, credit rationing, and all the reasons the economy did not live up to the textbook description.

Recall that this was happening at a time when much of the academic macroeconomics profession was eschewing the Keynesian in favor of the frictionless, perfectly competitive, complete information, real business cycle theories. Joe was decidedly swimming against the tide. But with his enthusiasm, passion, and conviction, you'd never have known it.

Some perspective on this situation is useful. Back in the mid-1960s, when Joe started his research career, there was a growing appreciation that financial markets and the economy did not conform to the Arrow-Debreu ideal. This is reflected in the Fed's own macroeconometric model, the MPS model developed by Franco Modigliani at MIT, Albert Ando at the University of Pennsylvania, and Fed economists in the late 1960s.[1] The model featured a detailed accounting of the balance sheets of financial institutions and included important roles for credit rationing in the monetary transmission mechanism to housing and household wealth on consumption. Admittedly, the primary justification for credit rationing was not market failure, but the extensive regulations, including Regulation Q, that led to bouts of disintermediation and credit constraints in housing finance.

During the ensuing years, academic macroeconomic theory increasingly jettisoned these complications and confined itself to the fundamental determinants of financial conditions and aggregate spending, such as changes in technology. In the real business cycle (RBC) and related approaches, researchers fully took on board the arbitrage-free approach to pricing assets and delinking asset prices from economic decisions. This process culminated in the development and widespread use in central banks of dynamic stochastic general equilibrium (DSGE) models. Early DSGE models wholly abstracted from asset pricing, bank lending, and all other aspects of the financial system.[2] All financial flows were assumed to circulate effortlessly.

At the Fed, we were slow to abandon our tried-and-true models and jump on this bandwagon. In large part, this reflected the need to have models that are empirically relevant—that "fit the data"—so they are useful for forecasting and quantitative analysis. But it also reflected the human capital developed in the institution that valued insights and perspectives that were no longer in vogue.

In the early 1990s, around the time I joined the Fed, the staff at the Board of Governors developed a new macroeconometric model, dubbed FRB/US.[3] It eliminated most of the balance sheet apparatus designed to deal with Regulation Q and the explicit modeling of the banking sector. However, it did incorporate links between imperfections in financial markets and economic decisions. For example, the central role of internal financing was recognized through a corporate cash flow channel on investment. Similarly, household credit constraints were modeled as rule-of-thumb consumers. Although asset price risk premia were modeled in very stylized ways, they did feed into consumer and business spending decisions.

This was the state of play when financial markets started to set off alarms in 2007. To an outside observer, it might appear that we at the Fed were armed with macro models that were simply ill-equipped to diagnose the ills that beset the economy or devise effective treatment plans. And that would be half true. But, it would ignore the most important asset we had (well, besides the monopoly franchise to create unlimited amounts of reserves): The in-depth knowledge of the theories of financial market imperfections that Joe and many others had developed over the preceding forty years. Many economists and policy makers at the Fed—including then-Chairman Ben Bernanke and Janet Yellen—were steeped in the literature that had its intellectual roots in this research.

As events unfolded, I was struck by the immediate translation of abstract theoretical models to the real world—Despite the fact that the trend in macro for decades was to abstract from these issues; Despite the fact that many of the early problems were in capital markets or the shadow banking system, rather than traditional commercial banking; Despite the fact that many theoretical models focused on the nonfinancial business sector's decisions to invest and produce, while, at least in the early stages, the real-world problems were centered in financial firms. I could imagine Ben Bernanke thinking, "I have seen this before and I know what it means." Almost overnight, Fed economists and policy makers pivoted to applying the insights and tools they were taught—in many cases, back in graduate school—to understand what was going wrong, why, and what could be done to fix it.[4]

Three insights of the theoretical literature were key. First, owing to various information and market imperfections, the degree of credit rationing and its effect on the economy depends on the state of the world. Constraints that in "good" times may not bind and therefore may be invisible can have huge consequences during a period of stress. Second, financial and economic decisions depend on perceived probabilities of default. When those probabilities rise, panic sets in and everyone hunkers down—even those who should, in principle, feel safe—and economic activity collapses. Third, under extreme circumstances, these effects are so acute that credit is unavailable at any market price.

All of these ideas owe their intellectual roots to the research on asymmetric information and financial market frictions that started back in the 1960s and was developed over the subsequent forty years.[5] The details and names differed—whether it was called "the financial accelerator" or "credit rationing"—but the insights that grew out of this extensive line of decades-long research shaped our understanding of events and the policy responses that followed.

Three policies are particularly noteworthy in this regard. First, in addition to discount window lending to banks, the Fed used its emergency lending powers to provide liquidity to primary dealers and commercial paper markets, money market mutual funds, and securitization markets in response to parts of our credit markets shutting down.[6] Second, working with the other key regulatory agencies and the U.S. Treasury, the Fed's first stress tests, or Supervisory Capital Assessment Program, forced the largest banks to have adequate capital reserves in a severely adverse economic environment. This program was designed to overcome the private interest in avoiding stock dilution and assure that banks were far away from risk of insolvency, and thereby ready and able to get credit flowing again.

Third is monetary policy. Standard textbook theories saw little benefit from balance sheet policies. But, going back to the work of Jim Tobin, some economists had highlighted the potential for balance sheet policies to affect the economy in the presence of financial market imperfections. The aggressive use of purchases of mortgage-backed securities (MBS) and longer-term Treasury securities, more commonly referred to as quantitative easing (QE), became a critical and powerful tool of monetary policy.[7] These purchases worked by pushing up prices of Treasuries and MBS and related assets, fostering financial conditions that supported stronger economic growth. Although these effects were not in our off-the-shelf models, economists at the Fed and elsewhere quickly ramped up analysis and found ways to incorporate these effects in models and to analyze the effects of policy actions.[8]

This period of seat-of-the-pants analysis and cobbling together models with financial frictions has morphed into an extensive research program on the theory and empirics of financial market imperfections. Indeed, Gilchrist and Zakrajšek (2012) find that financial risk premium shocks are a major driver of economic cycles. Macroeconomists are busy building models that incorporate these frictions in a variety of ways.[9] Much of this research is still fairly rudimentary. Nonetheless, it represents an exciting rediscovery of the importance of financial market frictions in macroeconomics.

To sum up, we have, to some extent, gone full circle in bringing institutional details and market imperfections into macro thinking and models in the past fifty years. That brings me to a conversation I had with a colleague a while ago. When I explained that my macro teachers at Stanford were Bob Hall, Tom Sargent, John Taylor, and Joe, not to mention my LSE professors Chris Pissarides, Charlie Bean, and Richard Layard, he quipped that he now understood why I was so confused about macroeconomic principles. But what I have learned in the past twenty years is that this eclectic approach to studying the economy is the greatest gift my teachers gave me. And we did end up using Blanchard and Fischer's book in a later class, so that investment paid off in the end as well. More generally, having economists with diverse perspectives at the Federal Reserve—who learned from inspiring teachers like Joe Stiglitz—has served us and our country well over these very difficult past eight years and will continue to do so in the future.

NOTES

1. Brayton et al. (1997).
2. See, for example, Christiano, Eichenbaum, and Evans (2005).
3. Reifschneider, Tetlow, and Williams (1999).
4. Bernanke (2015).
5. See, for example, Stiglitz and Weiss (1981), Bernanke and Gertler (1989), Greenwald and Stiglitz (1993), Kiyotaki and Moore (1997), and references therein.
6. See Williams (2011) for a summary.
7. See D'Amico et al. (2012) and Williams (2014) for summaries.
8. See, for example, Gagnon et al. (2011), Chung et al. (2012), Chen, Cúrdia, and Ferrero (2012), and references therein.
9. Christiano, Motto, and Rostagno (2010) and Clerc et al. (2015).

REFERENCES

Bernanke, Ben S. 2015. *Courage to Act: A Memoir of a Crisis and Its Aftermath.* New York: Norton.
Bernanke, Ben, and Mark Gertler. 1989. "Agency Costs, Net Worth, and Business Fluctuations." *American Economic Review* 79:14–31.
Blanchard, Olivier, and Stanley Fischer. 1989. *Lectures in Macroeconomics.* Cambridge, MA: MIT Press.
Brayton, Flint, Andrew Levin, Ralph Tryon, and John C. Williams. 1997. "The Evolution of Macro Models at the Federal Reserve Board." *Carnegie-Rochester Conference Series on Public Policy* 47 (December):43–81.
Chen, Han, Vasco Cúrdia, and Andrea Ferrero. 2012. "The Macroeconomic Effects of Large-Scale Asset Purchase Programmes." *Economic Journal* 122 (564):289–315.

Christiano, Lawrence J., Martin Eichenbaum, and Charles L. Evans. 2005. "Nominal Rigidities and the Dynamic Effects of a Shock to Monetary Policy." *Journal of Political Economy* 113 (1):1–45.

Christiano, Lawrence J., Roberto Motto, and Massimo Rostagno. 2010. "Financial Factors in Economic Fluctuations." European Central Bank Working Paper 1192 (May). http://www.ecb.europa.eu/pub/pdf/scpwps/ecbwp1192.pdf.

Chung, Hess, Jean-Philippe Laforte, David Reifschneider, and John C. Williams. 2012. "Have We Underestimated the Probability of Hitting the Zero Lower Bound?" *Journal of Money, Credit and Banking* 44:47–82.

Clerc, Laurent, Alexis Derviz, Caterina Mendicino, Stephane Moyen, Kalin Nikolov, Livio Stracca, Javier Suarez, and Alexandros P. Vardoulakis. 2015. "Capital Regulation in a Macroeconomic Model with Three Layers of Default." *International Journal of Central Banking* 11 (3):9–63. http://www.ijcb.org/journal/ijcb15q3a1.htm.

D'Amico, Stefania, William English, David López-Salido, and Edward Nelson. 2012. "The Federal Reserve's Large-Scale Asset Purchase Programmes: Rationale and Effects." *Economic Journal* 122 (564):F415–F446.

Gagnon, Joseph, Matthew Raskin, Julie Remache, and Brian Sack. 2011. "The Financial Market Effects of the Federal Reserve's Large-Scale Asset Purchases." *International Journal of Central Banking* 7 (1):3–43. http://www.ijcb.org/journal/ijcb11q1a1.htm.

Gilchrist, Simon, and Egon Zakrajšek. 2012. "Credit Spreads and Business Cycle Fluctuations." *American Economic Review* 102 (4):1692–1720.

Greenwald, Bruce C., and Joseph Stiglitz. 1993. "Financial Market Imperfections and Business Cycles." *Quarterly Journal of Economics* 108 (1):77–114.

Kiyotaki, Nobuhiro, and John Moore. 1997. "Credit Cycles." *Journal of Political Economy* 105 (2):211–248.

Reifschneider, David, Robert Tetlow, and John Williams. 1999. "Aggregate Disturbances, Monetary Policy, and the Macroeconomy: The FRB/US Perspective." *Federal Reserve Bulletin* (January):1–19. http://www.federalreserve.gov/pubs/bulletin/1999/0199lead.pdf.

Stiglitz, Joseph E., and Andrew Weiss. 1981. "Credit Rationing in Markets with Imperfect Information." *American Economic Review* 71 (3):393–410.

Williams, John C. 2011. "Two Cheers for Bagehot." In *Challenges to Central Banking in the Context of Financial Crisis*, edited by Subir Gokarn, 333–347. New Delhi: Academic Foundation.

Williams, John C. 2014. "Monetary Policy at the Zero Lower Bound: Putting Theory into Practice." Working Paper, Hutchins Center on Fiscal and Monetary Policy. Washington, DC: Brookings Institution (January 16). http://www.brookings.edu/research/papers/2014/01/16-monetary-policy-zero-lower-bound-williams.

CHAPTER 11

Ambiguity and International Risk Sharing

Brian Hill and Tomasz Michalski

ABSTRACT

We address the problem of risk sharing in international finance in a novel way. Instead of studying investors with standard risk-averse preferences that allocate capital across different countries we consider a portfolio choice problem when investors exhibit ambiguity aversion and perceive ambiguity in assets issued in foreign locations. Firms issue contracts that can have an equity (participation in the risky project) and debt component (fixed payment). We find that increases in the variance of their risky production process cause firms to issue assets with a higher variable payment (equity). Hikes in investors' perceived ambiguity have the opposite effect, and lead to less risk sharing. Entrepreneurs from capital-scarce countries finance themselves relatively more through debt than equity. They are thus exposed to higher volatility per unit of consumption. Increases in perceived ambiguity lead to lower across-border capital flows.

1. INFORMATIONAL BARRIERS AND CAPITAL FLOWS

Capital stocks differ enormously between countries. Why would this be the case? One answer is that there are severe market imperfections in international capital markets. Neoclassical theory, however, points typically to other explanations. Under standard neoclassical models, if all countries had the same technology and there were unrestricted flows, capital stocks in all countries would be the same as rates of the return on capital would equalize. So, perhaps there are differences in total factor productivity (TFP) or institutions that explain the existing discrepancies.

The influential study of Caselli and Feyrer (2007) seems to indicate that this is the case, as they find that rates of return on capital are roughly equalized across a large set of countries, which one would expect if the allocation of capital was efficient. However, supposing even that this question is settled, there are other phenomena—such as the lack of international risk sharing or the home bias—which suggest that imperfections in the international capital market are alive and well. This is the point of departure of our analysis.

Suppose that investors are ambiguity averse, and cannot assess well the probabilities of various events affecting firms in foreign economies that issue risky securities. For example, they may be unsure about what is the proper distribution from which production shocks are drawn. In such a case, they may not invest as eagerly abroad as in their domestic economy and it is well known that this may cause a home bias to arise as in Uppal and Wang (2003), Benigno and Nistico (2012), or with information acquisition as in Nieuwerburgh and Veldkamp (2009). Empirically, for example, Gelos and Wei (2005) show that funds invest less in less transparent countries. What does this imply for the asset structure when issuers take this into account? What can be said then about international risk sharing, investment, and asset holdings from this perspective? How does the asset structure depend on the distribution of world wealth?

We argue that the answers to these questions in Hill and Michalski (2014) shed a light on important regularities found in data and the stylized facts about international finance. For example, despite the fact that developing countries' gross domestic products (GDPs) are perceived as being more volatile, they cannot obtain a high degree of risk sharing—insurance from different shocks provided by well-diversified investors—which would be predicted by a standard model of portfolio choice with risk. There is also a large home bias. Capital flows seem to be rather procyclical to emerging markets (see, for example, Kaminsky, Reinhart, and Vegh 2004). Such countries (and firms located there) often issue foreign-denominated fixed-rate bonds even if they have what Reinhart, Rogoff, and Savastano (2003) call "debt intolerance," i.e., run into sovereign debt crises under debt burdens significantly lower than developed countries. Firms with foreign-denominated debt face ballooning liabilities in the case of adverse exchange rate movements. There is a long-lasting concern that too much of international financing relies on fixed-rate debt but proposals to introduce output-linked securities such as Schiller (1993) have not been successfully implemented so far.

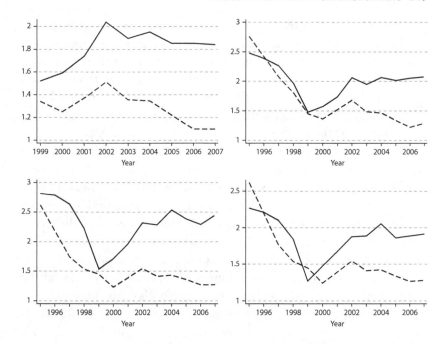

Figure 11.1   Ratios of Debt to Equity External Liabilities Among Net Capital Importers (solid line) and Capital Exporters (dashed line)

Upper left panel: A sample of all 177 countries available for years 1999–2007. *Upper right panel*: A sample of 29 OECD members (as of the end of 1996). *Lower left panel*: 15 European Union members as of the end of 1995. *Lower right panel*: 11 Eurozone members as of the beginning of 1999.

Source: Lane and Milesi-Ferretti (2007) dataset.

The available data on the issue, in figure 11.1 show that the share of debt in all public and private external liabilities of capital importers (countries with negative net foreign assets) is markedly higher than that of capital exporters in various subsamples of the Lande and Milesi-Ferretti (2007) data for the most recent years characterized by the freest capital flows. This is not necessarily driven by the "emerging" countries in the sample as the same patterns are observed for Organization for Economic Cooperation and Development (OECD) countries.

We propose a simple (albeit algebraically intense) model that is able to account for these phenomena. Firms have access to a risky production technology as well as investors' own productive capital that they would like to invest. Entrepreneurs issue contracts that promise a share in the risky outcome and a fixed payout (bond payment). Investors make their portfolio choices after observing the contract terms. Both the firms and the investors are risk averse, and maximize their utility of consumption (the residual of the payout to investors) and the net proceeds from capital, respectively. However, investors also perceive ambiguity in foreign-issued assets, to which they are averse. The problem is static with no default. We analyze the problem under different assumptions on investor ambiguity aversion and the distribution of worldwide capital ownership.

Our focus is different from the existing research on portfolio selection under ambiguity in that we are interested in the asset structure (which is typically assumed to be exogenous); capital allocation among countries with unequal wealth and the risk-sharing and consumption volatility implied by the contracts. A crucial assumption concerns the difference in the ambiguity perception of investors when considering foreign assets. More precisely, we assume that both home and foreign private investors perceive the same (reduced) distribution of productivity shocks for the asset offered by an entrepreneur, but that foreign investors perceive the asset as ambiguous whereas home investors do not. On the operational side, we use the smooth ambiguity model proposed by Klibanoff, Marinacci, and Mukerji (2005), in a specification provided by Gollier (2011). As shown by Maccheroni, Marinacci, and Ruffino (2013), this specification is an exact case of the equivalent of the Arrow-Pratt approximation for the case of ambiguity, and can be thought of as a generalization of mean-variance preferences to cover ambiguity. The advantage of this model is that the role of risk attitude, ambiguity, and attitude to ambiguity (e.g., ambiguity aversion) on portfolio decisions can be neatly decomposed. These ingredients allow us to have a tractable model that can be solved and analyzed analytically.

Main insights. In our model, each entrepreneur has a monopoly on her production process, but faces the following trade-offs. The higher the risk sharing (the share in the proceeds of the production process offered to outside investors), the lower risk that the firm carries, but also the lower the potential gains. As the entrepreneur promises a higher fixed payout, his consumption becomes more volatile.

We find that increases in the riskiness of the production process cause entrepreneurs to offer contracts with a higher risky share and a lower fixed payout—they effectively seek insurance from investors that are better able to diversify risk (by investing in many non correlated assets). This is as predicted by standard models of portfolio choice with risk (for example, the workhorse CARA-normal model). By contrast, increases in the perceived ambiguity, or in the investors' ambiguity aversion, cause firms to lower the variable part therefore insuring (or rather assuring) investors. The effect on the fixed payout can be both positive and negative, depending on other factors. Therefore, increases in risk and ambiguity concerning the firms' processes lead to different outcomes.

We also show that the contract an entrepreneur issues depends on the total wealth of his home investors. In countries with low levels of investor wealth (relative to others), firms issue contracts with higher fixed payouts and lower variable parts. Therefore, *ceteris paribus*, entrepreneurs in capital-scarce countries obtain less risk sharing than their counterparts in capital-abundant countries.

If we interpret the fixed payouts as bonds and the variable parts as equity, the model can thus reproduce the patterns observed in figure 11.1: agents in net capital-importing countries would on average issue relatively more debt. Investor ambiguity aversion can also solve the puzzle of why the observed degree of international risk sharing may be lower than what standard models predict. Firms in countries with a higher volatility of GDP may prefer to issue fixed-rate securities rather than obtain risk-sharing schemes if (a) investors are ambiguity averse to foreign-issued assets and (b) their domestic markets are relatively capital scarce. This explanation relies solely on ambiguity perception and aversion, and does not require that foreign investors possess less information than locals. It thus differs from another explanation that the characteristics of the productivity-generating processes of a country's firms are relatively less known in the outside world.

Firms in countries with lower domestic-based wealth attract less capital. Moreover, when ambiguity aversion of investors is not too high, firms in countries with relatively lower wealth issue assets with lower overall expected returns. Even with a lower installed capital stock, the marginal effective product of capital can be thus lower in countries with fewer domestic investors but not because the marginal return on *physical* capital is low (as for example, in Matsuyama 2004, due to low contract enforcement). So, in a world with ambiguity and ambiguity aversion, we can have equalized marginal returns of capital as measured by Caselli and Feyrer (2007), even in the presence of output gains from reallocating capital. Financial market imperfections may stem solely from ambiguity aversion and prevent capital flows from "rich" to "poor" countries.

Contract issuance under ambiguity causes the entrepreneur's consumption to become more volatile per unit of consumption as they promise higher fixed payouts to investors. The model thus offers a complementary story from the existing ones about why developing countries (i.e., associated with low investor wealth) may have more volatile consumption streams. Moreover, increases in ambiguity (opposite to increases in risk) can generate "capital flight," and increase the home bias. As a side gain, the model can deliver tractable expressions for the home bias or consumption correlations between agents in different countries and match their values obtained in the empirical literature for reasonable parameters.

Our work in context. The question of the composition of the contracts offered by emerging countries has been a subject of concern for a long time in international economics as witnessed by the long-time policy debates. There are several studies on the macroeconomic trade-offs of issuing various types of (fixed versus floating, short-versus long-term) debt or GDP-linked securities in calibration exercises after imposing a financial structure. Caballero and Krishnamurthy (2003) study why firms in emerging markets might prefer foreign currency—rather than local currency-denominated debt financing. Note that for firms, the standard moral hazard argument against governments issuing local currency-denominated contracts does not apply. Broner, Lorenzoni, and Schmukler (2007) and Jeanne (2009) investigate the maturity composition of debt issues. The asset issuance patterns discussed in these papers could be potentially also explained by investor ambiguity aversion either toward foreign currency-denominated bonds or long-term bonds.

The fact that there is limited international risk sharing between countries has attracted significant attention. Joseph Stiglitz pointed out many of his lectures that the standard models of portfolio choice with risk fail with the task of explaining the observed international capital allocation. Kose, Prasad, and Terrones (2007) examine empirically the patterns and possible causes. They find that industrial countries do attain a higher degree of risk sharing than developing countries. Emerging countries that had large cross-border capital flows have seen little change in their ability to share risk. The authors claim that this was due to the prevalence of portfolio debt financing. Bengui, Mendoza, and Quadrini (2013) investigate how well a standard business cycle model with different frictions can explain both the (low) extent of risk sharing (in the short run) that is observed in the data and the increase in international cross-holdings of assets since the opening of international markets. Both the canonical model with complete markets and perfect capital mobility and the one with the most severe form of incomplete asset markets (only bonds traded) fail to emulate the low degree of observed risk sharing. A model with port-folio rigidities (modeled as a convex cost of changing the stock of foreign assets) improves greatly the match with the data. This points to the direc-tion taken in this paper—that the extent of risk sharing may be affected by portfolio rigidities. Atkeson (1991) constructs a model with moral haz-ard and enforcement in lending and shows that countercyclical flows (and hence a lack of risk sharing) may be an outcome of an optimal insurance contract in the presence of the aforementioned frictions. Risk sharing in Mendoza, Quadrini, and Rios-Rull (2009) can also be affected by different levels of financial development (modeled as depending on the extent of an enforcement problem). In particular, a country with a well-developed financial system would have a positive net position in equity while having a negative position in bonds. Aguiar and Gopinath (2007) argue that shocks in emerging markets are perceived to be permanent to the trend of growth while they are transitory in developed countries. This helps to explain countercyclical current account behavior, consumption volatility that exceeds income volatility and sudden stops in emerging markets in an otherwise standard business cycle model of a small open economy with one-period risk-free bonds. In our main paper (Hill and Michalski 2014), we point to a complementary, preference-based explanation for some of these phenomena.

2. SKETCH OF THE MODEL

There are two countries, called country 1 and country 2, M entrepreneurs, or firms, of which M_c reside in country c. There is a measure N of inves-tors, each of which resides in a single country (with N_c investors residing in country c), and each with the same productive capital or wealth $w > 0$.

There is one period within which the timing of events is as follows. First, each entrepreneur communicates to investors the contract terms of hiring capital that they will irrevocably honor. They do this noncoop-eratively, and they compete monopolistically for funds. Investors observe these contract terms and make their portfolio decisions. Then capital is transferred, productivity draws are realized, output produced, and payouts and consumption take place.

Entrepreneurs. Each entrepreneur residing in a particular country has access to a technology that is governed by an i.i.d. stochastic process; for an entrepreneur n, the risky project which he can run has stochastic return x_n.

A typical entrepreneur issues a contract containing two elements. The first, $v_n \in [0,1]$, describes the share of the proceeds (or participation in losses) from his risky project. The second is riskless in terms of return (or payment demanded) of R_n. One interpretation of this capital structure is the standard distinction between debt (the R_n payment) and equity (the v_n term).

Once a firm n obtains capital k_n on the market, it invests in a risky production process. The outcome is given by $y_n = x_n f(k_n)$ where $f(k_n) = k_n$ and x_n is stochastic productivity that is unknown prior to investment. We assume that the firm has the same information as home investors and perceives no ambiguity with respect to its stochastic process; hence, it treats the stochastic return as being distributed according to the normal distribution with $x_n \sim N(\mu_n, \sigma_n^2 + \tau_n^2)$. Finally, we assume that productivity draws across firms in a particular country are independent, and that this is common knowledge.

The entrepreneur (firm) chooses contract terms so as to maximize his expected utility from consumption. The entrepreneur acts as a standard Bayesian decision maker with a CARA utility function with degree of absolute risk aversion A.

Investors. An investor l will allocate a fraction of his endowed wealth $0 \leq \alpha_{ln} \leq 1$ into assets issued by firm n, with $\sum_n \alpha_{ln} \leq 1$. Any uninvested capital yields zero return. Given that the most interesting situations are where there is scarcity of and hence competition for capital, we focus on these cases, and assume that investors invest all of their wealth in the existing firms.

Investors often feel surer in their judgments about assets from their own country rather than foreign assets. This intuition can be translated by the fact that investors perceive more *ambiguity* with respect to events concerning foreign assets (such as the realization of the stochastic return x_n) than events concerning domestic firms. To capture this we adopt the smooth ambiguity model proposed by Klibanoff, Marinacci, and Mukerji (2005). Rather than assuming that agents have a single ("known") probability distribution P for the returns of an uncertain asset x, the model allows uncertainty about the "true" distribution governing returns, which is represented by a (second-order) probability distribution over the possible distributions. Letting π denote this second-order distribution, decision makers choose assets x to maximize:

$$V(x) = \int_\Delta \varphi\big(\mathbb{E}_P\big(u(x)\big)\big) d\pi = \mathbb{E}_\pi \varphi\big(\mathbb{E}_P\big(u(x)\big)\big) \qquad (11.1)$$

where u is a standard von Neumann-Morgenstern utility function, φ is a strictly increasing real-valued function, and Δ is the space of probability distributions over values of x. As standard, u represents the decision-maker's risk attitude; by contrast, φ represents the decision-maker's *ambiguity attitude* (in the sense of Klibanoff, Marinacci, and Mukerji 2005, §3). Concave φ corresponds to *ambiguity aversion*.

This decision model has a natural interpretation in terms of model uncertainty (see, e.g., Klibanoff, Marinacci, and Mukerji 2005; Hansen 2007). The set Δ can represent the set of possible parameter estimates for a particular model of the stochastic process determining asset returns. The decision maker may be unsure as to which of the parameter values is correct: there may be a set in which all are plausible given the data. This *model uncertainty* is represented by the second-order distribution π. The functional form, with a concave φ, can be thought of as one way of incorporating considerations of robustness of one's choice across the possible parameter values.

We assume that an investor considers that there are several possible distributions for the stochastic return x_n ran by a firm n in a foreign country. For simplicity, we posit that he is sure that the returns follow a normal distribution. He is sure about the variance (volatility) of the return, but not about the expected return. So he considers plausible only distributions $\tilde{x}_n \sim N(m, \sigma_n^2)$ for some fixed σ_n^2, and some set of possible means m. His second-order prior over this set of distributions is itself normally distributed, with mean μ_n and variance $\tau_n^2 : \tilde{m}_n \sim N(\mu_n, \tau^2)$. Following the standard terminology, we shall call σ_n^2 (the variance of the underlying stochastic process) the *risk*. In this specification, the "extent" of the (model) uncertainty about the parameters of the stochastic process is summarized by τ_n^2, which we call the *ambiguity*.

Solution. To obtain a tractable model we use the specification of Gollier (2011). Each investor has a constant absolute risk aversion utility function of the form $u(z) = -(1/\theta)e^{-\theta z}$ where $\theta > 0$ represents the degree of (absolute) risk aversion. Each investor is ambiguity averse and has constant relative ambiguity aversion; the transformation function is thus of the form $\varphi(U) = -\frac{(-U)^{1+\gamma}}{1+\gamma}$, where $\gamma \geq 0$ represents the degree of (relative) *ambiguity aversion*. Risk aversion and ambiguity aversion are the same for all investors.

There exists a general solution for contract terms that are offered by entrepreneurs:

$$v_{i,1} = \frac{\dfrac{A}{\theta}\left(N_1 + \dfrac{\sigma_1^2 + \tau_1^2}{\sigma_1^2 + \tau_1^2(1+\gamma)}N_2\right)}{\left(2 + \dfrac{A}{\theta}\left(N_1 + \dfrac{\sigma_1^2 + \tau_1^2}{\sigma_1^2 + \tau_1^2(1+\gamma)}N_2\right)\right)} \tag{11.2}$$

$$R_{i,1} = \mu(1 - v_{i,1}) - w\theta\Upsilon_{i,1} \tag{11.3}$$

where $\Upsilon_{i,1}$ is an (involved) function of the parameters of the model. The expected return to investors on a unit of capital is then $R_{i,1} + v_{i,1}\mu = \mu - w\theta\Upsilon_{i,1}$.

Given this solution, one can find the capital allocation, calculate expected returns and the home bias, etc. We shall concentrate on the main differences between the "standard model with risk" and the model with ambiguity.

3. LESSONS

In what follows, we assume that all agents (investors and firms) use the same σ_n^2 and τ_n^2 for all firms in a given country: this corresponds to them perceiving the same values for the risk and ambiguity of all assets in that country (although their treatment of these values differs depending on whether it is a home or foreign country). We also set the means of the stochastic process to be equal across firms and countries $\mu_i = \mu_j = \mu$.

3.1. THE STANDARD MODEL WITH RISK
AND NO AMBIGUITY AVERSION

In the benchmark case with no ambiguity aversion $\gamma = 0$, investors act like expected utility maximizers and the portfolio choice problem collapses to a standard CARA-normal problem. This constitutes what we call "the standard model with risk."

The implications are immediate and unsurprising. All firms issue assets with the same contract terms irrespective of their residence, and investors hold identical portfolios. End capital allocation does not depend at all on where investors or entrepreneurs reside, but only on the risk of the firm's stochastic process: there are no frictions in the capital market. If firms in one country have more risky production processes, then they will choose to obtain less capital following the logic of the CARA-normal model. The level of equity offered does not depend on the variance of the firms' stochastic production process. In that sense, in equilibrium the entrepreneurs offload the same share of their idiosyncratic risk. If the stochastic processes are the same in terms of mean and variance, the entrepreneurs obtain the same level of consumption insurance and the same Sharpe ratio of consumption no matter the country in which they reside. Moreover, in this case, expected returns on all assets are the same in both countries.

Finally, as the environment becomes more risky (σ_1^2 or σ_2^2 increase), the interest rates offered by firms in equilibrium on their risk-free bonds fall (as investors value the sure return more and the demand for them increases). The overall effect of more risk on expected real asset returns is negative.

3.2. COUNTRIES ASYMMETRIC IN CAPITAL AND AMBIGUITY-AVERSE INVESTORS

Consider now the case of ambiguity-averse investors ($\gamma > 0$) and countries asymmetric in terms of capital endowments, i.e., the number of investors. To focus on the question of unequal capital endowments, we assume that the countries are identical as concerns risk, ambiguity and the number of firms ($\sigma_1^2 = \sigma_2^2 = \sigma^2$, $\tau_1^2 = \tau_2^2 = \tau^2$, and $M_1 = M_2 = \frac{M}{2}$), though may differ in the measure of investors. We assume that $N_1 > N_2$.

First, it can be shown that the capital invested in the country with a larger measure of investors is higher and the country with fewer investors is always a net capital importer. The latter allows us to identify the capital-importing country with the one with less domestic capital.

Contract characteristics and their consequences for asset composition. The situation in the presence of ambiguity is markedly different from the benchmark risk-only case considered in section 3.1. First, whereas in a world with no ambiguity aversion, all firms would offer the same contract irrespective of the initial investor distribution, in the presence of ambiguity, both contract terms are different between the two countries. We can prove that entrepreneurs from the country that is relatively scarce in capital, issue contracts that "insure" investors more, bearing more risk themselves (they offer securities with a lower equity participation). On the other hand, they pay a higher interest rate per unit of capital obtained. Both of these factors can be explained by the attempt to have access to the richer capital market in the foreign country.

This has two interesting immediate implications. First, entrepreneurs in the capital-scarce country issue relatively more bonds than equity. Hence, our model implies that capital importers will have a higher bond/equity ratio in outstanding assets; this is consistent with the patterns found in figure 11.1 and discussed in the first section of this chapter. Second, the nature of the contracts issued in the capital-scarce country renders entrepreneurial consumption there more variable when measured by the Sharpe ratio. This is a consequence of the ambiguity aversion of foreign investors, which renders it more difficult for firms in capital-importing countries to obtain insurance from shocks. Accordingly, to attract the desired capital, they must propose contracts that hinder risk sharing (with relatively low equity part v) and that exacerbate the variance of consumption (since more capital is obtained through bond issuance).

We would like to mention the links between this model to several important contributions of Joseph Stiglitz. First, let's frame the main assumptions in the Grossman and Stiglitz (1980) framework that studied informational market efficiency with fixed asset supply and greatly popularized the usage of the CARA-normal model. Looking at one country, we could map foreign investors into the group of less-informed investors considered there while the domestic investors to the well-informed ones. In the Grossman and Stiglitz (1980) model, if there are too many uninformed investors, the price system becomes less informative (and information can never be fully revealed). Perhaps a different set of contracts (also including risk-free debt) offered by entrepreneurs (as considered and suggested above) could partially minimize the problem: the better-informed investors could stock up on the risky (equity) assets. Although, of course, the Grossman and Stiglitz (1980) pessimistic result remains. Scarce information (in the sense of few well-informed investors) could lead to more debt financing. Second, Newbery and Stiglitz (1984) propose a pathbreaking model that argues that the opening of capital markets could be Pareto-inferior because of asset market incompleteness. In their production economy, both types of agents (producers and consumers) may be worse off than prior to integration (though for different reasons) as there are increases in risk for the producers and changes in the production allocation. In our model with market incompleteness, capital opening is Pareto-efficient and benefits the entrepreneurs no matter the parametrization; however, the volatility of their consumption increases *because* of the composition of contracts that are offered—and the increase in the share of debt financing. The latter effect exists unequivocally only in the capital-scarce country though it may occur also in the capital-abundant country (for the intuition, see the discussion in Hill and Michalski 2014).

Asset returns. As ambiguity aversion grows, entrepreneurs turn primarily to domestic investors for funds. In autarky, the expected returns are higher in the capital-scarce country as the competition for funds is fiercer. On the other hand, when ambiguity aversion is low, and foreign investors are ready to invest, the firms in the capital-scarce country compete with those from the capital-abundant country. In particular, when $N_2 = 0$ and country 2 firms compete with country 1 firms for capital then the expected return on assets is always higher in country 1. These patterns are in stark contrast to the case without ambiguity studied in section 3.1, where the expected returns are independent of the distribution of wealth. As such, it suggests another possible answer to the question of why the rates of return on capital found empirically may be lower than predicted by standard theories in capital-importing (typically also identified with "emerging") countries (see, for example, the discussion in Caselli and Feyrer 2007).

3.3. ONE COUNTRY WITH NO WEALTH

Further analytic results with asymmetric countries are possible for the case where one country has all the world wealth so that $N_2 = 0$.

It turns out that the end capital distribution between the two countries becomes more even with the increase in risk. Moreover, the interest differential between the two countries' representative firms' bonds decreases: $\frac{\partial}{\partial \sigma^2}(R_2 - R_1) < 0$. As risk increases and the effect of ambiguity gets "drowned out," the model comes close to the case where there is no ambiguity, and where there is no difference in capital distribution or contract terms between the two countries.

If the investors' ambiguity aversion (γ) changes it is as if they perceive foreign assets as carrying a higher effective variance. Then there is no change in the equity share offered in the capital-abundant country, but the interest rate R_1 declines. At the same time, as ambiguity aversion increases, entrepreneurs from the capital-importing country offer lower equity stakes and "insure" foreign investors by offering higher interest rates on the bond part of the contract. Moreover, the "weakening" of foreign competition allows the firms in the capital-rich countries to offer lower interest rates. In the end, the interest differential offered by firms in the two countries grows: $\frac{\partial}{\partial \gamma}(R_2 - R_1) > 0$. Despite this, the capital invested in the capital-scarce country decreases. The Sharpe ratio of entrepreneurial consumption in the two countries also diverges: entrepreneurs in country 2 need to accept more risk per unit of expected consumption.

The picture is more complex, however, as concerns changes in ambiguity (τ^2). Qualitatively, an increase in ambiguity is an intermediate scenario between an increase in risk and an increase in ambiguity aversion. As shown in the full paper, investors act as if they have different "effective" variances for domestic and foreign assets. It turns out that the "effective" variance of production processes perceived by investors increases for both home and foreign assets, though more strongly for the latter. Then $\frac{\partial v_1}{\partial \tau^2} = 0$, $\frac{\partial R_1}{\partial \tau^2} < 0$. As in the case of increased ambiguity aversion, firms from the capital-abundant country obtain lower interest rates as investors seek more "safety." However, the effect on the interest rate in the capital-scarce country cannot be signed. This is due to the interplay between the two forces. On the one hand, an increase in ambiguity leads to an increase in the variance perceived by all investors for all assets, so they are willing to accept a lower remuneration for holding bonds; this is the mechanism driving the interest rate down when the risk increases. On the other hand, the "effective" variance perceived by investors in country 1 toward firms in country 2 increases faster than the variance perceived toward firms in country 1, due to ambiguity aversion; this is the same as the mechanism that drives the interest rates in country 2 up when the ambiguity aversion increases. The interest differential $R_2 - R_1$ on the bond part of the contract may be nonmonotonic in ambiguity; for example, it may have a hump shape.

A "global" crisis interpretation of the model. Consider a general increase in risk and ambiguity. As long as the proportional increase in ambiguity is greater than that for risk, the discrepancy between the capital invested in the capital-abundant and capital-scarce country increases unequivocally. This observation suggests an interesting interpretation of global crisis events. If investors become suddenly less sure about the stochastic properties of productivity for *all* assets—if their ambiguity or "model uncertainty" increases—the model would predict a dramatically lower capital allocation in capital-importing countries. This could be an explanation for what happens during global crises, like the one in 2008, that does not assume some asymmetric shocks to peripheral capital importers, increases in risk, in ambiguity aversion, transaction or information costs: a general increase in ambiguity (or "model uncertainty") about the stochastic properties of economic fundamentals would produce the observed effects. Notice that, as observed above, such effects do not follow from a general increase in risk alone, but it does occur whenever the proportional increase in ambiguity is larger than that of risk. Arguably, situations of the sort just mentioned correspond more precisely to environments that have not gotten significantly more risky in the technical sense—of having higher variances for the underlying stochastic processes—but that do have large increases in ambiguity which means economic agents are less sure about the parameters of the stochastic processes driving economies.

CONCLUDING REMARKS

Inclusion of ambiguity and ambiguity aversion changes the properties of the standard model with risk and may be able to account for the reduced risk sharing and the existence of the home bias. Increases in risk, ambiguity, and ambiguity aversion have radically different, and in many cases, opposite effects on the capital invested internationally, the extent of risk sharing given by v and the interest rates R. This allows us to rationalize stylized facts about international capital flows with a simple model; in fact, the model can explain the different patterns of debt/equity issuance at the macroeconomic level.

The firms in our model can be interpreted as different idiosyncratic sources of risk in a country. The case where $M_1 = M_2 = 1$ can be interpreted as one source of risk or alternatively in terms of an assumption that all stochastic production processes within that country are perfectly correlated: one could have several separate entities issuing assets with the same characteristics (this would be the equilibrium outcome) that would be treated by investors as if they were the same asset. An alternative interpretation of the case $M_1 = M_2 = 1$ is in terms of holding a market portfolio of equity and bonds from that country. Generalizing this interpretation, a version of the model can be developed with several (that is, more than two) individual countries that noncooperatively compete for funds, yielding qualitatively similar results to those reported above.

In our base model described above, we assumed that assets from both countries are "ambiguous" to foreign investors to the same extent. We also analyzed a version of the model where investors are ambiguity averse toward all assets—domestic ones with the same degree as toward the foreign ones and one country's assets exhibit a higher ambiguity (τ^2) in the minds of investors. This corresponds to a situation where one country would be less transparent than the other one, for example, because of differing degrees of confidence in official statistics. The more "ambiguous" firms will then issue contracts with a higher fixed payment and a lower equity part. This provides another explanation why international risk sharing is limited in general.

Finally, let's discuss briefly how models with transaction costs or market imperfections such as informational asymmetries would work differently from ours. Analyzing models with transaction costs in international transactions yields, in principle, the home bias. But unless they are asymmetric across assets they should not affect the asset composition. There is no evidence that transaction costs increase in international crises leading to capital flight. On the other hand, pure moral hazard or adverse selection models have a difficulty in explaining the existence of the home bias. There needs to be a mechanism that differentiates the behavior between home and foreign investors to deliver differences in asset issuance between capital-rich and capital-scarce countries as well. While we by no means wish to suggest that such effects are absent, the ability of ambiguity to explain, such a diverse collection of phenomena, in tandem with the robust underlying intuition, leads in favor of further research into its possible consequences for international economics.

NOTE

This is a nontechnical summary of the paper "Risk Versus Ambiguity and International Security Design" (working paper), HEC Paris, 2014.

REFERENCES

Aguiar, Mark, and Gita Gopinath. 2007. "Emerging Market Business Cycles: The Cycle Is the Trend." *Journal of Political Economy* 115 (1):69–102.

Atkeson, Andrew. 1991. "International Lending with Moral Hazard and Risk of Repudiation." *Econometrica* 59 (4):1069–1089.

Bengui, Julien, Enrique G. Mendoza, and Vincenzo Quadrini. 2013. "Capital Mobility and International Sharing of Cyclical Risk." *Journal of Monetary Economics* 60:42–62.

Benigno, Pierpaolo, and Salvatore Nistico. 2012. "International Portfolio Allocation Under Model Uncertainty." *American Economic Journal: Macroeconomics* 4:144–189.

Broner, Fernando A., Guido Lorenzoni, and Sergio L. Schmukler. 2007. "Why Do Emerging Countries Borrow Short Term?" NBER Working Paper No. 13076.

Caballero, Ricardo J., and Arvind Krishnamurthy. 2003. "Excessive Dollar Debt: Financial Development and Underinsurance." *Journal of Finance* 58 (2):867–893.

Caselli, Fabio, and James Feyrer. 2007. "The Marginal Product of Capital." *Quarterly Journal of Economics* 122 (2):535–568.

Gelos, R. Gaston, and Shang-Jin Wei. 2005. "Transparency and International Investor Behavior." *Journal of Finance* 60 (6):2987–3020.

Gollier, Christian. 2011. "Portfolio Choices and Asset Prices: The Comparative Statics of Ambiguity Aversion." *Review of Economic Studies* 78 (4):1329–1344.

Grossman, Sanford J., and Joseph E. Stiglitz. 1980. "On the Impossibility of Informationally Efficient Markets." *American Economic Review* 70 (3):393–408.

Hansen, Lars P. 2007. "Beliefs, Doubts and Learning: Valuing Macroeconomic Risk." *American Economic Review* 97 (2):1–30.

Hill, Brian, and Tomasz Michalski. 2014. "Risk versus Ambiguity and International Security Design." Working Paper. Paris: HEC.

Jeanne, Olivier. 2009. "Debt Maturity and the International Financial Architecture." *American Economic Review* 99 (5):2135–2148.

Kaminsky, Graciela L., Carmen M. Reinhart, and Carlos A. Vegh. 2004. "When It Rains, It Pours: Procyclical Capital Flows and Policies." In *NBER Macroeconomics Annual 2004 Technical Report*, edited by Mark Gertler and Kenneth S. Rogo. Cambridge, MA: National Bureau of Economic Research.

Klibanoff, Peter, Massimo Marinacci, and Sujoy Mukerji. 2005. "A Smooth Model of Decision Making Under Ambiguity." *Econometrica* 73:1849–1892.

Kose, M. Ayhan, Eswar Prasad, and Marco Terrones. 2007. "How Does Financial Globalization Affect Risk Sharing? Patterns and Channels." Working Paper 07/238, International Monetary Fund.

Lane, Phillip, and Gian-Maria Milesi-Ferretti. 2007. "The External Wealth of Nations Mark II: Revised and Extended Estimates of Foreign Assets and Liabilities, 1970–2004." *Journal of International Economics* 73:223–250.

Maccheroni, Fabio, Massimo Marinacci, and Doriana Ruffino. 2013. "Alpha as Ambiguity: Robust Mean-Variance Portfolio Analysis." *Econometrica* 81 (3).

Matsuyama, Kiminori. 2004. "Financial Market Globalization, Symmetry-Breaking, and Endogenous Inequality of Nations." *Econometrica* 72:853–884.

Mendoza, Enrique G., Vincenzo Quadrini, and J.-V. Rios-Rull. 2009. "Financial Integration, Financial Development, and Global Imbalances." *Journal of Political Economy* 117 (3):371–416.

Newbery, David M. G., and Joseph E. Stiglitz. 1984. "Pareto Inferior Trade." *Review of Economic Studies* 51 (1):1–12.

Nieuwerburgh, Stijn Van, and Laura Veldkamp. 2009. "Information Immobility and the Home Bias Puzzle." *Journal of Finance* 64 (3):1187–1215.

Reinhart, Carmen M., Kenneth S. Rogoff, and Miguel A. Savastano. 2003. "Debt Intolerance." *Brookings Papers on Economic Activity* 1:1–74.

Schiller, Robert J. 1993. *Macro Markets: Creating Institutions for Managing Society's Largest Economic Risks*. Oxford: Clarendon Press.

Uppal, Raman, and Tan Wang. 2003. "Model Misspecification and Underdiversification." *Journal of Finance* 58:2465–2486.

PART IV

Networks

CHAPTER 12

Use and Abuse of Network Effects

Hal Varian

ABSTRACT

The term "network effects" has a clear meaning in the context of economic models, but it is sometimes confused with other concepts like increasing returns to scale and learning-by-doing. This essay is an attempt to clear up some of this confusion.

The basic idea of network effects was introduced into economics by Rohlfs (1974) over forty years ago. His original motivation was to understand why AT&T's Picture Phone flopped. Since then, there have been many other contributions to the theory of network effects. Shapiro and Katz (1994), Economides (1996), Shy (2001), and Rohlfs (2003) provide useful surveys and overviews.

Carl Shapiro and I helped to popularize the term in our 1998 book *Information Rules* (Shapiro and Varian 1998). Nowadays, the term "network effects" is used not only by economists, but also by lawyers, journalists, regulators, and the business community.

The concept is easy to describe: a good exhibits network effects if the value to a new user from adopting the good is increasing in the number of users who have already adopted it. This generates a positive feedback loop: the more users who adopt the good, the more valuable it becomes to potential adopters. This positive feedback loop also works in reverse: if adoption fails to reach a critical mass of users, the good or service may fall into a "death spiral" and ultimately disappear.[1]

A simple graphical model can be helpful in fixing ideas, so I will outline a model based on Rohlfs (1974, 28). Assume the value of adopting a product to consumer v is vx where $x \in [0, 1]$ is the number of consumers

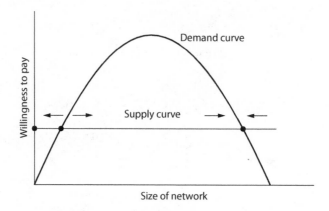

Figure 12.1 Supply and Demand for a Good That Exhibits Network Effects

Note: There are three equilibria, two stable and one unstable

who have already adopted the product and v is uniformly distributed over [0, 1]. Suppose the product is sold at price p. Then the marginal consumer has a value just equal to the price: $vx = p$. Everyone with a value greater than v will also adopt, which means $x = 1 - v$. Putting these two expressions together gives us the equilibrium condition

$$(1 - x)x = p.$$

The expression $(1 - x)x$ can be thought of as an inverse demand curve, as it tells you the price at which a fraction x of the market would adopt. On the supply side, we will assume that any amount of the good can be supplied at a constant marginal cost c. Plotting demand and supply together gives us figure 12.1, which is essentially the same as Rohlfs (1974).

We see that there are three equilibria: an equilibrium where no one adopts the good, an equilibrium where a small fraction adopts, and an equilibrium where a large fraction adopts.

We can add a simple dynamic adjustment process that says x increases when the demand price is greater than the supply price and decreases when the demand price is less than the supply price. With this dynamic, the zero equilibrium and the high equilibrium are stable, while the middle equilibrium is unstable.

The adoption rate associated with the middle equilibrium is known as the *critical mass*. An adoption rate higher than this leads to a virtuous circle of growth, while an adoption rate smaller than the critical mass leads to a vicious circle of extinction.

The concept of network effects is one of those economic ideas that you can explain to a regulator in five minutes and they can talk about it for five months. Unfortunately, in my experience, people often misunderstand the idea and attribute industry phenomena to network effects when it is inappropriate to do so. In this chapter I describe some of the misconceptions I have encountered involving network effects and the internet search industry.

1. DEFINITIONS

We start with three definitions:

Demand side economies of scale. The value of adopting a service to an incremental user is larger when more users have already adopted. (Network effects, network externalities.)

Supply side economies of scale. The cost of producing incremental output (or an incremental quality improvement) is smaller at larger levels of output. (Increasing returns to scale.)

Learning by doing. The cost per unit is lower (or quality is higher) the more output has been produced. (Learning curve, experience curve.)

I like the terms "demand side" and "supply side" economies of scale since they make the source of the positive feedback explicit. Network effects are due to value increasing with the number of units sold, while increasing returns to scale have to do with the cost declining or the quality improving as production increases.

The distinction between supply side economies of scale and learning by doing has to do with timing: learning by doing is usually viewed as depending on *cumulative* output, as in the original paper by Arrow (1962); while economies of scale have to do with the production level in a particular time period.

These forms of increasing returns to scale are driven by different forces. *Share* is relevant for the network effects story. In fact, it is built into the model as an assumption: a consumer's value for a product depends on its market share. By contrast, *size*, meaning the level of production, is what matters for returns to scale, not share per se. In the case of learning by doing, it is *experience* that matters.

In the economics literature, experience is often measured by cumulative output. Though this is a convenient modeling shorthand, it can be somewhat misleading as it suggests that "learning" is a passive activity that automatically happens as more output is produced. Nothing could be further from the truth. Learning by doing necessarily requires investment in data collection, analysis, and action.

As Stiglitz and Greenwald (2014) emphasize, learning is critically important to economic progress. Furthermore, learning doesn't "just happen," it requires investment at the level of the individual, the organization, and society at large. Gathering data is only the first step. In order to be useful that data must be turned into information, knowledge, and understanding.

Demand side and supply side economies of scale are important economic forces, to be sure. But they pale in significance compared to learning by doing, which, in my view, is the major source of competitive advantage in technology industries.

2. DEMAND SIDE AND SUPPLY SIDE ECONOMIES OF SCALE

Armed with the concepts described above, we can ask whether search engines, such as Google, Bing, Yandex, and Baidu exhibit network effects. Do you care how many other people use the same search engine that you use? Of course not. What matters is how well your search engine performs, not how many people use it. This means there are no traditional network effects in search.

In the early 2000s, there were a number of general purpose internet search engines: Alta Vista, Lycos, Inktomi, Yahoo, Microsoft Live, and Google.[2] In those days, it was common for people to use multiple search engines. As time went on, some search engines were able to improve their performance while others lagged behind. There was no apparent advantage to size. Indeed, the newest and smallest search engine appeared to perform the best and improve most rapidly. The result was an industry consolidation that resulted in only a few general purpose search engines.

During this same period of consolidation, we also saw the emergence of many *special purpose* search engines for local search, shopping search, travel search, and so on. These search engines tend to be focused on commercial topics, since that is where the money is. If we look at commercial search, rather than general purpose search, the industry structure looks very different. According to Soper (2015), 44 percent of product searches start on Amazon, 34 percent on a search engine, and 31 percent at a specific retailer. This observation is particularly relevant since the only searches that make money on general purpose search engines are commercial searches, since those are the searches that attract advertising revenue.

If classic demand side economies of scale are not relevant to search, what about supply side economies of scale?

Large internet companies such as Amazon, Google, Facebook, Microsoft, and IBM have data centers around the world. Several of these companies lease out part of their computing and networking infrastructure. This "cloud computing" technology has the advantage that new entrants can scale their computing infrastructure needs as their scale of operation increases. Data centers, which were previously a fixed cost, have now become a variable cost, leading to a dramatic increase in entry into technology businesses.

The hardware side of computing is now essentially a constant returns to scale industry. Customers can order compute cycles on demand. Suppliers—those who operate the data centers—can scale computing up by adding central processing units (CPUs) with more cores, adding more CPUs to the motherboards, adding more motherboards to the racks, adding more racks to the data center, or adding more data centers. At each level of aggregation, replication allows computing power to scale more or less linearly with demand.

The software side of computing is different, of course. Once you spend money to develop software, you can essentially replicate it at zero-marginal cost. In this respect, software is an embodiment of learning as described in Stiglitz and Greenwald (2014).

3. INDIRECT NETWORK EFFECTS

Some observers have claimed that search engines exhibit direct network effects since advertisers want to be where there are more users, and users want to be where there are more advertisers. However, it is hard to take this latter claim seriously, given the fact that consumers do not typically choose a search engine because of its ads. If anything, given a choice between two search engines, consumers would likely prefer the one with fewer ads.

If classic direct network effects are not at work with search engines, what about *indirect* network effects? This concept involves a somewhat more complex positive feedback loop. Think of an operating system where there are three relevant parties: the seller of the operating system, the developers of applications for the operating system, and the customers who buy both the operating system and the applications.

Suppose that two operating system vendors compete. Developers might find it attractive to develop applications for that system with the most users, and the users might find the operating system attractive that has the most applications. This leads to a positive feedback loop: more users leads to more developers leads to more applications leads to more users. The result is a winner-take-all market.

This is an appealing model, but it is not always in accord with the facts. After all, there are three major operating systems for PCs (Linux, Windows, and Mac OS), and there are two major operating systems for mobile devices (iOS and Android). So for both desktop and mobile devices there is room for more than one operating system. It appears that indirect network effects are not as powerful as commonly believed. Indeed, Bresnahan, Orsini, and Yin (2014) show that developers typically multihome and offer apps for both of the major operating systems for mobile devices.

4. NETWORK EFFECTS AND SEARCH

Here is a statement meant to illustrate how indirect network effects allegedly work in the search industry:

> . . . the online search and search advertising markets are characterized by "network effects:" the more users and advertisers use a given search engine, the more it is able to leverage data to improve its product and, by extension, attract more users and advertisers.

The key claim here is that "more users lead to more data leads to more product improvements which leads to more users."

This is not really a network effect, direct or indirect. It is a supply side effect: more data allows the search engine to produce higher quality products which in turn attract more users.

As we have already observed, more data does not automatically lead to a better product. Data is the raw material that serves as input into learning, but the learning itself requires an investment. If firms invest in learning they may achieve a competitive advantage over those that don't but there are no guarantees. Mere data by itself doesn't confer a competitive advantage; that data has to be translated into information, knowledge, and action.

Here is another claim that attempts to describe a positive feedback loop in the search engine industry.

> The higher the number of **advertisers using an online search advertising service**, the higher the revenue of the **general search engine platform**; revenue which can be reinvested in the maintenance and improvement of the **general search service** so as to attract more **users**. [Emphasis added]

Here, the feedback loop runs through the advertisers: more advertisers generate higher revenues, which can then be used to improve the service in order to attract more users. To see the problem, we just make a few substitutions for the bold words in the quote.

> The higher the number of **customers a business** has, the higher the revenue of the **business**, revenue which can be reinvested in the maintenance and improvement of the **business** so as to attract more **customers**.

Who would have guessed that building a successful business was so easy? Just get more revenue and everything else takes care of itself! This is silly, of course. But there are two separate reasons why it is silly.

The first is that serving more customers is generally costly. Sure, if you produce a very high quality product at a low price, you may attract many of the customers. But serving all those customers a high quality product may be expensive. When we account for costs, things look a little different.

> The higher the number of customers a business has, the higher the **costs** of the business, **costs** which must be **spent** in the maintenance and improvement of the business if **it is to serve that higher number of customers**.

So which is it that matters, revenue or costs? The answer is "both." As every economist knows, marginal revenue and marginal costs are both important in determining output. If you can produce more and better incremental output and sell it so as to generate incremental revenue that exceeds incremental cost, your profits will increase. But this has nothing to do with network effects.

This leads us to the second problem with the passage; when the concept is expressed correctly—using profit rather than revenue—it applies to any business.

> The higher the profit a business has, the more it can invest in the improvement of its business in order to attract more customers.

That hardly seems profound. The way to build a profitable business to . . . be profitable. Even if we view this truism as a profound insight, it is by no means clear that investment in improving a business is guaranteed to succeed. Every business wants to learn how to build better products at a lower cost, but not every business can succeed in doing so. Creating a learning organization—or a learning society—requires commitment and investment.

Finally, we consider the following passage about network effects.

> The network effects on the online search advertising side are due to the link between the number of users of a general search service and the value of the online search advertisements shown by that general search engine. The higher the number of users of a general search service, the greater the likelihood that a given search advertisement is matched to a user and converted into a sale. This in turn increases the price that a general search engine can charge advertisers if their search advertisements are clicked on.

As in the previous example, the passage ignores costs, so we will do this as well. The central claim is that a search engine that has more users can charge a higher cost per click (CPC). To investigate this claim, we need to carefully distinguish between advertisers and users, the two sides of this two-sided market. Let v be the value of a click to an advertiser and let $D(v)$ be the number of clicks from users that have a value greater or equal to v. If the search engine sets the cost of a click to be p, the number of clicks purchased will be $D(p)$—all of those clicks that have a value greater than p.

The search engine offers a cost per click p that maximizes expected revenue, $pD(p)$. By inspection, the revenue-maximizing price only depends on the distribution of advertiser values for clicks; it has nothing to do with the number of users. A search engine with twice as many users (and clicks) as another will have twice as much revenue, but will charge the same CPC to the advertisers, as long as the characteristics of the users are the same.

In actuality, most search engines use an auction rather than setting a price. However, the same analysis applies in setting the optimal reserve price.

5. DIMINISHING RETURNS TO DATA

One variation on the arguments advanced above is what is sometimes called the "data barrier to entry." The idea is that a large incumbent has a larger amount of customer data that allows it to build better products than potential entrants, giving incumbents an unassailable competitive advantage over entrants.

The first and most obvious point to make is that if there is a data barrier to entry, it must apply in all industries. After all, the incumbents are actually producing a product while the potential entrants are not producing that product. So virtually by definition, the incumbents must have more data than the entrants. Thousands of new businesses start up every year. The fact that they have less data than their incumbent competitors doesn't seem to discourage them.

But in starting a new business, is the problem with data or with knowledge? For example, I would like to enter the automobile manufacturing industry. Unfortunately, I know nothing whatsoever about how to build an automobile. Should that be considered a barrier to entry?

Knowledge is a critical part of production. In economic models, knowledge is embedded in the production function but in the real world, knowledge is embedded in people. If you want to start an automobile company, but know nothing about how to build a car, the first thing you should do is to hire some automotive engineers.

In the search engine industry new entrants—which started with no data—have often competed successfully with incumbents. Google wasn't the first search engine, but it had a better algorithm than the incumbents. Furthermore, Google was able to build an organization that continuously improved on that initial algorithm. The dot-com crash of 2000 was hugely important to Google since it allowed the company to hire experienced and highly capable engineers who were willing to work for options.

Today's successful businesses had no data when they started, but nevertheless they were able to acquire sufficient expertise to gain a foothold, gather what data they could, and extract information and knowledge from that data to create a competitive advantage over the incumbents.

Consider, for example, how Google acquired expertise in voice recognition in 2006. The first thing it did was to hire leading researchers in that area—they provided the knowledge. These researchers developed GOOG411, a service that used voice recognition for telephone directory services. The key insight the team had was to implement the voice recognition algorithm in the cloud rather than in individual devices. This allowed the algorithm to learn from the millions of directory requests. Within a few months, the algorithm became very good, and by the end of the year it became one of the best voice recognition systems available. A few years later, the Google Brain team was able to apply neural nets to the voice recognition problem and improve the performance by even more.

But other companies are making similar improvements. Amazon developed the Echo and set the explicit goal of reducing latency—recognizing and responding to the voice request more quickly than was previously possible. When the Echo was first developed, the average response time for voice recognition was around 2.5–3 seconds. The team set their goal at 2 seconds. But that wasn't good enough for Jeff Bezos, who demanded 1-second latency. They didn't hit that target but were able to get the latency down to 1.5 seconds, better than the other technologies available at that time.[3]

The lesson is clear: knowledgeable people can usually figure out a way to acquire data, but data can't acquire people, no matter how big it is.

6. DIMINISHING RETURNS TO DATA

Most inputs to production exhibit diminishing marginal returns and data is no exception. Consider the simplest statistical model:

$$y_i = \mu + e_i \quad \text{for } i = 1, \dots, n,$$

where y_i is some outcome, μ is an unknown constant, and e_i is some random noise with mean zero and variance σ^2. The parameter μ could itself be a function of p other covariates, in which case we would write $\mu(x_{i1}, \dots, x_{ip})$, but we avoid that complication for now.

Suppose that we estimate the parameter μ on a training set with n observations using the sample mean $\bar{x} = \sum_{i=1}^{n} x_i / n$. Now consider a new value of y that is generated by the same process, $y_{n+1} = \mu + e_{n+1}$. A natural estimate of this new value is $\bar{x}$. The error of this estimate is

$$y_{n+1} - \bar{x} = \mu + e_{n+1} - \bar{x}.$$

It is not hard to see that the expected value of this error is zero and its variance is given by

$$\text{var}\,\bar{x} + \text{var}\,e_{n+1} = \frac{\sigma^2}{n} + \sigma^2 = \text{estimation error} + \text{irreducible error}.$$

The estimation error goes down as $1/n$. The irreducible error is constant. A larger sample helps you get a better estimate of the parameter μ, but that effect dies out rather quickly, leaving you with the irreducible uncertainty that does not decline with the size of the dataset.

The relationship between the training set size can be visualized using a simple simulation. I construct a test set of 100 observations drawn from a $N(0, 1)$ distribution. I then estimate μ using 100 training sets with 100 generated observations. Figure 12.2 shows the estimated variance for the 100 training sets, along with the theoretical variance.

What about the more complex model where μ depends on some other features $(x_{i1}, \dots, x_{ip})$? Additional features may well aid in prediction,

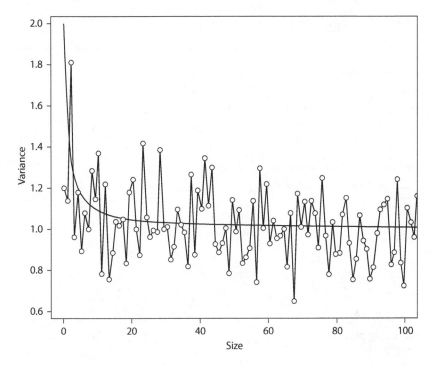

Figure 12.2   How the Variance of the Prediction Error Changes as the Training Set Size Changes

but a larger entity is not automatically able to observe more or better features. Indeed, a smaller entity that is clever about collecting features may well be able to outperform an entity with more data in terms of predictive accuracy.

SUMMARY

I have described three concepts: network effects, returns to scale, and learning by doing. Network effects are a demand side phenomenon (value depends on share) while the other two effects are supply side phenomenon (cost depends on the current or cumulative output).

The distinction is important since if value is positively related to share, the most value comes from a 100 percent share—a natural monopoly. On the other hand, firms with different cost functions depending on experience or other factors does not necessarily imply monopolization. Firms with different costs of production for quantity or quality can easily coexist.

Table 12.1 Competition Among Internet Companies

Product	Amazon	Apple	Google	Facebook	Microsoft
Operating systems	x	x	x		x
Browsers		x	x		x
Productivity tools		x	x		x
E-mail and messaging		x	x	x	x
E-books	x	x	x		
Smartphones and devices	x	x	x		x
Video and music distribution	x	x	x		
Streaming video	x		x	x	
Videoconferencing		x	x	x	x
Home delivery services	x		x		
General purpose search engines			x		x
Special purpose search engines	x	x	x		x
Digital assistants	x	x	x	x	x
Social networks			x	x	
Advertising platforms	x		x	x	x
Maps		x	x		x
Cloud services	x		x		x

In fact, if we look at the major high-tech online firms today, we see intense competition among the firms. As table 12.1 shows, they are all competing against each other in many different industries. This competition is why we see such rapid innovation and such low prices in the technology industries. It is also remarkable that these internet firms are competing with each other using different business models. For example, Microsoft sells an operating system to original equipment manufacturers (OEMs), Google gives away an open source OS, Amazon has adapted the Google OS for its proprietary hardware, and Apple sells its hardware and OS together as a bundle.

All these firms invest heavily in learning. At any particular time, they may have different capabilities, but they can overcome deficiencies by learning rapidly. At one time, Google knew little about operating systems or voice recognition, Facebook knew little about streaming video and image search, and Amazon knew little about selling cloud computing. But they learned quickly, and the knowledge that they have accumulated is the fundamental source of competitive advantage.

NOTES

The views expressed are solely the opinions of the author and do not necessarily represent the views of his employer.

1. One common confusion among noneconomists is that this latter effect is (erroneously) described as "negative feedback." With positive feedback, the big get bigger and the small get smaller, while with negative feedback, the big get smaller and the small get bigger.

2. Three of these (Lycos, Inktomi, and Google) grew out of the National Science Foundation (NSF)/Defense Advanced Research Projects Agency (DARPA) Digital Libraries research program, a prime example of how government research funding can contribute to innovation and productivity growth.

3. Eugene Kim, "The Inside Story of How Amazon Created Echo, the Next Billion-Dollar Business No One Saw Coming," *Business Insider*, April 2, 2016, http://www .businessinsider.com/the-inside-story-of-how-amazon-created-echo-2016-4.

REFERENCES

Arrow, Kenneth. 1962. "The Economic Implications of Learning by Doing." *Review of Economic Studies* 29 (3):155–173.

Bresnahan, Timothy, Joe Orsini, and Pai-Ling Yin. 2014. "Platform Choice by Mobile App Developers." Technical Report, Stanford University. http://www .law.northwestern.edu/research-faculty/searlecenter/events/internet/documents /Yin_multihoming%20v12py.pdf.

Economides, Nicholas. 1996. "The Economics of Networks." *International Journal of Industrial Organization* 14 (6):673–699.

Rohlfs, Jeffrey. 1974. "A Theory of Interdependent Demand for a Communications Service." *Bell Journal of Economics and Management Science* 5 (1):16–37.

Rohlfs, Jeffrey. 1994. *Bandwagon Effects in High-Technology Industries*. Cambridge, MA: MIT Press.

Shapiro, Carl, and Michael Katz. "Systems Competition and Network Effects." *Journal of Economic Perspectives* 8 (2):93–115. https://www.aeaweb.org/articles?id=10.1257 /jep.8.2.93.

Shapiro, Carl, and Hal R. Varian. *Information Rules*. Cambridge, MA: Harvard Business School Press.

Shy, Oz. 2001. *The Economics of Network Industries*. Cambridge: Cambridge University Press.

Soper, Taylor. 2015. "Amazon's Dominance of Online Shopping Starts with Product Searches, Study Shows." *Geek Wire*. http://www.geekwire.com/2015 /amazon-dominates-the-online-shopping-world-survey-shows/.

Stiglitz, Joseph E., and Bruce C. Greenwald. *Creating a Learning Society*. New York: Columbia University Press.

CHAPTER 13

Financial Contagion Revisited

Franklin Allen and Douglas Gale

INTRODUCTION

The financial crisis of 2007–2009 has demonstrated the importance of dislocation in the financial sector as a cause of economic fluctuations. The prevalence of financial crises has led many to conclude that the financial sector is unusually susceptible to shocks. One theory is that small shocks, which initially only affect a few institutions or a particular region of the economy, spread by *contagion* to the rest of the financial sector and then infect the larger economy. There is a growing literature on this phenomenon. An excellent survey is provided in Benoit et al. (2017). In this paper, we focus on contagion through interbank markets. Allen and Gale (2000) developed a stylized model with simple networks of four banks to consider the trade-off between risk sharing through interbank markets and the possibility of contagion originating from small shocks. They show that complete networks where every bank is connected with every other bank are more robust than incomplete markets where not all banks are connected. Recent literature has focused on more general models and a range of sizes of shocks. Elliott, Golub, and Jackson (2014) consider the role of integration and diversification. The former is concerned with how much banks rely on other banks while the latter is the number of banks a particular bank's liabilities are spread over. In the context of different models, Gai and Kapadia (2010) and Acemoglu, Ozdaglar, and Tahbaz-Salehi (2015) show that connected networks where all banks are connected to each other, at least indirectly, are more robust to shocks because of risk sharing than networks where they are not all connected. However, large shocks are more likely to make all institutions fail in connected networks.

In this paper, we again focus on the role of small shocks in bringing down the financial system through interbank market connections. We are able to show that general complete networks are more robust than incomplete networks. As before, we take as our starting point the model presented in Allen and Gale (1998). The assumptions about technology and preferences have become standard in the literature since the appearance of the Diamond and Dybvig (1983) model. There are three dates $t = 0, 1, 2$ and at the first date there is a large number of identical consumers, each of whom is endowed with one unit of a homogeneous consumption good. At the beginning of the second date, the consumers learn whether they are early consumers, who only value consumption at date 1, or late consumers, who only value consumption at date 2. Uncertainty about their preferences creates a demand for liquidity. In order to provide for future consumption, consumers have to save their endowment. Two assets are available for this purpose, a safe, short-term asset and a risky, long-term asset. We refer to these as the short and long assets, respectively. Uncertainty about their preferences creates a demand for liquidity. The long asset has a higher return, but it pays off only in the last period and is therefore not useful for providing consumption to early consumers.

Banks have a comparative advantage in providing liquidity. At the first date, consumers deposit their endowments in the banks, which invest them in the long and short assets. In exchange, depositors are promised a fixed amount of consumption at each subsequent date, depending on when they choose to withdraw. Early consumers withdraw at the second date while late consumers withdraw at the third date. The banking sector is perfectly competitive, so banks offer risk-sharing contracts that maximize depositors' *ex ante* expected utility, subject to a zero-profit constraint.

Bank runs occur in some states because the returns to the risky asset are so low that the banks cannot make the payments promised to their depositors. Depositors also have access to the short asset. If late consumers anticipate that their payout at date 2 will be less than depositors will receive at date 1 they will withdraw early, pretending to be early consumers, and save the proceeds using the short asset until the final date.

In Allen and Gale (1998), the returns to the risky asset are perfectly correlated across banks, so a low return causes insolvency in all banks simultaneously. A bad shock is thus tantamount to an economy-wide financial crisis. In the present paper, by contrast, we are explicitly interested in constructing a model in which small shocks lead to large effects by means of contagion. The question we address is whether and under what circumstances a shock within a single (small) sector can spread to other sectors and lead to an economy-wide financial crisis by contagion.

The economy consists of a number of sectors or regions. For simplicity, it is assumed that the long asset can be liquidated at date 1 or at date 2. The risk-free returns are $r < 1$ and $R > 1$, respectively. The number of early and late consumers in each region is assumed to be random. These liquidity shocks are imperfectly correlated across regions, thus providing the potential for insurance against the liquidity shocks. Regions with high liquidity shocks can obtain liquidity from low consumers. One way to provide this liquidity insurance is by exchanging deposits. Suppose that region A has a large number of early consumers when region B has a low number of early consumers, and vice versa. Since regions A and B are otherwise identical, their deposits are perfect substitutes and the banks can exchange deposits at the first date without affecting their net wealth. After the liquidity shocks are observed, one region will have a high demand for liquidity and one will have a low demand. Suppose region A has a higher than average number of early consumers. Then banks in region A can meet their obligations by liquidating some of their deposits in the banks of region B. Region B is happy to oblige, because it has an excess supply of liquidity in the form of the short asset. Later, banks in region B will want to liquidate the deposits they hold in the banks of region A to meet the above-average demand from late consumers in region B. The banks in region A can meet this demand because they have a below-average number of late consumers, that is, an excess supply of the long asset.

In general, whenever the liquidity shocks in different regions are less than perfectly correlated, banks can improve the risk sharing they offer to depositors through cross holdings of deposits. In certain circumstances, it can be shown that complete risk sharing can be achieved in this way: as long as all the regions are connected in a particular way and there is no aggregate uncertainty across all regions, then the first-best allocation can be decentralized through a competitive banking sector.

Inter-regional cross holdings have another role: they create an interdependency among the regions that is one of the ingredients needed for financial contagion. Financial contagion is a complicated phenomenon and it requires several preconditions. The first one has already been mentioned, the financial interconnectedness that arises from cross holdings of deposits or other financial claims. The second element is that there must be an aggregate shortage of liquidity. To understand what this means, we need to be more precise about the conditions of individual banks. We distinguish three conditions in which banks can find themselves at the second date, after uncertainty has been resolved. A bank is solvent if the demand for withdrawals is less than the value of liquid assets (the short asset plus net holdings of deposits in other banks). A bank is insolvent if it can meet the demand for withdrawals, but only by liquidating the long asset at date 1. It can reduce the payout to late consumers as long as it pays them as much as the early consumers (otherwise there will be a run). The value of the long asset that can be liquidated at the second date, consistently with the incentive constraint, is called the bank's buffer. This buffer, added to the value of liquid assets, is the maximum that the bank can provide in the second period, without provoking a run. Bankruptcy occurs when the demand for withdrawals is greater than the sum of the liquid assets and the buffer. Then the late consumers run and all the creditors cash in their claims. The bank is forced to liquidate all its assets and still cannot meet its promised payments.

Banks try to avoid insolvency, because liquidating the long asset reduces the value of the bank. Instead of getting a return of R per unit at date 2, they get a return of r per unit at date 1. As long as the bank has more of the short asset than it needs, it is happy to redeem its deposits by paying out the short asset. When the bank does not have an excess supply of the short asset, it tries to meet any shortfall by liquidating deposits in other banks. The problem arises when there is a global excess demand for the short asset. Cross holdings of deposits can be used to redistribute excess supplies of the short asset among regions but they cannot increase the total amount of the short asset in existence at date 1. So, when there is an economy-wide excess demand for the short asset, it can only be met by liquidating the long asset, but banks will only do this if they are forced to do so, that is, if the demand for withdrawals is greater than the liquid assets the bank holds.

Suppose that the global excess demand for liquidity is attributable to an extremely high demand for liquidity (number of early consumers) in one region. While the excess demand for liquidity may be small by comparison to the entire economy, it may be very large in relation to the region's assets, large enough to cause bankruptcy in that region. If the banks in this region were able to call upon the other regions, by withdrawing the deposits held in those regions, then it could possibly avoid bankruptcy. But the banks in other regions do not want to provide liquidity and they can avoid doing so by using their extra-regional deposits strategically. For example, suppose that region A has a high demand for liquidity and region B has an average demand for liquidity. Region B has just enough of the short asset to meet the demands of its own depositors, without giving anything to banks in region A. The two regions have the same number of extra-regional deposits. If region A tries to liquidate its deposits in region B to get more liquidity, then region B will avoid liquidating the long asset by liquidating its claims on banks in region A instead. These two transactions cancel out, leaving region A no better off. Even if there are many regions and the pattern of cross holdings is complicated, the same principle applies. As long as region A is merely insolvent, it cannot force the other regions to provide liquidity.

Things are different once banks in region A become bankrupt, because then a deposit in region A is worth less than a deposit in region B. If the banks in various regions simultaneously try to liquidate their cross holdings, there will be a transfer of value to the bankrupt regions. This spillover is what allows for the possibility of contagion, but whether contagion occurs or not depends crucially on the form of connectedness between regions as well as the other parameters of the model.

If every region is connected to every other region, then there may be no contagion at all. Suppose that markets are complete, in the sense that a bank in one region can hold deposits in all other regions. Then bankruptcy in one region will put pressure on all of the banks. However, if there are many regions, so that the number of bankrupt banks is small relative to the total number of banks, the transfer that each region has to make will be small and that region's buffer will be big enough to cover the transfer demanded. As a result, there may be insolvency but no bankruptcy outside the troubled region.

The impact of insolvency in one region is quite different if markets are incomplete, in the sense that the banks in one region are able to hold deposits in only a few of the other regions. In this case, the transfer occasioned by bank runs in one region fall initially on a few regions outside the initially troubled region. The total size of the buffer held by these regions may not be enough to sustain the demands made on it and those regions directly connected to the initially troubled region may be driven into bankruptcy. Once this happens, it is easier for the contagion to spread. There is now a group of bankrupt regions, in which the run by depositors has forced the banks to liquidate all their assets, with a consequent loss in value. Furthermore, their claims on the remaining solvent regions may be smaller in proportion to their liabilities than in the original region where the contagion began. This is because their claims on each other are now of less value. And so it may be easier, under certain conditions, for the contagion to spread. We provide conditions under which insolvency will spread to all the regions by contagion when markets are incomplete, and there would be no contagion if markets were complete.

It is important to note the importance of the free-rider problem in explaining the difference between complete and incomplete markets. With complete markets, every bank in every region suffers a loss from the troubled region. There is no way to avoid paying one's share. With incomplete markets, the banks in the troubled region have a direct claim only on the banks in a small number of regions. The banks in those regions have claims on banks in other regions and indirectly on all the regions. But as long as the regions are solvent, they can decline to offer liquidity if it means liquidating the long asset. They do this by liquidating their deposits in other regions instead. The effect of this policy is to make things worse for the regions that are directly connected to the troubled region, to the point where they too become insolvent. At that point, some of the regions that refused to provide liquidity find themselves on the frontline, holding claims on insolvent regions. The attempt to protect oneself by hoarding liquidity and refusing to liquidate costly assets proves ultimately self-defeating and makes the situation worse.

The rest of the paper is organized as follows.

1. LIQUIDITY PREFERENCE

In this section, we describe a simple model in which liquidity preference leads to a demand for risk-sharing contracts. The framework borrows from the models in Diamond and Dybvig (1983) and Allen and Gale (1998), with some significant differences.

Dates. There are three dates $t = 0, 1, 2$.

Goods. At each date there is a single consumption good, which serves as a numeraire. This good can also be invested to provide for future consumption. Each consumer is endowed with one unit of the good at date 0 and nothing at the subsequent dates.

Assets. There are two types of assets, a liquid asset (the *short asset*) and an illiquid asset (the *long asset*).

- The short asset is represented by a storage technology. An investment of one unit of the good at date $t = 0, 1$ yields one unit of the good at date $t + 1$.

- Investment in the long asset can only be made at date 0. One unit of the good invested in the long asset at date 0 produces R units of the good at date 2. The long asset can be prematurely liquidated at date 1, in which case it yields a liquidation value of r per unit. We assume that $0 < r < 1 < R$. The decision whether to liquidate the asset at date 1 or to let it mature at date 2 is made at the beginning of date 1.

Regions. There are n (*ex ante*) identical regions $i = 1,...,n$. In each region there is a continuum of (*ex ante*) identical consumers. Let $0 < \omega^i < 1$ be the random fraction of early consumers in region i and $1 - \omega^i$ be the random fraction of late consumers.

Uncertainty. The (finite) set of states of nature is denoted by Ω with generic element $\omega = (\omega^1,...,\omega^n)$ and probability density $p(\omega) > 0$. The random variables $\{\omega^i\}$ are *exchangeable*: for any permutation $\pi : \{1,...,n\} \rightarrow \{1,...,n\}$ and any state $\omega = (\omega^1,...,\omega^n)$, the state ω' defined by putting

$$\omega' = (\omega^{\pi(1)},...,\omega^{\pi(n)})$$

also belongs to Ω and satisfies $p(\omega) = p(\omega')$. In particular, this implies that the random variables $\{\omega^i\}$ have the same marginal distributions.

Information. All uncertainty is resolved at date 1 when each consumer observes the state of nature ω and learns whether he is an early or late consumer. A consumer's type is not observable, so late consumers can always imitate early consumers.

Preferences. A typical consumer's utility function in region i can be written as

$$U^i(c_1,c_2) = \begin{cases} u(c_1) & \text{with probability } \omega^i \\ u(c_2) & \text{with probability } 1 - \omega^i, \end{cases} \tag{13.1}$$

where c_t denotes consumption at date $t = 1,2$. The period utility functions $u(\cdot)$ are assumed to be twice continuously differentiable, increasing and strictly concave.

Since ω^i is also the probability of being an early consumer at date 1, the welfare of a consumer at date 0 is given by the expected utility

$$\sum_{\omega \in \Omega} p(\omega)\{\omega^i u(c_1(\omega)) + (1 - \omega^i)u(c_2(\omega))\}.$$

The role of banks is to make investments on behalf of consumers. We assume that only banks can distinguish the genuine long assets from assets that have no value. Any consumer who tries to purchase the long asset faces an extreme adverse selection problem, so in practice only banks will hold the long asset. This gives the bank an advantage over consumers in two respects. First, the banks can hold a portfolio consisting of both types of assets, which will typically be preferred to a portfolio consisting of the short asset alone. Second, by pooling the assets of a large number of consumers, the bank can offer insurance to consumers against their uncertain liquidity demands, giving the early consumers some of the benefits of the high-yielding risky asset without subjecting them to the volatility of the asset market.

Free entry into the banking industry forces banks to compete by offering deposit contracts that maximize the expected utility of the consumers. Thus, the behavior of the banking industry in each region can be represented by an optimal risk-sharing problem. The behavior of banks will be discussed in more detail later, when we describe an equilibrium with decentralized banking. First, however, we look at a benchmark case where a central planner makes optimal decisions on behalf of the consumers in all regions.

2. OPTIMAL RISK SHARING

The planner is assumed to maximize the sum of the consumer's expected utilities. The planner holds a portfolio (x_t, y_t) at the end of date $t = 0,1$, where x_t is the total amount of the long asset and y_t is the total amount of the short asset. Consumption in region i at date $t = 1,2$ is denoted by $c_t^i(\omega)$ and depends on the state, which is revealed at the beginning of date 1. The general problem can be written as follows:

$$(P1) \begin{cases} \max & \sum_{i=1}^{n} \sum_{\omega \in \Omega} p(\omega) \left\{ \omega^i u\left(c_1^i(\omega)\right) + \left(1 - \omega^i\right) u\left(c_2^i(\omega)\right) \right\} \\ \text{s.t.} & \text{(i)} \quad x_0 + y_0 \leq n; \\ & \text{(ii)} \quad \sum_{i=1}^{n} \omega^i c_1^i(\omega) \leq y_0 - y_1(\omega) + r\left(x_0 - x_1(\omega)\right); \\ & \text{(iii)} \quad \sum_{i=1}^{n} \left(1 - \omega^i\right) c_2^i(\omega) \leq y_1(\omega) + R x_1(\omega); \\ & \text{(iv)} \quad c_1^i(\omega) \leq c_2^i(\omega). \end{cases}$$

The objective function is the sum of expected utilities. Conditions (i), (ii), and (iii) are the budget constraints at dates 0, 1, and 2, respectively. The last constraint, condition (iv), is the incentive constraint, which says that late consumers do not wish to imitate early consumers in any region and in any state.

We begin by studying a modified problem in which the incentive constraint (iv) is omitted. The set of attainable consumption allocations $\{(c_1^i, c_2^i)\}$ in the modified problem is convex and the utility function $u(\cdot)$ is concave. It follows from general risk-sharing principles that consumption will be uniform across regions and that aggregate consumption depends only on the aggregate shock $\hat{\omega} \equiv \sum_{i=1}^n \omega^i$. Then we can write the planner's problem in a simpler form, treating consumption $(c_1(\hat{\omega}), c_2(\hat{\omega}))$ as a function of $\hat{\omega}$ and the date only. With a slight abuse of notation, we write $p(\hat{\omega})$ for the probability of $\hat{\omega}$. Then the planner has to choose a total investment x_0 in the long asset, a total investment y_0 in the short asset, an amount of the long asset $x_1(\hat{\omega})$ to carry through to date 2, an amount $y_1(\hat{\omega})$ of the short asset to carry through to date 2, the consumption $c_1(\hat{\omega})$ of an early consumer, and the consumption $c_2(\hat{\omega})$ of a late consumer in order to maximize the typical consumer's expected utility. Note that the initial investment portfolio (x_0, y_0) does not depend on $\hat{\omega}$ because the planner does not yet know the value of $\hat{\omega}$. However, all the decisions made at date 1 and date 2 depend on $\hat{\omega}$, which is revealed at the beginning of date 1.

The modified risk-sharing problem can be written in per capita terms as follows:

$$
(P2) \begin{cases}
\max & \sum_{\hat{\omega}} p(\hat{\omega}) \left\{ \hat{\omega} u \left(c_1(\hat{\omega}) \right) + (1 - \hat{\omega}) u \left(c_2(\hat{\omega}) \right) \right\} \\
\text{s.t.} & \text{(i)} \quad x_0 + y_0 \leq n; \\
& \text{(ii)} \quad \hat{\omega} c_1(\hat{\omega}) \leq y_0 - y_1(\hat{\omega}) + r\left(x_0 - x_1(\hat{\omega}) \right); \\
& \text{(iii)} \quad (1 - \hat{\omega}) c_2(\hat{\omega}) \leq y_1(\hat{\omega}) + R x_1(\hat{\omega}).
\end{cases}
$$

This problem is easy to solve and it turns out that it satisfies the first-order condition

$$
u'(c_1(\hat{\omega})) \geq u'(c_2(\hat{\omega})).
$$

If this condition were not satisfied for some aggregate shock $\hat{\omega}$, the objective function could be increased by using the short asset to shift some consumption from early to late consumers. Thus, a solution to (P2) satisfies the incentive constraints of (P1) and hence must be a solution to (P1). In particular, this means that a solution to (P1) achieves the first best because the incentive constraints are nonbinding.

Theorem 1. *The planner's risk-sharing problem (P1) is equivalent to the modified problem (P2). From this it follows that the solution to the planner's problem is first-best efficient, that is, the incentive constraints do not bind.*

It is worth noting the special case in which there is no aggregate uncertainty, that is, $\hat{\omega}$ is a constant across all states of nature. In that case, the optimum consumption profile (c_1, c_2) is nonstochastic. This case is of particular interest in the sequel because, when there is no aggregate uncertainty, the first best can be decentralized using standard (noncontingent) deposits.

3. EQUILIBRIUM

In this section, we describe the working of a decentralized banking system. But first, we need to specify the banks' investments.

The central planner in section 2 can insure consumers against liquidity shocks by reallocating goods across regions. Unlike the central planner, the banks cannot directly allocate goods across regions. Instead they must operate through an *interbank market* in financial claims. The kinds of claims allowed in this model are deposits, that is, banks can trade bank deposits in different regions in order to provide insurance against liquidity shocks. Since deposits are homogeneous within a region, we can assume that a bank in region i is only interested in holding deposits in a representative bank in any other region j. To allow for the possibility that markets are not complete, we introduce the notion of a market structure.

Market structure: For any region i there is a set of neighboring or adjacent regions $N^i \subset \{1, \ldots, i-1, i+1, \ldots n\}$. A bank in region i is allowed to hold deposits in a representative bank in the regions $j \in N^i$ and is not allowed to hold deposits in banks in regions $j \notin N^i$. Consumers can only hold deposits in a bank in their own region.

The interbank deposit market is said to be *complete* if banks are allowed to hold deposits in all other regions, that is,

$$N^i = \{1, \ldots, i-1, i+1, \ldots n\}$$

for each region i. Otherwise the interbank market is said to be *incomplete*. Whether the interbank market is complete or incomplete, we always assume that all the regions are connected in an intuitive sense. Region i is *directly connected* to region j if $j \in N^i$. Region i is *indirectly connected* to region j if there exists a sequence $\{i_1, ..., i_K\}$ such that $i_1 = i$, $i_K = j$, and i_k is directly connected to region i_{k+1} for $k = 1, ..., K - 1$. Finally, the deposit market is said to be *connected* if, for every ordered pair of regions (i, j) with $i \neq j$, region i is (indirectly) connected to region j.

In each region i there is a continuum of identical banks. All banks in a given region are assumed to behave in the same way and all consumers in a given region are assumed to behave in the same way. Thus, we can describe an equilibrium in terms of the behavior of a representative bank and representative consumer (or one early and one late consumer at dates $t = 1, 2$) in each region.

At the first date, consumers in region i can deposit their endowment of the consumption good with a bank in exchange for a *deposit contract* that promises them either c_1^i units of the good at date 1 or c_2^i units of the good at date 2. The bank will not necessarily keep this promise and a lot of attention will be paid in what follows to the rules governing the bank when it is unable to meet its commitments.

Each bank in region i takes the resources deposited by the consumers and invests them in a portfolio (x_0^i, y_0^i, z_0^i) consisting of $x_0^i \geq 0$ units of the short asset, $y_0^i \geq 0$ units of the short asset and an admissible portfolio of deposits $z_0^i \geq 0$ held in other regions. A deposit portfolio for region i is an $(n-1)$-tuple $z_0^i = (z_1^i, ..., z_{i-1}^i, z_{i+1}^i, ..., z_n^i)$, where z_{0j}^i is the number of deposits in region j held by the bank in region i. The portfolio z_0^i is admissible if $z_{0j}^i = 0$ for any region j that is not adjacent to i, that is, $j \notin N^i$. Let Z^i denote the admissible set of portfolios for region i.

At the beginning of the second period, the state of nature ω is observed and individual consumers learn whether they are early consumers or late consumers. Late consumers can calculate whether they are better off withdrawing their deposits immediately or waiting to withdraw their deposits in the last period. If it is weakly optimal to wait we assume that they do so in equilibrium; otherwise they withdraw immediately. In the latter case, there is a run and the bank is forced to liquidate all its assets in order to meet the demands of the depositors. The banks choose a portfolio $(x_1^i(\omega), y_1^i(\omega), z_1^i(\omega))$ of assets to carry forward into the next period.

In the final period, there are no decisions to make. The banks liquidate all their assets and distribute the proceeds to the depositors who consume them.

The equilibrium is defined recursively, beginning with the last period.

3.1. EQUILIBRIUM IN THE FINAL PERIOD

In the final period, banks liquidate all of their assets and distribute the proceeds to their depositors. The typical bank in region i has a portfolio $(x_1^i(\omega), y_1^i(\omega), z_1^i(\omega))$ at the beginning of date 2 in state of nature ω. There are two cases to be considered, depending on whether or not the banks were bankrupt at date 2.

When banks go bankrupt, they have to liquidate all of their assets immediately. Thus, if the banks in region i were bankrupt at date 1 then

$$(x_1^i(\omega), y_1^i(\omega), z_1^i(\omega)) = 0.$$

The value of the banks' deposits in this case is $q_2^i(\omega) = 0$.

In the other case, the banks in region i are not bankrupt at date 1, so they have assets to dispose of at date 2. Since these assets include deposits in other regions' banks, we have to take account of the value of deposits in other regions when calculating the value of deposits in region i. In other words, we have to determine the value of deposits in all regions simultaneously.

Without loss of generality, we can assume that all banks are bankrupt at date 2. At date 0, each bank will choose a value of c_2^i high enough so that

$$q_2^i(\omega) \le c_2^i$$

in every state ω. This is a zero-profit condition resulting from perfect competition among the banks in each region. If it were violated, it would mean that some assets were left over in some state of nature and that would violate the assumption that banks choose deposit contracts to maximize consumer welfare.

The assets of the typical bank in region i are valued at

$$\sum_{j \ne i} q_2^j(\omega) z_{j1}^i(\omega) + y_1^i(\omega) + R x_1^i(\omega),$$

which is equal to the bank's claims on banks in regions $i-1$ and $i+1$ *plus* the bank's holding of the short asset *plus* the bank's holding of the long asset. The bank's liabilities are the number of deposits outstanding, each valued at the market price $q_2^i(\omega)$

$$\left(\sum_{j \neq i} z_{i1}^j(\omega) + (1-\omega^i) \right) q_2^i(\omega).$$

The equilibrium value of $q_2^i(\omega)$ is determined by the condition that the bank's assets just equal its liabilities, thus,

$$\left(\sum_{j \neq i} z_{i1}^j(\omega) + (1-\omega^i) \right) q_2^i(\omega) = \sum_{j \neq i} q_2^j(\omega) z_{j1}^i(\omega) + y_1^i(\omega)) + Rx_1^i(\omega)). \quad (13.2)$$

The equilibrium values of the deposits are determined simultaneously by the n equations (13.2), one for each region, involving n unknowns, one price $q_2^i(\omega)$ for each region.

[It is easy to see that there is a solution to this system of equations for every non-negative specification of portfolios. For regions in which banks were insolvent at date 1 put $q_2^i(\omega) = 0$. For regions in which banks were solvent at date 1 we can obtain a lower bound by assuming $q_2^j(\omega) = 0$ on the right-hand side of (13.2) and solving for $q_2^i(\omega)$. Next substitute these values into the right-hand side of (13.2) and continue to perform this algorithm indefinitely. The values of $q_2^i(\omega)$ obtained at each iteration are nondecreasing. They are also bounded above, because denoting the left- and right-hand values by $q_2'(\omega)$ and $q_2(\omega)$, respectively, and summing (13.2) over i yields

$$\sum_{i=1}^{n}(1-\omega^i)q_2^{i'}(\omega) = \sum_{i=1}^{n} \left(\sum_{j \neq i} q_2^j(\omega) z_{j1}^i(\omega) - \sum_{j \neq i} q_2^{i'}(\omega) z_{i1}^j(\omega) \right)$$

$$+ \sum_{i=1}^{n} \left(y_1^i(\omega)) + Rx_1^i(\omega)) \right)$$

$$\leq \sum_{i=1}^{n} \left(y_1^i(\omega)) + Rx_1^i(\omega)) \right),$$

since $q_2'(\omega) \geq q_2(\omega)$. Thus, convergence is assured and by continuity the limiting values will satisfy (13.2) for $i = 1,...,n$.]

3.2. EQUILIBRIUM IN THE INTERMEDIATE PERIOD

At the beginning of date 1, the banks in region i have the portfolio (x_0^i, y_0^i, z_0^i) chosen at date 0. These are their assets. The liabilities of the bank are the potential claims from depositors. The total deposits outstanding from depositors in region i are one unit and from banks in other regions are $\sum_{j \neq i} z_{i0}^j$. The bank has promised each depositor c_1^i units of consumption on demand, but not all depositors will demand this payment in period 1. Early consumers have no choice but to withdraw their deposits at date 1. Late consumers can withdraw at date 2 or withdraw at date 1 and store the goods until date 2. It is optimal for the late consumers to wait and withdraw at the final date if and only if

$$q_2^i(\omega) \geq q_1^i(\omega).$$

Otherwise they would be better off withdrawing at date 1 and storing the deposit until date 2.

The next task is to determine the conditions under which the bank will be able to meet the claims made by the depositors. Suppose that the bank is not bankrupt. The bank needs to choose a new portfolio $(x_1^i(\omega), y_1^i(\omega), z_1^i(\omega)) \geq 0$ that satisfies the following condition:

$$\sum_{j \neq i} q_1^i(\omega)(z_{i0}^j - z_{i1}^j(\omega)) - \sum_{j \neq i} q_1^i(\omega)(z_{j0}^i - z_{j1}^i(\omega)) + \omega^i q_1^i(\omega)$$

$$\leq (y_0^i - y_1^i(\omega)) + r(x_0^i - x_1^i(\omega)). \tag{13.3}$$

The left-hand side represents the value of the deposits being redeemed at date 1 (where it is implicitly assumed that $q_1^i(\omega) = c_1^i$ since the bank is nonbankrupt).

The set of portfolios that satisfy the constraint (13.3) is compact and convex. If it is nonempty, then the bank should choose the portfolio from the set of portfolios that maximize the value of the deposits at date 2 (the bank cannot pay out more than c_1^i at date 1 but has chosen c_2^i large enough that additional assets can always be distributed at date 2). Let $\zeta_1^i(a_0, q, \omega)$ denote the set of optimal portfolios at date 1. It depends on the action $a_0^i = (x_0^i, y_0^i, z_0^i, c_1^i, c_2^i)$ chosen at date 0, on the prices q, and on the state ω.

If the set of feasible portfolios at date 1 is empty, then we put $\zeta_1^i(a_0, q, \omega) = \{0\}$ and force the bank to liquidate at date 1. In this case, both the banks in other regions and the late consumers in region i will withdraw their deposits in the current period and the value of the deposits is determined by the equation

$$\left(\sum_{j\neq i} z_{i0}^j + 1\right) q_{i1}(\omega) = \sum_{j\neq i} q_{j1}(\omega) z_{j0}^i + y_0^i + r x_0^i.$$

The left-hand side is the number of deposits outstanding multiplied by the liquidation value; the right-hand side is the liquidation value of the assets, including the value of deposits in banks in other regions.

Where late consumers are indifferent between withdrawing their deposits at date 1 and date 2, we assume that they withdraw at the final date. We make this assumption because we want to avoid runs if at all possible. Under this assumption, it turns out that there are only two possibilities: either $q_2^i(\omega) \geq q_1^i(\omega) = c_1^i$ or $0 = q_2^i(\omega) \leq q_1^i(\omega) < c_1^i$ and there is a run that forces the bank to liquidate all its assets at the first date. To see this, suppose that $q_1^i(\omega) = c_1^i$. Then if $q_2^i(\omega) < c_1^i$ it must be optimal for all late consumers to withdraw at the first period and get c_1^i. But since consumption can be stored from date 1 to date 2, there must exist a set of decisions by the bank that provide $q_2^i(\omega) \geq c_1^i$, that is, $\zeta_1^i(a_0, q, \omega) \neq \{0\}$, contradicting the equilibrium conditions. The other case that needs to be considered is $q_1^i(\omega) < c_1^i$. In that case, the bank is unable to meet its obligations and must liquidate all assets. This implies that $q_2^i(\omega) = 0$ as required.

3.3. EQUILIBRIUM IN THE INITIAL PERIOD

At the first date, banks choose investment portfolios and deposit contracts to maximize the expected utility of the typical depositor, taking as given the behavior of the banks in other regions. So far we have described the equilibrium behavior of the banks at dates 1 and 2, assuming that all the banks in region i behave identically. But in order to describe the choice of the bank's optimal portfolio at the first date, we have to allow for the possibility that the bank chooses a different portfolio from the others and consequently will have a different liquidation value. In other words, we cannot take the liquidation value $q_t^i(\omega)$ as given when the bank is changing its initial portfolio. Similarly, we cannot assume that the bank can sell deposits to other banks; if the portfolio chosen by the bank is unattractive to other banks, they may not be willing to buy them at a price $q_0^i = 1$. Selling them at a price less than 1 means that depositors are subsidizing the banks, of course. We therefore assume that it is illegal to sell deposits in this way; all depositors, both consumers in region i or banks from other regions, must be treated in the same way. Therefore, $q_0^i \equiv 1$ and bank deposits can be issued to banks in other regions only if it is optimal for other banks to accept them. In equilibrium, deposits held by banks from other regions are demand-determined.

To begin with, we consider a single bank in region i, and assume that the bank does not issue any deposits to other banks. The choices of the distinguished bank are marked by a 94 and the usual notation is used for the other banks, in region i and in other regions. Suppose then that the bank has issued one unit of deposits and used the proceeds to invest in a portfolio $(\hat{x}_0^i, \hat{y}_0^i, \hat{z}_0^i)$. It also chooses a deposit contract $(\hat{c}_1^i, \hat{c}_2^i)$. Let $\hat{a}_0^i = (\hat{x}_0^i, \hat{y}_0^i, \hat{z}_0^i, \hat{c}_1^i, \hat{c}_2^i)$ denote the bank's action at date 1. The other banks in region i choose a portfolio (x_0^i, y_0^i, z_0^i) deposit contract (c_1^i, c_2^i) and banks in regions $j \neq i$ choose the portfolio (x_0^j, y_0^j, z_0^j) and deposit contract (c_1^j, c_2^j). The liquidation values of the other banks are given by q, which is determined in the usual way.

Once ω is realized at date 1, the bank learns whether it is insolvent or not, that is, whether there is a feasible portfolio choice that allows it to pay $\hat{c}_1^i$ to withdrawers at date 1. In any case, there is a well-defined liquidation value of deposits $\hat{q}_t^i(\omega)$ at date t and the payoff to depositors is $u(\hat{q}_1^i(\omega))$ if the bank is insolvent at date 1 and

$$\omega^i u(\hat{q}_1^i(\omega)) + (1 - \omega^i) u(\hat{q}_2^i(\omega))$$

if the bank is solvent at date 1. It is important to remember here that $\hat{q}_t^i$ is a function of the initial action $\hat{a}_0^i$ as well as the actions of the representative banks in each region. Let $U^i(\hat{a}_0^i, \omega)$ denote the expected utility in state ω given the action $\hat{a}_0^i$ at date 0. Then the expected utility of the depositors is

$$U(\hat{a}_0^i) = \sum_{\omega \in \Omega} p(\omega) U(\hat{a}_0^i, \omega).$$

The bank is assumed to choose $\hat{a}_0^i$ to maximize $U(\hat{a}_0^i)$.

4. DECENTRALIZATION OF THE SOCIAL OPTIMUM

The optimal risk-sharing problem (P1) discussed in section 2 maximizes the unweighted sum of expected utilities. There are other efficient allocations besides the solution to this problem but given the symmetry of the model—regions are *ex ante* identical—makes this is a natural benchmark for the efficiency of risk sharing. In this section, we show that under certain conditions the first best can be decentralized by a competitive banking sector issuing standard deposit contracts. The main assumption we need is that there is no aggregate uncertainty.

- The size of the aggregate shock $\hat{\omega} = \sum_{i=1}^{n} \omega^i$ is the same for every state $\omega \in \Omega$.

This assumption implies that the consumption allocation corresponding to the solution of (P1) is a constant (c_1, c_2), independent of the state ω. This is necessary to allow banks to implement the optimal risk sharing through noncontingent deposit contracts.

4.1. COMPLETE MARKETS

There are no bank runs in an equilibrium that decentralizes the solution of the planner's problem (P1). Each bank has enough assets to provide consumers with the optimal consumption allocation (c_1, c_2). Deposits in different banks are perfect substitutes and hence have the same value at date 0.

At date 0, an individual bank in region i chooses a portfolio (x_0^i, y_0^i) subject to the feasibility constraint $x_0^i + y_0^i \leq 1$ and offers the depositors in his bank a deposit contract $(c_1^i, c_2^i) = (c_1, c_2)$.

Let z_{jt}^i denote the number of deposits held by the typical bank in region i in banks in region j at the end of date $t = 0, 1$. Suppose that each bank chooses a symmetrical portfolio z_0^i at date 0, where

$$z_{j0}^i = \begin{cases} \zeta & j \neq i \\ 0 & j = i \end{cases},$$

where $\zeta > 0$ is a large number. Each bank in region i chooses the same portfolios

$$(x_t^i, y_t^i) = n^{-1}(x_t, y_t)$$

at dates $t = 0, 1$ where (x_t, y_t) denotes the planner's portfolio at date t in the solution to (P1). Since there is no aggregate uncertainty in the planner's problem, we know that $\hat{\omega} c_1 = y_0$ and $(1 - \hat{\omega}) c_2 = R x_0$, that is, consumption in the intermediate period is financed through the short asset and consumption in the final period is financed through the long asset. This implies that the budget constraint at date 1 requires

$$\left[\sum_{j\neq i}(z_{i0}^{j} - z_{i1}^{j}(\omega)) - \sum_{j\neq i}(z_{j0}^{i} - z_{j1}^{i}(\omega))\right]c_{1} \leq (y_{0}^{i} - y_{1}^{i}(\omega)) + r(x_{0}^{i} - x_{1}^{i}(\omega))$$

$$= y_{0}^{i}. \tag{13.4}$$

Let $\gamma \equiv n^{-1}\hat{\omega}$ denote the average number of early consumers in each region and note that $y_{0}^{i} = \gamma c_{1}$, so the deficit in region i is $\omega^{i} - \gamma$ deposits. The budget constraint (13.4) will be satisfied if and only if

$$\left[\sum_{j\neq i}(z_{i0}^{j} - z_{i1}^{j}(\omega)) - \sum_{j\neq i}(z_{j0}^{i} - z_{j1}^{i}(\omega))\right] = \omega^{i} - \gamma.$$

In region i put $z_{1}^{i}(\omega) = z_{0}^{i}$ if $\omega^{i} - \gamma \leq 0$. For any region i such that $\omega^{i} - \gamma > 0$ let $\eta^{i}(\omega)$ denote the ratio of region i's excess demand to total excess demand:

$$\eta^{i}(\omega) = \frac{\omega^{i} - \gamma}{\sum_{i}\max\{\omega^{i} - \gamma, 0\}}.$$

Then define region i's portfolio $z_{1}^{i}(\omega)$ by putting

$$z_{j1}^{i}(\omega) = \begin{cases} 0 & \text{if } \omega^{j} - \gamma > 0 \\ z_{0}^{i} - \eta^{i}(\omega)(\omega^{j} - \gamma) & \text{if } \omega^{j} - \gamma \leq 0. \end{cases}$$

In words, if the banks in region i need extra liquidity, they do not draw down deposits in banks in regions j that are liquidity-constrained ($\omega^{j} - \gamma > 0$). Instead, they proportionately draw down their deposits in regions that have excess liquidity ($\omega^{j} - \gamma \leq 0$). It is clear that the portfolios defined satisfy the budget constraint (13.4). Obviously, there are many other ways of defining a portfolio $z_{1}^{i}(\omega)$ to satisfy the budget constraint.

Summing the budget constraints (13.4) and making use of the planner's budget constraint for date 1 we end up with the interbank deposit market-clearing condition at date 1

$$\sum_{i}\left[\sum_{j\neq i}(z_{i0}^{j} - z_{i1}^{j}(\omega)) - \sum_{j\neq i}(z_{j0}^{i} - z_{j1}^{i}(\omega))\right] = 0.$$

At date 2, the budget constraint for a bank in region i will be

$$\left[\sum_{j\neq i}z_{i1}^{j}(\omega)-\sum_{j\neq i}z_{j1}^{i}(\omega)+(1-\omega^{i})\right]c_{2}\leq y_{1}^{i}(\omega))+Rx_{1}^{i}(\omega)). \quad (13.5)$$

Summing (13.5) across i we obtain the planner's budget constraint for date 2 if and only if

$$\sum_{i}\left[\sum_{j\neq i}z_{i1}^{j}(\omega)-\sum_{j\neq i}z_{j1}^{i}(\omega)\right]=0.$$

The market-clearing condition in deposits for date 2 is identically zero. It is easy to check that if banks satisfy the budget constraint (13.4) then the budget constraint (13.5) is automatically satisfied. Given a sequence of portfolios (z_{0}^{i},z_{1}^{i}) satisfying the budget constraints (13.4) and (13.5) for each region i, the banks can achieve the same investment portfolios and consumption allocations for their depositors as the central planner. It remains to check that this is an equilibrium.

At date 2, there are no decisions to be made. The value of deposits in region i will be $q_{2}^{i}(\omega)=c_{2}^{i}=c_{2}$ in every state of nature ω.

At date 1, the value of deposits will be $q_{1}^{i}(\omega)=c_{1}^{i}=c_{1}$ in every state of nature ω and since $c_{1}\leq c_{2}$ it is optimal for early and late consumers to withdraw at date 1 and date 2, respectively.

Once the state ω is revealed at date 1, it is clear that each bank cannot do better than to meet its obligations under the deposit contract (c_{1},c_{2}). There is no portfolio decision that allows the bank to meet its obligations and achieve a surplus in either period. At date 0, things are more complicated. We assume that each bank wants to maximize the expected utility of the typical consumer subject to the budget constraints at dates $t=1,2$. The question then is whether it can do better than the choice of portfolios and deposit contract described above.

For the case of an equilibrium with complete risk sharing, it is easy to characterize the optimality of banks' behavior. Suppose that all banks in region i choose the deposit contract (c_{1}^{i},c_{1}^{i}) and the sequence of portfolios $\{(x_{t}^{i},y_{t}^{i},z_{t}^{i}\}_{t=0,1}$ and a single bank in some region k deviates by choosing a contract (c_{1}',c_{1}') and a sequence of portfolios $\{(x_{t}',y_{t}',z_{t}')\}_{t=0,1}$. We can treat the resulting reallocation as the result of a trade between the deviating bank and a fully insured representative bank in each region i. The effect of the deviating bank choosing a different portfolio and deposit contract is to effect a contingent transfer of consumption between the deviating bank and the representative banks in each region. The equilibrium deposit contract (c_1, c_2) solves the maximization problem

$$
\begin{aligned}
\hat{\omega}u(c_1)+(1-\hat{\omega})u(c_2) &= \sup_{\hat{\omega}c_1+(1-\hat{\omega})R^{-1}c_2 \leq 1} \{\hat{\omega}u(c_1)+(1-\hat{\omega})u(c_2)\} \\
&= \sup_{\omega^i c_1(\omega^i)+(1-\omega^i)R^{-1}c_2(\omega^i)\leq 1} \sum_{\omega} p(\omega)\{\omega^i u(c_1(\omega)) \\
&\qquad\qquad\qquad\qquad +(1-\omega^i)u(c_2(\omega)\}.
\end{aligned}
$$

The representative bank in region i will not accept deposits in the deviating bank unless they leave depositor welfare at least as high as before. This means that

$$
\begin{aligned}
\sum_{\omega} p(\omega)\{\omega^i u'(c_1)\frac{\Delta_1^i(\omega)}{\omega^i}+(1-\omega^i)u'(c_2)\frac{\Delta_2^i(\omega)}{1-\omega^i}\} \\
= u'(c_1)\sum_{\omega} p(\omega)\{\Delta_1^i(\omega)+R^{-1}\Delta_2^i(\omega)\} \geq 0,
\end{aligned}
$$

where $\Delta_t^i(\omega)$ is the net transfer to region i at date t as a result of the deviating bank's trade. But this means that

$$
\begin{aligned}
\sum_{\omega} p(\omega)\{\omega^k u'(c_1)\frac{\Delta_1(\omega)}{\omega^k}+(1-\omega^k)u'(c_2)\frac{\Delta_2(\omega)}{1-\omega^k}\} \\
= u'(c_1)\sum_{\omega} p(\omega)\{\Delta_1(\omega)+R^{-1}\Delta_2(\omega)\} \leq 0,
\end{aligned}
$$

where

$$
\Delta_t(\omega) = -\sum_{i=1}^{n}\Delta_t^i(\omega),
$$

for $t=1,2$. In other words, the depositors of the deviating bank cannot be made better off by any feasible state-contingent transfers that are acceptable to the other banks. The fact that the deviating bank cannot make arbitrary state-contingent reallocations, but has to use deposit contracts, simply restricts its ability to increase welfare. The Pareto-optimality of (c_1, c_2) makes it clear that it is impossible for a deviating bank to make itself better off through trade with the representative bank.

Theorem 2. *Let $(x_0, y_0, x_1(\omega), y_1(\omega), c_1, c_2)$ be the solution to the planner's problem (P1) and suppose that the representative bank in each region i chooses a deposit contract $(c_1^i, c_2^i) = (c_1, c_2)$, a sequence of portfolios $(x_0^i, y_0^i, z_0^i, x_1^i(\omega), y_1^i(\omega), z_1^i(\omega))$ satisfying*

$$(x_0^i, y_0^i, x_1^i(\omega), y_1^i(\omega)) = n^{-1}(x_0, y_0, x_1(\omega), y_1(\omega)),$$

and the budget constraints (13.4) and (13.5). Then the equilibrium of the decentralized banking system described above implements the first-best allocation.

4.2. INCOMPLETE MARKETS

In constructing an equilibrium in which the social optimum could be decentralized, it was assumed that each bank can hold a complete portfolio of deposits. In practice this is unlikely to be true, because of the complexity of such a strategy or because of the informational requirements. However, complete markets are not necessary in order to decentralize the first best as long as the regions are connected in an appropriate sense. As an illustration, consider the case where regions are arranged clockwise in a circular network. Each region i is directly connected to the next region $i+1$ in the clockwise direction, that is, for each region i the neighboring set is $N^i = \{i+1\}$ where region $n+1$ is identified with region 1. With this restriction, the overall structure of equilibrium is similar to that described in the previous section.

To show that social optimum can be decentralized with this market structure, it is sufficient to show that the banks can satisfy their budget constraints. At date 0, each bank chooses an admissible portfolio

$$z_{j0}^i = \begin{cases} \zeta & \text{if } j = 1+1; \\ 0 & \text{otherwise.} \end{cases}$$

At date 1, the bank has to choose an admissible portfolio $z_1^i(\omega)$ such that

$$\left[\sum_{j=i\pm1}(z_{i0}^j - z_{i1}^j(\omega)) - \sum_{j=i\pm1}(z_{j0}^i - z_{j1}^i(\omega)) + \omega^i \right] c_1 \le y_0^i.$$

If this constraint is satisfied then the constraint at date 2 is automatically satisfied. The aggregate budget constraint at date 1, $\hat{\omega}c_1 = y_0$, ensures that we can find portfolios $\{z_1^i\}$ satisfying the regional budget constraints if ζ is chosen large enough. This is all one needs to decentralize the social optimum.

For the general case of an arbitrary, connected collection of neighborhoods $\{N^i\}$, we can show that it is possible to decentralize the social optimum by constructing a set of deposit portfolios $\{z_t^i\}$ that will satisfy the budget constraints above. The easiest way to do this is to begin with the equilibrium portfolios for the economy with complete markets and then construct an equivalent profile of portfolios for the economy with neighborhoods $\{N^i\}$. Let $\{z_t^i\}$ denote the portfolios for the complete markets economy and let $\{\hat{z}_t^i\}$ denote the corresponding portfolios for the incomplete markets economy. To construct $\{\hat{z}_t^i\}$ we proceed as follows. Take $i = 1$ and some $t = 0$ and consider the smallest index $j \neq i$ such that $z_{j0}^i \neq 0$ and region i cannot hold deposits in region j. Then the connectedness assumption implies that there exists a chain $\{i_1, ..., i_K\}$ such that i_k is directly connected to i_{k+1} and $i_1 = i$ and $i_K = j$. Then let $\hat{z}_{j0}^i = 0$ and put $\hat{z}_{i_{k+1}0}^{i_k} = z_{i_{k+1}0}^{i_k} + z_{j0}^i$ for every $k = 1, ..., K - 1$. Replace z_0^i with $\hat{z}_0^i$ and apply the same procedure again until the portfolio for region i is admissible. Then move on to the next index $i = 2$, and so on, until all the regions have admissible portfolios at date 0. Then go through the same procedure at date $t = 1$ for each state ω and region i.

This procedure clearly results in a set of admissible profiles $\{z_t^i\}$ for all regions and dates $t = 0, 1$. Also, it is easy to see that these portfolios are equivalent to the original portfolios, in the sense that each region has the same number of deposits as before in every state and at every date. For this reason, the new portfolios must satisfy the budget constraints at each date. Another way to see that the budget constraints must be satisfied is to note that the changes we have made simply create a series of "pass throughs," where region $i = i_1$ holds a deposit in region j indirectly by holding a deposit in region i_2 which holds an offsetting deposit in region i_3 . . . which holds an offsetting deposit in region $i_K = j$.

Thus, the decentralization argument given in the first part of this section extends easily to any connected family of neighborhoods $\{N^i\}$.

5. CONTAGION

To illustrate the possibility of contagion, we use the decentralization theorems from section 4 to show the existence of an equilibrium with complete risk sharing. Then we perturb the model to show that for some states a small excess demand for liquidity can lead to an economy-wide crisis. In other words, the equilibrium with complete risk sharing suffers from financial fragility.

In section 4, we showed that complete risk sharing could be decentralized using standard deposit contracts if (a) there is no aggregate risk, that is, if $\hat{\omega}$ was constant, and (b) the economy is connected, that is, the family of neighborhoods $\{N^i\}$ is connected. As an illustration of the contagion problem, we take a particular structure of the admissible deposit portfolio sets, namely, the case in which each region i can hold deposits only in region $i+1$, where we identify region $n+1$ with region 1. This would be the case if the regions were arranged clockwise in a circle, with banks in region i being able to hold deposits in the neighboring region in the clockwise direction.

Let (c_1, c_2) denote the optimal consumption profile chosen by a central planner when there is no aggregate uncertainty. Let (x, y) denote the per capita investments in the long and short assets, respectively, chosen by the planner. The symmetry of the model implies that there will be an equilibrium, in which every region behaves symmetrically in the first period. The optimal deposit contract in region i will be

$$(c_1^i, c_2^i) = (c_1, c_2).$$

The initial portfolio will be

$$(x_0^i, y_0^i, z_0^i) = (x, y, z_0^i)$$

where

$$z_{j0}^i = \begin{cases} \zeta & j = i+1 \\ 0 & j \neq i+1 \end{cases}$$

and ζ is an appropriately chosen constant. We choose ζ to be as small as possible, but assuming that there is nondegenerate uncertainty, ζ must be positive in equilibrium.

At date 1, the state ω is observed and all the early consumers (and only the early consumers) withdraw their deposits worth c_1 each. In order to satisfy the budget constraint, banks in region i choose (x_1^i, y_1^i, z_1^i) so that

$$(x_1^i(\omega), y_1^i(\omega)) = (x_0^i, 0)$$

(there is no need to liquidate the long asset and it is never optimal to carry the short asset over to the last period) and

$$\omega^i c_1 = y_0^i + (z_{i+1,0}^i - z_{i+1,1}^i(\omega))c_1 - (z_{i0}^{i-1} - z_{i1}^{i-1}(\omega))c_1.$$

In the last period, the budget constraint is

$$(1 - \omega^i)c_2 = Rx_0^i + z_{i+1,1}^i(\omega)c_2 - z_{i1}^{i-1}(\omega)c_2.$$

The budget constraint at date 2 is satisfied if the budget constraint at date 1 is satisfied, so it is enough to show that there exists a choice of z_1^i for each i that satisfies the budget constraint at date 1. The existence of these portfolios $\{z_1^i\}$ follows from arguments provided in section 4. Here we note that there is an essentially unique way of defining the portfolios. Suppose that $z_{2,1}^1(\omega)$ is given for some state ω. Then the second-period budget constraint for $i = 2$ determines $z_{3,1}^2(\omega)$. Continuing in this way, we can show that if $z_{i+1,1}^i$ is given then the second-period budget constraint for $i + 1$ determines $z_{i+2,1}^{i+1}$. When we get back to region $i = 1$, the value of $z_{2,1}^1(\omega)$ determined by the budget constraint must agree with the value initially given, because summing the budget constraints from $i = 2, ..., n$ gives

$$\sum_{i=2}^{n} \omega^i c^1 = (n-1)y_0 + (z_{1,0}^n - z_{1,1}^n(\omega))c_1 - (z_{2,0}^1 - z_{2,1}^1(\omega))c_1$$

which implies, on substituting $\hat{\omega} = \sum_{i=1}^{n} \omega^i$,

$$(\hat{\omega} - \omega^1)c^1 = (n-1)y_0 + (z_{1,0}^n - z_{1,1}^n(\omega))c_1 - (z_{2,0}^1 - z_{2,1}^1(\omega))c_1$$

or equivalently

$$\omega^1 c^1 = y_0 + (z_{2,0}^1 - z_{2,1}^1(\omega))c_1 - (z_{1,0}^n - z_{1,1}^n(\omega))c_1.$$

This shows that the originally given value of $z_2^1(\omega)$ satisfies the budget constraint for region $i = 1$.

We have not shown that the portfolios defined in this way satisfy the non-negativity constraint. However, by choosing $z_{2,1}^1$ sufficiently large, all of the other values will be non-negative. So, choose $z_{2,1}^1$ to be the smallest value that is consistent with the non-negativity constraint.

It is straightforward to check that the portfolio defined in this way is the (essentially) unique portfolio that satisfies the budget constraint in both periods.

Note that there is an indeterminacy in the definition of the portfolio in the initial period because we have not specified ζ. Clearly, ζ has to be big enough to allow for the definition of a non-negative z_1^i at date 1. Let ζ be chosen to be the smallest value of ζ that is consistent with a non-negative z_1^i. With this convention, the equilibrium is uniquely defined. Theorem 2 shows that this is in fact an equilibrium.

Now, let us take the equilibrium as given and consider what happens when we "perturb" the model. By a perturbation, I mean the realization of a state $\bar{\omega}$ that was assigned zero probability at date 0 and has a demand for liquidity that is very close to that of the states that do occur with positive probability. Specifically, define the state $\bar{\omega}$ by putting

$$
\bar{\omega}^i = \begin{cases} \gamma & i \neq k \\ \gamma + \varepsilon & i = k \end{cases}.
$$

Thus, at date 0 the choices of deposit contract (c_1^i, c_2^i) and initial portfolio (x_0^i, y_0^i, z_0^i) are the same as in the equilibrium with complete risk sharing. Furthermore, for any of the states ω that occur with positive probability, the equilibrium proceeds at dates 1 and 2 in the way described above. For the distinguished state $\bar{\omega}$ things are different, as we show in a number of steps.

Step 1. In state $\bar{\omega}$ there must be at least one region in which the banks are insolvent. The proof is by contradiction. Suppose, contrary to what we want to prove, that banks in all regions are solvent. Then $q^i(\bar{\omega}) = c_1$ for all i. However, the demand for deposits from early consumers is γ in each region and the stock of the short asset is $y_0^i = \gamma c_1$, so there is an excess demand for liquidity that can only be met by liquidating the long asset in some region. Any bank that liquidates the long asset will lose value. More precisely, the bank has just enough of the short asset to meet the demands of its local depositors (early consumers), so it has to liquidate some of the long assets if it allows other banks to withdraw more from it than it withdraws from them. For every unit of the long asset it liquidates, it gives up R future units of the good and gets r present units of the good. For every unit of deposits it retains, it gets c_2 future units of the good and gives up c_1 present units of the good. So it is costly to liquidate the long asset if

$$\frac{R}{r} > \frac{c_2}{c_1}. \tag{13.6}$$

This inequality will hold, for example, if $u'(c)c$ is decreasing because that implies that

$$\frac{u'(c_1)c_1}{u'(c_2)c_2} > 1 \tag{13.7}$$

and the optimal deposit satisfies

$$u'(c_1) = Ru'(c_2) \tag{13.8}$$

so using the inequalities (13.7) and (13.8) we have

$$\frac{c_2}{c_1} < \frac{u'(c_1)}{u'(c_2)} = R < \frac{R}{r}$$

as required. The assumption (13.6) is maintained in what follows, so no bank will willingly liquidate the long asset.

To avoid liquidating the long asset, banks must redeem at least as many deposits as are withdrawn by banks from other regions. But this implies that no region is able to get extra liquidity from other regions. The only equilibrium is one in which all banks simultaneously withdraw their deposits in banks in other regions at date 1 and these mutual withdrawals offset each other and so have no effect. The result is that banks in region k are forced to be self-sufficient. Then solvency in region k requires

$$\begin{aligned} (\gamma + \varepsilon)c_1 &\geq y_0^k + r(x_0^k - x_1^k(\bar{\omega})) \\ (1 - \gamma - \varepsilon)c_1 &\geq Rx_1^k(\bar{\omega}). \end{aligned} \tag{13.9}$$

The demand for deposits is $\gamma + \varepsilon$ and solvency requires that each agent should get c_1. The short asset y_0^k will be used first and then some of the long asset will be liquidated to yield an additional $r(x_0^k - x_1^k(\bar{\omega}))$. At the last date, the late consumers must be given at least c_1 to prevent a run, so the amount paid out will be at least $(1 - \gamma - \varepsilon)c_1$, and the liquidation value of the bank's portfolio will be $Rx_1^k(\bar{\omega})$. The conditions in equation (13.9) are necessary and sufficient for solvency at date 1, so if these conditions are violated then banks in region k must be insolvent and a bank run (crisis) occurs. In what follows we assume that equation (13.9) is violated.

Note that we have not yet shown that region k must be insolvent; only that some region must be insolvent. However, it is easy to see that in any region other than region k, the banks can protect themselves against insolvency by liquidating all their deposits in other regions' banks at date 1, on the assumption that the late consumers do not run unless there is no equilibrium in their region in which it is optimal for them to withdraw late. Hence the only equilibrium will be one in which banks in region k (and possibly other regions) are insolvent.

Step 2. Having established that banks in region k must be insolvent, we next show that the financial crisis must be extend to other regions. We assume to the contrary that all regions $i \neq k$ are solvent. Since the banks in region k are insolvent, they must liquidate all their holdings of deposits in region $k+1$ and the banks in region $k-1$ will find it optimal to liquidate their deposits in the banks of region k. The value of the deposits in region k are determined by the condition that the value of liabilities equals the value of assets:

$$(1+\zeta)q_1^k(\bar{\omega}) = y_0^k + rx_0^k + \zeta c_1$$

since the value of deposits in region $k+1$ equals c_1 as long as they are solvent. Then

$$q_1^k(\bar{\omega}) = \frac{y_0^k + rx_0^k + \zeta c_1}{1+\zeta}$$

and the transfer from banks in region $k+1$ to banks in region k is

$$
\begin{aligned}
\zeta(c_1 - q_1(\bar{\omega})) &= \frac{\zeta(1+\zeta)}{1+\zeta}c_1 - \frac{\zeta}{1+\zeta}(y_0^k + rx_0^k + \zeta c_1) \\
&= \frac{\zeta(c_1 - y_0^k - rx_0^k)}{1+\zeta}.
\end{aligned}
$$

By a previous argument, the banks in regions $i \neq k, k-1$ will not want to liquidate the long asset, so without loss of generality, we can assume that they all liquidate their holdings of deposits in other regions in the current period. This means that banks in region $k-1$ have to remain self-sufficient. Solvency in this region is only possible if there is a solution to

$$\gamma c_1 \leq y_0^j + r(x_0^j - x_1^j(\bar{\omega})) - \frac{\zeta(c_1 - y_0^k - rx_0^k)}{1+\zeta}$$

$$(1-\gamma)c_1 \leq Rx_1^j(\bar{\omega}).$$

for $j = k - 1$. Since $\gamma c_1 = y_0^j$ and $(1-\gamma)c_2 = Rx_0^j$, these conditions can be satisfied if and only if

$$\frac{\zeta(c_1 - y_0^k - rx_0^k)}{1+\zeta} \leq r(x_0^j - x_1^j(\bar{\omega})) \leq \frac{r(1-\gamma)(c_2 - c_1)}{R}.$$

The last expression on the right is the amount of liquidity that we can get at date 1 without violating the incentive constraint at date 2. Making similar substitutions, the first expression on the left can be rewritten as

$$\frac{\zeta((1-\gamma)c_1 - r(1-\gamma)c_2/R)}{1+\zeta}$$

so the inequality becomes

$$\frac{\zeta(c_1 - rc_2/R)}{1+\zeta} \leq \frac{r(c_2 - c_1)}{R}$$

or

$$\frac{\zeta(Rc_1 - rc_2)}{1+\zeta} \leq r(c_2 - c_1)$$

which is certainly violated for r small enough, for example.

Step 3. The preceding step has shown that under certain conditions we must have bank runs in equilibrium in region $k-1$. To ensure that the process continues to infect the other regions we only need to show that the value of the bank deposits in region $k-1$ will be even lower than we assumed in region k. To see this, note that once a run has occurred, the banks in region $k-1$ have even less assets than the banks in region k in the previous step. Whereas the banks in region k could call upon the solvent banks in region $k+1$, whose deposits are worth c_1, the banks in region $k-1$

can only call on the insolvent banks in region k, whose deposits are worth $q_1(\overline{\omega}) < c_1$. Their demand for liquidity is the same, so they are in a worse position than the banks in region k. As a result, $q_{k-1}(\overline{\omega}) < q_k(\overline{\omega}) < c_1$, so region $k + 2$ must be insolvent. As we continue to argue by induction, at each step the value of deposits in the marginal insolvent regions gets lower and it is easier to prove that the marginal solvent regions cannot satisfy the conditions for solvency. We conclude that all regions must be insolvent. Note that this implies that the values of deposits in all regions are the same: $q^i(\overline{\omega}) = y_0^i + rx_0^i$.

6. ROBUSTNESS OF COMPLETE MARKETS

The incompleteness of markets is essential to the contagion result in the following sense. There exist parameter values for which any equilibrium with incomplete markets involves runs in state $\overline{\omega}$ (this is the set of parameter values characterized in section 5). For the same parameter values, we can find an equilibrium with complete markets that does not involve runs in state $\overline{\omega}$.

To see this, we go back to the complete markets equilibrium in section 4 under the assumption that $\hat{\omega}$ is a constant. In that case, the non-contingent deposit contract (c_1, c_2) is the first best and we have seen that there is a sequence of portfolios $\{(x_0^i, y_0^i, z_0^i), (x_1^i, y_1^i, z_1^i)\}$ that implements this contract as an equilibrium. Now suppose that we introduce the small probability state $\overline{\omega}$ that led to contagion in section 5. Of course, several restrictions on the parameter values were required in order to generate runs and those restrictions are assumed to be satisfied here. The question is whether there exists an equilibrium for state $\overline{\omega}$ in which runs do not occur, even though those conditions are satisfied? To answer this question in the affirmative, we have to show that it is possible to liquidate deposits without violating the conditions

$$q_1^i(\overline{\omega}) = c_1^i \le q_2^i(\overline{\omega}), \tag{13.10}$$

for $i \ne k$. As long as these conditions are satisfied, there will not be any runs in the regions $i \ne k$.

Without loss of generality, we consider the case in which $q_1^k(\overline{\omega}) < c_1^k$. Otherwise, there is no difficulty in showing that every region is solvent. Then banks in region k will liquidate all of their claims against banks in regions $i \ne k$ and banks in regions $i \ne k$ will liquidate all their deposits in region k. In order to satisfy the condition (13.10), banks in regions $i \neq k$ must be able to find a portfolio $(x_1^i(\overline{\omega}), y_1^i(\overline{\omega}), z_1^i(\overline{\omega}))$ such that

$$(\gamma + \zeta)c_1^i \leq y_0^i + r(x_0^i - x_1^i(\overline{\omega})) + q_1^k(\overline{\omega})\zeta$$

and

$$(1 - \gamma)c_1^i \leq Rx_1^i(\overline{\omega}).$$

We have already seen that these inequalities cannot be satisfied for the value ζ required in the equilibrium with incomplete markets. But the value of ζ required here is different. With incomplete markets, the typical bank holds deposits in two regions; with complete markets it holds deposits in $n-1$ regions. Therefore, the value of ζ in equilibrium with complete markets is $2/(n-1)$ times the value required in equilibrium with incomplete markets. Since there is no constraint on how large n can be, we can certainly find parameter values for which the solvency conditions (13.10) are satisfied for complete markets but not for incomplete markets.

Another way of stating this is that for any definition of $\overline{\omega}$ (any feasible choice of $\varepsilon > 0$), the complete markets equilibrium is robust for n large enough, whereas for some parameter values, the incomplete markets equilibrium will not be.

7 CONTAINMENT

The critical ingredient in the example of contagion analyzed in section 5 is that any two regions are connected by a chain of overlapping bank liabilities. Banks in region i have claims on banks in regions $i-1$ and $i+1$, which in turn have claims on banks in regions $i-2$ and $i+2$, respectively, and so on. If we could cut this chain at some point, the contagion that begins with a small shock in region k would be contained in some connected component of the set of regions. The structure of claims is endogenous, however, so we cannot simply assume that the whole economy is not enmeshed in a single web of claims. Some restrictions on the structure of the model are required in order to ensure that the economy can be broken down into small independent clumps of regions. One way to do this is to assume a special structure of liquidity shocks, which does not require much interconnectedness of claims in order to achieve complete risk sharing.

As an illustration, consider the special case in which adjacent pairs of regions can achieve complete risk sharing. More precisely, assume that for some constant γ

$$\omega^i + \omega^{i+1} = 2\gamma \tag{13.11}$$

for every region i and almost every state ω. Equation (13.11) implies that the number of regions n is an even number, of course. An equilibrium is defined by analogy with the equilibrium in section 5 except that claims are exchanged between pairs of regions only. Let (x_0, y_0) be the initial portfolio and (c_1, c_2) be the deposit contract chosen by the central planner as the solution to (P1). This allocation can be decentralized with incomplete markets as follows. At date 0, the representative bank in each region i chooses a portfolio (x_0^i, y_0^i, z_0^i) and a deposit contract (c_1^i, c_0^i), where

$$(x_0^i, y_0^i) = n^{-1}(x_0, y_0)$$

and

$$(c_1^i, c_0^i) = (c_1, c_2).$$

The main difference from the equilibrium described in section 5 is that the deposits are exchanged between pairs of regions: if i is an even number, then regions i and $i+1$ exchange claims, but regions i and $i-1$ do not. Thus,

$$z_{j0}^i = \begin{cases} \zeta & i \text{ is even and } j = i+1; \\ \zeta & \text{if } i \text{ is odd and } j = i-1; \\ 0 & \text{otherwise.} \end{cases}$$

At date 1, the state ω is observed and each pair of regions $(i, i+1)$, where i is an even number, adjust their holdings of deposits so that the optimal consumption allocation can be achieved. Specifically, $q_1^i(\omega) = c_1$ for every region i and any state ω and

$$(x_1^i(\omega), y_1^i(\omega), z_1^i(\omega)) = (x_0^i, 0, z_1^i(\omega)),$$

where $z_1^i(\omega)$ is chosen so that

$$z_{j1}^i(\omega) = \begin{cases} Z_{j0}^i - (\omega^i - \gamma) & \text{if } i \text{ is even and } j = 1+1; \\ Z_{j0}^i - (\omega^i - \gamma) & \text{if } i \text{ is odd and } j = i-1; \\ 0 & \text{otherwise.} \end{cases}$$

At date 2, the banks liquidate their remaining portfolios and it is easy to see from the banks' budget constraint that the value of deposits will be $q_2^i(\omega) = c_2^i$ in every region.

It is straightforward to show, in the same way as in section 5, that these choices are optimal and feasible, in other words, that they constitute an equilibrium.

Now suppose that we perturb the equilibrium by introducing a small probability state $\bar{\omega}$ in which there is an excess demand for liquidity in some state k:

$$\bar{\omega}^i = \begin{cases} \gamma + \varepsilon & \text{if } i = k; \\ \gamma & \text{if } i \neq k. \end{cases}$$

Without loss of generality we can assume that k is even; the other case is exactly symmetric. Then regions k and $k+1$ are linked by overlapping claims to deposits, but there are no claims linking regions $k-1$ and k or linking regions $k+1$ and $k+2$. Thus, the component $(k, k+1)$ is independent of the remainder of the regions. In fact, it is clear that *whatever happens in regions k and $k+1$*, we can define an equilibrium for regions $i \neq k, k+1$ in which $q_t^i(\bar{\omega}) = c_t^i$ for $t = 1, 2$. In words, in state $\bar{\omega}$ there may be bank runs in region k and they may spill over to region $k+1$, but this will have no effect on other regions. The effects of the disturbance associated with state $\bar{\omega}$ will be contained in the component $(k, k+1)$.

The same general result will hold whenever we can establish that a set of regions $C \subset \{1, \ldots, n\}$ is disconnected from its complement in equilibrium.

CONCLUSION

In this paper, we have considered a more general version of the model in Allen and Gale (2000), which only considered the networks of four banks. We show that similar results hold in much more general contexts with an unlimited number of banks. In particular, shocks that are small relative to the economy as a whole can cause a collapse of the financial system. There are two main differences with the Diamond-Dybvig model. The first is the assumption that the illiquid, long-term assets held by the banks are risky and perfectly correlated across banks. Uncertainty about asset returns is intended to capture the impact of the business cycle on the value of bank assets. Information about returns becomes available before the returns are realized and when the information is bad it has the power to precipitate a crisis. The second is that we do not make the first-come, first-served assumption. This assumption has been the subject of some debate in the literature as it is not an optimal arrangement in the basic Diamond-Dybvig model (see Wallace 1988 and Calomiris and Kahn 1991). In a number of countries and historical time periods, banks have had the right to delay payment for some time period on certain types of accounts. This is rather different from the first-come, first-served assumption. Sprague (1910) recounts how in the United States in the late nineteenth century people could obtain liquidity once a panic had started by using certified checks. These checks traded at a discount. We model this type of situation by assuming the available liquidity is split on an equal basis among those withdrawing early. In the context this arrangement is optimal. We also assume that those who do not withdraw early have to wait some time before they can obtain their funds and again what is available is split between them on an equal basis.

A number of authors have developed models of banking panics caused by aggregate risk. Wallace (1988, 1990), Chari (1989), and Champ, Smith, and Williamson (1996) extend Diamond and Dybvig (1983) by assuming the fraction of the population requiring liquidity is random. Chari and Jagannathan (1988), Jacklin and Bhattacharya (1988), Hellwig (1994), and Alonso (1996) introduce aggregate uncertainty which can be interpreted as business cycle risk. Chari and Jagannathan (1988) focus on a signal extraction problem where part of the population observes a signal about future returns. Others must then try to deduce from observed withdrawals whether an unfavorable signal was received by this group or whether liquidity needs happen to be high. Chari and Jagannathan are able to show panics occur not only when the outlook is poor but also when liquidity needs turn out to be high. Jacklin and Bhattacharya (1988) also consider a model where some depositors receive an interim signal about risk. They show that the optimality of bank deposits compared to equities depends on the characteristics of the risky investment. Hellwig (1994) considers a model where the reinvestment rate is random and shows that the risk should be borne both by early and late withdrawers. Alonso (1996) demonstrates using numerical examples that contracts where runs occur may be better than contracts which ensure runs do not occur because they improve risk sharing.

Another important feature of the model is the fact that connections between regions take the form of interbank deposits rather than investments in real assets. Of course, since the motive for investing in other regions is to provide insurance against liquidity shocks, it is natural to assume that banks have claims on each other. But there might also be a motive for spreading investments across regions if the long assets were risky and the returns were imperfectly correlated across regions. In this case, investing directly in real assets in other regions would be an alternative to investing in deposits in the banks of other regions. The effects would be quite different, however. When a bank becomes insolvent, it is forced to liquidate its assets, with a consequent loss of value. Another bank which has a claim on the first suffers from this loss of value too, even if the second bank is solvent. If the second bank had invested in a real asset instead, it would have had another option. It could have held the real asset until maturity and thus avoided the loss of value that results from liquidation.

PROOFS

Theorem 1. *The planner's risk-sharing problem (P1) is equivalent to the modified problem (P2). From this it follows that the solution to the planner's problem is first-best efficient, that is, the incentive constraints do not bind.*

Proof. Consider first the consumption of early consumers. For any state ω with $\hat{\omega} > 0$, concavity of the utility function $u(\cdot)$ implies that

$$\frac{\sum_{i=1}^{n} \omega^i u(c_1^i(\omega))}{\sum_{i=1}^{n} \omega^i} \leq u(\hat{c}_1(\omega))$$

where

$$\hat{c}_1(\omega) \equiv \frac{\sum_{i=1}^{n} \omega^i c_1^i(\omega)}{\sum_{i=1}^{n} \omega^i}.$$

So there is no loss of generality in assuming that

$$c_1^i(\omega) = \hat{c}_1(\omega),$$

for every i and every ω. A similar argument shows that there is no loss of generality in assuming that

$$c_2^i(\omega) = \hat{c}_2(\omega),$$

for every i and every ω. Finally, suppose that there exist two states ω and ω' such that $\hat{\omega} = \hat{\omega}'$. Then define

$$(c_1(\omega), c_2(\omega)) = (c_1(\omega'), c_2(\omega')) = \frac{1}{2}\left[(\hat{c}_1(\omega), \hat{c}_2(\omega)) + (\hat{c}_1(\omega'), \hat{c}_2(\omega'))\right].$$

It is easy to see that $(c_1(\omega), c_2(\omega))$ and $(c_1(\omega'), c_2(\omega'))$ satisfy the feasibility constraints and, because the objective function satisfies

$$\hat{\omega}u(\hat{c}_1(\omega)) + (1 - \hat{\omega})u(\hat{c}_2(\omega)) = \hat{\omega}'u(\hat{c}_1(\omega')) + (1 - \hat{\omega}')u(\hat{c}_2(\omega')),$$

it follows from the concavity of $u(\cdot)$ that

$$
\begin{aligned}
\hat{\omega}u(c_1(\omega)) + (1 - \hat{\omega})u(c_2(\omega)) &= \hat{\omega}'u(c_1(\omega')) + (1 - \hat{\omega}')u(c_2(\omega')) \\
&\geq \hat{\omega}u(\hat{c}_1(\omega)) + (1 - \hat{\omega})u(\hat{c}_2(\omega)) \\
&= \hat{\omega}'u(\hat{c}_1(\omega')) + (1 - \hat{\omega}')u(\hat{c}_2(\omega')).
\end{aligned}
$$

With a slight abuse of notation we write $p(\hat{\omega})$ for the probability of $\hat{\omega}$. Then the planner has to choose a total investment x_0 in the long asset, a total investment y_0 in the short asset, an amount of the long asset $x_1(\hat{\omega})$ to carry through to date 2, an amount $y_1(\hat{\omega})$ of the short asset to carry through to date 2, the consumption $c_1(\hat{\omega})$ of an early consumer, and the consumption $c_2(\hat{\omega})$ of a late consumer in order to maximize the typical consumer's expected utility. Note that the initial investment portfolio (x_0, y_0) does not depend on $\hat{\omega}$ because the planner does not yet know the value of $\hat{\omega}$. However, all the decisions made at date 1 and date 2 depend on $\hat{\omega}$, which is revealed at the beginning of date 1.

The modified risk-sharing problem can be written in per capita terms as follows:

$$(P2)\begin{cases}
\max & \sum_{\hat{\omega}} p(\hat{\omega})\{\hat{\omega}u(c_1(\hat{\omega})) + (1 - \hat{\omega})u(c_2(\hat{\omega}))\} \\
\text{s.t.} & \text{(i)} \quad x_0 + y_0 \leq n; \\
& \text{(ii)} \quad \hat{\omega}c_1(\hat{\omega}) \leq y_0 - y_1(\hat{\omega}) + r(x_0 - x_1(\hat{\omega})); \\
& \text{(iii)} \quad (1 - \hat{\omega})c_2(\hat{\omega}) \leq y_1(\hat{\omega}) + Rx_1(\hat{\omega}).
\end{cases}$$

Suppose that we solve the problem for a particular state $\hat{\omega}$, that is, we solve the problem

$$\max \quad \hat{\omega}u(c_1(\hat{\omega}))+(1-\hat{\omega})u(c_2(\hat{\omega}))\}$$

$$\text{s.t.} \quad \text{(ii)} \quad \hat{\omega}c_1(\hat{\omega}) \le y_0 - y_1(\hat{\omega}) + r(x_0 - x_1(\hat{\omega}));$$

$$\text{(iii)} \quad (1-\hat{\omega})c_2(\hat{\omega}) \le y_1(\hat{\omega}) + Rx_1(\hat{\omega}).$$

A necessary condition for an optimum is that

$$u'(c_1(\hat{\omega})) \ge u'(c_2(\hat{\omega})),$$

with strict equality if $y_1(\hat{\omega}) > 0$, which implies that

$$c_1(\hat{\omega}) \le c_2(\hat{\omega})$$

for every $\hat{\omega}$. So the incentive constraint (iv) in the original problem P1 in the text is automatically satisfied. ∎

REFERENCES

Acemoglu, D., A. Ozdaglar, and A. Tahbaz-Salehi. 2015. "Systemic Risk and Stability in Financial Networks." *American Economic Review* 105 (2):564–608.

Allen, F., and D. Gale. 1998. "Optimal Financial Crises." *Journal of Finance* 53 (4): 1245–1284.

Allen, F., and D. Gale. 2000. "Financial Contagion." *Journal of Political Economy* 108:1–33.

Alonso, I. 1996. "On Avoiding Bank Runs." *Journal of Monetary Economics* 37:73–87.

Benoit, S., J. Colliard, C. Hurlin, and C. Perignon. 2017. "Where the Risks Lie: A Survey on Systemic Risk." *Review of Finance* 21:109–152.

Calomiris, C., and C. Kahn. 1991. "The Role of Demandable Debt in Structuring Optimal Banking Arrangements." *American Economic Review* 81:497–513.

Champ, B., B. Smith, and S. Williamson. 1996. "Currency Elasticity and Banking Panics: Theory and Evidence." *Canadian Journal of Economics* 29:828–864.

Chari, V. 1989. "Banking without Deposit Insurance or Bank Panics: Lessons from a Model of the U.S. National Banking System." *Federal Reserve Bank of Minneapolis Quarterly Review* 13 (Summer):3–19.

Chari, V., and R. Jagannathan. 1988. "Banking Panics, Information, and Rational Expectations Equilibrium." *Journal of Finance* 43:749–760.

Diamond, D., and P. Dybvig. 1983. "Bank Runs, Deposit Insurance, and Liquidity." *Journal of Political Economy* 91:401–419.

Elliott, M., B. Golub, and M. Jackson. 2014. "Financial Networks and Contagion." *American Economic Review* 104:3115–3153.

Gai, P., and S. Kapadia. 2010. "Contagion in Financial Networks." *Proceedings of the Royal Society of London A: Mathematical, Physical and Engineering Sciences* 466 (2120):2401–2423.

Gorton, G. 1988. "Banking Panics and Business Cycles." *Oxford Economic Papers* 40:751–781.

Hellwig, M. 1994. "Liquidity Provision, Banking, and the Allocation of Interest Rate Risk." *European Economic Review* 38:1363–1389.

Jacklin, C., and S. Bhattacharya. 1988. "Distinguishing Panics and Information Based Bank Runs: Welfare and Policy Implications." *Journal of Political Economy* 96:568–592.

Sprague, O. 1910. *A History of Crises under the National Banking System.* Washington, DC: U.S. Government Printing Office.

Wallace, N. 1988. "Another Attempt to Explain an Illiquid Banking System: The Diamond and Dybvig Model with Sequential Service Taken Seriously." *Federal Reserve Bank of Minneapolis Quarterly Review* 12 (Fall):3–16.

Wallace, N. 1990. "A Banking Model in Which Partial Suspension Is Best." *Federal Reserve Bank of Minneapolis Quarterly Review* 14 (Fall):11–23.

CHAPTER 14

The Economics of Information and Financial Networks

Stefano Battiston

1. ECONOMIC NETWORKS AND ECONOMICS OF INFORMATION

The literature on economic networks has been developing since the late 1990s and early 2000s (Kirman 1997; Jackson and Wolinsky 1996; Bala and Goyal 2000; Allen and Gale 2001; Jackson and Watts 2002; Stiglitz and Greenwald 2003; Ballester et al., 2006; Jackson et al. 2006). In particular, since the Great Recession a consensus has formed around the idea that financial interlinkages play an important role in the emergence of financial instability (Henry et al. 2013), and that, in order to understand and tame financial instabilities, a mathematical formulation in terms of financial networks is useful and often necessary (Battiston et al. 2007; Haldane 2009; Stiglitz 2010; Gai et al., 2011; Haldane and May 2011; Battiston et al. 2012a; Elliott et al., 2014; Acemoglu et al., 2015; Battiston et al. 2016). It is common to observe how the economic networks field builds both upon notions and methods from other disciplines such as graph theory in mathematics (Bollobas 1998), social networks in sociology (Bonacich 1987; Granovetter 1978, 1973), and the physics of complex networks (Dorogovtsev and Mendes 2003; Newman 2003; Barabáasi 2009; Schweitzer et al. 2009; Barrat et al. 2004; Caldarelli 2007; Caldarelli et al., 2007), as well as upon some other branches of economics such as game theory, or input-output analysis.

However, it is less commonly understood that many relations exist between the ongoing research program in complex financial networks, in which Stiglitz has made important contributions in recent years (Stiglitz and Greenwald 2003; Battiston et al. 2007; Delli Gatti et al. 2010; Stiglitz 2010; Battiston et al. 2012a,b, 2013, 2016; Roukny et al., 2016), and economics of information, i.e. the vast and long-standing literature on the role of externalities in the presence of imperfect and asymmetric information in market economies, in which Stiglitz has been the central figure for several decades (see, e.g., Stiglitz 2000, for an overview). Not enough attention has been devoted so far to clarify and formalize the relations between these two streams of literature. Hence, the aim of this paper is twofold. We want to start filling in this gap by offering some reflections that will hopefully stir up the discussion. We also want to review some of Stiglitz's contributions to the financial network literature in order to familiarize the rest of the economic profession with these kind of research methods and the results that can be obtained.

1.1. WHY FINANCIAL NETWORKS?

An important question that often arises is why, precisely, we should care about networks in economics and finance. The answer we offer in this paper stems from the relations between economics of information and financial networks. In brief, in this paper we argue that because asymmetric information is associated with important externalities, the impact of actors on the system and the way they are affected by others depend on their positions in a network of relations. While standard approaches are inadequate to capture these dependences, the network approach allows to characterize the microeconomic mechanics of how externalities emerge and how they lead to systemic effects. As a result, the financial networks field succeeds in delivering a number of policy insights in various areas that could not be obtained otherwise.

There are two specific areas in which financial networks matter. The first is financial stability. Linkages, represented by financial contracts can have ambiguous effects: on the one hand, they increase individual profitability and reduce individual risk, but on the other hand, they propagate financial distress either on the assets side or on the liability side or both, thus increasing systemic risk. On this topic several issues remain open but much work has already been done in recent years (Allen et al. 2012; Allen and Gale 2001; Battiston et al. 2012a,b; Beale et al. 2011; Amini et al. 2012; Gai, Haldane, and Kapadia 2011; Gai and Kapadia 2010; Haldane and May 2011; Stiglitz 2010; Gai et al., 2011).

The second area, is macroprudential policy. Institutions have an incentive to become too connected to fail and too correlated to fail Acharya and Yorulmazer 2007; Acharia 2009. Empirically, they are observed to form tightly knit structures (Boss et al. 2004; Cajueiro and Tabak 2008;

Craig and Von Peter 2010; Iori et al. 2008; Soramäki et al., 2007; Upper and Worms, 2004; Vitali et al., 2011) and to gain exposure to similar risks (Gai and Kapadia 2010). Once these structures emerge in the financial system, they alter the incentives of each institution with respect to risk taking. Indeed they induce a collective moral hazard (Farhi and Tirole 2012) whereby groups of institutions are altogether too-big-to-fail. In turn, this gives institutions greater market power and increases the risk of regulatory capture.

1.2. ASYMMETRIC INFORMATION AND NETWORKS

The fundamental legacy of the economics of information is the recognition that information is typically costly, imperfect, and asymmetric and that this "deeply affects the understanding of . . . the fundamental welfare theorem and some of the basic characterization of a market economy, and provides explanations of economic and social phenomena that otherwise would be hard to understand" (Stiglitz 2000, 1). One of the reasons why information matters are externalities, since it turns out that most of the interesting or problematic externalities arise in the presence of imperfect or asymmetric information (Stiglitz 1996, page 23). Indeed, when information, and in particular the information on the origins and the effects of the externalities is perfect, the problem of internalizing the externalities can be formalized as a simple coordination problem. In contrast, imperfect and asymmetric information poses a broader range of qualitatively different challenges that arise when agents happen to have different information sets, in particular about the origin or the magnitude of the externalities and can play strategically on other agents' lack of information. As a result, asymmetric information is associated with important externalities and many of these externalities do not simply affect all actors at the same way or at the same time. Instead, they take effect along the relations (e.g., financial or trade contracts) in a *network*. In this way, externalities may affect specific actors at specific times and along specific *pathways* (e.g., chains of actors and contracts).

1.3. EXTERNALITIES AND NETWORKS

Externalities are usually defined as positive or negative effects imposed by agents on others for which they do not pay a cost or get a return. The relation between externalities and networks results from how externalities "travel" from one player to another. Some externalities are like air pollution: everybody is exposed at the same time and in a similar way. Other types of externalities exert impact only along specific relations between players, i.e. through direct and indirect counterparties. Notice that if the network is *connected* and there is no dampening of the effect (the effect does not decrease moving along pathways, i.e. sequences of actors and relations), eventually everybody in the market is affected. However, in general the network could be *disconnected*, so that some players are never affected by the externality. Moreover, effects could decrease at every step so that indirect counterparties are less affected than the direct ones.

The presence and the structure of a financial network can work as conduit of both positive and negative externalities. An example of positive externality is the following. If A diversifies over a number of assets that are uncorrelated with other players' portfolios, it reduces its own risk. While this decision could be driven by the intention of A to increase its own creditworthiness vis-à-vis its counterparty B, it happens to also improve B's creditworthiness, which A did not take into account in its decision.

An example of negative externality is the following. If A is exposed to B, B's decisions to gain exposure to C may propagate financial distress to A or even to indirect counterparties, i.e. A's creditors, without B paying for this. In the classic case of *default contagion* (Allen and Gale 2001), the default of C could induce the default of B and, further, the default of A. However, it has been recently recognized also the importance of the case of *distress contagion*, in which financial distress can propagate even in the absence of default and solely due to increases in the default probability of the players in the chain (Battiston et al. 2012c, 2016a).

1.4. MARKETS AND NETWORKS

Any market can be graphically represented as two networks (see Network Glossary in Appendix). The first is the network of players, in which nodes and trades between two players correspond edges. The second is the network of players and securities. This is a *bipartite* network in which one type of nodes corresponds to players and another type to securities, while an edge connecting a player and a security represents the fact that the players hold the securities (by an amount specified by the weight of the edge).

The specific added value that we can gain from this modeling approach depends on the structure of the market, which may differ substantially across contexts. For instance, when selling a share of a quoted company in the stock market, one typically does not care about the identity of the buyer and its ability to pay. The reason is that the trade goes through a central counterparty who guarantees its completion. In other markets, however, the identity of the counterparty in a trade or in a contract matters. For instance, in a credit market that is not fully collateralized, there is a nonzero counterparty risk, which is not the same with every counterparty. If one defaults on its obligations may cause losses in its counterparty. In turn, this may cause losses to the counterparties of the counterparty. As a result, losses may travel along chains of contracts, and if they do, they do not affect players who are not part of the chain.

In network terms, in the first example of the stock market all sellers and buyers are connected only to the central clearing counterparty. Every seller is thus indirectly connected to any buyer. This can be represented as a *star* network (see Appendix), which is one of the simplest network architecture. In this case, the position of all buyers is equivalent. The second example, could instead be any complex architecture emerging from the decentralized decisions of agents in establishing contracts with each other.

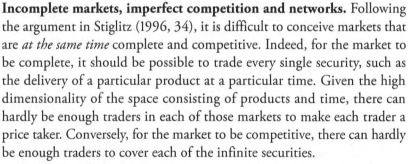

Incomplete markets, imperfect competition and networks. Following the argument in Stiglitz (1996, 34), it is difficult to conceive markets that are *at the same time* complete and competitive. Indeed, for the market to be complete, it should be possible to trade every single security, such as the delivery of a particular product at a particular time. Given the high dimensionality of the space consisting of products and time, there can hardly be enough traders in each of those markets to make each trader a price taker. Conversely, for the market to be competitive, there can hardly be enough traders to cover each of the infinite securities.

We can conclude that:

- If markets are not competitive there are securities that are only traded by a small subset of the players. This implies that the network of players is not a *complete graph*.
- If markets are not complete there are securities that are not traded at all or traded only by subsets of traders. This means that the network players-securities is not a *complete bipartite graph*.

- When networks are not complete and are not particularly simple, then actors hold *asymmetric* positions in the network, meaning that their *network centrality* is heterogeneous across actors.

The last point is particularly relevant in market with externalities because the position of the players in the network becomes important to determine to what extent (1) a given player is affected by externalities from other players and (2) to what extent she affects other players directly or indirectly (i.e. what is her systemic importance).

1.5. THE FINANCIAL SYSTEM AS A NETWORK

Notice that when two or more securities are traded by market players, whereby some *but not all* market players trade both securities, then the set of trades is better represented by a *multiplex network*, i.e. nodes are connected by edges of different types each corresponding to a given security. More in detail, and following (Battiston and Caldarelli 2013; Battiston, Caldarelli, D'Errico 2015), the financial system can be regarded as a *multiplex network* in the following way. Financial institutions can be represented as nodes and financial dependencies due to contracts between counterparties can be represented as links. Whenever the identity of the counterparties, their past relations and their financial fragility matter, thinking the system as a network improves our understanding (e.g., in comparison to thinking it as a market where prices incorporate all the relevant information). Moreover, it is crucial to add securities to this picture, represented as a second type of node. The fact that institutions invest in a given security or are exposed to its price variation via some (publicly traded) derivative contract can also be represented as a second type of link. This general network representation covers for instance the case of a system consisting of an interbank market (where banks are connected via balance-sheet interlocks because the assets of one are the liabilities of some other ones) and an external assets market (where banks are connected through financial instruments issued outside the financial network). In particular, examples of classes of external assets are: (1) mortgage-backed securities, which played a role in the subprime crisis in 2008–2009; (2) sovereign bonds, that played a role in the period 2011–2012; (3) links arising through underlying real assets, e.g., the price of assets in the real-estate sector. It is very important to notice that distress propagates not only via institution-institution linkages but also via institution-security linkages.

For instance, the fire-selling of one institution has negative externalities on those institutions that are exposed to the same asset or asset class. This institution may then propagate distress both to the institutions that are exposed to them and to the securities they are exposed to. Many of the effects that are relevant for systemic instabilities can be described within the above general network representation.

Overall then, in this setting, there are two types of connections among banks, both conducive for the spreading of financial distress. On the one hand, shocks move from one bank to another via the direct interlocks between balance sheets. That is, since the liabilities of one bank are the assets of some other banks, the default of the obligor implies a loss for the creditors (see, e.g., Battiston et al., 2012b). However, as studied in Battiston et al. (2012a), for example, even if the obligor does not default, some distress spreads to the creditors anyway. Indeed, the fact that the equity of the obligor is being depleted implies that the market value of its obligations decreases. Notice that complementary to contagion, but not less important, is the issue of liquidity provision. Indeed, in the case creditors decide to hoard liquidity rather than providing it to other market players, this has negative externalities to the other institutions and to the system hampering its functionality (Gai, Haldane, and Kapadia 2011). Accordingly, the identification of the institutions that are systemically important has to account not only for the potential contagion an institution may cause but also for their role as liquidity providers.

On the other hand, there are indirect connections among banks due to the fact that they invest in common assets. This implies that, for instance, if as a result of a shock on the price of an asset, a bank sells a quantity of that asset sufficient to move down the price, the other banks holding the same asset will experience both the initial shock and the secondary shock and may start in turn to sell the asset themselves, triggering a devaluation spiral.

It has been argued that many financial crises originate from bubbles in some asset market, typically assets associated with the housing sector (Alessi and Detken 2011). Accordingly, in the banking crisis of 2008, the overlapping portfolios channel played a major role in triggering the downturn. Therefore, the ultimate objective of contagion models should be to incorporate both the effects coming from overlapping portfolios and balance sheet interlocks (Allen et al. 2012, Caccioli et al. 2014). However, more attention should be devoted to the fact that the interlocking balance sheet channel can greatly amplify the effects of shocks acting along the overlapping portfolio channel. Moreover, from a mathematical point of view, the network of banks and assets is a bipartite network meaning that there are no edges between the nodes in the same class—indeed assets do not invest in another assets. This network can be "projected" into a network of banks in which the relations now represent the fact that two banks hold one or more assets in common, the weight of the edge reflecting the magnitude of the overlap. As will be argued more in detail later, although the economic mechanism behind is completely different, there are formal analogies in the spreading of contagion in the two types of networks and lessons to be learned on one can provide insights for the other. In light of these considerations, in the following we will focus on the contagion along the balance sheet interlock and we will give insights on how the overlapping portfolios issue can be incorporated.

2. DEFAULT PROBABILITY IN FINANCIAL NETWORKS

2.1. TOWARD A GENERAL EQUILIBRIUM THEORY OF CREDIT

As argued in Stiglitz and Greenwald (2003, chap. 8), credit is a more pervasive phenomenon in modern economy than we tend to think. Essentially, any time a payment is not executed exactly at the same time as the delivery of a product or service, this is equivalent to extending credit. This means for instance that firms extend credit to each other along a supply chain whenever they accept a delayed payment. If there are shocks on these payments and this cause any cost to the parties, there are externalities that arise and the possibility of cascades of default as investigated in (Battiston et al. 2007). Therefore banks are not the only actors who extend credit, although they enjoy the special status of being allowed to create credit endogenously.

In all cases, the central question about credit is what is the probability for the future payment to be fulfilled. This is where information comes in. Not only information about the financial liquidity and solvency of the counterparty matter but also information about its incentives. As soon as information is imperfect, precisely because agents cannot observe nor anticipate the financial solvency and liquidity of their counterparties' counterparties, they are exposed to losses caused by those indirect counterparties without the latter being charged the cost of the losses.

In other words, the externalities described earlier such as default contagion and distress contagion may emerge. Further, if information is asymmetric and/or markets are incomplete the network structure matters and actors are better off or worse off depending on their position in the network.

One of the first works investigating the properties of a credit network, and in particular the emergence of multiple equilibria is in Stiglitz and Greenwald (2003, chap. 8). The model considers a closed chain of firms, i.e. a *ring network* architecture. Each firm in the ring receives goods from the previous one and supplies credit. The interesting case is the presence of bankruptcy costs, i.e. in case of default, what a firm can repay is potentially significantly less than what it owes, due for instance to legal costs or disruption of social capital, which are in many cases a consequence of imperfect information. In this case, the default of one firm, due to a real shock, can cause a domino effect down the ring.

If a bank lends to all firms in the ring, and information is imperfect in the specific sense that actors can only ascertain the creditworthiness of their own counterparties, then several interesting phenomena may arise.

Confidence crises versus Real crises. The first phenomena is confidence crises akin to sunspot crises. If there is a common belief in a downturn of the economy, firms and the bank charge high interest rates in the expectation of high risk of default and expectations are self-fulfilling. The second phenomena is the existence of multiple equilibria in the presence of a real shock. In one equilibrium, the real shock to one of the firm does not trigger any bankruptcy. In another equilibria, some or all the firms default depending on the bankruptcy costs.

The insights from this analysis on monetary policies are as follows. The effects of monetary policies on banks can be amplified in the economy through the trade credit relations among firms giving rise to a new form of *credit multiplier*, which is usually not considered and whose magnitude depends on the financial linkages along the production network.

2.2. THE PRICE OF COMPLEXITY IN FINANCIAL NETWORKS

The question raised in the previous section is taken up and analyzed more systematically in two recent connected papers (Battiston et al., 2016a; Roukny, Battiston, and Stiglitz 2016) that share the same basic model but analyze complementary questions. Battiston et al. (2016a) analyze the probability of systemic default in a network of financial contracts and shows that it can be very sensitive on imperfect information about contracts.

Model setup. We consider a set of lending contracts among n banks ("interbank contracts") and a set of contracts of banks on securities outside the banking system ("external contracts"). We refer to these two sets as the financial network.

Model timing. At time 1, banks raise funds and make investments in external and interbank assets. At time 2, the values of the external assets are shocked and updated. While the shock distribution is known at time 1, shocks are only observed at time 2. At time 2 the interbank contracts mature and their value is also updated depending on the shocks that have occurred. For each bank i, the main quantities are the following.

Assets and liabilities. Assets and liabilities of i on the external markets are denoted as a_i^E and ℓ_i^E. Assets and liabilities of i on the interbank credit market are denoted as a_i^B and ℓ_i^B. Total liabilities are denoted as ℓ_i. At time 1, each bank i allocates its external assets in a portfolio of securities on the external market, E_{ik} denoting the fraction of i's external assets invested at time 1 in the security k. The unitary value of the external security k is x_k^E. Without loss of generality: at time 1, $x_k^E(1) = 1$ for all k, while $x_k^E(2)$ is a random variable drawn from a given distribution. At time 2, then the external assets of bank i, is a sum of random variables, $a_i^E(2) = a_i^E(1)\sum_k E_{ik}x_k^E(2)$. For our purposes, it is sufficient to assume that we can express the external assets of bank i as follows: $a_i^E(2) = a_i^E(1)(1 + \mu + \sigma u_i)$, where u_i is a random variable drawn from a given distribution with mean zero and variance one, the parameter μ is the expected return of the portfolio and σ its standard deviation. We also assume to know the joint probability distribution $p(u_1,...,u_n)$.

At time 1, each bank i allocates its interbank assets among the other banks, B_{ij} denoting the fraction of i's interbank assets invested at time 1 in the liability of bank j. These investments are secured via collateralization, i.e. bank j posts as collateral for the loan an asset that bank i will collect in case bank j defaults. In spirit, this approach is similar to Gai, Haldane, and Kapadia (2011), although for the purpose of our study, we exclude re-hypothetication, i.e. assets used as collateral are kept aside and cannot be reused. The collateral is also assumed to be risk free in the time horizon of the model, i.e. its value stays constant during the two periods and it can be ignored in the default condition further below.

The unitary value of the interbank liability of bank j to other banks is x_j^B. Without loss of generality: at time 1, $x_j^B(1) = 1$ for all j. The liabilities of bank j are constant in value from the perspective of bank i, i.e. the debt agreed upon in the contract at time 1. However, from the point of view of counterparties of j, $x_j^B(2) = 1$ if bank j honors its obligation, $x_j^B(2) = R$ otherwise, where R is the recovery rate, i.e. the fraction of the interbank asset that is covered by the collateral and that the lender can recover after the default of j. Accordingly, at time 2, the interbank assets of bank i is $a_i^B(2) = a_i^B(1)\sum_j B_{ij}x_j^B(2)$. Notice that this approach differs from previous models (Eisenberg and Noe 2001; Rogers and Veraart 2013) based on the determination *ex-post* of the clearing vector of payments.

Default condition. The standard balance sheet identity in financial accounting states that equity of bank i, e_i, is the difference between assets and liabilities. Hence $e_i(2) = a_i^E(2) + a_i^B(2) - \ell_i = a_i^E(1)(1 + \mu + \sigma u_i) + a_i^B(1)\sum_j B_{ij}x_j^B(2) - \ell_i$. It is also standard to assume that the default of bank i occurs when equity becomes negative, i.e. if $e_i(2) < 0$. In the following, we are interested in the probability of default of individual banks. Notice that we assume $e_i(1) > 0$, thus $e_i(2) < 0$ iff $\frac{e_i(2)}{e_i(1)} < 0$. It is then convenient to write the default condition as $\varepsilon_i(1 + \mu + \sigma u_i) + \beta_i \sum_j B_{ij}x_j^B(2) - \lambda_i < 0$, where the parameter $\varepsilon_i = \frac{a_i^E(1)}{e_i(1)}$ measures the magnitude, per unit of initial equity of bank i, of the investments of bank i in external assets. Similarly, the parameter $\beta_i = \frac{a_i^B(1)}{e_i(1)}$, also called interbank leverage, measures the magnitude, per unit of initial equity, of i's investments in interbank assets and the parameter $\lambda_i = \frac{l_i(1)}{e_i(1)}$ measures the magnitude, per unit of initial equity, of i's total liabilities. Let us define a default indicator χ_i, with $\chi_i = 1$ in case of default of bank i and $\chi_i = 0$ otherwise. Because the only variable that is exogenously stochastic is the shock u_i on each bank's external assets, we finally write the default condition as follows

$$u_i < \theta_i \equiv \frac{1}{\varepsilon_i \sigma}(\lambda_i - \varepsilon - \varepsilon\mu_i - \beta_i \sum_j B_{ij}x_j^B(\chi_j)), \tag{14.1}$$

where θ_i denotes the default threshold. Notice that we have dropped the time in the notation, while we have emphasized in the formula that the value of the interbank liability of a counterparty j, x_j^B, depends on the default indicator of j, χ_j, to recall that it is $x_j^B(\chi_j = 0) = 1$ and $x_j^B(\chi_j = 1) = R$. Thus, depending on the magnitude and sign of the shocks u_i that hit all banks, some of them can default on their obligations, possibly causing other banks to default. We can now express the default indicators χ_i of all banks as a system of equations

$$\forall i \quad \chi_i = \Theta(u_i - \theta_i(\chi_1,...,\chi_n)), \tag{14.2}$$

where Θ denotes the step function or Heaviside function (i.e. equal one if the argument is positive, zero otherwise). A solution of the system, denoted as χ^*, depends on the vector of shocks u and on the initial condition χ^0, which represents the initial belief of the banks in other banks' defaults. The existence and uniqueness of the solution is discussed further below.

The determination of the fixed point of this system of equations can become computationally cumbersome if we want to sample at a fine resolution the shock space of an arbitrary number of banks. However, in the default condition of the counterparties j of bank i, we can simplify the computation by replacing the value of the second-order counterparties' credit obligations (i.e. the obligations of neighbors of order 2 in the contract network) with their expected value. In other words, we replace the stochastic variable x_k^B with its expected value $\mathbb{E}[x_k^B] = RP_k + (1 - P_k)$, where P_k is the default probability of bank k. This is a legitimate approximation since expected values are commonly used in the banking practice to estimate the future value of assets. Notice also that this approximation does not remove the effects of correlations across shocks on banks.

Default probability. The probability P_i of default at time 2 of bank i is then simply the integral over the shock space of the default indicator:

$$\forall i \quad P_i = \int \chi_i^*(u, \chi^0) p(u) du, \tag{14.3}$$

where $p(u)$ denotes the joint density function of the shocks and accounts for possible correlations across shocks. Finally the probability of systemic default is

$$P^{sys} = \int \chi^{sys}(\chi^*(u, \chi^0)) p(u) du, \tag{14.4}$$

where χ^{sys} is the systemic default indicator. The choice of the systemic default identification can vary and there is no consensus on what should be defined as a systemic event. For the sake of clarity, in the following we consider the extreme but intuitive case of all banks defaulting, i.e. $\chi^{sys} = \Pi_i \chi_i^*$.

Main results. The two main results of (Battiston et al. 2016a) are as follows. Not only imperfect information on financial contracts imply imperfect information on systemic risk (more precisely, on the probability of systemic default) but the imperfection of information is typically amplified by the network of contracts. Moreover the specific structure of contracts matters, meaning that not all network structures behave the same way.

For the purpose of this section and for didactical purposes, it is enough to focus on errors in a single parameter, namely the recovery rate R, and to consider three basic architectures with three nodes: a star, a chain and a ring. Based on the model setup described earlier, one can then compute analytically the sensitivity $\partial P^{sys} / \partial R$ of the default probability on the recovery rate R as a function of the ratio between interbank leverage β and the maximal loss $\varepsilon\sigma$ that a bank can withstand on the external assets. In a wide range of parameters, the sensitivity is shown to be highest for the ring network architecture, followed by the chain and the star architectures. The intuition behind this result is that the systemic default probability in an interbank network depends on the multiplicative interplay among the parameters that matter for the default thresholds. In particular, the multiplication involves the banks located along chains of lending. As a result, more numerous and longer chains lead to stronger amplification of the errors on the parameters. Indeed, $\partial P^{sys} / \partial R$ is a polynomial in the interbank leverage β, where the leading power depends on the presence of chains or cycles in the network. This result, shown in Battiston et al. (2016a) and not reported before in the literature, illustrates concretely the impact of the complexity of the financial network on the determination of systemic risk.

2.3. UNCERTAINTY AS A SOURCE OF SYSTEMIC RISK IN FINANCIAL NETWORKS

In the previous section we showed how the structure of the financial network can amplify the imperfections of information. In this section, we show that even in the presence of perfect information, the structure of financial networks, and in particular cyclical interdependences, can lead to an endogenous form of uncertainty.

We summarize the results obtained in Roukny, Battiston, and Stiglitz (2016), which build on the same model described earlier and show how the financial network implies the existence of multiple equilibria, even with perfect information on the financial contracts. More precisely, in this case, all characteristics of contracts are known including the distributions of returns on investments. The only unknown variables are the individual returns at time 2. Notations and assumptions are as in the previous section. Let us further refer to a *cycle* as an arrangement of contracts on a closed chain, such as in the ring structure analyzed in Section 2.1. Consider the case of N banks, with recovery rate strictly smaller than one and with non-negative interbank leverage. A necessary and sufficient condition for the system to display multiple equilibria is that there exists a simple cycle C_k of credit contracts along $k \geq 2$ banks, such that for each bank i and its borrowing counterparty $i+1$ along the cycle, the default threshold of i changes with the default state of i's borrower. In simple terms, the theorem states that as soon as there is an interbank market with some cycle of contracts there will be multiple equilibria. Two typical equilibria are the one in which all banks default and the one in which no bank defaults.

Mathematically speaking, the existence of multiple equilibria on bank defaults simply means that there are multiple configurations of default/no default that solve the system of equations defining the default conditions. The economic meaning of multiple equilibria in this model is that, even if information about contracts and counterparties is perfect, the cyclic interdependence of the balance sheets of banks leaves room for an endogenous indetermination of the default states. Depending on their beliefs, agents could rationally coordinate to one of several economic outcomes, which for simplicity can be thought of as a good equilibrium and a bad one. There are several possible mechanisms that could make agents coordinate on the bad equilibrium, including for instance the combination of liquidity hoarding and asset fire sales. If agents come to believe that external assets held by their counterparties are overpriced they will hoard liquidity and sell part of those assets, thus inducing counterparties to do the same, effectively causing a systemic crisis. In the presence of multiple equilibria of the default state χ for a given combination of shocks, the probability of default is not well-defined any longer, because, when integrating over the shock space, the integrand can take several values for the same shock. A simple way to overcome this problem, is to resort to the idea of scenarios. Depending on the chosen scenario, for any given shock for which multiple equilibria exist, one equilibrium is selected according to a predefined rule. More precisely, we define the worst (best) equilibrium as the function that for any given shock u, selects the solution in which the largest (smallest) number of banks default.

Given the set $\{\chi_k^{sys}(u)\}$ of all the possible solutions for the default conditions of Equation (14.2) for any given shock u, the *worst equilibrium* is defined as the function of the shock $u : \chi^{sys+}(u) = max_k\{\chi_k^{sys}(u)\}$. Similarly, the *best equilibrium* is the function of the shock $u : \chi^{sys-}(u) = min_k\{\chi_k^{sys}(u)\}$.

In the following we will refer to the best (worst) scenario as the one in which the best (worst) equilibrium is selected. Accordingly, we define the *systemic default probability* in the worst (+) ("pessimistic") scenario and best (−) ("optimistic") as:

$$P^{\pm} = \int \chi^{sys\pm}(u)\, p(u)\, du. \tag{14.5}$$

We then define as *uncertainty on the systemic default probability* the difference between the systemic default probability in the two scenarios:

$$\Delta P = P^{+} - P^{-}. \tag{14.6}$$

By measuring the difference between the probabilities of systemic default in the best and the worst scenario, the quantity ΔP is also a measure of the uncertainty in the assessment of P^{sys}, due to the presence of multiple equilibria. One can derive analytical expressions for the uncertainty ΔP in simple network structures. For instance, uncertainty increases going from a ring market to a star market with double linkages (i.e. in which the center of the star lends to and borrows from each of the nodes in the periphery).

Overall, this model allows to investigate how uncertainty as defined above depends on crucial quantities such as leverage, volatility, interbank market structures and correlation across external shocks (Roukny et al., 2016). Results show that leverage both on the interbank market and the external assets increase uncertainty, while volatility in external assets has ambiguous effects. Correlation across shocks can also have nonmonotone effects on uncertainty. However, complete correlation in a set of homogenous banks univocally increases uncertainty with respect to the uncorrelated case. In terms of network structure, uncertainty decreases with the length of the credit chain. When analyzing a market composed of multiple cycles (i.e., star market), uncertainty increases compared to single-cycle structures.

In terms of policy, this analysis offers a new way to estimate the systemic impact of too-big-to-fail institutions in a network context (Haldane and May 2011; BoE 2013). By showing how cyclical structures in the network imply more uncertainty over default probability, the analysis also contributes to the discussion on regulatory financial data disclosure (Alvarez and Barlevy 2015).

2.4. DEFAULT CASCADES AND RISK DIVERSIFICATION IN NETWORKS

A dominant belief in recent decades, both in the finance academic literature and in practice, has been that diversification of investment opportunities is always beneficial, as long as the marginal gain of a new investment exceeds the monitoring costs. In other words, risk diversification never entails adverse external effects. The intuition for this belief comes from the following argument. If shocks are uncorrelated, then the central limit theorem ensures that the fluctuation decrease with the number of sources of shocks, i.e. the number of different assets in the portfolio. As a result, in case of a shock to a counterparty, the exposure of everyone is small enough that financial contagion does not spread.

However, there is a misleading use of the notion of contagion in this argument. To understand why, consider an example often made by Joseph Stiglitz in his lectures: if 50 people infected with Ebola arrived on a plane at the JFK airport, then a full diversification strategy would imply sending one person to each different state. Obviously, this does not sound like a very good strategy. Indeed, in the field of epidemiology, where contagion refers to the transmission of a disease, it is well known that a larger number of contacts leads to higher levels of epidemics in a population. In fact, one crucial contribution of network science to epidemiology has been to show that the network structure matters and that a network with a skewed distribution of number of contacts is more conducive to epidemics than a homogenous network (Barrat et al. 2008). So what is the difference in terms of mathematical structure between "contagion" in financial networks and "contagion" in the context of epidemic spreading in social networks?

An entire stream of works has been investigating the conditions under which risk diversification in finance may have undesired effects at the system level (see, e.g., Brock, Hommes, and Wagener 2009; Wagner 2010; Stiglitz 2010; Battiston et al. 2012a; Beale et al. 2011). Stiglitz has played a central role in the development of a research program in this direction by writing, contributing to, or by inspiring directly a series of papers (Battiston et al. 2007; Lorenz and Battiston 2008; Stiglitz 2010; Delli Gatti et al. 2010; Battiston et al. 2012a,b; Roukny et al. 2013; Tasca and Battiston 2016; Tasca et al. 2017; Vitali, Battiston, and Gallegati 2016; Battiston et al. 2016a,b; Bardoscia et al. 2017).

The detailed mathematical mechanism by which diversification can be detrimental differs across the various works cited above and some examples are detailed in the following sections. However, in the retrospective, from all these works and from the numerous works of other research groups, the following meta-theory has been emerging. As long as losses are conservative in nature, then it is true that diversification is always beneficial. By conservative, we mean that the loss does increase when passing from a counterparty to the next. For instance, if A defaults on its payment of $10 to its creditors, this translates, in equilibrium, into a loss of no more than $10 for B. By "in equilibrium," we mean here that, net of all possible externalities resulting from the default of A, the total effect for B is no more than $10.

However, in the presence of imperfect information and associated externalities, there are many economic contexts in which losses are not conservative in the sense defined above. For instance, contingent upon the loss on its asset side, B faces either a tightening of its credit conditions (as analyzed in Battiston et al., 2012a), or a run on its short-term liabilities (as analyzed in Battiston et al. 2012b; Roukny et al. 2013). Both cases lead to additional costs for B that accrue to the initial loss from the default of B. As a result, having more numerous financial interlinkages comes at some point with an increase in systemic risk.

Incidentally, it is a trivial mathematical fact that the probability of systemic default conditional to one actor defaulting, cannot decrease with diversification and approaches the value one with full diversification and with homogenous actors. Indeed, when everybody has fully diversified, all portfolios are identical and thus if one defaults then all must default at the same time. In most models and in policy discussions, It is usually assumed that, in contrast, the unconditional probability of systemic default decreases with diversification. In other words, although the conditional systemic risk increases by construction with diversification, the unconditional systemic risk decreases so fast that diversification is always good. In fact, it has been shown that in presence of nonconservative losses, even the unconditional systemic risk increases with diversification (Battiston et al. 2012a,b, 2016a; Roukny et al. 2013).

The work of Battiston et al. (2012a) contributes to the debate on the resilience of financial networks by introducing a dynamic model for the evolution of financial robustness. It shows that, in the presence of financial acceleration and persistence—i.e. when the variations in the level of financial robustness of institutions tend to persist in time or get amplified—the probability of default does not decrease monotonically with diversification. As a result, the financial network is most resilient for an intermediate level of connectivity.

This is a very simplified, reduced form, model. In order to capture the interdependence among banks that arises from financial ties, we model the evolution of the levels of financial robustness—meant as an equity ratio—of different agents as coupled stochastic processes. Because this model is dynamic and in continuous time, it allows to consider the effect of variations in financial robustness from one bank to the other, rather than focusing solely on bankruptcy events. Moreover, in this model, the reason why the failure probability increases with connectivity is more subtle than in earlier contagion models and emerges from a milder assumption.

In a nutshell, we assume that counterparties of a bank are able to observe quarterly variations in its financial robustness (or some proxy) and when these variations are more negative than "normal," they take actions which penalize the bank. What is perceived as normal by the counterparties is the typical magnitude of the fluctuations of bank's robustness, as measured by its standard deviation σ (in the absence of previous penalizations). When counterparties react, this translates in an immediate, further, drop in the bank's financial robustness by a magnitude α. This assumption is meant to capture the adverse effect that may arise, for instance, because those providing credit increase the interest rate charged, or when short-term creditors decide to hoard liquidity and not to roll over their funds, forcing the agent to fire-sell assets in order to pay back the debts. The ratio α/σ between the amplitude of the adverse effect and the fluctuation amplitude plays a crucial role. If $\alpha > \sigma$, then it is likely that in the next time step the counterparties will observe another variation more negative than normal, and will react again. This chain of events may continue for several quarters in a row. We call *trend reinforcement* this particular form of persistence of financial distress. Notice that because of the random fluctuations, the chain will break as soon as the bank is hit by a shock that is positive and large enough to overcome the effect of the previous penalization. In summary, fluctuations have a beneficial role, that is to push the bank out of the trend reinforcement. Diversification, by reducing fluctuations entails an unanticipated external effect.

2.5. DEFAULT CASCADES

We have further investigated the issue of the effect of diversification in a series of other papers that use different mathematical setting. In Battiston et al. 2012b we have focused on cascades of defaults and considered the effect of the cost of fire-selling in presence of short-term lenders, that decide to run on the bank that experiences a loss if the core capital of the bank is small. This is a dynamic, discrete-time model, where the law of motion is derived from balance-sheet considerations very much in line with Gai and Kapadia, 2010.

The economy consists of N banks with the following balance sheet structure. The assets of each bank i include interbank assets A_i^B (i.e. mid and long-term investments in obligations of other banks) and external assets A_i^E (assets not directly related to any bank in the system). Similarly, liabilities include interbank liabilities and external liabilities. The external assets include short-term and thus liquid assets A_i^{ES} and less liquid ones, denoted as A_i^{EM}. The latter can be liquidated but, potentially, at a loss that depends on how illiquid the market for those assets at the moment of the sale. Liabilities include interbank liabilities that have a mid- to long-term maturity and external liabilities, denoted as L_i^{ES} that instead are short term and are owed to creditors external to the banking system under focus.

Following the standard approach in the literature, we define as default of bank i at time t, the event of the equity of bank i becoming negative. We are interested in investigating how the number of banks defaulting in the system depends on the structure of the balance sheet interlock among banks as well as on the liquidity of the market of external assets. In the following, it turns out that it is mathematically convenient to focus on a capital ratio that measures the equity of bank i relative to its total interbank asset, defined as $\eta_i = \frac{A_i - L_i}{A_i^B}$, where A_i and L_i are the total assets and liabilities of bank i.

We consider the usual mechanism by which a bank faces losses due to the default of some of its borrowers. As benchmark, we consider the case of zero-recovery rate, although this condition can be easily relaxed in the model. In addition, after suffering from losses due to the default of some borrowers, the short-term creditors of the bank may decide to run on their loans and refuse to roll over the short-term funding. As a result, bank i sells the assets necessary to pay back those liabilities. First, the bank sells the liquid ones. If needed it also sells part of the less liquid ones. Depending on how illiquid the market is, in order to sell the latter assets the bank is forced to sell them below the market price ("fire-selling") incurring additional losses.

The quantities that matter in the above sequence of events are the following: the difference $L_i^S - A_i^S$ between the amount that bank i has to repay and the amount that can be liquidated promptly; the ratio q between the market price for the less liquid assets and the fire-selling price at which those assets have to be liquidated in order to find a buyer. As a result, the parameter $b_i = (q-1)\frac{L_i^S - A_i^S}{A_i^L}$ represents the loss incurred by bank i in the process, measured in relative terms with respect to its total interbank assets.

The sequence of events in the model is as follows. There is a number of initial defaults that can, in turn, induce the default of others and the process stops when no more default events are observed. In the end, the size of the cascade, i.e., the total amount of defaulted agents, is recorded. The default is determined by the equity of a bank becoming negative. The equity of each bank may decrease over time as a result of two mechanisms. First, bank i faces the default of a counterparty, which implies the loss of the corresponding asset A_{ij}, while liabilities of i remain the same. Second, bank i incurs in a credit run from its short-term external creditors whenever the number of failures among the counterparties of i, relative to the system size, raises above a certain threshold that depends on bank i capital ratio. Formally, the condition reads as $\frac{k_{fi}(t)}{N} > \frac{\eta_i(0)}{\gamma}$, where γ is a parameter that measures the sensitivity of the external creditors. Notice that the bank run could be modeled as a game among the short-term creditors in line with an established stream of works. However, here we model it in reduced form in light of the fact that the macroscopic behavior of the default cascade depends on the conditions that trigger the bank run and not so much on the way the bank run unfolds.

In this model, the size of the cascade, i.e., the total amount of defaulted banks, can be computed analytically under some approximation regarding the structure of the network and correlations across defaults in the neighborhood of each bank (Battiston et al. 2012b). The analytical results are confirmed by simulations and extended to the case of heterogeneous networks. Here we summarize the results that are most relevant for the policy debate on capital ratio requirements.

Even in a minimal model as the one considered here, if we want to investigate the resilience of different network architecture, there are several degrees of freedom to consider: the type of shock (e.g., random vs targeted); the correlation between capital ratio (e.g., the structure of the balance sheet can be assigned across banks in a way that the capital ratio depends or not on the number of contracts the bank holds); the degree distribution (e.g., comparing scale-free networks with random graphs); the market illiquidity.

The insight from models of default cascades in presence of illiquidity is that looking at capital ratios only is not enough, but also looking at topology is not enough. We actually need to look at the interplay of topology, liquidity and capital buffers. When liquidity is high, the architecture of the market does not play any role: different networks provide similar stability profiles. When liquidity is low, it makes a big difference whether the network is very heterogeneous (scalefree) or homogenous (regular graph). However, the distribution of capital buffers (e.g., whether the hubs are more capitalized or less capitalized) can reverse the results. Given the current context where banking regulation remains mainly at the individual level, those results show that the way claims and liabilities are intertwined within financial markets, creating highly complex financial networks, should not be neglected. Therefore, the findings suggest the need for regulators and policy makers to acquire sufficiently detailed map, not only of the individual balance sheet but also of the structure of mutual exposures and market conditions they are confronted in order to make better decisions.

3. FINANCIAL NETWORKS: POLICY INSIGHTS AND FUTURE AVENUES

Some of the fundamental insights from the body of works in financial networks, reviewed in this paper, can be summarized as follows. On the one hand, as usually thought of, financial interlinkages help players to diversify their individual risk. On the other hand, financial linkages may (1) increase systemic risk in a variety of situations, in particular when financial losses are not conservative, but get amplified during the propagation of distress from a bank to another one; (2) amplify information imperfection, in particular by increasing the relative errors on the probability of systemic default; (3) generate endogenous uncertainty, even if information is perfect and symmetric.

Remarkably, all the above results, concern networks of simple lending contracts. In the presence of financial derivatives the effects can generally be stronger although it is more difficult to obtain analytical results and the formulation of models of financial networks in the presence of derivative contracts is only at the beginning. The model described in

Battiston et al. (2016a,b) can be extended to the case of derivative contracts. In a recent extension of the clearing model of Rogers and Veraart (2013) to the case in which players can also trade credit default swaps. Schuldenzucker et al., (2017) has shown that closed chains of derivative contracts can disrupt the uniqueness and even the very existence of consistent solutions for the payoffs of the players.

Despite recent regulatory attempt to move derivative contracts through centrally cleared counterparties, a large portion of the volume of these contracts are still traded over the counter with limited disclosure. There are several on-going initiatives at financial supervision authorities, or policy making institutions to collect derivative contract data in central repository (see, e.g., the EMIR platform in the European Union). Yet, access to data is limited to regulatory bodies and in general derivative markets are characterized by information being highly asymmetric. As argued in Battiston et al. (2013), paradoxically, this information asymmetry is one of the main incentives for market players to engage in a derivatives market that is so complex. Derivatives, especially OTC derivatives, are not easy to price, and their evaluation relies on models. This makes it harder to estimate the risk of the deal, resulting in an information asymmetry that can be exploited at the expense of other parties. Another way that financial institutions profit from complexity stems from their need to be perceived as systemically important, to guarantee governmental rescue in the face of crises. And there remains an even less savory use of complexity. Derivatives can be used to manipulate accounts to make things seem better at one moment, at the cost of making things look worse at another. A notorious example is the one of financial institutions using derivatives to make Greece's financial position appear strong enough to qualify for membership in the eurozone. The fact that the complexity of financial networks, including derivatives, may not only hamper the assessment of systemic risk, but also foster its emergence, has spurred a debate in recent years about the global financial architecture and its possible regulation. Several reforms have been proposed in recent years, emphasizing the need for transparency and exchange markets, targeting the implicit subsidies that government-insured entities receive from the public and removing the priority given to derivative instruments in bankruptcy. Enforcing the use of exchange markets will make information on prices, volumes and exposure available to regulators and the public, making the network structure more transparent. It is also likely to limit the intrinsic problems associated with network interdependence, because the failure of an individual party would be absorbed by the exchange market, rather than being transmitted through the network. However, these markets, if undercapitalized, could also lead to a heightened systemic risk.

In general, well-designed regulatory systems must focus simultaneously on regulating the derivatives network, and mediating the influence of market participants on future policies. It is clear that banks profit from being regarded as too connected, too correlated—and even too complex—to fail, giving them an incentive to engage in excessive risk taking and amplifying the degree of systemic instability. A prudent strategy would therefore not only tame interdependencies and risk taking, but also restrict the power of the financial sector. Unfortunately, lobbying has played—and continues to play—an important role in limiting the development of regulatory structures designed to enhance systemic stability. In any case, reform must be approached dynamically, as market players— pursuing their individual incentives—find ever new ways to circumvent existing regulations at the expense of systemic stability and social welfare. This certainly amounts to a formidable challenge, from the point of view of both network science and political economy theory, with significant societal implications.

Overall, the network economics literature has been providing rigorous mathematical evidence that financial complexity (both the complexity of individual contracts and the complexity of the structure of the network of contracts) can increase systemic risk. In this respect, for instance the idea of "ring-fencing" (e.g., the separation of commercial and investment arms of banks) may fail in taming systemic risk because its does not necessarily reduce interconnectedness and complexity in the network of the commercial arms of banks among each other (and similarly for the investment arms). In turn, in order to reduce the complexity of the financial system one promising idea is to foster a more diverse market ecology (Battiston et al. 2013, 2016; Haldane and May 2011) and a more balanced allocation of bargaining power between the public interest versus the financial industry

The growing field of financial networks has been offering both theoretical insights and practical tools such as network-based metrics to assess systemic importance. As we argued here, many of these results relate to issues of imperfect information and incompleteness of markets. We believe that the connections between information economics and network economics are deep and articulated and deserve the attention of a stream of future work.

A NETWORK GLOSSARY

We report a list from Battiston and Caldarelli (2013) of network theory definitions that could be useful to the reader. Consider a simplified banking system composed of n banks and m assets.

- In our context, an interbank **network** G is the pair (N, E) consisting of the set of **nodes** or **vertexes** $N(G) = 1, \ldots, n$ representing banks, and a set of edges $E(G)$, or links, representing financial contracts among banks.
- If the network is directed, an **edge** is an ordered pair of nodes (i, j) representing in our context that bank i lends to bank j. A weight A_{ij} can be associated with the edge indicating, for instance, the nominal value of the contract. If the network is undirected the order of the pair is not relevant, $(i, j) = (j, i)$ indicate the same edge.
- The **adjacency matrix**. A of size $n \times n$ where n is the **order** of the graph is defined as follows. The element A_{ij} is not zero if an edge goes from i to j. The component i, j of A_{ij} is the weight of the edge.
- A network is said to be *bipartite* if the nodes can be grouped in two classes such that no edge exists between any two node of the same class. In our context the network of banks and assets is a bipartite network.
- The **neighborhood** of a node i is the set $N_i = j \in N : (ij) \in E$.
- The (connectivity) **out-degree**, or out-degree of a node i in G, denoted as k_i, is the number of edges outgoing from i. Similarly we can define the **in-degree**. If nonspecified, we mean the **total degree** or the degree in the case edges are undirected.
- **Hub**. A vertex with large degree.
- A **path** between two nodes i_1 and i_k is a sequence of nodes $(i_1, i_2, \ldots, i_k)$ such that $(i_1, i_2), (i_2, i_3), (i_{k-1}, i_k) \in E$. In other words it is a set of edges that goes from i_1 to i_k.
- The **distance** between two vertices is the number of edges in a shortest path connecting them.
- The **diameter** is the maximum value of **distance** among all the possible pairs of nodes in the network.
- A **cycle** is a closed **path**, that is in which the first and last vertices coincide.
- A **tree** is a subgraph of G without **cycles**. If it encompasses all the nodes (but not all the edges) is called spanning tree. The root is the

only vertex with no incoming edges. A **leaf** is a vertex of degree one that is not the **root**.

- A **connected component** in G is a maximal set of firms such that there exists a path between any two of them. We will say that two components are disconnected if there is no path between them. A connected graph is a graph consisting of only one connected component.
- There are several measures of **centrality** that capture in different ways the importance of a node or an edge. For instance, the **betweenness** centrality of a node capture the number of paths that have to go through node i in order to connect all the pairs of nodes in the network. The feedback centrality is in itself a class of centrality measures that capture the importance of a node in a recursive way, based on a linear combination of the importance of the nodes in its neighborhood. **Eigenvector** centrality belongs to this class and it is the solution, if it exists and is unique and positive, of the eigenvalue equation associated with the adjacency matrix, $Ax = \lambda x$.
- The **clustering** coefficient measures the fraction of neighbors of node, averaged across the set of nodes, that are also neighbors. In other words, it measures the number of triangles that are realized in the network, relative to the total number of possible triangles that could exist in the network.
- A **community** is an intentionally underspecified notion indicating a group of nodes that are more densely connected among each other than with the nodes that are not in the group.
- **Motifs.** All the possible **graphs** of a given "little" (e.g., 3,4,5 order. Their statistics contribute to characterizing the topological properties of the network.
- Three classes of network are relevant to this paper, based on the degree distribution:
  1. *regular* where directed edges between nodes are assigned randomly under the constraint that all nodes have the same degree k.
  2. *random* where the degree distribution follows a Poisson distribution: $P(k) = \binom{n-1}{k} p^k (1-p)^{n-1-k}$.
  3. *scalefree* where the degree distribution follows a power law distribution: $P(k) \sim k^{-\alpha}$.
- The simplest way to visualize the difference is to look at where two distinct kinds of graphs are shown for the same set of vertices and the same number of edges.

REFERENCES

Acharya, V. V, and T. Yorulmazer (2007) "Too Many to Fail: An Analysis of Time-Inconsistency in Bank Closure Policies." *Journal of Financial Intermediation* 16:1–31.

Acharya, V. V. 2009. "A Theory of Systemic Risk and Design of Prudential Bank Regulation." *Journal of Financial Stability* 5:224–255.

Acemoglu, D., A. Ozdaglar, and A. Tahbaz-Salehi. 2015. "Systemic Risk and Stability in Financial Networks." *American Economic Review* 105 (2):564–608.

Alessi, L., and C. Detken. 2011. "Quasi Real Time Early Warning Indicators for Costly Asset Price Boom/Bust Cycles: A Role for Global Liquidity." *European Journal of Political Economy* 27 (3):520–533.

Allen, F., and D. Gale. 2001. "Financial Contagion." *Journal of Political Economy* 108 (1):1–33.

Allen, F., A. Babus, and E. Carletti. 2012. "Asset Commonality, Debt Maturity and Systemic Risk." *Journal of Financial Economics.* 104:519–534.

Alvarez, F., and G. Barlevy. 2015. "Mandatory Disclosure and Financial Contagion." *Working Paper Series of National Bureau of Economic Research*, w21328.

Amini, H., R. Cont, and A. Minca. 2012. "Stress Testing the Resilience of Financial Networks." *International Journal of Theoretical and Applied Finance* 15 (1).

Bala, V., and S. Goyal. 2000. "A Noncooperative Model of Network Formation." *Econometrica* 68 (5):1181–1230.

Ballester, C., A. Calvó-Armengol, and Y. Zenou. 2006. "Who's Who in Networks. Wanted: The Key Player." *Econometrica* 74 (5):1403–1417.

Barabási, A. L. 2009. "Scale-Free Networks: A Decade and Beyond." *Science* 325 (5939):412–413.

Barrat, A., M. Barthélemy, R. Pastor-Satorras, and A. Vespignani. 2004. "The Architecture of Complex Weighted Networks." *Proceedings of the National Academy of Sciences of the United States of America* 101 (11):3747–3752.

Barrat, A., M. Barthélemy, and A. Vespignani. 2008. *Dynamical Processes on Complex Networks.* New York: Cambridge University Press.

Bardoscia, M., S. Battiston, F. Caccioli, and G. Caldarelli. 2017 "Pathways Towards Instability in Financial Networks." *Nature Communications* 7.

Battiston, S., and G. Caldarelli. 2013. "Systemic Risk in Financial Networks." *Journal of Financial Management Markets and Institutions* 2:129–154.

Battiston, S., G. Caldarelli, C.-P. Georg, R. May, and J. Stiglitz. 2013. "Complex Derivatives." *Nature Physics* 9 (3):123–125.

Battiston, S., G. Caldarelli, and M. D'Errico. 2015. "The Financial System as a Nexus of Interconnected Networks." In *Interconnected Networks*, edited by A. Garas, 195–229. New York: Springer.

Battiston, S., G. Caldarelli, R. May, T. Roukny, and J. E. Stiglitz. 2016a. "The Price of Complexity in Financial Networks." *Proceedings of the National Academy of Science* 113, 10031–10036..

Battiston, S., G. Caldarelli, M. D'errico, and S. Gurciullo. 2016b. "Leveraging the Network: a Stress-Test Framework Based on DebtRank." *Statistics and Risk Modeling* 33:1–33.

Battiston, S., D. Delli Gatti, M. Gallegati, B. Greenwald, and J. E. Stiglitz. 2007. "Credit Chains and Bankruptcy Propagation in Production Networks." *Journal of Economic Dynamics and Control* 31 (6):2061–2084.

Battiston, S., D. Delli Gatti, M. Gallegati, B. Greenwald, and J. E. Stiglitz. 2012a. "Liaisons Dangereuses: Increasing Connectivity, Risk Sharing, and Systemic Risk." *Journal of Economic Dynamics and Control* 36 (8):1121–1141.

Battiston, S., D. Delli Gatti, M. Gallegati, B. Greenwald, and J. E. Stiglitz. 2012b. "Default Cascades: When Does Risk Diversification Increase Stability?" *Journal of Financial Stability* 8 (3):138–149.

Battiston, S., M. Puliga, R. Kaushik, P. Tasca, and G. Caldarelli. 2012c. "DebtRank: Too Central to Fail? Financial Networks, the Fed and Systemic Risk." *Scientific Reports* 2:1–6.

Beale, N., D. G. Rand, H. Battey, K. Croxson, R. M. May, and M. A. Nowak. 2011. "Individual versus Systemic Risk and the Regulator's Dilemma." *Proceedings of the National Academy of Sciences* 108 (31):12647–12652.

BoE, 2013. "A Framework for Stress Testing the UK Banking System." Bank of England discussion paper.

Bollobas, B. 1998. *Modern Graph Theory: Graduate Texts in Mathematics*. New York: Springer.

Bonacich, P. 1987. "Power and Centrality: A Family of Measures." *American Journal of Sociology* 92 (5):1170–1182.

Boss, M., H. Elsinger, M. Summer, and S. Thurner. 2004. "Network Topology of the Interbank Market." *Quantitative Finance* 4:677–684.

Brock, W. A., C. H. Hommes, and F. O. O. Wagener. 2009. "More Hedging Instruments May Destabilize Markets." *Journal of Economic Dynamics and Control* 33 (11):1912–1928.

Caccioli, F., M. Shrestha, C. Moore, and J. D. Farmer. 2014. "Stability Analysis of Financial Contagion due to Overlapping Portfolios." *Journal of Banking Finance* 46:233–245.

Caldarelli, G. 2007. *Scale-Free Networks: Complex Webs in Nature and Technology*. Oxford: Oxford University Press.

Caldarelli, G., A. Capocci, and D. Garlaschelli. 2007. "Self-Organized Network Evolution Coupled to Extremal Dynamics." *Nature Physics*. 3 (11):813.

Cajueiro, D. O. and B. M. Tabak. 2008. "The Role of Banks in the Brazilian Interbank Market: Does Bank Type Matter?" *Physica A* 387:6825–6836.

Craig, B., and G. Von Peter. 2014. "Interbank Tiering and Money Center Banks." *Journal of Financial Intermediation* 23:322–347.

Delli Gatti, D., M. Gallegati, B. Greenwald, A. Russo, and J. E. Stiglitz. 2010. "The Financial Accelerator in an Evolving Credit Network." *Journal of Economic Dynamics and Control* 34 (9):1627–1650.

Dorogovtsev, S. N., and J. F. F. Mendes. 2003. *Evolution of Networks—From Biological Nets to the Internet and WWW*. Oxford: Oxford University Press.

Eisenberg, L., and T. H. Noe. 2001. "Systemic Risk in Financial Systems." *Management Science* 47 (2):236–249.

Elliott, M., B. Golub, and M. O. Jackson. 2014. "Financial Networks and Contagion." *American Economic Review* 104 (10):3115–3153.

Farhi, E., and J. Tirole. 2012. "Collective Moral Hazard, Maturity Mismatch and Systemic Bailouts." *American Economic Review* 102 (1):60–93.

Gai, P., and S. Kapadia. 2010. "Contagion in Financial Networks." *Proceedings of the Royal Society A: Mathematical, Physical and Engineering Sciences* 466 (2120):2401–2423.

Gai, P., A. Haldane, and S. Kapadia. 2011. "Complexity, Concentration and Contagion." *Journal of Monetary Economics* 58 (5):453–470.

Galeotti, A., S. Goyal, M. O. Jackson, F. Vega-Redondo, and L. Yariv. 2010. "Network Games." *Review of Economic Studies* 77:218–244.

Granovetter, M. S. 1973. "The Strength of Weak Ties." *American Journal of Sociology* 78:1360–1380.

Granovetter, M. S. 1978. "Threshold Models of Collective Behavior." *American Journal of Sociology* 83 (6):1420.

Greenwald, B. C. N., and J. E. Stiglitz. 1993. "Financial Market Imperfections and Business Cycles." *Quarterly Journal of Economics* 108:77–114.

Haldane, A. G. 2009. "Rethinking Financial Networks." Speech delivered at the Financial Student Association, Amsterdam.

Haldane, A. G., and R. M. May. 2011. "Systemic Risk in Banking Ecosystems." *Nature* 469 (7330):351–355.

Henry, J. and C. Kok, eds. 2013. "A Macro Stress Testing Framework for Assessing Systemic Risks in the Banking Sector." *European Central Bank Occasional Paper Series* no. 152.

Iori, G., G. De Masi, O. V. Precup, G. Gabbi, and G. Caldarelli. 2008. "A Network Analysis of the Italian Overnight Money Market." *Journal of Economic Dynamics and Control* 32:259–278.

Jackson, M. O., and A. Watts. 2002. "The Evolution of Social and Economic Networks." *Journal of Economic Theory* 106 (2):265–295.

Jackson, M. O., and A. Wolinsky. 1996. "A Strategic Model of Social and Economic Networks." *Journal of Economic Theory* 71 (1):44–74.

Kirman, A. 1997. "The Economy as an Evolving Network." *Journal of Evolutionary Economics* 7 (4):339–353.

Lorenz, J., and S. Battiston. 2008. "Systemic Risk in a Network Fragility Model Analyzed with Probability Density Evolution of Persistent Random Walks." *Networks and Heterogeneous Media* 3 (2):185–200.

Newman, M. 2003. "The Structure and Function of Complex Networks." *SIAM Review* 45.

Rogers, L. C. G., and L. A. M. Veraart. 2013. "Failure and Rescue in an Interbank Network." *Management Science* 59 (4):882–898.

Roukny, T., S. Battiston, and J. E. Stiglitz. 2016. "Interconnectedness as a Source of Uncertainty in Systemic Risk." *Journal of Financial Stability*, in press.

Roukny, T., H. Bersini, H. Pirotte, G. Caldarelli, and S. Battiston. 2013. "Default Cascades in Complex Networks: Topology and Systemic Risk." *Scientific Reports* 3:1–31.

Schuldenzucker, S., S. Seuken, and S. Battiston. 2017. "Default Ambiguity: Credit Default Swaps Create New Systemic Risks in Financial Networks." Working paper ssrn n. 3043708.

Schweitzer, F., G. Fagiolo, D. Sornette, F. Vega-Redondo, A. Vespignani, and D. R. White. 2009. "Economic Networks: The New Challenges." *Science* 325 (5939):422–425.

Soramäki, K., M. L. Bech, J. Arnold, R. J. Glass, and W. E. Beyeler. 2007. "The Topology of Interbank Payment Flows." *Physica A* 379:317–333.

Stiglitz, J. E. 1996. *Whither Socialism?* Cambridge, MA: MIT Press.

Stiglitz, J. E. 2000. "The Contributions of the Economics of Information to Twentieth Century Economics." *Quarterly Journal of Economics* 115 (4):1441–1478.

Stiglitz, J. E., and B. C. N. Greenwald. 2003. *Towards a New Paradigm in Monetary Economics*. Cambridge: Cambridge University Press.

Stiglitz, J. E. 2010. "Risk and Global Economic Architecture: Why Full Financial Integration May Be Undesirable." *American Economic Review* 100 (2):388–392.

Tasca, P., and S. Battiston. 2016. "Market Procyclicality and Systemic Risk." *Quantitative Finance* 16:1219–1235.

Tasca, P., A. Deghi, and S. Battiston. 2017 "Portfolio Diversification and Systemic Risk in Interbank Networks." *Journal of Economic Dynamics and Control* 82:96–124.

Upper, C., and A. Worms. 2004. "Estimating Bilateral Exposures in the German Interbank Market: Is There a Danger of Contagion?" *European Economic Review* 48:827–849.

Vitali, S., J. B. Glattfelder, and S. Battiston. 2011. "The Network of Global Corporate Control." *PLoS One* 6 (10).

Vitali, S., S. Battiston, and M. Gallegati. 2016. "Financial Fragility and Distress Propagation in a Network of Regions." *Journal of Economic Dynamics and Control* 62:56–75.

Wagner, W. 2010. "Diversification at Financial Institutions and Systemic Crises." *Journal of Financial Intermediation* 19 (3):373–386.

PART V

Development

CHAPTER 15

Joseph Stiglitz and China's Transition Success

Justin Yifu Lin

ABSTRACT

China is the most successful transition economy in the world. Joseph Stiglitz is the most influential and respected foreign economist in China. In this short article, I will first briefly discuss the achievements of China's transition since 1979, the reasons for China's success, the unaccomplished transition agenda, and the contributions Professor Stiglitz made to China's transition success.

1. THE ACHIEVEMENTS OF CHINA'S TRANSITION

Before China's transition from a planned economy to a market economy at the end of 1970s, China had been trapped in poverty for centuries. Its per capita income was US$154 in 1978, less than one-third of the average in Sub-Saharan African countries.[1] China was an inward-looking country as well. Its trade dependence (trade-to-GDP) ratio was only 9.7 percent. China's growth since then has been miraculous. Annual gross domestic product (GDP) growth averaged 9.7 percent over the thirty-six-year period in 1979–2014, and annual growth in international trade, 16.0 percent. China is now an upper middle-income country, with a per capita GDP of US$7400 in 2014, and more than 600 million people have escaped poverty. Its trade dependence ratio reaches around 50 percent, the highest among the world's large economies. China overtook Japan as the world's second largest economy in 2009, replaced Germany as the world's largest exporter of merchandise in 2010, overtook the United States as the world largest trading country in 2013, and became the world's largest economy in purchasing power parity in 2014. The spectacular growth over the past three decades has made China not only a driver for world development but also a stabilizing force in the world economy, as demonstrated by China's role during the East Asian financial crisis in late 1990s and recent global crisis that erupted in the United States in 2008. This extraordinary performance far exceeded the expectations of anyone at the outset of the transition, including Deng Xiaoping, the architect of China's reform and opening-up strategy.[2]

2. THE CAUSE OF TRANSITION SUCCESS IN CHINA AND FAILURES IN OTHER ECONOMIES

The reason China started the transition to a market economy in 1979 was because it suffered from poor economic performance due to various distortions and interventions inherited in the planning system. Like other socialist economies and many other developing countries in post–World War II, China aimed to accelerate the building of modern advanced industries similar to those in high-income countries with a series of ambitious plans. But China was a poor agrarian economy at that time and did not have a comparative advantage in those industries. Chinese firms in those industries were not viable in an open competitive market.[3]

To achieve its strategic goal, the Chinese government needed to protect the priority industries by giving firms in those sectors a monopoly and by subsidizing them through various price distortions, including suppressed interest rates, an overvalued exchange rate, and lower prices for inputs. The price distortions created shortages, and the government was obliged to use administrative measures to mobilize and allocate resources directly to nonviable firms (Lin 2009; Lin and Li 2009).

These interventions enabled China to quickly establish modern advanced industries, test nuclear bombs in the 1960s, and launch satellites in the 1970s. But the resources were misallocated, the incentives were distorted, and the labor-intensive sectors in which China held a comparative advantage were repressed. As a result, economic efficiency was low. China remained to be a poor country.

All other socialist countries and many developing countries after World War II adopted a development strategy similar to that of China. Most colonies gained political independence after the 1950s. Compared with developed countries, these newly independent developing countries had extremely low per capita income, high birth and death rates,

low average educational attainment, and very little infrastructure—
and were heavily specialized in the production and export of primary
commodities while importing most manufactured goods. The development of modern advanced industries was perceived as the only way
to achieve rapid economic takeoff, avoid dependence on the Western
industrial powers, and eliminate poverty (Prebisch 1950).

It became a fad after the 1950s for developing countries in both the
socialist and the non-socialist camps to adopt a development strategy
oriented toward heavy industry and import substitution (Lal and Mynt
1996). But the capital-intensive modern industries on their priority
lists defied the comparative advantages determined by the endowment
structure of their low-income agrarian economies. To implement their
development strategy, many socialist and non-socialist developing countries introduced distortions and government interventions like those in
China.[4] This strategy made it possible to establish some modern industries and achieve investment-led growth for one or two decades in the
1950s to the 1970s. Nevertheless, the distortions led to pervasive soft budget constraints, rent seeking, and misallocation of resources. Economic
efficiency was unavoidably low. Stagnation and frequent social and economic crises began to beset most socialist and non-socialist developing
countries by the 1970s and 1980s. Liberalization from excessive state
intervention became a trend in the 1980s and 1990s.

The symptoms of poor economic performance and social and economic crises, and their root cause in distortions and government interventions, were common to China and other socialist transition economies
as well as other developing countries. But the academic and policy communities in the 1980s did not realize that those distortions came from
second-best institutional arrangements, endogenous to the needs of providing protections to firms in the priority sectors. Without such protection, those firms would not have been viable. As a result, policy makers
and academics recommended that socialist and other developing countries immediately remove all distortions by implementing simultaneous
programs of liberalization, privatization, and marketization with the aim
of quickly achieving efficient, first-best outcomes.

But if those distortions were eliminated immediately, many nonviable firms in the priority sectors would collapse, causing a contraction
of GDP, a surge in unemployment, and acute social disorders. To avoid
those dreadful consequences, many governments continued to subsidize
the nonviable firms through other, disguised, less efficient subsidies and

protections (Lin and Tan 1999). Transition and developing countries thus had even poorer growth performance and stability in the 1980s and 1990s than in the 1960s and 1970s (Easterly 2001).

During the transition process, China adopted a pragmatic, gradual, dual-track approach. The government first improved the incentives and productivity by allowing workers in collective farms and state-owned firms to be residual claimants and to set the prices for selling at the market after delivering the quota obligations to the state at fixed prices (Lin 1992). At the same time, the government continued to provide necessary protections to nonviable firms in the priority sectors and simultaneously, liberalized the entry of private enterprises, joint ventures, and foreign direct investment in labor-intensive sectors in which China had a comparative advantage but that were repressed before the transition. This transition strategy allowed China both to maintain stability by avoiding the collapse of old priority industries and to achieve dynamic growth by simultaneously pursuing its comparative advantage and tapping the advantage of backwardness in the industrial upgrading process. In addition, the dynamic growth in the newly liberalized sectors created the conditions for reforming the old priority sectors. Through this gradual, dual-track approach China achieved "reform without losers" (Lau, Qian, and Roland 2000; Lin, Cai, and Li 2003; Naughton 1995) and moved gradually but steadily to a well-functioning market economy.

A few other socialist economies—such as Poland[5] and Vietnam, which achieved outstanding performance during their transitions—adopted a similar gradual, dual-track approach (Lin 2009). Mauritius adopted a similar approach in the 1970s to reforming distortions caused by the country's import-substitution strategy and became Africa's success story (Subramanian and Roy 2003).[6]

3. THE UNACCOMPLISHED TRANSITION IN CHINA

The gradual, dual-track approach to transition is a double-edge sword. While it enables China to achieve enviable stability and growth in the transition process, it also brings with it a number of structural problems, particularly the disparities in income distribution, consumption and savings, and widespread corruption.[7] When the transition started in 1979, China was a relatively egalitarian society. With rapid growth, income distribution has become increasingly unequal. The Gini coefficient, a measurement of income inequality, increased from .31 in 1981 to .47 in 2008 (Ravallion and Chen 2007). Meanwhile, household consumption as a percentage of GDP dropped from about 50 percent in the early stage of transition down to about 35 percent in the first decade of the new century, whereas the fixed asset investment increased from around 30 percent to more than 45 percent of GDP. Such trends are the by-products of the dual-track approach to transition.

During the transition process, the Chinese government retained some distortions as a way to provide continuous support to nonviable firms in the priority industries. Major remaining distortions include the concentration of financial services in the four large state-owned banks, the almost zero royalty on natural resources, and the monopoly of major service industries, including telecommunications, power, and banking.[8]

Those distortions contributed to the stability in China's transition process. They also contributed to the rising income disparity and other imbalances in the economy. This is because only big companies and rich people had access to credit services provided by the big banks and the interest rates were artificially repressed. As a result, big companies and rich people were receiving subsidies from the depositors who had no access to banks' credit services and were relatively poor. The concentration of profits and wealth in large companies and widening income disparities were unavoidable. The low royalty levies of natural resources and the monopoly in the service sector had similar effects.

In general, the marginal propensity to consume decreases with income. Therefore, if wealth is disproportionately concentrated in the higher-income group, the nation's consumption-to-GDP ratio will be lower and the savings ratio will be higher. The concentration of wealth in the large firms has a similar effect. A consequence of such an income distribution pattern is relatively high household savings and extraordinarily high corporate savings in China, as shown in figure 15.1. The high household and corporate savings in turn lead to a high rate of investment and quick building up of production capacity.

Those distortions also created huge economic rents. The rent-seeking activities led to widespread corruption, undermining the government's legitimacy.

It is imperative for China to address the above transition issues by removing remaining distortions in the finance, natural resources, and service sectors in order to complete the transition to a well-functioning

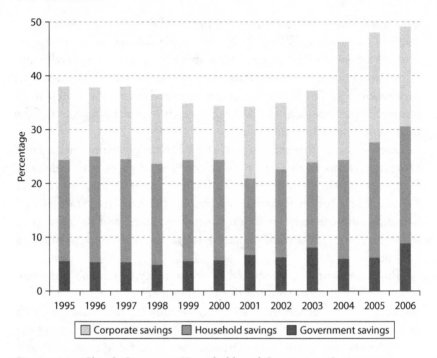

Figure 15.1   China's Corporate, Household, and Government Savings as a Percentage of GDP

Source: National Bureau of Statistics, *China Statistical Yearbook (1998–2009)*.

market economy. The necessary reforms include: (1) Removing financial repression and allowing the development of small and local financing institutions, including local banks, so as to increase financial services, especially access to credit, to household farms as well as small- and medium-sized enterprises in the manufacturing and service sectors; (2) Reforming the pension system, removing old retired workers' pension burdens from the state-owned mining companies and levying appropriate royalty taxes on natural resources; and (3) Encouraging entry and competition in the telecommunications, power, and financial sectors. It is also timely for China to remove remaining distortions to complete the transition to a well-functioning market economy. China has changed from a poor, capita-scarce country at the onset of the transition to an upper middle-income country. As a result, most firms in the old priority industries have become viable and competitive in domestic and global markets.

4. JOSEPH STIGLITZ'S CONTRIBUTION
TO CHINA'S ECONOMIC TRANSITION

Professor Stiglitz's involvement in China's policy discussions started from the very beginning of China's transition. In the early days, the Chinese government sent delegations of policy researchers to learn basic economic principles and solicit advice from leading economists in the advanced countries about how to establish a well-functioning market economy. In addition to educating Chinese students, Professor Stiglitz, as a Clark Medalist in 1979, was one of the economists to be consulted at that time. Professor Stiglitz's interactions with China expanded and intensified from students and policy researchers to senior leaders in China after he joined the Council of Economic Advisers in 1993, and especially after he became the Chief Economist of the World Bank in 1997. He visited China several times, attending conferences, giving public lectures, and directly advising senior policy makers annually during the past twenty years. His textbooks, including *Economics, Principles of Macroeconomics*, and *Economics of the Public Sectors*, were translated into Chinese and used widely in undergraduate and graduate courses in Chinese universities. The Chinese editions of his monographs, such as *Whither Socialism*; *Globalization and Its Discontents*; *Fair Trade for All*; *Making Globalization Work*; *The Three Trillion Dollar War*; *Creating a Learning Society*; *The Great Divide*; and several others were the best sellers in China.

Based on his decades of research on the role of the state, Professor Stiglitz advocated a "third way:" a view of the market and the state that neither puts excessive trust in markets nor in governments, but that sees the government and market as strategic complements to be used to achieve social economic goals (1989). His "third way" view was in conflict with the prevailing neoliberalism in the 1980s and 1990s. The dominant neoliberal view of the right way to transition from a socialist planning economy to a market economy in the global academic community was shock therapy, removing all government interventions and distortions by implementing privatization, marketization, liberalization, and stabilization simultaneously and immediately as encapsulated in the Washington Consensus.[9] Professor Stiglitz has questioned in his 1990 Wicksell Lectures, the free market doctrine (Stiglitz 1994); and in his 1998 WIDER Lecture, he pointed out that "all too often, the dogma of liberalization became an end in itself not a means to a better financial system" (Stiglitz 1998a). The spirit of China's approach for transition was close to Professor Stiglitz's "the third way" and his critique of the Washington Consensus. Therefore, Professor Stiglitz was among the first to appreciate the merit of China's pragmatic dual-track approach of transition. In his lecture on "Second Generation Strategies for Reform for China" delivered at the occasion of Peking University's Centennial Celebration in 1998, he compared the experiences of transition in China and Russia and "suggests two lessons about the pace and sequencing of reforms. The first is that introducing competition does more to improve performance and productivity than privatizing in a non-competitive environment. The second that it is crucial to maintain social organization during these transitions and to create the institutional infrastructure that a market economy requires" (Stiglitz 1998b).

Professor Stiglitz does not only appreciate the achievements of China's transition, but also draws from his knowledge of the function of economy and broad experiences in other countries to actively advise the Chinese government about how to deepen reforms and handle emerging challenges in China. In his "Second Generation Strategies for Reform for China," he suggested to the Chinese government to reform the tax system to reverse the declining tax revenue, to create an effective social safety net, to privatize housing, to separate the bad debts so as to commercialize the banking system, and to shed the responsibility for social services so as to impose hard budget constraints on state-owned enterprises. Premier Zhu Rongji highly appreciated these proposals and recommended the full text of this lecture to be published in *People's Daily*, which is read by every official in China. Those proposals formed the core of Zhu Rongji's reform programs.

In March 2000, the Development Research Center of the State Council inaugurated the Annual China Development Forum. The Forum is an annual event, held right after the People's Congress, for Chinese leaders, leading foreign and Chinese enterprises, and renowned scholars to exchange views about the policy and reform agenda in China. Professor Stiglitz has been a key participant for each edition of this Forum since 2000. He used those occasions to advise Chinese policy makers to move toward balanced growth (2004); to pursue a green net national product (2006); to institute a new national innovation system (2007); to control imported inflation (2008); to warn of the possibility of a protracted crisis due to an ineffective policy response in the United States and to introduce early intervention for children as an antipoverty measure (2009); to advocate a new global reserve system to address global imbalance (2010); to suggest that China adopt a new growth pact by investing in education, health, and green growth to increase domestic demand (2011); to use fiscal policy to invest in areas for supporting redistribution, restructuring, and inclusive and sustainable growth (2012); to improve corporate and public governance for harmonious growth (2013); to forge a new system of an open economy in knowledge, finance, and trade (2014); and to avoid the middle-income trap by using China's fiscal capacity to invest in education, health, and the environment in order to build an inclusive and sustainable growth model with Chinese characteristics (2015).[10] The Chinese leaders paid close attention to the above policy proposals and integrated many of Professor Stiglitz's recommendations in China's policies.

The Chinese media interviewed Professor Stiglitz frequently to solicit his views on the global economy and policy issues in China. For example, in his interview in *Economic Daily* on April 1, 2013, he advocated that the quality of growth was more important than the speed of growth;[11] his interview in *Diyicaijing* (a Chinese financial newspaper) on March 25, 2010, advised that the appreciation of the Chinese yuan would not reduce China's trade surplus with the United States but would increase the income disparity in China.[12] His interview on November 11, 2014, with the *China News Net*, warned of the possibility a new global financial crisis due to the asset bubble as a result of loose monetary policies in developed countries.[13] These interviews help shape public opinion in China about the direction of policies for reforms and responses to crises. Professor Stiglitz also helps the outside world to understand the achievements, challenges, and opportunities of China's transition and development by writing op-eds for major international media. For example, his op-eds entitled "A Trade War with China Isn't Worth It" in *Project Syndicate* on April 6, 2010,[14] "China's Reformers Can Triumph Again, If They Follow the Right Route" in the *Guardian* on April 2, 2014,[15] and the "Chinese Century" in the January 2015 issue of *Vanity Fair*.

CONCLUDING REMARKS

Overall, China's pragmatic approach to transitioning from a planning economy to a market economy benefited greatly from Professor Stiglitz's active advice, analysis of a world with imperfect information, and view about the need for a third way that allows the state and market to function complementarily to achieve social, economic goals. China's success of transition in turn provides a best testing ground for many of his economic insights and ideas.

I would like to conclude this paper by sharing three personal stories that I had with Professor Stiglitz.

I met Professor Stiglitz at a World Bank reception in 1993 and asked why he had not received the Nobel Prize, although all my classmates in Chicago in the early 1980s had thought he deserved one. He replied that only those economists whose theories proved to be wrong would receive the Nobel Prize, and his theories were right so he would not receive the Nobel Prize. There is some truth to his reply, especially from the viewpoint of developing countries. So far, I have not found any developing countries that have been successful using mainstream economic theories to guide their development or transition.

The second story was in 1997 after he delivered a lecture on economic development at the China Center for Economic Research at Peking University of which I was the founding director. I asked him why the East Asian economies were so successful and the Latin American economies performed so poorly. His answer was that the Latin America students who came to study economics in the United States returned to their home countries to become ministers, and those who came to study engineering stayed in the United States to become engineers; whereas the East Asian students did just the opposite, those who studied economics stayed in the United States to teach, and those who studied engineering returned to their home countries to become ministers. This was a keen observation and there is some truth to it as well. The applicability of an economic theory depends on the similarity of the preconditions embedded in the theory. Most prevailing theories today are developed by economists in high-income countries who draw from the experiences in high-income countries and are based on the social, economic conditions in high-income countries. The social, economic conditions in developing countries differ substantially from those of high-income countries. The direct application of theories developed in high-income countries to form policies in developing countries most likely will not work. Influenced by economic education in the United States, the ministers in Latin America might faithfully and ideologically apply the economic theories they learned from school to address the problems in their home countries without examining the differences in the preconditions between the United States and their own countries. By contrast, an engineer is trained to achieve a certain goal within a certain budget and constraints.

Therefore, the policy designed by a minister with an engineering background and a good grasp of the economic reality in his/her country is most likely to be effective. His/her approach to policy making conforms closely to the true spirit of an economic approach.

The third story happened at the China Development Forum in 2002 after Professor Stiglitz received the Nobel Prize in 2001. I chaired and moderated his luncheon, and before his speech, I asked him whether his theory was still right now that he had received the Nobel Prize. He shied away from my question in his response. I would like to take this occasion to say that his theories of incomplete information and view of the third way are most useful for understanding the challenges of development and transition in developing countries and provide a very useful framework for making policies to achieve inclusive and sustainable development in developing countries. In fact, the new structural economics, of which I advocate as the third edition of development economics, is inspired by his third way view and emphasizes the need for an effective market with an enabling state to facilitate the structural transformation in the process of economic development in a developing country (Lin 2012).

NOTES

This chapter was prepared for the Festschrift in honor of Professor Joseph Stiglitz's fiftieth anniversary of teaching. The first two sections draw heavily on "Demystifying the Chinese Economy" (Lin 2013).

1. Unless indicated otherwise, the statistics on the Chinese economy reported in the this chapter are from the *China Statistical Abstract 2015*, *China Compendium of Statistics 1949–2008*, and various editions of the *China Statistical Yearbook*, published by China Statistics Press.

2. Deng's goal at that time was to quadruple the size of China's economy in twenty years, which would have meant an average annual growth of 7.2 percent. Most people in the 1980s, and even as late as the early 1990s, thought that achieving that goal was a mission impossible.

3. While the policy goal of France, Germany, and the United States in the late nineteenth century was similar to that of China in the mid-1950s, the per capita incomes of the three countries were about 60–75 percent of Britain's at the time. The small gap in per capita incomes indicated that the industries on the governments' priority lists were the latent comparative advantages of the three countries (Lin, Monga et al. 2011).

4. There are different explanations for the pervasive distortions in developing countries. Acemoglu, Johnson, and Robinson (2005), Engerman and Sokoloff (1997), and Grossman and Helpman (1996) proposed that these distortions were caused by the

capture of government by powerful vested interests. Lin (2009, 2003) and Lin and Li (2009) propose that the distortions were a result of conflicts between the comparative advantages of the economies and the priority industries that political elites, influenced by the dominant social thinking of the time, targeted for the modernization of their nations.

5. In spite of its attempt to implement a shock therapy at the beginning, Poland did not privatize its large state-owned enterprises until very late in the transition.

6. In the 1980s, the former Soviet Union, Hungary, and Poland adopted a gradual reform approach. However, unlike the case in China, their state-owned firms were not allowed to set the prices for selling at markets after fulfilling their quota obligations and the private firms' entry to the repressed sectors were subject to severe restrictions, but the wages were liberalized (while in China, the wage increase was subject to state regulation). These reforms led to wage inflations and exacerbated shortages. See the discussions about the differences in the gradual approach in China and the former Soviet Union and Eastern Europe in Lin (2009, 88–89).

7. Many of China's problems today including environment degradation and the lack of social protections are generic to developing countries. In this section, I will only focus on a few prominent issues that arose specifically from China's dual-track approach to transition. The collective volume edited by Brandt and Rawski (2008) provides excellent discussions of other development and transition issues in China.

8. Before the transition, state-owned enterprises (SOEs) obtained their investment and operation funds directly from the government's budgets at no cost. The government established four large state banks in the early 1980s, when the fiscal appropriation system was replaced by bank lending. The interest rates have been kept artificially low in order to subsidize the SOEs. Prices of natural resources were kept at an extremely low level so as to reduce the input costs of heavy industries. In return, the mining firms' royalty payments were waived. After the transition, the natural resource prices were liberalized in the early 1990s but royalties remained nominal to compensate for the transfer of pension provisions for retired workers from the state to the state-owned mining companies. However, the private and joint-venture mining companies, which did not enter until the 1980s and thereafter, did not have any pension burdens. The low royalty payment was equivalent to a direct transfer of natural resource rents from the state to these companies, which made them extraordinary profitable. The rationale for giving firms in telecommunications and power sectors a monopoly position before the transition was because they provided public services and made payments on large capital investments. Because of the rapid development and fast capital accumulation after the transition, capital is less of a constraint now, but the Chinese government continues to allow the service sector to enjoy monopoly rents (Lin, Cai, and Li 2003).

9. Summers (1994, 252–253) wrote, when it comes to reforming a socialist economy, there is a surprising consensus among mainstream economists for adopting shock therapy based on the Washington Consensus.

10. The above highlights were based on Professor Stiglitz's slides presented at the China Development Forum.

11. See http://finance.sina.com.cn/review/hgds/20130401/135315017391.shtml.

12. See http://www.aastocks.com.cn/News/2010/3/24/c6165a5b-8e0a-4034-8596-47b3a43470d0.shtml.

13. See http://economy.caijing.com.cn/20141110/3745188.shtml.

14. See Joseph Stiglitz, "A Trade War with China Isn't Worth It," The Guardian, April 7, 2014, http://www.theguardian.com/commentisfree/cifamerica/2010/apr/07 /united-states-china-currency-manipulation.

15. See Joseph Stiglitz, "China's Reformers Can Triumph Again, If They Follow the Right Route," *The Guardian*, April 2, 2014, http://www.theguardian.com/business /economics-blog/2014/apr/02/china-reformers-triumph-follow-right-route.

REFERENCES

Acemoglu, D., S. Johnson, and J. A. Robinson. 2005. "Institutions as the Fundamental Cause of Long-Run Growth." In *Handbook of Economic Growth, Vol. 1A*, edited by P. Aghion and S. N. Durlauf, 385–472. Amsterdam: Elsevier.

Brandt, L., and T. G. Rawski (eds.). 2008. *China's Great Economic Transformation*. Cambridge: Cambridge University Press.

Easterly, W. 2001. "The Lost Decades: Developing Countries' Stagnation in Spite of Policy Reform, 1980–1998." *Journal of Economic Growth* (6):135–157.

Engerman, S. L., and K. L. Sokoloff. 1997. "Factor Endowments, Institutions, and Differential Paths of Growth among New World Economies: A View from Economic Historians of the United States." In *How Latin America Fell Behind*, edited by S. Haber, 260–304. Stanford, CA: Stanford University Press.

Grossman, G. M., and E. Helpman. 1996. "Electoral Competition and Special Interest Politics." *Review of Economic Studies* 63 (2):265–286.

Lal, D., and H. Mynt. 1996. *The Political Economy of Poverty, Equity, and Growth: A Comparative Study*. Oxford: Clarendon Press.

Lau, L. J., Y. Qian, and G. Roland. 2000. "Reform without Losers: An Interpretation of China's Dual-Track Approach to Transition." *Journal of Political Economy* 108 (1):120–143.

Lin, J. Y. 1992. "Rural Reforms and Agricultural Growth in China." *American Economic Review* 82 (1):34–51.

Lin, J. Y. 2003. "Development Strategy, Viability and Economic Convergence." *Economic Development and Cultural Change* 53 (2):277–308.

Lin, J. Y. 2009. *Economic Development and Transition: Thought, Strategy, and Viability*. Cambridge: Cambridge University Press.

Lin, J. Y. 2012. *New Structural Economics: A Framework for Rethinking Development and Policy*. Washington, DC: World Bank.

Lin, J. Y. 2013. "Demystifying the Chinese Economy." *Australian Economic Review* 46 (3): 259–268.

Lin, J. Y., and F. Li. 2009. "Development Strategy, Viability, and Economic Distortions in Developing Countries." Policy Research Working Paper 4906. Washington, DC: World Bank.

Lin, J. Y., C. Monga et al. 2011. "Growth Identification and Facilitation: The Role of the State in the Dynamics of Structural Change." *Development Policy Review* 29 (3): 264–290.

Lin, J. Y., and G. Tan. 1999. "Policy Burdens, Accountability, and Soft Budget Constraints." *American Economic Review* 89 (2):426–431.

Lin, J. Y., F. Cai, and Z. Li. 2003. *The China Miracle: Development Strategy and Economic Reform.* Hong Kong: Chinese University Press.

National Bureau of Statistics. 2009. *China Compendium of Statistics 1949–2008.* Beijing: China Statistics Press.

National Bureau of Statistics. 2009. *China Statistics Yearbook (1998–2009).* Beijing: China Statistics Press.

National Bureau of Statistics. 2015. *China Statistical Abstract 2015.* Beijing: China Statistics Press.

Naughton, B. 1995. *Growing Out of the Plan: Chinese Economic Reform, 1978–1993.* New York: Cambridge University Press.

Prebisch, R. 1950. *The Economic Development of Latin America and Its Principal Problems.* New York: United Nations. Reprinted in *Economic Bulletin for Latin America* 7 (1/1962):1–22.

Ravallion, Martin, and Shaohua Chen. 2007. "China's (Uneven) Progress against Poverty." *Journal of Development Economics* 82 (1):1–42.

Stiglitz, Joseph E. 1989. *The Economic Role of the State.* Oxford: Wiley-Blackwell.

Stiglitz, Joseph E. 1994. *Whither Socialism?* Cambridge, MA: MIT Press.

Stiglitz, Joseph E. 1998a. "More Instruments and Broader Goals: Moving Toward the Post-Washington Consensus." WIDER Annual Lecture. Helsinki, Finland.

Stiglitz, Joseph E. 1998b. "Second Generation Strategies for Reform for China." Address given at Peking University (July 20).

Stiglitz, Joseph E. 2015. "Chinese Century." *Vanity Fair* (January).

Subramanian, A., and D. Roy. 2003. "Who Can Explain the Mauritian Miracle? Mede, Romer, Sachs, or Rodrik?" In *Search of Prosperity: Analytic Narratives on Economic Growth*, edited by D. Rodrik, 205–243. Princeton, NJ: Princeton University Press.

Summers, Larry. 1994. "Comment." In *The Transition in Eastern Europe, Vol. 1*, edited by Oliver Jean Blanchard, Kenneth A. Froot, and Jeffrey Sachs, 252–253. Chicago: Chicago University Press.

CHAPTER 16

The Sources of Chinese Economic Growth Since 1978

Lawrence J. Lau

ABSTRACT

China has made tremendous progress in its economic development since it began its economic reform and opened to the world in 1978. It is currently the fastest-growing economy in the world—averaging 9.72 percent per annum over the past thirty-six years. What are the sources of this Chinese economic growth? Chinese economic growth since 1978 may be attributed to the following sources: (1) the realization of the surplus potential output from the initial economic slack that resulted from the mandatory central planning prior to 1978 (12.65 percent); (2) the growth of tangible capital (55.71 percent) and labor (9.67 percent) inputs; (3) technical progress (growth of total factor productivity [TFP]) (7.97 percent); and (4) the effect of economies of scale (13.99 percent). In the context of China, an important way in which self-fulfilling expectations can be created and changed is through the pronouncement of policy changes and actual actions by a government with credibility. Episodes in which the government was instrumental in changing both the direction and the magnitude of public expectations, and thus enhancing the growth of aggregate demand, are identified and presented.

INTRODUCTION

It is my great honor and pleasure to participate in this conference in honor of my old friend Professor Joseph Stiglitz. Joe has made path-breaking contributions in almost all areas of economics—macroeconomics, microeconomics, monetary theory, public finance, international economies,

economic development, economic growth, the economics of information, the economics of risk and uncertainty, you name it. His breadth
and versatility are unique and unparalleled. He is interested in the most
minute, some would almost say arcane, details of theory, but at the same
time he has the most insightful and practical policy advice to offer. He is
also most original—he always has something new and interesting to say
on an old and supposedly tired subject.

I first met Joe when he joined the Department of Economics at Stanford
in the early 1970s. Joe, Eytan Sheshinsky, and I collaborated on an article
together. We have since kept in touch—every time I meet Joe, I always
learn something new. He became very interested in economic development in general and in China in particular, and involved me in a number
of his projects on economic growth in East Asia and on Chinese economic
reform. Joe was instrumental in China being granted most-favored-nation
status in the mid-1990s, which was the forerunner to Chinese accession
to the World Trade Organisation (WTO) in 2001. Throughout the years,
Joe has provided very helpful advice to the highest levels of the Chinese
government. This is one reason I decided to contribute a paper on the
Chinese economy to this conference in his honor.

China has made tremendous progress in its economic development
since it began its economic reform and opened to the world in 1978.
It is currently the fastest-growing economy in the world—averaging
9.72 percent per annum over the past thirty-six years. It is historically
unprecedented for an economy to grow at such a high rate over such a
long period of time. However, the Chinese economy has begun to slow
down, to an annual rate of growth of around 7 percent, in a process of
transition to a "New Normal." Why has China been able to grow at such
a high rate and for such a long period of time? What are the sources of
Chinese economic growth since 1978? These are the questions explored
in this paper.

It is interesting to compare the growth of Chinese and U.S. real
gross domestic products (GDPs) in both aggregate and per capita terms
(figures 16.1 and 16.2). The line with circles and the line with squares represent the levels of real GDP and real GDP per capita of China and the United
States, respectively. The gray bars and black bars represent the annual rates
of growth of China and the United States, respectively. Figure 16.1 shows
that between 1978 and 2014, Chinese real GDP grew from US$369 billion
to US$10.4 trillion (in 2014 prices), to become the second largest economy
in the world, after the United States. Chinese economic growth began to

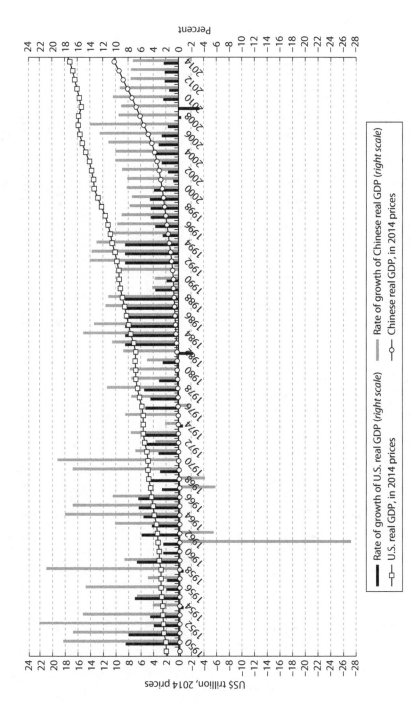

Figure 16.1 Chinese and U.S. Real GDP and Their Rate of Growth Since 1949 (US$ Trillion 2014)

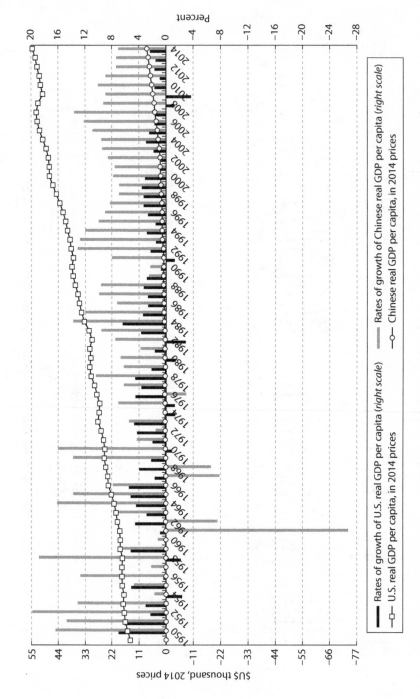

Figure 16.2   Chinese and U.S. Real GDP per Capita and Their Rate of Growth Since 1949 (US$ Thousand 2014)

take off after China began its economic reform in 1978, and accelerated in 2001, when China acceded to the World Trade Organisation. The rate of growth of Chinese real GDP has been higher than that of the United States in every single year since 1978, sometimes significantly so. By comparison, the U.S. GDP of approximately US$17.4 trillion was approximately 1.7 times the Chinese GDP in 2014.

However, despite the rapid growth of the Chinese economy in the aggregate, in terms of its real GDP per capita, China is still very much a developing economy. Figure 16.2 shows that in 1978, the Chinese real GDP per capita was only US$383 (in 2014 prices), approximately 1.25 percent of the U.S. then real GDP per capita of US$30,472. By 2014, the Chinese real GDP per capita had grown to US$7604, still less than one-seventh of the U.S. GDP per capita of US$54,575.

1. THE CHINESE ECONOMIC FUNDAMENTALS

What are the sources of this Chinese economic growth? Long-term economic growth of a country depends on the rates of growth of its primary inputs—tangible (or physical) capital and labor—and on technical progress (also known as the growth of total factor productivity)—that is, the ability to increase output without increasing inputs. The rate of growth of tangible or physical capital depends on the rates of investment on structure, equipment, and basic infrastructure, which in turn depends on the availability of national savings. The rate of technical progress depends on investment in intangible capital, which includes human capital and research and development (R&D) capital.

Chinese economic growth since 1978 has been underpinned by a consistently high domestic investment rate, enabled by a national savings rate of over 35 percent except for a brief start-up period in the early 1950s (see figure 16.3). The Chinese national savings rate rose to around 40 percent in the early 1990s, and at times approached or even exceeded 50 percent in more recent years. The high Chinese savings rate means that the Chinese economy can finance all of its domestic investment needs from its own domestic savings alone, without having to depend on the more fickle foreign capital inflows (including foreign direct investment, foreign portfolio investment, foreign aid, or foreign loans). In particular, it does not need to borrow abroad and bear the potential risks of a large, short-term and often interruptible foreign currency-denominated debt. Thus, the Chinese economy is always assured of a high rate of growth of

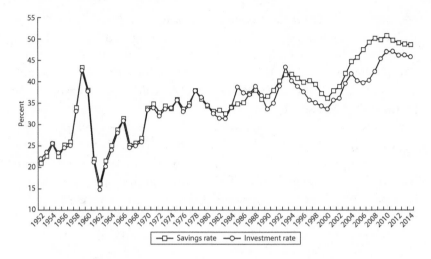

Figure 16.3   Chinese National Savings and Gross Domestic Investment as a Percent of GDP Since 1952

its tangible capital stock. It is therefore also more immune from external disturbances than most other economies.

China, like Japan, Taiwan, and South Korea in their respective early stages of economic development, has an unlimited supply of surplus labor—there is therefore no shortage of and no upward pressure on the real wage rate of unskilled, entry-level labor over an extended period of time. The distribution of Chinese GDP by production-originating sectors in 2014 was approximately: Primary (agriculture), 9.2 percent; Secondary (manufacturing, mining, and construction), 42.6 percent; and Tertiary (services), 48.2 percent (see figure 16.4). (Note that mining is normally included in the primary sector in most other economies.)

The distribution of employment by sector in 2014 was: Primary, 29.5 percent; Secondary, 29.9 percent; and Tertiary, 40.6 percent (see figure 16.5). The agricultural sector employed 29.5 percent of the Chinese labor force but produced only 9.2 percent of the Chinese GDP in 2014. Thus, labor can be productively transferred to the other two sectors where labor productivity and wage rates are higher as long as complementary capital and demand are available.

The huge size of the domestic market with 1.37 billion consumers and their pent-up demands for housing and transportation and other consumer goods and services (e.g., education, health care, and more recently, elderly care) enables the realization of significant economies of scale in

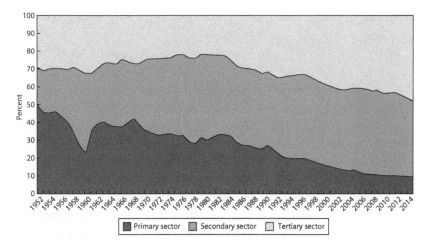

Figure 16.4   The Distribution of GDP by Sector

production, based entirely on the domestic demand in China. The huge domestic market also greatly enhances the productivity of intangible capital (e.g., R&D capital and goodwill, including brand building) by allowing the fixed costs of the R&D for a new product or process or advertising and promotion in brand building to be more easily amortized and recovered. In addition, the huge domestic market also enables significant "learning by doing," so that the unit costs of production decline

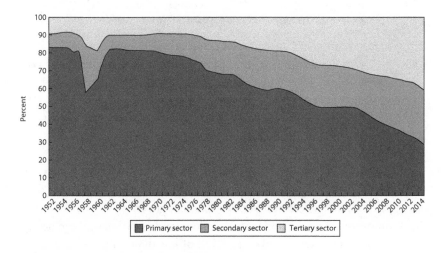

Figure 16.5   The Distribution of Employment by Sector Since 1952

with rising cumulative output. This is yet another form of manifestation of economies of scale.

Another important implication of the huge size of the domestic economy is the relatively low external dependence. Thus, while the quarterly rates of growth of Chinese exports and imports fluctuate like any other economy (see figures 16.6a and 16.6b for the rates of growth of exports and figures 16.7a and 16.7b for the rates of growth of imports, respectively, for selected Asian economies), the quarterly rates of growth of the Chinese real GDP, represented by the black circles in figures 16.8a and 16.8b, can be clearly seen to be relatively much more stable than those of other economies. It never turned negative whereas many of the other Asian economies would experience absolute declines in their real GDPs. This is of course also due in part to the fact that China does not have to depend on the inflow of foreign savings for its investment.

Finally, China also had the additional "advantage" of having been a centrally planned economy for more than a quarter of a century before it undertook its economic reform and opened its economy to the world in 1978. A centrally planned economy is well known to have inherent economic inefficiency, or equivalently, economic slack, which implies that China had surplus potential output prior to its economic reform, which could be realized under appropriate economic reform policies. This prior economic inefficiency or surplus potential output thus also constituted an additional source of Chinese economic growth since 1978.

2. THE MONOPSONISTIC LABOR MARKET IN CHINA

Figure 16.3 shows that China has an extraordinarily high national savings rate. This rate would be considered high even by the standards of East Asian economies.[1] Why is this the case, especially considering that the Chinese GDP per capita is still significantly below those of other East Asian economies? One explanation is that the Chinese government was and still is the largest single employer of nonagricultural workers in China and therefore has both the ability and the incentive to keep wage rates low. Before the economic reform of 1978, the Chinese government was the sole employer for all workers in the urban areas of China and set their wage rates. As the sole employer, the Chinese government could exercise its monopsonistic power and pursued a low (and egalitarian) wage policy, resulting in a low share of labor in GDP of less than 50 percent over the past several decades compared to a share of between 60 and 70 percent in the developed economies of the West.

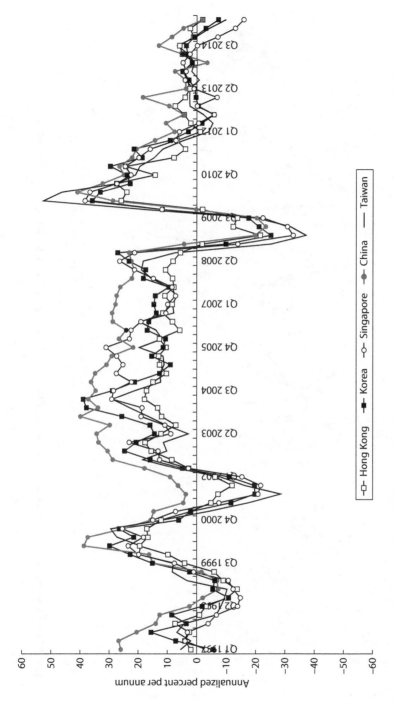

Figure 16.6a   Quarterly Rates of Growth of Exports of Goods: China and the Four East Asian Newly Industrialized Economies

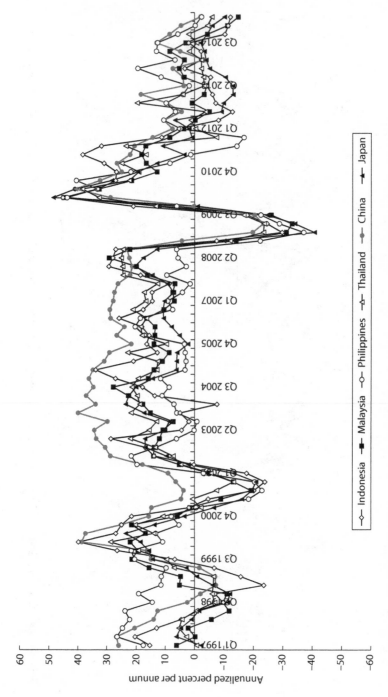

Figure 16.6b Quarterly Rates of Growth of Exports of Goods: China, Japan, and Selected ASEAN Economies

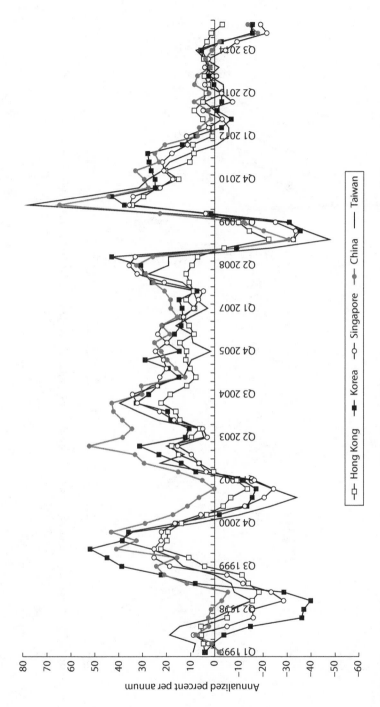

Figure 16.7a   Quarterly Rates of Growth of Imports of Goods: China and the Four East Asian Newly Industrialized Economies

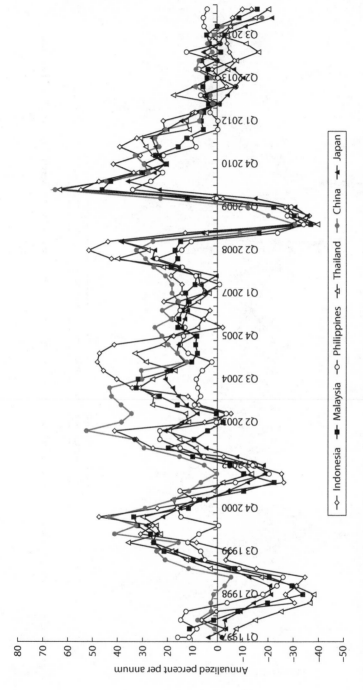

Figure 16.7b Quarterly Rates of Growth of Imports of Goods: China, Japan, and Selected ASEAN Economies

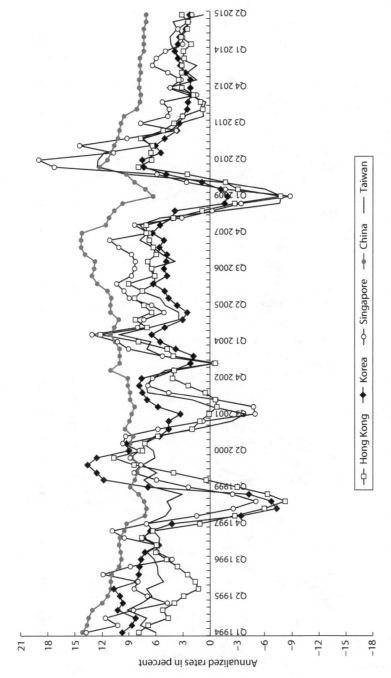

Figure 16.8a   Quarterly Rates of Growth of Real GDP, Year Over Year (YOY): China and the Four East Asian Newly Industrialized Economies

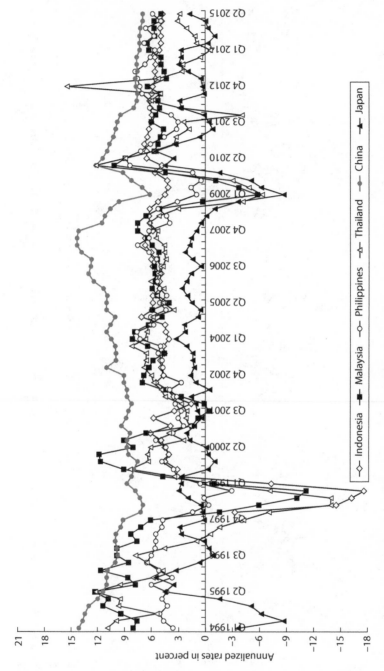

Figure 16.8b   Quarterly Rates of Growth of Real GDP, Year Over Year (YOY): China, Japan, and Selected ASEAN Economies

The low-wage policy reflected three considerations. First, it was designed to increase national savings through higher profits of the enterprises, most of which are state owned, so that the needed domestic investments could be readily financed. This objective of the low-wage policy is similar to the "price scissors" policy of maintaining a large gap between industrial and agricultural prices, practiced in the former Soviet Union in the early twentieth century and in China in the 1950s. Second, a low-wage policy helped to maximize employment, and in particular, the absorption of surplus labor from the agricultural sector into the industrial and service sectors. Third, it was compatible with the ideological preference of the Chinese Communist Party for thrift and egalitarianism in the distribution of income. Note that if the government is the sole employer, the wage and individual income tax policies can be de facto integrated—no separate individual income tax is necessary. In this context, a low-wage (and low- or no-tax) policy has a similar economic effect as a high-wage and high-tax policy but is politically easier to adopt, implement, and sustain.

Even as recently as 2010, the share of Chinese public sector employment, including the employees of central and local governments and their affiliated units, state-owned enterprises (SOEs), and publicly financed educational and health care institutions, was still over 50 percent of all urban employment (see figure 16.9). The government could therefore

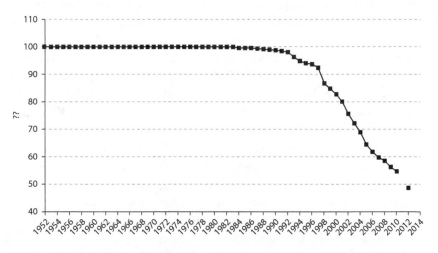

Figure 16.9 The Share of Public Sector Employment in Total Nonagricultural Employment in China

exercise a decisive influence on not only the wage rates of the public-sector employees, but also the level of wage rates in the economy as a whole. Today, a government job is still the preferred choice for many Chinese workers because of the job and income security and the significant fringe benefits that it offers. Many married couples would adopt the strategy of having one spouse working in the public sector and the other working in the private sector.

This low-wage policy has had two major effects. First, it has kept the labor share (and the household share) of GDP low; and second, it has created large profits for state-owned (and other) enterprises. The disposable household income share of GDP in China may be estimated at around 50 percent in 2014, much lower than the corresponding share in a developed economy, where it would typically be above 60 percent, and also lower than those of other developing economies with a comparable real GDP per capita. The Chinese share of labor is likely to be lower than the share of household disposable income, as the latter includes, in addition to wages and salaries, the net proprietor's income, net asset income, and net transfers (which amounted to 43 percent of the total household disposable income), but excludes direct taxes and other mandatory charges such as social security contributions. As Chinese households have less disposable income to spend relative to Chinese GDP, China also has a lower household consumption to GDP ratio than others. This ratio, as well as the total final consumption (which is the sum of government consumption and household consumption) to GDP ratio, have been declining over time (see figure 16.10). As of 2014, the total final consumption ratio was just over 50 percent and the household consumption ratio was approximately 38 percent, both significantly lower than most other economies with a comparable real GDP per capita. The Chinese household savings rate may be estimated at around 30 percent from survey data, comparable to those of ethnically Chinese households in Hong Kong and Taiwan. What all of this means is that the high Chinese savings rate is not due to a particularly high household savings rate but instead to high enterprise profits and reinvestment rates. Thus, Chinese household consumption cannot be expected to be a major source of growth of Chinese aggregate demand in the short or medium term, even though it has been growing in real terms at 1.5 times the rate of growth of GDP, as long as household disposable income remains relatively low.

The high Chinese national savings rate of between 40 and 50 percent should therefore be attributed to the high propensity to save on the part

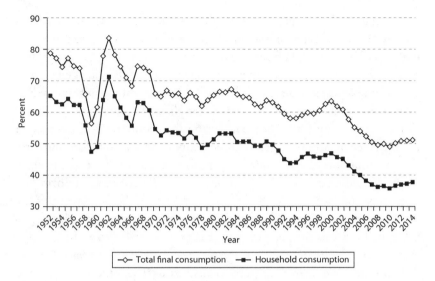

Figure 16.10   Total Chinese Final and Household Consumption as a Percent of Its GDP

of Chinese enterprises out of their profits, especially since they distribute very little in terms of cash dividends to their shareholders, which include the Chinese government (the majority shareholders of SOEs) and the households. Household income and government revenue can both be increased if the SOEs are required to distribute a greater proportion of their profits as cash dividends to their shareholders, which may in turn lead to higher household and government consumption.

3. THE SOURCES OF CHINESE ECONOMIC GROWTH

The rates of growth of Chinese real output, real tangible capital stock, and labor (employment) over the past thirty-six years are presented in table 16.1. It is clear that the tangible capital stock has grown much more rapidly than labor over the past thirty-six years.

Table 16.1   The Rates of Growth of Real Output, Capital Stock, and Labor

Rates of growth of real output (1978–2014)	9.72 percent
Rates of growth of inputs (1978–2013)	
Tangible or physical capital	10.83 percent
Labor	1.88 percent

Chinese economic growth since 1978 could have come from several sources: (1) the realization of the surplus potential output from the initial economic slack that resulted from mandatory central planning; (2) the growth of tangible capital and labor inputs (and the growth of the intangible inputs such as human capital and R&D capital[2]); (3) technical progress (growth of total factor productivity [TFP]); and (4) the effect of economies of scale.

Lau and Zheng (2017), by comparing the economic performance of the Province of Anhui and the Municipality of Shanghai before and after the introduction of economic reform, found that the preexisting slack in the Chinese economy before it undertook its economic reform and opened to the world in 1978 could be estimated to be 50 percent of the actual output in 1978. Based on the assumption that the Chinese real GDP in 1978 was 50 percent higher than it actually was, the implied average annual rate of growth of the Chinese economy between 1978 and 2014 would have been 8.49 percent instead of 9.72 percent. Thus, the reduction of the economic slack that existed before 1978 would account for approximately 1.23 percentage points of the economic growth over the past thirty-six years, or approximately 12.5 percent of the post–1978 economic growth. The remaining economic growth of 8.49 percent per annum can be attributed to the growth of primary inputs, technical progress or growth of TFP, and economies of scale.

The degree of economies of scale cannot be estimated in a straightforward way. In fact, it is underidentified with time-series aggregate data from only a single country—the effects of economies of scale are confounded with the effects of technical progress. However, a meta-production function approach, first introduced by Lau and Yotopoulos (1989) and extended by Boskin and Lau (1992), based on the transcendental logarithmic production function introduced by Christensen, Jorgenson, and Lau (1973), can be used to identify and separate the effects of economies of scale and technical progress under fairly general and testable assumptions. Boskin, Guo, and Lau (2015) have recently estimated the degrees of returns to scale for the Group-of-Seven (G-7) Countries using the meta-production function approach. They found the degree of local returns to scale of the United States to be 1.20 in 1960 and 1.11 in 2007. The average degree of returns to scale for the United States over this period would be 1.155, almost the same as the 1.15 estimated by Denison (1974)[3] but somewhat larger than the assumption of 1.10 used by Denison (1961).[4] Assuming that this estimate of the returns to scale also applies to the Chinese economy on average, it would mean that over a thirty-six-year period, from 1978 to 2014, the average rate of growth would have been 8.36 percent if there were only constant returns to scale, instead of the actual 9.72 percent. This difference would have accounted for 36.1 percent of the Chinese real GDP in 2014. It also means that out of the rate of growth of 9.72 percent, economies of scale account for 1.36 percentage points, or 13.99 percent of the measured economic growth over this period.

As pointed out in section 2, the actual share of labor in GDP in China is low relative to other economies. It may be estimated to be around 50 percent.[5] However, it is believed that the production elasticity of labor is probably higher than the labor share, somewhere between 0.55 and 0.6, as labor has been systematically underpaid due to the low-wage policy maintained by the Chinese government. Since there exist increasing returns to scale, capital as the residual claimant, cannot in general be paid its marginal product; but because labor is actually underpaid, capital can be either underpaid or overpaid relative to its marginal product. With returns to scale assumed to be 1.155, and the production elasticity of labor estimated as between 0.55 and 0.6, the production elasticity of capital may be estimated as (1.155–0.55) or (1.155–0.6), or between 0.555 and 0.605, as the capital and labor elasticities should sum to the degree of returns to scale. Thus, the relative weights of capital and labor may be estimated as 0.48 versus 0.52, or vice versa. Since they are almost equal, we shall use 0.5 as the relative weight of capital and labor for the purpose of the growth-accounting exercise.

The results of the growth-accounting exercise are presented in table 16.2. We note that the elimination of the preexisting economic slack and economies of scale account for respectively 1.23 and 1.36 percentage points, or a total of 2.59 percentage points, of the Chinese economic growth of 9.72 percent between 1978 and 2014. If we subtract 2.59 percent from 9.72 percent, we obtain 7.13 percent. This average annual rate of growth has been achieved by quite a few other economies over a couple of decades in the past. We also note that the growth of tangible capital accounts for more than half of the growth in real output, whereas the growth of labor and technical progress each account for less than 10 percent of the economic growth. If we take out the contributions of the elimination of the prior economic slack and economies of scale, the growth of tangible capital accounts for the bulk of the remaining economic growth, 5.42 percent out of 7.13 percent, or 76 percent. This is similar to the findings of Kim and Lau (1994) on the sources of economic growth of

Table 16.2 The Sources of Chinese Economic Growth (Monopsonistic Labor Market Case)

Sources of Chinese Economic Growth, 1978–2014	Percentage Points	Percent
Elimination of preexisting economic slack	1.23	12.65
Growth of tangible capital	5.42	55.71
Growth of labor	0.94	9.67
Technical progress	0.78	7.97
Economies of scale	1.36	13.99
Total	*9.72*	*100.00*

the East Asian Newly Industrialized Economies (NIEs). If a more conventional growth accounting exercise is done under the assumption of constant returns to scale, the effects of the elimination of the preexisting economic slack and economies of scale would have been captured as part of technical progress or the growth of TFP. If this is done, technical progress or growth of TFP would have accounted for 34.61 percent of Chinese economic growth since 1978.

4. THE ROLE OF EXPECTATIONS

Expectations of the future are important determinants of the behavior of enterprises and households, which in turn determine whether and how much they invest and consume, respectively. For a large economy such as China, the domestic investment and consumption together determine the level of aggregate demand and ultimately whether the economy grows or stagnates and not net exports. There are many ways in which expectations about the future may be formed. Expectations may be based on past experience, such as "tomorrow will be the same as today," but they may also not be based solely on past experience, for example, they may be based on the views of so-called opinion leaders. Expectations may also be affected by the occurrence of some important event, such as the breakout of a war, the election of a new government, the rise of an epidemic, or some specific government pronouncement or action, which can credibly cause changes in the public expectations of the future. Moreover, expectations can often, but not always, and certainly not consistently, be self-fulfilling, if they are sufficiently strongly held by a sufficiently large number of people.

One well-known manifestation of self-fulfilling expectations is in the asset markets. If investors expect the price of an asset, for example, real estate or stock, to go up, and act accordingly by buying real estate or stock, the price of real estate or stock will indeed be driven up by the concerted buying, because the increase in demand in real estate or stock is not and cannot be immediately met by an increase in supply. Thus, the expectations of the investors can be self-fulfilling. There are many such examples in which asset price bubbles are created around the world.

The run-up in the price of Chinese residential real estate between October 2012 and October 2013 was an example of self-fulfilling expectations. The more recent Chinese stock price run-up between November 2014 and July 2015 may also be considered as another such example. But self-fulfilling expectations do not always have to be bullish. If all investors believe that the price of residential real estate is likely to be stable, and act accordingly, that is, they do not try to outbid one another since they know they can always buy a similar property later, then the price of residential real estate will indeed be quite stable. This was what occurred in Singapore, where the government was believed by the public to adjust the rate of release of new lots for residential construction upward and downward in the same direction as the price of residential real estate, thus dampening the price changes.

However, the prices of assets cannot continue to go up forever. All asset price bubbles are sustained by new investors with new buying power coming into the market. At some point, the available potential new buying power will be exhausted with the price levels significantly exceeding what can reasonably be supported by the underlying economic fundamentals in a steady state. When this happens, the asset prices will begin to fall and fall precipitously. So ultimately, the rosy expectations may fail to be fulfilled. And this will lead to a collective downward revision of the expectations.

In the context of China, an important way in which self-fulfilling expectations can be created and changed is through the signaling by the Chinese government. A government with credibility can use its pronouncement of policy changes and actual actions as instruments for changing the macroeconomic expectations of the public about the future of the economy. In fact, Keynesian countercyclical fiscal policies often work because they have the ability to change expectations. In a country such as China, expectations are often formed not only from directly experienced market outcomes but also from the pronouncements and actions of its senior government leaders. The government, because of the many potential instruments at its disposal, is widely believed to have the power to turn around the economy, and is thus a credible authority that can play the coordinating role. The following examples drawn from the Chinese experience show how the Chinese government was able to change negative expectations credibly through its pronouncements and actions.

In 1989, in the aftermath of the June 4 incident, the Chinese economy became quite depressed, in part because of foreign sanctions, but mostly because of generally negative expectations about the future on the parts of enterprises and households. As a result, enterprises did not invest and households did not consume. The years 1990 and 1991 were similarly slow, despite an abundance of liquidity. The rates of growth of real GDP in 1989 and 1990 were the lowest since economic reform began in 1978 (see figure 16.11) and the rates of growth of fixed asset investment in 1989 and 1990 were negative—the only years with a negative rate of growth of fixed asset investment since 1978 (see figure 16.12), which showed how negative the expectations were.

Then in early 1992, Deng Xiaoping, the paramount Chinese leader at the time, undertook his famous southern inspection tour. Everywhere he went, he urged the people to seize the moment and grasp the opportunities. His words changed expectations in the entire country almost overnight. Enterprises began investing and households began consuming once again. As a result, the rest of 1992, as well as 1993 and 1994, were boom years with double-digit rates of economic growth (and relatively high rates of inflation) and high rates of growth of fixed asset investment (see figures 16.11, 16.12, and 16.13).

In mid-1997, the East Asian Currency Crisis broke out, first in Thailand, and then in South Korea until it engulfed almost all of the East Asian economies, with the exception of Japan. Almost all of the East Asian currencies, with the exception of the Hong Kong dollar, which was (and still is) pegged to the U.S. dollar, devalued significantly. The quarterly rates of growth of exports and imports of all East Asian economies fell precipitously (see figures 16.6 and 16.7). Premier Zhu Rongji of the People's Republic of China decided to hold the renminbi/US$ exchange rate steady amid the chaos of the East Asian currency crisis, and thus managed to maintain the confidence of the domestic investors and consumers about China's economic future, keeping the Chinese economy growing (see figure 16.14). In so doing, he also helped to stabilize the exchange rates of the other East Asian currencies and facilitated the

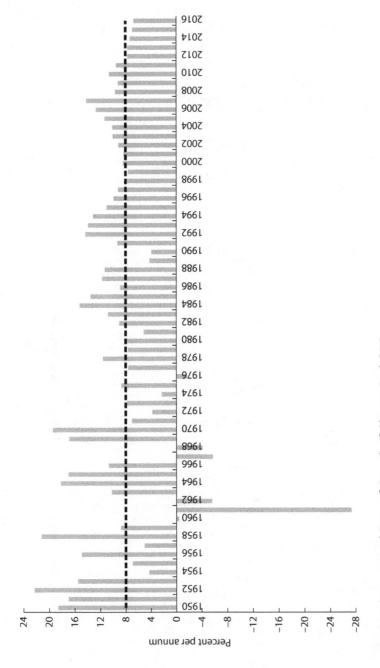

Figure 16.11　Annual Rates of Growth of Chinese Real GDP

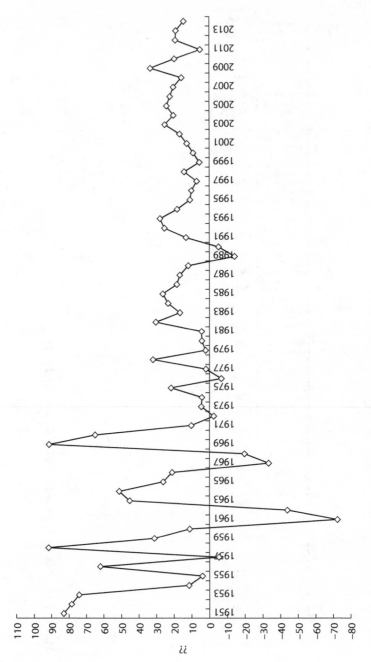

Figure 16.12 Annual Rates of Growth of Chinese Fixed Assets Investment

recovery of the other East Asian economies. Had China also devalued at that time, it would have led to another cycle of competitive devaluation among the East Asian economies, with unimaginably negative economic and social consequences.

In 2000, the whole world was suffering from the burst of the internet bubble, this was no exception in the United States and China (the negative expectations then were reflected in the exceptionally low rates of growth of fixed asset investment). Then in December 2001, China became a member of the WTO. The Chinese accession to the WTO also changed expectations in a dramatic way, which also reflected the expected expiration of the Multi Fibre Agreement which governed global trade in textiles in 2005. It had a significant effect on the rates of growth of both real GDP (see figure 16.13) and fixed asset investment (see figure 16.14). In 2005, the renminbi began to be allowed to appreciate relative to the U.S. dollar, which adversely affected the growth of exports, and the rate of growth of fixed asset investment fell back to more normal levels.

In 2008, in the immediate aftermath of the collapse of Lehman Brothers in the United States, all credit dried up in the United States as well as the other developed economies. Overnight, importers in the United States and other developed economies could no longer place their import orders to China and other trading partner countries because their banks were not in a position to issue acceptable letters of credit. As a result, export orders received by Chinese enterprises declined by approximately 50 percent (see figures 16.6 and 16.7). There was real panic in the air. Fortunately, barely six weeks later, Chinese Premier Wen Jiabao unveiled the 4 trillion yuan (approximately 6 percent of the then Chinese GDP) economic stimulus program, which once again managed to maintain the confidence of Chinese enterprises and households in their economy. Actually, the economic stimulus program did not really take effect until at least a year later, but the announcement of the program itself alone managed to restore positive expectations among the Chinese public (see figures 16.14 and 16.15).

In all of these cases, the Chinese government was able to turn around the very negative domestic expectations about the future of the Chinese economy into positive ones, and in so doing, greatly reduced the uncertainty pertaining to the future and increased general business as well as consumer confidence. These changes in turn fueled investment booms that resulted in the subsequent economic growth.

However, with the bursting of the Chinese stock market bubble in July 2015 and the slight but unexpected devaluation of the renminbi of

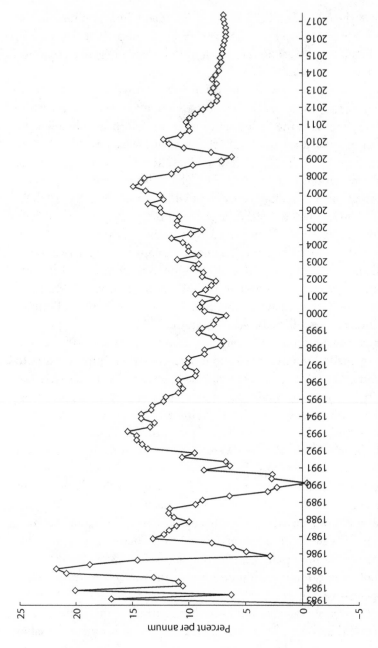

Figure 16.13   Quarterly Rates of Growth of Chinese Real GDP, Year Over Year (YOY)

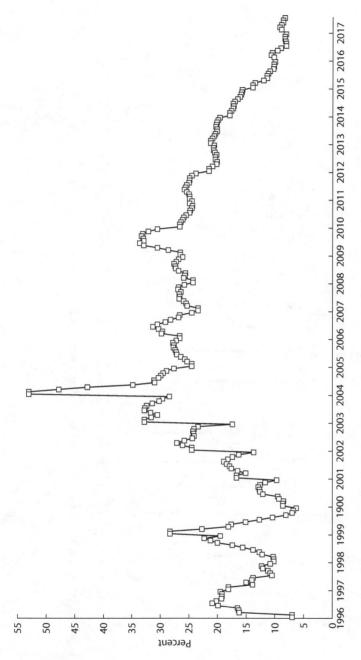

Figure 16.14 Monthly Rates of Growth of Chinese Fixed Assets Investment, Year Over Year (YOY)

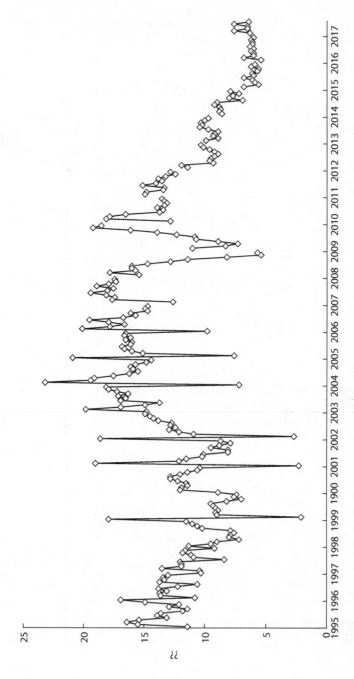

Figure 16.15 Monthly Rates of Growth of Real Value-Added of Chinese Industry, Year Over Year (YOY)

approximately 4 percent in August 2015, the confidence of the Chinese enterprises and households has been somewhat shaken. At the same time, reacting to these developments in China, the world markets have also panicked and doomsayers have been coming out in droves, predicting the imminent collapse of the Chinese economy. Perhaps this is the time for the Chinese government to take more decisive and visible actions to increase domestic aggregate demand so as to reduce uncertainty, shore up confidence, and change expectations of the Chinese public about the future.

CONCLUDING REMARKS

Chinese economic growth during the past thirty-six years can be attributed to the growth of tangible inputs—tangible capital and labor, and in particular, tangible capital—rather than the growth in intangible capital or technical progress, just as the past economic growth of other East Asian economies at a similar stage of economic development. The successful Chinese experience strongly reaffirms the fundamental importance of having and maintaining a high investment rate, enabled by a high national savings rate, and surplus labor. A low-wage policy was instrumental in a high national savings rate and a rapid rate of absorption of surplus labor. In addition, the size of the Chinese domestic economy is a favorable factor allowing the ready realization of economies of scale and reducing vulnerability to external disturbances. The prior economic slack, inherent in any previously centrally planned economy, has also been a significant source of economic growth upon Chinese transition to a market economy.

Expectations will continue to play an important role in the Chinese economy. A strong Chinese central government with the unique power to mobilize domestic aggregate demand can credibly change expectations from negative to positive at critical junctures to keep the economy growing.

NOTES

This chapter was originally a paper presented at the conference, "A Just Society: Honoring Joseph Stiglitz," held at the Columbia Business School, Columbia University, New York, October 16–17, 2015. Lawrence J. Lau wishes to thank Michael Boskin, Ayesha Macpherson Lau, Joseph Stiglitz, Yanyan Xiong, Huanhuan Zheng, and Wentong Zheng for their invaluable advice, comments, and suggestions, but retains sole responsibility for any remaining errors. All opinions expressed herein are the author's own and do not necessarily reflect the views of any of the organizations with which the author is affiliated.

1. Among East Asian economies, only Singapore has a comparably high national savings rate.

2. In this chapter, the contributions of the growth of human capital and R&D capital to Chinese economic growth are not estimated separately but subsumed in the contribution of technical progress or growth of TFP.

3. See Denison (1974, 75).

4. See Denison (1961, 75).

5. One possible estimate of the share of household disposable income in Chinese GDP is 43 percent in 2014, based on officially published data. However, the labor share can differ from the above because of net proprietor's income, net household asset income, and direct taxes and transfers. The data on the household consumption share of GDP, which are probably less prone to errors, indicate a share of around 38 percent in 2014 (see figure 16.10). However, a household consumption share of 38 percent does not seem to be consistent with a household income share of 43 percent, which would imply an exceptionally low household savings rate out of disposable income. A more reasonable estimate of the household disposable income share or labor share in GDP in 2014 is probably around 50 percent or even a little higher.

REFERENCES

Arrow, Kenneth J. 1962. "The Economic Implications of Learning by Doing." *Review of Economic Studies* 29 (3):155–173.

Boskin, Michael J., and Lawrence J. Lau. 1992. "International and Intertemporal Comparison of Productive Efficiency: An Application of the Meta-Production Function Approach to the Group-of-Five (G-5) Countries." *Economic Studies Quarterly* 43 (4):298–312.

Boskin, Michael J., Haiqiu Guo, and Lawrence J. Lau. 2015. "Technical Progress and G-7 Economic Growth." Working Paper, Institute of Global Economics and Finance, Chinese University of Hong Kong, Shatin, New Territories, Hong Kong.

Christensen, Laurits R., Dale W. Jorgenson, and Lawrence J. Lau. 1973. "Transcendental Logarithmic Production Frontiers." *Review of Economics and Statistics* 55 (1):28–45.

Denison, Edward F. 1961. *The Sources of Economic Growth in the United States and the Alternatives Before Us.* Committee for Economic Development, New York.

Denison, Edward F. 1974. *Accounting for United States Economic Growth, 1929–1969.* Washington, DC: Brookings Institution.

Kim, Jong-Il, and Lawrence J. Lau. 1994. "The Sources of Economic Growth of the East Asian Newly Industrialized Countries." *Journal of the Japanese and International Economies* 8 (3):235–271.

Lau, Lawrence J., and Pan A. Yotopoulos. 1989. "The Meta-Production Function Approach to Technological Change in World Agriculture." *Journal of Development Economics* 31 (2):241–269.

Lau, Lawrence J., and Huanhuan Zheng. 2017. "How Much Slack Was There in the Chinese Economy Prior to Its Economic Reform of 1978?" *China Economic Review* 45:124–142.

CHAPTER 17

Knowledge as a Global Common and the Crisis of the Learning Economy

Ugo Pagano

INTRODUCTION

Almost by definition, a move of knowledge from the public to the private sector increases inequality: everyone has equal rights of access to a public good. By contrast, the privatization of knowledge entails that only the monopolistic owner has full access to it. Increased rents are likely to cause both declining growth and increasing inequality.

Knowledge is by far the most important global common of humankind and, since the dawn of human history, its production and accumulation has been the distinctive feature of our species. However, its weight in production processes has greatly increased in recent decades. The roots of the modern knowledge-intensive society can be found in the Enlightenment[1] movement, which formulated the basic values of a liberal and democratic society:

> The uber-ideology of the Enlightenment—the questioning of authority, and the belief in meritocracy, the notion that is possible and desirable, the respect extended to science and technology have created preconditions that are favorable to the creation of a learning society and to learning institutions (firms) within our society. (Stiglitz and Greenwald 2014, 11 percent Kindle version)

The increasing privatization of knowledge raises important political and moral issues. Moreover, the fact that learning may generate different competing theories (Elkana 2000) entails that we need procedures and institutions to falsify theories. This has important implications for the organization of a learning society.

In this chapter, we will focus on the effects that learning has on inequality and development. We will try to analyze two main interrelated problems that characterize a learning society. On the one hand, there is a tension between the nonrival nature of knowledge and its private appropriation. On the other hand, there is an institutional mismatch between the global nature of the public good that is knowledge and the fragmentation of political power among different nations. We will argue that these two contradictions can provide an explanation of economic stagnation and of inequality.

The structure of the chapter is as follows. The next section focuses on the ways in which the institutions of a learning society deal with the two contradictions that we have considered. Section 2 examines the relation between the private appropriation of knowledge and inequality. Section 3 analyzes the relation between the monopolization of knowledge and the recent dynamics of the global economy, which has witnessed the boom of the roaring nineties and, after that, several years of economic stagnation. Finally the concluding section suggests some possible policies aiming at a just learning society.

1. THE INSTITUTIONS OF THE LEARNING SOCIETY

The institutions by which learning activities are organized have much to do with the nature of knowledge—the fundamental input as well as the fundamental output of learning activities. In a famous passage, President Jefferson observed how knowledge is like the flame of a candle: other candles can be lit without decreasing the flame of the candle used to transmit the fire. In the language of economics, knowledge is a nonrival good: enlightening others does not decrease our light and, in this sense, the use by others of the same piece of knowledge occurs at zero-marginal cost. While a piece of bread is a rival good that can be eaten only by one person, in the case of knowledge the gospel story of the multiplication of the loaves and fishes can become a real experience of ordinary life. Unsurprisingly, ever since Arrow's (1962) fundamental contribution, learning (and learning to learn) has been considered to be the engine of economic development.

However, even if knowledge is a nonrival good, the exclusion of others from the use of a certain piece of knowledge is well possible. This exclusion involves a monopoly on knowledge which restricts nonowners' rights much more than other forms of private property. Thus, a knowledge economy is characterized by a *fundamental paradox*.

On the one hand, since knowledge is a nonrival good, open access to its benefits could greatly contribute to global freedom and equality. Small firms and workers' cooperatives, using freely available knowledge—according to Arrow (1996) a "fugitive resource"—should become increasingly widespread (Hodgson 1999; Bowles 2004).

On the other hand, the privatization of knowledge restricts others' freedom and increases inequality to a much greater extent than other forms of enclosure (such as the closures of land which preceded the Industrial Revolution. The ownership of physical assets does not entail that similar (or even equal) assets are unavailable. Thus, individuals are not necessarily deprived of their freedom to pursue those patterns of self-development and growth requiring their use. By contrast, intellectual monopoly entails that no other similar resource is available to other individuals. The potential freedom entailed by nonrival use can evolve into an extreme restriction of others' liberties. Since the same piece of knowledge can be used an infinite number of times and its value increases with complementary pieces of knowledge, giant firms endowed with substantial portfolios of intellectual property rights can easily outcompete small firms. Thus, once knowledge becomes part of firms' private capital, big corporations are likely to enjoy the fruits of intellectual monopoly (Pagano 2014) and the knowledge-intensive economy becomes a very hostile environment for small firms.

Thus, we must face what may be called *the paradox of the knowledge economy*: it is potentially democratic and egalitarian but, at the same time, it is offering corporations and financial capital unprecedented opportunities to concentrate on wealth and monopoly power.

The dark side of the knowledge economy has attracted little attention among economists. According to much standard economic theory, intellectual monopoly and a patent system are necessary evils required to stimulate an adequate level of innovative investments.

The orthodox argument can be challenged on two grounds.

First, inventors may be compensated by the first mover advantages entailed by their discovery. Intellectual monopoly is not the only possible extrinsic reward for innovation, and its net benefits should be compared with the benefits of other incentive systems. Rewards, career advancement, and prizes can be alternative extrinsic motivations that stimulate innovations. Moreover, some knowledge is also produced for intrinsic motivations: humans are endowed with a natural curiosity that can only be satisfied by discovering new things.

Second, the incentive effect is often obtained at the expense of some blockage of others' opportunities. Since innovation and scientific discovery are cumulative processes, the availability of some knowledge may be an essential input for the production of new knowledge. Thus, the intellectual monopoly of one individual may decrease the incentives of other individuals to invest in innovation capabilities. For society at large, the blocking effect is likely to be much larger than the incentive effect.

No realistic system for rewarding the production of new knowledge is optimal, and there are trade-offs among alternative institutional arrangements. Rewarding individuals for the production of new knowledge and allowing everyone to use it would, in principle, be the optimal solution, but estimating the value of the new knowledge is a very difficult task. Some of the benefits may only become evident after a very long time. However, rough systems of rewards for the production of open science, such as those offered by academic advancement based on peer reviews, have allowed remarkable advances of human knowledge (especially when the extrinsic motivation for prestige and money is accompanied by intellectual integrity and intrinsic human curiosity). Limited rewards for exceptional discoveries have been compensated by some payments for failed lines of investigation. This redistribution of rewards may have acted as a form of insurance that is very useful for stimulating an inevitably risky activity like scientific research.

In the case of open science, there is no blockage of similar or complementary discoveries. By contrast, in the case of intellectual property rights, while the rewards are high, the blocking effects may also be astronomically high. A comparative normative analysis of rewards and intellectual property rights should take into account the fact that their net benefits are different for different pieces of knowledge. It should also consider the related "institutional complementarities" among politics, law, and corporate governance (Aoki 2010). For some pieces of knowledge, the blocking effects are more relevant than the incentive effects while, in other cases, the opposite may be true.

The complexity of the problem entails that a rich mix of institutions should be used by a learning society:

> Every country should have a portfolio of instruments. The nature of the portfolio will affect the extent to which the country is successful in creating a learning society; it will affect the innovativeness and the efficiency of the system—including the uncertainty and transaction costs facing market

participants. In our view, too much weight has been assigned to patents in the current portfolio of the United States. (Stiglitz and Greenwald 2014, 57 percent Kindle version)

The excessive use of the patent system is also due to the lobbying and the rent-seeking activities of (potential) patent holders. Basu points out that:

Not all but most of the rich got there by mastering the art of barter through nods and winks as well as the extensive use of the exchange of favors—activities that we were told had ended in the medieval age. (Basu 2011, 27)

The patent attribution system is hardly an exception to this rule.

The excessive weight of the patent system is exacerbated by the fact that most knowledge is not only an impure public good. It is also a global common in the sense that its benefits are not limited geographically: "a mathematical theorem is as true in Russia as it is in the United States as it is in the United States, in Africa as it is in Australia." The fact that many scientific truths "are universal in nature" (Stiglitz 1999) raises two problems for the patent system.

(i) "Every innovation makes use of previously accumulated knowledge—it draws on the global commons of preexisting knowledge. How much of the returns to the innovation should be credited to this use of the global commons? Current practice says zero—because it is a commons, there is no price. But this is not the way things need be. In many parts of the world, there is a recognition that charges can and should be imposed for the use of commons (whether they are forests, grazing lands, or fisheries)." Such charges can be justified on both efficiency and equity grounds. The international community could similarly claim the right to charge for the use of the global knowledge commons (Stiglitz 1999).

As long as it is not clear how much firms draw from the global knowledge commons, it is not possible to establish their real contributions. The firm stands on the shoulders of giants (and also of many ordinary people) without paying for their services. Patents may be overused because no patent holder pays for the use of the global knowledge commons. While owners of privatized intellectual property prosper, universities and other public institutions (as well as all the producers of traditional knowledge, often in developing countries) receive no compensation. Ironically, they are even criticized for their "economic inefficiency." By contrast, even in the cases in which knowledge owners take the unpleasant form of patent trolls and inhibit economic development, their rent-seeking activities are seen as a form of efficient profit maximization. Indeed, the only way in which universities and other public institutions can prosper is by betraying their mission of advancing open science. In many cases, they become the worst patent trolls (Lemley 2008).

(ii) If knowledge is a global common, each country has an incentive to use the public knowledge of other countries and to overprivatize the knowledge that it is producing. This free-riding problem is greatly exacerbated by the present institutions of the world economy. The institution of the World Trade Organization (WTO), with the associated Trade-Related Aspects of Intellectual Property Rights (TRIPS) Agreement, has created an international regime of strong intellectual property rights whereby the holders of each country's patented knowledge can reap their profits around the globe. By contrast, the public knowledge produced by a country is used without any compensation by the other countries. Hence, each country is pushed toward a portfolio of instruments for intellectual property management that increases the weight of patenting well beyond what would happen in a closed economy.

2. INCREASING INEQUALITY AND THE ADVENT OF INTELLECTUAL MONOPOLY CAPITALISM

In his much acclaimed book, Piketty (2014) uses a figure (see figure 17.1), which underlies his criticism of the Kuznets curve. A rate of profit r greater than the rate of growth g involves redistribution in favor of capitalist owners and an increase in inequality.

Unfortunately, this has been the case only for a limited period of capitalism, and since the 1980s, there has been a marked shift of capitalism toward a more unequal and unjust society. According to Piketty, Kuznets's hypothesis (that the initial increase in inequality was a price to be paid for a richer and more equal future society) is discredited by the recent divergence between higher rates of profits and lower rates of growth. By contrast, Piketty (figure 17.1) advances the idea that capitalism has an inbuilt tendency toward increasing inequality that was tamed by the two World Wars, which forced the ruling classes of each country to reach

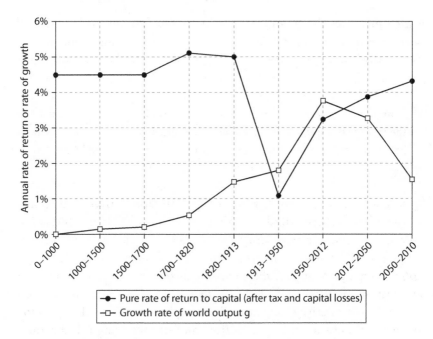

Figure 17.1   Rate of Return to Capital Compared to Growth Rate

Note: The rate of return to capital (after tax and capital losses) fell below the growth rate during the twentieth century, and may again surpass it in the twenty-first century.

Source: See Piketty (pse.ens.fr/capital21c).

a compromise with its own working class. During the 1980s, the institutional compromises resulting from the two wars were dismantled, and capitalist economies resumed their natural trends of increasing inequality.

While factor prices and quantities usually move in opposite directions, Piketty's increasing inequality trend is justified by the fact that capital accumulation and the return to capital move in the same direction—a real puzzle for economic theory. To solve this puzzle, Stiglitz has introduced two useful definitions of capital and wealth, which are not properly distinguished in Piketty's work. Capital is the productive capacity of the nonhuman factors employed in production. By contrast, wealth is the value of these assets. Wealth and capital do not necessarily move in the same direction. For instance, wealth may increase because the price of land goes up but this does not signify that productive capacity has increased. In other words, since in Piketty, *r* is the return to wealth, it may have little to do with the *r* of standard growth theory, which measures the (marginal) productivity of capital. It includes all sorts of "exploitation rents" including those related to monopoly power. When these rents increase, wealth increases as well (even if capital is unchanged):

> If monopoly power of firms increases, it will show up as an increase in the income of capital, and the present discounted value of that will show up as an increase in wealth (since claims on the rents associated with that market power can be bought and sold). (Stiglitz 2015, 24)

Stiglitz (2015) considers various types of exploitation rents. Some of them have characterized capitalism ever since the British Industrial Revolution. The increasing rent on land was already the major preoccupation of David Ricardo. Consequently, exploitation rents can hardly offer a convincing explanation for the increasing inequality of recent decades. By contrast, in the 1980s and 1990s, the new learning economy was characterized by the massive emergence of new exploitation rents. The growing intensity of knowledge in production, and its increasing privatization, greatly increased the rents arising from intellectual monopoly:

> Knowledge that is freely available increases output, but doesn't show up in anybody's balance sheet and therefore would not normally be reflected in the national accounts as wealth. But changes in the intellectual property regime (what Boyle (2003) refers to as the enclosure of the knowledge commons) have resulted in an increase in the wealth of those who are given these property rights. (Stiglitz 2015, 27)

The years 1982–1999 witnessed a great mutation in the nature of the assets used in production. By the end of the millennium, the wealth of corporations was generated not so much by their machines and buildings as by their intellectual monopolies. Patents, copyrights, and trademarks now constitute the bulk of the big corporations' assets. Figure 17.2 offers a rough idea of the revolution of the assets structure that took place in 1980s and 1990s. In less than twenty years, the percentage of tangible assets (houses, machines, etc.) in the capital of the first 500 business corporations decreased dramatically, becoming about one-quarter of what it had been at the beginning of the 1980s.

The U.S. 1980 Bayh-Dole Act and the 1994 TRIPS Agreement (an annex to the institution of the WTO) allowed a massive privatization of

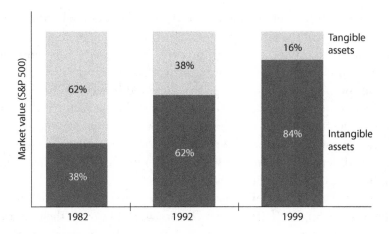

Figure 17.2   Assets Structure, 1982–1999

Source: Juergen H. Daum, *Intangible Assets and Value Creation*, Hoboken, NJ: John Wiley & Sons, 2002.

knowledge. Financial claims could now also be held on a massive quantity of intangible assets related to knowledge and information.

Corporations have exploited the huge economies of scale and of scope that arise when knowledge becomes a private input. Because of the strong international regime of intellectual property, they have also been able to decentralize production to firms located in low–labor-cost countries without the fear that independent competitors in those countries could also use their knowledge. The nonrival nature of knowledge, which could in principle favor small, and even self-managed, firms, is used to create artificial economies of size which make the cheap acquisition and defense of property rights possible only for big business. In the absence of knowledge privatization, the need to provide incentives to invest in human capital would be an argument in favor of the labor-hiring-capital solution. Because of the monopolization of intellectual capital, the knowledge economy can become a prohibitive environment for small labor-managed firms and an ideal setting for big corporations. The monopolistic ownership of intellectual property encourages investment in skills necessary to improve the knowledge that one already owns. In turn, the skills that are developed make it even more convenient to acquire and produce more private knowledge. Thus, big business corporations are more likely to enjoy a virtuous circle between firms' capabilities and their intellectual property. By contrast, other firms may often be trapped in vicious circles of underinvestment in human capital where the lack of intellectual property discourages the acquisition of skills and the lack of skills discourages the acquisition of intellectual property. This hypothesis is consistent with a substantial body of recent research showing that the divergence of returns on invested capital has greatly increased in recent times (even if the analysis is restricted to nonfinancial firms) and the fact that the well-performing firms have shared their rents with their employees. As a result, at least in the United States, inequality has not been driven by growing income differentials within the same firm but by the dramatic divergence in the earnings of different firms.

Figure 17.3, taken from a paper also presented at the conference in honor of Joe Stiglitz (Furman and Orszag 2015), illustrates the increased divergence between the return on invested capital in publicly traded nonfinancial firms.[2]

The high relative earnings of the best-performing firms are also shared by the workers, and they are the main factor explaining increasing wage inequality. As Barth, Bryson, and Freeman (2014, 21) point out, the "distribution of earnings across establishments widened markedly during the 1970s–2000s period of increasing inequality of individual

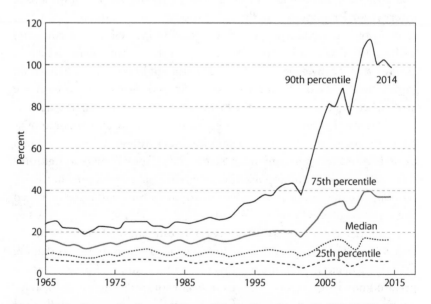

Figure 17.3   Return on Invested Capital Excluding Goodwill, U.S. Publicly Traded Nonfinancial Firms.

earnings." It accounted for most of the increased inequality among workers "most tellingly accounting for the 79 per cent among the stayers—workers who continued from one year to the next in the same establishments" (2014, 22).

Song et al. (2015) find strong evidence that *within-firm* pay inequality has remained mostly flat over the past decades. They observe that

> even if individuals in the top 1 percent in 2012 are paid much more than the top one per cent in 1982, they are now paid less, relative to their firms' mean incomes, than they were three years ago. Instead of top incomes rising within firms, top-paying firms are now paying even higher wages. This may tend to make inequality more invisible, as individuals do not see rising inequality among their peers. More research needs to be done to understand why inequality between firms has increased so much more than inequality within them. But this fact of stable inequality within firms should inform our understanding of the great increase in inequality within the United States over the last three decades. (2015, 30)

There is no doubt that "more research needs to be done to understand why inequality between firms has increased so much more than inequality within them." However, we believe that the reinforcement of intellectual property rights is likely to be a strong candidate to explain the nature of these growing inequalities. We have seen that in a regime of strong property rights some firms are likely to find themselves in virtuous self-reinforcing circles between skills and intellectual property whereas some other firms suffer from a vicious interaction between lack of skills and lack of intellectual property. These mechanisms explain why firms diverge not only in the rate of returns on their invested capital but also in the wages that they pay. The firms endowed with a greater amount of intellectual capital not only earn much greater returns on the capital that they invest but also, by investing more in the firm-specific skills of their workers, they pay higher wages. In turn, the possibility of making investments in human capital specific to private intellectual property is an important reason for the high return on invested capital.

Employees' skills specificity in firms owning much intangible proprietary intellectual capital (patents, trademarks, proprietary projects, and design) is likely to be much greater than that existing in firms employing a great deal of physical capital. Physical capital can be replicated whereas proprietary intellectual capital cannot, and it involves a high specificity of the employees that utilize and improve this type of capital. Moreover, the strength of intellectual property rights also allows widespread outsourcing of the activities that do not require firm-specific skills. Intellectual monopoly limits the possibility of imitating the firm outsourcing its activities. Massive outsourcing has occurred both abroad in low-wage countries and within advanced economies, contributing to the growing inequality in the returns of capital and labor in the different firms.

The literature, which we have examined, limits the analysis of growing interfirm inequality to nonfinancial firms. However, the overall increase in inequality is even greater if we include financial firms in the analysis. According to Philippon (2012, 1605), workers in finance "earn the same education-adjusted wages as other workers until 1990, but by 2006 the premium is 50 per cent on average" with executives in finance earning "250 percent more than executives elsewhere."

Philippon argues that, similarly to the 1920s, the absence of regulations may have favored financial innovation (in this case with little intellectual property rights [IPR] protection) and a demand for particularly skilled workers. Another possibility, consistent with the thesis advanced in our paper, is that the change of underlying assets, considered in figure 17.3, has contributed to the recent dramatic change in the composition of the financial industry.

Intangible assets are more firm-specific than tangible assets, and the degree of specificity of the assets influences the nature of the financial industry and the mix of financial instruments (Williamson 1988; Nicita and Pagano 2016). Tangible assets can be more easily redeployed to other uses and have a thicker market with a fairly well-known price that can offer an easy guide for safe lending protected by collateral. Traditional banking can do very well in this situation. By contrast, intangible assets such as patents, reputation, and trademarks do not have the same thick liquid markets of tangible assets and known market prices to be used in the case of default by the organization. In the case of default, the financiers cannot be easily compensated with the sale of the organization's assets. Traditional banking is not a useful financing tool for companies of this type. Financiers can only gain by sharing the gains of the company. However, this is a much riskier business involving much more sophisticated skills.

The increasing commodification of knowledge has enlarged the set of assets over which financial claims can be defined and enforced. It has, in this way, contributed to remarkable growth of the financial industry in the past three decades (Philippon 2015). The knowledge embodied in human beings and the knowledge available as public goods cannot provide a significant basis for the growth of financial assets. By contrast, the knowledge privatized and transformed into firms' intellectual monopolies increases their stock market values and furnishes a powerful engine for the expansion of financial assets. Note that the growth of the financial assets can be completely disentangled from the growth of the economy. This may be simply due to a redefinition of rights on assets that could otherwise have been part of the workers' human capital or a collective good belonging to the entire society. By contrast, this change in the nature of the assets may often hamper the development of economic opportunities. In some cases, knowledge would have been more productive if it had been embodied in the workers' minds or if it had been owned as a public good instead of a private monopoly. Increased financial wealth may come together with a decrease in the wealth of society and with an increase in the share of wealth owned by financial capital.

While the reinforcing of intellectual property favors financialization, the financialization of the economy induces companies to commodify their intellectual capital even more. In an economy in which strong competitive pressure requires the ability to attract cheap finance, the company's structure of assets evolves in this direction. The higher the intensity of private commodified knowledge, relative to other types of knowledge, the easier it becomes to attract cheap finance. Thus, the financialization of the economy and the commodification of knowledge reinforce each other, and they jointly induce a mutation in the nature of the business corporation. The typical corporation becomes characterized by pervasive financial control and by the high intensity of intangible assets.

The "intangible corporation" has become a thing responsible to financial markets, and otherwise an irresponsible thing. Thanks to strong IPRs, production can be outsourced. In this way, many stakeholders have lost their rights in the corporation while they are still dependent on it in highly monopolized markets. Moreover, since profits derive mainly from intellectual monopoly, the knowledge-intensive corporation is also a litigation-intensive one, ready to use all possible ways to defend and expand its intellectual monopolies against competing public and private claims.

The main advantage of big corporations now consists in their possibility to assemble large packages of complementary knowledge, partially overcoming the "anti-commons tragedies" of knowledge privatization. However, this partial solution of the anti-commons problem comes together with an even greater monopoly power of the modern corporation that owns large bundles of complementary pieces of knowledge and, as a result, some future technological paths.

Paradoxically, the monopoly power of the modern corporation shares some characteristics with that of the old chartered corporations, such as the East India or the Hudson Bay Companies. Chartered corporations had a monopoly on a limited (but fairly vast) territory. New corporations have a monopoly on a limited (but increasingly large and potentially global) field of knowledge. In some ways, their power is greater than that of the old corporations because nation-states now find it difficult to regulate their global intellectual monopolies. There is a growing asymmetry between the power of the nation-states, with a monopoly power in many fields but on a restricted territory, and the power of the business corporations, which is restricted to few fields but is not geographically limited.

Financial firms and corporations are creating a new legal framework independent of any democratic control. The Transatlantic Trade and Investment Partnership (TTIP) is completing the process of introducing a "Lex Corporatoria" that has the same private character as the "Lex Mercatoria" existing in the Middle Ages. However, the "Lex Corporatoria" is enforced with the help of the public authorities. Since firms can choose to incorporate in different countries, the latter compete to have the privilege (and the fees) of global enforcement. The United Kingdom is only too ready to become the Delaware of the global economy (perhaps also with the help of the TTIP treaty), unconstrained by the interferences of federal democratic government. By contrast, a just society requires some form of genuine global governance. It cannot be founded on the judicial system of a single nation willing to outcompete its rivals to attract corporate legal business. The founding principles of a just society should take into due account that knowledge has always been the most important global common of our species, and that its unequal distribution can generate an unjust global society.

3. THE ROARING NINETIES AND THE GREAT DEPRESSION

The monopolization of the economy has not only favored increasing inequality. It has also been a major cause of the Great Depression. In his 2003 book, Stiglitz already showed that the seeds of a subsequent crisis had been planted during the "roaring nineties." He observed that, in the dot-com bubble of the 1990s, the *irrational exuberance of investors* played an important role in planting the seeds of future destruction. However, the exuberance was not completely irrational. Both the roaring nineties and the subsequent dramatic economic crisis can also be, at least partially, explained by a rational (even if eventually self-defeating) investment dynamic induced by the reinforcement of intellectual property, which started with the 1980 Bayh-Dole Act and culminated with the 1994 TRIPS Agreement.

However, the time profiles of the incentive and blocking effects are very different. The incentive effect is immediate. As soon as the reinforcement of intellectual property is introduced (and even before, when it is expected to happen), firms are induced to invest in innovations that can be patented. By contrast, the blocking effect comes later, when many innovations have been patented and many technological paths are forbidden, or too costly, for nonowners.

Thus, the introduction of stronger property rights is likely to favor an initial boom and later to cause a depression of innovative investments—an investment pattern consistent with the boom of the "roaring nineties" as well as with the following investment crisis culminating in the great depression (see figure 17.4, taken from Belloc and Pagano 2012). After the reinforcement (and also immediately before, when the reinforcement was widely expected) of intellectual property rights achieved with the 1994

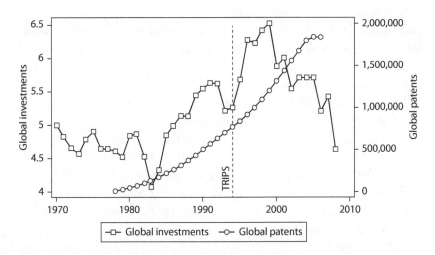

Figure 17.4   Global Patents and Global Investments

Source: Figure 2 from Belloc and Pagano, "Knowledge Enclosures, Forced Specializations and Investment Crisis." *European Journal of Comparative Economics* 9 (3):445–483.

TRIPS Agreement, there was a total world increase in investments for about five years. However, after this initial boom, a continuous decline of global investments occurred in the first decade of the new millennium, culminating in the recent global financial crisis. The roaring nineties were not only followed by the great depression; they also contained its seeds.

It is a commonly accepted wisdom that the financial crisis was due to an excess of savings with respect to investments. While this situation has been described as a "savings glut," the data show that the crisis was due more to a famine of good investment opportunities than to an increase in the propensity to save. The monopolization of the global economy has contributed to this famine of investment opportunities.

In the crisis of the 1930s, protectionism was considered one of the worst consequences of the financial crisis. By contrast, in the recent downturn, protectionism (in its new form of global IPR tariffs) may have been a cause instead of a consequence of the financial crisis. Intellectual property rights may restrict investments more than tariffs. Even the highest tariff can, at most, protect the national industry against foreign competitors. By contrast, intellectual property can offer global protection to a national firm. When a coordinated cluster of firms of a nation-state (and often with its important, even if usually unrecognized, support) owns a patent thicket covering a particular sector of the economy, intellectual property rights can become a very powerful form of economic protectionism and limit the development opportunities for poor countries (Chang 2002). The other economies are forced to specialize either in sector where they are endowed with similar patent thickets or in the mature, and competitively overcrowded, sectors where no intellectual protectionism is available.

However, even global intellectual protectionism for wealthy countries and free competition for poor countries were not considered to be satisfactory. The United States "pushed other countries to open up their markets to areas of our strength, such as financial services, but resisted, successfully so, efforts to make us reciprocate" (Stiglitz 2003, 206).

There is an interesting difference between standard protectionism and intellectual property protection. The former limits international trade: goods that could be cheaply imported are produced in the protected country. The latter stimulates international trade and may have been one of factors driving globalization: goods can only be produced in the protected country (or under a license in others) and they must be imported by the other countries. However, both types of protectionism limit valuable investment opportunities and can have a depressive effect on global development.

The Council of Economic Advisors opposed the growing intellectual protectionism that, according to Joe Stiglitz (2003, 208–209), was negotiated during the Clinton administration especially under the pressure of the drug companies. It was indeed difficult to resist that pressure for two reasons. First, even if the term "intellectual property" rests on a misconception, it can nevertheless camouflage monopoly by identifying it with ordinary private property. The private ownership of knowledge is very different from ordinary private ownership. Knowledge is a nonrival good. The use of a chemical formula does not crowd out other uses in the same way as the use of a chair entails that others cannot sit on that chair. The private property of a chair is not depriving others of other freely available uses, as it happens in the case of knowledge. "Stealing" knowledge is like depriving some individuals of a chair on which they can, however, continue to sit. Indeed, the term "intellectual property" is a recent ideological construct. There is no trace of it even in the relatively recent work of Schumpeter, who contributed so much to our understanding of the relations between innovative activities and entrepreneurial profits. However, this misleading ideological construct is rather powerful. It has given intellectual monopoly the same status as ordinary property. It was perhaps because of this ideology that American negotiators of the TRIPS agreements (for instance, Kantor, mentioned in Stiglitz 2003, 208) believed that fair international intellectual treaties prescribed a respect for private property that included what was in fact an intellectual monopoly and involved a policy similar to tariff protectionism.

Second, even if the (mis-)conception of intellectual monopoly as ordinary private property may lead to frustrating long-run results, it may be reinforced by its short-run effects on reality. For social actors, the term *intellectual property* has not only a cognitive but also a manipulative function. The cognitive and manipulative functions are interdependent, generating what Soros (2010, 2013) calls "reflexivity." The problem with reflexivity is that, for some time, wrong conceptions may appear to be right only because they involve a manipulation of reality that seemingly confirms them. In the case of the (mis-)conception of intellectual property, this perverse reflexivity is particularly evident. The agents expect from intellectual property the usual benefits that derive from the private ownership of rival goods. In the roaring nineties, the manipulation of reality arising from this (mis-)conception seemed to confirm the optimistic expectations. This is hardly surprising. We have seen that, when property rights are reinforced, the immediate effect is an investment boom. This helped to confirm the idea that one was getting from intellectual property the usual advantages of well-defined and secure private property rights.

For these reasons, countering the reinforcement of intellectual property rights in the roaring nineties was particularly difficult. Even now, in spite of the fact that we have gone through a major depression, it is not easy to limit this form of protectionism. After all, the advantages of intellectual property seem to be proved by the fact that firms and nations more endowed with this type of property do much better than those which lack it. Even if it is well known that what is (relatively) good for a single entity may be bad for all the entities, many people are tempted by easy and misleading generalizations. The fallacy of composition may still be a powerful obstacle to an understanding of the economy.

CONCLUSION

For the great recession to be overcome, it is necessary that more knowledge becomes available in the global public domain. In the absence of a world government, each nation-state should invest in public knowledge. However, there is an evident free-rider problem. For each nation-state, it is convenient that other nations sustain the costs of these investments in public knowledge. The widespread underfunding of universities and of other public research institutions is an evident expression of these free-riding policies involving a huge underinvestment in the most important global common produced by humankind.

To overcome this global underinvestment in the production of new public knowledge, some international institutions must change. The global enforcement of IPRs, coupled with the national fragmentation of public investments, has induced each nation to free ride on the production of the global pool of knowledge. Ironically, these policies are often defended by (mis)using the holy name and the well-established ideology of unfettered competitive markets. By contrast, free riding on the production of public knowledge should be seen as a damaging form of unfair competition where one reaps the benefits of others' costly investments. The WTO should be reformed in such a way that this unfair competition is tamed. The charter of the WTO should include rules stating that a fair participation in international trade requires a gross national product (GNP) fraction (increasing more than proportionally with national wealth) of each member state to be invested in open science and to be made available to all countries as a global common.

The modern knowledge economy offers great opportunities for the multiplicative effects of public investments. In recent years, much knowledge has been privatized and monopolized. The multiplier could be increased when government expenditure helps to transfer knowledge from the private to the public sphere. Knowledge is a nonrival good whose uses are often inefficiently restricted by existing monopolies. Public research can have a beneficial role in lifting these restrictions. In some cases, public buyouts of IPRs could also be useful. They could leave the former monopolies with more money and more competition. In this way, they could greatly stimulate their investments. At the same time, competitors could now enter the markets and increase their investments, marshaling additional resources. For many potential uses, knowledge is presently an idle resource and, in the present circumstances, a super-multiplier is likely to exist. The standard multiplicative properties of public investments would be reinforced by the intrinsic multiplicative properties of a public good like knowledge. Open science and open markets are institutional complements. They should replace a world that is increasingly characterized by a perverse complementarity between closed science and closed markets.

We need some courageous policies of asset redistribution. Even in the case of tangible assets, some policies of asset redistribution can decrease agency costs and enhance the efficiency of the economy (Bowles, Gintis, Olin Wright 1999). Some redistribution and collective sharing of intellectual assets would not only involve these standard advantages of efficiency-enhancing redistributions; they could also generate additional benefits due to the nonrival nature of knowledge. Many people could simultaneously enjoy the use of an asset moved from the private to the public sphere of the economy. What is redistributed as public knowledge can be a multiple of the amount taken away from the present private owners.

The learning society can take different forms. Potentially, the nonrival nature of knowledge can make it a fast-growing and just society. However, the same knowledge, when privatized, can cause more stagnation and inequality than the standard tangible production factors. This second unfortunate possibility is what underlies the current crisis of the learning society. Moving more knowledge into the public space can however open unprecedented possibilities for our species. We may conclude with the title of the last chapter of the *Price of Inequality*: "Another World Is Possible"!

NOTES

I thank Joe Stiglitz and David Donald for very useful comments.

1. This view may understate the importance of the many early "enlightenments" that had occurred in other parts of the world. The Italian Renaissance, which was accompanied by the development of the first universities (Berman 1985), had given great impetus to natural science. Science and technology were also shining in China during different periods, especially the Song dynasty (Lin 2013). Confucian culture did not block but instead stimulated the advancements of science and technology, and the influence of Confucius on the French Enlightenment (in particular, Voltaire) is a well-known early chapter in the history of global cultural interdependencies. However, there is no doubt that the Enlightenment marked an unprecedented acceleration of these processes and a dramatic break with unproven religious beliefs, vindicating the right of humans to learn without constraints and prejudices.

2. The data including goodwill are less dramatic. However, Furman and Orszag (2015) show that even on this basis, the variance has increased over time. Moreover, they point out that, since their focus is on the emergence of the high returns in the first place, excluding goodwill seems more appropriate.

REFERENCES

Aoki, M. 2010. *Corporations in Evolving Diversity: Cognition, Governance and Institutions.* New York: Oxford University Press.

Arrow, K. J. 1962. "The Economic Implications of Learning by Doing." *Review of Economic Studies* 29 (2):155–173.

Arrow, K. J. 1996. "Technical Information and Industrial Structure." *Industrial and Corporate Change* 5:645–652.

Barth, E., A. Bryson, and David J. Freeman. 2014. "It's Where You Work. Increases in Earnings Dispersion across Establishments and Individuals in the U.S." IZA Discussion Paper No. 8437.

Basu, K. 2011. *Beyond the Invisible Hand. Groundwork for a New Economics.* Princeton, NJ: Princeton University Press.

Belloc, F., and U. Pagano. 2012. "Knowledge Enclosures, Forced Specializations and Investment Crisis." *European Journal of Comparative Economics* 9 (3):445–483.

Berman, H. J. 1985. *Law and Revolution.* Cambridge, MA: Harvard University Press.

Bowles, S. 2004. *Microeconomics: Behavior, Institutions, and Evolution.* Princeton, NJ: Princeton University Press.

Bowles, S. and H. Gintis. 1999. *Recasting Egalitarianism: New Rules for Communities, States and Markets.* New York: Verso.

Boyle, J. 2003. "The Second Enclosure Movement and the Construction of the Public Domain." *Law and Contemporary Problems* 66 (33):33–73.

Chang, H. J. 2002. *Kicking Away the Ladder. Development Strategy in Historical Perspective.* London: Anthem Press.

Elkana, Y. 2000. "Rethinking—Not Unthinking—The Enlightenment." In *Debates on Issues of Our Common Future,* edited by W. Krull. Weilerswist, Germany: Velbruck Wissenschaft. Also available at http://www.ceu.hu/yehuda rethinking enlightnment.pdf.

Furman, J., and P. Orszag. 2015. "A Firm-Level Perspective on the Role of Rents in the Rise in Inequality." Paper presented at "A Just Society" Centennial Event in Honor of Joseph Stiglitz, Columbia University.

Gellner, E. 1997. *Postmodernism, Reason and Religion*. New York: Routledge.

Hodgson, G. M. 1999. *Economics and Utopia. Why the Learning Economy Is Not the End of History*. New York: Routledge.

Lemley, M. A. 2008. "Are Universities Patent Trolls?" *Fordham Intellectual Property, Media and Entertainment Law Journal* 18 (3):611–631.

Lin, J. Y. 2013. "China's Economic Development and Cultural Renaissance in the Multipolar Growth World of the 21st Century." *China Economic Journal* 6 (1):1–11.

Nicita, A., and U. Pagano. 2016. "Finance-Technology Complementarities: An Organizational Equilibria Approach." *Structural Change and Economic Dynamics* 37:43–51.

Pagano, U. 2014. "The Crisis of Intellectual Monopoly Capitalism." *Cambridge Journal of Economics* 38:1409–1429.

Pagano, U., and M. A. Rossi. 2009. "The Crash of the Knowledge Economy." *Cambridge Journal of Economics* 33 (4):665–683.

Philippon, T. 2015. "Has the U.S. Finance Industry become Less Efficient? On the Theory and Measurement of Financial Intermediation." *American Economic Review* 105 (4):1408–1438.

Philippon, T., and R. Ariell. 2012. "Wages and Human Capital in the U.S. Finance Industry." *Quarterly Journal of Economics* 127 (4):1551–1609.

Philippon T. 2015. "Has the US Finance Industry Become Less Efficient? On the Theory and Measurement of Financial Intermediation." *American Economic Review* 105 (4):1408–1438.

Piketty, Thomas. 2014. *Capital in the Twenty-First Century*. Cambridge, MA: Harvard University Press.

Rowthorn, R. 2014. "A Note on Piketty's Capital in the Twenty-First Century." *Cambridge Journal of Economics* 38 (5):1275 –1284.

Song, J., D. Price, F. Guvemen, and N. Bloom. 2015. "Firming Up Inequality." CEP Discussion Paper No. 1354.

Soros, G. 2010. *The Soros Lectures at the Central European University*. Public Affairs, New York.

Soros, G. 2013. "Fallibility, Reflexivity and the Human Uncertainty Principle." *Journal of Economic Methodology* 20 (4):309–329.

Stiglitz, J. E. 1999. "Knowledge as a Global Public Good." http://p2pfoundation.net /Knowledge_as_a_Global_Public_Good.

Stiglitz, J. E. 2003. *The Roaring Nineties*. New York: Norton.

Stiglitz, J. E. 2012. *The Price of Inequality*. New York: Norton.

Stiglitz, J. E., and B. C. Greenwald. 2014. *Creating a Learning Society*. New York: Columbia University Press.

Stiglitz, J. E. 2015. "New Theoretical Perspectives on the Distribution of Income and Wealth among Individuals." NBER Working Paper No. 21189.

Williamson, O. 1988. "Corporate Finance and Corporate Governance." *Journal of Finance* 43 (3):567–591.

PART VI

Law and Economics

———

CHAPTER 18

Conservatism and Switcher's Curse

Aaron Edlin

ABSTRACT

This chapter formally models the virtues of Edmund Burke's conservatism, characterizes the optimal level of conservatism, and applies the model to management, law, and policy. I begin by introducing "switcher's curse," a trap in which a decision maker systematically switches too often. Decision makers suffer from switcher's curse if they forget the reason that they maintained incumbent policies in the past and if they naively compare rival and incumbent policies with no bias for incumbent policies. Conservatism emerges as a heuristic to avoid switcher's curse. The longer a process or policy has been in place, the more conservative one should be. On the other hand, the more conservative were past decision makers, the more progressive one should be today.

INTRODUCTION

Consider a CEO that rarely if ever changes a long-standing policy, even when she cannot identify a good reason to stick with the status quo. For her, the fact that things have always been done a certain way is reason itself not to change.

In management, this CEO would be seen as a dinosaur and a clear victim of status-quo bias. But in political philosophy, this CEO's position has a long tradition. Edmund Burke wrote in 1790:

> You see, Sir, that in this enlightened age I am bold enough to confess that we [the English] . . . instead of casting away all our old prejudices, we cherish them . . . and, to take more shame on ourselves, we cherish them

because they are prejudices; and the longer they have lasted, and the more generally they have prevailed, the more we cherish them.

This chapter formally models the virtues of Burkean conservatism, characterizes the optimal level of conservatism, and applies the model in management, law, and government policy to individuals and to organizations. The fact that things have always been done a certain way can be a perfectly good reason not to change, *particularly* if one doesn't know why they have always been done that way.

Not everyone would agree. Oliver Wendell Holmes (1897), for example, wrote that "[i]t is revolting to have no better reason for a rule of law than that so it was laid down in the time of Henry IV." Many judges no doubt wish they could ignore precedent and simply cite to Holmes.

Likewise, it is surely tempting to a *new* CEO to channel Holmes and announce: "We will look at everything with fresh eyes." But, the problem with such an approach is that if past rationales have been forgotten, or are simply unknown to a new decision maker, as they often will be to a new CEO, then this progressive approach will lead to too much switching. The new CEO will be a victim of what I call "switcher's curse."

Looking at alternative policies with fresh eyes ignores the fact that a long-standing policy has likely competed against other policies in the past and only survived because it won those competitions. Perhaps it even competed against the very rival it faces today. A policy's longevity testifies to its virtue, and those with imperfect recall should only switch to policies that appear substantially better. The new CEO could run into switcher's curse if she applies her decision-making philosophy and if she (and her organization) can't remember the reasons that the policies were put in place and stayed in place.[1]

Switcher's curse is a trap for the unwary, inexperienced, or boundedly rational decision maker. The trap is that a new policy looks better than it actually is, or an existing policy looks worse than it is.

Two colleagues have provided examples which I hope ring bells for the reader. One pointed out that he has frequently wasted days, weeks, and even months pursuing ideas for simpler proofs of a theorem in a years-old working paper only to finally realize that he had tried these approaches before, sometimes many times before. Perhaps he should have put weight on the idea that his proof was the way it was for good reason, even if he did not remember the reason, and been more skeptical of new approaches.

Another colleague recently changed an important grading policy in a course he had taught for many years. To alleviate student worries about exams and to improve his teacher ratings, this colleague decided to put more weight on problem sets and ceased grading them on a "check/no-check" basis (whereby nearly everyone got a check). This switch turned out poorly when it emerged that some students had access to the problem sets and solutions from earlier years through fraternities and the like. This was a big problem now that there was substantial weight on problem sets. The irony was that this colleague had early in his teaching career adopted the check/no-check, low-weight grading policy for problem sets exactly so that he could reuse his perfected problem sets year after year without worrying about some students having solutions. He had kept the policy for many years for exactly that reason. Eventually though, he forgot the reasons for his own grading policy and changed it to improve ratings only to have his ratings plummet.

The experiences of Company X, a technology company, serve as another illustration of switcher's curse.[2] During the dot-com boom, a few individuals who created and consumed intellectual property ("content"), concluded that both creators and consumers of content were poorly served by existing systems of production and distribution. They invented a radical new model. Established organizations, though, were far too conservative to try their approach, so they founded Company X.

As entrepreneurs and innovators, they evaluated everything with fresh eyes and never privileged the status quo. They were constantly changing the systems that they put into place at Company X. At the outset, their flexibility and progressivism paid off and they rarely regretted switching to a new policy.

After about five years, however, "improvements" to their system began to go awry. The new systems they put in place had flaws that they did not anticipate and old systems had virtues they had forgotten. Frequently, they decided to switch back to their old system. Sadly, even this full circle was not necessarily the end. Several years later, this cycle might be repeated as the whole lesson was forgotten and someone again had a new clever idea or even the same clever idea. Once switching began to go awry at Company X the problem seemed to get worse with time.

This story raises a question. Why did Company X profit from early switches but eventually suffer switcher's curse? It is not simply that X's managers ran out of good ideas. That would simply mean a slower arrival rate of good ideas and less switching. Instead, the problem was that over time, Company X began to switch when it shouldn't, suffering from switcher's curse.

This chapter presents a very simple model that provides a possible answer. Policies compete sequentially after signals of their quality are drawn. The decision maker has limited information in that she does not know the past signals of a policy's quality or the past performance of a policy. What she does know is how long a policy has been in place.

I begin by comparing a "naive" decision maker who does not take into account the past at all (including the longevity of a policy) with a fully rational Bayesian updater who, even though she does not remember past signals, makes the most of the fact that a status-quo policy must have won past contests.

In a simple two-period example with no switching cost, the naive decision maker switches if contemporaneous information about a new policy is better than that for a status-quo policy, and is indifferent to switching if information is the same and there are no switching costs. Such a decision maker will switch too often, suffering switcher's curse.

In contrast, I find that a fully rational decision maker who compares a status-quo policy that appears otherwise equal (or close) to an alternative policy should not switch even if there are no switching costs. The reason is straightforward. The incumbent policy competed against another policy last year (or might have done so) and its incumbency is itself a signal that it is a good policy, even if the specific reasons that the policy was kept are forgotten.

Given that an incumbent policy was judged good in the past, it is likely that the reason that it looks relatively bad today is either because today's evaluation study drew a relatively pessimistic signal of the policy's quality or a relatively optimistic signal of the alternative. I find that the longer an incumbent policy has survived, the more pronounced these effects and the heavier the thumb should be on the scale in favor of the incumbent policy.

Conservatism is a heuristic that addresses switcher's curse. A conservative decision maker will hesitate to make changes, particularly to a long-standing policy, even when she can't articulate or pinpoint reasons not to switch. Only if some new policy is truly compelling will she switch, and the longer a policy has been in place, the more compelling any alternative must be. A naive decision maker, by contrast, estimates with "fresh eyes" the virtues of a new policy and the status-quo policy and switches if the estimated virtues of switching justify the transition cost. She will suffer switcher's curse. Although Holmes finds conservatism "revolting," conservatism has a big virtue: it avoids switcher's curse.

In practice, of course, conservatism is a matter of degree and different people and organizations display different degrees of conservatism. In this chapter's model, as in life, it is possible to be too conservative. How conservative one should be depends on many factors. One factor turns out to be how conservative past decision makers were. If past decision makers were extremely conservative, little is learned from their decision to keep a policy and it will therefore pay to be relatively progressive today. In contrast, if a policy survived a long time despite being subject to the vicissitudes of progressive management, which is exactly what happened at Company X, then the policy is very likely good and a great degree of conservatism is warranted today. Thus, the innovators at Company X eventually needed to change their progressive approach and become extremely conservative, or they needed to be replaced with conservative management. In turn, extremely conservative decision makers might enjoy success for a while but should eventually moderate or be replaced with progressives.

To summarize, our main propositions state:

1. Conservatism and Switcher's Curse. A naive decision maker switches too often because she puts existing and alternative policies on the same footing. It is frequently optimal to be conservative and stick to the status quo even when contemporaneous information suggests switching.
2. The older the policy, the more conservative one should be today. This is true regardless of a decision-maker's level of conservatism in the past.
3. The more progressive were past decision makers, the more conservative it is optimal to be today, and conversely, the more conservative were past decision makers, the more progressive it is optimal to be today.

Propositions 1 and 2 formalize Burke's intuition. Proposition 3 is new, as far as I know.

Section 1 discusses related literature. Section 2 presents a simple two-period example that captures the intuition of switcher's curse and its cure, conservatism. Subsequently, Section 3 explores a multiperiod model with variable switching costs where conservatism is a matter of degree. After developing the main model, the chapter applies its basic lesson to several contexts: the system of *stare decisis* in which courts are loath to change legal rules; administrative law; venture capital; separation of powers; the evolution of a firm; the cases of a new CEO and a new employee; cycles of metapolicy and policies; and finally, the decision to stay married or to divorce. Appendix B presents a case study of Company X, providing further motivation for the model.

1. RELATED LITERATURE

Conservatism is closely related to the well-known psychological phenomenon of status-quo bias (Samuelson and Zeckhauser 1988; Kahneman, Knetsch, and Thaler 1991; Burmeister and Schade 2007; Porter and McIntyre 1984). Status-quo bias is generally understood to be a flaw, but this chapter's analysis suggests that far from a flaw, status-quo bias could be a healthy psychological adaptation that helps avoid "switcher's curse."

In turn, switcher's curse in this paper's model, can be understood to arise from either of two other well-documented psychological phenomena, the "availability bias" (Tversky and Kahneman 1973) or "prior neglect" (Kahneman and Tversky, 1973, 1982; Bar-Hillel 1980). The availability bias means that agents may overemphasize recent or contemporaneous information and deemphasize past information which is less available. Even without memory loss, this would explain our naive agent's mistakes. Likewise, the naive agent in our model can be seen as a victim of prior neglect because she neglects the difference in priors between an incumbent policy and a proposed alternative.[3] In sum, then, this chapter shows that status-quo bias may actually compensate for two other biases, prior neglect and the availability bias, which would otherwise cause switcher's curse.

Several economics papers have explored various aspects of conservatism. Prendergast and Stole (1996) and Zwiebel (1995) explore how conservatism can emerge when managers' talents are unobservable and they seek to increase their pay by protecting or improving their reputations. Conservatism protects the managers in these models at the expense of the companies they serve. In this chapter, by contrast, managerial conservatism protects companies and might be undertaken by wise principals not just by misbehaving agents.

Other related papers are Rasmusen (1992), Hirshleifer and Welch (2002), and Baliga and Ely (2011). Rasmusen argues, based on reversion to the mean, that when the status quo has a known payoff and an innovation receives a particularly good signal, reversion to the mean suggests that the innovation is not as good as it appears. Rasmusen's reversion to the mean argues for caution when estimating any uncertain return, not for prioritizing the status quo; in fact, in contrast to this chapter's model, Rasmusen points out that "[i]f the true profitability of the status quo were unknown, the conservative bias would disappear."

Hirshleifer and Welch (2002) consider a setting of limited memory. They are interested, however, in fully rational decision making. This chapter, in contrast, studies the impact of potentially irrational rule-of-thumb decision-making styles, characterized on a spectrum of progressivism to conservatism, and asks what metapolicy or heuristic makes most sense given the level of progressivism or conservatism of prior decision makers. Switcher's curse only arises when decision makers are irrationally progressive and cannot arise for the rational agents of Hirshleifer and Welch (2002).

Baliga and Ely (2011) also explore the consequences of limited memory. They argue that "sunk cost bias is an optimal heuristic that compensates for the constraints of limited memory." Their point is closely related to this chapter in that sticking with a project ("sunk cost bias") can be seen as a form of conservatism. Their paper differs in a couple of ways. First, I study a multiperiod model in a stationary environment, whereas they study a single project that will be at a different state at date 2; this means that while their conclusion can be seen as a form of this chapter's proposition 1, this chapter's proposition 2, which states that the longer a policy has been in place the more conservative the decision maker should be does not have a counterpart in their paper. Second, they are studying rational behavior, so nothing analogous to switcher's curse arises, whereas this chapter compares rational and irrational behavior in a setting where past decision makers deviated from rationality. This distinction leads to the discovery that past progressivism makes conservatism today more sensible (proposition 3), which also has no counterpart in their model.

2. A SIMPLE TWO-PERIOD EXAMPLE OF SWITCHER'S CURSE AND CONSERVATISM

Here, I present a simple two-period example that illustrates switcher's curse and its cure, conservatism. Policies are either good ("G") or bad ("B"), with good policies having a higher expected payoff than bad policies. A good policy is always good, and a bad policy always bad. For a court, a policy could be that the court and its lower courts only enforce liquidated damages for breach of contract if the damages are a reasonable estimate of expectation damages. For Congress, the Affordable Care Act is a policy. For a company, a policy might be requiring managers to confer with their own bosses before firing employees or it could be using Microsoft Windows instead of Apple computers. For an individual, a policy might be being single or being married.

A decision maker does not directly observe whether a policy is good or bad, but instead observes a noisy contemporaneous signal of its quality. Past signals are forgotten, but a decision maker knows that a status-quo policy was used in the past. The fact that a policy was used in the past means that it won some contest with another policy.

The basic question in this paper is how naive decision making compares with optimal decision making under limited information. By "naive," I mean that the decision maker assumes that the base rate probability that the incumbent policy is good is the same as that for the general population from which a competing policy is drawn. This captures the idea of comparing policies with "fresh eyes," as the founders of Company X did. It also captures the well-known phenomenon in which people ignore differences in base rates (the base-rate fallacy or prior neglect).

Every policy is independently drawn with probability $p \in (0,1)$ of being good ("G") and $1-p$ of being bad ("B").

2.1. TIME 0

At time 0, a decision maker must choose whether to use policy A or policy D. She does not observe whether either policy is good or bad. Instead she observes independent signals $d_0 \in \{g,b\}$ of D and $a_0 \in \{g,b\}$ of A. A signal "g" indicates that the associated policy *appears* good and a signal "b" indicates that the policy *appears* bad.

Every signal is statistically independent of every other signal. The signals are accurate with probability $s > 1/2$, which represents signal strength. Thus, the chance that any good policy appears to be good or that any bad policy appears to be bad is s; the chance that any good policy appears to be bad or any bad policy appears to be good is $1-s$. Formally,

$$\Pr(a_0 = g \mid A = G) = s = \Pr(a_0 = b \mid A = B) \tag{18.1}$$

$$\Pr(d_0 = g \mid D = G) = s = \Pr(d_0 = b \mid D = B). \tag{18.2}$$

The time 0 decision rule is:

1. If $a_0 = d_0$, then flip a coin to choose between A and D.
2. Otherwise, choose the policy that appears to be good.

This decision rule is fully rational because the prior probability that A is good equals the probability that D is good. It is also what a naive decision maker would do who simply assumed that the base rates were identical for the two policies.

2.2. TIME 1

Without loss of generality, assume that policy A was chosen at time 0 and so A is the status-quo policy at time 1. The question is whether to switch to some other policy $E \in \{G, B\}$.

The time 1 decision maker does not directly observe whether E or A are good or bad but instead observes a signal $e \in \{g, b\}$ of E and signal $a \in \{g, b\}$ of A, where

$$\Pr(a = g \mid A = G) = s = \Pr(a = b \mid A = B) \tag{18.3}$$

$$\Pr(e = g \mid E = G) = s = \Pr(e = b \mid E = B). \tag{18.4}$$

The time 1 decision maker either has limited recall or is a new decision maker without records of the time 0 contest. Either way, she does not know a_0 or d_0.

After comparing a with e, the decision maker chooses whether to keep A or switch to E. I compare "naive" and "conservative" decision-making approaches as specified below:

Naive	$e = b$	$e = g$
$a = b$	flip coin	switch to E
$a = g$	keep A	flip coin

Conservative	$e = b$	$e = g$
$a = b$	keep A	switch to E
$a = g$	keep A	keep A

The two decision makers differ on the diagonal when signals are equal. The naive decision maker is indifferent between policy A and E in that case and flips a coin to choose between them. In contrast, the conservative decision maker favors the status quo and so keeps A when signals are equal. She puts a thumb on the scales in favor of the status quo and wouldn't switch in that case even if you paid her a small amount to do so.

Which approach is better? The conservative approach turns out to be better because positive information is embedded in incumbency as shown by the following lemma.

Lemma 1. $\Pr(A = G \mid A \text{ won at time } 0) > \Pr(A = G) \equiv p.$

Proof. See Appendix A.

The intuition for Lemma 1 is straightforward. Winning at time 0 is a good signal and Bayesian updating implies that once A wins at time 0, the probability that it is good increases above P.

In the example, incumbency entails a certainty that a prior contest occurred. In reality, it only entails a positive probability of a prior contest. Lemma 1 would hold in either case.

Lemma 1 is the basis for concluding that the conservative approach dominates the naive approach.

Observation 1. *The conservative approach is strictly better than a naive approach in the two-period example.*

Proof. See Appendix A.

The key to the observation is that the conservative and naive decision maker only disagree on the diagonals when both policies appear bad or both appear good. The naive decision maker is indifferent to the policies in these cases, but should not be.

According to Lemma 1, the incumbent policy is likely better (prior to time 1 signals), so the naive decision maker errs by flipping a coin when time 1 signals are equal. This is an example of what I call switcher's curse. Just as *winner's curse*, in an auction, involves a failure to take into account the negative information entailed in another party's lower bids, and can lead a bidder to bid too high and win an auction too often, here *switcher's curse* involves a failure to take into account the positive information entailed in winning past contests, and can lead a decision maker to switch too often.

The naive decision maker fails to take account of the fact that A being a status-quo policy is itself a good signal about A. The conservative approach incorporates this information by not switching in cases where contemporaneous signals indicate that the two policies are equally good.

In practice, of course, conservatism comes in degrees and entails more than just refusing to switch when contemporaneous information is in equipoise. A true conservative will often refuse to switch to policies that appear better, and sometimes even significantly better. That turns out to be equally sensible. If we generalize the example to allow the rival policy to appear slightly better than the incumbent policy, the best decision rule would be to keep the incumbent policy provided the rival policy did not appear to be too much better.

Below, I generalize the example in a slightly different direction. I explore contests where switching costs may be positive and are a continuous random variable. This allows me to study a continuum of conservatism. At the same time, I extend the model to a multiperiod model. These two changes allow me more fully to explore the phenomenon observed at Company X. Switcher's curse was not a big factor early on there, but it eventually bit severely for two reasons. First, switcher's curse is larger for older policies, and second, switcher's curse is larger when past decision makers were highly progressive as were the innovators at Company X. Each of these factors suggests that an optimal decision maker should have become highly conservative at Company X over time.

3. MULTIPERIOD MODEL: CONSERVATISM ON A CONTINUUM

I consider here the decision problem of choosing between a status-quo policy A and an alternative policy E^t at time t ("today") in a multiperiod model. First, I will ask how the optimal choice depends upon the length of time that an incumbent policy has been in place. Second, what kinds of mistakes would be made by a naive decision maker who ignored the importance of incumbency? And third, how are the answers to the above two questions affected by the extent of prior or future decision-makers' conservatism or progressivism? This third question asks how a decision maker today should optimally account for past and future nonoptimal decision making (either by others or by herself).

In order to assess degrees of conservatism, I introduce a cost of switching to E^t given by x^t. Each period this cost is independently drawn from the uniform distribution $U[0, x_{max}]$ and is observable.[4] A conservative person switches from a policy that appears bad to one that appears good only if x^t is low. A more progressive (or impulsive) decision maker will have a higher threshold for switching costs. The decision-maker's level of progressivism or conservatism defines a rule of thumb for decision making.

At time 0 a policy is drawn that has probability p of being good and $1 - p$ of being bad. At each subsequent time t, there is a contest: an alternative policy E^t is drawn (also with probability p of being good) and a decision maker draws a signal e^t of E^t, a new signal a^t of the status-quo policy A, and a new switching cost x^t; each signal is statistically independent of all others. The signals each have strength s, as described in the two-period example above.

Below, I will suppress the time superscripts whenever confusion is unlikely to result. As in the two-period example, while the decision maker prefers a good policy, she does not know whether a policy is of type G or B, and so must form probability estimates. Because the model now has switching costs, even a naive decision maker won't switch if signals are equal.

Switching is tempting only if A appears bad and E appears good (i.e., if $a = b$ and $e = g$) and if the switching cost x is sufficiently low. The decision-maker's problem is to figure out how low constitutes "sufficiently low."

Define a decision-maker's threshold for switching as x^*, which is to say that the decision maker switches only if $a = b$, $e = g$, and $x < x^*$.

This framework admits a continuum of conservatism or progressivism as follows.

Definition 1. *The greater is the switching threshold x^* the more **progressive** is the decision maker.*

Definition 2. *The lower is the switching threshold x^* the more **conservative** is the decision maker.*

Definition 3. *A decision maker is **completely conservative** if $x^* = 0$.*

The idea behind these definitions is that a conservative decision maker is relatively skeptical that a new policy is better and therefore will only switch under a relatively low switching cost. A progressive decision maker is open to the idea that a new policy is better than the status quo and willing to switch even at a relatively high switching cost if an alternative policy appears better. An extremely conservative decision maker switches only if switching costs are very low (and alternative policies appear good). The higher is x^* the more prone is a decision maker to switch and the more progressive and less conservative we say she is.

Let us begin by considering an optimal decision rule today at time $t > 1$ taking as given the level of conservatism of past and future decision makers. I study the optimal decision rule today given the following Information Set.

Information Set: *The decision maker knows (1) current signals, (2) the longevity of the status-quo policy, and (3) the conservatism or progressivism of past and future decision rules.*

The motivation for studying such an optimum, rather than optimal behavior today assuming past and future optimal behavior, is that in practice, it is likely that past decision makers behaved nonoptimally (they were human), and the current decision maker cannot depend upon future decision makers to behave optimally.[5]

The current decision maker does not know past signals either because she was not the past decision maker or because she has imperfect recall. The assumption is extreme in many settings where at least a signal of the signal is available—in law, for example, past opinions constitute an imperfect signal of the signal. The model highlights the value of preserving institutional memory, such as through written judicial opinions or corporate management information systems. Because a conservative philosophy emerges as a substitute for good memory, the value of institutional memory is higher for progressive decision makers.

The current decision maker also does not know whether the alternative policy "*E*" has ever been tried in the past or is entirely new. Future research might explore what happens if a decision maker knows that an alternative policy "*E*" was used in the past and for how long.

In this model, a rational decision will depend upon the probability that *A* is good, the probability that *E* is good, the switching cost *x*, and the difference in the present discounted value between having a good and bad policy, a difference that I study in the next section.

3.1. THE PRESENT DISCOUNTED VALUE OF GOOD AND BAD POLICIES

The present discounted values of a good policy, denoted $V(G)$, and of a bad policy, denoted $V(B)$, depend upon flow payoffs and the frequency of switching, which in turn depends upon the degree of conservatism or progressivism of future decision makers. For tractability, I shall assume that the level of conservatism of future decision makers does not vary with time.

Let the expected per-period payoff of a good policy be π_G and of a bad policy be π_B. The decision maker does not observe the expected payoff, or equivalently whether the policy is good or bad, but only observes the realized payoff which takes values of 0 or 1 with probability $1-s$ and s for a good policy G and with probability s and $1-s$ for a bad policy B. The realized payoff is simply the signal of the policy's quality and has strength $s > 1/2$.

Policies follow a Markov process with the state G, B being unknown to the decision maker and transition probabilities $P_{G \to B}$ and $P_{B \to G}$ depending upon the degree of conservatism of future decision makers. A future decision maker will inadvertently switch away from a good policy to a bad one if and only if (1) the incumbent good policy A appears to be bad; (2) the alternative policy E is bad but appears to be good; and (3) a switching cost below the decision-maker's threshold is drawn. Likewise, a future decision maker who unknowingly has a bad policy will switch and luck into a good policy if and only if (1) the incumbent bad policy appears to be bad, (2) the alternative policy E is good and appears to be good, and (3) the switching cost is below the decision-maker's threshold.

Let x^*_{future} be the threshold for switching of future decision makers, so that they switch when $x < x^*_{future}$. Then, these transition probabilities are as follows:

$$P_{G \to B} = (1-s)[(1-p)(1-s)]\left[\frac{x^*_{future}}{x_{max}}\right], and \qquad (18.5)$$

$$P_{B \to G} = s[ps]\left[\frac{x^*_{future}}{x_{max}}\right]. \qquad (18.6)$$

Then the expected present discounted value of the random future stream of payoffs from having a good policy G can be calculated as follows. A flow payoff of π_G is earned. Then with probability $P_{G \to B}$, the policy will be switched to a bad policy next period so that a payoff of π_B would be earned in the following period. Of course, in the case of switching, a switching cost will be incurred that will on average be $x^*/2$. With probability $1 - P_{G \to B}$ the good policy will be maintained and π_G will again be earned in the following period. Assuming a discount factor $\delta < 1$ for future payoffs, $V(G)$ and $V(B)$ are found by solving the following pair of simultaneous equations:

$$V(G) = \pi_G + \delta\left[P_{G \to B}(V(B) - x^*/2) + (1 - P_{G \to B})V(G)\right]$$
$$V(B) = \pi_B + \delta\left[P_{B \to G}(V(G) - x^*/2) + (1 - P_{B \to G})V(B)\right]. \qquad (18.7)$$

3.2. OPTIMAL DECISION MAKING AT TIME t

Below I characterize the optimal switching rule for a decision maker today, where "optimal" means the best decision given the limited information available (i.e., that past signals are forgotten) and given that past and future decision makers have rule-of-thumb switching thresholds that may not be optimal. I will then compare the decisions of an optimizing decision maker at time $t > 1$ to one who is naive and ignores the information embedded in incumbency. I will also explore how optimal decisions depend upon the progressivism or conservatism of past and future decision makers.

Given that switching costs are positive, the decision maker will consider switching only when the incumbent policy appears bad and an alternative appears good: i.e., when $a = b$ and $e = g$ (where I have suppressed the time t superscripts on a and e). The question is how low switching costs x must be to make switching worthwhile.

Consider any time $t > 1$. Let I denote the event that $a = b$ and $e = g$. The expected value of policy E given I is

$$V(E \mid I) = \Pr(E = G \mid I)V(G) + [1 - \Pr(E = G \mid I)]V(B) \qquad (18.8)$$

and the expected value of policy A is

$$V(A \mid I) = \Pr(A = G \mid I)V(G) + [1 - \Pr(A = G \mid I)]V(B). \qquad (18.9)$$

Hence, the expected amount by which E is better than the status quo A equals

$$V(E \mid I) - V(A \mid I) = [\Pr(E = G \mid I) - \Pr(A = G \mid I)][V(G) - V(B)]. \qquad (18.10)$$

This makes sense: the extra expected value of policy E over A equals (1) the increased probability that policy E is good over the baseline probability that policy A is good, times (2) the expected extra value derived from a good policy.

For a decision maker who seeks to maximize the expected value of the policy, it is optimal to switch if and only if the switching cost is less than the above quantity: i.e., if and only if $x < x^*_{optimal}$, where

$$x^*_{optimal} \equiv [\Pr(E = G \mid I) - \Pr(A = G \mid I)][V(G) - V(B)] \qquad (18.11)$$

The above expression defines the optimal switching threshold, $x^*_{optimal}$, at any time $t > 1$. If prior to receiving signals at time t, the decision maker thought it much more likely that A is good than that E is good, then it is possible that the right-hand side of the above expression is negative. That would mean that it is optimal to ignore time t signals so that even if E appeared good, A appeared bad, and $x = 0$, it would still be optimal not to switch. For fully rational decision makers that would imply being in an informational cascade (see Bikhchandani, Hirshleifer, and Welch 1992).

Let P_A denote the prior probability that the decision maker believes that A is good and P_E denote the prior that E is good, where each prior is formed immediately before seeing the period t signals about the quality of the policies. I assume that $p_A < 1$ and $p_E < 1$.

The decision maker can form posteriors according to Bayes' rule. Thus, for example, if E appears to be good and A appears to be bad, the posteriors are as follows:

$$\Pr(E = G \mid e = g, p_E) = \frac{sp_E}{p_E s + (1 - p_E)(1 - s)} \tag{18.12}$$

$$\Pr(A = G \mid a = b, p_A) = \frac{(1 - s)p_A}{p_A(1 - s) + (1 - p_A)s}. \tag{18.13}$$

These posteriors are the relevant probabilities to use to find $x^*_{optimal}$ using equation (18.11).

It is intuitive that the posterior probability that A is good despite receiving a bad signal will be increasing in the prior probability that A is good. This intuition is confirmed by the following lemma.

Lemma 2. $\Pr(A = G \mid a = b, p_A)$ *is increasing in* P_A, *the probability that* $A = G$ *prior to the signal a.*

Proof. From equation (18.13) we have that

$$\Pr(A = G \mid a = b, p_A) = \frac{(1 - s)}{(1 - s) + s(1 - p_A)/p_A}, \tag{18.14}$$

which is increasing in P_A because $\frac{1 - p_A}{p_A}$ is decreasing in P_A. ∎

Corollary 1 follows directly from the lemma above, the formula for $x^*_{optimal}$, the fact that A and E are statistically independent, and the fact that the event under consideration is the event where A appears bad and E appears good.

Corollary 1. *The optimal switching-cost threshold $x^*_{optimal}$ is decreasing in P_A.*

3.3 SWITCHER'S CURSE FROM NAIVE DECISION MAKING AND CONSERVATISM AS A CURE

I will now show that a naive decision maker who ignores the information embedded in incumbency will switch too often, suffering what I dub "switcher's curse." At the same time, I will show that conservatism is a heuristic that can eliminate switcher's curse.

Formally, I define a naive decision maker as follows.

Definition 4. *A **naive** decision maker does not consider the importance of past decisions for the probability that A is good; she instead assumes that $P_A = P_E = P$ and then computes the optimal switching threshold given these beliefs.*

A naive decision-maker's switching threshold is:

$$x^*_{naive} = [\Pr(E = G \,|\, e = g, p_E = p) - \Pr(A = G \,|\, a = b, p_A = p)][V(G) - V(B)]$$

$$= \left[\frac{sp}{ps + (1-p)(1-s)} - \frac{(1-s)p}{p + s - 2ps} \right][V(G) - V(B)]$$

$$> 0. \tag{18.15}$$

As in the two-period model, a naive decision maker does not consider the possibility that incumbent policies have a higher base rate of being good than new policies. Perhaps, the naive decision maker commissions a study of the incumbent policy and of the alternative without telling those doing the study which is the incumbent policy (perhaps to avoid status-quo bias) and switches whenever the new policy appears better than the old, taking into account transition costs.

I will now argue that a naive decision maker will switch too often. Too often, the naive decision maker will switch to a bad E when A is good, and this will not be compensated for by the increased chance of abandoning a bad status-quo A and getting a good alternative E. This is what I mean by switcher's curse and why I say that naive decision makers will suffer switcher's curse.

I demonstrate switcher's curse in several steps. The first is to observe that if A wins a contest against E under an arbitrary switching threshold $x^* > 0$, then the probability that A is good increases as a result of the win. I formally state this in the following lemma.

Lemma 3. *If at any time t, (1) A wins a contest with E, (2) the decision maker is not completely conservative, and (3)* $p_A \in (0,1)$*, then the posterior probability that A is good will exceed the prior: i.e.,* $\Pr(A = G \mid A \text{ wins at } t, x^* > 0, p_A) > p_A$ *for any* $p_A \in (0,1)$*. When the decision maker is completely conservative, then winning does not increase the likelihood that A is good: i.e.,* $\Pr(A = G \mid A \text{ wins at } t, x^* = 0, p_A) = p_A$ *for any* P_A*.*

Proof. See Appendix A.

The intuition behind Lemma 3 is that when $x^* > 0$, winning is a good signal of A's quality. Of course, A might have won even though $a = b$, but it is more likely to win if $a = g$, and a good signal g is more likely to occur if $A = G$. This observation leads a fully rational decision maker to a positive updating of P_A after a win. Of course, in the extreme case that a decision maker is completely conservative, winning provides no information and so the posterior equals the prior.

Because a naive decision maker is boundedly rational and neglects the fact that the prior P_A should reflect the updating from past victories of the status-quo policy, a naive decision maker does not appreciate how good the status quo is before observing signals. A naive decision maker treats A and E symmetrically and starts with the unupdated probability p. If prior decision makers were completely conservative, refusing to switch under all circumstances, then the naive decision maker's belief that $p_A = p$ would be unbiased.

The optimality of being more conservative than a naive decision maker follows from Lemma 3.

Proposition 1 *The optimal decision-making rule is more conservative than the naive one—i.e.,* $x^*_{optimal} < x^*_{naive}$—*provided that at least one earlier decision maker was not completely conservative.*

Proof. When A was first drawn, it had probability p of being good. Winning with a completely conservative decision maker does not update the probability that A is good. However, Lemma 3 shows that each time A wins a contest in which $x^* > 0$, the probability that $A = G$ increases. Thus, $p_A > p$.

The naive switching-cost threshold would be optimal by construction if $p_A = p$. Now recall that Corollary 1 states that $x^*_{optimal}$ is decreasing in P_A. It follows that $x^*_{optimal} < x^*_{naive}$.

The above proposition states that naive decision makers switch too often. This phenomenon, I call switcher's curse because the decision maker too often switches away from a good policy because she failed to account for the good signal embedded in incumbency. Even if she cannot remember the reasons that past decision makers stuck with A (or that she herself did in the past), the fact that they did is informative: A is better on average than the contemporaneous signal suggests.

Switcher's curse can be caused by the "base-rate fallacy" also known as "prior neglect," a well-known phenomenon that has been documented in the psychology literature by Kahneman and Tversky (1973, 1982) and Bar-Hillel (1980). In experiments, people often ignore the differences in base rates for two choices A and E, and focus on specific information, even when told explicitly that A and E have different base rates.[6] Our decision-maker's problem is harder than those in the Kahneman-Tversky laboratory because no one tells our decision maker that status-quo policies are very likely to be good. Somehow he needs to figure out that status-quo policies tend to be good. Because this problem is subtle, even someone not subject to the base-rate fallacy in those experiments might still be subject to switcher's curse.

Switcher's curse also can result from the "availability bias," another well-known heuristic discovered by Tversky and Kahneman (1973). The availability bias is a tendency to overemphasize current information and underemphasize past information. Our naive agent suffers from the availability bias.

The fact that it is optimal to resist change, even when change seems good, shows that conservatism is a heuristic that can avoid switcher's curse. Status-quo bias is not so much a bias as it is a useful adaptation to counterbalance other biases, namely prior neglect and the availability bias. Of course, more conservatism is not always better, for there is an optimal degree of conservatism given by equation (18.11).

3.4. SWITCHER'S CURSE AND THE NEED FOR CONSERVATISM GROW FOR OLDER POLICIES

Below, I show an important fact about switcher's curse. Switcher's curse becomes a bigger problem, the longer the status-quo policy has been in place.

Proposition 2. *Suppose that prior decision makers were not completely conservative and had identical levels of conservatism* $x^* > 0$. *Then, the optimal decision rule becomes more conservative the longer the status-quo policy A has been in place—i.e., $x^*_{optimal}$ is decreasing in the longevity of the incumbent policy A.*

Proof. As observed in the proof of the prior proposition, when *A* was first drawn, it had probability *p* of being good. And, Lemma 3 shows that each time *A* wins a contest in which $x^* > 0$, the probability that $A = G$, which is the P_A for next period, increases. Corollary 1 then shows that every time *A* wins a contest in which $x^* > 0$, the optimal switching-cost threshold $x^*_{optimal}$ decreases in the next period. Hence, $x^*_{optimal}$ decreases over time with the longevity of *A*; it pays to be more conservative the longer *A* has been in place.

Proposition 2 implies that the optimal conservative policy is not just to be resistant to change, but to be particularly resistant to switching away from long-standing policies. All change is not equal. Switcher's curse is larger for older policies, because these policies will have survived more past contests. A wise decision maker avoids switcher's curse by being conservative, and according to Proposition 2, the longer *A* has been in place the more conservative she should be.

3.5. WHY IT IS OPTIMAL TO BE MORE CONSERVATIVE IF PAST DECISION MAKERS WERE PROGRESSIVE

Here I explore the effects of past decision-makers' degree of conservatism or progressivism.

The posterior that a winning policy is good will increase with the progressivism of a decision maker. This is put precisely in Lemma 4.

Lemma 4. *After the status-quo policy A wins at any time t, where $x^* > 0$, the posterior that A is a good policy increases with the progressiveness of a decision maker and decreases with her conservatism: i.e.,* $\frac{\partial \Pr(A=G|A \, wins)}{\partial x^*} > 0.$

Proof. See Appendix A.

The intuition behind Lemma 4 is straightforward. If a decision maker is extremely conservative then very little is learned from the fact that a policy won. Even if signals were bad, it would be likely to win, so updating won't be strong. On the other hand, if the decision maker is progressive (a large x^*), then winning becomes meaningful and leads to substantial updating of the prior that $A = G$.

I will now explore how the conservatism or progressivism of past decision makers affects the level of conservatism that is appropriate today. As a preliminary, I state a straightforward lemma.

Lemma 5. *For a policy A, where the prior* $p_A \in (0,1)$*, the posterior probability that A is good conditional on winning at t is increasing in the prior probability that A is good: i.e.,* $\frac{\partial \Pr(A=G|A \text{ wins}, p_A)}{\partial p_A} > 0$ *for any* $p_A \in (0,1)$.

Proof. See Appendix A.

Proposition 3. *Suppose that past decision makers all had the same* $x^* > 0$*. Then, the more conservative they were, the more progressive the current period-t decision maker should be, and the more progressive they were, the more conservative the current decision maker should be: i.e.,* $x^*_{optimal}$ *is decreasing in the switching-cost threshold* x^* *that past decision makers applied.*

Proof. See Appendix A.

The basic logic of the proposition's proof is that increases in x^* at any time t directly increase the posterior at that time t that A is good, holding time t's priors fixed, according to Lemma 4. There is an indirect effect as well that moves in the same direction: Increases in x^* in still earlier periods will increase the priors at time t that A is good, and higher priors increase posteriors as shown in Lemma 5. These two effects combine to ensure that higher x^* prior to time t increases the time t priors that A is good. Higher priors at time t, according to Corollary 1, increase the optimal level of conservatism thereby proving the theorem.

The intuition for the proposition is that if the past decision makers who chose to keep A were very progressive then A very likely survived past contests by getting a lot of good signals. This suggests that A is probably good and that even if A appears bad according to contemporaneous information, abandoning A would be a mistake unless switching costs are very low.

For ease of exposition in the proof, avoiding extra subscripts, the proposition is stated assuming that past decision makers had the same level of conservatism. The reader can check that levels can differ and that increasing, or decreasing, the level of conservatism of a single past decision maker rather than all at once leads to the same results. The situation would be more complex in a model where signal strength varied, though it would continue to be the case that progressive decision makers keeping a policy for a long time is a very strong signal that a policy is good.[7]

Proposition 3 explains why switcher's curse became so severe at Company X over time. Because Company X was run by entrepreneurs, they were extremely progressive, looking at all policies with fresh eyes and always coming up with new ideas. If a policy survived a long time in that environment it was very likely to be good. Switching a long-standing policy was almost always a mistake, so Company X faced switcher's curse again and again.

4. APPLICATIONS AND INTERPRETATION

Here I interpret the lessons from the model and suggest a variety of applications. Each application is brief and intended to be stimulating and provocative, not a thorough treatment of the issues. Hopefully, the applications suggest avenues for further research, whether empirical, experimental, or theoretical. First though, a few comments on general interpretation.

4.1. GENERAL INTERPRETATION

Imperfect information, limited memory, and processing limitations (bounded rationality) all play roles in this chapter's model. Information is imperfect in that decision makers do not observe the actual quality (i.e., expected payoff) of a given policy; instead, they observe a signal of quality, possibly a realization of payoff. Second, decision makers do not remember prior signals, though they may know how long a policy has been in place. Third, I consider decision makers that follow rule-of-thumb behavioral rules characterizing a degree of conservatism or progressivism. Naive decision makers ignore all information embedded in incumbency which leads them to suffer switcher's curse and to be too progressive as compared with an optimal fully rational decision maker (who is still handicapped by imperfect information and limited memory).

For simplicity, I have assumed that there is a contest every period, so that a decision maker can infer that a status-quo policy has definitely won prior contests. A richer model would have a probability of a contest at each stage. This complexity would not affect the existing results (switcher's curse would remain and grow with time, but just be smaller).

I have emphasized that naive decision makers will be subject to switcher's curse and that conservatism emerges as a remedy for switcher's curse, or viewed differently, a substitute for full memory. Of course, it is entirely possible to be too conservative and the multiperiod model encompasses that possibility. Conservatism, like most things, has an optimal level and should be practiced in moderation.

The model highlights the value of memory. If decision makers knew why they had kept a policy in the past, they would not be subject to switcher's curse, at least not so long as they were able to process and properly use that information. If processing were overly costly or complex, a conservative rule of thumb might still be a useful heuristic.

Environmental changes were also not considered. The model has a stationary environment. If the environment changed radically, so that what was a good policy in the past is no more likely than any other policy to be good today, then conservatism loses all its value and a naive approach is optimal. In less extreme cases, it is reasonable to suppose that the results are moderated but not eliminated. Note also that if a policy has survived many environmental changes, it is reasonable to imagine it is very robust and a good deal of conservatism is called for.

Finally, I note that experimentation played no role in the discussion. Because signals are not remembered, there is actually no role to experiment in the model. Experimentation is an interesting issue when past signals are remembered, an issue that has been explored in the multiarm bandit literature among others. Likewise if past signals were remembered there would be a real option value of not switching.

4.2. LAW AND *STARE DECISIS*

Oliver Wendell Holmes (1897, at 469) had a point when he complained of laws that are maintained merely because they have been maintained since Henry IV. Yet, under the common law, and many other systems as well, courts continue to believe in *stare decisis*, which means that prior court decisions are not lightly overturned. Moreover, older decisions, at least if continuously applied, are even less apt to be overturned. This system is perhaps most commonly defended because it provides "uniformity of treatment to litigants, and . . . stability and certainty in the law."

In the words of the U.S. Supreme Court in *Kimble v. Marvel* (2015), "[I]t is not alone sufficient that we would decide a case differently now than we did then." Although Kimble argued that (the Brulotte Court) "just made the wrong call," the Court says "[t]hat claim, even if itself dead-right, fails to clear *stare decisis*'s high bar."

The Burkean conservatism that this chapter develops would assert that however revolting this seemed to Holmes, and even apart from the benefits of predictability and stability, putting weight on the decisions of the past, even if they seem wrong, makes a current court more likely to be right.

To be sure, the legal system differs from our model because decisions are written down and reasons are given for past decisions in court opinions. However, not all the reasons for past decisions are contained in the opinions. Sometimes the most important reasons are absent; indeed, legal realists often argue that opinions are reverse engineered with decisions made first and opinions constructed as *ex-post* rationalizations. Regardless, it is clear that *stare decisis* means more than simply considering the arguments made in the past. *Stare decisis* does not require that courts read prior courts' opinions before deciding, but instead directs them to follow prior decisions. Even without *stare decisis*, advocates could bring forward sound arguments found in past cases and current judges could take them for what they are worth independent of precedential value. But *stare decisis* means abiding by past decisions even when they seem wrong, so long as they are not too wrong.

A court is not "inexorably bound by its own precedents," and can overrule them if the court is "clearly convinced that the rule was originally erroneous or is no longer sound because of changed conditions" (see Moore and Oglebay 1943, 539–540). The model indirectly provides strong support for overruling precedents when the situations that lead to them no longer exist. If the arguments to switch are tied to changed circumstances then switcher's curse is not likely to bite. This point is consistent with Holmes who found adherence to an old rule "still more revolting if the grounds upon which it was laid down have vanished long since, and the rule simply persists from blind imitation of the past." I would, however, put the matter somewhat differently than Holmes. If you are truly blind, then adherence to the past is sound. If on the other hand, you know the prior grounds for the rule and know they no longer hold, then abandoning the rule is reasonable.

This chapter can be understood as formally modeling one reason why precedent matters, and why old precedents carry more weight than newer ones. Likewise, because the chapter's conservative conclusions evidently depend upon a stationary environment, it suggests that those seeking to overturn a precedent should demonstrate that overruling the precedent is complementary with environmental changes.

Of course, different judges give different weight to precedent. The idea that progressive judges who give less weight should follow conservative ones who give more weight and vice versa is a new claim coming out of the model.

4.3. ADMINISTRATIVE LAW

Administrative law appears broadly to incorporate the conservative philosophy modeled here. For example, "a court is not to substitute its judgment for that of the agency" (*Motor Vehicle Mfrs. Assn. of United States, Inc. v. State Farm Mut. Automobile Ins. Co.*, 463 U.S. 29, 43, 103). *Chevron* deference is a form of conservatism in that a thumb is on the scale in favor of agency judgments and these judgments are not revisited with fresh eyes.

A recent decision by the Supreme Court in *FCC v. Fox Television* (129 S. Ct. 1800, 2009), however, runs counter to what this chapter advocates. The U.S. Federal Communications Commission (FCC) had changed its rules for what constituted indecent broadcasting over the radio waves. The Second Circuit overruled the Commission relying "in part on Circuit precedent" and on the Circuit's interpretation of Supreme Court precedent in *State Farm* that required "a more substantial explanation for agency action that changes prior policy," including making clear "why the original reasons for adopting the [displaced] rule or policy are no longer dispositive" (Ibid. at 1810). The Supreme Court, in an opinion by Scalia, overturned the Second Circuit's conservative rule that guarded against switcher's curse with respect to agency decisions. Scalia argued that the FCC didn't need to provide "a more detailed justification than what would suffice for a new policy created on a blank slate."

Breyer dissented in *Fox Television* joined by Ginsberg, Stevens, and Souter. Breyer championed a heightened burden on agencies that change policy. Breyer argued that the FCC had not met its burden to change a rule under *State Farm* because the FCC's explanation of its policy change largely discussed factors "well-known to it the first time around" which provide "no significant justification for a *change* in policy." Breyer's view of the FCC's change of position is similar to his view of the Supreme Court's change of position on vertical price fixing in *Leegin Creative Leather Products v. PSKS* (551 U.S. 877, 2007). In *Leegin*, Breyer, again joined by Ginsberg, Stevens, and Souter, argued that the Court was unwise to overturn a 100-year-old precedent against vertical price fixing given that all the majority's arguments could as easily have been made thirty or forty years ago and there had been no significant new learning that justified a change of Supreme Court antitrust policy.

This chapter's arguments favor the Breyer-Ginsberg-Stevens-Souter conservative philosophy over their progressive brethren.

4.4. VENTURE CAPITAL

Venture capitalists get a lot of proposals. How should they identify those with potential? A common first question is whether there is competition already. Venture capitalists seek green fields, not crowded fields.

If there is no competition, a good follow-up is: "Why is there no competition?" A strong version of conservatism would say that if there is no competition, then it is a bad idea because there must be good reasons that no one has entered or that those who entered exited.

A more nuanced follow-up would ask if anything dramatic changed that makes this business possible now where it would have been impossible a decade or two earlier. If the business proposal would have been equally possible a decade earlier, then conservatism suggests putting it at the bottom of the pile. After all, a great deal of negative information is contained in the fact that no firm in a related business has started this business already, or started it and survived.

Consider Netflix. Netflix proposed in 1998 to distribute rental movies by mail. There was no competition so it passed the venture capitalist's first screen. However, neither mail nor the movie rental business were new in 1998, which might suggest this was a bad idea according to the model here. The absence of competition at that point was a very bad signal about the idea. But let's consider the nuanced question.

The emerging DVD standard made movies much cheaper to mail than the old bulky VHS tapes. Moreover, the internet allowed people, even with the low bandwidth available in those days, to easily choose a movie, store and update a ranked list, and communicate their orders to Netscape. This made Netflix a valuable investment in 1998, even though a pure mail order movie rental business would have failed in the 1980s. Prophesies of future broadband and future streaming made Netflix a golden opportunity.

The point is that environmental changes meant that Netflix could not have been successful in the past, but could be successful in 1998. In the face of environmental changes that were complementary with the idea, there was no reason to be conservative. And, progressivism paid off big.

4.5. SEPARATION OF POWERS

Although America's founders were revolutionary and sought fundamental change, they had the prescience to set up a system of government with separation of powers. The consequence is that it is frequently extremely hard to get anything changed. The system is conservative.

The difficulty of achieving change in Washington, DC, is supremely frustrating to anyone who works there and can lead presidents to dream of a parliamentary system where the prime minister and ruling legislative party are unified. Even when both parties of Congress and the president manage to agree on new legislation, the courts may declare it unconstitutional. Yet, despite its obvious frustrations, a conservative system has virtues. Perhaps it is good that little gets done. Switcher's curse might be worse.

4.6. EVOLUTION OF A FIRM

A new firm needs to create a business model and many policies to effectuate that model. Likely enough, the firm will not get anything right on its first try. Conventional wisdom has it that the business plan will itself survive (at most) until it hits its first customer. And, this is much as it should be according to the model: Initially, the model suggests that the firm should be relatively flexible and progressive. If an alternative business model appears better, why not switch? If someone suggests abandoning cubicles in favor of an open floor plan, and the benefits appear to justify the costs of switching, by all means switch. The mind-set of the entrepreneur, which is naturally progressive, is well suited to managing such a firm.

Eventually though, the business model and policies will have longevity. Longevity means that they will have survived many past contests with alternative policies. Unless times have changed, their age should not stand against them, but rather in their favor. There are reasons, and likely sound reasons, that the business model or operating policies survived prior contests and are the way they are. These reasons should be respected even if they are forgotten. One way to respect them is to require as in the model that switching costs be very low before switching. Another would be to require that a new alternative policy appears extremely good (in a model with variable goodness) or be very sure to be good (in a model where a more precise signal of E might be possible).

One benefit of bringing in senior managers later in a firm's evolution could be that they are naturally more conservative.[8]

4.7. THE NEW CEO AND THE NEW EMPLOYEE

A new CEO comes to a firm. Should he fire the senior management team? The answer is: it depends.

No doubt, the new CEO will have some impulse to make changes and prove himself to the board, and no doubt he would like to have a new team loyal to him, but firing the senior managers could subject the new CEO to switcher's curse.

If the firm has been successful, the existing management team is of long standing, and the CEO retired because she was getting older, the new CEO should proceed with caution. The existing team knows a lot about why the firm came to do things the way it does. In the model, the existing team will remember many of the rationales behind incumbent policies (older signals). That will no doubt help him avoid switcher's curse as one cause of switcher's curse is lack of memory. As long as the CEO respects their judgment and doesn't push too hard for change he could avoid a lot of switcher's curse.

On the other hand, suppose that the old CEO was extremely conservative and fired by the board because she refused to adapt to an evolving world. If she surrounded herself with extremely conservative managers, perhaps it is time for them to go. But if the existing managers are prudent people who have been frustrated by the old CEO's absolute refusal to make any changes, the existing managers may be the perfect partners for the new CEO, as their memories will help her sort out the good incumbent policies from the bad ones.

Similar issues arise with any new employee. The employee will come with fresh eyes, but that is not necessarily a good thing, however. After all, a lack of institutional memory will subject him to switcher's curse if he is not conservative by nature. So when the employee comes to his boss and suggests a change in the first week on the job, a wise reply would be: "wait a year." Watch and consider over the next year how things would be with the alternative policy. If it still seems a good idea, then it is worth considering. This is the policy Company X came to after leniently letting many new employees pursue their ideas.

4.8. CYCLES OF POLICIES AND CYCLES OF METAPOLICIES LIKE CONSERVATISM ITSELF

Political cycles are common with conservatives followed by progressives, and in turn, progressives followed by conservatives. Such cycles of metapolicy may be sensible, at least in the following sense. Once one has a long sequence of conservatives, it is likely time for a progressive. Likewise, once one has a long sequence of progressives, it is likely time for a conservative. Similarly, if the judiciary has been dominated by conservatives and strict adherents to *stare decisis*, then it may be time for some activist judges.

A different kind of cycle is when policy A switches to E and then back to A. This is a policy cycle rather than a metapolicy cycle. Such policy cycles could easily result from switcher's curse, limited memory, and decision makers who are too progressive. Companies, universities, and other organizations may go through cycles of centralization and decentralization. When purchasing is decentralized to departments, for example, eventually someone may observe that costs could be reduced with centralized purchasing. After a period of centralized purchasing, departments may rebel because they perceive the centralized purchasing services as too slow or unresponsive to idiosyncratic needs of departments. It is possible, of course, that such changes reflect optimal adjustment to changed technology or circumstances. Frequently, though they are like a dog chasing its tail, but more costly.

Company X recently almost suffered a cycle but was saved by the conservatism it had adopted after suffering switcher's curse. Four years ago, it had formed an outreach group, whose purpose was to evangelize for its software-as-a-service (SAAS) product. The outreach group wrote blogs, newsletters, and conducted webinars, each one-to-many marketing activities. It also did certain one-to-one customer service activities for individual customers. Recently, the CEO contemplated an internal reorganization in which he put all the one-to-one services into another group, the customer support group, that specialized in one-to-one interactions. The rationale for the switch seemed clear-cut. Having one group do all one-to-one activities and another do only one-to-many ones was logical and efficient, and having each customer have a single point of contact would minimize confusion.

In the end, though, the CEO decided to stick with the status quo even though he admitted he had no reason to do so other than conservatism. Only later, long after he decided to maintain the status quo, did the CEO remember a key virtue of the existing structure, a virtue that was part of why he himself had set things up this way years before. Only through their one-on-one interactions with live customers, helping them with concrete issues, could the outreach group gain the texture and wisdom it needed to write meaningful one-to-many marketing materials. Without that experience, the marketing materials would be generic and off-point marketese. Had the CEO switched, he would eventually have switched back.

Company X's CEO was saved by his conservative management philosophy from entering a wasteful policy cycle. He developed the conservative philosophy after suffering switcher's curse one too many times.

4.9. DIVORCE

Consider what this model has to say about the following situation.

Baseline facts. Harold has been married ten years to his wife, Wilma. Harold is miserable in his marriage, which makes him just plain miserable. He can't remember why he married Wilma and can't see any good reason to stay in this marriage.

4.9.1. VARIATION 1

Assume also that Harold is a level-headed rational decision maker. This chapter suggests that Harold should likely not leave his wife. If it had always been this bad he would *rationally* have probably left one or two years into his marriage. So there must be good times Harold has simply forgotten. This chapter's advice to Harold is: "Hang in there, Harold. Probably, you and Wilma are at each other's throats now only because each of you has unusual stress at work, and the baby has been sick for so long, keeping you sleepless. This too shall pass."

4.9.2. VARIATION 2

Assume instead that Harold tends to be impulsive and confident when it comes to decision making.

Now the inference above is much stronger. If the past had all been as bad as the present, he would surely have left her long ago given how impulsive he is and how confident he is in his opinions.

4.9.3. VARIATION 3

Assume finally that Harold is extremely conservative and cautious by nature and avoids big changes.

Sadly, in this case, this chapter implies that it could easily be that the past of this marriage is like the present. Miserable. Why did Harold stick with it so long? It takes an avalanche of negative signals to get an extremely conservative person to make a change. If he forgets past signals, he may never leave unless he changes his decision-making philosophy. Perhaps it is time to do that.

CONCLUSIONS

Many expressions capture the essential intuitions of this chapter. We say, "If it ain't broke, don't fix it;" "The grass is always greener;" and "The devil you know is better than the devil you don't." Each maxim became a mantra at Company X after switcher's curse had bitten enough times.

These age-old expressions suggest that the wisdom of conservatism has long been recognized, no doubt even before Edmund Burke. They also suggest that many people have overly progressive tendencies and need urging to be more conservative, else there would be no need for the maxims.

This chapter has studied problems in which a decision maker decides between a status-quo policy and another policy. Naively looking at the two policies with fresh eyes will lead the decision maker to switch too often, suffering what I call switcher's curse. Switcher's curse arises if the status-quo policy may have competed against (and won against) other policies before to achieve its incumbent status, and if there was a tendency for the better policy to win the prior contest(s). In such circumstances, if a decision maker does not give adequate weight to the positive information embedded in incumbency she will suffer switcher's curse. Very progressive people, such as the innovators who started Company X are likely to do just that. Limited memory and either prior neglect or the availability heuristic, two widely documented psychological phenomena, can lead agents to be naive and overly progressiveness so that they suffer switcher's curse in our model.

I show that conservatism is a rule-of-thumb antidote for switcher's curse. Decision makers should put a thumb on the scale in favor of a status-quo policy. They should be more conservative the longer a policy has been around. I also show that if past decision makers were progressive, then it pays to be especially conservative today. If past decision makers were extremely conservative, progressivism is called for today.

One lesson of the analysis is that what psychologists describe as status-quo bias (see, e.g., Burmeister and Schade 2007 and Kahneman, Knetsch, and Thaler 1991) is often not a bias but a heuristic that can compensate for these other biases. The analysis also points to what may be the best arguments to overturn a long-standing policy. Instead of just arguing that some other policy is better than the incumbent policy, it is more convincing to show that the other policy is better now, but only because of environmental changes, and that absent those changes, the incumbent policy would have been better in the past. Such an argument strikes at the heart of Burkean conservatism and truly justifies change.

APPENDIX A: PROOFS

PROOF OF LEMMA 1

For brevity, we write "A won" in place of "A won at time 0." Bayes' rule implies:

$$\Pr(A = G \mid A \text{ win}) = \frac{\Pr(A \text{ win} \mid A = G)}{\Pr(A \text{ win})} \Pr(A = G) \qquad (18.16)$$

The numerator can be calculated as follows:

$$\begin{aligned} \Pr(A \text{ won} \mid A=G) = &\ 1/2 \Pr(a_0 = g \mid A=G)\Pr(d_0 = g) \\ &+ 1/2 \Pr(a_0 = b \mid A=G)\Pr(d_0 = b) \qquad (18.17) \\ &+ \Pr(a_0 = g \mid A=G)\Pr(d_0 = b). \end{aligned}$$

To simplify the expression, let $w = \Pr(a_0 = g \mid A=G)$ and $z = \Pr(d_0 = b)$. We then have

$$\begin{aligned} \Pr(A \text{ won} \mid A = G) \ &= 1/2\, w(1-z) + 1/2\,(1-w)z + wz \\ &= w/2 + z/2 \qquad (18.18) \\ &= 1/2 \Pr(a_0 = g \mid A=G) + 1/2 \Pr(d_0 = b). \end{aligned}$$

A similar derivation shows that

$$\Pr(A \text{ won}) = 1/2 \Pr(a_0 = g) + 1/2 \Pr(d_0 = b). \qquad (18.19)$$

Bayes, equation can then be rewritten as

$$\Pr(A = G \mid A \text{ won}) = \frac{\Pr(a_0 = g \mid A=G) + \Pr(d_0 = b)}{\Pr(a_0 = g) + \Pr(d_0 = b)} \Pr(A = G). \qquad (18.20)$$

Since $\Pr(a_0 = g \mid A = G) > \Pr(a_0 = g)$, this establishes that

$$\Pr(A = G \mid A \text{ won}) > \Pr(A = G). \tag{18.21}$$

∎

PROOF OF OBSERVATION 1

Define $p_A \equiv \Pr(A = G \mid A \text{ won at time } 0)$, and $p_E \equiv p$. These are the probabilities that A and E, respectively, are good immediately prior to receiving the time 1 signals a and e of their quality.

The naive and conservative decision maker only disagrees when signals are equal.

Consider first the case: $a = b, e = b$.

Observe that

$$
\begin{aligned}
\Pr(A = G \mid a = b) &= \frac{\Pr(a = b \mid A = G)p_A}{\Pr(a = b)} \\
&= \frac{(1-s)p_A}{(1-s)p_A + s(1-p_A)} \\
&= \frac{1-s}{1-s+s\dfrac{1-p_A}{p_A}}
\end{aligned}
\tag{18.22}
$$

which is increasing in p_A. By symmetry and the fact that $p_A > p_E = p$, we therefore have

$$\Pr(A = G \mid a = b) > \Pr(E = G \mid e = b), \tag{18.23}$$

so that being conservative and keeping A is better in this case.

Consider now the case: $a = g, e = g$.

The logic in this case is similar. Observe that

$$
\begin{aligned}
\Pr(A = G \mid a = g) &= \frac{\Pr(a = g \mid A = G)p_A}{\Pr(a = g)} \\
&= \frac{sp_A}{sp_A + (1-s)(1-p_A)} \\
&= \frac{s}{s+(1-s)\dfrac{1-p_A}{p_A}}
\end{aligned}
\tag{18.24}
$$

which is increasing in p_A. By symmetry and the fact that $p_A > p_E = p$, we therefore have

$$\Pr(A = G \mid a = g) > \Pr(E = G \mid e = g). \tag{18.25}$$

This implies that $\Pr(A = G \mid a = g, e = g) > \Pr(E = G \mid a = g, e = g)$, so that being conservative and keeping A is better in this case as well. ∎

PROOF OF LEMMA 3

We abbreviate "A wins at t" with "A wins." According to Bayes' rule

$$\Pr(A = G \mid A \text{ wins}) = \frac{\Pr(A \text{ wins} \mid A = G) p_A}{\Pr(A \text{ wins})}. \tag{18.26}$$

Let's unpack the updating ratio $u \equiv \dfrac{\Pr(A \text{ wins} \mid A = G)}{\Pr(A \text{ wins})}$. We can rewrite the numerator as follows:

$$
\begin{aligned}
\Pr(A \text{ wins} \mid A = G) &= 1 - \Pr(A \text{ loses} \mid A = G) \\
&= 1 - \Pr(a = b, e = g, x < x^* \mid A = G) \\
&= 1 - \Pr(a = b \mid A = G)\Pr(e = g)\frac{x^*}{x_{max}}.
\end{aligned} \tag{18.27}
$$

In words, A wins only if it didn't lose and it loses only if (i) A appears bad (i.e., if $a = b$), (ii) E appears good (i.e., $e = g$), and (iii) switching costs are below the switching-cost threshold (i.e., $x < x^*$).

Similarly, we can rewrite the denominator as follows:

$$
\begin{aligned}
\Pr(A \text{ wins}) &= 1 - \Pr(A \text{ loses}) \\
&= 1 - \Pr(a = b)\Pr(e = g)\frac{x^*}{x_{max}}.
\end{aligned} \tag{18.28}
$$

Comparing (18.27) and (18.28), and observing that $\Pr(a = b \mid A = G) < \Pr(a = b)$, we find that whenever $x^* > 0$ it follows that $u > 1$. In contrast, when $x^* = 0$, then expression (18.27) equals expression (18.28) and $u = 1$. ∎

PROOF OF LEMMA 4

Recall that

$$\Pr(A = G \mid A \text{ wins}) = \frac{\Pr(A \text{ wins} \mid A = G) p_A}{\Pr(A \text{ wins})}$$

$$\equiv u \, p_A. \tag{18.29}$$

We will now show that

$$\frac{\partial u}{\partial x^*} > 0. \tag{18.30}$$

Observe that (explanation follows the equations)

$$sgn\left(\frac{\partial u}{\partial x^*}\right) = sgn\left(\frac{\partial \dfrac{\Pr(A \text{ wins} \mid A = G)}{\Pr(A \text{ wins})}}{\partial x^*}\right)$$

$$= sgn[-\Pr(A \text{ wins})\Pr(a = b \mid A = G)\Pr(e = g)\frac{1}{x_{max}}$$

$$+ \Pr(A \text{ wins} \mid A = G)\Pr(a = b)\Pr(e = g)\frac{1}{x_{max}}]$$

$$= sgn[-\Pr(A \text{ wins})\Pr(a = b \mid A = G)$$

$$+ \Pr(A \text{ wins} \mid A = G)\Pr(a = b)]$$

$$= 1 \tag{18.31}$$

where $sgn(w)$ takes the value "1" when w is positive and "–1" when w is negative.

The second equality above follows by (i) substituting into the right-hand expression of the top line using equations (18.28) and (18.27), (ii) evaluating the derivative using the quotient rule, and then (iii) eliminating the squared term in the denominator, which is of necessity positive.

The third inequality follows by eliminating the positive quantities $\Pr(e = g)$ and $\frac{1}{x_{max}}$.

The fourth inequality follows because

$$\Pr(a = b) > \Pr(a = b \mid A = G) \tag{18.32}$$

and

$$\Pr(A \text{ wins} \mid A = G) > \Pr(A \text{ wins}). \tag{18.33}$$

∎

PROOF OF LEMMA 5

$$\Pr(A = G \mid A \text{ wins}; p_A)$$

$$= \frac{\Pr(A \text{ wins} \mid A = G) p_A}{\Pr(A \text{ wins})} \tag{18.34}$$

$$= \frac{\Pr(A \text{ wins} \mid A = G) p_A}{\Pr(A \text{ wins} \mid A = G) p_A + \Pr(A \text{ wins} \mid A = B)(1 - p_A)}$$

Hence

$$sgn\left(\frac{\partial \Pr(A = G \mid A \text{ wins})}{\partial p_A}\right) = sgn\left(\frac{\partial}{\partial p_A}\left(\frac{1}{1 + \dfrac{(1 - p_A)\Pr(A \text{ wins} \mid A = B)}{p_A^{'}\Pr(A \text{ wins} \mid A = G)}}\right)\right)$$

$$= -sgn\left(\frac{\partial \dfrac{(1 - p_A)}{p_A}}{\partial p_A}\right)$$

$$= 1. \tag{18.35}$$

∎

PROOF OF PROPOSITION 3

Suppose that A is a status-quo policy that has been in place for T periods at time t.

For any time m, let p_A^m denote the probability that $A = G$ immediately prior to the time m contest and prior to receiving any time m signal about A.

Updating is special in the first period for policy A and so our proof will depend upon whether policy A began at time 0 or at a later time.

Case #1: A began at time 0.

We suppose that A began at time 0 and had probability p of being good and $1 - p$ of being bad, $p \in (0,1)$. At time 1, A faced its first contest. The prior probability that A is good at time 1 equals p: i.e.,

$$p_A^1 = p. \tag{18.36}$$

Let x^* be the decision rule applied at times $m = 1,...,T - 1$. Observe that p_A^1 does not depend upon x^*, directly or indirectly, so that

$$\frac{dp_A^1}{dx^*} = 0. \tag{18.37}$$

Let $g(p_A^m, x^*) \equiv \Pr(A = G \mid A \text{ wins}, p_A^m, x^*)$ be a function that maps priors p_A^m at any given time m for a status-quo policy A into a posterior that $A = G$ given that A wins at time m under the switching threshold x^*.

An equation of motion of p_A^m is then given by

$$p_A^m = g(p_A^{m-1}, x^*), \text{ for } m = 2,...,T. \tag{18.38}$$

We can now show by induction that

$$\frac{dp_A^m}{dx^*} > 0, m = 2,...,T. \tag{18.39}$$

First, we establish inequality (18.39) for $m = 2$. Observe that

$$\frac{dp_A^2}{dx^*} = g_1 \frac{dp_A^1}{dx^*} + g_2, \tag{18.40}$$

where g_1 and g_2 denote the first and second partial derivatives of g. Since $\frac{dp_A^1}{dx^*} = 0$, we can simplify the above to yield:

$$\frac{dp_A^2}{dx^*} = g_2. \tag{18.41}$$

Observe that $g_2 > 0$ because of Lemma 4. This establishes inequality (18.39) for the case $m = 2$. To complete our inductive proof, assume that

$$\frac{dp_A^{k-1}}{dx^*} > 0. \tag{18.42}$$

Differentiating (18.38) yields

$$\frac{dp_A^k}{dx^*} = g_1 \frac{dp_A^{k-1}}{dx^*} + g_2. \tag{18.43}$$

Observe now that $\dfrac{dp_A^k}{dx^*} > 0$ because

- $g_2 > 0$ (see Lemma 4)
- $g_1 > 0$ (see Lemma 5), and
- the inductive hypothesis that $\frac{dp_A^{k-1}}{dx^*} > 0$.

This establishes inequality (18.39), and in particular that $\frac{dp_A^T}{dx^*} > 0$. Now Corollary 1 proves the proposition for case #1.

Case #2. A is first chosen at some time m > 0.

The only meaningful difference from case #1 is that the formula for p_A^{m+1} differs from what the formula was for p_A^1 above. We need to ensure that

$$\frac{dp_A^{m+1}}{dx^*} = 0. \tag{18.44}$$

Let policy F be the status-quo policy at time m, let p_F be the prior that F is good, and let f be the signal of F's quality.

$$
\begin{aligned}
p_A^{m+1} &= \Pr(A = G \mid A \text{ wins at time } m; x^*, p_F) \\
&= \frac{\Pr(A \text{ wins at time } m \mid A = G; p_F, x^*) p}{\Pr(A \text{ wins at time } m \; p_F, x^*)} \\
&= \frac{\Pr(a = g, f = b, x < x^* \mid A = G; p_F, x^*) p}{\Pr(a = g, f = b, x < x^* \; p_F, x^*)} \\
&= \frac{\Pr(a = g \mid A = G) p}{\Pr(a = g)}.
\end{aligned} \tag{18.45}
$$

The last equality follows because a^m, f, x^m are independent and f and x^m are unaffected by whether A is good or bad. This implies that

$$\frac{dp_A^{m+1}}{dx^*} = 0. \tag{18.46}$$

The remainder of the proof in case #2 follows that of case #1.   ∎

APPENDIX B: COMPANY X—A CASE STUDY IN SWITCHER'S CURSE AND CONSERVATISM

As mentioned in the introduction, Company X began with innovations and an entrepreneurial mind-set. For a while all went well and changes were mainly for the better, but eventually the firm began to suffer switcher's curse. Changes often went haywire and had unintended consequences. Frequently, the virtues of an existing policy had been forgotten and only became evident after a switch.

B.1. LOG-IN SCREENS

A simple example is log-in screens. Company X developed its own software. When Company X began, the internet was young and log-ins were especially frustrating to users. Many users turned off upon seeing a log-in screen. As usage meant success, the company had a strong interest in minimizing log-in hassles. Early on, the company had a smart innovation (independently invented by many firms) to put a "Remember me" box under a log in so that users could click it and never have to log in again from that computer (so long as the user's browser allowed the system to place a cookie on his machine). This was a valuable early switch in policy. Unfortunately, most users did not bother clicking that box so Company X continued to worry about how to make logging in easier.

Eventually, one executive had an epiphany. Why not make the "Remember me" box be default "on" so that a user needed to click it to turn it off? Defaults matter a lot (see Madrian and Shea 2001, and Thaler and Sunstein 2003), so this switch was expected to dramatically increase usage and to be well worth the effort of reprogramming legacy software.

Although the switch seemed a no-brainer, it went wrong. Librarians, who were Company X's paying customers and are especially concerned with privacy issues, complained vociferously, because some patrons when using public computers did not uncheck the box so that other patrons later found themselves in another person's account when sitting down at the same commonly used machine. The complaints were sufficient that Company X had to switch back quickly; again this required programming effort because the old code needed to be regression tested again to make sure it was compatible with other independent changes that were concurrently made.[9]

The reader may wonder if this was a good gamble that went awry for an unforeseeable reason. In a sense that is right, but here is the catch. This same executive had had this same idea a couple of years earlier and the firm had tried it with the same "unforeseeable" result. In fact, every year or two the executive regularly had the same epiphany. Usually he got lucky and was saved by the memory of a long-standing employee. Company X's managers believe they only made the mistake of switching the log-in default twice before, but cannot be sure.

Eventually, the once progressive executive became more conservative and even if no one could remember the reason that the default was "off" was best, trusted that if it weren't, the firm would have switched long ago.

Company X may seem quite a mess. The question though, is "compared to what?" Compared to perfection, surely. But, despite its bobbles, Company X has grown and thrived in a difficult market. Other companies must suffer similar issues, or Company X could not thrive. This model is intended to explain why firms can have such troubles. A few more examples will help to motivate the model.

B.2. COMPANY Y'S SWITCH IN SALES STRATEGY

Company X licensed its software but faced reputational barriers as an early software-as-a-service company. It therefore entered a partnership with Company Y, a large established company, as the exclusive distributor of its software service. Company Y had a large sales force with hundreds of salespeople around the world selling to libraries, but its reputation was more important to the partnership. After consideration, Company Y decided not to use this established organization to sell Company X's software service and instead started a specialized sales force. The reasons were sound: Company Y's products were content, not software, and X's software product would also have been lost among much higher ticket items in the portfolio of the main sales force. Company Y therefore started a specialized sales force which did quite well arguably proving the decision sound.

After management changes at Company Y, it switched tactics and decided to expand sales not by hiring more specialized salespeople but by jettisoning the specialized sales model and using Y's main sales force. Sales slowed rather than rose, tensions ensued between X and Y, and the partnership ended. Company X bought the rights back to sell its software services, returned to a specialized sales force, and sales grew strongly.

In short, Company Y, after management changes, forgot the reasons for its original policy and suffered switcher's curse. It lost a great deal of money from this mistake.

B.3. AN OUTSIDE CEO

A few years later, Company X hired an experienced successful outside CEO from the same industry. This executive made a great many changes at Company X. Most of these were to conform with her own experience at other companies. In a sense, one might think that these changes were conservative in that they conformed to outside norms. But they did not work. Unnoticed was that Company X was idiosyncratic and its policies fit together and worked tolerably well. Changing to industry norms was an option that had always been available to X's managers and a student of this chapter's model might surmise that perhaps they had not switched for good reason. One example: Company X had found it difficult to sell subscriptions to new content and therefore early on decided to sell subscriptions to its content together as a bundle. Company X's bundled subscription system worked well and so X kept the system. Unlike many other firms in the industry, however, as it added new content to its portfolio it added that content to the bundled subscriptions of existing customers and raised the price accordingly.

The new CEO decided to switch from this policy to those of her previous firm's, which created a new content bundle each year without upgrading old subscriptions. There were two problems. The first was one of organization. It was difficult for a small firm to build new systems to keep track of different customers subscribing to different packages—the 2007, 2008, or 2009 bundle of content, depending upon the year of original purchase and whether the customer upgraded to a subsequent year—and to build systems to provide electronic access to arbitrary collections of content. The bigger problem was that content could not be sold effectively a la carte by Company X (which is what led Company X to bundle in the first place) and few existing customers wanted to upgrade their packages to include new content when they now had the option not to. Company X consequently suffered switcher's curse and lost substantial revenue and profit.

B.4. THE SWITCHES OF COMPANY Z, AN ACQUIRER

Company X eventually sold its content business. Company Z, a much larger firm in the industry, bought it. For six months all was well. Then the acquirer changed a number of policies, including ceasing to use Company X's software. In doing so, it failed to appreciate that Company X's policies were not chosen randomly but refined over time and kept when they worked. It failed to appreciate that X's managers could at any time have switched to industry standard practices or software if those would have made sense. It is not that industry standard practices are wrong, nor that X's policies were, but Company X had a niche and its policies worked for that niche. The result of the acquirer's changes was that many critical content producers quit. Company Z suffered switcher's curse because it did not give sufficient weight to the idea that Company X's policies were there for a sound reason, even if that reason was not apparent to Company Z.

All these examples are of course open to other interpretations, like any case study. The interpretations above, however, serve to motivate the model in this chapter and to illustrate the ideas of this chapter. The reader is encouraged to check this chapter's ideas against her own experience, or even better, to develop empirical tests of these ideas.

NOTES

Thanks to Oxford University Press for permission to republish. Originally published as "Conservatism and Switcher's Curse," *American Law and Economics Review* 2017 (49–95).

I thank George Akerlof, Jonathan Carmel, Stefano Dellavigna, Daniel Hemel, Benjamin Hermalin, Louis Kaplow, Brent McDonnell, David Kennedy, Barry Nalebuff, Mitch Polinsky, Catherine Roux, Alan Schwartz, Carl Shapiro, Joseph Stiglitz, Philipp Strack, Eric Talley, Abraham Wickelgren, Justin Wolfers, Jeffrey Zwiebel, and seminar participants at Columbia, the University of Chicago, the University of California Berkeley, NHH in Bergen, Norway, the University of St. Gallen in Switzerland, the American Law and Economics Association Meetings, and the National Bureau of Economic Research Summer Institute for helpful conversations. I owe particular thanks to George Akerlof and Benjamin Hermalin for encouraging me to write my ideas about conservatism and the switcher's curse.

1. Organizations have difficulty remembering the past because employees come and go, because even when they stay, they suffer from human frailties of poor memory, and because information can become siloed. Hirshleifer and Welch (2002) provide an extensive review of psychological literature to the effect that actions will be easier to remember than the reasons for actions. In this chapter's vernacular, actions are policies and I assume that the CEO can tell the difference between a new policy and an incumbent one even though she can't remember why the incumbent policy was put in place. Anand, Manz and Glick (1998) provide an instructive example in which managers at a major aerospace company after "another wave of changes in management" decided that a technology was critical but "no one remembered that there was an expert already on staff."

2. The real name of Company X is withheld.

3. In our context, such prior neglect is even more likely to arise than in the experiments where it is discovered, because sophisticated inference is required in our context even to figure out that a status-quo policy is likely good. In contrast in many prior neglect experiments, the difference in base rates is either stated or supposed to be common knowledge to subjects.

4. The difficulty of knowing the cost of switching prior to any switch is another important source of switcher's curse that I will explore in a different paper. If Kahneman and Tversky's (1979) "planning fallacy" applies, then, people will have a tendency to underestimate switching costs.

5. The decision maker may only have beliefs about the conservatism or progressivism of past and future decision rules in which case the optimal decision rule should be understood to be optimal conditional on these beliefs.

6. In a famous example, a decision maker who thinks she sees a blue cab typically ignores the base rate that almost all cabs are green and concludes that in fact she probably saw a blue cab because that is how it appeared. Remarkably, the base-rate fallacy occurs in the lab even when people are told that cabs are mostly yellow (that is the Kahneman and Tversky experiment). Such mistakes can cause switcher's curse.

7. In a model where signal strength varied, immediately after a policy A was chosen, the probability that it was good would depend upon the strength of the signal saying it was good. A more conservative decision maker would tend to switch only after seeing very strong signals, so immediately after a switch, a new policy is more apt to be good the more conservative was the person deciding to switch. From that point forward, progressive decision makers deciding to keep the policy will most quickly and strongly update the priors that A is good. Thus, *conservative* decision makers switching to a policy tends to suggest it is good, while *progressive* ones maintaining the policy tends to suggest it was good. It is a reasonable hypothesis that over a sufficiently long period of time, the latter effect would dominate in a model of varying signal strength, but that hypothesis is left for future research.

8. It is common in Silicon Valley to bring in older, more experienced, and likely more conservative managers to run a company after a point. "Once a company takes off, the next round of staffing often involves bringing in people with experience— "grown-ups" as they are sometimes called—who know how to manage a maturing

business . . ." (Bernstein 2015). As one example, Eric Schmidt (age 46) was brought in to be CEO of Google in 2001 succeeding Larry Page (age 28), who continued with the firm, serving as president under Schmidt. See http://googlepress.blogspot .com/2001/08/google-names-dr-eric-schmidt-chief.html.

9. According to Wikipedia (downloaded August 28, 2014, and available from the author), regression testing is needed because "Experience has shown that as software is fixed, emergence of new faults and/or re-emergence of old faults is quite common."

REFERENCES

Anand, Vikas, Charles C. Manz, and William H. Glick. 1998. "An Organizational Memory Approach to Information Management." *Academy of Management Review* 23:796–809.

Baliga, Sandeep, and Jeffrey Ely. 2011. "Mnemonics: The Sunk Cost Fallacy as a Memory Kludge." *American Economic Journal: Microeconomics* 3:35–67.

Bar-Hillel, Maya. 1980. "The Base-Rate Fallacy in Probability Judgments." *Acta Psychologica* 44:211–233.

Bernstein, Mark F. 2015. "Over the Hill in Silicon Valley?" *Princeton Alumni Weekly* (March 18):24–27.

Bikhchandani, Sushil, David Hirshleifer, and Ivo Welch. 1992. "A Theory of Fads Fashion, Custom, and Cultural Change as Informational Cascades." *Journal of Political Economy* 100:992–1026.

Burke, Edmund. 1790. *Reflections on the Revolution in France.* London: J. Dodsley.

Burmeister, Katrin, and Christian Schade. 2007. "Are Entrepreneurs' Decisions More Biased? An Experimental Investigation of the Susceptibility to Status Quo Bias." *Journal of Business Venturing* 22:340–362.

Dertouzos, Michael, Richard K. Lester, and Robert M. Solow. 1989. *Made in America, Regaining the Productive Edge.* Cambridge, MA: MIT Press.

Hirshleifer, David, and Ivo Welch. 2002. "An Economic Approach to the Psychology of Change: Amnesia, Inertia, and Impulsiveness." *Journal of Economics and Management Strategy* 11:379–421.

Holmes, Oliver Wendell. 1897. "The Path of the Law." *Harvard Law Review* 10:457–478.

Kahneman, Daniel, and Amos Tversky. 1973. "On the Psychology of Prediction." *Psychological Review* 80:237–251.

Kahneman, Daniel, and Amos Tversky. 1979. "Intuitive Prediction: Biases and Corrective Procedures." In *Forecasting: TIMS Studies in the Management Sciences, Vol. 12*, edited by S. Makridakis and S. C. Wheelwright. Amsterdam: North Holland.

Kahneman, Daniel, and Amos Tversky. 1982. "Evidential Impact of Base Rates." In *Judgment under Uncertainty: Heuristics and Biases*, edited by Daniel Kahneman, Paul Slovic, and Amos Tversky, 153–160. New York: Cambridge University Press.

Kahneman, Daniel, Jack L. Knetsch, and Richard H. Thaler. 1991. "Anomalies: The Endowment Effect, Loss Aversion, and Status Quo Bias." *Journal of Economic Perspectives* 5:193 206.

Kimble v. Marvel Enterprises 135 S.Ct. 1697 (2015).

Madrian, Brigitte C., and Dennis F. Shea. 2001. "The Power of Suggestion: Inertia in 401(k) Participation and Savings Behavior." *Quarterly Journal of Economics* 116:1149–1187.

Moore, James, and Robert Oglebay. 1943. "The Supreme Court, *Stare Decisis* and Law of the Case." *Texas Law Review* 21:514–553.

Porter, Maureen, and Sally McIntyre. 1984. "What Is, Must Be Best: A Research Note on Conservative or Deferential Responses to Antenatal Care Provision." *Social Science and Medicine* 19:1197–1200.

Prendergast, Canice, and Lars Stole. 1996. "Impetuous Youngsters and Jaded Old Timers: Acquiring a Reputation for Learning." *Journal of Political Economy* 104:1105–1134.

Rasmusen, Eric. 1992. "Managerial Conservatism and Rational Information Acquisition." *Journal of Economics and Management Strategy* 1:175–201.

Samuelson, William, and Richard Zeckhauser. 1988. "Status Quo Bias in Decision Making." *Journal of Risk and Uncertainty* 1:759.

Thaler, Richard, and Cass Sunstein. 2003. "Libertarian Paternalism." *American Economic Review* 93:175–179.

Tversky, Amos, and Daniel Kahneman. 1973. "Availability: A Heuristic for Judging Frequency and Probability." *Cognitive Psychology* 5:207–232.

Zwiebel, Jeffrey. 1995. "Corporate Conservatism and Relative Compensation." *Journal of Political Economy* 103:1–25.

_____

CHAPTER 19

The "Inner Logic" of Institutional Evolution

TOWARD A THEORY OF THE RELATIONSHIP BETWEEN FORMAL
AND "INFORMAL" LAW

Antara Haldar

INTRODUCTION

This chapter will take an initial step in the direction of trying to systematize a theory of the *relationship* between formal and "informal" law (social norms, conventions, and other nonformal rules that influence behavior). Following a well-established strain of the literature on institutions (e.g., Aoki 2001; Greif 2006), "law" will be defined as any set of underlying rules that systematically influence patterns of behavior—since it is *effect*, rather than *source*, that is relevant for economic outcomes (the capacity of institutions to enable agents to enter into mutually beneficial transactions), the focus of this project in the first instance.[1] Thus, it will concern itself with the entire gamut of institutions that present themselves as successful solutions to collective action problems, whether formal or informal.

The significance of this project derives not only from the fact that a majority of the world's population (particularly in the Global South, but also in substantial pockets around the globe—what has sometimes been described as the "South in the North") effectively lives outside the ambit of formal law—but also that it represents a significant gap within mainstream legal scholarship that we still lack an adequate theory of "informal law" and its relationship with formal legal systems. The paper will also make a contribution by putting a range of theoretical traditions concerned with institutions—ranging from law and development to sociological approaches (like legal pluralism) to economic approaches (like New Institutional Economics, and social capital theory)—in dialogue. It will rely, in particular, on the theoretical frames offered by Polanyi (1944).

The conventional wisdom has been that—just as the progression from a pre-legal to a legal order has been conceived of as a *linear* one[2]—so too, is the evolution from institutional informality to formal institutions, involving arriving at a steady-state end point. This is the story that is told both about the legal evolution of the Global North, as well as the prescription underlying the policy advice provided to the Global South. This chapter will critically examine the conventional wisdom, and explore an alternative hypothesis: that the logic of institutional evolution is less about the shift from informal to formal as a binary, than it is about the optimal balance being struck between the formal and informal elements in the system.

Specifically, the chapter will attempt to explore three propositions that flow out of this reconceptualization.

First, informal institutions may have a critical role to play at earlier stages of institutional evolution: Building on a growing literature that argues that informal institutional structures can be much more efficient than predicted by standard theory (Ostrom 1990; Haldar and Stiglitz 2013), the paper will explore whether certain characteristics inherent to informal institutions (endogenous evolution, information economies, tapping into preexisting social capital, flexibility, etc.) make them more suitable in certain settings in terms of both external factors of adaptation to local conditions (*context*) and factors internal to agents within the system, like familiarity with institutional structures (*cognition*).

Second, informal institutions will often exhibit a tendency toward formalization (e.g., into formal law): While some informal institutions are extremely resilient in their informality,[3] several others will often display a tendency to evolve into formal ones. This is often driven by the pressures of "scaling up," i.e., the bid to amplify economic gains by increasing the institutional radius through rapid institutional replication, a process facilitated by codification. Indeed, it is this tension that frames the "inner logic" of institutional evolution: formal law may be seen as a means of capturing (or encoding in a durable form that lends itself to replication) "learning" or information about successful strategies that emerge at the local level to solve collective action problems, i.e., formal institutions can be seen as a mechanism for embedding informal ones; formalization will, however, inevitably introduce new rigidities and a loss of responsiveness.

Third, formality may not be a steady end state: While the tendency toward formalization may be inherent in the "logic of institutional evolution," it may not represent a steady-state equilibrium that is completely divorced from informal institutions.

The next section will summarize the current theory on institutions and its account of the trajectory of institutional evolution. The following section will consider evidence of whether this theory adequately describes the empirical reality in the context of three case studies—land titling in Peru, microfinance in Bangladesh and India, and the global financial crisis. In light of the empirical evidence, the penultimate section will suggest an alternative description of institutional evolution may be in terms of a *Polanyian* "double movement" rather than as a linear progression. The final section will conclude the discussion.

THE CURRENT THEORY OF INSTITUTIONAL EVOLUTION

Nearly all the dominant strains of scholarship have posited that the process of institutional evolution is characterized by informal structures mutating into formal ones. This is seen to represent a transition to a superior state—both normatively, in the sense of the "rule of persons" being succeeded by the "rule of law," but also, and more significantly for the present discussion, in economic terms, in the sense of the radius for economic transitions being widened from those premised on personalistic ties (where "names and faces" matter) to one in which anonymous economic agents can enter into mutually beneficial transactions not on the basis of any personal knowledge of each other but acting, instead, in reliance on a third party able to enforce the contract, typically the state legal system.

Thus, for North (1990) whether a state will progress toward "growth, stagnation or decline" is fundamentally a function of whether cooperative institutions that facilitate these transactions emerge or not—particularly in the context of advanced industrial economies where the bulk of economic activity is based primarily not on production, but trade and exchange—where the quantum of profits (and hence growth) is determined essentially by transaction costs (which are, in turn, a function of how effective institutions are). The theory of growth here—broadly accepted by institutional analysts across the spectrum—is simple: the more effective institutions are, the more they will reduce transaction costs per trade; the lower the transaction costs, the greater the profits per exchange; and, consequently, the higher the levels of growth. North's account does not specify that the cooperative institutions need necessarily be formal rather than informal—yet, the assertion across the swathe on institutional scholarship has been that it must be. The preference for formal institutions is not difficult to understand; where these institutions are effective, they provide an effective lever for exercising a decisive—and systemic—influence on social and economic policy. Indeed, this bias toward formality permeates the spectrum of scholarship—ranging from "developmentalists" to conventional institutional theorists working in the New Institutional Economics (NIE) tradition.

For a majority of scholars working in the NIE tradition the focus on formal institutions is explicit. Acemoglu, Johnson, and Robinson (2002) trace the "reversal of fortunes" in the current era between the "New World" colonies and others like the Mughals in India and the Aztecs and Incas of South America—far more prosperous in the 1500s—to the evolution of institutions of "private property" rather than "extractive" ones in these regions. La Porta et al. (1998) find that pedigree, in the sense of the "legal family" that a set of institutions belong to, is an important determinant of legal effectiveness and the growth prospects of an economy. The World Bank in its *Doing Business* and *World Governance Indicators* measures only formal aspects of a legal system as a predictor of how effective the institutional structure will be in underpinning economic transactions.[4] De Soto (2000) explicitly attributes "underdevelopment" to the failure of a functional formal legal system to unleash the "invisible potential" of "dead capital" in these regions of the world—the very basis, he argues, of growth and development in the capitalist model. At the risk of oversimplifying somewhat, the cumulative effect of this scholarship is the prescription that a formal, Western-style legal system designed to protect private property rights and enforce contracts is a necessary and sufficient condition for economic growth and development.[5]

Interestingly—coming at the issue from a very different perspective—the "developmentalists" from the "first law and development movement" of the 1960s onward (i.e., the era of the post–Cold War zeal of the U.S. Agency for International Development [USAID] and other such organizations to "export" the model of the U.S. legal system as part of the developmental effort) share a very similar amalgam of assumptions. Trubek and Galanter (1974) describe this as "liberal legalism:" a position characterized by paramount faith in the legal system that sees law as both the end and means of development. In particular, this centered on four main beliefs—that the state is central, that the focus of the discourse should be on the higher echelons of the legal system, that legal rules can be assumed to be effective as instruments of social change and, crucially, that there is a natural tendency for legal systems to evolve into more formal ones.

That is not to say that current scholarship lacks an account of informal norms in entirety. The law and society tradition—going back as far as Macaulay (1963)—provides an account of how the "handshake" in a business transaction may be more important than the formal contract. Even more noteworthy is that Macaulay's study is not set in the markets of Asia, Africa, or Latin America, but instead in the automobile industry in Midwestern America—against the backdrop of a fully developed state infrastructure for contract enforcement. Similarly, Friedman (1969) emphasizes the importance of the interactive dynamics between law and culture, while Engle Merry (1988) describes the complexities of legal pluralism.

These ideas are not restricted to the law and society school. Economists, building on the insights of sociologists like Coleman (1988) and political scientists like Putnam (1995, 2000), acknowledge the economic importance of networks, norms, and social trust that facilitate solutions to collective action problems. Even within NIE, pathbreaking work by Ostrom (1990) demonstrates that "informal" solutions to the collective action problems presented by common pool resources can be much more effective on a sustained basis than predicted by standard theory. Themes of institutional plurality, hybrid institutions (part-public, part-private), and endogeneity are central to this strain of work.

Along these lines, Berkowitz, Pistor, and Richards (2003a,b) offer an account of the differential performance of the colonies that is quite distinct from the one offered by Acemoglu, Johnson, and Robinson (2002). The key factor, for them, in determining the success (legal effectiveness) of institutional importation—or "transplantation"—is the degree of adaptation of those institutions to local conditions and the degree of familiarity of agents within the system with the legal principles being introduced. Thus, in the colonies of the "New World" (i.e., the United States, Australia, and New Zealand), imported institutions were much more likely to fare better both because of reduced competition from competing institutional structures as a result of being less densely populated as well as the fact that, being "settler" colonies, the individual agents in these regions were far more familiar with the institutional structures being imposed as a result of these being a cultural continuum.

There are several problems with the scholarship on institutions as it currently exists. The first is that the portrayal of the legal evolution of the Global North in the simplistic terms of a frictionless development from pre-legal and/or informal to legal and formal is unsubstantiated, ahistorical, and largely inaccurate. The second is that to extrapolate from this ahistorical account of the development of the Global North to a prescription for the Global South with regard to the institutional prerequisites of growth is likely to yield erroneous results—both on account of providing an account of institutional evolution in the North that is too simplistic, but also due to its lack of engagement with both the stage of development and the specificities of the context of the Global South.

Most fundamentally, however, the current scholarship is lacking in its capacity to provide a satisfactory account of the interactive dynamics between the formal and informal elements of an institutional system; central to this discourse is the idea of law as a repository of information. This shortcoming manifests itself in two different ways. The first is a limitation associated with the formalist school: the standard theory does not provide an account—either descriptively, in the context of the Global North, or prescriptively, in the case of the Global South—of the *mechanics* by which the informal mutates into the formal. Indeed, the analytics for standard institutional theory in the case of the Global North begins at a point where the "end state" of formality has already been achieved, while, in the case of the Global South, the injunction to formalize is issued without any engagement with the process by which this will come about. The second is a limitation associated with those who tend to fetishize the "informal." From the very earliest theorists of the collective action problem (Olson 1965) onward, it has been clear that the alignment of individual and group interest bears an inverse relationship to the size of the group. Indeed, an explicit premise of Ostrom's work was a limit to the size of the units that she studied. The ideas of "thresholds" and "tipping points" (Granovetter 1978) are useful here. Threshold models of behavior are premised on the idea that group behavior is a critical determinant of individual behavior—and that, at a critical point of general conformity, individual behavior will tip. The concept of the "threshold"—the number or proportion of others who must take one decision before a given actor does so—is key, i.e., this is the point at which net benefits start to exceed net costs for a given actor. This idea of a "magic number" or "tipping point" is of enormous significance in policy terms—it suggests that relatively small shifts in the behavior of individual actors can play a role in shifting group outcomes—representing a domain of opportunity for strategic intervention that may be both more effective and economical than the tectonic shifts attempted by formal legal reform efforts.

EMPIRICAL CHALLENGES TO THE CONVENTIONAL ACCOUNT

To probe the efficacy of the current theoretical frames in accounting for a spectrum of empirical experience, this section will examine three case studies: the land titling program initiated in Peru and replicated in various parts of the Global South; microfinance, originating in Bangladesh and subsequently acquiring global reach; the credit crisis, radiating out of the United States, and spawning a global recession. While an in-depth analysis of each of these case studies is beyond the scope of this chapter, the discussion will focus on certain key elements that each of these cases have in common. In each of these three cases, an attempt was made to use the "law" to widen credit access and property ownership, with a view to achieving certain social and economic ends. Indeed, central to the discussion will be *the role of law as the basis for the creation of capital*, i.e., that alchemy that enables the law to tease out of a finite pot of physical assets capital that is many times its value.[6] The focus in each of the three cases will be on the interplay of formal and informal elements in determining the health—or pathology—of the institutional structures; and on the question of whether this elasticity that the law enables is infinite.

THE PERUVIAN LAND TITLING PROGRAM

In the late-1990s and early-2000s, land titling emerged as one of the most prominent and popular programs on the international development horizon. The immediate impetus for the program was the enormous intellectual influence of the work of De Soto (2000)—discussed above— whose ideas were operationalized not only through his own Lima-based think tank, the Institute for Liberty and Democracy (ILD), but also through international organizations like the World Bank and the United Nations (especially through the work of the Commission for Legal Empowerment of the Poor). At the peak of its influence, the ILD was advising over forty governments around the world—but it had its greatest impact in Peru. Under its direction, the Peruvian government undertook a large-scale land titling program involving two of its key agencies, the Comisión de Formalización de la Propiedad Informal (COFOPRI) and the Superintendencia Nacional de los Registros Públicos (SUNARP).

The Peruvian land titling program presents a high-profile instance of an attempt to achieve the formalist ideal. The idea behind the project was simple: informal landholdings were titled in the names of the squatters occupying them in the hope that these holdings could then be collateralized to raise credit through the formal banking sector, i.e., assets hitherto relegated to the category of "dead capital" could be folded into the system of capital creation through formalization with the intent of stimulating the economy and creating economic opportunities to be shared widely. Indeed, "dead capital" was held to be the primary cause of underdevelopment:

> houses built on land whose ownership rights are not adequately recorded, unincorporated businesses with undefined liability, industries located where financiers and investors cannot see them. Because the rights to these possessions are not adequately documented, these assets cannot readily be turned into capital, cannot be traded outside of narrow local circles where people know and trust each other, cannot be used as collateral for a loan and cannot be used as a share against investment.[7]

The economic intuition behind the program goes back to the core ideas of law and economics (Demsetz 1967; Coase 1990): property rights are essential to provide the security and certainty required to incentivize the use of resources in their most efficient way. Thus it was a straightforward application of the conventional wisdom that institutional evolution involves a linear progression toward formalization, or that of going from an inferior (informal) state to a superior (formal) one.

The empirical evidence on the program, however, finds no appreciable increase in access to credit as a result of the distribution of over 3.5 million titles (Field and Torero 2004), i.e., formalization failed to have the effect of capital creation. Indeed, as discussed at length elsewhere (Haldar and Stiglitz 2013), this result should not have come as a surprise: as with a range of other formalization programs, it points to a range of deep institutional pathologies associated with "legal transplantation" that is maladapted to its new host environment in terms both of *context* and *cognition*. With regard to context, the average value of the landholdings is so low that the transaction costs associated with litigation often exceeds the value of the land, making it unviable as collateral; a range of market imperfections, particularly acute in the case of the Global South (like "missing markets"), mean that the mere fact of land titling will not overcome the problem of "dead capital;" state-enforcement is a particularly costly means of enforcement (especially in terms of information costs) for such a low-value contract and—most importantly—legal capacity (in the sense of state-enforcement of the contract) cannot be trivially assumed. The failings of the program in terms of cognition factors is even more acute: the sheet of paper that is presented to the squatters has little socio-logical significance for them, the banks and the courtrooms in which the deeds acquire significance are too remote and far removed from their everyday experience to be meaningful, or even accessible—the rigidity and remoteness of these institutions making the entire process of formal-ization either too daunting for it to be effective, or just irrelevant.

MICROFINANCE IN BANGLADESH AND INDIA

The forty-year history of microfinance can broadly be divided into three phases: the 1970s to the late 1980s, the late 1980s to around 2006, and the mid-2000s to the present.

Microfinance began as a series of lending experiments in the villages of Bangladesh in the 1970s—associated in particular with Yunus and the Grameen Bank,[8] but also with other major Bangladeshi microfi-nance institutions (MFIs) like BRAC.[9] As mythologized, this was the era of "bicycle bankers" and basket weavers—marked by a small group of makeshift bankers (economics professor Yunus and his students) trying a social experiment on a group normally excluded entirely by formal banking institutions (women involved in a variety of "cottage" industries, who needed loans for their raw materials, etc.), with surprisingly positive results. The initial impetus for microfinance was to provide respite from the dominance of traditional moneylenders—the only source of credit available to the demographic being targeted by MFIs—who were viewed as exploiting poor borrowers, often charging usurious interest rates.[10] The resulting reluctance to deal with traditional moneylenders reduced credit, thereby negatively impacting productive investments and livelihoods.[11]

As per its original vision, microfinance entailed providing small loans, mostly to women—for productive purposes. The core of the original microfinance model was "the group:" borrowers at most MFIs were orga-nized into groups comprising five to ten members. In theory, at least, lending was based on joint liability—the idea that a second member of the group could not get a loan until the first paid back—thereby creating incentive for peer-monitoring and an alternative mechanism to prompt repayment. These groups served certain crucial social purposes in the functioning of microfinance as an institution—and it has been a matter of endless academic debate what precisely their economic function was.[12]

Whatever lay at the heart of the success of the incipient institutional experiment, there were several remarkable features of microfinance in its early years. First, repayment rates were extraordinarily high, well over 90 percent.[13] Second, these rates were achieved despite a credit contract that was almost entirely informal in nature—characterized by the absence of either collateral or any formal contract between the microfinance institution and borrower—and, until recently, any governmental regulation of the MFIs themselves.[14] These accomplishments were particularly impressive in the context of a region where repayment rates on loans to the rural and agricultural sectors have historically been woefully low, and attempts at institutional formalization have not typically met with great success. Finally, there were a variety of "rituals" associated with lending: the lenders cultivated close personal relationships with the borrowers, while close personal relationships between borrowers was fostered by organizing them into groups and requiring regular attendance and group meetings, etc.

By the 1980s, microfinance had become well-known in development circles. The borrower bases of Grameen and BRAC alone extended to several million, flourishing in the context of one of the most dynamic nongovernmental organization (NGO) sectors in the world in Bangladesh. Grameen now lends to approximately 8.4 million women and has replicas in eighty-four different countries, while BRAC boasts 7 million borrowers in Bangladesh alone and a global reach of over 100 million. A defining characteristic of this period in the development of microfinance is that although the model went "global," replicas maintained fidelity—in the main—to the original (lending without collateral or contracts, social ritual around lending in groups, a high degree of social contact both between borrowers and borrowers and bankers), and modifications did not compromise its core character.

Another characteristic of this period was a switch—at least among the old, more-established MFIs—from lending on a joint-liability basis or group lending to individual lending (in the case of the Grameen, this was identified as the shift from Grameen I to Grameen II). While the terms with longer-standing borrowers was shifted to individual lending, the original model was often retained for new regions or branches even by the older MFIs and was usually the model adopted by the new MFIs and, thus, persisted as the "learner" model. The organization of borrowers into groups was retained irrespective of the lending arrangements. It is significant that this shift in lending patterns did not lead to any perceptible drop in repayment rates: that MFIs globally—and certainly in

Bangladesh—were able to retain the high repayment rates of the early years of the microfinance experience indicated that it may, indeed, be a replicable—and scalable—model.

Through the 1990s, microfinance emerged as one of the—if not *the*—most important development program on the horizon. It was lent widespread support by international organizations like the United Nations and the World Bank, and further replicas of it of all sizes sprang up all over the world. The crowning glory, vis-à-vis the recognition of microfinance, came in 2006 when Yunus and the Grameen Bank were jointly awarded the Nobel Peace Prize, leading Yunus to comment that microfinance would put "poverty in museums." But while the data surrounding the poverty-alleviating effects of the institution sometimes seemed less convincing than its most ardent advocates thought,[15] there was much evidence of its socially transformative effects—including with regard to women's empowerment.[16]

The period from the mid-2000s onward represented a very different era in the microfinance experience. As a development initiative, microfinance became ubiquitous—and, in Bangladesh as elsewhere, the sector saw a period of "irrational exuberance." MFIs already in existence sought to widen their borrower base, while new MFIs struggled to establish themselves in an already-crowded market. The glut of credit supply meant that it was easy for borrowers to get caught in a phenomenon that has been described as "overlapping" (Haldar and Stiglitz 2013): borrowers taking loans from one MFI to pay another back, thereby getting caught in a debt trap. Another corollary of this phenomenon was, of course, the increasing incidence of fraudulence, etc. The cumulative effect of this was an increasing push for formalization of the sector—resulting, in Bangladesh, in the establishment of the *Palli Karma Shayak Foundation* (PKSF) and the Microcredit Regulatory Authority (MRA). What is noteworthy is that it was the very success of the microfinance experiment in its informal iteration that led to widespread replication—and resultant formalization.

While microfinance was spreading rapidly globally—an Indian MFI, SKS Microfinance that had emerged as the second-most important in the world (after Grameen)—decided to take the replication experiment to the next level, by developing the "universalizable" version of microfinance. On its own terms, it looked for inspiration not to conventional MFIs but rather to fast-scaling consumer businesses with an assembly line of mechanized processes and standardized products streamlined for rapid scaling, i.e., the attempt was explicitly to develop the "Starbucks" version of microfinance. The trade-off was clear: the more streamlined and clearly codified the institution, the easier and more seamless the process of replication. After building its reputation based on more conventional microfinance practice, it launched an extremely successful IPO in 2010—making it appear that the seamlessly scalable version of microfinance had been found. In November 2011, however—in what has been described as the equivalent of the fall of Lehman Brothers in the context of microfinance history—SKS faced a statewide repayment crisis, requiring instant government intervention and setting in motion a global contagion in the world of microfinance (Haldar and Stiglitz 2016).

The early experience of microfinance is a prominent example of a relatively informal, trust-based institutional intervention: distributing credit to the poor not against collateral and with any formal contracts, but based on peer monitoring. For thirty years, microfinance worked extremely successfully on the basis of these informal networks, accruing a borrower base of close to 1.2 billion globally and reporting repayment rates of over 90 percent. The reasons for this good performance lie—by analogy with Ostrom's work on common pool resources—in the information economies (*context* factors) and astute use of reputation (*cognition* factors) that are inextricably linked to its informal institutional character. The model may also, however, reveal the limits of informality: the rapidly expanding microfinance sector in Bangladesh has shown evidence of increasing formalization. Indeed, the current crisis in microfinance, radiating out of India, is associated with rapid expansion (indeed, an attempt at "universalization") and the shift to for-profit lending—but, even more fundamentally, a basic misinterpretation of what lay at the heart of the model (Haldar and Stiglitz 2015; Haldar and Stiglitz 2016). The crisis demonstrates the limits of "scale" encountered by informal institutions: its roots can be traced to its attempt to transcend the institutional history of microfinance as one based, fundamentally, on social ties.

THE FINANCIAL CRISIS

The Financial Crisis of 2008—leading to the Great Recession that is ongoing—was the product of a complex chain of events. The proximate cause for the broader crisis was subprime lending—an increase in the percentage of lower-quality mortgages (a large proportion of these being adjustable-rate mortgages) that was symptomatic of a wider trend of lowered lending standards or higher risk lending. The inferior quality of financial instruments combined with a general increase in indebtedness of the population (fueled by the easy availability of credit including significant elements of predatory lending) meant that when the period of "irrational exuberance" yielded to a decline in housing prices in the mid-2000s, the combination of the difficulty in refinancing mortgages and higher interest rates on adjustable-rate mortgages resulted in high rates of mortgage delinquency or default, leading to widespread foreclosures (further depressing the housing markets by augmenting supply). The value of housing-backed securities—widely held by global financial organizations—declined dramatically in value leading to the collapse of several major financial institutions and a crisis of confidence in the U.S. credit and financial markets.[17] The reluctance to invest further led, in turn, to a tightening of credit around the world and an economic slowdown—initially in the United States and Europe, and then globally. The deeper roots of the crisis are more hotly contested, with explanations ranging from flawed government policies to regulatory failures (particularly of the shadow banking system) to systematic "gaming" of the financial markets.

One—relatively simplistic—account of the root causes of the crisis stresses government policy encouraging a wider distribution of credit. For instance, the Housing and Community Development Act of 1992 required that a certain percentage of the loan purchases made by Fannie Mae and Freddie Mac be related to affordable housing, leading to the establishment of programs worth trillions to purchase affordable housing loans—thereby, allegedly, encouraging lenders to slacken underwriting standards with respect to these loans. The policies outlined in the "National Homeownership: Partners in the American Dream" document of 1995—have been accused, in a bid to broaden credit access and property ownership, of excessively relaxing lending standards. Similarly, the Community Reinvestment Act—originally enacted by the Carter administration in the 1970s and revived by the Clinton administration that aimed at ending lending discrimination and increasing flexibility by, for instance, explicitly including in the lending decisions of banks factors like responsiveness to community activists—has been said to have encouraged higher risk lending. Finally, additional policies associated with the 1995 Clinton package encouraged state and local organizations to broaden the base of affordable housing by providing loans with either a minimal down payment or no down payment at all—or by providing unsecured second loans to borrowers to defray down-payment costs; these second loans were typically "off the record" as far as the traditional lender was concerned.

While some of these governmental policies may have been at play in the broader ecosystem, the crisis may be understood differently on an institutional analysis, i.e., in terms of one of the key factors contributing to the crisis being the excessive mechanization of lending practices. The key economic function of formal law has been identified as the creation of capital—and the recent era of financialization pushed the limits of this process. Financial innovations like mortgage-backed securities (MBS), collateralized debt obligations (CDOs), and credit default swaps (CDS), as well as the complicated functioning of the shadow banking sector (with their off balance sheet derivatives and securitizations) allowed *many* times the value of an asset to be teased out of it on the basis of complex algorithms—concepts developed in the domains of mathematics and physics. This not only enabled capital creation on an unprecedented basis, but also widened the radius of transactions on to historic levels. Yet these opaque risk-pricing formulas were based on the faulty assumption of the strict independence of individual component mortgages. The functioning of the banking system became excessively mechanized in other ways as well—automated loan approvals became the norm without appropriate review or documentation.

Whereas institutions embedded in the social structure (e.g., where a personal relationship exists between the bank and the manager) offer certain inbuilt safeguards, complete formalization (i.e., reliance on formal rules rather than personal ties)—while well-suited to rapid expansion— also encourages "gaming" on the part of agents within the system. An important aspect of the argument traditionally put forward to establish the superiority of formal legal rules over informal codes has been that legal rules are considered to be more efficient in "informational" terms, i.e., as a means of capturing knowledge, or "learning," about efficient social processes. It has been claimed, in particular, that formal legal rules are easier to replicate than informal norms, and thereby better promote economic efficiency. However, the recent experiences of the U.S. mortgage markets may suggest that if this process of "shorthand" recording becomes too detached from social processes, the benefits associated with legal formalization may start to be undermined. Thus, in the case of the continuing crisis in the United States, in addition to breaches of procedure (for instance, the "robo-signers"), excessively formal and legalistic approaches may also be partially to blame—enabling rampant "gaming" at the margins of financial regulations, or a deliberate attempt to limit conformity to the "letter" of the law while ignoring its "spirit." Moreover, the pursuit of the economies of scale traditionally associated with formal systems, or the drive to maximize the volume of transactions, may have been a significant factor contributing to the crisis. Finally, if financial institutions had adopted a less formalistic and more communitarian view of the law, the implicit knowledge that lenders would have possessed about borrowers may have acted as a bulwark against many of the problems that have arisen.

Indeed, a variety of social movements that have emerged in the wake of the Financial Crisis that began in 2008—whether the advent of bailouts, the tightening of the regulatory framework, the "Occupy" movement or the backlash against austerity—are calling for a return of institutions to a more socially embedded position.

AN INSTITUTIONAL "DOUBLE MOVEMENT?"

While the conventional discourse on institutional evolution—as discussed above—is firmly grounded in linearity, this section—based on the locus traced by the case studies above—will suggest that an alternative conceptualization might be more akin to an institutional analogue of the Polanyian "double movement."

Polanyi (1944) famously analyzed the resilience of the market economy in terms of the "double movement"—the laissez-faire movement to expand the scope of the market, and the protective countermovement that emerges to resist the disembedding of the economy. Polanyi's concept of "embeddedness"—of course—expresses the idea that, in fact, the economy is not autonomous as portrayed in economic theory, but essentially subordinated to politics, religion, and social relations. It is the dual dynamic of the movement and countermovement, according to Polanyi, that establishes the stability of the market economy. Thus, on this view, far from undermining the market economy, the countermovement—that pulls away from full-blown self-regulation— is fundamental to its sustainability. Block (2001) compares this to the stretching of a giant elastic band:

> . . . one might say that disembedding the market is similar to stretching a giant elastic band. Efforts to bring about greater autonomy of the market increase the tension level. With further stretching, either the band will snap—representing social disintegration—or the economy will revert to a more embedded position.[18]

While the evidence from the microfinance experiment appears to suggest that the pressures of institutional replication—and scaling—of successful informal institutions may give rise to increasing formalization, the failure of the attempts at "universalizing" the model and the cautionary tale of the forces behind the financial crisis indicate that this formalization may not represent an end state. Indeed, while the failure of legal formalization through land titling to lead to capital creation in the Global South may reveal inadequacies in the process of institution building to engage with factors of context and cognition; equally, the orgy of capital creation in the recent history of financialization of the Global North may expose the inherent institutional limits to this process.

The implications of this altered conception are many. First, the context-cognition framework builds into the discourse on institutions—perhaps explicitly for the first time—a narrative of the relationship between individual agents at the micro-level and macro-level institutional change. Second, the overt focus on size and scale may go some of the way in explaining legal dualism in the Global South: the reason, for instance, that commercial codes, etc., are so much more effective than the legal system in general may be due to the fact that it is easier to set up an alternative rule system with the smaller number of actors at play in such types of formal reform. Finally, the idea of the institutional "double movement" collapses the fundamental institutional distinction that has been posited as existing between the Global North and the Global South. Within this framework, the difference in institutional structures is not one of kind but of degree, with institutional systems in all geographical regions being consciously theorized as containing elements of both the formal and the informal.

CONCLUSION

While an extensive literature exists on formal institutions (and its economic importance), and there is an emergent literature on informal institutions—there is relatively little scholarship putting the two in dialogue with each other.

This paper makes two substantive contributions. It suggests, first, that two factors (a) context and (b) cognition are critically important in determining the success of institutions, and may account for why transplants have, historically, met with such limited success. Second, it argues that while the "inner logic" of institutional evolution may gravitate toward formalization, formality may not necessarily represent a steady-state equilibrium.

Indeed, while the gaze of the bulk of scholarship on institutions has been trained on its formal surface, it is really working in sync with informal institutions on which the health of an institutional structure rests. This implies that just as informal institutions may tend toward formalization—by analogy with the Polanyian "double movement"— excessive formality may make institutions both rigid and brittle. Thus, while the evolution of institutions appears to be driven by an "inner logic"—complete formality may not be its logical conclusion.

NOTES

1. For Aoki (2001), the defining feature of an institution is that it is a part of the collective expectations that shape social behavior; for Greif (2006), institutions define regularized patterns of behavior. This is a very different approach, for instance, to that of the legal positivists who traditionally define law in terms of its "pedigree" (e.g., Hart 1961).

2. For Hart (1961), for instance, the union of primary and secondary rules marks this moment of transition.

3. The role of informal institutions—like *quanxi*—in the context of the Chinese economy attests to this. See, for example, Upham (2009) and Haldar and Stiglitz (2013).

4. See, for instance, Kaufmann, Kraay, and Mastruzzi (2006).

5. For a relatively crude articulation of this perspective, see Posner (1998).

6. As discussed above, De Soto (2000, 6) describes this as the "representational" system that allows the "invisible potential" of physical assets and labor to be extracted, and that makes for a "parallel economic life" allowing the conversion of physical assets into the highly malleable form that is capital. This characterization is not entirely new: as De Soto acknowledges, it underpinned Marx's idea of property rights as the means of extracting surplus value.

7. De Soto (2000, 6).

8. For a history of the Grameen Bank, see http://www.grameen-info.org/.

9. See http://www.brac.net/.

10. This makes the recent accusation, discussed below, that the new MFIs have degenerated into playing exactly the same role as traditional moneylenders particularly ironic.

11. As Emran, Morshed, and Stiglitz (2007) show, one of the consequences (given imperfections of labor markets) was that rural labor was vastly underemployed.

12. This literature starts with Stiglitz (1990).

13. The exact figure is disputed, but it is broadly accepted that repayment rates in the microfinance industry have traditionally been extremely high especially when compared with conventional banks. For an early estimate of Grameen repayment rates, see Hossain (1988).

14. The factors that sustained these repayment rates are discussed at length below. For a detailed analysis of the merits of an informal contract over a formal one, see Haldar and Stiglitz (2013).

15. Khandker (2005), for instance, estimates that microfinance in Bangladesh has only reduced poverty in Bangladesh by 1 percent per year—still, that means that over the thirty years since the beginning of Grameen, the poverty rate has been reduced significantly.

16. One very obvious manifestation of this repeatedly reported in interviews was an observable increase in female mobility, or women being seen outside the home. For other instances, see Pitt, Khandker, and Cartwright (2006) and Schuler, Sidney, Hashemi and Riley (1997).

17. See further information, Stiglitz (2010).

18. Block (2001, xxv).

REFERENCES

Acemoglu, D., S. Johnson, and J. A. Robinson. 2002. "Reversal of Fortune: Geography and Institutions in the Making of the Modern World Income Distribution." *Quarterly Journal of Economics* (117):1231–1294.

Aoki, M. 2001. *Towards a Comparative Institutional Analysis*. Cambridge, MA: Cambridge University Press.

Berkowitz, D., K. Pistor, and J. F. Richards. 2003a. "The Transplant Effect." *American Journal of Comparative Law* (51):163–203.

Berkowitz, D., K. Pistor, and J. F. Richards. 2003b. "Economic Development, Legality and the Transplant Effect." *European Economic Review* (47):165–195.

Block, F. 2001. "Introduction." In *The Great Transformation*, edited by Karl Polanyi. Boston: Beacon.

Coase, R. 1990. *The Firm, the Market and the Law*. Chicago: Chicago University Press.

Coleman, J. 1988. "Social Capital in the Creation of Human Capital." *American Journal of Sociology* 94 (Supplement):S95–S120.

Demsetz, H. 1967. "Toward a Theory of Property Rights." *American Economic Review* 57 (2):347–359.

De Soto, H. 2000. *The Mystery of Capital*. London: Bantam.

Engle Merry, S. 1988. "Legal Pluralism." *Law and Society Review* (22):867–896.

Field, E., and M. Torero. 2004. "Do Property Titles Increase Credit Access among Urban Poor? Evidence from a Nationwide Titling Program." Unpublished.

Emran, S., A. K. M. M. Morshed, and J. E. Stiglitz. 2007. "Microfinance and Missing Markets". Working paper. SSRN: https://papers.ssrn.com/sol3/papers.cfm?abstract_id=1001309.

Friedman, L. 1969. "Legal Culture and Social Development." *Law and Society Review* (4):29–44.

Granovetter, M. 1978. "Threshold Models of Collective Behavior." *American Journal of Sociology* 83 (6):1420–1443.

Greif, A. 2006. *Institutions and the Path to the Modern Economy: Lessons from Medieval Trade (Political Economy of Institutions and Decisions)*. Cambridge, MA: Cambridge University Press.

Haldar, A., and J. E. Stiglitz. 2013. "Analysing Legal Formality and Informality." In *Law and Economics with Chinese Characteristics: Institutions for the Twenty-First Century*, edited by D. Kennedy and J. Stiglitz. Oxford: Oxford University Press.

Haldar, A., and J. E. Stiglitz. 2015. "Taking Stock of Microfinance." *World Economics Journal* 16 (2):1–10.

Haldar, A., and J. E. Stiglitz. 2016. "Group Lending, Joint Liability, and Social Capital: Insights from the Indian Microfinance Crisis." *Politics and Society* 44 (4):459–497.

Hart, H. L. A. 2012 [1961, 1994]. *The Concept of Law.* Oxford: Oxford University Press.

Hossain, M. 1988. "Credit for Alleviation of Rural Poverty: The Grameen Bank in Bangladesh." International Food Policy Research Institute Report No. 65.

Khandker, S. R. 2005. "Microfinance and Poverty: Evidence Using Panel Data from Bangladesh." *World Bank Economic Review* 19 (2):263–286.

Kaufmann, D., A. Kraay, and M. Mastruzzi. 2006. "Governance Matters V: Aggregate and Individual Governance Indicators for 1996–2005." World Bank Policy Research Paper No. 4012.

La Porta, R., F. Lopez-de-Silanes, A. Shleifer, and R. W. Vishny. 1998. "Law and Finance." *Journal of Political Economy* (106):1113–1156.

Macaulay, S. 1963. "Non-Contractual Relations in Business: A Preliminary Study." *American Sociological Review* 28 (1):55–67.

North, D. C. 1990. *Institutions, Institutional Change and Economic Performance.* Cambridge, MA: Cambridge University Press.

Olson, M. 1965. *The Logic of Collective Action.* Cambridge, MA: Harvard University Press.

Ostrom, E. 1990. *Governing the Commons: The Evolution of Institutions for Collective Action.* Cambridge, MA: Cambridge University Press.

Pitt, M., S. R. Khandker, and J. Cartwright 2003. "Does Micro-Credit Empower Women: Evidence from Bangladesh." Policy Research Working Papers 2998, The World Bank.

Polanyi, K. 2001 [1944, 1957]. *The Great Transformation: The Political and Economic Origins of Our Time.* Boston: Beacon.

Posner, R. 1998. "Creating a Legal Framework for Economic Development." *World Bank Research Observer* 13 (1):1–11.

Putnam, R. 1995. "Bowling Alone: America's Declining Social Capital." *Journal of Democracy* 65–78.

Putnam, R. D. 2000. *Bowling Alone: The Collapse and Revival of American Community.* New York: Simon & Schuster.

Schuler, S.R., R. Sidney, S. Hashemi, and A. Riley. 1997. "The Influence of Women's Changing Roles and Status in Bangladesh's Fertility and Contraceptive Use." *World Development* 31 (3):513–534.

Stiglitz, J. E. 1990. "Peer Monitoring and Credit Markets." *World Bank Economic Performance* (4):351–366.

Stiglitz, J. E. 2010. *Freefall.* New York: Norton

Trubek, D., and M. Galanter. 1974. "Scholars in Self-Estrangement: Some Reflections on the Crisis in Law and Development Studies in the United States." *Wisconsin Law Review* 4 (1):1062–1103.

Upham, F. 2009. "From Demsetz to Deng: Speculations on the Implications of Chinese Growth for Law and Development Theory." Unpublished.

PART VII

Public Policies

Joe Stiglitz and Representative and Equitable Global Governance

José Antonio Ocampo

ABSTRACT

This chapter analyzes Joe Stiglitz's contributions to the debates on globalization and global economic governance. It refers first to his major books on the subject: *Globalization and Its Discontents* and *Making Globalization Work*. It then focuses on two issues on which I have interacted with him in the past: the creation of an apex mechanism of global economic governance within the United Nations system, and the need to strengthen cooperation on international corporate taxation. Two common features of his ideas are the need to fill major gaps in global cooperation, and to do so through representative institutions and fair and effective international judicial systems.

The contributions of Joe Stiglitz to the debates on globalization and global economic governance mostly follow his term as Chief Economist of the World Bank (1997–2000). They include two of his most popular books: *Globalization and Its Discontents* (Stiglitz 2002) and *Making Globalization Work* (Stiglitz 2006). They also include the major report of the UN Commission of Experts on Reforms of the International Monetary and Financial System convened by the president of the United Nations after the worldwide shocks generated by the North Atlantic financial crisis,[1] which Stiglitz headed; I will simply refer to it as the Stiglitz Commission (United Nations 2009a,b). Numerous other contributions could be added to the list.

In this chapter, I focus on two issues in which I have had the opportunity to work with him very closely: the need for an apex mechanism of global economic governance and for new rules for international corporate taxation. Two common features of Stiglitz's ideas in these areas are the need to fill major gaps in international cooperation, and to do so through representative institutions. As these and a broader set of ideas are also developed in his well-known books, I start with a brief analysis of their contributions to the globalization debate.

1. THE INDICTMENT OF GLOBALIZATION AND THE GLOBAL REFORM AGENDA

The major difference between Stiglitz's two major books on globalization relate to their focus: whereas *Globalization and Its Discontents* is an indictment of globalization as it has taken place; *Making Globalization Work*, as its title suggest, is a reform agenda for improving the global order. The first also focuses to a greater extent on the emerging and developing world, and it is highly inspired by the 1997 East Asian crisis, in which Stiglitz was involved as Chief Economist of the World Bank but had a very critical view of the management of the crisis by the International Monetary Fund (IMF). It is not surprising, therefore, that the book is highly critical of the IMF. The second book has a broader focus, as some of the discussions are also relevant for developed countries, and it is therefore truly a global agenda.

An interesting feature of both books is the view that globalization as potentially a force for good that has failed, however, to bring about those benefits because of the way it has been managed. In particular, he underscores in both books how it has been plagued by the incapacity of policies—or the lack of them—to manage some of the major problems of global markets. In the Preface to his first book (Stiglitz 2002), he emphasizes the prevalence of both market and government failures in the management of globalization, in particular the incapacity to design policies to manage the asymmetries of information that plague the functioning of markets—one of his major academic contributions—the fact that the interests that dominate the global agenda lack democratic attitudes, and the admonition that the globalization agenda is based on a curious blend of an ideology of "market fundamentalism" and "bad economics." In his view, this agenda also ignored the fact that capitalism is not uniform and that there are "varieties of capitalism"—to use a term that came into the academic literature at the turn of the century (see, for example, Hall and Soskice 2001)—with some institutional arrangements being able to handle the market and governance failures much better than others. This implies that there is not a single market model, but several that mix in different ways markets and government interventions, with democratic institutions allowing society to choose among them (Stiglitz 2002, 217–222). Beyond that, and making a bridge to his second book, he argues that most of these problems originate in the deficiencies of global governance: a system that is dominated by a few major industrial countries and, particularly, by the commercial and financial interests of these countries, generating a system of governance in which the most affected countries and people are left almost voiceless (Stiglitz 2002, 18–22).

This indictment of globalization also reflects, in Stiglitz's view, the "colonial mentality" of the major international financial institutions, and particularly of the IMF: the presumption that they knew much better than developing countries what was good for them (Stiglitz 2002, 24). This was reflected in what he identifies as the three major pillars of the "Washington Consensus:"[2] fiscal austerity, privatization, and market liberalization. There were negative elements of all three that were ignored in the design of the agenda: fiscal austerity led to unemployment and the shredding of the social contract; privatization faced missing markets, uncompetitive practices and, in the worst cases (which he underscores was a major problem in Russia), asset stripping; trade liberalization was inadequately sequenced to guarantee positive results, whereas financial liberalization without adequate regulation was a recipe for economic instability. The latter issue is particularly critical for Stiglitz's analysis of the mismanagement of the East Asian crisis by the IMF in his first book, which he argues was largely associated to the financial liberalization agenda of this institution. In contrast, he is less harsh in the book on the World Bank. It must be underscored, however, that for many developing country analysts, it was the World Bank more than the IMF that was the center of "market fundamentalism" and the worldwide spread of the Washington Consensus agenda in the 1980s.

Whereas the last chapter of the first book (*Globalization and Its Discontents*) proposes some of the elements of a global agenda, it is *Making Globalization Work* that develops in full that agenda. The first chapter of this volume summarizes his major areas of concern: the unfair rules that characterize globalization, the fact that it has put one type of capitalism over all others, that it has placed economics over other values (e.g., environmental sustainability), that it has generated many losers, and has taken away the sovereignty of nation-states with essentially nothing in return. This last issue is crucial, as in his view, globalization has increased demands on nation-states but at the same time have weakened their capacity to act, failing also to create democratic global institutions to replace or support their actions; in short, "economic globalization has outpaced political globalization" (Stiglitz 2006, 21).

Leaving some issues aside, the global agenda that Stiglitz proposes encompasses six major areas:

- Fair trade rules, which should include differential treatment for poorer countries, capping agricultural subsidies, eliminating tariff escalation, reducing the asymmetries between the liberalization of capital and labor, and designing international tribunals that use similar rules for managing international unfair trade practices to those that have been developed at the domestic level to limit the use of those practices. Stiglitz also proposes that multilateral trade agreements should be preferred to bilateral ones.
- A radically new agenda for intellectual property rights (IPRs), which would enhance the public good character of knowledge over the monopoly power granted by IPRs. This would require a stronger boundary of the "novelty" criterion for granting patents, and avoiding IPRs for knowledge that can be used to generate further knowledge. He indeed expresses the view that an open architecture for all forms of knowledge should be preferred to IPRs, as in science, and therefore that governments should give priority to the promotion of research that generates open knowledge. In his view, at least the IPR agenda should be applied in a weaker form in poorer countries, allowing for a broader use of compulsory licensing, and stronger recognition of traditional knowledge.
- A strong agenda to combat climate change, which would include commitments by all developed countries, but also by developing nations, to reduce the costs of compliance—allowing countries to choose between emission targets and carbon taxes—paying for avoided deforestation (and, more generally, for environmental services) and introducing in this area strong enforcing mechanisms.
- To manage the growing market power of multinationals, design global competition laws overseen by a global competition authority, restrict

in some areas (e.g., damages to the environment) the limited liability that corporations enjoy, and limit bank secrecy and other practices that promote corruption.

- Designing international sovereign debt-restructuring legislation that is more debtor friendly and guarantees, in particular debt restructuring that is done fairly, effectively, and rapidly. The major principle in this case is reducing the probability that countries would be back in default. This would require in the long term the creation of an international bankruptcy organization, and in the meanwhile an international mediation service. In turn, international financial institutions would play a more active countercyclical role in supporting countries facing debt crises, which would require more risk absorption by them.

- Finally, reforming the global reserve system, allowing in particular the regular issuance of "global greenbacks" (which could be the IMF's Special Drawing Rights/SDRs), possibly by a global central bank. This would reduce the high costs of building up foreign exchange reserves by developing countries. However, in his view, this system would also be good for the United States, as it allows the major reserve-issuing country to avoid running external deficits to satisfy the global demand for dollar reserves, with their associated contractionary effects on domestic economic activities.

The institutional requirements of this reform agenda are not equally developed in this book. An essential element of the agenda, which is highlighted in the last chapter, is a need for a new social contract between developed and developing countries, which is included in his agenda on trade, IPRs, control of global monopolies, payment of environmental services, debt, and the new global reserve system. As indicated, this may require the creation of a series of new institutions to manage global policy gaps, including global judicial authorities in some areas. Stiglitz also proposes several ways of reducing the democratic deficit of current arrangements, including changing the voting structure of the Bretton Woods Institutions (BWIs) and fairer representation of developing countries in general, greater transparency and increased accountability. Finally, he proposes a stronger UN Economic and Social Council (ECOSOC) to manage the interrelation between the different issues and cross, therefore, the "silos" that characterize existing international economic decision making.

2. THE NEED FOR AN APEX INSTITUTION
OF GLOBAL ECONOMIC GOVERNANCE

The Stiglitz Commission deepened the analysis of several of these issues. Beyond the recommendations on the immediate measures to overcome the North Atlantic financial crisis and an agenda of global financial reform, which were the major focuses of the Commission, it proposed a comprehensive agenda for systemic reforms of the global monetary and financial institutions.[3] They included (i) the creation of a global financial regulatory authority or at least a college of supervisors overseeing the systemically relevant financial institutions; (ii) a new global reserve system that could be based on the expanded role for SDRs; (iii) the creation of a global competition authority; and (iv) the design of an equitable sovereign debt-restructuring mechanism that guarantees that indebted countries are given a "fresh start," which should preferably be managed by an international bankruptcy court. The last three recommendations are in line with the proposals by Stiglitz (2006).

They also included institutional recommendations to enhance the representation of developing countries in the BWIs, as well as the Bank for International Settlements and the Financial Stability Forum (now Board), and to enhance the transparency of all these institutions. There was also specific mention of increasing the basic votes in the BWIs (those allocated equally to all member countries, independently of quotas) and introducing double or multiple majority voting. However, I will concentrate here on the proposal to create a new apex institution for global economic governance that would constitute a "democratically representative alternative to the G-20" (United Nations 2009b, para. 24).[4]

As this statement makes clear, this proposal was made as an alternative to the G-20, which had transformed itself into a leaders' forum after the outbreak of the North Atlantic financial crisis and self-designated itself in its September 2009 summit in Pittsburgh as "the premier forum for our international economic co-operation" (G-20 2009, paras. 19, 50). The starting point for this proposal should, therefore, be an evaluation of the G-20. In this regard, Ocampo and Stiglitz (2011) have suggested that the G-20 should be evaluated on the basis of five criteria. On leadership, it has shown a positive record, notably in terms of steering change in financial regulation, putting in place a new mechanism of macroeconomic cooperation (the Mutual Assessment Progress) and avoiding a new wave of protectionism to respond to the crisis. On effectiveness, it had a good start, but it deteriorated rapidly. In particular, in light of the uncertainties that continue to surround the global economy until the present, it is clear that macroeconomic cooperation in the G-20 was unable to generate a strong recovery and to avoid building up new global payment imbalances. On a third criterion, the contribution to the coherence of the global system of governance, it was able to coordinate some institutional reforms and actions (see also Woods 2013), but some reforms were left unfulfilled.

According to two other criteria, democratic representativeness and an effective independent secretariat, performance has been rather poor. Representation would be subject to more discussion below. Independent secretariats play a fundamental role in the international system by providing neutral technical support detached from the interests of the most powerful countries, as well as independent monitoring of decisions, advancing initiatives, helping mediate disputes, and identifying common ground for agreements. The rotating secretariats of ad hoc grouping are incapable of fulfilling these tasks and tend to generate mission creep or, even more, lack of a clear orientation. This may be one of the major reasons why the expectation that it could shift from a "crisis committee" to a "steering committee" of the global economy (Dervis and Drysdale 2014) has remained an unfulfilled promise.

The alternative proposal by the Stiglitz Commission was to create a Global Economic Coordination Council (GECC) (United Nations 2009, chap. 4). This idea belongs, of course, to the long history of proposals to create an Economic Security Council and similar institutions, such as an L-27 that could evolve out of the current ECOSOC (Rosenthal 2007; Dervis 2005, chap. 3). But it has three essential differences: (i) its central focus would be to coordinate the UN *system*, understood in a very broad sense to include all its specialized agencies, including the BWIs and the World Trade Organization (WTO), which according to the Commission should formally become part of the UN system; (ii) it would be based on a system of representation based on constituencies, and in this sense, similar to that of the BWIs rather than the "one country, one vote" system of the United Nations;[5] and (iii) it would be a new Council at the leaders' level, and therefore similar in this way to the G-20.

The first of these features is, in a sense, the most obvious and essential to guarantee the coherence of the system of global economic cooperation, which should be understood as encompassing the economic, social, and environmental areas—i.e., the broad concept of "sustainable development" in UN terminology. It would also help identify the interactions in the mandates of different organization (for instance, environmental effects of trade policies, or social effects of budgetary policies) and propose ways by which they might be addressed, thus crossing the current "silos" of existing international economic decision making. The GECC would, nonetheless, leave to the more specialized bodies the specific decisions in their area of work, though it could convene ministerial meetings of its own. The Council would also help to identify the multiple gaps in the current system of global economic cooperation, and take steps to overcome them.

The second feature, weighted vote, would mix the two ingredients now incorporated in the voting structure of the BWIs—basic votes and economic weight—with a greater weight for the first of these factors and a more appropriate measure of the second that is currently used in the determination of the capital/quota in the BWIs. It could also eventually include a third criterion: population. Weighted vote would, of course, be difficult to accept by those countries that defend the UN voting principle. However, this recognizes the fact that the apex institution of the system of global economic government cannot operate without the voice of the most important actors being strong and, furthermore, without them sitting at the table. Otherwise, they would simply ignore the decisions of that body. A system of constituencies and weighted vote is, in a sense, the only way to mix the universality of the proposed decision-making body with the recognition of power imbalances, and it is much better than the alternative system in which the less powerful players are excluded altogether (e.g., the G-7 and G-20) or powerful players are granted veto power (the UN Security Council).

This feature makes the GECC proposal different from the traditional proposal to transform ECOSOC into an "Economic Security Council."[6] The basic reason is that such transformation would fail to meet the previous criterion of guaranteeing a system of representation in which the most powerful players have a strong voice and are sitting at the table. According to the Stiglitz Commission, ECOSOC would continue to function as the coordinator of the UN *organization* (understood as the UN Secretariat, Funds, and Programs), though not the UN *system*. Although the latter is formally a function of ECOSOC according to the UN Charter, it is unclear whether it has ever really exercised it, except in a marginal way—and particularly, ECOSOC has historically exercised, at best, a limited coordination of the activities of the BWIs despite the character of the latter as specialized agencies of the UN system.

It is interesting to note that with regard to the design of an apex economic institution, the Palais Royal Initiative has made some proposals that are in some ways similar to those of the Stiglitz Commission. This initiative was convened by Michel Camdessus, Alexandre Lamfalussy, and Tommaso Padoa-Schioppa, and presented its proposals in February 2011 (Boorman and Icard 2011). These proposals included a three-level governance structure for the global economy, which would have at the top a reformed G-20 designed on the basis of a constituency system (Palais Royal Initiative 2011, 24). However, this proposal centered on the international monetary system, the major concern of that initiative, and thus that body would have more limited reach than the proposed GECC.

The Stiglitz Commission also recommended the creation of an additional instrument of economic policy coordination, which it saw as less difficult for countries to agree on than on the creation of the GECC: an expert panel that would follow the successful experience of the Intergovernmental Panel on Climate Change. The new panel would help evaluate the functioning of the global economic and social system and identify gaps in the international architecture, thus helping improve global economic decision making. It would be composed of academics and representatives of the international social movements and would help foster a fruitful dialogue with policy makers and international organizations.

3. INTERNATIONAL CORPORATE TAXATION

On international taxation, our common work with Joe Stiglitz has taken place in 2015–16 in the Independent Commission for the Reform of International Corporate Taxation (ICRICT), to which we both belong. What the Commission underscored in its main report, launched in June 2015 (ICRICT 2015a), is that the primary enabler of international corporate tax abuse is the separate entity principle, which allows major corporations to detach vast amounts of taxable income from the underlying business operations, reporting large parts of their profits in subsidiaries located in low-tax jurisdictions or in tax havens. On that basis, ICRICT's major proposal is that the system for taxing multinational corporations' subsidiaries as separate entities should be replaced in the long term by one in which multinational corporations are taxed as single and unified firms, using formulary apportionment to estimate their tax liabilities of the specific jurisdictions where they operate. This system would replicate, therefore, that which is partially used today by a few federal states to distribute some tax liabilities. The apportionment of (taxable) income to different jurisdictions would be based upon objective factors, which could include, among others, sales, employment, and the use of local natural resources. The latter is critical to guarantee an adequate tax share for developing countries, as the long history of controversies surrounding the models for double-taxation treaties indicate.

This ambitious long-term proposal has been accompanied by the Commission's recommendations in other areas. They include (i) proposals to curb tax competition, which include establishing a minimum corporate income tax by developed countries that would then serve as a standard for developing nations, and the commitment of all governments to examine the spillover effects of the tax benefits they grant to international investors, and the commitment to eliminate those that facilitate tax avoidance in other countries; (ii) increasing transparency, by requiring multinationals to file reports on revenues and taxes paid in all the countries in which they operate; these country-by-country reports would then become freely available to all tax administrators and (with a lag) to the public; (iii) strengthen enforcement, including through information exchanges among countries, and cooperation with developing nations to strengthen their capacity to inspect the operations of large international firms; and (iv) expanding the objectives of model tax treaties to include preventing double nontaxation, curbing abusive tax practices, and enabling information exchange to facilitate effective tax administration.

Another set of proposals refer to the need to build adequate representation of all countries into the system of international tax cooperation—"inclusiveness" in the terminology of the ICRICT Report. The major proposal in this regard is to establish an intergovernmental tax body within the United Nations, which would evolve out of the current expert committee on tax matters that is part of the ECOSOC system. This was the proposal presented by developing countries through their major representative group, the G-77, to the Third International Conference on Financing for Development held in Addis Ababa, Ethiopia, in July 2015, but it was rejected due to the opposition of major developed countries.[7] We both strongly defended the proposal of the G-77 at the conference. ICRICT has also proposed drafting a UN convention to combat abusive tax practices, which will eventually adopt a consolidation and apportionment system for taxing global corporate profits.

ICRICT also participated in the discussion of the first recommendations of the G-20/OECD Base Erosion and Profit Shifting (BEPS) Initiative that were launched at the annual meetings of the BWIs that took place in Lima, Peru, in October 2015. ICRICT (2015b) defended this initiative as a step in the right direction, particularly the system of country-by-country reporting by major international firms, which is a major advance in terms of transparency and coincides with one of the major ICRICT recommendations. However, it underscored two fundamental problems. The first is substantive: BEPS maintained the separate entity principle, and also postponed the proposals to improve the "profit-splits" methodology under the transfer pricing scheme, which can be understood as a step in the application of the principle of apportionment of revenues and expenses of international firms to specific jurisdictions. The second lies in the area of governance: although the G-20/OECD BEPS process has included forty-three counties (the thirty-four OECD countries plus the nine non-OECD G-20 countries), assigning the initiative to an organization that is essentially made up of developed countries (OECD) essentially takes away decision-making power from developing countries, making it subject to the preponderance of national concerns of developed countries—and, even worse, of special interests within them.

Equally problematic was the decision of several developed countries[8] to require mandatory arbitration through the Mutual Agreement Procedure (MAP) in their bilateral tax treaties as a mechanism to guarantee that treaty-related disputes will be resolved within a specified time frame. The problem is that, as in current investment treaties, arbitration involving government with private parties is not considered by many analysts as a good judicial mechanism—in contrast, to dispute settlement among governments that takes place in the WTO. The major problem is that the decisions of arbitration processes may generate conflicts with domestic law and judicial powers, including with the top national judicial authorities (Constitutional of Supreme Courts), and therefore do not constitute a real attempt to make domestic and international law compatible. In a sense, the problem is that arbitration sidetracks two essential democratic institutions: national parliaments and judicial systems.

An alternative, which has been discussed at ICRICT based on Stiglitz's recommendations, would be to design a system with the following characteristics:

- The creation of a public International Tax Court in which only national authorities have a direct voice (just like in the WTO dispute settlement), even if private parties are involved in the dispute, which implies that their participation is only through negotiations with their own national authorities. The court would help build up a set of precedents and interpretations, which would then be given considerable weight in subsequent proceedings.

• If there is a dispute about the interpretation of a treaty (e.g., the treatment of a particular category of income), then the judicial process should be entirely public.

• If there is a dispute about the facts and circumstances of a specific case, then the two courts of the different jurisdictions should delineate their interpretations in a precise way (e.g., how a particular source of revenue should be classified). The International Tax Court should then resolve the dispute with recommendations for changes in tax codes toward harmonization. Either party may apply for confidentiality on the grounds of commercial secrets, but a high bar should be established, and in any case the decision, set forth in clear enough terms as to provide a guide to similar disputes, should be made public.

• The governments of the two countries must respond within one year to the proposal of harmonization.

These proposals on tax matters, as well as those analyzed in the previous sections, underscore the two major concerns that have been at the center of Stiglitz's work on global governance. First, on the substance of the global agenda, filling the gaps in the system of international cooperation to overcome the problems that the current globalization process has faced. Second, on institutional arrangements, the need to design adequate global institutions, to guarantee fulfilling the democratic principle of representation in decision making, and the guarantee of fair and effective judicial processes that are essential for prevalence of the rule of law at the international level.

NOTES

1. I use this term rather than that of global financial crisis, because the crisis had global effects but its epicenters were the United States and Western Europe.

2. I use this term, as Stiglitz does, in the broad sense of market reforms, rather than the specific agenda that the more specific views that Williamson (1990) proposed were at the center of Washington's policies when he introduced that term, which then came to be widely used in the literature.

3. See a summary of the recommendations in United Nations (2009b). They also included some less central to the reform agenda proposed by the report, on development finance and a development-focused trade round.

4. I focus on this because of my active participation in drafting these recommendations, as a member of the Stiglitz Commission, and the fact that we later wrote a joint paper on the subject.

5. Excluding, of course, the vetoes that the permanent members of the Security Council have in the decisions of that body.

6. This term is used in the literature to underscore that the powers of the apex economic decision-making body should be as strong as in the UN Security Council, but it is not meant to imply in any sense any concept of "economic security."

7. As Under-Secretary-General for Economic and Social Affairs of the United Nations, I introduced this proposal in 2004 as part of a set of recommendations by the UN Secretariat to redefine the functions of what was still an *ad hoc* committee of experts. The proposal was not accepted but the committee was made a regular one within the ECOSOC system, and its functions were broadened beyond the traditional focus on the design of a fair model double-taxation treaty.

8. Australia, Austria, Belgium, Canada, France, Germany, Ireland, Italy, Japan, Luxembourg, the Netherlands, New Zealand, Norway, Poland, Slovenia, Spain, Sweden, Switzerland, the United Kingdom, and the United States.

REFERENCES

Boorman, Jack T., and André Icard (eds.). 2011. *Reform of the International Monetary System: The Palais Royal Initiative.* New Delhi: Sage.

Dervis, Kemal. 2005. *A Better Globalization: Legitimacy, Governance and Reform.* Washington, DC: Brookings Institution Press for the Center for Global Development.

Dervis, Kemal, and Peter Drysdale. 2014. "G-20 Summit at Five: Time for Strategic Leadership." In *The G-20 Summit at Five: Time for Strategic Leadership*, edited by Kemal Dervis and Peter Drysdale, chap 1. Washington, DC: Brookings Institution Press.

G-20 (Group of Twenty). 2009. *Leaders' Statement, the Pittsburgh Summit.* September 24–25.

Hall, Peter A., and David Soskice (eds.). 2001. *Varieties of Capitalism: The Institutional Foundations of Comparative Advantage.* New York: Oxford University Press.

ICRICT (Independent Commission for the Reform of International Corporate Taxation). 2015a. "Declaration of the Independent Commission for the Reform of International Corporate Taxation" (June). www.icrict.org.

ICRICT. 2015b. "Evaluation of the Independent Commission for the Reform of International Corporate Taxation for the Base Erosion and Profit Shifting Project of the G20 and OECD" (October). www.icrict.org.

Ocampo, José Antonio, and Joseph E. Stiglitz. 2011. "From the G-20 to a Global Economic Coordination Council." *Journal of Globalization and Development* 2 (2): article 9.

Palais Royal Initiative. 2011. "Reform of the International Monetary System: A Cooperative Approach for the 21st Century." In *Reform of the International Monetary System: The Palais Royal Initiative,* edited by Jack T. Boorman and André Icard, chap. 2. New Delhi: Sage.

Rosenthal, Gert. 2007. "The Economic and Social Council of the United Nations." In *The Oxford Handbook on the United Nations,* edited by Thomas G. Weiss and Sam Daws, chap. 7. New York: Oxford University Press.

Stiglitz, Joseph E. 2002. *Globalization and Its Discontents.* New York: Norton.

Stiglitz, Joseph E. 2006. *Making Globalization Work.* New York: Norton.

United Nations. 2009a. *Report of the Commission of Experts Convened by the President of the UN General Assembly on Reforms of the International Monetary and Financial System* (Stiglitz Commission) (September). United Nations, New York. http://www .un.org/ga/econcrisissummit/docs/FinalReport_CoE.pdf.

United Nations. 2009b. *Recommendations of the Commission of Experts Convened by the President of the UN General Assembly on Reforms of the International Monetary and Financial System.* UN General Assembly Document A/63/838 (April 29). http:// www.un.org/ga/search/view_doc.asp?symbol=A/63/838&Lang=E.

Williamson, John. 1990. "What Washington Means by Policy Reform." In *Latin American Adjustment: How Much Has Happened?* edited by John Williamson. Washington, DC: Institute for International Economics.

Woods, Ngaire. 2013. "The G20 and Global Governance." In *The Quest for Security: Protection without Protectionism and the Challenge of Global Governance,* edited by Joseph E. Stiglitz and Mary Kaldor, chap. 14. New York: Columbia University Press.

CHAPTER 21

The Fiscal Opacity Cycle

HOW AMERICA HID THE COSTS OF THE WARS IN IRAQ AND AFGHANISTAN

Linda J. Bilmes

ABSTRACT

Between 2006 and 2013, Joseph E. Stiglitz and Linda J. Bilmes co-authored a series of papers, articles, congressional testimonies, and a best-selling book[1] investigating the budgetary and economic costs of the U.S. wars in Iraq and Afghanistan. The full scale of those costs exceeded $3 trillion, including long-term disability benefits and medical care for veterans, war-related increases in the Pentagon base budget, social-economic burdens on veterans and costs to the economy.

Most of this amount was hidden from public view. This chapter examines how it was possible for the United States to commit trillions of dollars to the "post–9/11" conflicts with almost no public debate or accounting for the expenditures. The chapter shows that the methods used to pay for these conflicts differed from the methods used in previous U.S. wars such as Vietnam and Korea. The current wars have been funded through emergency and other mechanisms that circumvented congressional budget rules and kept war spending outside regular budget caps; bypassing standard systems of reporting that ensure transparency and accountability. The chapter examines several contributory factors to this lack of fiscal transparency, including (a) a disengaged public who neither fought in the military nor bore the cost of the conflicts in the form of higher taxes; (b) a military that relied on private contractors to an unprecedented degree; and (c) weak oversight that failed to provide accountability for spending. This led to a "fiscal opacity cycle" in which Congress and the executive branch were able the fund the wars without making budgetary trade-offs against other national priorities.

The lack of accountability for war spending had a real and significant impact on policy choices and outcomes. The impact included increased overspending, waste, profiteering and corruption, poor provision for military veterans of these wars, and nonstrategic military spending.

INTRODUCTION

The United States wars in Iraq and Afghanistan are the longest and most expensive conflicts in U.S. history. Since 2001, U.S. expenditures for military operations in Afghanistan, Iraq, and the surrounding region have amounted to $4.4 to $6 trillion,[2] taking into account medical care and disability compensation for veterans, structural increases to the military health care system, replenishment of equipment and weaponry, restoring the Reserves and National Guards to pre-war levels of readiness, social and economic costs, and conservative estimates for maintaining a long-term military and diplomatic presence in the region.

Direct budgetary outlays for the conflicts exceeded $2 trillion in the period 2001–2016, not including war-related spending in the U.S. Departments of Energy, State, Labor, Social Security, Medicare, Homeland Security, and the National Security Agency; state and local governments; and indirect costs at the Pentagon. The large sums borrowed to finance operations in Iraq and Afghanistan will also impose substantial long-term debt servicing costs. Future interest on money borrowed to finance the wars is excluded in these figures.[3]

Apart from the huge sums involved, there are three striking features of this spending.

First, the largest portion of that bill is yet to be paid. Since 2001, the United States has expanded the quality, quantity, availability, and eligibility of benefits for military personnel and veterans. This has led to unprecedented growth in the Department of Veterans Affairs (VA) and the Department of Defense budgets. In addition to the immediate requirements to provide medical care, there is at least $1 trillion in accrued liabilities for providing lifetime medical costs and disability compensation for those who have survived injuries. These benefits will increase further over the next forty years as veterans' age and require medical attention and disability compensation.[4] Long-term deferred costs also include structural increases to military personnel and health care systems; depreciation of military equipment; and maintaining a long-term military and diplomatic presence in the region. There are also far-reaching social costs, including the costs of impaired quality of life; as well as economic and financial costs.[5]

Second, this spending has taken place "off-budget." Unlike any other war in U.S. history, these conflicts have been funded almost entirely through extraordinary budget mechanisms that circumvent the regular congressional budget process, either partially or entirely. Between 2001 through 2015, Congress enacted some $2 trillion in direct appropriations for the wars in twenty-seven separate bills.[6] All but two of them were designated as "emergency" or "Overseas Contingency Operations" (OCO).[7] Unlike the regular defense and domestic budgets, these types of appropriations were not subject to congressional budget caps; therefore Congress did not have to choose between war funding and other spending.

Third, there is no official record of total expenditures or accounting for how money has been spent. Estimates of total budgetary costs[8] range from $1.7 trillion to more than $4.4 trillion but the constant among those who have attempted to tally it up is that no one really knows[9] (Belasco 2009, 2011, 2014; Stiglitz and Bilmes 2008, 2012; Edwards 2010; Watson Institute/Brown University 2011, 2015). The Congressional Budget Office (CBO), Congressional Research Service (CRS), Government Accountability Office (GAO), Inspector Generals, and auditors have reported that they cannot fully account for where the money has been spent. The Pentagon has reported "lost visibility" over tens of billions of dollars. Defense analysts have been unable to explain why the direct operating costs have risen from $1 million per troop in 2008 to $4.9 million per troop in FY 2017[10]—a 490 percent increase. Even taking into account the "known factors" such as operating tempo of the war, the size of the troop force, and the use of equipment and weapons, the CRS noted that "none of these factors appear to be enough to explain the size of and continuation in increases in cost" (Belasco 2011). Nor can this increase be explained by the small amounts to date appropriated for military activities to fight ISIL (Heeley and Wheeler 2016).

How can it be that there is no official record, explanation, or even a framework for tallying the full costs for America's most expensive war?

The absence of any account for war expenditures is contrary to the global push for transparency.[11] As Stiglitz observes, "There is, in democratic societies, a basic right to know, to be informed about what the government is doing and why . . . there should be a strong presumption in favor of transparency and openness in government" (Stiglitz 1999). This idea has taken root worldwide, promoted by the World Bank, the

International Monetary Fund (IMF), and the United Nations. In the past thirty years, more than 100 countries have enacted "right to freedom of information (RTI)" laws[12] (Mendel 2014). Transparency is linked to better accountability, civic engagement, and reduced corruption (Fung, Graham, and Weil 2007; Khagram, Fung, and De Renzio 2013). Some have even hailed transparency as a "basic human right" (Birkinshaw 2006).

The United States has been at the forefront of this effort. The public "right to know" is enshrined in popular culture, based on several articles of the U.S. Constitution (Wiggins 1956). Over the past half-century, the United States has enacted the Freedom of Information Act (FOIA 1966), the "Sunshine Act" (1976), and numerous laws and executive orders that expanded the public's access to government information.

Presidents George W. Bush and Barack Obama both took steps to expand the disclosure of government spending.[13] President Bush signed the Federal Funding Accountability Act in 2006, which required full disclosure to the public of all entities receiving federal funds, and established the "USAspending.gov" website. On taking office, President Obama signed two executive orders further expanding fiscal transparency, calling on the Office of Management and Budget to promote openness throughout the executive branch and pledging that his administration would be "the most open in history" (Obama 2009).

This chapter will show that despite a nominal U.S. desire to foster "transparency" in government, the executive and legislative branches adopted policies that effectively hid the costs of the post–9/11 wars. The spending for these wars was concealed by a variety of budget tricks, including circumventing regular appropriations pathways, deferring payments, combining war and non-war expenditures, underestimating depreciation and financing operations through debt. Hence unlike any previous U.S. war, the budget for the Iraq and Afghanistan wars is nearly invisible—a "ghost budget."

Three main factors played out during these conflicts that enabled the United States to continue funding the war in this unprecedented manner. These were

1. Historically low levels of public participation and engagement, in terms of both military service and financial contribution
2. Unprecedented use of private defense contractors to conduct the war
3. Limited oversight and monitoring of war spending

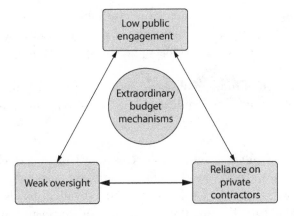

Figure 21.1 Fiscal Opacity Cycle

These three factors were self-reinforcing and emerged as a circular process (the "fiscal opacity cycle") shown in figure 21.1.

EXTRAORDINARY BUDGET MECHANISMS

Hiding trillions of dollars in government spending is not easy. To do this, Congress and the executive branch used the structural mechanisms of paying for the war as an "emergency," conflating war and non-war military appropriations, and deferring much of the spending to the future.

These practices were known to be a budget ruse. During the 2008 presidential campaign, Barack Obama criticized the use of hidden appropriations and pledged to end them if elected. In his first presidential address to Congress, Obama said: "For seven years, we have been a nation at war, No longer will we hide its price" and called for "an honest, more accurate and fiscally responsible estimate of federal spending [on the wars] . . . that would end "budget gimmicks and wasteful spending."

Yet, the Obama administration continued the same practices with only minor adjustments. Funding for the wars was designated as "Overseas Contingency Operations" in the FY 2011 budget, but this was a distinction without a difference. Like emergency funds, "OCO" was exempt from budget caps and sequestration requirements. The Pentagon was required to designate a "placeholder" amount for OCO funding in advance, but this could be changed when it was actually submitted. OCO evolved into an extra, separate military budget, containing a mixture of war funding and non-war funding that was subject to its own set of rules and virtually impossible to question. The process continued to be an end-run around the congressional apparatus for controlling and vetting appropriations.

This method of funding obscured fiscal accountability in three main ways: (1) off-budget funding; (2) co-mingling of war and non-war monies; and (3) deferred spending.

1. *Off-budget funding*: Funding designated by Congress as "emergency" or "OCO" does not count against government spending caps[14] and bears a lower threshold for justifying and providing details about the money requested. The statutory definition of emergency spending is "unanticipated . . . sudden . . . urgent . . . unforeseen . . . and temporary"[15]— where the intent is to disburse money quickly in dire situations such as earthquakes, or similar conditions in which detailed budgetary reviews would cause an unacceptable delay. Congress has used special supplemental emergency/OCO bills to pay for nearly all the expenditures related to Iraq and Afghanistan since 2001. By contrast, during the Korean and Vietnam wars, Congress quickly shifted from the initial use of "emergency" supplemental funding to integrate most war appropriations into the regular defense budget (Martin 2011).[16]

2. *Co-mingling of war/non-war monies*: The purpose of supplemental war funding, according to Congress is for *incremental* expenses related to the war.[17] However, there is no specific definition of "incremental" and the OCO and emergency designations can be applied to *any* account. In practice this means that war spending is deeply buried among hundreds of thousands of individual line item expenditures in the defense budget with no straightforward way to disaggregate these costs. Expenditures for Iraq and Afghanistan were intermingled (e.g., money was appropriated for construction, equipment, and personnel in both theaters) so as to make the two conflicts inseparable from a fiscal viewpoint.

The Department of Defense grew by $1 trillion between 2001 and 2014 (Belasco 2014) in addition to receiving at least $1.7 trillion in extra war spending. Some line items were clearly related to the war even though they were not categorized as such, including increased medical costs for troops deployed to the war theater, recruiting bonuses, and expenses related to the National Guards and Reservists participating in the wars (Stiglitz and Bilmes 2006, 2008; Bilmes 2007, 2013). However, much of the increased regular appropriations were supporting equipment, weapons, technology, and other procurement where it was not possible to determine the war versus non-war breakdown.

Compared to the Korean and Vietnam wars, the post–9/11 period was distinctive because war spending was not integrated into the regular defense appropriations process. In both previous eras, the president, the Pentagon, and Congress had debated the need for war funding, and had paid for the war through a combination of tax increases, nondefense spending cuts, and deferred routine defense spending (all of which were robustly debated). Since 2001, however, the additional money needed to fight the wars was appropriated through the last-minute emergency supplemental bills (with virtually no debate); or in the OCO budget, in which the need to be "war-related" was applied inconsistently.

The Pentagon and Congress have changed the definition of "war-related" several times. Initially, war requests were supposed to be directly related to the operations in Iraq and Afghanistan. In FY 2007, the Pentagon expanded "war-related" to include the "longer" war on terror, which meant that nearly anything could be requested this way. In 2009, the Office of Management and Budget (OMB) restored parts of the earlier "war-related" criteria, but adopted a broader geographic span, to include not only Iraq and Afghanistan but Pakistan, Kazakhstan, the Horn of Africa, the Persian Gulf, the Indian Ocean, and other countries. Given that a high percentage of military spending is multiyear funding for activities that take place over a period of time, it became almost impossible to disentangle war and non-war spending.

3. *Deferred spending.* Third, the government significantly expanded programs, benefits, and eligibility rules that will increase the long-term costs of the wars. Compensation and benefits were raised by 47 percent for Reservists and National Guards, primarily in the form of long-term deferred benefits (GAO 2007). Veterans' benefits (including eligibility, rate of compensation, physical and mental health care, and other benefits) were expanded significantly. These include "accrued" costs which have been promised, but not yet paid. Stiglitz and Bilmes have estimated that higher survival rates from injuries, better medical treatments, more generous disability compensation, and near-epidemic levels of physical and mental health conditions among returning troops mean that the cost of providing lifetime disability and health care benefits will surpass $1 trillion (Bilmes 2013; Stiglitz and Bilmes 2012). Other deferred spending includes $40 billion in concurrent military benefits, adjustments to Social Security Disability Insurance, and payments for contractor disability claims (Bilmes 2013).

The sheer volume of money, contracts, and off-budget financing of the wars and the commitments to large future expenditures that were not accounted for represent "constructed barriers" to fiscal transparency (Heald 2012). The question remains as to why this historically unprecedented pattern has persisted over fifteen years, with little serious opposition or questioning.

The literature on war finance does not provide a satisfactory answer. Budgets are usually described as being incremental, providing in a normative sense both a framework for society to reconcile competing demands for scarce resources and ensuring fiscal stability. Both the Korean and Vietnam wars followed this pattern (Wildavsky 1974). By contrast, the post–9/11 wars have been funded outside of the regular budget negotiation process, thus avoiding the need to reconcile competing demands. The economic environment (low interest rates, high demand for U.S. debt, and low inflation) has allowed the government to finance these expenditures entirely through debt, pretending that money is not scarce.

This chapter focuses on one aspect of this situation, which is the lack of transparency and accountability for these expenditures. There were three important factors that contributed to this fiscal opacity: (1) a disengaged public, (2) increased participation by private contractors, and (3) weak oversight. These factors were interrelated and reinforced each other, creating the fiscal opacity cycle.

HISTORICALLY LOW LEVELS OF PUBLIC PARTICIPATION AND ENGAGEMENT IN TERMS OF BOTH MILITARY SERVICE AND FINANCIAL CONTRIBUTION

The absence of conscription and the use of an all-volunteer force and private contract support combined with historically low taxes reduced public interest in the wars, lowered media attention, and took pressure off Congress to demand accountability. This made it easier for Congress and the executive branch to choose the politically expedient method of funding the wars using "emergency" off-budget money financed by debt.

The wars in Iraq and Afghanistan were the first major U.S. conflicts fought entirely by a combination of an "all-volunteer" military force (AVF) and large-scale use of private contractors.[18] The percentage of the population mobilized in the armed forces is small relative to the population in comparison to previous conflicts.[19] Less than 1 percent of the U.S. adult population was deployed to the combat zones with no threat of conscription for the remainder. The only time the nation had a lower percentage of its young people serving was during a brief period between World War I and World War II.

The Afghanistan and Iraq conflicts were also the only significant U.S. wars in which the (current) general population was not obliged to bear the financial burden in the form of higher taxes. Hormats (2007) and Webber and Wildavsky (1986) have documented that taxes were raised during the Spanish-American War, War of 1812, Civil War, World Wars I and II, and the Korean and Vietnam wars.[20] These taxes were significant. For example in 1914, Congress enacted a progressive income tax, with the top rate hitting 77 percent for incomes over $500,000. During World War II, Congress increased the top income tax rate to 91 percent, expanded the number of people required to pay taxes, and launched a massive war bond program. No previous war has been financed entirely through debt.[21]

The tax burden of the post–9/11 wars was significantly lower than during the wars in Korea and Vietnam. Not only were *top* marginal rates much higher (table 21.1), but the threshold for paying higher rates was lower. For example, the threshold for paying the top marginal rate of 39.6 percent for a household today is $417,000. Households earning the dollar equivalent of $417,000 during the Korean and Vietnam wars would have paid at least 71 percent and 63 percent, respectively (figure 21.2). In 1953, the threshold for paying a similar rate of 41 percent was merely $103,000 in today's dollars. Households earning $103,000 in today's dollars would pay 25 percent, whereas the equivalent taxpayers during the Korea and Vietnam wars would have paid 41 percent and 32 percent, respectively.[22]

Table 21.1   Comparison of Top Marginal Tax Rates During Korea, Vietnam, and Post–9/11 Wars

War (and final year)	Top Marginal Tax Rate (%)
Korea (1953)	92
Vietnam (1969)	77
OEF/OIF (2003–2013)	35.0
OEF/OIF (2014–2016)	39.60

Note: OEF: Operation Enduring Freedom (Afghanistan); OIF: Operation Iraqi Freedom (Iraq).

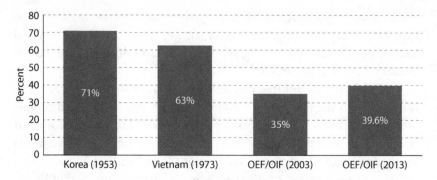

Figure 21.2 Comparison of Wartime Tax Rates During Korea, Vietnam, Afghanistan, and Iraq Wars

Note: Comparison of wartime tax rates for households earning the equivalent of $417,000 (the threshold for paying top marginal tax rates in 2013). OEF: Operation Enduring Freedom (Afghanistan); OIF: Operation Iraqi Freedom (Iraq).

Source: "Federal Individual Income Tax Rate Adjusted for Inflation." *Tax Foundation*.

By contrast, the period of Iraq/Afghanistan conflicts saw a series of tax cuts. In 2001 and 2003, the top four marginal income tax rates were reduced, the tax rate on capital gains and dividends was cut, the estate tax virtually phased out, the child tax credit increased, and taxes on married couples were lowered. Taxes were not raised again until 2011, when the deal to avoid the "fiscal cliff" restored top marginal income tax rates to their pre-2001 levels. However, unlike Presidents Truman and Johnson, respectively, the 2011 President Obama did not link tax policy to the costs of the wars (Miller 2007).

Moreover, the current wars were paid for by deficit spending, which meant that the financial burden of the wars was not borne by current taxpayers but rather deferred to the next generation. This led to the illusion that the war was free. Financing the war entirely through debt is an intergenerational trade-off, which is difficult to quantify, because the current generation may apply a different discount rate to futures ones.

The combination of low participation in the military and low tax obligations to pay for the war helped create an environment in which the costs of the war could be hidden. Russett (1990) and Parks (1957) provide support for this argument, showing that Americans are most interested in foreign policy when it has the greatest potential to affect them directly; and that public opinion can influence the level of military spending. There is a phenomenon in the literature of "rallying around the flag" during national crises which, unless the crisis is sustained, dissipates quickly and the public returns to its previous levels of attention and support (Russett 1990).

The U.S. public overwhelmingly supported the 2001 invasion of Afghanistan and a majority favored the 2003 effort to topple Saddam Hussein, but in both cases, polls show that public attention and enthusiasm for the conflicts tapered off after the initial period, and public awareness of the wars remained at low levels throughout the conflicts. Research on longitudinal public opinion surveys and shares of the "newshole" devoted to the wars show low and declining public interest and knowledge about the wars. For example, in April 2004, 55 percent of Americans were able to identify correctly the approximate number of U.S. fatalities in Iraq but by March 2008, only 28 percent could do so, with declines across every demographic group. Moreover, a majority of respondents *under*estimated the number of U.S. fatalities, which by that point had reached nearly 4000.[23] News coverage of the Iraq War fell during this period from 15 percent to 3 percent of the "newshole." By 2011, it had fallen to 0.6 percent on this metric.

Apart from a brief spike in public awareness at the onset of the "surge," public attention to the wars (measured by relative importance) has remained below 20 percent. This contrasts with the Vietnam era, when 45 percent of the public said that foreign affairs, focusing on Southeast Asia, was "the most important problem facing the country" from early 1965 through 1973 (Russett 1990).

UNPRECEDENTED RELIANCE ON PRIVATE CONTRACTORS

Throughout the Afghanistan and Iraq conflicts, the U.S. military has relied heavily on private contractors to supplement the "all-volunteer force." Contractors were hired for virtually every military function, including deterrence, combat operations, stabilization, and civil governance. The number of paid contractors working in the war zone exceeded the number of military troops during most years of the conflict. The ratio of private contractors per uniformed U.S. personnel was 1.2:1; by comparison, the ratio was 0.005:1 in the Gulf War and 0.02:1 in Vietnam.[24]

Reliance on contractors forms an "intrinsic" barrier (Heald 2012) to transparency by increasing the complexity of the process and number of participants in the conflicts. The integration of private firms into the conflicts also blurs the lines of financial accountability. FOIA law permits an exemption for "trade secrets and commercial or financial information obtained from a person and privileged or confidential." Many companies interpreted this to mean that they were not obliged to disclose their financial data, on the basis that it could jeopardize their competitive position. This led to a lack of compliance with financial reporting requirements as well as lax enforcement by the government in collecting this information. In many cases, it was impossible to know if money was being well spent or not.

The U.S. government bore the cost of compensating the vast contract workforce for insurance, injuries, and compensation, despite having little or no control over the individuals involved. However, the United States does not collect data on how many individuals work on any given contract, nor on casualties that occur in this workforce. Nevertheless, the Department of Labor reimburses U.S. companies for hazard insurance, which they are required to purchase for their own and subcontracted staff. The Labor Department also pays the insurance companies that underwrite the claims for the cost of actual outlays for disability and injury awards.

Numerous reports by congressional and external investigators focus on the inadequate accountability and lack of oversight for money spent on contract support, leading to wasteful spending, profiteering from contracts, and corruption. According to a top-level Pentagon report, the Department of Defense paid $573.7 billion to more than 300 contractors involved in civil fraud cases during the first decade after 9/11. Another $255 billion was paid to 54 contractors convicted of criminal fraud.[25]

A number of scholars have explored how the participation of the private sector changes the nature of the armed forces in terms of incentive structures, managerial complexity, chain-of-command structures, and other aspects. Martha Minow specifically focuses on the "lack of transparency" in the use of private contractors, writing that "The large sums of money involved [in private contracting] jeopardize the effectiveness of military activities, the professionalism of the military, the integrity of the legislative process and foreign policy decision making, public confidence in the government, national self-interest, and the stability of the world order" (Minow 2005).

WEAK OVERSIGHT AND ACCOUNTABILITY FOR WAR EXPENDITURES
DURING OR AFTER THE PERIOD

During a conflict, the priority is to win. It is understandable that the military may need to withhold the details of some operations, and that not every penny can be accounted for. However, in the literature addressing how to trade-off the need for secrecy in national security versus transparency for public accountability, one of the recurrent themes is the importance of oversight. Stiglitz (1999), Florini (2007), Hood and Heald (2006), Sagar (2013), Kitrosser (2015), Berman (2014), Colaresi (2014), and others have pointed out that oversight is vital in situations where disclosure may conflict with national security needs. Most espouse the need for *retrospective oversight*, such that the details may be examined *ex post* (Colaresi 2014; Sagar 2013; Kitrosser 2015).

Nominally, the United States has a robust standing fiscal oversight structure for both real time and *ex-post* oversight. This includes congressional subcommittees, budget and evaluation agencies (CRS, CBO), audit agencies (e.g., GAO), as well as Inspector Generals, accountants, and quasi-governmental agencies. Since 2003, the United States has also convened special oversight agents including the Commission on Wartime Contracting; the Special Inspector Generals for Iraq (SIGIR), Afghanistan Reconstruction (SAGAR),[26] and numerous other commissions and consultants hired to review specific topics.

By and large, this method was not effective from the perspective of tracking post–9/11 war costs. Budget overseers were thwarted because their processes relied on having access to standard data inputs, such as budget justification materials and cost and operational details. Many of these inputs were simply not produced in the emergency and OCO budgets. The Pentagon effectively ceded control of costs to its private contractors, so many databases are incomplete.[27] Accounting oversight thus failed due to the combination of weak systems and lack of information from private contractors who played a significant role in wartime operations. The key oversight agencies have expressed frustration, anger, and exasperation with the lack of information.[28]

Weak government accounting systems make it easier to hide the true costs of a war, if the system ignores deferred spending and indirect costs. U.S. government accounting systems do not document most items in a way that enable an easy accounting of the resources directly used or the full budgetary impact. For example, the CBO uses short-term funding conventions that do not account for costs that occur beyond a ten-year time horizon (thus ignoring deferred veterans benefits), and the Pentagon ignores the long-term costs of depreciating equipment.[29] The U.S. Treasury did not reflect the financing costs of the war in terms of how much the war contributed to the growing national debt or to interest payments.

However, the weak oversight for war spending was exacerbated by the U.S. government wishing to hide the costs of the wars—which were becoming increasingly unpopular—from the electorate. There is evidence that the government deliberately withheld information that was needed for fiscal oversight. For example, Senator James Webb, a member of the Commission on Wartime Contracting, said: "One of the eye-openers for me as a member of the Senate Foreign Relations Committee was when we had testimony from the State Department discussing $32 billion of programs that were going into Iraq reconstruction. As someone who spent a good bit of time as a bean-counter in the Pentagon, I asked if they would provide us . . . a list of the contracts that had been let, the amounts of the contracts, a description of what the contracts were supposed to do, and what the results were. And they could not provide us that list. For months we asked them. And they were unable to come up with a list of the contracts that had been let."[30]

CONSEQUENCES

The net result that the war costs as presented to the U.S. public were a partial snapshot, based on faulty accounting and incomplete budget and financial data. Public disengagement, private contractors, and an erosion of the oversight system created a "fiscal opacity cycle" in which the costs of war were largely hidden from view and the public had little incentive to press for fiscal transparency.

Even assuming that the government did not deliberately set out to hide the costs of the war from public view—the resulting lack of fiscal transparency produced many of the outcomes predicted by those who champion transparency. Fiscal transparency is held to promote accountability, civic engagement, and to decrease corruption. In this case, there was less accountability for taxpayer money, the population was disengaged from major decisions about the war, and there was widespread profiteering, waste, and fraud. Moreover the lack of controls over war expenditures led to specific negative consequences for veterans and for the regular military.

CONSEQUENCES FOR VETERANS

From 2007 to 2010, Stiglitz and Bilmes argued that the Department of Veterans Affairs (VA) was "overwhelmed" and unprepared for the demands of the conflicts (Bilmes and Stiglitz 2010; Bilmes 2007). This prediction was based on their discovery that the Pentagon was keeping two sets of casualty reports: a complete list of "non-mortal" casualties (for internal purposes only); and an abridged list, which reported only a subset of injuries sustained in combat, as narrowly defined. This second list, which excluded injuries incurred during training accidents, transport, accidents, disease, etc., was one-third the size of the total list. Yet, this second list was being shared with the media and the VA—resulting in the VA requesting inadequate funds for planning, medical care, and staffing.[31]

Stiglitz and Bilmes argued that all of these service members would be receiving costly health care and compensation, regardless of how they came by their injuries. Indeed, they pointed out that post–9/11 troops would require higher levels of disability compensation and medical care than previous generations of veterans due to the higher survival rates from injuries, better medical treatment, more generous disability compensation, and incidence of physical and mental health conditions among returning service members. They testified to Congress in 2010 that the cost of meeting obligations to the current veterans would be extremely high—and that it was being concealed.[32]

Since then, the demand has risen even faster than Stiglitz and Bilmes's estimates. The number of veterans seeking care in the VA system has risen from 4.2 million in 2001 to 6.6 million in 2014 (Baggalmen 2014)—despite the decline in the total number of U.S. veterans from 26 to 21.5 million in this time period. The VA budget has tripled (from $70 billion to $185 billion), nearly doubled its workforce to 353,000, and it has become the fastest-growing department in the federal government.

Yet, the VA has struggled to meet demand—and largely fallen short. The problems include lengthy waiting times at some VA hospitals, inability to fill thousands of vacancies for medical staff, and a lack of funding to pay for badly needed infrastructure repairs. The VA's efforts to meet its own revised patient targets has led to widespread falsification of data related to patient access to doctors and other data manipulation. There is a chronic backlog of disability claims arising from the overwhelming number of veterans seeking benefits. Efforts to expedite the processing of claims have produced an expensive secondary backlog in the number of legal appeals.

Many of these problems would have been lessened if basic information about veterans' injuries and the costs of treatment and compensation had been shared—both within the government and with the public. This situation persists today. As of July 2016, the Department of Defense reports that 52,442 troops have been "wounded in action" in and around Iraq and Afghanistan. However, more than one million veterans of Iraq and Afghanistan have been treated at VA hospitals and clinics, representing 59 percent of all eligible service members.[33] By hiding the true number of service members who are wounded or injured, the government minimizes the scale of medical problems and shifts much of the burden to the veterans and their families.

CONSEQUENCES FOR NATIONAL SECURITY

Costly promises made during the war have reduced the flexibility of the Department of Defense to fund other priorities. These decisions extend far beyond the initial choices made to invade Afghanistan and Iraq and to expand U.S. military involvement in both countries; they include growing the defense medical system; increasing military pay, benefits, and retirement pensions; mobilizing National Guards and Reservists and granting them military benefits, supplementary pay increases, expansion of TRICARE subsidies, allowing "concurrent receipt" for veterans; and constructing new state-of-the-art medical facilities, such as the $4.5 billion Walter Reed National Military Medical Center in Bethesda, Maryland.

These decisions may be necessary to sustain the all-volunteer force, which depends on a pipeline of recruits, and is sensitive to economic inducements (Simon and Warner 2007). But from a budgetary standpoint, these have been hidden costs of the war, in which cumulatively hundreds of billions of dollars of long-term costs have been added into the system without any discussion about how to pay for them. The military is already reeling under the large and rapidly growing cost of the TRICARE health care system, which has grown from $19 billion to $58 billion since 2001, and has become the fastest-rising cost in the entire defense budget. Additionally, Congress has refused to allow the Pentagon to rescind its "temporary" military pay raises enacted during the war years. The diversion of defense budget dollars to support these activities, as well as veterans, will dominate future defense spending and are set to continue, with much of this growth now "baked in" to the consolidated national security budget. Assuming this pattern continues, there will be a much smaller amount of an already-shrinking defense budget available for core military functions. As a consequence of these wartime spending choices, the United States will face constraints in funding investments in personnel and diplomacy, training, research and development, energy efficiency, and new military initiatives. One likely result is that the United States will tilt in the direction of fewer military personnel in the forces, due to the long-term "baked-in" cost of maintaining active-duty troops. Budget considerations will favor greater investment in unmanned weaponry, robotics, and other technological solutions—which may or may not be a wise choice over the longer term. The legacy of decisions taken during the Iraq and Afghanistan wars will dominate future federal budgets for decades to come.

CONCLUSION

One of Joe Stiglitz's most famous speeches was his 1999 Keynote Address to Amnesty International, "On Liberty, the Right to Know, and Public Discourse: The Role of Transparency in Public Life." He argued that the consequences of secrecy can be grave, citing for example, the Cold War and the arms race, which were exacerbated by the military concealing information about Soviet economic weakness. He included fiscal transparency as an important element of the democratic process, referencing the U.S. Savings and Loan crisis as a consequence of flawed accounting. The post–9/11 wars are another example of how damaging a lack of transparency can be, both to our economy and to our democratic system of government. Joe's contribution to this work has been profound.

NOTES

1. *The Three Trillion Dollar War: The True Cost of the Iraq Conflict* (by Joseph E. Stiglitz and Linda J. Bilmes; New York: Norton, 2008) was a *New York Times* best seller and has been translated into more than twenty languages. See also Linda J. Bilmes and Joseph E. Stiglitz, "The Long-Term Costs of Conflict: The Case the Iraq War" in *The Handbook on the Economics of Conflict* (edited by Derek L. Braddon and Keith Hartley; Cheltenham, UK: Edward Elgar, 2011) and Joseph E. Stiglitz and Linda J. Bilmes, "Estimating the Costs of War: Methodological Issues, with Applications to Iraq and Afghanistan" in *The Oxford Handbook of the Economics of Peace and Conflict* (edited by Michelle Garfinkel and Stergios Skaperdas; Oxford: Oxford University Press, 2012).

2. Based on the estimate of $4.8 trillion by the Watson Institute/Brown University "Cost of War" study (April 2016) and other economic and social costs.

3. These financing costs are estimated at $8 trillion (Watson Institute/Brown University 2015).

4. Spending for veterans' benefits peaks decades after a war. WWI veterans' benefits peaked in 1969 and for WWII in the 1980s (see Edwards 2010, 2014). See also Bilmes (2007).

5. Any estimation of macroeconomic costs, such as the link between oil prices and decisions of the Federal Reserve to loosen monetary and regulatory policy prior to the financial crisis, would raise the costs of the wars, even if only a small fraction of the "blame" is attributed to the decision to invade Iraq.

6. Including funds designated for Operation Enduring Freedom (OEF), Iraqi Freedom (OIF), Operation New Dawn (OND), and Noble Eagle; and appropriations related to the war effort for the Departments of State and Veterans Affairs.

7. The Overseas Contingency Operation (OCO) designation was introduced in 2010 to replace the terminology of "emergency" and adopted for the FY 2011 budget. The OCO budget requests were submitted with the regular defense request, but OCO funding continued to be exempt from budget caps and separate from the regular defense budget.

8. Based on the Stiglitz and Bilmes (2012) taxonomy for estimating war costs.

9. Not including debt service or economic costs.

10. Direct OCO spending per troop has risen from $1 million in 2008 to $5.9 million in FY 2017, of which $1 million could be explained by known factors (Heeley 2016). Belasco (2014) reports that per-troop costs in Afghanistan increased by 345 percent from $870,000 in FY 2011 to $3.9 million in FY 2015.

11. Transparency involves more than simply disclosing information. It also requires the "access, comprehension and use of it by the public" (Ginsberg et al. 2012).

12. Paraguay was the one-hundredth country to adopt freedom-of-information laws in September 2014 (Open Government Partnership).

13. Transparency, openness, and disclosure are related but slightly different concepts, in that "openness" might be a characteristic of the organization, and disclosure is the act of disseminating information, whereas transparency also requires external receptors capable of processing information made available (Heald 2006).

14. Each committee in Congress is allocated a specific amount of budget authority; funds designated as emergency or OCO do not count within these statutory budget limits.

15. See § 102(4) (20).

16. Other possible explanations (for example, that the military could not plan ahead sufficiently to request funds during the regular budget cycle) are not persuasive because in each year, the administration announced the supplemental war request months ahead of the budget submission.

17. The regular defense budget covers ordinary expenses such as salaries for service members, which are paid regardless of whether they are deployed. Troops are paid supplemental "hardship pay" and other benefits during wartime which may be considered an "incremental" expense.

18. The AVF was introduced in 1973. Although the military has employed contractors since the Revolutionary War, private contractors were engaged more extensively and in roles traditionally performed by the military during recent years.

19. To place participation in perspective, over 9 million military personnel served on active duty in the Vietnam era (August 1964 to May 1975). In the current conflicts, 2.8 million Americans have served over 15 years, since October 2001.

20. The 1991 Gulf War was mostly financed by U.S. allies.

21. Possibly excepting the Revolutionary War, during which the Colonies borrowed from France.

22. Calculated using "U.S. Federal Individual Income Tax Rates History, 1862–2013 (Nominal and Inflation-Adjusted Brackets)," Tax Foundation (October 2013) and the IRS's Tax Statistics database. "SOI Tax Stats—Individual Statistical Tables by Tax Rate and Income Percentile," IRS. https://www.irs.gov/uac/SOI-Tax-Stats-Individual-Statistical-Tables-by-Tax-Rate-and-Income-Percentile (2016).

23. Project for Excellence in Journalism "News Content Index" (February 2008).

24. Defense Science Board, "Contractor Logistics in Support of Contingency Operations," June 2014.

25. Report to Congress on Contracting Fraud, Under Secretary of Defense for Acquisition, Technology and Logistics (October 2011).

26. These were set up to investigate the $110 billion (Afghanistan) and $62 billion (Iraq) appropriated for reconstruction spending.

27. For example, "SPOT" or "Synchronized Pre-Deployment Operational Tracker" set up in 2008, which was supposed to track spending information on contracts awarded in the State Department, U.S. Agency for International Development (USAID), and the Pentagon. In 2010, GAO reported that "SPOT still cannot reliably track information on contracts, assistance instruments and associated personnel in Iraq and Afghanistan." GAO further stated that the data on personnel was unreliable due to "significant over- and undercounting."

28. See for example, GAO-11-886, "DOD, State, and USAID Cannot Fully Account for Contracts, Assistance Instruments, and Associated Personnel"; GAO-11-355, "U.S. Efforts to Vet Non-U.S. Vendors Need Improvement"; GAO-11-1, "DOD, State and USAID Face Continued Challenges in Tracking Contracts, Assistance Instruments, and Associated Personnel."

29. These structural flaws did not always increase the costs of war—in some cases, they obscured cost *savings*. For example, the United States reported that it saved some $12 billion per year that had been required to enforce the Northern and Southern "No-Fly" zones over Iraq for a decade prior to the U.S. invasion (Stiglitz and Bilmes 2008).

30. August 31, 2011—Final Commission on Wartime Contracting in Iraq and Afghanistan News Briefing about its Final Report to Congress.

31. Using the "Freedom of Information Act (FOIA), Bilmes and Stiglitz uncovered this discrepancy in 2007.

32. Stiglitz and Bilmes (2008) predicted that by 2012, some 41 to 46 percent of new veterans would be enrolled in the VA health care system and that 39 to 43 percent would have applied for disability benefits. The percentage of Iraq and Afghanistan veterans receiving government medical care has grown to 59 percent of the total.

33. "Analysis of VA Health Care Utilization among Operation Enduring Freedom (OEF), Operation Iraqi Freedom (OIF), and Operation New Dawn (OND) Veterans," VHA, U.S. Department of Veterans Affairs (June 2014).

REFERENCES

Baggalmen, Erin. 2014. "The Number of Veterans that use VA Healthcare Services: A Factsheet." Congressional Research Service, June 3.

Belasco, A. 2014 (Updated: 2005, 2006, 2007, 2008, 2009, 2010, 2011). "The Cost of Iraq, Afghanistan, and Other Global War on Terror Operations Since 9/11." Congressional Research Service. United States Defense Technical Information Center No. CRS-7-5700, CRS-RL33110.

Berman, E. 2014. *An Enduring Tension: Balancing National Security and Our Access to Information*. New York: International Debate Education Association.

Bilmes, L. 2007. "Soldiers Returning from Iraq and Afghanistan: The Long-Term Costs of Providing Veterans Medical Care and Disability Benefits." *Faculty Research Working Paper Series*, RWP07-001 Ed. Cambridge, MA: John F. Kennedy School of Government, Harvard University.

Bilmes, L., and J. Stiglitz. 2008. "Hidden Wounds and Accounting Tricks: Disguising the True Costs" In *Lessons from Iraq: Avoiding the Next War*, edited by Miriam Pemberton and William D. Hartung. Boulder, CO: Paradigm Publishers.

Bilmes, L., and J. E. Stiglitz. 2010. "Statement to the U.S. House of Representatives Committee on Veterans Affairs Hearing on the True Cost of War." Washington, DC (September 30).

Bilmes, L., and J. Stiglitz. 2011. "The Long-Term Costs of Conflict: The Case of the Iraq War." In *Handbook on the Economics of Conflict*, edited by Derek L. Braddon and Keith Hartley. Cheltenham, UK: Edward Elgar.

Bilmes, L. 2013. "The Financial Legacy of Iraq and Afghanistan: How Wartime Spending Decisions Will Constrain Future National Security Budgets." *Faculty Research Working Paper Series*, 13-006 Ed. Cambridge, MA: John F. Kennedy School of Government, Harvard University.

Birkinshaw, P. 2006. "Transparency as a Human Right." In *Transparency: The Key to Better Governance?*, edited by Christopher Hood and David Heald. Oxford: Published for the British Academy by Oxford University Press.

Colaresi, M. P. 2014. *Democracy Declassified: The Secrecy Dilemma in National Security*. Oxford: Oxford University Press.

Edwards, R. D. 2010. "A Review of War Costs in Iraq and Afghanistan." NBER Working Paper Series 16163. Cambridge, MA: National Bureau of Economic Research.

Edwards, R. D. 2014. "U.S. War Costs: Two Parts Temporary, One Part Permanent." *Journal of Public Economics* 113:54–66.

Florini, A. 2007. *The Right to Know: Transparency for an Open World*. New York: Columbia University Press.

Fung, A., M. Graham, and D. Weil. 2007. *Full Disclosure: The Perils and Promise of Transparency*. Cambridge: Cambridge University Press.

Ginsberg, W., M. P. Carey, L. E. Halchin, and N. Keegan. 2012. "Government Transparency and Secrecy: An Examination of Meaning and Its Use in the Executive Branch." Washington, DC: *Congressional Research Services (CRS) Reports and Issue Briefs*.

Heald, D. 2006. "Varieties of Transparency." In *Transparency: The Key to Better Governance?*, edited by C. Hood and D. Heald. Oxford: Published for the British Academy by Oxford University Press.

Heald, D. 2012. "Why Is Transparency about Public Expenditure So Elusive?" *International Review of Administrative Sciences* 78 (1):30–49.

Heeley, L., and A. Wheeler. 2016. "Defense Divided: Overcoming the Challenges of Overseas Contingency Operations." Washington, DC: Stimson Center.

Hood, C., and D. Heald (eds.). 2006. *Transparency: The Key to Better Governance?* Oxford: Published for the British Academy by Oxford University Press.

Hormats, R. D. 2007. *The Price of Liberty: Paying for America's Wars,* 1st ed. New York: Times Books.

Khagram, S., A. Fung, and P. De Renzio. 2013. *Open Budgets: The Political Economy of Transparency, Participation, and Accountability.* Washington, DC: Brookings Institution Press.

Kitrosser, H. 2015. *Reclaiming Accountability: Transparency, Executive Power, and the U.S. Constitution.* Chicago: University of Chicago Press.

Martin, Aaron L. 2011. "Paying for War: Funding for U.S. Military Operations Since 2001." Dissertation, Pardee RAND Graduate School. ProQuest.

Mendel, T. 2014. *Right to Information Series: Recent Spread of RTI Legislation.* Policy Note. Washington, DC: World Bank.

Miller, R. 2007. *Funding Extended Conflicts: Korea, Vietnam, and the War on Terror.* Westport, CT: Praeger Security International.

Minow, M. 2005. "Outsourcing Power: How Privatizing Military Efforts Challenges Accountability, Professionalism, and Democracy." *Boston College Law Review* 46 (5):989–1026.

Obama, B. 2009. "Memorandum on Transparency and Open Government." *Weekly Compilation of Presidential Documents* (January 21).

Parks, W. 1957. "Secrecy and the Public Interest in Military Affairs." *George Washington Law Review* 26:23.

Russett, B. M. 1990. *Controlling the Sword: The Democratic Governance of National Security.* Cambridge, MA: Harvard University Press.

Sagar, R. 2013. *Secrets and Leaks: The Dilemma of State Secrecy.* Princeton, NJ: Princeton University Press.

Simon, C. J., and J. T. Warner. 2007. "Managing the All-Volunteer Force in a Time of War." *Economics of Peace and Security Journal* 2 (1):20–29.

Stiglitz, J. E. 1991. "On Liberty, the Right to Know, and Public Discourse: The Role of Transparency in Public Life." Oxford Amnesty Lecture, Oxford, United Kingdom.

Stiglitz, J., and L. Bilmes. "The Economic Costs of the Iraq War: An Appraisal Three Years After the Beginning of the Conflict." NBER Working Paper No. 12054. http://www.nber.org/papers/w12054.

Stiglitz, J. E., and L. J. Bilmes. 2008. *The Three Trillion Dollar War: The True Cost of the Iraq Conflict.* New York: Norton.

Stiglitz, J. E., and L. J. Bilmes. 2012. "Estimating the Costs of War: Methodological Issues, with Applications to Iraq and Afghanistan." In *The Oxford Handbook of the Economics of Peace and Conflict,* edited by M. R. Garfinkel and S. Skaperdas, 275–315. New York: Oxford University Press.

U.S. GAO (Government Accountability Office). 2007. *Military Personnel: DOD Needs to Establish a Strategy and Improve Transparency Over Reserve and National*

Guard Compensation to Manage Significant Growth in Cost. Washington, DC: U.S. Government Accountability Office.

U.S. GAO. 2011. *Iraq and Afghanistan DOD, State, and USAID Cannot Fully Account for Contracts, Assistance Instruments, and Associated Personnel: Report to Congressional Committees*. Washington, DC: U.S. Government Accountability Office.

Watson Institute/Brown University. 2011 (Updated: 2013, 2015). Costs of War.org.

Webber, C., and A. Wildavsky. 1986. *A History of Taxation and Expenditure in the Western World*. New York: Simon & Schuster.

Wiggins, J. 1956. *Freedom or Secrecy?* New York: Oxford University Press.

Wildavsky, A. 1974. *The Politics of the Budgetary Process*, 2nd ed. Boston: Little, Brown.

CHAPTER 22

It Works in Practice, But Would It Work in Theory?

JOSEPH STIGLITZ'S CONTRIBUTION TO OUR UNDERSTANDING
OF INCOME CONTINGENT LOANS

Bruce Chapman

BACKGROUND

What follows is an account of an important input from Joseph Stiglitz regarding the debate and evolution of the theoretical and policy potential of income contingent loans (ICLs). An important contextual issue is that ICLs have a remarkable capacity to influence the way that a particular form of government intervention can improve the workings of economies, and it is a potential that has yet to be properly and formally recognized in the profession. The contribution of Joseph Stiglitz to this issue occurred in 2013, through the auspices of a workshop organized through the International Economic Association (IEA) and held at Dhurajik Pundit University in Bangkok, and has been written in Stiglitz (2015) and Stiglitz and Yung (2014).

As background it is interesting to note that what is curious about the development of a general understanding of ICLs is that even though the first nationally based loan system of this type had been introduced in Australia nearly twenty-five years before the 2013 workshop, and the conceptual understanding of the economics of ICLs had been progressing, the theoretical underpinning of the instrument lacked a critical insight related to the role of the public sector in loan collection, and this (arguably) final piece of the jigsaw was provided by Joseph Stiglitz. This chapter provides both the background to, and the context for, an appreciation of his insights.

We begin with a definition: an ICL is a form of debt in which repayments depend on a borrower's future income, and thus their capacity to pay; this is a critical difference to normal "mortgage-type" loans in which repayments are agreed on the basis of fixed obligations with respect to time. ICLs began on a national scale in Australia in 1989 with the introduction of a college tuition loan program known as the Higher Education Contribution Scheme (HECS), in which charges were to be financed through loans to students and repaid depending on future incomes (collected through the income tax system, the Australian equivalent of the U.S. Internal Revenue Service [IRS]). Over time, variations of the system have been adopted in essence (although with parameter and design differences) in around seven countries, with the international spread of ICLs being documented in section 1.

Since the adoption of the scheme, considerable research has been done on the potential for the use of ICLs in a wide and disparate array of possible social and economic policy reforms well beyond student loans, with just about all of these being related to Australian case studies in institutional and empirical terms. There has been a small revolution in the social science research agenda in Australia with respect to ICLs, which is documented in section 2. While it is accurate to describe the spread of nonstudent loan ICL research beyond Australia as limited, there is no obvious reason for this to be true in the future.

Section 3 outlines briefly the progression of the theoretical underpinnings of the essence of ICLs over the initial fifteen years or so after HECS, a discussion that illustrates a highly unusual evolution of economic reasoning. What made this process rare, even odd, is that while the general theory of ICLs was incomplete when HECS was adopted, the Australian (and followed by other countries') ICLs operated as planned, with university enrollments progressing satisfactorily, debts being paid in an administratively efficient way, and there being no apparent adverse effects on the access of the relatively poor. We were thus in a situation pertinent to the old joke concerning academic economics and policy manifested in the question: "Well, it works in practice but would it work in theory?"

The contribution of the IEA Bangkok Workshop, and in particular the perspicacity of Joseph Stiglitz in a conceptually critical area of our understanding of ICLs, helped square the circle. The essential insight was to explain and promote the extraordinary significance of the effectiveness of government-operated ICLs; Joseph Stiglitz endorsed and supported arguments for ICLs generally, but also explained the importance for social welfare of controlling ICLs by governments. This contribution is examined in detail in section 4.

1. INTERNATIONAL ICL POLICY HISTORY

As noted, in 1989, Australia introduced a student ICL, HECS, which involved domestic higher education students being charged tuition but with the obligation to pay being deferred until debtors earned above a particular threshold of personal income (which is currently around A$54,000 per annum), at a fixed proportion of income which is (now) set at a maximum of between 4 and 8 percent. A critical aspect of the reform was that the debt would be collected by employers and remitted to the Australian Tax Office (that is, this country's equivalent to the U.S. IRS) in much the same way that personal income taxes are.

Twenty-nine years later, HECS (now known as HECS-HELP) now exists in different forms in more than a handful of countries, although scheme design, eligibility, interest rate, and debt forgiveness regimes differ widely between systems, and have changed over time in most national jurisdictions. Critically, however, the essential characteristics of the loans, income contingency and collection through the auspices of the equivalent of each country's IRS, have not been compromised.

ICLs in other countries typically take forms that are similar to the scheme initiated in Australia. Debts to cover tuition costs (and in most cases, income support) are recorded while a person is studying, and the relevant income tax authority is informed of the individual's future repayment obligation. A typical tuition debt in Australia is about 45–50 percent of the recurrent cost of higher education (which amounts to about US$5,000 per full-time equivalent annual year of study on average, although in other countries the obligation can be quite different (for example, in England the charge is close to 100 percent of the recurrent costs).

Countries other than Australia that have adopted (or likely soon will adopt) ICLs, and the year in which the arrangement first began, are as follows: New Zealand (1991), England (1998), Hungary (2001), Thailand (for 2006 only), South Korea (2011), the Netherlands (2016), and Japan. The higher education reform debate is alive and well in Ireland, where a paper explaining the problems with mortgage-type loans and offering a suggested ICL is receiving public attention (Chapman and Doris 2016). Similarly, the governments of Colombia and Brazil are currently exploring student loan reforms, away from a mortgage-type arrangement and toward an ICL.

Further, a bill was put to the U.S. Congress in 2013, which could have meant the adoption in that country of an ICL as the default option in an array of student loan choices. So-called income-based repayment options exist in the U.S. student loan provisions, but they are generally thought to be poorly designed and characterized by extraordinary complexity and other problems; take-up rates are very low. While the 2013 bill did not pass, it is widely regarded in the United States that the reform impetus toward ICLs remains (Dynarski 2014).

2. THE AUSTRALIAN INNOVATION AND ICL RESEARCH APPLICATIONS

2.1. GOVERNMENT AS A RISK MANAGER

In the Australian debate, ICLs were seen to fit easily into a conceptual framework in which a major role recognized for government involves the management and distribution of risks (Chapman 2006). The concept of risk plays a central and unifying role in current analyses of a wide range of social and political issues, and has been argued to be similar to that performed by the concept of globalization in the 1990s (Quiggin 2003).

The role of government, and particularly of the welfare state, has been reinterpreted with an increasing emphasis on risk and uncertainty, and across the social sciences there are different analytical approaches. Neoclassical economists have stressed the extent to which risk can be rationally managed using the tools of expected utility theory. Psychologists, sociologists, and various groups of other economists have stressed the limitations of expected utility theory.

When government is considered in its role as a risk manager, new aspects of both existing policies and future policy options are revealed. In *When All Else Fails*, for example, David Moss (2003) provides a fine historical analysis of the role of the state as the ultimate risk manager. Through analysis of U.S. government legislative reforms over the last 200 years, Moss promotes an understanding of the risk management role of the state, which can take many diverse forms, such as laws associated with limited liability, the application of speed limits for automobiles, national health insurance, occupational health and safety legislation, disaster relief, and Social Security.

Barr (2001) has written a similar treatment of the welfare state as that promoted by Moss, in which the potential role of government is analyzed in the context of insurance failure, which is conventionally seen in the economics literature to be a consequence of asymmetric information. In the absence of markets providing accessible and affordable insurance, Barr argues that government has a unique role to play as a "piggy bank," an efficient institution to manage and decrease the costs to citizens of the unavoidable uncertainties associated with human events. As stressed by many, there are disparate ways in which government intervention can help manage the risk of citizens, an obvious instrument outside the United States, being universal health care insurance.

In the current context, it is critical to realize that ICLs for higher education are simply a subset of the many risk management instruments available to government, a point made most explicitly in Shiller (2003). What ICLs offer, after all, is insurance against consumption hardship and protection against the costs of default that arise with mortgage-type loans when the incomes of debtors are low. To begin to tease this out in the journey toward a general theoretical framework, what now follows are brief notes on several applications of ICLs beyond student loans. Through this process, we are seeking to address the question for policy: under what circumstances are ICLs appropriate and inappropriate instruments for governments to use for social welfare improvement?

2.2. ICL CASE STUDIES BEYOND HIGHER EDUCATION TUITION

Since the introduction of HECS, there has been an intriguing development in economic research in Australia that has been motivated by the administrative success of the policy. The basis to this analysis is the notion that if an ICL works in practice for the financing of student loans, it might be that the instrument has the potential to be used in other areas of social and economic policy reform. To date, there have now been as many as around twenty quite different ICL research applications, and what now follows involves a selective presentation of just a few,[1] to offer a taste of the many possibilities.

2.2.1. INCOME SUPPORT FOR ALL TERTIARY EDUCATION FINANCING

It is critical to understand that while HECS concerns the collection of tuition charges only, the basic idea can and does apply to the financing of all costs associated with studying, including income support. Indeed, in just about all countries with student loans, the finances distributed are designed to cover living expenses as well as the payment of up-front fees. In at least two of the countries with ICLs—England and New Zealand—the loans have a means-tested component incorporating financial support for student living expenses; and in the Australian context, there have been various attempts to both model and promote for policy consideration the use of HECS for living costs as well (Chapman, Higgins, and Taylor 2009).

2.2.2. ICLS FOR PAID PARENTAL LEAVE

The majority of Organization for Economic Cooperation and Development (OECD) governments have grants-based paid parental leave (PPL) systems, in which parents of infants are provided with income support for short periods to allow time-off paid work for the purposes of child rearing. However, the time involved to cover the expenses is typically quite short[2] because of the costs to government.

Higgins (2010) and Chapman and Higgins (2009) illustrate that there might be a solution to the lack of preparedness of governments and businesses to finance PPL beyond very short periods. Similar to the situation associated with higher education financing, it is recognized that there is a fairly clear market failure, in that in the absence of collateral the private commercial bank sector would not be interested in providing loans for this activity; asymmetric information and the associated adverse selection and moral hazard loom large for this issue.

The main contribution of the research in the area of the application of ICLs to PPL is to explain and present simulations of revenue streams of debt repayments with respect to different household and expected lifetime income streams. Higgins (2010) highlights that there are critical design issues in order to minimize the potential for both adverse selection and moral hazard to undermine the financial basis of the potential policy. Clarification is offered as to what such an approach might mean for government subsidies for particular groups and what the financial implications for PPL borrowers might be.

The PPL analysis involving an optional supplement to a grants system suggests that an ICL approach has the potential to satisfy key policy objectives: it can introduce flexibility and choice without requiring major further contributions from the government; it provides a solution to a financing impasse that would not be solved by commercial banks; and, because repayments of the loan are only required when households are in a position to do so, it provides significant consumption smoothing and income distribution advantages over alternatives. Higgins (2010) and Higgins and Sinning (2013) show the sensitivity of collection of ICLs on the basis of different approaches to the modeling of fluctuations in estimates of future incomes.

2.2.3. LOW-LEVEL CRIMINAL FINE REPAYMENTS

A quite different application of the basic principles of ICLs came from a suggestion by John Quiggin in the context of the collection of low-level criminal fines. The basic idea that ICLs could apply to this area was motivated by the facts that current collection processes for low-level criminal activity are inefficient and expensive for the public purse—a large proportion of fines remain uncollected—and with the current fine collection arrangements there can be significant social costs. The latter might even involve the imprisonment of offenders for low-level criminal activity to meet their fine repayment obligations.

Chapman et al. (2004) propose the Fine Enforcement Collection Scheme (FECS), which would use the tax and/or social security systems to collect fines for low-level criminal activity that were not recovered within a grace period (of say, a month); most of these would be in the order of $1000. The repayments would depend on the offender's future income, and would thus be paid back at a level that would fluctuate with capacity to pay. There would need to be relatively low-income thresholds for repayment to make the scheme viable, implying that the HECS parameters would not be suitable.[3]

FECS can be seen as balancing risks for the individual and the community. For the individual, it almost eliminates the risk of a fine turning into something more costly such as the seizure of a car or even imprisonment. On the other hand, it reduces offenders' chances of avoiding paying some or all of the debt. For the community, it ensures that the loss of revenue through nonpayment of fines is minimized, and the unnecessary costs associated with penalty escalation are avoided. For magistrates, FECS would likely produce a greater certainty that fines imposed would be collected, and this would enhance the credibility of the sanction.

2.2.4. THE "BRAIN DRAIN TAX"

One of the most transparent examples of regressive outcomes in international labor markets is the fact that very significant numbers of skilled immigrants trained in poor countries emigrate to more developed countries in search of higher incomes. For example, many engineering graduates from Haiti move to the United States and other rich countries after completion of their degrees, and the situation is very similar with respect to young Indian doctors and nurses trained in the Philippines. A policy approach using the basic concepts of an ICL could be used to redress some of this injustice.

In this ICL application, skilled immigrants trained in poor countries might be able to contribute to the costs of their education to compensate the government of their country of origin for part of the investments. An associated and essentially the original idea comes from Bhagwati (1972), who suggested the use of an ICL collection mechanism using the income tax system of the developed countries to which the graduates of poor countries typically migrate. Chapman et al. (2016) explain the issue and the possible solution with respect to emigrants to Australia from developing countries. A broader solution would involve internationalization of the collection of a financial contribution from the graduates of developing countries who emigrate to more wealthy destinations, but only if and when their incomes exceed a given threshold. In Australia, New Zealand, and England, for example, the use of the existing ICL collection systems would seem to be ideally suited to such a task.

2.2.5. OTHER POTENTIAL APPLICATIONS OF ICLS

As well as the above examples, over about the last twenty years there has been considerable research output related to the application of the basic principles of ICLs to a large number of other areas of social and economic policy. These examples are as follows, for the financing of or payment of

    i. R & D investments (Denniss, Yuan, and Withers 2009)
    ii. White collar crime and insider trading offenses (Chapman and Denniss 2005)
    iii. Income smoothing for the agricultural sector (Chapman and Botterill 2004, 2009)
    iv. Housing cost relief for low-income households (Gans and King 2006)
    v. Social investment community projects (Chapman and Simes 2006)
    vi. Elite athlete training (Denniss, Fear, and Milane 2012)
    vii. Solar energy devices (Baldwin, Chapman, and Umbu 2015)
    viii. Nursing homes and aged care (Chomit and Piggott 2014)
    ix. Unemployment insurance (Stiglitz and Yung 2014)
    x. Climate change adaptation policies (Dobes and Chapman 2013)

2.3. SUMMARY

The introduction of HECS encouraged, indeed motivated, a plethora of economics research in Australia involving the application of ICLs to a diverse range of social and economic policy reform suggestions. While this was going on, theoretical insights with respect to the conceptual basis of ICLs were emerging, and this is the subject of what now follows.

3. THEORETICAL DEVELOPMENTS WITH RESPECT TO ICLS

In the beginning of national ICL policy, that is the late 1980s, there was some clear understanding of the benefits of such an instrument. Specifically, there is little doubt that one part of the insurance payoffs to student debtors—insurance against default—was well understood (Barr 1989; Chapman 1997). But other benefits and difficulties associated with ICLs, now well integrated into this area of research, emerged more clearly over time.

In the Australian context, the clearest early exposition of the ICL benefit of intertemporal consumption smoothing can be found in Quiggin (2003, 2014) that provides a more general exposition of the major costs and benefits involved in comparisons of alternative approaches to student loan financing. The first of these papers was the beginning of a more formal economic modeling approach to ICLs, explaining rigorously the insurance benefits of ICLs.

It is of interest to record that the evolution of critical aspects of ICL theory arose, or at least was clarified by, attempts to make practicable applications of ICLs to particular problems. An important example comes from the work that formed the basis of the idea of the earliest analysis and policy design exercise involving the use of ICLs outside of student loans. This provided an explanation of the use of revenue contingent loans as a substitute for government grants designed to relieve the financial stress for Australian farmers experiencing drought (Botterill and Chapman 2004).

An integral aspect of the revenue contingent loan idea related to the need to design a system in which repayments of the debt could not easily be avoided, and this required the input of an astute rural accountant who helped make the policy plan close to foolproof in terms of debt collection (Botterill and Chapman 2009). In retrospect, the policy analysis can be seen as addressing an issue basic to all economic policy design, the need to minimize moral hazard.

Similarly, the thinking involved in the design of the PPL ICL (Higgins 2009) was focused on the very difficult problem of the system not being undermined by the noncollection of the debt from people choosing to take an ICL to help finance child rearing knowing that they were unlikely to rejoin the labor force. Another way of describing this, of course, is the requirement that this form of an ICL policy minimizes the costs associated with the classic problem of adverse selection. The importance of avoiding both moral hazard and adverse selection in an ICL policy design have been analyzed in detail with respect to four case studies examined in Chapman (2010).

These developments meant that before the 2013 IEA Workshop, many of the puzzles behind the conceptual basis of ICLs had been sorted out, and the significance of the policy approach can be characterized as follows. An ICL is a risk management instrument that can be used to deliver both intertemporal consumption smoothing and insurance against default; the challenge involved in the efficacious application of ICLs requires parameters and rules to be designed to minimize the noncollection costs inherent in both moral hazard and adverse selection.[4] While these understandings are a very long way from the conceptual underpinnings related to the original introduction of HECS, there remained an issue that had only been partially thought through, the importance of understanding the institutional basis for the operation of ICLs.

4. ENTER JOSEPH E. STIGLITZ, STAGE LEFT: TRANSACTIONAL EFFICIENCIES AND ICLS

The 2013 IEA Workshop was designed to address outstanding issues related to the conceptual basis of ICLs. As explained above, there had been an evolution in the thinking that lay behind an understanding of ICLs, yet the analytical framework seemed somewhat incomplete. It is hard to be precise about what was missing, but it seemed to be related to the broad public policy issue concerning the role of the public and private sectors. Specifically, an important question that had yet to be fully addressed seemed to be: Is it important that ICLs are operated through the public sector?

This is addressed comprehensively in Stiglitz (2015), which provides an expansive list of the conceptual case for governments operating ICLs.

The first two issues had already been considered in the literature, and these are that

i. Governments are able to take advantage of the highly significant economies of scale involved in the collection of income taxes. Indeed, it is reported in Chapman (2006) that an estimate of the Australian Tax Office HECS collection costs were no more than about 3–4 percent of annual revenue, and that this experience seemed to be about the same for the ICLs operating in England.

ii. Government has access to the best information concerning the true income situation of debtors. Further, it is possible that the public sector has a legal jurisdictional monopoly in knowing the true incomes of citizens, an issue that has yet to be tested constitutionally in any country.

Stiglitz (2015) considers four additional reasons why ICLs can be argued to be the realm of government, and these are as follows:

i. Because governments are not interested in making a return (profit) on individual borrowers a public sector ICL can be universal and not discriminatory on the basis of expected individual incomes. On the other hand, if private agents were involved in the design and operation of ICLs, they would engage in cherry-picking with adverse consequences with respect to both transaction costs and equity.

ii. There will be a higher spread between borrowing and lending rates with private sector ICLs because these will reflect the costs of financial transactions faced by the customers. The costs are argued to be higher for the private sector as agents engage in marketing and higher levels of complexity related to likely discriminatory pricing behavior.

iii. Actions in one market affect outcomes in others, and government engagement in ICLs could be such as to minimize unintended consequences associated, for example, with the disruption to the pecuniary externalities from optimal investments in education.

iv. As illustrated by the events and lead-up to the global financial crisis, the financial sector has considerable potential to manipulate and undermine markets with major attendant social costs.

In Stiglitz (2015), these benefits are labeled as "transactional efficiencies" arising from government engagement in ICLs, with the issue being accorded further accessible examination in Denniss (2014). While both authors focus on public-sector operational issues, there is a further aspect of transactional efficiencies inherent in the simplicity of loan collections as far as the debtors—students—are concerned, which is touched on or implied in their analyses. This is that the administrative burdens for borrowers faced with high variances in their individual capacities to repay an ICL are close to zero; this has to be a major issue for student debtors and seems to motivate myriad complaints about the current highly complex U.S. student loan system.

The notions explained and developed under the rubric of transactional efficiencies come close to finalizing a general theory of ICLs, an instrument with great potential for progressive economic reform, able to deliver insurance benefits with minimal social costs if made operational through the public sector. Of course, all of these potential benefits can only be delivered through proper attention in ICL design to the critical concerns related to moral hazard and adverse selection, themselves economics of information issues given much relevance and credibility from earlier Joseph Stiglitz contributions.

ICLs are a potentially critical development in economic thought, and add to the array of risk management instruments operated through government. Under some circumstances, many of them commonplace, it seems to be the case that the use of ICLs to improve social welfare, even without the market failures associated with asymmetric information (Long 2014). Joseph Stiglitz has provided critical input into these developments, most significantly, through an explanation of the importance of transactional efficiencies that are available with the use of the public sector to deliver ICLs.

NOTES

The author is grateful to Richard Denniss, Tim Higgins, Ali Khan, Idione Meneghel, John Quiggin and Joseph Stiglitz for conceptual insights. All errors and omissions are the responsibility of the author. The support of the Australian Research Council (ARC, LP110200496) is acknowledged with gratitude.

1. The discussion here follows Chapman (2014) quite closely.

2. This is typically quite short and of the order of four to six months duration.

3. Recent developments in this area highlight the potential to have the collection of fines operate directly through the social security system (Chapman, Ronalds, and Rydgeway 2016).

4. For insightful analysis of the likelihood that the importance of these issues is often overstated, see Palacios (2014).

REFERENCES

Baldwin, K., B. Chapman, and U. Raya. 2014. "Improving Access to Solar Energy Systems Using Income Contingent Loans." *Optics for Solar Energy*, Optical Society of America (OSA), USA: 1–3.

Barr, N. 2001. *The Welfare State as Piggy Bank: Information, Risk, Uncertainty and the Role of the State.* Oxford: Oxford University Press.

Bhagwati, J. 1972. "The Brain Drain and Income Taxation: A Proposal." Massachusetts Institute of Technology Working Paper 92. http://dspace.mit.edu/bitstream / handle/1721.1/63416/braindrainincome00bhag.pdf?sequence=1.

Botterill, L., and B. Chapman. 2004. "An Income-Related Loan Proposal for Drought Relief for Farm Businesses." *Australian Journal of Public Administration* 63 (3):10–19.

Botterill, L., and B. Chapman. 2009. "A Revenue Contingent Loan Instrument for Agricultural Credit with Particular Reference to Drought Relief." *Australian Journal of Labour Economics* 12 (2):181–196.

Chapman, B. 2006. *Government Managing Risk: Income Contingent Loans for Social and Economic Progress.* London/New York: Routledge/Taylor & Francis Group.

Chapman, B. 2010. "Policy Design Issues for Risk Management: Adverse Selection and Moral Hazard in the Context of Income Contingent Loans." In *Risk, Welfare and Work*, edited by G. Marston, J. Moss, and J. Quiggin. Melbourne, Australia: Melbourne University Press.

Chapman, B. 2014. "Income Contingent Loans: Background." In *Income Contingent Loans: Theory, Practice and Prospects*, edited by B. Chapman, T. Higgins, and J. E. Stiglitz, 12–28. New York: Palgrave Macmillan.

Chapman, B., and R. Denniss. 2005. "Using Financial Incentives and Income Contingent Penalties to Detect and Punish Collusion and Insider Trading." *Australian and New Zealand Journal of Criminology* 38 (1):122–140.

Chapman, B. and A. Doris. 2016. "Modelling Higher Education Financing Reform for Ireland."Working Paper, Department of Economics, Finance and Accounting, Maynooth University.

Chapman, B., and T. Higgins. 2009. "An Income Contingent Loan for Extending Paid Parental Leave." *Australian Journal of Labour Economics* 12 (2):197–216.

Chapman, B., T. Higgins, and D. Taylor. 2009. "Income Contingent Loans for Mature Aged Training." *Australian Journal of Labour Economics* 12 (2):167–179.

Chapman, B., C. Ronalds and G. Rydgeway. 2016. "Repaying low-level criminal fines through income contingent debts." Mimeo, Australia National University.

Chapman, B., and R. Simes. 2006. "Profit Contingent Loans for Social Community Investment Projects in Disadvantaged Regions." *Public Policy* 1 (2):93–102.

Chapman, B., A. Freiberg, J. Quiggin, and D.Tait. 2004. "Using the Tax System to Collect Fines." *Australian Journal of Public Administration* 63 (3):20–32.

Chomit, A., and J. Piggott. 2014, "Elderly Support Policies as Resource Contingent Loans." In *Income Contingent Loans: Theory, Practice and Prospects*, edited by B. Chapman, T. Higgins, and J. E. Stiglitz, 172–179. New York: Palgrave Macmillan.

Denniss, R. (2014), "Utilizing the Transactional Efficiencies of Contingent Loans—A general Framework." In *Income Contingent Loans: Theory, Practice and Prospects*, edited by B. Chapman, T. Higgins, and J. E. Stiglitz, 248–259. New York: Palgrave Macmillan.

Denniss, A., M. Yuan, and G. Withers. 2009. "Innovation Financing and the Use of Income Contingent Loans." *Australian Journal of Labour Economics* 12 (2):145–165.

Denniss, R., J. Fear, and E. Milane. 2012. "Justice for All: Giving Australians Greater Access to the Legal System." Australia Institute Paper No. 8. http://www.tai.org.au/node/1831.

Dobes, L., and B. Chapman. 2013. "Financing Adaptation to Climate-Induced Retreat from Coastal Inundation and Erosion." CCEP Working Paper 1113. Crawford School of Public Policy, Australian National University.

Dynarski, S. 2014. "An Economist's Perspective on Student Loans." Washington, DC: Brookings Institution.

Gans, J., and S. King. 2006. "The Housing Lifeline: A Housing Affordability Policy." *Agenda* 11 (2):143–155.

Higgins, T. 2009. "Essays in the Development and Costing of Income Contingent Loans." PhD thesis, College of Business and Economics, Australian National University.

Higgins, T., and M. Sinning. 2013. "Modelling Income Dynamics for Public Policy Design: An Application to Income Contingent Student Loans." *Economics of Education Review* 37:73–285.

Long, Ngo Van. 2014, "Income Contingent Loans: Towards a Piecemeal Linear Scheme In *Income Contingent Loans: Theory, Practice and Prospects*, edited by B. Chapman, T. Higgins, and J. E. Stiglitz, 49–62. New York: Palgrave Macmillan.

Moss, D. 2003. *When All Else Fails*. Cambridge, MA: Harvard University Press.

Palacios, M. 2004. *Investing in Human Capital: A Capital Markets Approach to Higher Education Funding*. Cambridge, MA: Cambridge University Press.

Palacios, M. 2014 "Over-emphasized Costs and Under-emphasized Benefits of Income Contingent Financing." In *Income Contingent Loans: Theory, Practice and Prospects*, edited by B. Chapman, T. Higgins, and J. E. Stiglitz, 207–215. New York: Palgrave Macmillan.

Quiggin, J. 2003. "The Welfare Effects of Income-Contingent Financing of Higher Education." Working Paper No.428, Faculty of Economics, Australian National University.

Quiggin, J. 2014. "Income Contingent Loans as a Risk Management Device." In *Income Contingent Loans: Theory, Practice and Prospects*, edited by B. Chapman, T. Higgins, and J. E. Stiglitz, 39–48. New York: Palgrave Macmillan.

Shiller, R. 2003. *The New Financial Order: Risk in the 21st Century*. Princeton, NJ: Princeton University Press.

Stiglitz, Joseph E. 2015. "Income-Contingent Loans: Some General Theoretical Issues, with Applications." In *Contemporary Issues in Microeconomics*, edited by J. E. Stiglitz and M. Guzman, 129–136. New York: International Economics Association Series.

Stiglitz, J., and J. Yung. 2014. "Income Contingent Loans for the Unemployed: A Prelude to a General Theory of the Efficient Provision of Social Insurance." In *Income Contingent Loans: Theory, Practice and Prospects*, edited by B. Chapman, T. Higgins, and J. E. Stiglitz. New York: Palgrave Macmillan.

CHAPTER 23

The Public Economics of Long-Term Care

Pierre Pestieau and Gregory Ponthiere

ABSTRACT

With the rapid increase in long-term care (LTC) needs, the negligible role of the market and the declining role of informal family care, one would hope that the government would take a more proactive role in the support of dependent elderly, particularly those who cannot, whatever the reason, count on assistance from their family. The purpose of this paper is to analyze the possibility of designing a sustainable public LTC scheme integrating both the market and the family.

INTRODUCTION

Due to the aging process, the rise in long-term care needs constitutes a major challenge of the twenty-first century. Long-term care (LTC) concerns individuals who are no longer able to carry out basic daily activities such as eating, washing, dressing, etc. Nowadays, the number of persons in need of LTC is substantial. According to Frank (2012), in 2010 nearly 10 million Americans required ongoing help through LTC. This number is expected to grow to reach 15 million by 2020. Similarly in Europe, the number of persons in need of LTC is expected to grow from 27 million in 2013 to 35 million by year 2060 (see EC 2015).

The expected rise in the number of persons in need of LTC raises the question of the provision of care. As stressed by Norton (2000), about two-thirds of LTC is generally provided by informal caregivers (mainly the family, i.e., spouses, daughters, and stepdaughters). Recent figures in Frank (2012) show that about 80 percent of dependent individuals in the United States receive informal care from relatives and friends. The remaining LTC is provided formally, that is, through services that are paid on the market. Formal care can be provided either at the dependent's home, or in an institution (care centers or nursing homes).

Whereas LTC services do not require high skills, they are nonetheless extremely expensive. The average " private pay" rate for a single room in a nursing home exceeds $75,000 per year. Home-based LTC costs an average of $18 per hour[1] These large costs raise the question of the funding of formal LTC. This question will become increasingly important in the future, where it is expected that the role of the informal LTC provision will decrease. The implication of this is that financial risks associated with meeting LTC needs will grow and therefore the development of mechanisms for absorbing these risks will gain in importance.

Given that each person has a large probability (between 35 and 50 percent) to enter a nursing home when becoming old (see Brown and Finkelstein 2009), and given the large costs related to LTC, one would expect that private LTC insurance markets would expand, in order to insure individuals against the—quite likely—substantial costs of LTC. However, although markets for private LTC insurance exist, these remain thin in most countries. According to Brown, Coe, and Finkelstein (2007), only about 9 to 10 percent of the population at risk of facing future LTC costs have purchased private LTC insurance in the United States. This is the so-called "long-term care insurance puzzle."[2] Because of various reasons, lying both on the demand side (myopia, denial of LTC, crowding out by the family, etc.) and on the supply side of that market (high loading factors, unattractive reimbursement rules, etc.), only a small fraction of the population buys LTC private insurance. One can thus hardly rely only on the development of private LTC insurance markets to fund the cost of LTC.

In light of the expected decline in informal care, and of the difficulties faced by the market for private LTC insurance, one would hope that the public sector will play a more important role in the provision and funding of LTC. Nowadays, in most advanced economies, the state is involved either in the provision or in the funding of LTC services, but to an extent that varies strongly across countries. Note, however, that the involvement of the public sector in LTC is, in most countries, not as comprehensive and generous as it is for the funding of general health services. The LTC "pillar" of the welfare state remains quite thin in comparison with other pillars of the social insurance system.

The goal of this chapter is to examine some challenges raised by the design of an LTC social insurance system. In discussing the design of a social insurance scheme for LTC, we will follow the public economics approach that was initiated by Atkinson and Stiglitz (1980). This approach allows us to identify some important features of an optimal public LTC insurance, and, in particular, to pay attention to the articulation of efficiency and equity concerns in the design of such a public insurance system.

The remainder of the chapter is organized as follows. Section 1 briefly explains why informal care is expected to decline and why the private market fails to play a role in covering LTC needs. Then, section 2 develops a simple model of two-sided altruism to identify some key features of the optimal LTC public insurance scheme. Section 3 examines some additional difficulties raised by the design of public LTC insurance. Section 4 concludes the discussion.

1. INFORMAL CARE AND LTC PRIVATE INSURANCE

Before considering the design of LTC social insurance, let us first examine the main reasons why it is necessary to develop some kind of social insurance for LTC. The motivations are twofold: on the one hand, the expected decline in the future of the role of the family in LTC provision; on the other hand, the expectation that the factors explaining the LTC private insurance puzzle will remain at work in the next decades.

Let us first consider the role of the family.[3] It is expected that the family, which provides today the bulk of LTC, will be less active in the coming decades. A number of factors explain such a gloomy prospect. The drastic change in family values, the growing number of childless households, the increasing rate of participation of women in the labor market, and the mobility of children imply that the number of dependent elderly who cannot count on the assistance of either spouses or children is increasing.

At the same time, it is important to realize that, at least for heavy cases of dependence, informal care can be quite costly for caregivers.[4] There exists a growing literature trying to assess the collateral costs that informal caring can represent for the caregivers. Several studies highlight that caregivers bear large opportunity costs because of care responsibilities (e.g., Van Houtven, Coe, and Skira 2013). Informal care may have adverse effects on multiple dimensions of the health of caregivers.[5]

The detrimental effects related to the physical aspect are generally less intensive than the psychological effects. Schulz and Sherwood (2008), Hirst (2005), and Burton et al. (2003) showed that moving into a demanding caregiving role (more than twenty hours per week of help for dealing with basic activities of daily living) led to an increase of depression and psychological distress, impaired self-care, and poorer self-reported health. A conjecture that would need testing is that these costs depend closely on the motives underlying caring: altruism, exchange, or norm. In other words, one could expect that informal care that rests on norm as opposed to altruism would involve more collateral costs. But in any case, we can expect, given the increasingly large literature on the costs of informal care provision, that the size of informal care will go down in the future.

If the importance of informal care is likely to decrease in the next decades, then an important issue concerns the extent to which the LTC private insurance market can develop so as to cover the costs of formal LTC. The literature on the LTC private insurance puzzle questions the capacity of the market to cover a large part of the population at risk of LTC costs. Actually, although LTC costs are high, and despite large probabilities to become dependent at an old age, the LTC private insurance market remains underdeveloped, in contradiction with basic theoretical predictions.

Various factors were introduced to explain this puzzle.[6] First, empirical evidence shows that individuals tend, because of either myopia or ignorance, to underestimate the risk of dependence, and thus do not feel the need to be insured against LTC. For instance, Finkelstein and McGarry (2006) show, on the basis of AHEAD data, that about 50 and of people believe that they have a zero probability to enter a nursing home in the next five years (average age of respondents = 79 years). Another possible explanation as if LTC insurance exhibits high prices that can be the consequence of adverse selection or administrative costs; this can also explain the low demand for LTC insurance (see Brown and Finkelstein 2007). Third, a number of families prefer to rely on informal caring, which is generally warmer and cheaper. Parents can avoid insuring to force their children to assist them in case of dependence and children can incite their parents not to insure to increase their expected bequests (see Pauly 1990). Fourth, there is the Good Samaritan argument: some families know that they can rely on means-tested social assistance such as Medicaid in the United States. Even well-to-do families can resort to these programs through what has been called strategic impoverishment (see Brown and

Finkelstein 2008). Fifth, many insurance contracts have unattractive rules of reimbursement such as a monthly lump-sum compensation that is insufficient and unrelated to the real needs of the dependent (see Cutler 1993). Finally, there is often a denial of severe dependence; it is so awful that one prefers not to think about it, and thus does not consider purchasing private LTC insurance.[7]

Whereas these different factors may explain why the coverage of LTC private insurance is so low, a key question is whether or not these plausible causes of the LTC insurance puzzle will persist in the future. If the answer is positive, this means that the mounting needs of LTC will not be covered by the market, and that the construction of a social LTC insurance is definitely needed.

2. THE DESIGN OF LTC SOCIAL INSURANCE

The state already plays some role in most countries, but, as already mentioned, this role is still modest and inconsistent. In a recent report for the United Kingdom, Dilnot (2011) sketches the features of what can be considered as an ideal social program for LTC. This would be a two-tier program. The first tier would concern those who cannot afford paying for their LTC and do not benefit from family support. It would be a means-test program. The second tier would address the fears of most dependents in the middle class that they might incur costs that would force them to sell all their assets and prevent them from bequeathing any of them. These two concerns are not met by current LTC practices.

The design of a public LTC scheme is not an easy task. It depends on the objective of the government and the tools available; it also depends on the type of private insurance market that prevails and the structure of the families involved. In particular, a key issue is the assumptions concerning the motivations behind the behavior of family members. For instance, children may serve as informal caregivers because of altruism, or because of a strategic motive (e.g., getting a bequest), or because of a social norm.[8] Similarly, the dependent parent may either be altruistic toward his children, and purchase an LTC private insurance policy so as to minimize the cost imposed on his children, or, alternatively, behave in a more egoistic way and not purchase insurance, so as to force his children to provide informal LTC to him. Obviously, these different motivations lead to distinct behaviors at the laissez-faire, and, hence, invite different public interventions.[9]

To discuss these issues more formally, we focus here on a particular framework of two-sided altruism, based on Cremer, Pestieau, and Roeder (2016). We consider an economy composed of families wherein coexist a parent and a child. Parents are supposed to be purely altruistic, and thus care about the utility of the children, whereas the child is supposed to be imperfectly altruistic, and weighs the utility of the parent by a coefficient $\beta \in [0,1]$.

Individuals live two periods: young adulthood and old adulthood, during which dependence arises with a probability π. In period 1, individuals work, consume, and possibly provide an amount a of informal LTC to their parent in the case where the parent is dependent.[10] In period 2, individuals consume, leave some bequests b to their children, and, in case of dependence, receive informal LTC from their children.

Individual utility functions are supposed to be state dependent. In the case of good health, the utility of consumption is given by the function $u(c)$, with $u'(c) > 0$ and $u''(c) < 0$. In the case of dependence, the utility of consumption is given by $H(c)$, with $H'(c) > 0$ and $H''(c) < 0$. It is reasonable to suppose that, for a given c, we have $u(c) > H(c)$ and $u'(c) > H'(c)$.

Following the literature on the LTC insurance puzzle, we suppose that there is no private LTC insurance, and that dependence shock implies necessarily less inheritance and more care for children.

The utility of the child is:

$$U_c = \pi \left[u(w(1-a)+b) + \beta H(y+h(a)-L-b) \right]$$
$$+ (1-\pi) \left[u\left(w+\hat{b}\right) + \beta u\left(y-\hat{b}\right) \right] \tag{23.1}$$

while the utility of the parent is:

$$U_p = \pi \left[H(y+h(a)-L-b) + u(w(1-a)+b) \right]$$
$$+ (1-\pi) \left[u\left(y-\hat{b}\right) + u\left(w+\hat{b}\right) \right] \tag{23.2}$$

where w is the child's wage rate, b is the amount of bequest, y is the wealth of the parent, L is the cost of LTC, $h(a) \leq L$ is the product of informal care. We also use the ^ symbol to denote the variables when the parent is healthy.

Let us now write the problem of a utilitarian social planner, whose goal is to select all variables (consumption and care) in such a way as to maximize the sum of the utility of the parents and the children. For this purpose, we deliberately abstract here from altruistic motivations, and carry out a laundering of preferences, in such a way as to avoid double counting.[11] The planner's problem can be written as:

$$\max_{m,\, c,\, \hat{m},\, \hat{c},\, a} \quad \pi\left[H(m)+u(c)\right]+(1-\pi)\left[H(\hat{m})+u(\hat{c})\right]$$

$$\text{s.t.} \quad (1-\pi)\left(\hat{m}+\hat{c}-L\right)+\pi\left(m+c\right)$$

$$= \quad y+(1-\pi)w+\pi\left[w\left(1-a\right)+h\left(a\right)\right]$$

where c and $\hat{c}$ denote the consumption of the child (when the parent is, respectively, dependent and healthy), whereas m and $\hat{m}$ are the consumption of the parent (again when the parent is, respectively, dependent and healthy).

First-order conditions (FOCs) yield:

$$H'(m)=u'\left(\hat{m}\right)=u'(c)=u'\left(\hat{c}\right)=\mu \qquad (23.3)$$

$$w=h'(a) \qquad (23.4)$$

where μ is the Lagrange multiplier associated to the resource constraint of the economy. Thus, the first-best social optimum involves a full equalization of marginal utilities across all ages of life and all health states (dependent or not).

Let us now consider how this social optimum can be decentralized. For this purpose, we suppose the following timing. First, the government announces its policy; second, the state of nature is revealed (dependence or not of the parent); third, the parent chooses bequests (either b or $\hat{b}$); fourth, the child chooses informal care a. This timing amounts to consider the state as a Stackelberg leader, who plays first, anticipating the reactions of other players (here children and parents).

When children are imperfectly altruistic toward their parents, i.e., $\beta<1$, the decentralization of the first-best optimum requires lump-sum transfers $(\hat{D},D)$, a tax on labor τ_a, and a tax on bequests τ_b such that:

$$\pi D=(1-\pi)\hat{D}+\pi\left[\tau_a w(1-a^*)+\tau_b b^*\right] \qquad (23.5)$$

These four policy instruments suffice to decentralize the utilitarian social optimum.

Until now, we made the simplifying assumption that all individuals are identical *ex ante* (i.e., before knowing whether one is dependent or not at the old age). Let us now relax that assumption, and consider how the social optimum could be decentralized in an economy where families differ in terms of wages w_i and wealth y_i. The available policy instruments here only include a social LTC allowance g, a tax on labor τ_a, and a tax on bequests τ_b. The second-best problem can be expressed by means of the following Lagrangian:

$$\max_{\tau_a, \tau_b, g} \mathcal{L} = \sum_i n_i \left\{ \begin{array}{l} \pi\left[H\left[y_i - L - b_i + g + h(a_i) \right] + u\left[(1-\tau_a)w_i(1-a_i) + (1-\tau_b)b_i \right] \right] \\ +(1-\pi)\left[u\left(y_i - \hat{b}_i \right) + u\left[(1-\tau_a)w_i + (1-\tau_b)\hat{b}_i \right] \right] \\ -\mu\left[\pi g - \tau_a(1-\pi a_i)w_i - \tau_b\left(\pi b_i + (1-\pi)\hat{b}_i \right) \right] \end{array} \right\}$$

where n_i is the number of families of type i, and where μ is the Lagrange multiplier associated to the government's budget constraint. Let us denote $\Delta_i \equiv u'(c_i) - H'(m_i) \gtrless 0$ and $\hat{\Delta}_i \equiv u'(\hat{c}_i) - H'(\hat{m}_i) < 0$. From the FOCs of this problem, and assuming that cross effects are negligible (i.e., $\frac{\partial \tilde{a}^c}{\partial \tau_b} = 0$ and $\frac{\partial \hat{b}^c}{\partial \tau_a} = 0$), we obtain the following two formulas for the optimal tax on labor and the optimal tax on bequests:

$$\tau_a = \frac{\left[\begin{array}{l} \pi(1-\beta)E\left[H'(m)h'(a)\dfrac{\partial \tilde{a}^c}{\partial \tau_a} \right] - \pi cov(\Delta, w(1-a)) - (1-\pi)cov(\hat{\Delta}, w) \\ -\pi E\Delta Ew(1-a) - (1-\pi)E\hat{\Delta}Ew \end{array} \right]}{\mu Ew\dfrac{\partial \tilde{a}^c}{\partial \tau_a}} \quad (23.6)$$

and

$$\tau_b = \frac{-\pi cov(\Delta, b) - (1-\pi)cov(\hat{\Delta}, \hat{b}) - \pi E\Delta Eb - (1-\pi)E\hat{\Delta}E\hat{b}}{-\mu E\left[\pi\dfrac{\partial b^c}{\partial \tau_b} + (1-\pi)\dfrac{\partial \hat{b}^c}{\partial \tau_b} \right]} \quad (23.7)$$

where the operator E is used to denote the sum over individuals, and where $\frac{\partial b^c}{\partial \tau_b} \equiv \frac{\partial b}{\partial \tau_b} + \frac{\partial b}{\partial g}\frac{\partial g}{\partial \tau_b}$ denote the effect of a change in the tax on bequests on the amount of bequests when this change is compensated by a variation in the LTC allowance g in such a way as to maintain the government's balanced budget.[12] In a similar way, $\frac{\partial \tilde{a}^c}{\partial \tau_a} \equiv \frac{\partial \tilde{a}}{\partial \tau_a} + \frac{\partial \tilde{a}}{\partial g}\frac{\partial g}{\partial \tau_a}$ is the compensated effect of a change in the tax on labor leaving the government's budget balanced.

These formulae summarize the various determinants of the optimal taxes on bequests and labor. Let us first interpret the tax on labor τ_a. For this purpose, let us suppose that children are perfectly altruistic, so that $\beta = 1$. In this case, the first term of the numerator vanishes, and the tax formula includes an equity term at the numerator, and an efficiency term at the denominator, whose size depends on the extent to which increasing the tax on labor contributes, by reducing the opportunity cost of providing LTC, to make children raise their amount of informal aid to the dependent parents. Once we suppose that children are imperfectly altruistic, i.e., $\beta < 1$, another term is added at the numerator. This term is positive, and depends on how imperfect the altruism of children is. The less altruistic children are, the larger the optimal tax on labor should be. Note, however, that the size of this additional term depends also on the extent to which children's informal care reacts a lot or not to a compensated change in the tax on labor.

Turning now to the formula for the optimal tax on bequests, we can see that its numerator is a standard equity term. This term supports taxing bequests to the extent that this reduces inequalities in well-being across individuals. The denominator is an efficiency term, which captures the incidence of τ_b on the fiscal revenues, through its impact on the level of bequests left by parents in case of dependence and in case of nondependence. This term is more or less large, depending on how strongly parents react to a compensated change in the tax on bequests.

These formulae identify some important determinants in the design of optimal LTC social insurance. This insurance must be designed as a part of a global taxation system including also a taxation of bequests and a taxation of labor. The underlying intuition goes as follows. Taxing bequests is necessary here, in such a way as to redistribute from lucky families where the parent is healthy to unlucky families where the parent is dependent. Moreover, the decentralization of the social optimum also requires taxing labor, because of two distinct reasons. First, this is another way to reduce inequalities between lucky children having no dependent parent and unlucky children having dependent parents. Second, when children are imperfectly altruistic toward their parents, the laissez-faire amount of informal care is too low, and the tax on labor induces them to raise the amount of LTC by reducing its opportunity cost.

3. DISCUSSION

While the optimal taxation model developed in the previous section casts some light on the design of public LTC insurance, this framework relies on some simplifying assumptions, which may not be neutral at all for the issue at stake, and, as such, are worth examining here.

First, on the normative side, the above approach relies on a utilitarian social welfare function. Although this approach is quite standard in public economics, it should be stressed nonetheless, that this can be questioned in the present context of LTC because as we have seen, dependent parents do not have the same preferences as nondependent parents. Hence, at the first-best optimum, the equality $H'(m) = u'(\hat{m})$ implies, provided $H'(x) < u'(x)$ for a given x, that the optimal consumption of the healthy parent should be higher than the one of a dependent parent. This corollary is questionable. Obviously, the problems faced by utilitarianism in the context of heterogeneous preferences are not new (see Arrow 1971; Sen 1973), but these problems are raised in an acute way when considering the design of LTC public insurance.

Still on the normative side, another issue that has been raised concerns the treatment of altruistic motivations in the social planning problem. In the above formulation, the government deliberately rules out altruistic motivations, and takes these into account only insofar as these affect how parents and children react to fiscal instruments. We carried out this laundering of preferences in order to avoid any double counting, but one could argue that, from a welfarist perspective, these altruistic motivations would deserve to be taken into account. This would affect the design of the LTC public insurance scheme.

On the positive side, the above formulation also relies on some important assumptions, which can be questioned, and, as such, invite further developments.

First, we supposed, when considering the decentralization, that children and parents perfectly perceive the probability of old-age dependency, i.e., π. In light of the existing literature (see Brown and Finkelstein 2009), this constitutes an obvious simplification. Introducing myopia would definitely affect the form of optimal public intervention.[13]

Moreover, we considered here a simple framework where parents can, in case of dependence, rely for sure on the (imperfect) altruism of their children. This assumption is strong, since in real life, there exists a deep uncertainty regarding whether parents can, in case of dependence, really rely on children's informal care. Thus, introducing uncertain altruism seems to lead to a more realistic setting, but also a more complex one, since this introduces another motive for public insurance: insurance against having nonaltruistic children.[14]

Still concerning children, our framework simplified the picture, by considering families including only one parent and one child. This allowed us to abstract from strategic interdependencies among children, which can, when the dependent's health is a public good, lead to coordination failures among children, and hence, cause an underprovision of care to the dependent parent.[15] Our focus on a one parent/one child framework also allowed us to ignore differences in LTC provision among children of the same family, due for instance to different time constraints because of age differentials across children.[16] We also abstracted here from the spouses, who are often informal caregivers.[17] Moreover, it is increasingly frequent to introduce grandchildren in a sequential exchange game: grandparents take care of their grandchildren and when dependent they are assisted by their own children.[18]

Other important issues were not considered in the above framework. One of the concerns of the middle class is to avoid being forced to sell all their assets and thus to be unable to transmit anything to their heirs.[19] Another important issue, which is not discussed here, is whether or not one can restrict public benefits to those who really need them because of too few resources or because they cannot count on the assistance of their children or spouses. Ideally, we should distinguish between the case in which the public benefit is restricted to those who are not helped by their children (opting out) and the case in which such a restriction is not possible (topping up).[20]

Finally, a last simplification is that the above model was purely static. Although convenient, such a static approach involves several limitations. First, as the economy develops, wages and interest rates change as well, which modifies the opportunity costs of providing LTC.[21] Moreover, the characteristics of individuals in the economy, including their degree of altruism, may change over time, and may potentially be influenced by public intervention.[22]

CONCLUSIONS

This chapter began with an observation: LTC needs are increasing rapidly and neither the market nor the family seem to be able to meet such a mounting demand. From there, we analyzed the possibility of developing a full-fledged LTC public insurance scheme that would fulfill two objectives: redistribution and insurance, and that would rest, to the extent possible, the market and the family.

Our model allowed us to highlight some important determinants of the design of such an LTC public insurance system, with a particular emphasis on efficiency and equity concerns, and on the articulation between public intervention and informal care provided by the family. But our discussions also showed that our model—as any model—cannot capture all dimensions at work in the context of an LTC provision. As already mentioned, a major difficulty in studying LTC lies in the large number of agents playing a role in LTC: the dependent, informal caregivers (spouses and children), insurance companies, formal care givers, nursing homes, etc. Another source of difficulty lies in the large heterogeneity, among agents, in resources and in motivation.

All these difficulties reinforce the need for more research on LTC. Admittedly, the current budgetary crisis makes it difficult to develop what has been called the fifth pillar of a modern social protection. But given the increasing prevalence of LTC needs, our societies will sooner or later have to build that fifth pillar. Our modest task in this paper was to highlight some important dimensions and challenges that arise in the design of an LTC public insurance system.

NOTES

Financial support from the Chaire "Marché des risques et création de valeur" of the FdR/SCOR is gratefully acknowledged.

1. See U.S. Department of Health and Human Services (2016).
2. On this, see Cutler (1993), Brown and Finkelstein (2007, 2008, 2009, 2011), and Pestieau and Ponthiere (2011).
3. On the role of the family in LTC provision, see the survey by Cremer, Pestieau, and Ponthiere (2012).
4. See Klimaviciute et al. (2016) for an attempt to test the relative prevalence of caring motives.
5. See Schulz et al. (1995), Pinquart and Sörensen (2003), and Vitaliano, Zhang, and Scanlan (2003).

6. We summarize here some of the main plausible explanations. Further details can be found in the surveys by Brown and Finkelstein (2011), Pestieau and Ponthiere (2011), and Cremer, Pestieau, and Ponthiere (2012).

7. This explanation is close to the issue of denial of death explored by Kopczuk and Slemrod (2005).

8. On the strategic bequest motive, see Bernheim, Shleifer, and Summers (1985).

9. Note that, in case of altruism, a key issue is also whether governments should take altruistic motives into account in their social planning problem.

10. The amount of informal care here takes the form of time. On the study of social LTC insurance under money transfers from children to parents, see Pestieau and Sato (2008).

11. This point is further discussed in section 3.

12. Similarly, we have $\frac{\partial b^c}{\partial \tau_b} \equiv \frac{\partial b}{\partial \tau_b} + \frac{\partial b}{\partial g} \frac{\partial g}{\partial \tau_b}$.

13. On the design of LTC public insurance under myopia, see Cremer and Roeder (2015).

14. Optimal public policy under uncertain altruism is studied in Cremer, Gahvari, and Pestieau (2012, 2017).

15. On family games in the context of LTC, see Stern and Engers (2002) and Pezzin, Pollak, and Schone (2007, 2009).

16. On the interactions between informal LTC provision and the timing of births, see Pestieau and Ponthiere (2015).

17. See Pezzin, Pollak, and Schone (2009).

18. See Kureishi and Wakabayashi (2007).

19. On this, see Klimaviciute and Pestieau (2016).

20. On this distinction, see Cremer, Pestieau, and Ponthiere (2012).

21. See Canta, Pestieau, and Thibault (2016).

22. On the impact of public LTC insurance on the prevalence of altruism in the population, see Ponthiere (2013), who develops a dynamic model of socialization.

REFERENCES

Arrow, K. J. 1971. "A Utilitarian Approach to the Concept of Equality in Public Expenditures." *Quarterly Journal of Economics* 85:409–415.

Atkinson, A., and J. Stiglitz. 1980. *Lectures on Public Economics*. New York: McGraw-Hill.

Bernheim, B. D., A. Shleifer, and L. Summers. 1985. "The Strategic Bequest Motive." *Journal of Political Economy* 93 (6):1045–1076.

Brown, J., N. Coe, and A. Finkelstein, A. 2007. "Medicaid Crowd-Out of Private Long-Term Care Insurance Demand: Evidence from the Health and Retirement Survey." In *Tax Policy and the Economy* 21:1–34, NBER chaps. Cambridge, MA: National Bureau of Economic Research.

Brown, J., and A. Finkelstein. 2007. "Why Is the Market for LTC Insurance So Small?" *Journal of Public Economics* 91:1967–1991.

Brown, J., and A. Finkelstein. 2008. "The Interaction of Public and Private Insurance: Medicaid and the LTC Insurance Market." *American Economic Review* 98 (3):1083–1102.

Brown, J., and A. Finkelstein. 2009. "The Private Market for Long-Term Care in the U.S.: A Review of the Evidence." *Journal of Risk and Insurance* 76 (1):5–29.

Brown, J., and A. Finkelstein. 2011. "Insuring Long Term Care in the U.S." *Journal of Economic Perspectives* 25 (4):119–142.

Burton, L., B. Zdaniuk, R. Schultz, S. Jackson, and C. Hirsch. 2003. "Transitions in Spousal Caregiving." *Gerontologist* 43 (2):230–241.

Canta, C., and P. Pestieau. 2014. "Long-Term Care and Family Norm." *B.E. Journal of Economic Analysis and Policy Advances* 14 (2):401–428.

Canta, C., P. Pestieau, and E. Thibault. 2016. "Dynamics of Capital Accumulation with LTC Insurance and Family Norms." *Economic Theory.* Forthcoming.

Cremer, H., F. Gahvari, and P. Pestieau. 2012. "Endogenous Altruism, Redistribution, and Long Term Care." *B.E. Journal of Economic Analysis and Policy Advances* 14:499–524.

Cremer, H., F. Gahvari, and P. Pestieau. 2015. "Uncertain Altruism and the Provision of Long Term Care." Unpublished.

Cremer, H., P. Pestieau, and G. Ponthiere. 2012. "The Economics of Long-Term Care: A Survey." *Nordic Economic Policy Review* 2:108–148.

Cremer, H., P. Pestieau, and K. Roeder. 2016. "LTC Social Insurance with Two-Sided Altruism." *Research in Economics* 70:101–109

Cutler, D. 1993. "Why Doesn't the Market Fully Insure Long-Term Care?" NBER Working Paper No. 4301. Cambridge, MA: National Bureau of Economic Research.

Dilnot, A. 2011. *Fairer Care Funding: The Report of the Commission on Funding of Care and Support.* London: Commission on Funding of Care and Support.

EU. 2015. "The 2015 Ageing Report." *European Economics* 3.

Finkelstein, A., and K. McGarry. 2006. "Multiple Dimensions of Private Information: Evidence from the Long-Term Care Insurance Market." *American Economic Review* 96 (4):938–958.

Frank, R. G. 2012. "Long-Term Care Financing in the United States: Sources and Institutions." *Applied Economic Perspectives and Policy* 34:333–345

Hirst, M. 2005. "Carer Distress: A Prospective, Population-Based Study." *Social Science and Medicine* 61 (3):697–708.

Klimaviciute, J., and P. Pestieau. 2016. "Long-Term Care Social Insurance. How to Avoid Big Losses?" CORE Discussion Paper 2016-7. Center for Operations Research and Econometrics (Louvain-la-Neuve).

Klimaviciute, J., S. Perelman, P. Pestieau, and J. Schoenmaeckers. 2016. "Caring for Dependent Parents: Altruism, Exchange or Family Norm?" Unpublished.

Kopczuk, W., and J. Slemrod. 2005. "Denial of Death and Economic Behavior." *B.E. Journal of Theoretical Economics* 5 (1): article 5.

Kureishi, W., and M. Wakabayashi. 2007. "Why Do First-Born Children Live with Parents?" *Geography of the Family in Japan.* Osaka University (mimeo).

Norton, E. 2000. "Long Term Care." In *Handbook of Health Economics, Vol. 1b,* edited by A. Cuyler and J. Newhouse, chap. 17. New York: Elsevier.

Pauly, M. V. 1990. "The Rational Non-Purchase of Long-Term Care Insurance." *Journal of Political Economy* 98:153–168.

Pestieau, P., and M. Sato. 2008. "Long Term Care: the State, the Market and the Family." *Economica* 75:435–454.

Pestieau, P., and G. Ponthiere. 2011. "The Long-Term Care Insurance Puzzle." In *Financing Long-Term Care in Europe: Institutions, Markets and Models*, edited by J. Costa-Font and C. Courbage. London: Palgrave Macmillan.

Pestieau, P., and G. Ponthiere. 2015. "Long-Term Care and Births Timing." PSE Discussion Paper 2015–10.

Pezzin, L., R. Pollak, and B. Schone. 2007. "Efficiency in Family Bargaining: Living Arrangements and Caregiving Decisions of Adult Children and Disabled Elderly Parents." *CESifo Economic Studies* 53 (1):69–96.

Pezzin, L., P. Pollak, and B. Schone. 2009. "Long-Term Care of the Disabled Elderly: Do Children Increase Caregiving by Spouses?" *Review of Economics of the Household* 7 (3):323–339.

Pinquart, M., and S. Sörensen. 2003. "Differences Between Caregivers and Non-Caregivers in Psychological Health and Physical Health: A Meta-Analysis." *Psychology and Aging* 18 (2):250–267.

Ponthiere, G. 2013. "Long-Term Care, Altruism and Socialization." *B.E. Journal of Economic Analysis and Policy Advances* 14 (2):429–471.

Schulz, R., A. T. O'Brien, J. Bookwala, and K. Fleissner. 1995. "Psychiatric and Physical Morbidity Effects of Dementia Caregiving: Prevalence, Correlates, and Causes." *Gerontologist* 35 (6):771–791.

Schulz, R., and P. R. Sherwood. 2008. "Physical and Mental Health Effects of Family Caregiving." *Journal of Social Work Education* 44 (3):105–113.

Sen, A. K. 1973. *On Economic Inequality*. Oxford: Clarendon Press.

Stern, S., and Engers, M. 2002. "LTC and Family Bargaining." *International Economic Review* 43 (1):73–114.

U.S. Department of Health and Human Services. 2016. "How Much Care Will You Need?" http://longtermcare.gov/the-basics/how-much-care-will-you-need/.

Van Houtven, C., N. Coe, and M. Skira. 2013. "The Effect of Informal Care on Work and Wages." *Journal of Health Economics* 32 (1):240–252.

Vitaliano, P., J. Zhang, and J. Scanlan. 2003. "Is Caregiving Hazardous to One's Physical Health? A Meta-Analysis." *Psychological Bulletin* 129 (6):946–972.

CHAPTER 24

Jomo E. Stiglitz

KENYA'S FIRST NOBEL LAUREATE IN ECONOMICS

Célestin Monga

INTRODUCTION

At a conference on African economic development held in Ottawa, Canada, a few years ago, a group of scholars from Africa decided to have dinner together and get to know each other. They were all experts in various disciplines of the social sciences and the humanities. One of them stood up, said his surname and first name, and indicated that he was simply a human rights activist. Yet, his title on the official program for the conference was actually professor of economics at a reputable Canadian university. When asked why he would not mention that, he seemed embarrassed. He hesitated for a few seconds before saying: "Yes indeed, I teach there and I write academic articles and even books. But I have noticed that whenever I introduce myself in public as a Congolese economist, people just burst into laughter spontaneously . . . So I stopped saying those words. Nowadays I just tell everyone that I am a human rights activist. It seems to be more credible . . ."

That was shocking to me. Why on earth would anyone laugh at the idea of a Congolese economist? True, the Democratic Republic of Congo—his native country—still has a gross domestic product (GDP) per capita of less than $500 a year. But so what? Zambia has a GDP per capita of less than $2,000 a year but it is the native country of some pretty good economists—including the former U.S. Federal Reserve vice chair Stanley Fischer.

The puzzling story of a good researcher—good enough to be recruited to teach in a well-respected North American university—but who was to ashamed to juxtapose his suspicious Congolese name to the prestigious word "economist" led me to think of contributions to the discipline of economics by citizens from poor countries.

The most famous one that comes to mind is obviously Sir W. Arthur Lewis who was awarded the Nobel Prize, for "pioneering research into economic development . . . with particular consideration of the problems of developing countries." Of course, when he received the Nobel in 1979 he was a British citizen. But that doesn't change the fact that he was originally from Saint Lucia, a small island nation in the eastern Caribbean whose gross national income per capita was still less than $900.

But searching for heroes who may have emerged from any particular country could quickly become a meaningless exercise in essentialism. One needs to be mindful of the randomness of geographical significance and the mysteries of learning, which often take place in ways that cannot be traced in linear paths. It makes more sense to focus not on places of birth or on brain drain but on what Ghanaian economist Yaw Nyarko calls brain circulation. W. Arthur Lewis was certainly a great embodiment of that concept. I would argue in this essay that Joseph Stiglitz is an even better example of brain circulation, and that the people of Kenya, where he spent some of his most formative intellectual years, have the right to claim him as their own.

This essay outlines the philosophical itinerary of Joseph Stiglitz. It highlights his rebellious nature and thirst for discovery, which led him to use his incredible intellect not only to change the discipline of economics several times but also to make the world a better place. The essay argues that his inexhaustible quest for the truth and for justice has made him one of the most powerful spokesperson for developing countries, and certainly the voice of the African voiceless on issues of economic development and global governance. In fact, the Midwesterner named Joseph Stiglitz has converted himself into a Kenyan economist whom some of us, African intellectuals and professionals, simply refer to as Jomo Stiglitz—we gave him a typical Kenyan first name to acknowledge the fact that he has indeed become one of us. As you celebrate him here today, remember that you celebrate an African economist. We claim him proudly.

1. A REBEL WHO SUBVERTS MAINSTREAM ECONOMICS

There has always been something Kenyan about Joseph Stiglitz. True, he was born in Gary, Indiana (United States), on the southern shores of Lake Michigan. He was supposed to live the life of a typical Midwesterner:

both his parents were born within six miles of Gary, early in the twentieth century, and lived in that area most of their lives. At a young age he became footloose, going east to college, and quickly enjoying the challenges and joys of going out of his native perimeter to explore the world—and find his true self and his true calling in the process.

Joseph Stiglitz quickly defied tradition and geography and decided that he would be a rebel citizen of the world. Just like the people of the Rift Valley, who believe that you only gain wisdom and independence and become a true man when you emancipate yourself from the comforting chains of family and birthplace to move and conquer new people and new territories, he set himself up to confront unknown worlds.

The day he was born—Tuesday, February 9, 1943—the United States declared victory against Japan in the World War II campaign for Guadalcanal and nearby islands in the southwest Pacific. It had been a bloody fight: the Japanese lost 24,000, who were killed, while the U.S. sustained 1,653 deaths. February 9 was a pivotal moment: according to historians, the Guadalcanal defeat put Japanese forces on the defensive, never to regain their dominance in the war. American forces gradually proceeded toward Japan, reaching the Japanese Home Islands before dropping two atomic bombs that led to Japan's surrender. It would have been understandable that someone born that day and growing up with chilling stories of the war, of Hiroshima and Nagasaki, decided to become a historian, a social activist, a priest, or even an Indiana politician. Yet, Joe Stiglitz chose to try to change the world through the study of economics.

There was already something Kenyan about him . . .

In the 1940s and 1950s, Gary, Indiana, was a bit like Nairobi, Kenya, or Yaoundé, Cameroon, or any other African city: it was racially segregated. Joseph Stiglitz grew up and went to public schools in that environment. But racism is not only the source of economic distortions: it is also inefficient at achieving its own goals. That was the case in Gary, Indiana, where the proponents of segregated public schools did not realize that these same schools were socially integrated: they admitted both rich and poor white kids, which obviously brought some diversity into these institutions. As an elementary and high school student, the young Joseph Stiglitz quickly found himself surrounded with kids from affluent areas of the city and state.

That inadvertent, positive promiscuity actually helped him a lot: he quickly became fully aware of the social costs of poverty and intergenerational inequality. Although his own educational success could have allowed him personally to join the ruling class quietly and avoid the scars of poverty, he has always been concerned about injustice and big social, political, and moral issues. Exactly as if he had grown up and spent his entire life in Nairobi or Yaoundé.

Joseph Stiglitz has always been a sort of dilettante—one that has interest in so many things, that he believes one life may not be enough to pursue all his dreams—but a serious dilettante, a committed dilettante. Few people know that he left Amherst College where he attended as an undergraduate student without a degree! He simply did not care about diplomas: he was thirsty for knowledge and obsessed with the quest for new ideas. It is a bit ironic that he later received an honorary doctorate from Amherst College.

There has always been something Kenyan about him . . .

Like many people in Africa, Joseph Stiglitz has deep distrust of authority, and he doesn't hide it. He also doesn't mind being a minority. This was most evident when he first experienced political power. Not in the Clinton administration but when he was elected president of the Student Council during his sophomore year at Amherst College. Guess what: despite the fact that 90 percent of the students at the school belonged to a fraternity there, he decided to campaign for their abolition "because they were socially divisive, and contrary to the spirit of a liberal arts school and community." Needless to say, things did not go smoothly; a recall referendum was initiated to remove him from the post! Incidentally, that episode is typical of African politics: as soon as a president gets elected democratically there are always very good reasons to remove him from office.

Concerned with segregation and the repeated violation of civil rights, Joseph Stiglitz has always advocated the big-bang approach to social change. As a youngster, he was impatient with those (like President Kennedy) who took a cautious approach. He later wrote: "How could we continue to countenance these injustices that had gone on so long. (The fact that so many people in the establishment seemed to do so—as they had accepted colonialism, slavery, and other forms of oppression—left a life-long mark. It reinforced a distrust of authority which I had had from childhood.)" He marched on Washington the day Martin Luther King gave his "I Have a Dream" speech. He organized an exchange program between Amherst and a small, African American, southern school.

Joseph Stiglitz got very lucky when he moved to Massachusetts Institute of Technology (MIT). Among many assets there he had four Nobel laureates as teachers: Paul Samuelson, Robert Solow, Franco

Modigliani, and Kenneth Arrow. After his first year as a graduate student, he was offered the opportunity of editing Paul Samuelson's collected papers, which he did very well. But there was one problem: that work became so successful that people in the economics profession only thought of him as "the guy who edited Samuelson's papers . . ." Of course, that bothered him. He had his own ego and wanted to be known for his own work! By the way, it has been said that Samuelson (also from Gary, Indiana) once wrote in a recommendation letter that Joe was "the best economist" ever produced in that town.

While studying as a Fulbright Fellow at Cambridge in 1965–1966,[1] his research focused on growth, technical change, and income distribution, both how growth affected the distribution of income and how the distribution of income affected growth. Some people erroneously believe that he discovered these issues only in recent years, now that they have become almost fashionable. No. In fact, one of his early successes was his 1969 paper "The Distribution of Income and Wealth Among Individuals" (*Econometrica*), which emerged from his thesis.

Joseph Stiglitz has always been obsessed with the poor and with inequality, and issues of persistent unemployment. His choice of topics was not that of a renegade; he wanted to go beyond the business cycles to look at the interaction between macro and some deeper social issues. On the methodological front, he was even more daring: while most macroeconomic models in the mid-sixties assumed that wages and prices were fixed (as if the Great Depression never happened), he wrote a paper with Bob Solow on the dynamics of adjustment (1968) to explain the persistence of unemployment, and another with George Akerlof to show how such dynamics can give rise to cyclical behavior (1969). He was already not only a rebel but a defector—if not a traitor to "mainstream economics."

He was not deterred by the risk of taking on some of his MIT teachers. He was skeptical of the dominant theories in the economics of uncertainty, most notably that of Modigliani and Miller, which argued confidently that corporate financial structure—whether firms finance themselves with debt or equity—made no difference (other than as a result of taxes). The Modigliani-Miller theorem was based on assumptions of rational behavior, despite the overwhelming evidence of market irrationality, and the millions of people in financial markets around the world who are constantly concerned about corporate finance—but not for reasons having to do with taxation! In a 1969 paper, Joseph Stiglitz meticulously invalidated it, he showed the importance of two crucial assumptions ignored by Modigliani and Miller: their analytical framework rested on the illusory idea of perfect (or at least symmetric) information, and the deceptive notion that the corporate finance world had no bankruptcy. The failure of firms and financial institutions (including in the development industry) to analyze the consequences of these big assumptions probably explains at least some of the policy failures observed around the world for decades. Yet, I suspect that even today the Modigliani-Miller theorem is still being taught as an essential tool in corporate finance courses. I certainly remember learning about it myself as a student at MIT!

2. ON ECONOMIC THEORY:
CUTTING-EDGE MODELING OUT OF AFRICA

Joseph Stiglitz's obsessions only got worse with time, especially when he found himself at the Institute of Development Studies at the University of Nairobi in the summer of 1969. That new environment—much different from Cambridge, England, and Cambridge, Massachusetts—surreptitiously pushed him to move from working simply on the economics of uncertainty to the information asymmetries, and more generally, imperfect information.

Surprisingly, he confesses that he has been wondering why his stay there completely defined his intellectual itinerary. He once wrote: "The time I spent in Kenya was pivotal in the development of my ideas on the economics of information. I have often wondered why." I think I can all conjecture why: in Nairobi, he found himself in a place where almost nothing seemed to work as in the old economics textbooks. That forced him "to think everything through from first principles." And while the city was quite different from Gary, Indiana, the *problématique* of economics there was in fact quite reminiscent of the incongruities of the standard economic theory. For instance, he had seen discrimination in the labor market in Indiana, even though the textbook theories asserted that such situations could not exist in competitive equilibrium so long as there are some nondiscriminatory individuals or firms, since it would be profitable to any such firm to hire the lower-wage discriminated-against individuals. Wandering on the streets of the city he could also see with his own eyes similar discrepancies between economic theory and reality.

When he decided to explore the *logic* of economic models in Nairobi, he could not reconcile them with everyday observation. He was confronted with problems for which there was no obvious answer: What do firms actually maximize? What should they maximize? He quickly realized how sensitive not only were the *results* of the standard model to the (clearly unrealistic) assumptions posited, but even the reasonableness of the *assumed* behavior. The Masai rebel in him quickly took over and he felt compelled to challenge the analysis of competitive equilibrium, which was postulated by his teachers Arrow and Debreu. He later wrote: "As my work progressed, the discrepancies between the kind of behavior *implied* by the standard model and actual behavior also became increasingly clear. In the standard model, the only risk that firms should worry about was the correlation of the outcomes (profits) with the 'market'; in practice, businesses seem to pay less attention to that than they do to 'own' risk, the chance the project will succeed or fail. In the standard model, everyone agrees about what the firm should do; in practice, there are often heated disagreements. It seemed to me that any persuasive theory of the firm had to be consistent with these, and other, aspects of widely observed firm behavior."

Nairobi was therefore a pivotal moment in his intellectual development. It was almost an epiphany. He was forced to realize that models which suggested that there was no such thing as unemployment, or that it was at most short lived, were at least suspect—if not completely misleading. This is not conjecture on my part. Joseph Stiglitz said it in his Nobel lecture: "Models of perfect markets, as badly flawed as they might seem for Europe or America, seemed truly inappropriate for these countries. . . . I had seen cyclical unemployment—sometimes quite large—and the hardship it brought as I grew up, but I had not seen the massive unemployment that characterized African cities, unemployment that could not be explained either by unions or minimum wage laws (which, even when they existed, were regularly circumvented). Again, there was a massive discrepancy between the models we had been taught and what I saw."

These observations led him to intensify his research on the economics of uncertainty, which in turn, quickly led to the work on the economics of information. In Nairobi, only a few years after Kenya's independence, Joseph Stiglitz could reflect on the effects of colonialism, which neither delivered economic growth or democracy, and which was inconsistent with the principles in which he had been taught, and come to believe. The Kenyan market economy was plagued by repeated periods of unemployment, and left almost all of the population in poverty—he had seen comparable mysteries of capitalism in Gary, Indiana. He was forced to wrestle with the limitations of the market—the so-called market failures—that became one of the central foci of his research. He quickly came to the conclusion that economists should deal with the problems of gathering, analyzing, and disseminating information, and making decisions based on imperfect information.

Perhaps the biggest *systemic* failure associated with the market economy is the periodic episodes of underutilization of resources. Joseph Stiglitz has always been puzzled by the reasons why the labor market does not clear—why there is persistent unemployment. Starting with the work carried out with Robert Solow and George Akerlof, he sketched economic models that focused on the consequences of finite speeds of adjustment of wages and prices. ("Even if wages fall, if prices fall too, real wages may not adjust very quickly.") His paper on the exploration of "Alternative Theories of Wage Determination and Unemployment in Less Developing Countries," was completed while he was at the University of Nairobi. That paper was followed by a series of others on the efficiency wage theories, which explain why it may beneficial for firms to pay a wage higher than the market clearing wage; for instance, the increase in productivity often more than offsets the increase in wages.

The theory of equity rationing subsequently discussed by Joseph Stiglitz and co-authors helped explain why more "flexible" contractual arrangements are sometimes not adopted; "such arrangements (such as those where wages depend on firm profitability) in effect make the worker have an implied equity stake in the firm, and, given asymmetries of information, the value which workers are willing to assign to such contractual provisions is less than that which is acceptable to the firm." One can easily imagine labor markets in which firms also integrate their social responsibility—and the benefits of being perceived as "good citizens"—in their wage and contractual policies. Such theoretical approaches would allow for better analyses of labor markets in countries with a history of discrimination or ethnic tensions—and therefore suffering from peculiar forms of hysteresis. This would be true not only for South Africa but also for countries like India, Malaysia, and others.

I suspect that some of the things he saw in Kenya and in repressed financial markets elsewhere in the developing world also inspired his 1981 seminal paper with Andrew Weiss, in which he challenged the textbook model of credit markets. The established knowledge assumed that interest rates were the appropriate market instrument to balance the demand and supply of credit. Of course, that knowledge ignored the glaring strange behavior of some bank customers who would borrow money at much higher interest rates without the intention to ever pay back—either because they knew something about their business that bankers did not (asymmetric information) or because no legal economic activity could actually generate the necessary rate of return to pay back the loan—. The Stiglitz-Weiss paper offered a more realistic description of credit markets by showing why bankers might engage in credit rationing (i.e., limit the volume of loans) rather than raise the interest rate indefinitely to match the demand.

Even the work done by Joseph Stiglitz with Avinash Dixit, which is not directly related to the economics of information but instead to industrial organization, can be seen as providing the intellectual blueprint for developing countries that must enter global value chains in order to reap the full benefits of today's globalization of trade. I would argue that the famous 1997 Dixit-Stiglitz paper actually laid out the strongest theoretical foundations for understanding many important issues of international trade, and for designing the optimal trade strategy for a country like Kenya. Why? First, because international trade is the most important driver of growth for African countries. Second, the paper offers a general equilibrium model to examine how well the market actually works, and highlights the trade-offs between economies of scale and product diversity. This is obviously an important topic not only because of the large number of firms in almost all countries, and their heterogeneity, but also because of the puzzling issues of industrial structure. Even more than others, African economies are concerned with the challenges and opportunities of the changing patterns of industrial structure and technological upgrading across the world, the implications of alternative production bundles and innovation strategies for the economy's aggregate performance. Contrary to the unrealistic models of pure competition, pure monopoly, or oligopoly, the Dixit and Stiglitz model lays out the widely prevalent situation where there are so many firms in the economy that each can ignore its impact on others' actions, but still, firms face downward-sloping demand curves as there is monopolistic competition. The model shows quite clearly that there is only one borderline case in which the market makes the perfect trade-off between economies of scale and product diversity; but in general, the market was incompetent on such a critical question.

Because many of these remarkable insights were inspired by his stay in Kenya, one can confidently say that Joseph Stiglitz was the second black

Nobel laureate in economics, of course, after W. Arthur Lewis. I suspect Joe may secretly resent Lewis for having stolen that first spot from him in 1979 . . .

3. ON POLICY MATTERS: THE VOICE OF THE AFRICAN VOICELESS

African intellectuals have always been critical of mainstream economics and the dominant policy frameworks in vogue on the continent. That was certainly the case during the colonial period, and even more so after the independence wave. Even as most African countries recorded high rates of growth in the 1960s and 1970s, there was always a very strong group of dissidents. Not only from Marxist economists such as Samir Amin but also from people such as Joseph Tchundjang Pouémi or Mohamed Dowidar whose ideological affiliation was not clear-cut. In the 1980s and 1990s when the Washington Consensus became the framework for translating the Rational Expectations Revolution into development policies and practices, there was even more intellectual resistance from African economists: Adebayo Adedeji, Thandika Mkandawire, Mamadou Moustapha Kasse, and many others led the charge, pointing to the weaknesses and inconsistencies in the Bretton Woods model. Beyond economists, Africa produced quite a number of great social scientists who also challenged conventional economic thinking about the continent (sociologist Jean-Marc Ela and political scientist Adebayo Olukoshi, among others), and highlighted its devastating social consequences and its deleterious effects on the productive structure of African economies (especially in agriculture and manufacturing). Yet, even when that criticism was well formulated, it was dismissed with disdain as irrelevant.

It took the much stronger voice of Joseph Stiglitz to bring Africa's intellectual and policy perspective into the debate. As senior vice president and chief economist of the World Bank in 1997–2000, he witnessed the vicious ignorance or cynicism of some policy makers who refused to acknowledge the real negative side effects of the Washington Consensus. He observed negative effects of financial liberalization in Asian countries where speculators could come in and go out at will; he observed the economic, social, and human consequences of structural adjustment programs in Africa, where they favored privatization at all costs, even when they fostered the transfer of public assets into private hands, which led to widespread unemployment and cuts in basic services.

Not one to ever shy away from a fight, Joseph Stiglitz challenged the proponents of the Washington Consensus with intensity and vengeance. In March of 1997, barely a month into his tenure at the World Bank, he went to Ethiopia to meet with Prime Minister Meles Zenawi. Stiglitz later wrote: "During our discussions he showed a deeper and more subtle understanding of economic principles (not to mention a greater knowledge of the circumstances in his country) than many if not most of the international economic bureaucrats I would deal with in the succeeding three years."

At the time of Joe's visit to Ethiopia, the country's population was already almost 60 million but its GDP per capita was roughly only about $100—yes, one-hundred dollars. Moreover, Ethiopia's economic history had been marked by droughts, famines, suffering, and death on a large scale. Prime Minister Meles Zenawi, who had seized power in 1991, after a seventeen-year guerrilla war against an incompetent but brutal Marxist regime, was in a bitter fight with the International Monetary Fund (IMF) over macroeconomic strategy. He had basically balanced the government budget, cut military spending in favor of social expenditures, kept inflation under control, and engineered economic growth. But the IMF was not buying it; they only noticed that a large fraction of government revenue was from foreign aid, which they considered unsustainable. And since the Ethiopian government was unwilling to cut spending or raise taxes in anticipation of the potentially disastrous scenario of vanishing external assistance, the IMF had suspended its program. It also canceled a major credit, thereby signaling to other potential development financiers that Ethiopia was not open for business.

Recalling the almost two decades of civil war that his country suffered, Prime Minister Meles Zenawi blatantly told Joseph Stiglitz that they had not gone through bloodshed for seventeen years to be lectured by some Washington bureaucrats and be prevented from delivering better public services to their people once they had persuaded donors to pay for them. Those were powerful words. "I cannot adequately describe the emotional force of his words or the impact they had on me," Joseph Stiglitz later wrote. "I had taken the World Bank job with one mission in mind—to work to reduce poverty in the poorest countries of the world. I had known that the economics would be difficult, but I had not fathomed the depth of the bureaucratic and political problems imposed by the IMF."

There was also the issue of financial liberalization, which Washington experts wanted to see implemented immediately in Ethiopia. Conventional wisdom at the time was that all countries in the world, regardless of their level of economic and financial development, should deregulate and allow market forces to set the dynamics of interest rates and inflows-outflows of capital. The dominant policy makers in Washington did not seem to have learned any lesson from the U.S. Savings and Loan debacle. Prime Minister Zenawi was shocked at the intellectual rigidity of the Washington economists. He reminded Joseph Stiglitz that Kenya, the country next door, had gone through financial liberalization and experienced soaring interest rates. He also told him about the stories of many developing countries in the world that were not adequately equipped to handle the potential risks from orthodox macroeconomic policies. He pointed out that in Ethiopia, the situation was actually quite good, for a country that had just emerged from famine and civil wars. There was no inflation; in fact, prices were falling, and the economy was growing steadily.

On that same trip, Joseph Stiglitz also learned something sinister about the political economy of foreign aid. The previous year (1996), Ethiopia had repaid earlier than scheduled a loan to a U.S. bank using its reserves. The rationale for doing that was simple: the country was receiving lower interest rates on its reserves than it had to pay on the loan. Why wait? Yet, that totally rational financial and macroeconomic decision was heavily criticized by the U.S. Treasury and by the IMF, on the grounds that they had not been consulted . . . When told about it, Joseph Stiglitz wondered, with the pride that any African citizen would have: "Why should a sovereign country—one whose policies had convincingly demonstrated its capability—have to ask permission of the IMF for every action it undertakes?"

Finally, there was the political problem of conditionality, and its moral significance: as a native of a small town and as an honorary citizen of Kenya where he had really come to age as a great economic theorist, Joseph Stiglitz was shocked to learn about the true nature of the relationship between aid donors and political leaders in poor countries, and did not like it at all. He resented what he perceived to be the subordination between the IMF and its African clients. He felt the shame that an African prime minister or president would feel when: (a) being forced to grant an appointment in his busy schedule to an unknown, illiterate PhD holder whose only credential was to be a staffer at a Washington financial institution; (b) being dictated erroneous policy decisions as conditions for receiving balance of payment support; and (c) knowing well that when the disastrous consequences of such policies materialize and create economic and sociopolitical chaos in their country, the Washington bureaucrat who imposed them would have moved to another more lucrative job, immune to responsibility and chasing an even brighter career goal. He later wrote: "The processes themselves, with the numerous conditions that are often attached, not only infringe on national sovereignty but also tend to undermine democracy. I returned to Washington from Ethiopia gravely upset by what I had seen."

Thanks to his encounter with the Ethiopian leader, Joseph Stiglitz has become deeply immersed in the important economic policy issues facing all of Africa today. He has championed many causes that were only of interest to African economists. These include debt relief for poor countries—a highly pertinent issue when you know that a lot of the financial transactions were odious debt. He also spoke out forcefully against rich nations' agricultural subsidies to their minority of rich farmers, which hold back competition from poorer farmers in Africa and depress international prices of commodities that are the main source of income for large fractions of populations.

4. A PERMANENT THREAT TO OUR INTELLECTUAL QUIETUDE

When General de Gaulle forced himself back into power in France in 1958 after having inspired a military putsch in the French colony of Algeria, and when he adopted a new constitution that gave him full authority, his socialist nemesis François Mitterrand referred to him as "The Permanent Coup d'état." In a pamphlet with the same title, the socialist leader mocked de Gaulle as a man who would constantly use his past aura as France's war hero to impose himself into the public discourse and invalidate the normal functioning of democratic politics. I am not betraying any secret here by saying that some people at the IMF, the World Bank, or the U.S. Treasury, view Joseph Stiglitz the same way Mitterrand viewed de Gaulle—not only as an unmanageable troublemaker but as a permanent threat to peaceful, mainstream economic thinking.

There has always been something Kenyan about him . . .

Joseph Stiglitz is a combative fighter—one who never gives up. Again, this may be something he picked up from the Masai warriors during his time in Kenya. He loves politics and he loves arguing. Someone once said to me that a good indication that Joseph Stiglitz was actually an

African guy was his appetite for arguments and debates, including with his friends. If you have any doubt about that, ask Janet Yellen, the current Governor of the U.S. Federal Reserve, who still considers Joseph Stiglitz one of her best friends and mentors. Yet not too long ago, she was shocked to learn that Joseph Stiglitz did not just write op-ed pieces fiercely criticizing Fed policies and the notion that the central bank could even consider raising interest rates at this moment, instead of focusing on job creation and wage growth. After releasing an article with the not-so-subliminal title "Fed Up with the Fed" (an article published by Project Syndicate in 130 countries around the world), Joe actually led a demonstration at the Fed's annual policy summit in Jackson Hole, Wyoming. He was among fifty protestors who gathered there holding signs reading "Whose Recovery Is This?" and "How Many Jobs Do I Have to Work to Be Middle Class?"

I haven't asked Olivier Blanchard about his friendship with Joe during his tenure as IMF Chief Economist. But I can guess that he was never serene when he woke up every morning to deal with global macroeconomic crises while reading statements by Joe in the press about the misguided and cruel policies of the IMF. Kaushik Basu who currently occupies the position of World Bank Senior Vice President and Chief Economist that Joseph Stiglitz once held, once introduced him at a lecture in Washington. He said: "People often ask me what Joe Stiglitz accomplished when he was Chief Economist of the World Bank. I tell them: as Chief Economist of the World Bank, Joe Stiglitz changed . . . the IMF!" (Vintage Kaushik Basu, by the way).

I know for a fact that François Bourguignon, whom Joe brought to the World Bank in the 1990s as one of his protégés, was always nervous about the prospect of having to respond to controversies. When I worked as François's Economic Adviser, I would sometimes trick him by saying, in a matter-of-fact tone, that Joseph Stiglitz has just made a public statement about World Bank research. François would immediately raise his eyebrows, drop whatever he was reading, and ask almost frantically: "Oh yeah? What did he say? *Ah bon ? Qu'est-ce qu'il a dit ?*" Looking at François's always worried demeanor, I thought Joe Stiglitz was indeed a sort of permanent threat to our intellectual quietude as World Bank economists, one reminiscent of the "permanent coup d'état," as Mitterrand had said about de Gaulle.

Someone told me recently "Joseph Stiglitz never found an intellectual argument that he did not like, and that may make him prone to controversies and even conflicts. He is very talkative and has an opinion about every subject. Just like a typical African intellectual." Well, without commenting on the underlying negative essentialism in that statement, I would say that Joseph Stiglitz actually embodies the virtues of cosmopolitanism, which I see as the exact opposite of essentialism.

There has always been something Kenyan about him . . . How many Nobel laureates in economics have found time to travel to Africa and to speak at "obscure venues" for free, when they could command hefty speaking fees? His name is not Joseph Eugene Stiglitz. His real name is probably something like JOMO STIGLITZ—a typical Kenyan name. He just happens to live in New York like many Kenyans. He is Africa's pride, he is Africa's first Nobel laureate.

NOTE

1. As a Fulbright fellow at Cambridge, Joseph Stiglitz had Joan Robinson as his first mentor. Things did not go too well between the two of them. He later wrote: "We had a tumultuous relationship. Evidently, she wasn't used to the kind of questioning stance of a brash American student, even a soft-spoken one from the mid-west, and after one term, I switched to Frank Hahn."

Franklin Allen is professor of finance and economics and director of the Brevan Howard Centre at Imperial College London. His main areas of interest are corporate finance, asset pricing, financial innovation, comparative financial systems, and financial crises. He is a co-author, with Richard Brealey and Stewart Myers, of the eighth through twelfth editions of *Principles of Corporate Finance*.

Linda Bilmes is the Daniel Patrick Moynihan Senior Lecturer in Public Policy at the Harvard Kennedy School. Professor Bilmes is a leading expert on budgetary and public financial issues and a full-time faculty member at Harvard University. She has authored numerous books and publications regarding the cost of war and veterans' issues, including the *New York Times* best seller *The Three Trillion Dollar War: The True Cost of the Iraq Conflict* (with Joseph E. Stiglitz). She is the recipient of many awards and honors, including the "Speaking Truth to Power" prize by the American Friends Service Committee.

Bruce Chapman is a professor of economics at the College of Business and Economics at the Australia National University. He has worked directly on many labor market and education policies, and is an acknowledged world expert on income contingent student loans.

Giovanni Dosi is a professor of economics and director of the Institute of Economics at the Scuola Superiore Sant'Anna in Pisa; co-director of the task forces "Industrial Policy" and "Intellectual Property Rights," IPD—Initiative for Policy Dialogue at Columbia University; the continental European editor of *Industrial and Corporate Change*, and is included in "ISI Highly Cited Researchers." A selection of his works has been published in two volumes: *Innovation, Organization, and*

Economic Dynamics: Selected Essays (Edward Elgar, 2000) and *Economic Organization, Industrial Dynamics and Development: Selected Essays* (Edward Elgar, 2012).

Aaron Edlin holds the Richard Jennings chair and professorships in both the economics department and law school at University of California, Berkeley, and is a research associate at the National Bureau of Economic Research. He is co-author with P. Areeda and L. Kaplow of *Antitrust Analysis*, one of the leading casebooks on antitrust; and co-author with Joseph Stiglitz of *Economists' Voice* and *Economists' Voice 2.0*. He has also published in leading journals and periodicals such as the *American Economic Review, Econometrica, Journal of Political Economy, Harvard Law Review, Yale Law Journal*, the *New York Times*, and the *Wall Street Journal*.

Jason Furman is a professor of the practice of economic policy at the Harvard Kennedy School and a nonresident senior fellow at the Peterson Institute for International Economics. Furman served as a top economic advisor to President Barack Obama, including as the chair of the Council of Economic Advisers from 2013–2017, acting as both Obama's chief economist and a member of the Cabinet. In addition to numerous articles in scholarly journals and periodicals, Furman is the editor of two books on economic policy.

Douglas Gale is a Silver Professor and professor of economics at New York University and a fellow of the British Academy. His current research interests include general equilibrium theory and financial economics, with a focus on financial crises, banking regulation, and market illiquidity. His most recent book is *Understanding Financial Crises* (Oxford University Press, 2007) with Franklin Allen.

Antara Haldar is a tenured associate professor at the University of Cambridge, where she holds the inaugural position in Empirical Legal Studies and serves as the deputy director of Graduate Programs at the Faculty of Law. She is also a senior research associate at Cambridge's Judge Business School. She teaches law and economics, legal theory, and Cambridge's first-ever course on law and development. She has been a consultant to the United Nations on inclusive finance and was an invited member of the scholarly committee of the World Justice Project. She holds degrees in both law and economics, and is invited to speak and teach at universities around the world.

Benjamin E. Hermalin holds professorships in both the Economics Department and in Berkeley's Haas School of Business. He is currently

Berkeley's vice provost for the faculty. His areas of research include corporate governance, the study of organizations (especially leadership), industrial organization, and law and economics. He is co-editor of the *Handbook of the Economic of Corporate Governance* (North Holland, 2017) and a former co-editor of the *RAND Journal of Economics*.

Brian Hill is a research fellow at the French National Center for Scientific Research (CNRS) and CNRS Research Professor at HEC Paris. He has been an active researcher in philosophy, logic, and economics, with current interests particularly in the field of decision theory. Much of his recent research has focused on what counts as a rational reaction to severe uncertainty or ambiguity, and attempts to marry theoretical insights and tools from economics and philosophy, with an eye on practical consequences for the handling of uncertainty in concrete decisions, such as those involving environmental policy.

Arjun Jayadev is a professor of economics at Azim Premji University and a senior economist at the Institute for New Economic Thinking. His research focuses on the ways in which policy shifts that have occurred globally over the last three decades have impacted distributional outcomes (measured in terms of income, wealth, and power). He has been a fellow at Columbia University's Committee on Global Thought and a fellow at the Roosevelt Institute in New York. His work has appeared in a number of journals, including the *American Economic Journal: Macroeconomics*, *Journal of Development Economics*, *World Development*, the *Cambridge Journal of Economics*, *Health Affairs*, and several others.

Ravi Kanbur is a professor of world affairs and economics at Cornell University. He researches and teaches in development economics, public economics, and economic theory. He is well known for his role in policy analysis and engagement in international development. He is the former president of the Society for the Study of Economic Inequality, president of the Human Development and Capabilities Association, co-chair of the Scientific Council of the International Panel on Social Progress, past member of the High Level Advisory Council of the Climate Justice Dialogue, and a member of the OECD High Level Expert Group on the Measurement of Economic Performance.

Michael Katz is Sarin Professor Emeritus in Strategy and Leadership, professor emeritus of economics, University of California, Berkeley. He has been on the faculty of the Haas School of Business and Department of Economics at Berkeley since 1987. Katz has also served as the Harvey Golub Professor of Business Leadership at New York

University; deputy assistant attorney general for economic analysis in the Antitrust Division of the U.S. Department of Justice; chief economist of the Federal Communications Commission; and assistant professor of economics at Princeton University.

Anton Korinek is an assistant professor of economics at Johns Hopkins University and a faculty research fellow at the National Bureau of Economic Research (NBER). His area of expertise is macroeconomics, international finance, and inequality. His most recent research investigates the effects of artificial intelligence on macroeconomic dynamics and inequality. Korinek also focuses on capital controls and macroprudential regulation to reduce the risk of financial crises. He investigates the global spillover effects of such policy measures as well as their implications for income inequality. He has won several fellowships and awards for this work, including from the Institute for New Economic Thinking. He has also been a visiting scholar at Harvard, the Bureau of Industry and Security (BIS), the International Monetary Fund (IMF), World Bank, and numerous central banks.

Rahul Lahoti is an assistant professor of economics at Azim Premji University. He received a PhD in economics from the University of Gottingen. His work centers on issues of development and public policy. His work has appeared in several journals including the *Journal of Globalization and Development* and *World Development*.

Lawrence J. Lau is the Ralph and Claire Landau Professor of Economics at the Chinese University of Hong Kong and Kwoh-Ting Li Professor Emeritus of Economic Development at Stanford University. From 2004 to 2010, Professor Lau served as vice-chancellor (president) of the Chinese University of Hong Kong. From 2010 to 2014, he served as chairman of CIC International (Hong Kong) Ltd. Professor Lau published *Yes, Hong Kong Can!* (with Kenny Shui and Yanyan Xiong) in 2016 and *Shaping a New Society—Conversations on Economics, Education, and Peace* (with Daisaku Ikeda) in 2017.

Justin Yifu Lin is a professor and the director of the Center for New Structural Economics, dean of the Institute of South-South Cooperation and Development, and honorary dean of the National School of Development, Peking University. His recent books include *Going beyond Aids: Development Cooperation for Structural Transformation, Beating the Odds: Jump-Starting Developing Countries* with Célestin Monga (Princeton University Press, 2017), *Demystifying the Chinese Economy* (Cambridge University Press, 2012), and *New*

Structural Economics: A Framework for Rethinking Development and Policy (World Bank, 2012).

Tomasz Michalski is an associate professor of economics at HEC Paris. His research focuses on various barriers to international exchange and their effect on economic outcomes whether they are institutionally, information, uncertainty, or enforcement related. He has worked on various topics such as intermediation in international and inter-regional trade, international finance, industry location and product quality, or contract enforcement and open economy growth. He holds a PhD from Columbia University and previously worked at the National Bank of Poland and the European Central Bank.

Célestin Monga is the vice-president and chief economist of the African Development Bank Group. He previously served as managing director at the United Nations Industrial Development Organization (UNIDO), and senior economic adviser-director at the World Bank. He is also a pro bono visiting professor of economics at the University of Paris 1 Panthéon-Sorbonne and Peking University. His books include *Beating the Odds: Jump-Starting Developing Countries* (Princeton University Press, 2017), with Justin Yifu Lin; the *Oxford Handbook of Africa and Economics* (Oxford University Press, 2015), co-edited with J. Y. Lin; and *Nihilism and Negritude: Ways of Living in Africa* (Harvard University Press, 2016).

David Newbery, CBE, FBA, is the research director of the Cambridge Electricity Policy Research Group and emeritus professor of applied economics at the University of Cambridge. He is a fellow of the British Academy and of the Econometric Society. He was the 2013 president of the International Association for Energy Economics. His collaboration with Joe Stiglitz goes back to 1969 and they co-wrote *The Theory of Commodity Price Stabilization: A Study in the Economics of Risk at Stanford* (Oxford University Press, 1981).

José Antonio Ocampo is co-director of Banco de la República (Central Bank of Colombia), professor at Columbia University, and chair of the Committee for Development Policy, as well as an expert committee of the United Nations Economic and Social Council (ECOSOC). In 2012–2013, he chaired the panel created by the IMF Board to review the activities of the IMF's Independent Evaluation Office; in 2008–2010, he served as co-director of the United Nations Development Program/Organization of American States (UNDP/OAS) Project on the "Agenda for a Citizens' Democracy in Latin America;" and in

2009, he served as a member of the Commission of Experts of the UN General Assembly on Reforms of the International Monetary and Financial System. He has published extensively on macroeconomic theory and policy, international financial issues, economic and social development, international trade, and Colombian and Latin American economic history.

Peter R. Orszag joined Lazard as a managing director and vice chairman of Investment Banking in May 2016. He also serves as the global co-head of healthcare at Lazard, and is based in New York. Prior to joining Lazard, Orszag was with Citigroup (2011–2016), where he was vice chairman of Corporate and Investment Banking and chairman of the Financial Strategy and Solutions Group. Before that he was the director of the Office of Management and Budget (2009–2010), serving in President Barack Obama's Cabinet, and director of the Congressional Budget Office (CBO) from 2007–2008. Before leading the CBO, Orszag was a senior fellow in economic studies at the Brookings Institution. He previously served in the Clinton Administration, on both the Council of Economic Advisers staff and the National Economic Council.

Ugo Pagano is professor of economic policy at the University of Siena. He is the director of the Doctoral School in Economics organized jointly by the Universities of Florence, Pisa, and Siena. He taught at the Central European University. He received a PhD from the University of Cambridge where he was also a university lecturer and a fellow of Pembroke College. His research interests include bio-economics, institutional economics, law and economics, and the economics of knowledge.

Pierre Pestieau taught economics at Cornell University and then at the University of Liege until 2008. He is now professor emeritus at the University of Leige. He is also a member of CORE, Louvain-la-Neuve; an associate member of PSE, Paris; and a CESIfo fellow. His major interests are pension economics, social insurance, inheritance taxation, and redistributive policies. His articles have been published in a number of journals. He has published with Robert Fenge, *Social Security and Retirement* (MIT Press, 2005) and *The Welfare State in the European Union* (Oxford University Press, 2006).

Edmund Phelps, winner of the 2006 Nobel Prize in Economics, is the director of the Center on Capitalism and Society at Columbia University. He has written books on growth, unemployment theory, recessions, stagnation, inclusion, rewarding work, and the good economy. His work can be seen as a lifelong project to put "people as we know them" into economic theory. His most recent book, *Mass Flourishing: How Grassroots Innovation Created Jobs, Challenge, and Change* (Princeton University Press, 2013), examines how modernist values sparked the grassroots innovation that once drove economic growth, employment, and job satisfaction.

Gregory Ponthiere received a PhD from the University of Cambridge (2006). He has taught economics at the University of Liege and at the Ecole Normale Supérieure. Since 2014, he has been a professor of economics at the University of Paris-Est. He is also an affiliated professor at the Paris School of Economics and a junior chair at the Institut Universitaire de France. His major interests are population economics and long-run dynamics.

Sanjay G. Reddy is an associate professor of economics at the New School for Social Research. He is an affiliated faculty member of the Politics Department of the New School for Social Research and a research associate of the Initiative for Policy Dialogue at Columbia University. He holds a PhD in economics from Harvard University, an MPhil in social anthropology from the University of Cambridge, and an AB in applied mathematics with physics from Harvard University. He has previously taught at Columbia University, and been a visitor at diverse academic institutions in India, Europe, and the United States.

Gary Smith received a PhD in economics from Yale University and was an assistant professor at Yale for seven years. He is currently the Fletcher Jones Professor of Economics at Pomona College. He has won two teaching awards and written nearly 100 academic papers (mostly on statistics and finance) and 13 books, most recently, *The AI Deception* (Oxford University Press, 2018).

Hal R. Varian is the chief economist at Google. He started in May 2002 as a consultant and has been involved in many aspects of the company, including auction design, econometrics, finance, corporate strategy, and public policy. He is also an emeritus professor at the University of California, Berkeley, in three departments: business, economics, and information management. He received an SB degree from MIT in 1969, and an MA and PhD from UC Berkeley in 1973. He has published numerous papers in economic theory, econometrics, industrial organization, public finance, and the economics of information technology.

Maria Enrica Virgillito is an assistant professor at the Institute of Economic Policy, Catholic University of Milan. She received a PhD from the Institute of Economics, Scuola Superiore Sant'Anna, Pisa with a dissertation on "Essays on Economic Coordination and Change: From Industry and Labour Markets to Macroeconomic Regimes of Growth." Her research interests range from industrial dynamics, labor markets, macroeconomic dynamics, agent-based modeling, technology and labor relations to evolutionary economics. She is currently involved as a project member in the H2020 ISIGrowth project.

John Williams is president and CEO of the Federal Reserve Bank of San Francisco. In this role, he serves on the Federal Open Market Committee, bringing the Fed's Twelfth District's perspective to monetary policy discussions in Washington, DC. He was previously the executive vice president and director of research for the San Francisco Bank Fed, which he joined in 2002. He began his career in 1994 as an economist at the Board of Governors of the Federal Reserve System. Williams's research focuses on topics that include: monetary policy under uncertainty, innovation, productivity, and business cycles. He has collaborated with economists from throughout the country and across the globe to examine economic and policy issues from different perspectives, and has published numerous articles in leading research journals.

ABMs. *See* Agent-Based Models
accountability, 460, 462, 464, 470
Acemoglu, D., 240, 425, 426
Acharya, V. V., 278
Adedeji, Adebayo, 517
administrative law, 401
adoption rates, 228
advanced industrial economies, 424
adverse selection, 127, 201, 247
advertisers, 233
Affordable Care Act, 384
affordable housing, 434
Afghanistan, U.S. war in, 13, 457–460,
    463; taxation and, 465, *465*, 466,
    466; troops "wounded in action" in,
    472; U.S. public support for, 467
Africa: African intellectuals, 517;
    economic development and, 508;
    economic policy issues facing, 520;
    politics in, 511
Agent-Based Models (ABMs), 183
aggregate demand, 165, 342, 351
aggregate surplus, 122
agricultural industries, 34
agricultural subsidies, 446, 520
Aguiar, Mark, 213
airline industry, 37–38
Akerlof, George, 512
Algeria, 520
Allen, F., 240, 241, 245, 271

"all-volunteer" military force (AVF),
    464, 467, 472
Alonso, I., 272
"Alternative Theories of Wage
    Determination and Unemployment
    in Less Developing Countries"
    (Stiglitz), 515
altruism, 497, 499; caring and, 496;
    imperfect, 501, 503; two-sided
    altruism, 495, 498
Amazon, 230; Echo, 235
ambiguity, 210–211, 221, 222; ambiguity
    aversion, 215, 216, 219; general
    increase in, 220; increases in, 212
Amin, Samir, 517
Amnesty International, 473
analysts, 101, 102, 104
Anand, Vikas, 419*n*1
Ando, Albert, 202
anonymous pairing, 117, 118;
    idiosyncratic matching and, 121;
    welfare maximization and, 124
anti-commons tragedies, 365
antitrust cases, 6
Apple, 116
Aristotle, 64
Armstrong, M., 125
Arrow, K., 175, 178, 179, 197,
    229, 512
artificial scarcity, 24

assets, *361*; asset price bubbles, 343; asset price risk premia, 202; banks and assets as bipartite network, 284; external assets market, 282, 286, 291; fire sales of, 290, 296; fixed asset investment, 344, *346*, 347, *349*; high-yielding risky assets, 247; intangible, 364, 365; interbank assets, 286, 287, 295; investment in long assets, 246; long, 264, 265; real, 273, 282; shocks on price of, 283; types of, 245; uncertainty about asset returns, 271; used in production, 360. *See also* return on assets
Atkeson, Andrew, 213
Atkinson, A. B., 55, 175, 176, 495
AT&Ts Picture Phone, 227
austerity, 191; backlash against, 436; Washington Consensus and, 445
Australia, 480; Australian Tax Office, 481, 489; drought in, 487; economic research in, 483
autonomy, 116
availability bias, 407; switcher's curse and, 382, 395
AVF. *See* "all-volunteer" military force

balance sheet identity, 287
Baliga, Sandeep, 382, 383
Banerjee, A. V., 67, 69
Bangladesh, 424, 428, 430; irrational exuberance in, 432
Bank for International Settlements and the Financial Stability Forum, 448
bankruptcy, 243, 244; liquidity and, 251
banks, 202, 253, 434; assets and banks as bipartite network, 284; bank defaults, 290; banking industry, 247; banking system, 300; budget constraints and, 258; charging high interest rates, 285; consumers and, 241; deposits exchanged by, 242; equilibrium and, 256; holdings of, 252; insolvency and, 243, 244, 245, 252, 255, 264, 266, 268; interbank assets, 286, 287, 295; interbank deposits, 272; interbank liabilities, 286, 295; interbank market, 249–250; interdependence among, 294; investment and, 247; liabilities of, 283; liquidity-constrained, 257; located along chains of lending, 289; portfolio selection and, 254, 258; profiting from being perceived as too-big-to-fail, 299; regulation on, 297; risk sharing and, 241; shadow banking sector, 435; value of deposits of, 251
Bar-Hillel, Maya, 395
Barr, N., 482
Barth, Erling, 36, 37, 362
Base Erosion and Profit Shifting (BEPS), 453
base-rate fallacy, 395, 419*n*6
Basu, K., 357, 521
Battiston, S., 289, 293, 298, 300
Bayesian updater, 380, 386
Bayes' rule, 392
Bayh-Dole Act (U.S.), 360, 367
Becker, Gary S., 50
behavioral economics, 6
Bengui, Julien, 212
Benigno, Pierpaolo, 208
Benoit, S., 240
BEPS. *See* Base Erosion and Profit Shifting
bequests, 499, 501
Berkowitz, D., 426
Berman, E., 469
Bernanke, Ben, 203
Bezos, Jeff, 236
Bhagwati, J., 486
Bhattacharya, S., 272
bicycle bankers, 430
Bilmes, Linda J., 457, 463, 471
bipartite networks, 280, 284
Birdsall, Nancy, 68, 69, 70, 77
Blanchard, Olivier, 201, 521
Blank, R., 78
Block, F., 436

blocking effects, 367
bookstores, 116
Boskin, Michael J., 340
Bourguignon, F., 55, 521
BRAC, 431
brain circulation, 509
brain drain, 485–486, 509
Bresnahan, Timothy, 232
Bretton Woods Institutions (BWIs), 447, 453; developing countries and, 448; ECOSOC and, 451; in U.N. system, 449; voting structure of, 450
Breyer, Justice Stephen, 401
British Industrial Revolution, 360
Broner, Fernando A., 212
Brown, J., 494
Bryson, A., 362
budgetary trade-offs, 457
budget constraints, 257, 258, 260, 263–264, 500; regional, 261; value of deposits and, 271
Buffett, Warren, 109
Burke, Edmund, 12, 377; conservatism and, 378, 399
Burton, L., 496
Bush, George W., 460
business cycle, 271; fluctuations, 167; frequencies, 168. See also real business cycle
BWIs. See Bretton Woods Institutions

Caballero, Ricardo J., 212
Caldarelli, G., 300
Camdessus, Michel, 451
capacity: capacity auctions, 134, 142–143, 143, 150; capacity remuneration mechanisms, 131; coal capacity, 133; energy and, 132; reliability and, 139
Capacity Market Units, 145
Capacity Payment (CP), 138
Capacity Revenue Mechanisms, 134
capital: capital flight, 212, 222; capital flows, 208, 327; capital stock, 23, 24; China growth rates of real output, labor and, 339, 339; dead

capital, 425, 429; distribution, 219, 297; elasticities, 341; formalization and, 429; government capital expenditures, 198; growth rates and, 359; housing, 24; human capital, 54, 327, 362, 365; human capital of children, 52; importers of, 209, 211, 217, 221; income of, 22, 43n1; increasing share of income going to, 19; intangible, 327, 329; intellectual capital, 361; law and, 428; physical, 363; productivity of, 24, 360; returns to, 26, 30; share of capital income accruing to top one percent, 23; share of GDI, 25; supranormal returns on, 20; tangible, 323, 351; venture, 381; wages and returns on, 21; wealth and, 198, 199, 359; wealth owned by financial capital, 365. See also return on invested capital
capitalism, 181, 514; development and, 425; inequality and, 358–359; varieties of, 444; venture capitalists, 402
CARA. See constant absolute risk aversion
carbon price floors, 133, 142
Card, David, 37
caregivers, 495
Carter, Jimmy, 434
Caselli, Fabio, 207, 211
CBO. See Congressional Budget Office
CCGT. See combined cycle gas turbine
CDOs. See collateralized debt obligations
CDS. See credit default swaps
CEGB. See Central Electricity Generating Board
Census Bureau's Economic Census, 33
Center for Research in Security Prices (CRSP), 102
Central Electricity Generating Board (CEGB), 137
centrality, 301
centrally planned economy, 323, 330

central processing units (CPUs), 231
CEOs. *See* chief executive officers
CfDs. *See* Contracts for Differences
Champ, B., 272
Champernowne, David, 50, 53
Chan, K., 108
Chapman, B., 484, 485, 486, 488
Chari, V., 272
chartered corporations, 366
Chevron, 401
chief executive officers (CEOs),
    403–404; new, 417; status-quo bias
    and, 377
children, 49, 60, 497, 503; human
    capital of, 52; inequalities between,
    501–502; LTC and, 498; utility
    maximizers and, 499. *See also*
    parents, children, and luck
China, 313, 314; Academy of Social
    Sciences, 10; changing negative
    expectations, 344, 347; confidence
    of enterprises and households in,
    351; distribution of employment
    in, 328, *329*; *Diyicaijing* (Chinese
    financial newspaper), 317; domestic
    investment of, 327, *328*; dual-
    track approach of, 312; East Asian
    financial crisis and, 310, 444;
    economic development of, 323,
    327; economic growth of, 330,
    340, 344; environment degradation
    in, 320*n*7; exports of goods from,
    331, 332; GDP and household
    consumption in, 338, *339*; GDP by
    sector in, 328, *329*; GDP of, 309,
    314, 324, 340; growth rates of real
    GDP, *345, 348*; growth rates of real
    output, capital, and labor in, 339,
    339; growth rates of U.S. and, 324,
    325; imports of goods from, *333,
    334*; labor and, 323; learning by
    doing in, 329; liberalization and,
    312; monopsonistic power in, 330;
    national saving of, 327, *328*, 330,
    337, 338; People's Congress, 316;

policy discussions in, 315, 319*n*3;
    public sector employment in, *337*;
    real growth rate of U.S. and, *326,*
    327; real value-added of Chinese
    industry, *350*; reasons for success
    of, 11; residential real estate in, 343;
    statistics on Chinese economy, 319*n*1;
    stock market bubble of, 347; taxation
    in, 316, 338; transition from planned
    to market economy, 309, 310, 316;
    very rapid growth of, 71, 74; wage
    policy in, 330; wages of public-sector
    employees in, 338; in WTO, 324,
    327, 347
China Center for Economic Research,
    318
China Development Forum, 319
"China's Reformers Can Triumph Again,
    If They Follow the Right Route"
    (Stiglitz), 317
"Chinese Century" (Stiglitz), 317
Chinese Communist Party, 337
Christensen, Laurits R., 340
civic engagement, 460, 470
civil fraud, 468
clearing vector of payments, 287
climate change, 446; Intergovernmental
    Panel on Climate Change, 451
Climate Change Act 2008 (GB), 133
Clinton, Bill, 3, 369, 434, 511
cloud computing, 231
coal plants, 133
Coase conjecture, 180
codification, 423
Coe, N., 494
COFOPRI. *See* Comisión de
    Formalización de la Propiedad
    Informal
Colaresi, M. P., 469
Coleman, J., 426
collateralized debt obligations (CDOs),
    435
collective action problems, 422, 423,
    426
colonialism, 445, 511, 514

Columbia University, 2
combined cycle gas turbines (CCGT), 143, 147
Comisión de Formalización de la Propiedad Informal (COFOPRI), Peru, 428
Commission on Wartime Contracting, 469, 470
commodities: knowledge, commodification of, 364, 365; primary, 311; risky commodity markets, 131
common law, 399
communications networks, 112, 113
Community Reinvestment Act, 434
competition: competitive devaluation, 347; competitive equilibrium, 514; imperfect, 281; perfect, 251
complex networks, 277
CONE. See Cost of New Entry
confidence crises, 285
Confucius, 372n1
Congress, U.S., 457; direct appropriations for wars, 459; supplemental war funding by, 462; World War II and, 465
Congressional Budget Office (CBO), 459, 470
Congressional Research Service (CRS), 33–34, 459
connected networks, 280
conservatism, 12, 293, 386, 395; Burke and, 378, 399; complete, 394; degrees of, 387–388, 390, 396, 397, 398; Holmes and, 381; institutional memory and, 389; naive decision makers and, 385, 409; optimal conservative policy, 396, 397, 398; in practice, 387; progressivism and, 383, 396, 404; Silicon Valley and, 419n8; status-quo bias and, 382; strong version of, 402; switcher's curse and, 380, 381, 393
consolidation, 33

constant absolute risk aversion (CARA), 214, 216, 217, 218
Constitution, U.S., 460
constraints, 248
consumers, 250, 253; banks and, 241; confidence of, 347; early consumers, 257, 273; higher prices for, 35; marginal propensity to consume, 313; monthly real consumption, 70; persons responsible for constituting consumer markets, 66; preferences of, 246; welfare-maximizing for, 251
consumption hardship, 483
contract issuance, 211
Contracts for Differences (CfDs), 146, 148
Cooper, R., 182
coordination failures, 181
Corak, Miles, 52, 53
Corbae, Dean, 34
corporate earnings: between companies, 101; forecasts of, 95, 96, 100; imperfect information and, 109
corporate finance, 513
corporate income tax, 452
corporate management information system, 389
corruption, 312, 460, 468, 470
cosmopolitanism, 522
Cost of New Entry (CONE), 144, 147
cost per click (CPC), 234
Council of Economic Advisors, 1, 315, 369
counterparties, 286–287, 294; centrally cleared, 298; default condition of, 288; indirect, 284; shocks to, 292
Counter-Reformation tide, 178
CP. See Capacity Payment
CPC. See cost per click
CPUs. See central processing units
credit, 293; access to, 428; credit chain, 291; credit multiplier, 285; interest rates and, 294; pervasiveness of, 284; sensitivity of external creditors, 296; short-term, 295

credit crisis, 428
credit default swaps (CDS), 435
creditors, 283
credit rationing, 181, 201, 515–516; market failure and, 202
creditworthiness, 280
Creedy, J., 50
Cremer, H., 498
criminal fraud, 468
critical mass, 228
cross holdings, 242–243
CRS. *See* Congressional Research Service
CRSP. *See* Center for Research in Security Prices
Current Population Survey, 36

DAM. *See* day-ahead market
data barrier to entry, 234
Davis, Steven J., 38, 39, 41
day-ahead market (DAM), 138, 146
DC links, 149
Deaton, A., 78
debt: debt-equity mix, 31; debt financing, 219; debt forgiveness regimes, 481; fixed-rate, 208; foreign currency-denominated, 327; international sovereign debt-restructuring legislation, 447, 448; public debt, 197; ratios of equity to, *209*
DECC. *See* Department of Energy & Climate Change
decentralization, 260–261, 405, 502; of first-best optimum, 499; of social optimum, 501
decision makers, 380, 398, 407; current, 389; future, 388, 389, 390, 391; optimizing, 391; past, 12, 377, 381, 383, 387, 388, 389, 395, 397. *See also* naive decision makers
Decker, Ryan, 38
default: bank defaults, 290; correlations across defaults, 296; default contagion, 280; default risk, 10; initial, 296; systemic, 288, 289, 293;

systemic default probability, 291; uncertainty over default probability, 291
deferred spending, 463, 464
demand, 227, *228*; aggregate demand, 165, 342, 351; demand curves, 122, 123, 228; for deposits, 265; economies of scale, demand side, 229, 230; for liquidity, 243–244, 261, 264; negative demand shocks, 189; short-run increases in, 137; for withdrawals, 243
democratic representativeness, 449
Democratic Republic of Congo, 508
demographic changes, 41
Deng Xiaoping, 310, 319n2, 344
Denison, Edward F., 340
Denniss, A., 490
Department of Defense, U.S., 458, 462, 468, 472
Department of Energy & Climate Change (DECC), U.K., 139, 142, *144*, 144–145; *Final Impact Assessment*, 145–146
Department of Labor, U.S., 468
Department of Veterans Affairs (VA), U.S., 458, 471
dependence, 498
deposits, 249, 252, 253; banks exchanging, 242; demand for, 265; deposit contracts, 247, 251, 255; depositor welfare, 259; equilibrium deposit contract, 259; extra-regional, 244; interbank, 257, 272; liquidating, 243, 245; optimal, 265; optimal deposit contracts, 262; payoff to depositors, 255; value of, 251, 254, 271
D'Erasmo, Pablo, 34
deregulation, 37–38
derivative contracts, 298
De Soto, H., 425, 428
destitution, 59
devaluation, 347
developed economies, 347

developing countries, 310; BWIs and, 448; growth performance and stability of, 312; process of economic development in, 319; social, economic conditions in, 318

development, 310; capitalism and, 425; developmentalists, 425; inequality and, 10; learning and, 354; process of economic development in developing countries, 319; strategy of development leaning on heavy industry, 311; sustainable development, 450; Third International Conference on Financing for Development, 452. See also economic development

Diamond, D., 241, 245, 272

Diamond-Dybvig model, 271, 272

digital goods, 116

Dilnot, A., 497

disability benefits, 463

disconnected networks, 280

dislocation, 9

distress contagion, 280

"Distribution of Income and Wealth Among Individuals, The" (Stiglitz), 512

diversification, 292–295

dividends, 95

division of labor, 184

Dixit, Avinash, 516

Diyicaijing (Chinese financial newspaper), 317

Doing Business (World Bank), 425

domestic markets, 328–329

Dosi, G., 175, 184, 191

dot-com boom, 379

dot-com bubble of 1990s, 366

dot-com crash of 2000, 235

double-taxation treaties, 452

Dowidar, Mohamed, 517

drought, 487

DSGE. See dynamic stochastic general equilibrium

Duflo, E., 67, 69

Dupriez, O., 78

durable goods, 75

DVD standard, 402

Dworkin, R., 49, 59

Dybvig, P., 241, 245, 272

dynamic stochastic general equilibrium (DSGE), 7, 159–160, 161–162, 186; central banks use of, 202; complexity introduced by, 171, 172; conceptual restrictions of, 173; dynamic aspect of, 163; GE and, 187; general equilibrium aspect of, 163–164; models of, 168–170; New Keynesian, 166; stochastic aspect of, 163–164; typical approach to writing a paper in, 168; welfare experiments and, 167

dynamism, 41, 44n6

dynastic equality, 57

earnings, 103, 103, 105; accuracy of earnings predictions, 100; base-year earnings, 102; inequality, 36; interindustry differentials in, 20; predictors of actual earnings, 99; relative, 105. See also corporate earnings

East Asia, 74; currency crisis in, 344; financial crisis in, 310, 444; NIEs in, 341–342; recovery of economies in, 347

Easterly, W., 70

eBay, 115–116

economic development, 319; Africa and, 508; of China, 323, 327; early stages of, 328; learning and, 354; patent trolls and, 358

economic fluctuations, 9

economic governance, 443

economic growth: of China, 330, 344; of NIEs, 341–342

economic networks, 277

economic reform, 340

Economics of Information, 8, 179, 191, 192; financial networks and, 278; fundamental legacy of, 279

Economics of Invention and Innovation, 179

Economics of Knowledge, 191, 192

economic theory, 2

Economides, Nicholas, 227

economies of scale, 35, 229, 230, 323, 330, 340; formal systems and, 436; knowledge and, 361; product diversity and, 516

ECOSOC. *See* UN Economic and Social Council

educational attainment, 311

efficient rationing, 117, 121

Eigenvector centrality, 301

Einstein, Albert, 169

elasticity, 428

elderly people, 493

electricity industry, 132, 150

Electricity Market Reform (EMR), 133, 147

Elliott, M., 240

Ely, Jeffrey, 382, 383

emergent phenomena, 165

employment: China distribution of, 328, *329*; new employees, 404; public sector employment in China, *337*

EMR. *See* Electricity Market Reform

energy: capacity and, 132; energy-only markets, 139, 140; intermittent generation of, 142; liberalized electricity market, 134, 135; prices of, 136; renewable, 141–142

Energy Act 2013 (GB), 133, 142

Engel curve methodology, 78

Enlightenment movement, 353

entrepreneurs, 64, 211, 213–214; dot-com boom and, 379; Sharpe ratio of entrepreneurial consumption, 220

environment degradation, 320n7

epidemiology, 292

equilibrium, 112, 181, 217, 267, 270; banks and, 256; competitive equilibrium, 514; with complete risk sharing, 262, 264; critical mass and, 228; equilibrium assumptions, 174; equilibrium deposit contract, 259; existence of multiple equilibria, 289, 290; information and, 179; liabilities and, 252; maximizing behaviors in order to establish, 186; micro heterogeneity as equilibrium phenomenon, 178; in which social optimum could be decentralized, 260. *See also* general equilibrium

equity, 207; annual returns on, 30, *30*; debt-equity mix, 31; equity participation, 9; ratios of debt to, *209*

equity rationing, 515

estimation errors, 236, *237*

Ethiopia, 518, 519

EU. *See* European Union

Euler equation, 187

Eurelectric, 136, 149

Europe, 75

European Union (EU), 131, 133; liberalized electricity market of, 135; *Renewables Directive*, 136, 141

Evolutionary Economics, 191

exchange markets, 298

exchange rates: global middle classes defined by, 85, *85*; Zhu Rongji and, 344

expectations: China changing negative, 344, 347; formation of, 342; policies, expected value of, 391; rational, 165, 166, 170, 187; self-fulfilling, 343

Expected Energy Unserved, 143

externalities, 121, 282; access externalities, 113; importance of, 112; information and, 279; negative effects of, 279, 280, 283; network, 172; positive effects of, 279; role of, 278; usage externalities, 113, 114

extrinsic motivations, 355

Facebook, 238

fair trade rules, 446

Fama, E. F., 96, 107, 108
Fama-French model, 107, *108*
family, role of, 495
Fannie Mae and Freddie Mac, 434
FCC. *See* Federal Communications
    Commission
FCC v. Fox Television, 401
FECS. *See* Fine Enforcement Collection
    Scheme
Federal Communications Commission
    (FCC), 35, 401
Federal Funding Accountability Act,
    460
Federal Reserve, 202, 205, 210;
    Supervisory Capital Assessment
    Program, 204
"Fed Up with the Fed" (Stiglitz), 521
Feyrer, James, 207, 211
Final Impact Assessment (DECC),
    145–146
financial contagion, 240, 244;
    incompleteness of markets and, 268;
    possibility of, 261; preconditions for,
    242; spreading of, 284
financial contracts, 288
financial crises, 190, 266, 489; East
    Asian, 310, 444; global, 424; growth
    effects of, 168; investment and, 368;
    North Atlantic, 443, 448; policy
    solutions to, 172; social movements
    emerging from, 436; of 2008, 433
financial dependencies, 282
financial industry, 364
financial instability, 277
financial institutions, 513; colonial
    mentality of, 445; financial
    dependencies and, 282; law and,
    436
financial instruments, 364, 434
financial interlinkages, 277
financialization: commodification of
    knowledge and, 365; of Global
    North, 437
financial networks, 299; complex, 297;
    Economics of Information and, 278;

resilience of, 293–294; structure of,
    280, 289
financial repression, 314
financial robustness, 293–294
financial stability, 278
Fine Enforcement Collection Scheme
    (FECS), 485
Finkelstein, A., 494, 496
firm-specific idiosyncratic learning,
    178
first-order conditions (FOCs), 499
Fiscal Neutrality toward Economic Growth
    (Phelps), 197
fiscal opacity cycle, 13, 457, *461*; factors
    leading to, 460, 464, 470
fiscal revenues, 501
fiscal transparency, 457, 470
Fischer, Stanley, 201, 508
flexibilization, 191
Florini, A., 469
fluidity, 41
FOCs. *See* first-order conditions
FOIA. *See* Freedom of Information Act
Foley, Duncan, 197
forecasting, 103, *103*, 104, *105*, *106*;
    corporate earnings, 95, 96, 100;
    current-year forecasts, 105; measuring
    accuracy of, 102; year-ahead forecasts,
    105
formalization, 423; capital and,
    429; complete, 435; institutional
    evolution and, 437; irrelevant, 430
France, 139
Frank, R. G., 493
Freedom of Information Act (FOIA),
    460, 468
Freeman, Chris, 175, 189
Freeman, David J., 362
free market doctrine, 315
free-rider problem, 245
French, K. R., 96, 107, 108
French Enlightenment, 372n1
Friedman, L., 426
Fuglie, Keith, 34
Furman, J., 372n1

G-7, 340
G-20, 448, 449
G-20/OECD, 453
G-77, 452
Gai, P., 240, 286, 295
Galanter, M., 425
Gale, D., 240, 241, 245, 271
game theory, 277
GAO. *See* Government Accountability Office
Gaynor, Martin, 35
GB. *See* Great Britain
GCIP. *See* Global Consumption and Income Project
GDI. *See* Gross Domestic Income
GDP. *See* gross domestic product
GE. *See* general equilibrium
Geanakoplos, John, 15
GECC. *See* Global Economic Coordination Council
Gelos, R. Gaston, 208
general equilibrium (GE), 179, 185; DSGE and, 187
generality, loss of, 122, 251, 273, 286, 385
General Theory of Employment, Interest and Money, The (Keynes), 188
Gertz, G., 67
Gibbons, Robert, 37
Gibrat, R., 50, 53
Gilchrist, Simon, 204
Gini coefficient, 312–313
Ginsberg, Justice Ruth Bader, 401
Glaeser, Edward L., 27, 28
Glick, William H., 419*n*1
Global Consumption and Income Project (GCIP), 5, 63, 70
Global Consumption Dataset, 70
global cultural interdependencies, 372*n*1
Global Economic Coordination Council (GECC), 449, 450, 451
global elite, 85
global financial architecture, 298
global governance, 445, 454

Global Income Dataset, 70
globalization, 443; management of, 444; problems of, 454; of trade, 516
Globalization and Its Discontents (Stiglitz), 443, 444
global middle classes, 63, 65, 71, *84*; competing definitions of, 86; defined by exchange rates, 85, *85*; as defined by global median, *72*, *73*; emerging, 66; estimates of size of, 68, *68*; global elite and, 85; Global Middle-Class Concept 1, 67, 69; Global Middle-Class Concept 2, 67, 69; Global Middle-Class Concept 3, 67, 69; lower threshold for, 76; market-specific definition of, 82; story of, 75
Global North: financialization of, 437; legal evolution of, 423, 426
global reserve system, 447
global society, 366
Global South, 423, 427, 428; legal dualism in, 437
global trade, 64
GNP. *See* gross national product
Gollier, Christian, 210, 215
Golub, B., 240
goods, 78, 245; digital, 116; durable, 75; exports from China, *331*, *332*; imports from China, *333*, *334*; knowledge as public good, 365, 371; nonrival goods, 354–355, 361; public, 357; rival, 369, 371
GOOG411, 235
Google, 235, 238
Google Brain, 235
Gopinath, Gita, 213
Government Accountability Office (GAO), U.S., 459
government-insured entities, 298
Graham, C., 70
Grameen Bank, 430, 431, 432
graph theory, 277
Great Britain (GB), 131, 133, 138, 142; electricity industry of, 132, 147; scarcity pricing, *141*; VoLL in, 139

Great Depression, 366, 367

Great Financial Crisis: aftermath of, 160; macroeconomics and, 159

"Great Gatsby Curve," 4, 48, 52, 60

Great Recession, 277, 370, 433

Greece, 298

Greenwald, Bruce, 9, 230, 231, 284, 285

Gross Domestic Income (GDI): changes in shares of, *25*; labor and capital share of, *25*

gross domestic product (GDP), 208; of China, 309, *314*, 324, 340; of China, by sector, 328, *329*; contraction of, 311; of Democratic Republic of Congo, 508; GDP-linked securities, 212; growth rates of China real, *345*, *348*; growth rates of real, *335*, *336*, 344; household consumption GDP of China, 338, *339*; share of labor in, 330, 338; of U.S., 29, 324; of Zambia, 508

Grossman, S., 179

gross national product (GNP), 11, 370

growth rates, 103, 105; capital and, *359*; China, real growth rates of, *326*, 327; of China, 324, *325*; growth-accounting exercise, 341, *342*; long-term, 191; output, *191*; of real GDP, *335*, *336*, 344; of real GDP in China, *345*, *348*; of real output, capital and labor in China, 339, *339*; sustainable, 317; U.S., real growth rates of, *326*; of U.S., 324, *325*

Guadalcanal, 510

Gulf War, 467

Guo, Haiqiu, 340

Gyourko, Joseph, 27, 28

Hagiu, A., 115, 116

Haldane, A., 286

Haltiwanger, John, 38, 39, 41, 182, 183

Hart, Peter, 50, 51, 52, 53

hazard rates, 123

Heald, D., 469

health care, 34–35; benefits, 463; health insurance plans, 112; publicly financed, 337; universal health care insurance, 483

Heaviside function, 288

heavy industry, 311

HECS. *See* Higher Education Contribution Scheme

Hellwig, M., 272

Herfindahl-Hirschman Index (HHI), 35

Hermalin, B. E., 124

HHI. *See* Herfindahl-Hirschman Index

hidden appropriations, 461

Higgins, T., 484

Higher Education Contribution Scheme (HECS), 480, 481; collection costs of, 489; introduction of, 483, 487; for living costs, 484

high-income countries, 65, 318

Hill, Brian, 208

Hirshleifer, David, 382, 383, 419*n*1

Hirst, M., 496

Ho, Kate, 35

Hodrick-Prescott (HP) filter, 168

Holmes, Oliver Wendell, 378, 381, 399, 400

Hong Kong, 338

Hood, C., 469

hookup apps, 111, 120

Hormats, R. D., 465

Hotelling, H., 97, 98

household consumption, 338, *339*

housing: affordable housing, 434; capital, 24; construction costs, *27*, 28; prices, 434; values, 27, 29

Housing and Community Development Act of 1992, 434

housing-backed securities, 434

HP. *See* Hodrick-Prescott filter

Huanhuan Zheng, 352

Hudson Bay Companies, 366

human rights, 508

Hussein, Saddam, 467

Hyatt, Henry R., 38, 39, 41

IBES. *See* Institutional Brokers' Estimate System

ICLs. *See* income contingent loans

ICRICT. *See* Independent Commission for the Reform of International Corporate Taxation

identity matrix, 55, 57

idiosyncratic matching, 112, 121, 128

IEA. *See* International Economic Association

IGE. *See* Intergenerational Income Elasticity

"I Have a Dream" speech (King), 511

ILD. *See* Institute for Liberty and Democracy

ILO. *See* International Labor Organization

IMF. *See* International Monetary Fund

imperfect competition, 281

imperfect information, 6, 278, 279, 288, 299, 398; corporate earnings and, 109; structural rigidities associated with, 8

incentive effects, 367

income, 22, 24, 43n1; absolute, 66; changing distribution patterns of, 64; distribution of, 337; high-income countries, 65; household disposable income, 338; income distribution, 21; income polarization, 64; income security, 75, 77; income transition equation, 50; increasing share of income going to capital, 19; inequality, 312–313; log income, 51, 52; share of income accruing to top one percent, *23*; taxable, 452; of upper classes, 81

income-based repayment options, 482

income contingent loans (ICLs), 14, 479–483; basic principles of, 485, 486; brain drain and, 486; individual capacities to repay, 490; insurance benefits of, 487; PPL and, 484, 488; in private sector, 489; risk and, 488

incomplete markets, 268–269; imperfect competition and, 281

incomplete networks, 281–282

incumbency, 393; importance of, 387

Independent Commission for the Reform of International Corporate Taxation (ICRICT), 451, 452–453

India, 86, 424; middle class in, 77, 88n5

individual utility functions, 498

Industrial Emissions Directive (EU), 133

industrial organization, 516

Industrial Revolution, 175

industry norms, 417

inefficient rationing, 112

inequality, 3–4, 54, 267, 269, 371; capitalism and, 358–359; between children, 501–502; children and, 60; Corak on, 53; development and, 10; dynastic, 5, 56, 57, 61; earnings, 36; elasticity of, 51; establishing, 413, 414; income, 312–313; intergenerational, 510; learning and, 354; mobility and, 51–52; monopolies and, 366; of opportunity, 58, 61; rents and, 20, 21; rise in, 19–20; rise in, taxonomy of, 23; wage, 20; wages, rise in inequality of, 37; within-firm pay inequality, 363

infinite horizon, 197

inflation, 166, 316, 519

informal caregivers, 497, 503

informal family care, 493; laissez-faire amount of, 502; in U.S., 494

informal institutions, 423, 437

informality, 433

information, 427; asymmetrical, 174, 179, 181, 278, 279, 298; distribution of, 180, 188; embedded in incumbency, 393; equilibrium and, 179; externalities and, 279; financial contracts, imperfect information on, 288; limited, 384; negative, 386; overemphasis on current, 395; positive, 386; possessing distinction from processing of, 96; on prices, 298; uncertainty and, 246. *See also* imperfect information

information economies, 433

Information Rules (Shapiro and Varian), 227

infrastructure, 311

innovation, 185, 415; extrinsic motivations and, 355; financial, 364; knowledge and, 356, 357; Rasmusen on, 382

input suppliers, 114

insider trading, 486

insolvency, 204, 241, 243, 244, 252, 255, 264, 266; spreading, 245

Institute for Liberty and Democracy (ILD), 428

institutional arrangements, 445

Institutional Brokers' Estimate System (IBES), 101

institutional complementarities, 356

institutional evolution: formalization and, 437; informal institutions and, 423; inner logic of, 438; trajectory of, 424

institutional memory, 389

institutional replication, 437

insurance failure, 482

intangible corporations, 365

Integrated Electricity Market, 135

Integrated Emissions Directive, 142

intellectual monopolies, 355, 356, 360; on intellectual capital, 361; property rights and, 369

intellectual property rights (IPRs), 355, 356; ideological construct of, 369; management of, 358; monopolies, 446; outsourcing and, 364; protectionism and, 368–369; reinforcement of, 363, 367, 370; ROIC and, 363; TRIPS and, 367–368

interbank market, 241, 282, 291

interconnectors, 145–146, 150

interest rates, 285, 294

Intergenerational Income Elasticity (IGE), 4, 48, 50

intergenerational inequality, 510

Intergovernmental Panel on Climate Change, 451

International Economic Association (IEA), 14, 479, 488

international finance, 207

international financial integration, 64

International Labor Organization (ILO), 68

International Monetary Fund (IMF), 444, 518; colonial mentality of, 445; RTI and, 460

international sovereign debt-restructuring legislation, 447, 448

International Tax Court, 453–454

internet, 402, 415

internet companies, competition among, *238*

internet search engines, 229, 230, 232, 234; search engine industry new entrants, 235

inter-regional cross holdings, 242

investment, 208, 214; banks and, 247; China domestic investment, 327, *328*; contrarian investors, 97, 109; diversification of investment opportunities, 292; financial crises and, 368; fixed asset investment, 344, *346*, 347, *349*; global, *367*; Great Depression, investment crisis culminating in, 367; in intangible capital, 327; investor errors, 108; irrational exuberance of investors, 366; in long assets, 246; nation-states investment in knowledge, 370; "value" investment strategies, 96, 97

IPRs. *See* intellectual property rights

Iraq, U.S. war in, 13, 457–460, 463; news coverage of, 467; taxation and, 465, *465*, 466, *466*; troops "wounded in action" in, 472; U.S. public support for, 467

Ireland, 134
Italian Renaissance, 372n1
iTunes, 116

Jacklin, C., 272
Jackson, M. O., 240
Jagannathan, R., 272
Japan, 328
Jeanne, Olivier, 212
job creation, *39*
job flows, 41
Job Openings and Labor Turnover
    Survey (JOLTS), 39
John, A., 182
Johnson, Lyndon B., 466
Johnson, S., 425, 426
joint density function, 288
joint-liability lending, 431
JOLTS. *See* Job Openings and Labor
    Turnover Survey
Jorgenson, Dale W., 340
judges, 400

Kahneman, Daniel, 395, 419n4
Kalecki, M., 50, 53
Kanbur, Ravi, 48, 49, 56, 57, 58, 59,
    60, 61
Kapadia, S., 240, 286, 295
Kasse, Mamadou Moustapha, 517
Katz, Lawrence, 37, 227
Katz, M. L., 124
Kelley, Truman, 100, 101, 102
Kenya, 14–15, 509, 510, 513, 515
Keynes, John Maynard, 188
Keynesianism, 175, 180, 196; bastard
    Keynesians, 186; countercyclical
    fiscal policies and, 343; K + S
    family of models, 183, *183*, 184;
    New Keynesianism, 166, 181;
    strategic complementaries and,
    182
Kharas, H., 67, 69
Kim, Jong-Il, 341
Kimble v. Marvel, 399
King, Martin Luther, Jr., 511

Kitrosser, H., 469
Kleiner, Morris, 42
Klibanoff, Peter, 210
knowledge: commodification of,
    364, 365; economies of scale and,
    361; global knowledge commons,
    353, 357; innovation and, 356,
    357; learning activities and, 354;
    modern knowledge economy, 371;
    monopolies on, 354; nation-states
    investment in, 370; nonrival good
    of, 354–355, 371; nonrival nature
    of, 11; privatization of, 353, 355,
    360–361; production and, 235, 360;
    production of new knowledge, 356;
    public, 358; as public good, 365,
    371
knowledge economies, 354–355
Korean War, 457, 463, 464
Kose, M. Ayhan, 212
Krishnamurthy, Arvind, 212
Krueger, Alan B., 37, 42, 52, 53
K + S. *See* Schumpeter meeting Keynes
Kurz, Mordecai, 197
Kuznets curve, 358

labor, 19; China and, 323; China
    growth rates of real output, capital
    and, 339, *339*; dynamism of U.S.
    labor markets, 38; elasticities, 341;
    immobility in, 38; income of, 22,
    24, 43n1; labor force participation
    rates, 196; optimal tax on, 500, 501;
    rents and, 21; share of GDI, *25*;
    share of labor income accruing to
    top one percent, *23*; share of labor
    in GDP, 330, 338; surplus, 351;
    tangible, 351
labor market, 181; flexibilization, 191;
    Phillips curve on, 186
laissez-faire movement, 436
Lakonishok, J., 99, 108
Lamfalussy, Alexandre, 451
land titling, 424, 428
land-use restrictions, 24, 27–29

La Porta, R., 425
Large Combustion Plant Directive (EU) (LCPD), 133, 142
Latin America, 58, 318; economic security in, 77; nonpoor in, 67
Lau, Lawrence J., 341, 352
law: administrative, 401; capital and, 428; financial institutions and, 436; formal and "informal," 12, 422; patterns of behavior systematically influenced by, 422; as repository of information, 427; rule of law, 454
LCPD. See *Large Combustion Plant Directive*
learning, 354. *See also* technological learning
learning by doing, 178, 227, 229, 230, 237, 329
learning organizations, 233
learning society, 11; different forms of, 371; institutions in, 356; privatization of knowledge and, 353
Least Worst Regrets approach, 145
Lectures on Macroeconomics (Blanchard and Fischer), 201
Leegin Creative Leather Products v. PSKS, 401
legal dualism, 437
legal pluralism, 422
legal positivists, 438n1
legal realists, 400
legal reform, 427
legal system, 399–400; legal dualism and, 437; underdevelopment and, 425
Lehman Brothers, 347, 433
lending, 289
Levy Control Framework, 147
Lewis, W. Arthur, 509, 517
liabilities, 278; of banks, 283; equilibrium and, 252; interbank, 286, 295; short-term, 293; value of, 266

liberalization, 311; China and, 312; financial, 518, 519; implementing, 315; Washington Consensus and, 445
liberal legalism, 425
limited memory, 383, 398, 407
linear tariffs, 117
liquidation, 273
liquidity, 241, 242, 267; abundance of, 344; bankruptcy and, 251; demand for, 243–244, 261, 264; deposits, liquidating, 243, 245; hoarding, 290; liquidity-constrained banks, 257; liquidity shocks, 269, 273; market illiquidity, 297; provision, 283
living costs, 484
lobbying, 357
log-in screens, 415
LoLE. *See* Loss of Load Expectation
LoLP. *See* Loss of Load Probability
longevity, 403
Longitudinal Business Data Base, 36
Longitudinal Employer-Household Dynamics, 36
long-term care (LTC), 14; children and, 498; cost of, 494; middle classes and, 503; number of agents in, 504; optimal LTC social insurance, 501; private insurance for, 496, 497; public LTC scheme, 497, 502, 504; rapid increase in needs for, 493; severe dependence and, 497; social insurance system, 495
Lopez-Calva, L. F., 67, 69
Lorenzoni, Guido, 212
Loss of Load Expectation (LoLE), 136, 139
Loss of Load Probability (LoLP), 137, 149
LTC. *See* long-term care
Lucas, Robert, Jr., 165
Lucas critique, 165–166, 167
luck, 49, 59

Macaulay, S., 426
Maccheroni, Fabio, 210

macroeconomics, *160*; aggregate demand and, 165; bias in, 170; criterion to judge usefulness of models of, 172; DSGE and, 159–160, 161; emergent phenomena in, 165; Great Financial Crisis and, 159; macroeconomic fluctuations, 164; microeconomics and, 164; orthodox macroeconomic policies, 519; quantitative interrelationships of macroeconomic variables, 168; robustness and, 172–173; traditional macroeconomic models of the 1970s, 167

macroprudential policy, 278

MAE. *See* mean absolute error

Making Globalization Work (Stiglitz), 443, 444, 445

Malthus, Thomas Robert, 175

management changes, 417

Manz, Charles C., 419*n*1

MAP. *See* Mutual Agreement Procedure

marginal cost, 118, 119, 123, 125; output and, 233; social optimum prices and, 127

Marinacci, Massimo, 210

market concentration, 34, *34*, 35

market failure, 169, 202, 445, 515

market illiquidity, 297

market imperfections, 429

marketing materials, 405

market irrationality, 512

marketization, 311, 315

markets economy, 261

market structure, 249

Markov process, 390

marriage, 406

Marx, Karl, 175, 181; property rights and, 438*n*6

Massachusetts Institute of Technology (MIT), 511

Mauritius, 312

MBS. *See* mortgage-backed securities

McGarry, K., 496

mean absolute error (MAE), 102

means-testing, 483

Medicaid, 496

Mendoza, Enrique G., 212, 213

Mercer cost of living database, 78

Merry, Engle, 426

MFIs. *See* microfinance institutions

Michalski, Tomasz, 208

Microcredit Regulatory Authority (MRA), 432

microeconomics, 164, 165

microfinance, 424; early years of, 431; importance of, 432; repayment crisis in, 433; spread of, 432; three phases of, 430

microfinance institutions (MFIs), 430; regulation of, 431; repayment rates of, 431–432

microfoundations, 164, 167

micro heterogeneity, 178

middle classes, 5, *87*, 497; condition and prospects of, 64; contested understanding of, 65; definitions of, 69; goods and services required for, 78; in India, 77, 88*n*5; level of material attainment of, 79; LTC and, 503; OECD and, 86; Ravallion on, 67; as sociological category, 75; threshold for, 71, *80*, 81, *83*; urban, 81–82; in U.S., 65, 86. *See also* global middle classes

Midwestern America, 426

migration: decline in job and geographic mobility, 42; long-distance migration in U.S., 39; rates of, *40*

Milanovic, B., 67, 69

military, U.S., 457, 460, 467

Minow, Martha, 468

"missing market" problems, 135, 150, 429

"missing money" problems, 135, 150

MIT. *See* Massachusetts Institute of Technology

Mitterrand, François, 520

Mkandawire, Thandika, 517

mobility, 29; declines in, 42, 49–50; inequality and, 51–52; "perfect mobility," 55; standard mobility equation, 54

model uncertainty, 215, 220

Modigliani, Franco, 202, 511–512

Modigliani-Miller theorem, 512–513

Molloy, Raven, 27, 28, 39

moneylenders, 430

monopolies, 119, 313; China monopsonistic power, 330; inequality and, 366; on intellectual capital, 361; IPRs and, 446; on knowledge, 354; monopoly rents, 320n8; natural, 172; on power, 366; pricing decisions of, 117; pure, 516. *See also* intellectual monopolies

moral hazard, 201, 279, 487

mortgage-backed securities (MBS), 204, 282, 435

mortgage-type loans, 479, 481

Moss, David, 482

MRA. *See* Microcredit Regulatory Authority

Mukerji, Sujoy, 210

multiarm bandit literature, 399

Multi Fibre Agreement, 347

multinationals, 446, 451

multiplex network, 282

Mutual Agreement Procedure (MAP), 453

Nairobi, 513–514

naive decision makers, 380, 381, 384; bounded rationality and, 394; conservatism and, 385, 409; indifference to policies, 386; mistakes made by, 387; switching threshold of, 393

National Grid, 143, *144*, 145

"National Homeownership: Partners in the American Dream," 434

National Income and Product Accounts (NIPA), 22

national savings: of China, 327, *328*, 330, 337, 338; of Singapore, 352n1

national security, 469

nation-states: investment in knowledge by, 370; sovereignty of, 446

natural resources, 313, 320n8

Nelson, R., 175, 180, 188

neoclassical economists, 482

neoliberalism, 315

Netflix, 402

Netscape, 402

network effects, 9, 116, 234; cross-platform network effects, 113–114; idiosyncratic matching and, 128; indirect network effects, 113, 231; internet search engines and, 229, 230, 232; supply and demand and, 227, *228*; two-sided markets and, 113

network of players, 280

network structures, 9, 291

Newbery, D. M., 133, 218

New Classic Economics, 186

New Electricity Trading Arrangements, 132

New Institutional Economics (NIE), 422, 425

Newly Industrialized Economies (NIEs), 341–342

"newsholes," 467

"New World" colonies, 425, 426

New Yorker Belle Époque, 2

NGO. *See* nongovernmental organization

NIE. *See* New Institutional Economics

NIEs. *See* Newly Industrialized Economies

Nieuwerburgh, Stijn Van, 208

NIPA. *See* National Income and Product Accounts

Nistico, Salvatore, 208

Nobel Peace Prize, 432

Nobel Prize, 318, 319

"No-Fly" zones, 475n29

nonconvexities, *176*, 178, 179

nongovernmental organization (NGO), 431

nonprice strategies, 114

nonrival goods, 354–355, 361

North, D. C., 424
North Atlantic financial crisis, 443, 448
Norton, E., 493
nuclear bombs, 310
nuclear power, 133
Numbeo cost of living index, 78, 82, 83, 84
nursing homes, 494
nutritional adequacy, 77
Nyarko, Yaw, 509

Obama, Barack, 460, 461
objective function, 274
Occam's razor, 171
occupational licensing, 42–43
Occupy movement, 436
OCGTs. See open cycle gas turbines
OCO. See Overseas Contingency Operations
OECD. See Organization for Economic Cooperation and Development
OEF. See Operation Enduring Freedom
OEMs. See original equipment manufacturers
off-budget funding, 462
Office of Management and Budget (OMB), 460, 463
Ofgem, 133
OIF. See Operation Iraqi Freedom
older policies, 387
oligopoly, 516
OMB. See Office of Management and Budget
OND. See Operation New Dawn
"On Liberty, the Right to Know, and Public Discourse: The Role of Transparency in Public Life" (Stiglitz), 473
online commerce, 111
open cycle gas turbines (OCGTs), 147
operating systems, 231–232, 238
Operation Enduring Freedom (OEF), 474n6
Operation Iraqi Freedom (OIF), 474n6
Operation New Dawn (OND), 474n6

opinion leaders, 342
opportunity, 292; equality of, 48–49, 60; inequality of, 58, 61; luck and, 59
optimal behavior, 389
optimal consumption profiles, 262
optimal decisions, 388, 391, 394
optimal switching threshold, 392
Organization for Economic Cooperation and Development (OECD), 71, 74, 85, 209, 453; middle class and, 86; PPL and, 484
original equipment manufacturers (OEMs), 238
Orsini, Joe, 232
Orszag, P., 372n1
Ortiz-Juarez, E., 67, 69
Ostrom, E., 426, 427, 433
output, 23, 24; China growth rates of labor, capital and real output, 339, 339; cumulative output, 229, 330; marginal cost and, 233; output buyers, 114; output-linked securities, 208; surplus potential output, 323, 340
outsourcing, 364
overprocurement, 131, 148, 149, 150
Overseas Contingency Operations (OCO), 459, 461, 463
Ozdaglar, A., 240

Padoa-Schioppa, Tommaso, 451
Paes de Barros, Ricardo, 58
paid parental leave (PPL), 484, 488
Palais Royal Initiative, 451
Palli Karma Shayak Foundation (PKSF), 432
Palma ratio, 70
panel of technical experts (PTE), 144–145, 147
parents, 498; dependence, 503; nondependent, 502; utility maximizers and, 499
parents, children, and luck (PCL), 48, 49, 54, 57, 60
Pareto efficiency, 7, 131–132

Parker, G., 114
Parks, W., 466
parliamentary system, 403
patents: excessive use, 357; global, *367*; patent trolls, 358; rent seeking and, 357, 358
path-dependence, 177
payment-card networks, 111
PCL. *See* parents, children, and luck
pensions, 314
People's Congress (China), 316
People's Republic of China, 344
perturbation, 264
Peru, 424, 428
Pestieau, P., 498
Pettinato, S., 70
Phelps, Edmund, 197
Philippines, 485
Philippon, T., 364
Phillips curve, 186, 187
Piketty, Thomas, 22, 358, 359
Pistor, K., 426
PKSF. *See* Palli Karma Shayak Foundation
planning fallacy, 419*n*4
platforms, 111, 115; anonymous pairing by, 117, 118, 121; autonomy of, 116; central role of, 112; cross-platform network effects, 113–114; idiosyncratic matching, 121; platform pricing, 117; priced access to, 120; profit-maximizing, 118, 121, 124, 125; transactions on, 113
Poland, 312, 320*n*5
Polanyi, Karl, 422, 436
Polanyian "double movement," 436, 437
policies, 337, 408; countercyclical fiscal policies, 343; cycles of metapolicy and policies, 382; expected value of, 391; good and bad, 383, 384–385; incumbent bad, 390; long-standing, 398; monetary, 285; naive decision maker indifference to, 386; optimal switching threshold, 392; orthodox

macroeconomic policies, 519; status-quo, 380, 384–388, 389, 394–395, 396, 398, 407, 412–414; transition costs between, 393; virtues of an existing, 415; wasteful policy cycle, 406
political cycles, 404
pornography, 111
portfolio selection, 210; banks and, 254, 258; withdrawals and, 255
positive feedback loops, 227, 232–233, 239*n*1
posterior probability, 392
Pouémi, Joseph Tchundjang, 517
poverty line, 66, 67, 77
PPL. *See* paid parental leave
PPP. *See* purchasing power parity
Prasad, Eswar, 212
Prater, Marvin E., 35
precedent, 400
Prendergast, Canice, 382
prices, 118, 128*n*3, *140*; access-pricing, 125; asset price bubbles, 343; asset price risk premia, 202; control over, 115; of energy, 136; GB scarcity pricing, *141*; housing, 434; information on, 298; membership pricing, 124; of natural resources, 320*n*8; negative, 119; platform pricing, 117; platforms, priced access to, 120; price caps, 135, 148; relative, 177; reliability and, 149; setting, 119; shocks on price of assets, 283; social optimum, 126–127; welfare-maximizing, 120, 121, 123, 129*n*12
prior neglect, 395
private defense contractors, 457, 460, 467, 468
private sector: ICLs in, 489; move of knowledge from public to, 353
privatization, 311, 517; implementing, 315; of knowledge, 353, 355, 360–361; Poland and, 320*n*5; Washington Consensus and, 445

product diversity, 516
production, 356; assets used in, 360; costs of, 237; inputs to, 236; knowledge and, 235, 360; techniques of, 188
productivity: of capital, 360; shocks to, 164; stochastic, 214
profits: Kuznets curve and, 358; profit-maximizing platforms, 118, 121, 124, 125; quantum of, 424; of SOEs, 339; switcher's curse loss of, 418
progressivism, 383, 387–388, 391, 404; degrees of, 396, 398
property rights, 180, 429; intellectual monopolies and, 369; introduction of stronger, 367; Marx and, 438*n*6; reinforcement of, 370. *See also* intellectual property rights
protectionism, 368–369, 448
PTE. *See* panel of technical experts
Ptolemaic epicycles, 178
public institutions, 357–358, 370
Public Investment, the Rate of Return, and Optimal Fiscal Policy (Arrow and Kurz), 197
publicly traded corporations, 30
public policy, 12, 111
public sector, 353
purchasing power parity (PPP), 67, 71, 77–78, 82, 88
Putnam, R., 426

QE. *See* quantitative easing
Quadrini, Vincenzo, 212, 213
quantitative easing (QE), 204
Quiggin, John, 485
quotient rule, 411

racial segregation, 510
Radner, R., 179
railroad industry, 35
Ramsey, Frank, 197
random networks, 301
Rasmusen, Eric, 382
Rational Expectations Revolution, 517

rationality, 380, 383, 385, 389; bounded, 174, 378, 394; expectations, rational, 165, 166, 170, 187; *ex-post* rationalizations, 400; fully rational decision makers, 392, 394; imperfect, 96; investors, irrational exuberance of, 366; irrational exuberance, 432, 434
Ravallion, Martin, 67
Rawls, John, 49
RBC. *See* real business cycle
R&D. *See* research and development
real business cycle (RBC), 170, 202
real crises, 285
real estate, 282, 343. *See also* housing
recessions, effects of, *190*
recovery rates, 289
reflexivity, 369
regression testing, 420*n*9
regression to the mean, 97, 98, 101, 109
regular networks, 301
Regulation Q, 202
regulatory systems, 299
Reinhart, Carmen M., 208
reliability: capacity and, 139; prices and, 149; security and, 136; VoLL and, 138
Renewables Directive (EU), 136, 141
rents, 28, 362; creation of, 21; economic, 19, 20, 27, 35, 313; exploitation rents, 360; increased prevalence of, 26; inequality and, 20, 21; labor and, 21; monopoly rents, 320*n*8
rent seeking, 21, 357, 358
research and development (R&D), 327, 329
retrospective oversight, 469
returning troops, 463
return on assets (ROA), 98
return on invested capital (ROIC), 31, *31*, 44*n*3, 208; financial firms data on, 32; IPRs and, 363; of nonfinancial firms, *32*, 33; rates of, 219, *362*
returns to scale, 237

revenue, 233
Revolutionary War, 474*n*18, 475*n*21
Ricardo, David, 360
Richards, J. F., 426
right to freedom of information (RTI),
    460
ring network architecture, 285, 289
Rios-Rull, J.-V., 213
risk: asset price risk premia, 202;
    aversion to, 215; default risk, 10;
    diversification of, 292; exposure to
    similar risks, 279; general increase
    in, 220; high-yielding risky assets,
    247; ICLs and, 488; idiosyncratic
    sources of, 221; individual, 278, 485;
    management and distribution of,
    482; neutrality, 132; risk-free returns,
    242; risk premium, 107; risky
    commodity markets, 131; systemic,
    278, 293, 299. *See also* constant
    absolute risk aversion
risk sharing, 8–9, 213, 248–249, 273,
    274; banks and, 241; complete, 269–
    270; efficiency of, 256; equilibrium
    with complete risk sharing, 262,
    264; in international finance, 207;
    optimal, 255
ROA. *See* return on assets
roaring nineties, 354, 366–368, 369,
    370
Robinson, Joan, 186, 425, 426, 522*n*1
robustness, 172–173
Rochet, J.-C., 112, 114, 124
Roeder, K., 498
Roemer, John E., 48, 49, 53, 58
Rogers, L. C. G., 298
Rognlie, Matthew, 24
Rogoff, Kenneth S., 208
Rohlfs, Jeffrey, 227, 228
ROIC. *See* return on invested capital
Rosenberg, Nate, 175
Roukny, T., 289
RTI. *See* right to freedom of information
Ruffino, Doriana, 210
rule of law, 454

Russett, B. M., 466
Russia, 316
Rysman, M., 115

SAAS. *See* software-as-a-service
Saez, Emanuel, 22
Sagar, R., 469
Saint Lucia, 509
Saks, Raven, 27
sales force, 416
sales model, specialized, 417
Samuelson, Paul, 511, 512
Savastano, Miguel A., 208
savings, 368. *See also* national savings
scalefree networks, 301
Schiller, Robert J., 208
Schmukler, Sergio L., 212
Schuldenzucker, S., 298
Schulz, R., 496
Schumpeter, Joseph, 175, 188–189; IPRs
    and, 369
Schumpeter meeting Keynes (K + S)
    family of models, 183, *183*, 184
scientific research, 356
SDRs. *See* Special Drawing Rights
Secrist, Horace, 97, 98
securities, 212, 282, 434; mortgage-
    backed securities, 204, 282, 435;
    network players-securities, 281
security, 135; income, 75, 77; national
    security, 469; reliability and, 136;
    short-run increases in demand and,
    137
SEM. *See* Single Electricity Market
Senate Foreign Relations Committee,
    470
separation of powers, 382, 403
Seuken, S., 298
shadow banking sector, 435
Shang-Jin Wei, 208
Shapiro, Carl, 227
Sharpe ratio, 218, 220
Sherwood, P. R., 496
Sheshinsky, Eytan, 324
Shliefer, A., 99, 108

shocks, 240–242, 290; aggregate shock, 248; correlations across, 288, 291; to counterparties, 292; dependence shock, 498; joint density function of, 288; liquidity shocks, 269, 273; negative demand shocks, 189; on price of assets, 283

Shorrocks, A. F., 54–55

Short-Run Marginal Cost (SRMC), 139

Shy, Oz, 227

SIGAR. *See* Special Inspector General for Afghanistan Reconstruction

SIGIR. *See* Special Inspector Generals for Iraq

Silicon Valley, 419*n*8

simulations, 236

Singapore, 343, 352*n*1

Single Electricity Market (SEM), 137, 138

singles bars, 111, 120, 126–127; transactions in, 124, 125

Sinning, M., 484

SKS Microfinance, 432

slavery, 511

SMC. *See* System Marginal Cost

Smith, Adam, 175, 185

Smith, B., 272

SO. *See* System Operators

social assistance, 34–35

social behavior, 438*n*1

social capital theory, 422

social change, 425

socialism, 310, 311, 312; neoliberalism and, 315

social justice, 63

social networks, 111, 277

social norms, 497

social optimum, 260, 499; decentralization of, 501; prices, 126–127; utilitarian, 500

Social Security, 338, 482

Social Security Disability Insurance, 463

social welfare, 5, 48, 490

SOEs. *See* state-owned enterprises

software-as-a-service (SAAS), 405, 416

Solon, Gary, 50, 52, 54

Solow, Bob, 175, 186, 196, 511

solvency, 265, 266, 267, 284

Song, Jae, 36, 37, 363

Soper, Taylor, 230

Soros, G., 369

Souter, Justice David, 401

South Asia, 71, 74

South Korea, 328

sovereignty, 446, 447, 448

S&P 500, 30

Special Drawing Rights (SDRs), 447, 448

Special Inspector General for Afghanistan Reconstruction (SIGAR), 469

Special Inspector Generals for Iraq (SIGIR), 469

Spletzer, James R., 38, 39, 41

SRMC. *See* Short-Run Marginal Cost

stagnation, 371

stare decisis, 399–400, 405

star networks, 281

state-owned enterprises (SOEs), 320*n*8, 337, 339

status-quo bias, 377, 380, 407; conservatism and, 382; counterbalancing other biases, 395

Stevens, Justice John Paul, 401

Stiglitz Commission, 443, 448; Palais Royal Initiative and, 451

stock market: Chinese stock market bubble, 347; investors, 96; selling shares on, 281

stock returns, 104, 106; mean reversion in, 98; relative, 105

Stole, Lars, 382

strategic impoverishment, 496

strategic intervention, 427

student loans, 490; income-based repayment options, 482; reforms to, 481

subprime crisis, 282

Summers, Lawrence H., 37, 196

SUNARP. *See* Superintendencia Nacional de los Registros Públicos
sunk cost bias, 383
sunspot crises, 285
Superintendencia Nacional de los Registros Públicos (SUNARP), Peru, 428
supply, 227, *228*; economies of scale, supply side, 229, 230; short-term security of, 135
supply chains, 284
Supreme Court, U.S., 399, 401
sustainable development, 450
switcher's curse, 377, 378, 394, 397; availability bias and, 382, 395; avoiding, 396; causes of, 379; conservatism and, 380, 381, 393; older policies and, 387; profit lost from, 418; winner's curse and, 386
switching cost, 388, 390, 403; positive, 391; switching-cost threshold, 410
System Marginal Cost (SMC), 138
System Operators (SO), 132, 134, 135, 136, 143, 144, 148
systems theory, 165

Tahbaz-Salehi, A., 240
Taiwan, 328
Tan Wang, 208
Target Electricity Model (TEM), 131, 134; energy-only market envisaged by, 139
tatonnements, 185
taxation, 198, 454; Australian Tax Office, 481, 489; on bequests, 499, 501; brain drain tax, 485; in China, 316, 338; corporate income tax, 452; double-taxation treaties, 452; individual income tax policies, 337; international corporate taxation, 443; labor, optimal tax on, 500, 501; multinationals and, 451; war and, 465, *465*, 466, *466*
tax havens, 452

tax liabilities, 452
Taylor rule, 187
technological learning, 175, 176, 178
technology, *177*; change, technological, 175; multiplicative transaction technology, 122; rate of technical progress, 327; technical progress, 351; trajectories, technological, *176*, 177
telecommunications, 313
TEM. *See* Target Electricity Model
Terrones, Marco, 212
TFP. *See* total factor productivity
Theory of the Second Best, 169
Third International Conference on Financing for Development, 452
third way, 315
thresholds for operationalization and measurement, 67
Thurow, Lester, 70, 71
Tirole, J., 112, 114, 124
TNUoS. *See* Transmission Network Use of System
Tobin, Jim, 204
Tomes, Nigel, 50
too-big-to-fail, 279, 291, 299
total factor productivity (TFP), 207, 323, 340, 342
Towards a New Paradigm of Monetary Economics (Greenwald), 9
Town, Robert, 35
Trade-Related Aspects of Intellectual Property Rights (TRIPS) Agreement, 358, 360; IPRs and, 367–368
"Trade War with China Isn't Worth It, A" (Stiglitz), 317
training set size, 236, *237*
transactional efficiencies, 489, 490
transaction costs, 424
transactions, 117, 120; demand curve for, 122; incremental cost of, 118; inframarginal, 123; multiplicative transaction technology, 122; on platforms, 113; in singles bars, 124, 125; volume, 114

Transatlantic Trade and Investment Partnership (TTIP), 366

transition costs, 393

Transmission Network Use of System (TNUoS), 143

transparency, 460; fiscal, 457, 470; openness and, 474n13; private defense contractors and lack of, 468

Treasury, U.S., 204

trend reinforcement, 294

TRICARE subsidies, 472

TRIPS. *See* Trade-Related Aspects of Intellectual Property Rights

Triumph of Mediocrity in Business, The (Secrist), 97

Trubek, D., 425

Truman, Harry S., 466

TTIP. *See* Transatlantic Trade and Investment Partnership

Tversky, Amos, 395, 419n4

two-sided markets, 119, 234; access externalities and, 113; bookstores and, 116; cross-platform welfare effects and, 114; examples of, 111–112; network effects and, 113; no consensus on, 111; Rysman on, 115

"Two-Sided Network Effects: A Theory of Information Product Design" (Parker and Van Alstyne), 114

UBS cost of living database, 78

U.N. *See* United Nations

uncertainty, 246; aggregate, 249, 262; about asset returns, 271; over default probability, 291; model uncertainty, 215; in network structures, 291; nondegenerate, 262; systemic default probability, uncertainty on, 291

UN Commission of Experts on Reforms of the International Monetary and Financial System, 443

underdevelopment, 425, 429

UN Economic and Social Council (ECOSOC), 449; BWIs and, 451; transformation of, 450

unemployment, 167, 445, 517; involuntary, 181; persistent, 512

United Nations (U.N.): BWIs in U.N. system, 449; economic governance in, 443; global economic governance of, 13; RTI and, 460; sustainable development and, 450; WTO in U.N. system, 449

United States (U.S.), 468, 473; American Dream, 64; Bayh-Dole Act, 1980, 360, 367; bookstores in, 116; collapse of Lehman Brothers in, 347; cost of nutritional adequacy in, 77; credit crisis and, 428; dynamism of U.S. labor markets, 38; founders of, 402; GDP of, 29, 324; growth rates of China and, 324, *325*; IGE in, 50; informal family care in, 494; intellectual protectionism and, 368; legislative reforms in, 482; long-distance migration in, 39; Medicaid, 496; middle classes in, 65, 86; public support for war, 467; real growth rate of China and, *326*, 327; wages in, 196; war-related spending of, 457–458. *See also* Afghanistan, U.S. war in; Iraq, U.S. war in

universal health care insurance, 483

University of Nairobi, 513, 515

unmanned weaponry, 473

Uppal, Raman, 208

upper classes, 65, 79; income of, 81

U.S. *See* United States

U.S. Agency for International Development (USAID), 131

usaspending.gov, 460

U.S. dollar (USD), 79

utilitarianism, 502

utility maximizers, 216; children, parents, and, 499

VA. *See* Department of Veterans Affairs
value chains, 516
Value of Lost Load (VoLL), 135, 149, 150; in Great Britain, 139; reliability and, 138
Van Alstyne, M., 114
Varian, Hal, 227
Veldkamp, Laura, 208
venture capital, 381
venture capitalists, 402
Veraart, L. A. M., 298
veterans: total number of, 471; veterans' benefits, 463. *See also* Department of Veterans Affairs, U.S.
VHS tapes, 402
vicious circles, 361
Vietnam, 312
Vietnam War, 457, 463, 464
virtuous circles, 361
Visa cards, 113
Vishny, R. W., 99, 108
Vogt, William, 35
voice recognition, 235
VoLL. *See* Value of Lost Load
von Neumann-Morgenstern utility function, 215

wages, 363; China wage policy, 330; efficiency, 181; of public-sector employees in China, 338; returns on capital and, 21; rise in wage inequality, 37; in U.S., 196
Wagstaff, Adam, 49, 58, 59, 60
Wallace, N., 272
Walmart, 115–116
Walras, Leon, 185
Walter Reed National Military Medical Center, 472
"war-related" definition of, 463
Washington Consensus, 315, 518; austerity, privatization, market liberalization and, 445; critique of, 316; Rational Expectations Revolution and, 517

wealth: capital and, 198, *199*, 359; domestic-based, 211; owned by financial capital, 365
Webb, James, 470
Webber, C., 465
Weiss, Andrew, 127, 181, 515
Welch, Ivo, 382, 383, 419*n*1
welfare experiments, 167
welfare-maximizing: anonymous pairing and, 124; for consumers, 251; prices, 120, 121, 123, 129*n*12
welfare theorems, 180
Wen Jiabao, 347
Weyl, E. G., 115
Wharton Land Use Regulatory Index, 28
When All Else Fails (Moss), 482
white collar crime, 486
Wicksell Lectures, 315
Wildavsky, A., 465
Williamson, S., 272
winner's curse, 386
Winter, S., 180, 188
withdrawals, 266; demand for, 243; portfolio selection and, 255; time of, 241, 250, 253, 254
women's empowerment, 432
workers: average earnings of, 36; worker flows, 41–42
working classes, 359
World Bank, 3, 10, 315, 425, 517, 521; poverty line of, 67
World Conference of the International Schumpeter Society in Japan, 189
World Governance Indicators (World Bank), 425
world markets, 351
World Trade Organization (WTO), 11, 324, 327, 347; dispute settlement at, 453; reforming, 370; TRIPS Agreement and, 358; in U.N. system, 449
World War II (WWII), 184, 310, 465, 510

World Wealth and Income Database, 22
Wright, J., 116
WTO. *See* World Trade Organization
WWII. *See* World War II

Yellen, Janet, 203, 521
Yin, Pai-Ling, 232
Yitzhaki, S., 67
Yorulmazer, T., 278

Yotopoulos, Pan A., 340
yuan, 317

Zakrajšek, Egon, 204
Zambia, 508
Zenawi, Meles, 518, 519
zero-recovery rate, 295
Zhu Rongji, 316, 344
zoning regulations, 28
Zwiebel, Jeffrey, 382